THE OXFORD HANDB(

CONTEMPORARY
PHENOMENOLOGY

The Oxford Handbook of Contemporary Phenomenology presents twenty-eight essays by some of the leading figures in the field, and gives an authoritative overview of the type of work and range of topics found and discussed in contemporary phenomenology. The essays aim to articulate and develop original theoretical perspectives. Some of them are concerned with issues and questions typical and distinctive of phenomenological philosophy, while others address questions familiar to analytic philosophers, but do so with arguments and ideas taken from phenomenology. Some offer detailed analyses of concrete phenomena; others take a more comprehensive perspective and seek to outline and motivate the future direction of phenomenology.

The handbook will be a rich source of insight and stimulation for philosophers, students of philosophy, and for people working in other disciplines of the humanities, social sciences, and sciences, who are interested in the state of phenomenology today. It is the definitive guide to what is currently going on in phenomenology. It includes discussions of such diverse topics as intentionality, embodiment, perception, naturalism, temporality, self-consciousness, language, knowledge, ethics, politics, art, and religion, and will make it clear that phenomenology, far from being a tradition of the past, is alive and in a position to make valuable contributions to contemporary thought.

THE OXFORD HANDBOOK OF

CONTEMPORARY

PHENOMENOLOGY

Edited by

DAN ZAHAVI

UNIVERSITY PRESS

Great Clarendon Street, Oxford, OX2 6DP,
United Kingdom

Oxford University Press is a department of the University of Oxford.
It furthers the University's objective of excellence in research, scholarship,
and education by publishing worldwide. Oxford is a registered trade mark of
Oxford University Press in the UK and in certain other countries

Published in the United States of America by Oxford University Press
198 Madison Avenue, New York, NY 10016, United States of America

British Library Cataloguing in Publication Data
Data available

Library of Congress Cataloging in Publication Data
Data available

ISBN 978-0-19-959490-0 (Hbk.)
ISBN 978-0-19-875302-5 (Pbk.)

CONTENTS

PART III SELF AND CONSCIOUSNESS

PART IV LANGUAGE, THINKING, AND KNOWLEDGE

PART V ETHICS, POLITICS, AND SOCIALITY

PART VI TIME AND HISTORY

PART VII ART AND RELIGION

Contributors

Renaud Barbaras is Professor of Philosophy at the University Paris 1 Panthéon-Sorbonne and a Member of the Institut Universitaire de France. His publications include *De l'être du phénomène: Sur l'ontologie de Merleau-Ponty* (1991), *La perception: Essai sur le sensible* (1994), *Le tournant de l'expérience: Recherches sur la philosophie de Merleau-Ponty* (1998), *Le désir et la distance: Introduction à une phénoménologie de la perception* (1999), *Vie et intentionnalité: Recherches phénoménologiques* (2003), *Introduction à la philosophie de Husserl* (2004), *Le mouvement de l'existence. Etudes sur la phénoménologie de Jan Patočka* (2007), *Introduction à une phénoménologie de la vie* (2008), *L'ouverture du monde. Lecture de Jan Patočka* (2011), and *La vie lacunaire* (2011).

Rudolf Bernet is Emeritus Professor of Philosophy at the University of Leuven (Belgium) and President of the Husserl Archives. In 2008 he was awarded the *Alexander von Humboldt-Forschungspreis*. His books include *An Introduction to Husserlian Phenomenology* (with I. Kern and E. Marbach) (1993), *La vie du sujet* (1994), and *Conscience et existence* (2004). He has prepared critical editions of Husserl's posthumous writings on time (1985; 2001), and edited (with D. Welton and G. Zavota) *Edmund Husserl: Critical Assessments of Leading Philosophers* (2005).

John Brough is Emeritus Professor of Philosophy at Georgetown University. He has written essays on temporality, aesthetics, representation, and imaging, and is the translator of *Husserliana Volume X* and, more recently, of *Husserliana Volume XXIII*, which collects Husserlian texts on memory, image, consciousness, and phantasy. He is also the editor, with Lester Embree, of *The Many Faces of Time*.

David Carr received his PhD from Yale University in 1966. He has taught at Yale, the University of Ottawa (Canada), and, since 1991, at Emory University, where he was department chair and is now Charles Howard Candler Professor Emeritus. He is currently Visiting Professor of Philosophy at the New School for Social Research. His publications include *Phenomenology and the Problem of History* (1974, reissued in 2009), *Time, Narrative and History* (1986), *Interpreting Husserl* (1987), and *The Paradox of Subjectivity* (1999).

Edward S. Casey is Distinguished Professor at SUNY, Stony Brook. He is the author of *The World at a Glance* (2007) and *Getting Back into Place* (2nd edn., 2009), as well as a number of other books and many articles on topics of memory, time, imagination, aesthetics, and the philosophy of psychoanalysis.

David R. Cerbone is Professor of Philosophy at West Virginia University. He is the author of *Understanding Phenomenology* (2006) and *Heidegger: A Guide for the Perplexed* (2008), as well as numerous articles on Heidegger, Wittgenstein, and the phenomenological tradition. He is also the editor (along with Søren Overgaard and Komarine Romdenh-Romluc) of the *Routledge Research in Phenomenology* series.

Steven Crowell is Joseph and Joanna Nazro Mullen Professor of Philosophy at Rice University. He is the author of numerous articles on phenomenology and of *Husserl, Heidegger, and the Space of Meaning: Paths Toward Transcendental Phenomenology* (2001). He is editor of *The Cambridge Companion to Existentialism* (2012) and, with Jeff Malpas, *Transcendental Heidegger* (2007). He has served as Executive Co-Director of the Society for Phenomenology and Existential Philosophy, and is currently co-editor of *Husserl Studies*.

Nicolas de Warren is Professor of Philosophy at the University of Leuven, Belgium. He is the author of *Husserl and the Promise of Time* (2009) and numerous articles, including, most recently, 'Miracles of Creation: Bergson and Levinas' and 'Homecoming: Jan Patocka's Reflections on the First World War.' He is also co-editor of *Contributions to Phenomenology* book series.

John J. Drummond is Robert Southwell, S.J. Distinguished Professor in the Humanities and Professor of Philosophy at Fordham University. He received his PhD from Georgetown University, and he is the author of *Husserlian Intentionality and Non-Foundational Realism: Noema and Object*, as well as *Historical Dictionary of Husserl's Philosophy*. He has edited or co-edited five collections of articles on themes in phenomenology, and he has published numerous articles on phenomenology in collections and in journals such as *Philosophy and Phenomenological Research, Journal of Consciousness Studies, Husserl Studies, New Yearbook for Phenomenology and Phenomenological Philosophy*, and *Phenomenology and the Cognitive Sciences*.

Günter Figal is Professor of Philosophy at the University of Freiburg im Breisgau, and has been President of the Martin-Heidegger-Gesellschaft since 2003. He is the author of numerous publications on topics in phenomenology, hermeneutics, and aesthetics, including *Martin Heidegger. Phänomenologie der Freiheit* (2000), *Gegenständlichkeit: Das Hermeneutische und die Philosophie* (2006), *Verstehensfragen: Studien zur phänomenologisch-hermeneutischen Philosophie* (2009), and *Erscheinungsdinge: Ästhetik als Phänomenologie* (2010).

Shaun Gallagher is the Lillian and Morrie Moss Chair of Excellence in Philosophy at the University of Memphis and Research Professor of Philosophy and Cognitive Science at the University of Hertfordshire. He is the author of *How the Body Shapes* *the Mind* (2005) and, with Dan Zahavi, *The Phenomenological Mind* (2008), and is editor of *The Oxford Handbook of the Self* (2011).

Sara Heinämaa is Senior Lecturer in Theoretical Philosophy at the University of Helsinki, and works as Academy Research Fellow at the Helsinki Collegium for Advanced Studies. She is the author of *Toward a Phenomenology of Sexual Difference: Husserl, Merleau-Ponty, Beauvoir* (2003), co-author of *Death, Birth and Femininity: Essays in the Philosophy of Embodiment* (2010), and has co-edited *Consciousness: From Perception to Reflection* (2007) and *Psychology and Philosophy: Inquiries into the Soul from Late Scholasticism to Contemporary Thought* (2008).

Klaus Held is Emeritus Professor of Philosophy at the Bergische Universität Wuppertal. He is author of *Lebendige Gegenwart* (1966), *Heraklit, Parmenides und der Anfang von Philosophie und Wissenschaft* (1980), *Treffpunkt Platon. Philosophischer Reiseführer durch die Länder des Mittelmeers* (1990), *Phänomenologie der politischen Welt* (2010), *Phänomenologieder natürlichen Lebenswelt* (2012) and numerous articles on phenomenology, ancient philosophy, and political philosophy. He edited Heidegger's *Metaphysische Anfangsgründe der Logik* (1976) and a collection of Husserl's basic writings (1985/86), and is co-editor of *New Studies in Phenomenology*. During 1987–94 he was President of the Deutsche Gesellschaft für phänomenologische Forschung.

Walter Hopp received his PhD from the University of Southern California. He is Associate Professor of Philosophy at Boston University, and is the author of *Perception and Knowledge: A Phenomenological Account* (2011).

Dorothée Legrand is a researcher at "Archives Husserl" (ENS, CNRS, Paris). She holds a PhD in philosophy and is trained in clinical psychology. Thematically, her work focuses on the notion of selfhood and subjectivity. Her publications include 'Subjective and Physical Dimensions of Bodily Self-Consciousness, and their Dis-integration in Anorexia Nervosa' (*Neuropsychologia* 2010) and, with P. Ruby, 'What is Self Specific? A Theoretical Investigation and a Critical Review of Neuroimaging Results' (*Psychological Review* 2009). She is also the editor of *Dimensions of Bodily Subjectivity* (2009).

Dieter Lohmar is Professor of Philosophy at the University of Cologne. He is the author of *Phänomenologie der Mathematik* (1989), *Edmund Husserls Formale und Transzendentale Logik* (2000), *Erfahrung und kategoriales Denken* (1998), and *Phänomenologie der schwachen Phantasie* (2008).

Junichi Murata is Professor of Philosophy at Rissho University. He studied at the Department of History and Philosophy of Science, University of Tokyo. He was Lecturer and Associate Professor at Toyo University (Tokyo) (1981–91), and Associate Professor and Professor at the Department of History and Philosophy of Science, University of Tokyo (1991–2011). His major book publications include (in Japanese) *Perception and the Life-World* (1995), *Philosophy of Colour* (2002), *The Ethics of*

Technology (2006), *Philosophical Inquiry into Self* (2007), *Philosophy of Technology* (2009), and (in English) *Perception, Technology, and Life-Worlds* (2007).

Søren Overgaard is Associate Professor of Philosophy at the University of Copenhagen. He is the author of *Husserl and Heidegger on Being in the World* (2004) and *Wittgenstein and Other Minds* (2007), and a co-editor of *The Routledge Companion to Phenomenology* (2011).

Dominique Pradelle is Professor of Philosophy at the Blaise Pascal University (Clermont-Ferrand), France. His publications include *L'archéologie du monde: Constitution de l'espace, idéalisme et intuitionnisme chez Husserl* (2000), and *Par-delà la révolution copernicienne* (2012). He is the French translator of works by Einstein (1989), Husserl (1989), and, with J.-F. Courtine, Heidegger (2001) and Lask (2002). He is currently the editor of the journal *Philosophie (Editions de Minuit)*.

Komarine Romdenh-Romluc is Lecturer in Philosophy at the University of Nottingham. She is the author of *Merleau-Ponty and the Phenomenology of Perception* (2011), and has also written articles on topics such as action, self-knowledge, and perception. She is a co-editor of the *Routledge Research in Phenomenology* series.

Hans Bernhard Schmid is Professor of Philosophy at the University of Vienna. He received his PhD (1998) and Habilitation (2005) from the University of Basel. He is currently working on a project dealing with the metaphysics of the social world. He is the author of *Subjekt, System, Diskurs: Edmund Husserls Begriff transzendentaler Subjektivität in sozialtheoretischen Bezügen* (2000), *Wir-Intentionalität: Kritik des ontologischen Individualismus und Rekonstruktion der Gemeinschaft* (2005), *Plural Action* (2009), and *Moralische Integrität: Kritik eines Konstrukts* (2011).

Charles Siewert is Robert Alan and Kathryn Dunlevie Hayes Professor of Humanities and Professor of Philosophy at Rice University. He is the author of *The Significance of Consciousness* (1998), and of a number of articles on consciousness, introspective self-knowledge, perception, and phenomenology.

David Woodruff Smith is Professor of Philosophy at the University of California, Irvine. He is the author of *Husserl* (2007), *Mind World* (2004), *The Circle of Acquaintance* (1989), and other works on intentionality, consciousness, phenomenology, philosophy of mind, philosophy of language, ontology, and early twentieth-century philosophy (analytic and continental).

Anthony J. Steinbock is Professor of Philosophy and Director of the Phenomenology Research Center at Southern Illinois University, Carbondale. He is the author of *Home and Beyond* (1995) and *Phenomenology and Mysticism* (2007), and is the translator of Edmund Husserl's *Analyses Concerning Passive and Active Synthesis* (2001). He is also editor-in-chief of *Continental Philosophy Review*, and general editor of Northwestern University Press's Book Series, 'Studies in Phenomenology and Existential Philosophy.'

László Tengelyi is Professor of Philosophy and Director of the Institute of Phenomenology at the University of Wuppertal, Germany. From 2003 to 2005 he was the President of the German Society of Phenomenology. Besides four books in Hungarian, he has published *The Wild Region in Life-History* (2004; German original, 1998), *L'expérience retrouvée* (2006), *Erfahrung und Ausdruck* (2007), and, with Hans-Dieter Gondek, *Neue Phänomenologie in Frankreich* (2011).

Bernhard Waldenfels received his PhD from Munich University, and is Emeritus Professor of Philosophy at the Ruhr University Bochum. His main fields of research are phenomenology and contemporary French philosophy. He is the translator of Merleau-Ponty's writings and the author of several books, including *Phänomenologie in Frankreich* (1983), *Antwortregister* (1994), *Order in the Twilight* (1996), *Bruchlinien der Erfahrung* (2002), *Phänomenologie der Aufmerksamkeit* (2004), *Schattenrisse der Moral* (2006), *The Question of the Other* (2007), and *Phenomenology of the Alien: Basic Concepts* (2011).

Donn Welton is Professor of Philosophy at Stony Brook University. He is author of *The Origins of Meaning: A Critical Study of the Thresholds of Husserlian Phenomenology* (1983) and *The Other Husserl: The Horizons of Transcendental Phenomenology* (2002). Recently he has published articles on dimensions of perceptual sense and the structure of basic affects.

Dan Zahavi is Professor of Philosophy at the University of Copenhagen, Director of the *Center for Subjectivity Research*, and co-editor-in-chief of the journal *Phenomenology and the Cognitive Sciences*. He is also past President of the Nordic Society for Phenomenology (2001–2007). His publications include *Husserl und die transzendentale Intersubjektivität* (1996), *Self-awareness and Alterity* (1999), *Husserl's Phenomenology* (2003), *Subjectivity and Selfhood* (2005), *Phänomenologie für Einsteiger* (2007), and (with Shaun Gallagher) *The Phenomenological Mind* (2008).

INTRODUCTION

To some extent, the aim of *The Oxford Handbook of Contemporary Phenomenology* should be self-explanatory: to include contributions by some of the leading proponents and practitioners in the field in order to provide the reader with a representative overview of the type of work and range of topics found and discussed in contemporary phenomenology. In contrast to such volumes as, say, *The Oxford Handbook of Philosophy of Mind* or the *The Oxford Handbook of Philosophy of Economics*, however, the contributions in the present handbook are not unified in terms of their subject matter, but in terms of their methodological approach, which is indebted to and affiliated with a specific philosophical tradition. But is there really something like a phenomenological tradition, let alone a phenomenological method?

Opinions are divided. According to one view, phenomenology counts as one of the dominant traditions in twentieth-century philosophy, and is still a force to reckon with. Edmund Husserl (1859–1938) was its founder, but other prominent and well-known exponents include Max Scheler, Martin Heidegger, Jean-Paul Sartre, and Maurice Merleau-Ponty. Given that phenomenology has been a decisive precondition and persisting interlocutor for a whole range of later theory formations, including existentialism, hermeneutics, deconstruction, and post-structuralism, it rightly deserves to be considered as the cornerstone of what is frequently and somewhat misleadingly called 'Continental philosophy'.

Husserl is the founding father of phenomenology, but occasionally it has been claimed that virtually all post-Husserlian phenomenologists ended up distancing themselves from most aspects of Husserl's original program. Thus, according to a second competing view, phenomenology is a tradition by name only. It has no common method and research program. It has even been suggested that Husserl was not only the founder of phenomenology, but also its sole true practitioner.

In my view—which has also guided the editorial work on the current volume—the latter view is mistaken. It presents us with a distorted picture of the influence of phenomenology in twentieth-century and contemporary philosophy, and it conceals the extent to which post-Husserlian phenomenologists continued the work of the founder. Although phenomenology has in many ways developed as an heterogeneous movement with many branches, although, as Ricoeur famously expresses it, the history of phenomenology is the history of Husserlian heresies (Ricoeur 1987: 9), and although it would be an exaggeration to claim that phenomenology is a philosophical system with a clearly delineated body of doctrines, one should overlook neither the formative impact of Husserl's work, despite the at times rebellious rhetoric of his successors, nor the common themes and concerns that have united, and continue to unite, its proponents.

But what, then, is the core of phenomenology? Again, opinions differ, but we find one proposal in *Phénoménologie de la perception*, in which Merleau-Ponty declares that phenomenology is distinguished in all its characteristics from introspective psychology and that the difference in question is a difference in principle. Whereas the introspective psychologist considers consciousness a mere sector of being, and tries to investigate this sector in the same way in which the physicist tries to investigate his, the phenomenologist, according to Merleau-Ponty, has realized that consciousness ultimately calls for a transcendental clarification that goes beyond common-sense postulates and brings us face to face with the problem concerning the constitution of the world (Merleau-Ponty 1945: 72). The simplest way to understand Merleau-Ponty's claim is by acknowledging that phenomenology—despite all kinds of other differences—is firmly situated within a certain Kantian or post-Kantian framework. One way to interpret Kant's *Copernican turn* is by seeing it as amounting to the conviction that our cognitive apprehension of reality is more than a mere mirroring of a pre-existing world. Thus, with Kant the pre-critical search for the most fundamental building blocks of empirical reality was transformed into a transcendental philosophical reflection on what conditions something must satisfy in order to count as 'real'. Phenomenology shares the conviction that the critical stance proper to philosophy necessitates a move away from a straightforward metaphysical or empirical investigation of objects to an investigation of the very framework of meaning and intelligibility that makes any such straightforward investigation possible in the first place. Rather than engaging in first-order claims about the nature of things (which it leaves to various scientific disciplines), phenomenology concerns itself with the preconditions for any such empirical inquiries. Thus, rather than contributing to or augmenting the scope of our positive knowledge, phenomenology investigates the basis of that knowledge and asks how it is possible. This is also why Husserl, just like Merleau-Ponty, would deny that the task of phenomenology is merely to describe objects or experiences as precisely and meticulously as possible. As Scheler once remarked, to reduce phenomenology to such an enterprise would be to make do with a 'picture-book phenomenology' (Scheler 1927, vii). This also highlights an important contrast with a good part of the preoccupation with phenomenal consciousness found in recent analytic philosophy of mind. The phenomenological interest in the first-person perspective has not primarily been motivated by the conviction that we need to consider the first-person perspective if we wish to understand mental phenomena. Rather, the phenomenologists' focus on the first-person perspective has as much been motivated by an attempt to understand the nature of objectivity as by an interest in the subjectivity of consciousness. Indeed, rather than taking the objective world as the point of departure, phenomenology precisely asks how something like objectivity is possible in the first place. How is objectivity constituted? Thus—and this is yet another way of highlighting its transcendental preoccupation—phenomenology is not interested in consciousness *per se*. It is interested in consciousness insofar as consciousness is world-disclosing.

Phenomenology should consequently be understood as a philosophical analysis of the different types of world-disclosure (perceptual, judgemental, imaginative, recollective, and so on), and in connection with this as a reflective investigation of those structures of experience and understanding that permit different types of beings to show themselves as what they are. By adopting the phenomenological attitude, we pay attention to how public objects (trees, planets, paintings, symphonies, numbers, states of affairs, social relations, and so on) appear. But we do not simply focus on the objects precisely as they appear. We also focus on the subjective side of consciousness, thereby becoming aware of our subjective accomplishments and of the intentionality that is at play.

It is not as if this transcendental focus is evident in each and every phenomenological analysis, and it is by no means highlighted in all of the contributions in the present volume; but it is, I would claim, essential to bear in mind if one is to understand the distinctive philosophical vision and ambition of classical phenomenology.

Phenomenology did not come to an end with the passing of Sartre and Heidegger. Much has happened since then, particularly in French phenomenology. Thinkers such as Emmanuel Lévinas, Paul Ricoeur, Jacques Derrida, Michel Henry, and Jean-Luc Marion have all questioned the adequacy of some of the classical phenomenological investigations. In their attempts to radicalize phenomenology they have disclosed new types and structures of manifestation, and have thereby contributed to the continuing development of phenomenology.

During its history, phenomenology has made important contributions to most areas of philosophy, including transcendental philosophy, philosophy of mind, social philosophy, philosophical anthropology, aesthetics, ethics, philosophy of science, epistemology, theory of meaning, and formal ontology. It has provided ground-breaking analyses of such topics as intentionality, perception, embodiment, self-awareness, intersubjectivity, and temporality. It has delivered a targeted criticism of reductionism, objectivism, and scientism, emphasized the importance of the first-person perspective, and argued at length for a rehabilitation of the life-world. By presenting a detailed account of human existence, where the subject is understood as an embodied and socially and culturally embedded being-in-the-world, phenomenology has also provided important inputs to a whole range of empirical disciplines, including psychiatry, nursing, sociology, literary studies, architecture, ethnology, and developmental psychology.

The present volume does not focus on applied phenomenology—that is, on the kind of contribution phenomenology can make to various empirical disciplines, though this is an issue worthy of its own extensive treatment—but on the distinct contribution that contemporary phenomenology can make to philosophy.

A characteristic feature of much recent work in phenomenology is the extent to which it is developed in a continuing dialogue and conversation with the founding fathers of the tradition. During the initial discussions regarding the format and structure of the present handbook, it was, however, decided to not include scholarly essays that primarily focused on historical figures. To that extent, the aim of the volume is not to present the state of the art when it comes to studies of Husserl, Heidegger, Merleau-Ponty, and so on. In fact, the contributors were requested not to focus specifically on exegetical treatments, nor to provide overviews of existing results, but instead to articulate and further develop their own theoretical perspective. This is also reflected in many of the chapter headings.

The contributors are based in Austria, Belgium, Denmark, Finland, France, Germany, Japan, the United Kingdom, and the USA. In compiling the volume it was obviously necessary to make some choices. I found it important to include contributions by phenomenologists who during the past fifteen to twenty years have shaped and dominated the field because of their writings and their teaching at the universities of Bochum, Freiburg, Leuven, Paris, and Wuppertal, but who have hitherto remained less known in the Anglophone world. Other editors would most probably have made other choices, but I am confident that a large number of the contributors to the present volume would have been included in any handbook on contemporary phenomenology, regardless of who the editor would have been.

As the volume will make clear, contemporary phenomenology is a somewhat heterogeneous field. The different contributions differ widely in style and focus. Some are very much concerned with issues and questions typical and perhaps also distinctive of phenomenological philosophy, while others address questions familiar to analytic philosophers, but do so with arguments and ideas taken from phenomenology. Some offer detailed analyses of concrete phenomena, and others take a more comprehensive perspective and seek to outline and motivate the future direction of phenomenology. Hopefully, the volume as a whole might function as a representative sample of what is currently happening in phenomenology, and make it clear to philosophers from other traditions that phenomenology, far from being a tradition of the past, is quite alive and in a position to make valuable contributions to contemporary thought.

Let me end by thanking Peter Momtchiloff, at Oxford University Press, for originating the idea for this volume and inviting me to be in charge, and for himself being an ideal editor. I would also like to thank Claes Holmberg and Martin Grünfeld for helping me formatting the final version of the manuscript and Adam Farley for compiling the index.

PART I

SUBJECTIVITY AND NATURE

CHAPTER 1

....

PHENOMENOLOGICAL METHOD: REFLECTION, INTROSPECTION, AND SKEPTICISM

....

DAVID R. CERBONE

1 QUESTIONING PHENOMENOLOGICAL METHOD

There is a time-honoured tradition—as long as the phenomenological tradition itself—of declaring phenomenology to be, variously, unreliable, irrelevant, hopelessly muddled, or even outright impossible. Typically, the reasoning behind these negative verdicts is something like this. Phenomenology is primarily a descriptive enterprise. What it seeks to describe are the phenomena associated with, or making up, consciousness or experience. As such, phenomenology is really just descriptive psychology, and the method employed to obtain those descriptions is primarily (if not exclusively) introspection. And since introspection is an inherently problematic means for gathering data (it affords a poor grip on what it seeks to describe, there is no settled set of techniques for introspecting, it is irreducibly first-personal and so its 'results' are not subject to independent confirmation or verification, and so on), the whole enterprise is thereby called into question. This line of reasoning seems almost ineluctable: once it is acknowledged that phenomenology is indeed interested in describing consciousness or experience, nothing prevents drawing the kind of conclusions reached by the phenomenological nay-sayers. After all, what else could the method of phenomenology be, apart from introspection? What other way is there to obtain an 'inside view' on the 'stream of consciousness'?

The persistence of this basic line of reasoning—such declarations of irrelevance and impossibility—is especially striking in light of the equally frequent and vehement attempts by practitioners of phenomenology to block it, and to do so not by finding some way to demonstrate the reliability of 'introspection', but by showing this line of reasoning to be ill-conceived almost from the start. That is, while phenomenology typically acknowledges its interest in describing consciousness or experience, it also typically resists being branded as a branch or style of psychology, while at the same time refusing the identification of its methods with introspection. For example, in his 1911 manifesto, 'Philosophy as Rigorous Science', Husserl asserts that a proper understanding of phenomenological inquiry crucially 'depends on one's . . . not confounding phenomenological intuition with "introspection", with interior experience' (Husserl 1965: 115). Introspection, presumably, suggests turning one's gaze inward, hoping to find and study a parade of inner happenings—what is taking place 'inside' the mind. But such an astronomy of the mental, whatever its merits or shortcomings, is not the business of phenomenology. Rather than introspection, understood as a special form of inner observation, for Husserl phenomenology instead proceeds by means of reflection. The phenomenologist effects 'acts of reflection' which are directed toward and 'seize upon' our first-order mental activity; the phenomenologist thereby lives 'completely in such acts of the second degree'—those reflective acts directed toward first-order (or first-degree) consciousness (Husserl 1982: 114). Phenomenological method, according to Husserl, 'operates exclusively in acts of reflection' (Husserl 1982: 174).

But insisting on a distinction between introspection and reflection (a distinction to which we will return and try to cash out shortly) is only one component of phenomenology's complaint against its would-be skeptics. What these skeptics ignore is phenomenology's distinctively non-empirical aspirations; that is, phenomenology does not primarily seek to contribute a chapter to psychological theory but instead is interested in *essences*. In the Preface Husserl wrote for the English translation of *Ideas*—his first and most complete working-out of 'pure' phenomenology—he at one point characterizes his project as having as its 'goal a science which deals not with the factual data of this inner sphere of intuition but with the essence, inquiring, that is, after the invariant, essentially characteristic structures of a soul, of a psychical life in general' (Husserl 1972: 8). With the phrase 'inner sphere of intuition', Husserl is no doubt evincing some interest in consciousness or experience: phenomenology is a 'science', which in some way deals with the sphere of consciousness. But the way phenomenology deals with consciousness is special: notice the distinction Husserl draws between 'factual data' and 'essence'. Indeed, the appeal to essence is made twice over in this remark, as he also refers to the 'essentially characteristic structures of a soul'. So whatever interest phenomenology takes in consciousness, it is not in the business of collecting 'factual data', of cataloging the particularities of our actual, empirical psychological lives.

In many ways, Husserl's interest in consciousness is more akin to the logician's than to the psychologist's. Consider as an example Husserl's contemporary, Gottlob Frege. In one of his later writings Frege writes that the task of logic and mathematics 'could perhaps be represented . . . as the investigation of *the* mind; of *the* mind, not of minds' (Frege 1991: 368–9).[1] I would suggest that the distinction Frege draws here—between minds

---

[1] I am greatly indebted to the work of Cora Diamond for calling my attention to, and bringing home the importance of, this remark. See especially 'Introduction I: Philosophy and the Mind', in (Diamond 1991), which is organized explicitly around Frege's remark.

and *the* mind—is operative in Husserl as well, and with at least some overlap of motivation and import. After all, logic looms large in Husserl's phenomenology: the six Logical Investigations constituting his breakthrough work are preceded by a lengthy 'Prologomena to Pure Logic', and his subsequent work continues to display a concern with logic and logical structure. More importantly, Frege and Husserl are resolute in their commitment to *anti-naturalism*. Both are adamant that psychology has no business interfering with logic: logical laws and principles are not psychological laws, nor any other kind of empirical generalizations. But if logic is in this way independent of psychology, in what way is logic concerned with '*the* mind'? What Frege means here is that rather than being determined by psychology (as various forms of psychologism would have it), logic and logical structure are determinative for psychology. Insofar as psychology concerns itself with such notions as *thought*, *belief*, or any others that have what is sometimes called 'propositional content', then logical structure plays an essential role: insofar as there are thoughts and the like, then these involve contents which are logically structured. For a particular psychological episode or state to be the thought that *p*, then it has to be such that *what* is thought is something that can be true or false, whose truth excludes the truth of *not-p*, that implies various other things, and which can be inferred from other things in turn. These relations of exclusion, implication, and inference are not themselves psychological relations, but they inform psychological processes insofar as those processes involve categories such as thought, belief, and so on.

In its concern for limning the essential structure of 'psychical life', Husserl's phenomenology is likewise concerned with '*the* mind' rather than minds. This concern extends well beyond Frege's interest in logic and logical structure. I cite Frege here only to motivate the idea that there is a way of investigating *thought*—and, for Husserl, mental phenomena more generally—that is not thereby a part of psychology. Husserl wants to emphasize 'from the start *that pure phenomenology ... is not psychology* and that neither accidental delimitations of its field nor its terminologies, but *most radical essential* grounds, prevent its inclusion in psychology' (Husserl 1982: xviii). For this reason, it is a mistake to think of phenomenology 'as a sphere comprising "immanental" descriptions of psychical mental processes, a sphere comprising descriptions that—so the immanence in question is understood—are strictly confined within the bounds of internal *experience*' (Husserl 1982: xviii). Phenomenology is thus not introspective psychology, and so whatever shortcomings may be detected in the latter do not automatically apply to the former.

My interest in this paper is not historical (I will not, for example, be exploring the relation between Husserl and Frege). Rather, I cite these passages as illustrative of phenomenology's attempt to clarify at the start its principal methods and aspirations in order to head off an all too frequent form of condemnation. My primary aim in the discussion to follow is to tease out in considerable detail the crucial distinctions at work in this attempt: gathering factual data versus discovering essences, and introspecting versus reflecting. These are not two entirely separate pairs of distinctions; they are instead aligned with one another. The nature of that alignment is what I hope to clarify. And while I will not be concerned to document in detail the rich history of this interplay between would-be phenomenologist and would-be skeptic, I will draw on occasion from the relevant sources—especially from the writings of Husserl.

2 AN OPENING EXERCISE

In order to explore the distinctions that phenomenology declares to be crucial for distinguishing its methods from those of psychology and other empirical disciplines, consider a simple example of a kind familiar to readers of Husserl.[2] I hold my coffee cup in front of me and slowly turn it while keeping it before my gaze. Performing this simple task generates a stretch—or an episode—of visual experience—the experience of watching a cup being slowly turned. Even such a simple episode affords myriad questions that lead off in very different directions. For example, what takes place between the cup and myself (my eyes) that makes it possible for me to *see* the cup? Further, what takes place within my body (*viz.* my brain) that allows me to see the cup? What is the relation between my seeing the cup and my *believing* or *knowing* that there is a cup in front of me (and in what way does the former provide *grounds* for the latter)? The first two questions might concern someone investigating the physiology of perception, while the third veers off in a more epistemologically-oriented direction. But suppose we leave questions like these aside, even while respecting their legitimacy: we ignore all the complexities of the brain, the details of the organism-environment interface, and so on; we exclude worries about justification and knowledge. Instead, we concentrate just on that stretch of experience *in and of itself*. That is, we attend just to the experience of seeing the cup, without attending to any of the questions and worries that might arise about just how that experience is caused or generated by my bodily engagement with a surrounding environment or to any concerns about whether my beliefs pertaining to the real existence of the cup are warranted or well-founded. Notice here that we are *reducing* the range of the interest we might take in my experience by *excluding* or *bracketing* many of the questions we might typically ask about that experience in the course of being curious about that experience, but especially when the interest we take in it is of a more scientific sort. By imposing these limitations, I would suggest that we are on the way to doing phenomenology.

In saying that phenomenology comes into view when we concentrate on the experience 'in and of itself', it would seem that we are taking our first steps along the problematic path sketched out above: concentrating in this manner is just the kind of introspective turn the critic of phenomenology cites in developing his skeptical worries. I hold the cup before my gaze, and turn it slowly; all the while I see the cup. In seeking to *describe* that experience of seeing, do I turn my attention *inward*? While it is true that there is a

---

[2] Using such an example was suggested to me by Dan Zahavi in comments on an earlier—and very different—version of this paper. Whether the use to which I put the example is what Zahavi intended is another matter.

difference between just seeing the cup and looking at the cup while trying to describe that experience of seeing, since the latter is more self-conscious or self-aware, it does not follow that doing the second involves any kind of inward turn. In looking at my experience while looking at the cup, I am not 'looking inside', probing around in my 'stream of consciousness'. If anything, I am paying more attention to the *cup*, and so directing my attention outward at least as much in the second case as in the first. However, I am not paying more attention to the cup in the sense of inspecting it more carefully to determine more of its features in greater detail, in the way someone contemplating purchasing the cup or appraising it might. Rather, I am paying more attention to the way by the cup is *presented* or *given* in my experience. In doing so, I begin to notice more about that experience. For example, while it is true that the cup (or whatever object I happen to be holding before me) is given in my visual experience, it is also true that it is presented only *partially*: I do not see all of the cup all at once, but only one side at a time. Indeed, as I turn the cup around, each of my moments of experience is qualitatively different. If I could somehow 'freeze-frame' my experience and trace out pictures of the cup as it is presented in the various 'frames', those pictures would have markedly different shapes. Ordinarily we do not notice this very explicitly—which is one of the reasons why drawing objects with correct perspective can be so difficult. So we have a kind of sameness-in-diversity at work in our experience: the stretch of experience presents us with *one* object (*the* cup) through an ever changing series of 'looks' or 'perspectives'—what Husserl calls 'adumbrations'.[3] If I reflect more carefully on my experience, I may further notice that these 'looks' or 'perspectives' follow one another in a smooth, predictable manner: as each side of the object comes into view, it does so in a way that was already anticipated in the previous view. Nothing about seeing the back of the coffee cup surprises me when it comes into view after previously experiencing the front.

3 SKEPTICISM ABOUT PHENOMENOLOGY

I have at this point offered a simple phenomenological description of a short stretch of my experience that emphasizes what Husserl refers to as the adumbrative character of perceptual experience. In what ways might this description be challenged or called into question? Here is one way of generating a skeptical attitude toward phenomenological description: the stretch of experience described in our opening exercise took place *over time*; moreover, by the time the description is formulated and reported, that stretch of experience has come and gone. Thus, any endeavour to describe it *now* has to rely on

---

[3] There is also what Husserl calls a *categorial* dimension to this stretch of experience: informing and uniting the stretch of experience is not just *cup*, but its *being white, being cylindrical*, and so forth. The cup's *being* white is not analyzable solely in terms of the sensory content of the experience: what Husserl calls *categorial* intuition, and not just *sensory* intuition, is at work in the experience. Despite its importance for Husserl's phenomenological project as a whole, I will not here be discussing his notion of categorial intuition.

memories of the experience, and that opens the door to the question of how one knows that the experience *at the time* really was the way it is remembered to be now. And how do we go about answering *that* question? Since that stretch of experience has now come and gone, there is no possibility of *comparing* it with the current memory of it in the way that you could, for example, compare your memory of a scene in a film with the scene itself by watching the scene again (the doorknob to the basement was indeed red, the knife was in the left hand, and so on). Experiencing and describing would appear to be separated by a *gap*, and phenomenological skepticism exploits that very separation. As Daniel Dennett expresses it:

> If the experience you are reporting is a past experience, your memory—on which you rely in your report—might be contaminated by error. Perhaps your experience was actually one way, but you now misremember it as having been another way. It certainly could seem to you *now* to have seemed to you *then* to have been a horse— even if *in fact* it seemed to you *then* to have been a cow. The logical possibility of misremembering is opened up no matter how short the time interval between actual experience and subsequent recall. (Dennett 1992: 318)

Dennett's distrust is hardly new, as Husserl confronted such skepticism from contemporary psychologists and philosophers. In §79 of *Ideas*, Husserl quotes at length from a 1907 tract by the psychologist H. J. Watt.[4] Though Watt's polemic is directed against Theodor Lipps, rather than Husserl, between Lipps and Husserl there are 'in an appreciable measure congruences, which justify our taking into consideration Watt's objections' (Husserl 1982: 182) Husserl cites the following string of quotations from Watt's article as illustrative:

> [Watt writes:] 'One can indeed scarcely even inquire into the likelihood of how one arrives at the cognition of immediate mental living. For it is neither knowledge nor the object of knowledge; it is rather something else. It is not to be discerned how a report about the mental living of mental living, even when it is there, could be put down on paper.' 'But this is always the ultimate question of the fundamental problem of self-observation.' 'Today one designates this absolute description as phenomenology.' (Husserl 1982: 182)

What Watt refers to here as 'the fundamental problem of self-observation' is the problem of ascertaining the characteristics of 'immediate mental living'. Drawing a sharp distinction between *living* through one's own mental processes and *knowing* them, Watt sees the problem to lie mainly in the fact that self-observation is 'ever retrospective', and so 'is always knowledge about mental processes just *had* as objects' (Husserl 1982: 183). There always arises the question of how one can 'know that his mental living is in actuality absolutely thus as he thinks it is' (Husserl 1982: 183). As Watt sees it, in self-observation

---

[4] The article Husserl discusses is H. J. Watt, 'Über die neure Forschungen in der Gedächtnis und Assoziationspsy-chologie aus dem Jahre 1905', which appeared in the *Archiv für die gesamte Psychologie* in 1907. All quotations of Watt's article are taken from Husserl's discussion. See (Cerbone 2003) for a fuller discussion of Husserl's engagement with phenomenological skepticism and its relation to latter-day skepticism of the kind that motivates Dennett's 'heterophenomenology'.

'the relation to something objective pertaining to the mental processes to be described changes. Perhaps this change has a much greater signification than one is inclined to believe' (Husserl 1982: 185). One can never, as it were, catch one's awareness unawares: how one's awareness shows itself in the act of reflection is no guarantee, Watt thinks, of how it *was* prior to, and so independently of, the reflective act. Alterations of various kinds might take place, and since the pre-reflective *lived* mental process has now receded into the past, there is no real possibility of factoring out any such alterations so as to determine what the mental process was *at the time*—that is, pre-reflectively, really like.

Let us try to develop Watt's worries a little further. Suppose I could relive the stretch of experience where I am turning the cup while gazing at it. How would I know that I am reliving it *in exactly the same way* as I lived it before? Would I be able to select among slight variations on the original experience—slight shifts in the way things appear or how they are seen? Suppose that I am presented with a number of slight variations on that original stretch of experience, in the way suspects are presented to witnesses in a police line-up. In some variations the apparent colour might be slightly different; in others, spatial relations may be slightly altered, and so on. How likely is it that one of these variations will stand out as *the* way the experience was lived the first time around? And if it is not likely, if these are not differences that make a difference, what does that say about there being some way my experience really was? Notice with this last question that what started as a series of epistemological worries can quickly develop into ontological ones, since it raises the question of whether there is a *fact of the matter* about what my experience was like at the time you enjoyed it. If I would be unable to select among a range of variations on the 'original experience', then one has to wonder whether it was some definite way in the first place. It may seem to me now that my experience *then* was one way or another, but it does not follow from that that it really was (or even seemed) that way at the time. As Dennett expresses it: '*There seems to be phenomenology*', but from this, 'it does not follow from this undeniable, universally attested fact that *there really is* phenomenology' (Dennett 1992: 366). In this way, what started as epistemological skepticism about experience gives way to a more ontologically inflected variety: rather than an unknowable flow of experience, beyond the reach of any kind of attentive regard, there is instead nothing there to be known. As Derrida expresses it in 'Freud and the Scene of Writing', 'Everything begins with reproduction' (Derrida 1978: 211), and so there is no 'original' experience whose content and structure may or may not be accurately delineated.

In light of these considerations we may sort phenomenological skeptics into two basic camps, as follows:

i) *Epistemological skepticism.* The transience or ephemerality of ground-level or 'immediate' experience makes it an inherently problematic notion. Immediate experience is too fleeting to 'capture' in any way that allows it to be examined. Any attempt to examine it, any effort somehow to freeze the 'flow' of experience or pull something out of the 'stream', necessarily *distorts* it, or at least faces the question of whether and how that attempt has distorted it and how one knows that it has not. To answer this last question one would need to compare the pre- or unfrozen free experience with the frozen one, although making the comparison would require capturing the former, and that trivializes the endeavor. This form of phenomenological skepticism can be considered a kind of epistemological skepticism: we all have immediate experience all right, but we cannot know all that much about it. (There are further worries that can be raised in this vicinity concerning the possibility of comparing 'streams' of experience across different experiencing subjects ('How can I know what *your* stream of experience is like?', and so on), but the worry about distortion cuts deeper, as it applies even at the first-personal level.)

ii) *Ontological skepticism*. Transience and ephemerality are standard ways in which we describe our experience, but in offering such descriptions we are in fact expressing our *beliefs* about our experience. Whether anything really corresponds to such beliefs is another matter. Indeed, it does not matter all that much whether anything really does correspond—whether there is a 'fact of the matter' about experience—since the beliefs are all that we have to express, report, and so on: if one deleted what the beliefs are about (that murky stream of consciousness) while keeping the beliefs fixed, no one could tell the difference, even the one who took himself to be reporting about his own experience. Like anthropologists cautiously investigating the supernatural beliefs of an alien tribe, a scientifically respectable approach to consciousness should likewise 'bracket' the experience that beliefs about experience purport to describe. And those brackets need never be removed. I call this form of phenomenological skepticism *ontological* or *absolute* skepticism, because it does not so much challenge the possibility of knowledge concerning experience as it suggests that ultimately there is nothing really there to know. Although this form of skepticism is often offered in the service of developing a scientifically minded account of consciousness and the mind (most notably, with Daniel Dennett), there are versions that are not driven in any particular way by a conception of the demands of natural science. Derrida, with his alignment of phenomenology with the 'metaphysics of presence', is the most prominent example. (See especially Derrida 1973.)

4 ACCURACY, EXISTENCE, AND ESSENCE

To what extent is the kind of description I offered in our opening exercise really vulnerable to these sorts of skeptical worries? A great deal depends on the sorts of *claims* that phenomenology makes with respect to that description and, correspondingly, which of the claims scrutinized by the skeptic are of interest to phenomenology. It could very well be that the kinds of worries which the would-be skeptic raises are irrelevant to the phenomenological project.

Skepticism about phenomenology begins with questions concerning the accuracy or fidelity of descriptions of experience to the experience itself. The would-be skeptic exploits the *gap* between the two: the experience has come and gone, while the description persists, and so one then wonders how to ensure that the description gets it right. That *any* description can be offered strikes the would-be skeptic as remarkable. (Note Watt's incredulity: 'One can indeed scarcely even inquire into the likelihood of how one arrives at the cognition of immediate mental living.') There is something peculiar about these kinds of worries, as they treat the notion of 'immediate mental living' as though it were a kind of *blind* process, taking place 'under the radar' of any kind of attention on my part. The phenomenological skeptic treats experience as something that I undergo or endure, and then wonders how I can become aware of it (and whether that awareness can adequately capture and delineate 'what it is like', and so on). But 'immediate mental living' is not something happening unawares that I need to become aware of; it is *itself* already awareness, and so already self-awareness. The question 'How can I become aware of my awareness?' is only a bit of verbal cleverness: it does not raise a genuine question in need of an answer. Consciousness which is not conscious of itself is no less absurd than a non-extended spatial object: 'Just as an extended object is compelled to exist according to three dimensions, so an intention, a pleasure, a grief can exist only as immediate self-consciousness' (Sartre 1956: liv). Thus, Watt's insistence on a sharp distinction between *living through* one's experiences—immediate mental living—and *knowing* them is untenable: living through one's experiences already involves a kind of knowledge or self-awareness.

In light of these considerations, worries about the *general* availability of descriptions carry a certain trace of hysteria. To the question 'How can you know what your experience just now was (or was like)?', it seems appropriate to answer, 'Well, I just had it, didn't I? It is not like it took place behind my back.' And that the experience has come and gone does not on its own motivate a *general* worry about describing it accurately. *Events* occurring out in the world also come and go, and yet it is possible to describe them. If while walking in the woods I say that a deer just ran by, the claim is not *just like that* impugned by my companion's pointing out that the deer's running by is no longer happening. I *can* be wrong—maybe there was no deer, or I mistook something else's running by for a deer—but from the mere fact of fallibility it does not follow that there is a wholesale *problem of description* with respect to events. If anything, getting the description of events right would appear to be more difficult than describing my experience of those events: even if I am wrong about having seen a deer, I can feel pretty confident that I *seemed* to see a deer.

That the skeptic finds remarkable the very possibility of describing 'immediate mental living' is itself rather remarkable. I have already noted the way in which the skeptic's incredulity ignores the way such 'immediate' experience already involves some kind of awareness while the skeptic treats it as something more like a blind process. That the latter is mistaken is shown by the skeptic's very raising of worries concerning the fidelity of various descriptions in the first place. What I mean here is that the skeptic's own raising of doubts about the possibility of describing 'immediate mental living' betrays some *awareness* of that immediate experience in order then to worry that descriptions (necessarily) get *it* wrong. For Husserl, the kind of skepticism displayed by Watt and others turns out to be *self-refuting*. The problem facing the skeptic here is that he helps himself to so much in the way of talking about 'immediate mental living', 'reflectionally unmodified mental processes', and so forth. In raising worries about the potential for reflection to distort these 'living processes', the skeptic thereby displays a certain amount of knowledge concerning the domain in question: he knows enough to know that there is *something* which may or may not be distorted by reflection, but even *that* knowledge is itself gained through reflection. Again, the skeptic is relying upon reflection in order to challenge it: 'Therefore a *knowledge* of reflectionally unmodified mental processes, among them reflectionally unmodified reflections, is continuously presupposed, while at the same time the possibility of that knowledge is placed in question' (Husserl 1982: 186). Since doubts about the efficacy of reflection depend upon at least some *knowledge* of 'immediate mental living', maintaining such doubts is ultimately equivalent to maintaining that there is 'not the slightest ground of justification for the certainty that a reflectionally unmodified mental process and a reflection are given and can be given at all' (Husserl 1982: 186).

While the motivation for raising a general worry about accurately describing experience seems pretty thin, the question of accuracy is in many ways beside the point: when it comes to the kind of description I offered above, phenomenology is not especially interested in questions of accuracy or detail-by-detail fidelity. Consider again the police line-up worry raised above: suppose I could not tell which 'replay' of my experience 'lines up' with the original one, or I make a mistake and pick a replay where the cup is tilted ever so slightly more or the apparent colour is slightly different than when I first watched it. I would claim here that it is perfectly reasonable for the phenomenologist to respond with indifference to these kinds of worry, as nothing of importance to phenomenology hangs on this kind of fidelity. Recall that Husserl envisions phenomenology as devoted to determining the 'essentially characteristic structures of the soul'. The adumbrative character of perceptual experience is one such structural characteristic: insofar as perceptual experience is of or about spatial-material objects such as coffee cups, then that experience *must* be structured adumbratively; that is, there is no such thing as seeing all of a coffee cup all at once. Delineating that structure in the stretch of experience described in the opening exercise is insensitive to worries about perfect fidelity or precise replay-recognition: in *any* 'replay' of the cup-seeing experience, if it is indeed a replay of that *kind* of experience, its being adumbratively structured will be apparent (and any replay that is not adumbratively structured will be immediately weeded out as an impostor). Indeed, it does not matter whether or not I really even had the experience at all. According to Husserl, the phenomenologist need have no more interest in how he 'can make sure of the *existence* of those mental processes which serve him as foundations for his phenomenological findings than the geometer would be interested in how the existence of figures on the board or the models on the shelf could be methodologically established' (Husserl 1982: 183). So the question of what that experience of seeing the cup was really like, and even the question of whether I really had just now the experience of the cup, are ultimately beside the point for phenomenology. Its findings concerning essential structures are in a sense conditional: *if* what happened with me experientially was *seeing a rotating coffee cup, then* it was an adumbratively structured experience. (Notice the parallel to the observations above concerning Frege, logic, and *the* mind: if what that creature has are thoughts, beliefs, and so on, then their 'contents' must be logically structured in various ways, and this conditional holds whether or not the creature in question actually has a psychological life at all.)

5 EXPERIENCE AND OBJECTIVITY

The phenomenological skeptic raises a problem about description, where what it is to describe something is modelled on the act of describing something held in one's hand; that is, on the act of describing an *object*. Many objects are easily grasped in this literal sense, and so holding them before one's gaze offers little difficulty: the object can be held there for as long as one likes, returned to again and again, and so accurately, even if not exhaustively, characterized. With sufficient care and attention, the object can be described *as it really is*, where that means becoming clear about what features or properties it (objectively) has. Describing *experience* would appear to need some analogue of grasping an object in one's hand and subjecting it to one's gaze: if only an experience could be captured, held onto for closer inspection, *then* we could determine *its* features and properties—the features and properties my past experience *really* had (rather than, say, what I take it now to have had). As we have seen, experience turns out to be an elusive object that does not permit this kind of grasping and inspecting: unlike the objects grasped in the hand, experiences quickly fade, recede into the past, and do not admit of cross-checking or corroboration. Describing an experience turns out to be like describing an object that fades into thin air the moment it is as much as glimpsed.

The problem with this way of conceiving of phenomenological description lies not with where it ends—skepticism of various stripes about experience—but with where it begins, with its importation of a model of description based on the activity of describing an object. That is, the problem lies in thinking of the task of describing experience as one of ascertaining the *determinate features* of experience—the ones it really has (or had)— so as to validate one candidate description against any others. Recall the imagery deployed in the generation of skeptical worries concerning phenomenology. I asked how one could tell which 'replay' of one's past experience was faithful to the original version. Notice that such a question of fidelity assumes that there is *some definite way* the experience was the first time around, and so onto which one replay rather than others could be superimposed in some precise way. Perhaps the problem lies with that assumption, and perhaps challenging that assumption is not so much a concession to skepticism as a way of refusing its intrusions.

As long as we persist in casting experience as one more objective process among others, we will be nagged by the kinds of questions that give rise to skepticism about phenomenology. This is so because experience turns out to be a very peculiar sort of objective process—one whose features are not readily accessible or ascertainable, even to the one whose experience there is. The 'fish' that swim in the stream of experience are slippery indeed—so slippery that some skeptics doubt their existence altogether. But fish are objectively existing objects, denizens of the objective world, and so thinking of experience as consisting of so many fish imposes a model of determinacy (a fish has a determinate number of fins, is one colour rather than another, is flatter or rounder than another, and so on), foreign to the nature of experience. To refuse the category of objective thought is to 'recognize the indeterminate as a positive phenomenon' (Merleau-Ponty 1962: 6).

How does the recognition of the indeterminate bear upon the threat of skepticism about phenomenology? Consider the following example. I am out walking my two dogs in the field below my house. Half-way through the walk I realize that my younger dog, Polly, has disappeared from view. While I was not paying attention she started to lag behind, or veered off into the brush, or was lured to the river by some enticing smell. Since I like to keep my dogs in view, I set about trying to find her. Now, Polly has mostly black fur, with just a few splashes of white here and there, which makes her difficult to spot against dark backgrounds (dark foliage, long shadows, and so on), and she can all but disappear on an evening walk while being only a few feet away. As I conduct my search in the field, I carefully scan a shadowy stretch where I thought I heard a faint jingling of her collar tags. I stare intently, at first registering only foliage and shadows, then, just as I am about to begin looking elsewhere, I see Polly exactly where I have been looking for several seconds. Polly came into view not by running into the area where I had been looking, but by my noticing that she had been there all along. There is nothing unusual about this sort of experience—of something coming into view that was already there. Experiences of this kind can be produced more or less at will with the help of puzzle pictures of the *I Spy* and *Where's Waldo?* variety.

Despite their familiarity, if we try to describe these experiences, they become more rather than less puzzling. For example, once I have spotted Polly in the stretch where I have been looking, I cannot reproduce the Polly-less visual experience I had been having prior to spotting her. That is, I cannot make myself *not* see Polly once I have found her (except in a trivial way, by closing my eyes or turning away). More importantly, if I now try to think about my visual experience just prior to spotting Polly amidst the foliage, how am I to describe it? Was Polly *present* in my visual field? In one sense, the answer is clearly 'no'. If she were indeed present in my visual field, then I would have seen her all along. But does that mean that she was *absent* from my visual field? Although a negative answer to the question of presence would appear to necessitate a positive reply to the question of absence, drawing such a conclusion would render indistinguishable my experience of finding Polly where I have already been looking and finding her somewhere else. In the former case my discovery is accompanied by a sense of her already having been there to be seen, even prior to my noticing. My visual experience immediately prior to noticing Polly explicitly is *suspended* or *indeterminate* between Polly-there and Polly-not-there. (Notice that such suspension or indeterminacy does not apply to, say, my retinal image, which either includes Polly or does not, and someone else might be better positioned to ascertain that than I am.) Objective thought cannot countenance, let alone tolerate, this sort of indeterminacy, which is why it inevitably distorts the character of perceptual experience (or fails to grasp it at all).

The misalignment of consciousness and objective thought arises from the *belatedness* of the latter in relation to the former: objective thought is a *product* of perceptual experience, but one that effaces its perceptual origins. The hardened categories of objective thinking cannot 'grasp consciousness *in the act of learning*' (Merleau-Ponty 1962: 28). Such acts involving 'circumscribed ignorance', and 'still "empty" but already determinate' intentions cannot be resolved into a set of objective facts. Indeed, for Merleau-Ponty perceptual experience cannot be properly understood in terms of *facts* at all:

> There can be no question of describing perception itself as one of the facts thrown up in the world, since we can never fill up, in the picture of the world, that gap which we ourselves are, and by which it comes into existence for someone, since perception is the 'flaw' in this 'great diamond'. (Merleau-Ponty 1962: 207)

Notice, however, the proximity of Merleau-Ponty's notion of perception as the irremovable 'flaw' to the phenomenological skeptic's own position: if perceptual experience cannot be regarded 'as one of the facts thrown up in the world', then experience cannot be a proper object of *knowledge* (insofar as knowing something is a matter of knowing what is *objectively* the case). But that is just what the skeptic about phenomenology has maintained all along: the nature of experience is such that it cannot be properly or adequately known. In a way, Merleau-Ponty's emphasis on the indeterminacy of experience is grist for the skeptic's mill: the indeterminacy constitutive of experience makes it too elusive to be knowable in a way that might satisfy the skeptic. Indeed, even the ontological skeptic can glean some vindication from Merleau-Ponty's views, since both appear to agree that there is no *objective fact of the matter* regarding the character and content of perceptual experience. The ontological skeptic contends that consciousness does not consist of third-personally available objective facts, and Merleau-Ponty would appear to agree.

That there is a kind of truth in skepticism—that is, that the persistence of skepticism about phenomenology shows us something important about the nature of the things that phenomenology seeks to describe—shows that phenomenology always faces the challenge of establishing its *authority* as compared with more objectively oriented descriptions and conceptions of the world:

> The physicist's atoms will always appear more real than the historical and qualitative face of the world, the physico-chemical processes more real than the organic forms, the psychological atoms of empiricism more real than perceived phenomena, the intellectual atoms represented by the 'significations' of the Vienna Circle more real than consciousness, as long as the attempt is made to build up the shape of the world (life, perception, mind) instead of recognizing, as the source which stares us in the face and as the ultimate court of appeal in our knowledge of these things, our *experience* of them. (Merleau-Ponty 1962: 23)

Despite these challenges, the very end of Merleau-Ponty's remark suggests that what I have called here the truth in skepticism is not the end of the matter. Despite a kind of concession to the phenomenological skeptic, phenomenology can raise some challenges of its own.

6 Phenomenology's transcendental project

As we have seen, the skeptic challenges the legitimacy of phenomenology. The skeptic typically does so in order to motivate another, more objectively oriented way of investigating consciousness (or whatever is left of it following the ontological skeptic's manoeuvres). As Dennett puts it, 'the challenge is to construct a theory of mental events, using the data that scientific method permits' (Dennett 1992: 71), and what that method allows as data is what is in principle available to a third-person, neutral investigator. In this way, phenomenological skepticism is generally accompanied by a great deal in the way of *acceptance* regarding scientific data.[5] The availability of such facts for constructing 'a theory of mental events' is not something the phenomenological skeptic finds problematic or worrisome: skepticism about phenomenology is not equivalent to, or in the service of, a more thoroughgoing skepticism. Whatever problems are held by the skeptic to beset the project of describing experience are not ones that generalize to the gathering of scientific data: since the latter is a third-personal, intersubjectively verifiable set of procedures, none of the worries about 'introspection' so much as arise.

From the standpoint of phenomenology, this trust in, or acceptance of, scientific method and its resultant data invites the following question. Whence this confidence in scientific method? I do not mean to suggest that phenomenology challenges phenomenological skepticism by offering its own form of skepticism. Instead, what it interrogates is the *availability* of scientific facts and theories. In what way do such things become available *at all*? Notice, for example, how Merleau-Ponty's charge that science is 'dishonest' is based upon covering over or ignoring what it inevitably presupposes:

> Scientific points of view, according to which my existence is a moment of the world's, are always both naive and at the same time dishonest, because they take for granted, without explicitly mentioning it, the other point of view, namely that of consciousness, through which from the outset a world forms itself round me and begins to exist for me. (Merleau-Ponty 1962: ix)

Phenomenology is interested precisely in what Merleau-Ponty calls 'the other point of view'—the experience through which a world becomes available at all. By reflectively delineating the structure of that experience, phenomenology seeks to demonstrate how scientific objectivity is possible at all. These *transcendental* aspirations on phenomenology's part are generally coupled with a claim to the effect that they cannot be fulfilled by

---

[5] Not all forms of skepticism about phenomenology are accompanied by such a commitment to the general authority of science. Again, Derrida comes most readily to mind here.

scientific means: because science 'takes for granted' an objectively determinate world, it cannot account for how that world becomes available via pre-objective experience. Science can only study the latter objectively, and so must *use* the very methods whose possibility needs to be explained. In other words, phenomenology typically charges that science—in the guise of *scientific naturalism*—faces a problem of circularity: science cannot explain its own possibility scientifically.[6]

Taken on its own, the charge of circularity may be met by the committed naturalist with little more than a shrug of the shoulders. A philosophical naturalist of a Quinean stripe may simply *refuse* these sorts of transcendental questions regarding how science is possible: any general theory of what I am here calling 'availability' smacks of the kind of 'first philosophy' which the naturalist rejects. Any question of how we get from experience to scientific theories can be answered only by using precisely those same scientific theories: 'Analyze theory-building how we will, we all must start in the middle' (Quine 1960: 4). Rather than circularity, Quine and others speak instead of the 'containment' of epistemology within natural science (see Quine 1969: 83). Such containment precludes the kind of transcendental project that phenomenology envisages: there is no project of explaining how we get from here (experience) to there (science) that does not already make use of where we end up. Whatever kind of circularity phenomenology exposes is something which the Quinean more or less happily accepts as unavoidable.

Notice that at this point the stand-off between phenomenology and its critics does not turn on conflating phenomenology's methods with some form of 'introspection', nor even does it turn on questions concerning the accuracy or reliability of *any* method for describing experience. Instead, I would suggest that here the debate does not turn on some flagrant misunderstanding of what phenomenology is all about. The naturalist understands all too well what phenomenology is up to here, and questions the validity of that enterprise. Insofar as *methods* are at issue here, what the naturalist denies is the efficacy of the kind of *excluding* and *bracketing* to which I appealed in our opening exercise; what the naturalist denies is that such techniques leave something—the experience in and of itself—whose structure can be delineated *independently* of what we hold to be true about the world. Rather than some caricature-laden notion of introspection, *this* kind of phenomenological skeptic zeroes in on phenomenology's central methodological commitment: Husserl's famous *epoché*.[7] In 'Epistemology Naturalized', Quine asks at

---

[6] In addition to the Merleau-Ponty passage just cited, see also (Husserl 1965). After noting the questions and problems that arise in reflecting on the possibility of scientific knowledge in relation to 'the subjective flow of consciousness', Husserl writes: 'To expect from natural science itself the solution of any one of the problems inherent in it as such—thus inhering through and through from beginning to end—or even merely to suppose that it could contribute to the solution of such a problem any premises whatsoever, is to be involved in a vicious circle' (Husserl 1965: 88–9).

[7] Although later phenomenology is sometimes almost defined by its hostility to the *epoché* (for example, Taylor Carman writes that 'most of the major representatives of that movement rejected the *epoché* as a phenomenologically unmotivated dogma' (Carman 2005: 76)), I have argued elsewhere that this way of characterizing later phenomenology's relation to Husserl misses the way in which his original notion of *epoché* continues to inform their own procedures. See (Cerbone 2011) for further discussion.

one point: 'But why all this creative reconstruction, all this make-believe?' (Quine 1969: 75). A complete defence of phenomenology's methods requires not just a debunking of caricature-laden and misfiring critiques of introspection, but an answer to Quine's question. Phenomenology must show that its methods amount to a great deal more than the kind of 'make-believe' that scientific naturalism derides.

At the same time, phenomenology may very well level its own charge of make-believe at the scientific naturalist who questions the very possibility of phenomenology.[8] Consider again Quine's image of the 'mutual containment' of epistemology and natural science: insofar as epistemology is contained within natural science, it studies the human subject in a resolutely third-personal way. Epistemology, for Quine, studies 'how the human subject of our study posits bodies and projects his physics from his data.' In doing so, Quine continues:

> ... we appreciate that our position in the world is just like his. Our very epistemological enterprise, therefore, and the psychology wherein it is a component chapter, and the whole of natural science wherein psychology is a component book—all this is our own construction or projection from stimulations like those we were meting out to our epistemological subject. (Quine 1969: 83)

It is not clear how the investigator is to maintain the kind of appreciation which Quine invokes here. For one thing, the 'stimulations' Quine mentions here are themselves wholly physical and so no less 'constructions' or 'projections' than more commonplace objects such as tables and chairs. Thus, it is unclear just what the investigator is supposed to appreciate here. If stimulations are no less constructs or projections than any other denizen of the physical world, in what sense are they the *basis* for projecting the latter? The thought that 'All of this is projected from sensory stimulations' dissolves upon the realization that sensory stimulations are themselves among 'all of this' that is being projected. Indeed, the very idea of 'projection' or 'construction' breaks down here, and so it is not clear just what kind of explanatory project naturalized epistemology offers. That one kind of construct or projection has *any* kind of primacy, such that it constitutes 'what I have to go on' in forming a larger conception of the world, is, by the naturalist's own lights, a kind of make-believe.

But there is a further problem, a deeper level of make-believe, in the kind of appreciation that Quine's investigator is supposed to maintain: namely, that what we have or undergo or endure as 'human subjects' is properly understood *solely* in terms of 'stimulations'. Consider again our opening exercise. To be sure, there is a vast catalogue of

---

[8] I would suggest that Dennett's notion of *heterophenomenology* is a prime example of such naturalistic make-believe, as the entire method is predicated on initially 'bracketing' the idea that the research subjects are indeed conscious at all. That Dennett requires that 'we have to keep an open mind about whether our apparent subjects are liars, zombies, parrots dressed up in people suits, but we don't have to risk upsetting them by advertising the fact' (Dennett 1992: 83) would appear to invite Quine's question, but levelled from the perspective of phenomenology. See (Cerbone 2003) and (Zahavi 2007) for further discussion of Dennett's problematic relation to more traditional conceptions of phenomenology.

stimulations involved in my seeing the rotating coffee cup: light is reflecting off the surface of the cup and striking my retinas in intricate ways, nerves are thereby being stimulated, and so on. But none of this figures into the description of my experience of *seeing*: I see the coffee cup; I see it adumbratively, where further possible views make up the *horizon* of any momentary look; the back of the cup comes predictably into view as it rotates. What Quine and others' fixation on stimulations omits entirely is this kind of description, and so this sense of ourselves as not just human subjects in the sense of being objects of scientific study but as precisely *subjects of experience*. As Merleau-Ponty complains: 'Objective thought is unaware of the subject of perception' (Merleau-Ponty 1962: 207). Indeed, this lack of awareness constitutes a kind of forgetfulness on the part of the researcher, who

> describes sensations and their substratum as one might describe the fauna of a distant land—without being aware that he himself perceives, that he is the perceiving subject and that perception as he lives it belies everything he says of perception in general. For, seen from the inside, perception owes nothing to what we know in other ways about the world, about *stimuli* as physics describes them and about the sense organs as described by biology. (Merleau-Ponty 1962: 207)

As we have seen, phenomenological reflection seeks to describe how things are 'seen from the inside', though without thereby lapsing into introspection and without merely concerning oneself with the details of particular episodes of experience. Such descriptions do not traffic in 'stimuli', 'sensory irritations', or the various messy details of our physiology. While not discounting the reality of such details, phenomenology insists upon the legitimacy and significance of its modes of descriptions, which concentrate on what I have referred to throughout as the experience in and of itself. One avenue of defence against naturalistically inspired skeptical assaults on such modes of description is to expose what is perhaps naturalism's greatest feat of make-believe: that there is no such inside view at all.

References

Carman, T. (2005), 'On the Inescapability of Phenomenology', in D. W. Smith and A. Thomasson (eds.) *Phenomenology and the Philosophy of Mind* (Oxford: Oxford University Press).

Cerbone, D. R. (2003), 'Phenomenology: Straight and Hetero', in C. G. Prado (ed.) *A House Divided* (Amherst, NY: Humanity Books).

—— (2011), 'Methods in Phenomenology after Husserl', in S. Luft and S. Overgaard (eds.) *The Routledge Guidebook to Phenomenology* (London: Routledge).

Dennett, D. (1992), *Consciousness Explained* (Boston, MA: Little, Brown and Company).

Derrida, J. (1973), *Speech and Phenomena and Other Essays on Husserl's Theory of Signs* (Evanston, IL: Northwestern University Press).

—— (1978), *Writing and Difference* (Chicago: The University of Chicago Press).

Diamond, C. (1991), *The Realistic Spirit: Wittgenstein, Philosophy, and the Mind* (Cambridge, MA: MIT Press).

Frege, G. (1991), *Collected Papers on Mathematics, Logic, and Philosophy* (Oxford: Blackwell).

Husserl, E. (1965), *Phenomenology and the Crisis of Philosophy* (New York: Harper and Row).

——— (1972), *Ideas: General Introduction to Pure Phenomenology* (New York: Collier Books, 4th printing).

——— (1982), *Ideas Pertaining to a Pure Phenomenology and to Phenomenological Philosophy: First Book* (Dordrecht: Kluwer Academic Publishers).

——— (1995), *Cartesian Meditations* (Dordrecht: Kluwer Academic Publishers).

Merleau-Ponty, M. (1962), *Phenomenology of Perception* (London: Routledge).

Quine, W. V. O. (1960), *Word and Object* (Cambridge, MA: MIT Press).

——— (1969), *Ontological Relativity and Other Essays* (New York: Columbia University Press).

Sartre, J.-P. (1956), *Being and Nothingness: An Essay on Phenomenological Ontology* (New York: Philosophical Library).

Zahavi, D. (2007), 'Killing the Straw Man: Dennett and Phenomenology,' *Phenomenology and Cognitive Science* 6: 21–43.

CHAPTER 2

TRANSCENDENTAL PHENOMENOLOGY AND THE SEDUCTIONS OF NATURALISM: SUBJECTIVITY, CONSCIOUSNESS, AND MEANING

STEVEN CROWELL

1 NATURE AND SPIRIT

In the 1920s Edmund Husserl turned his attention to issues that he would group under the heading 'Nature and spirit'. With Wilhelm Dilthey in mind, Husserl conceived these investigations as contributions to the philosophical grounding of the natural and human sciences. Transcendental phenomenology would clarify the sense and achievement of these sciences, defending the distinctive rationality of each while refusing to grant them the foundational status they take on in philosophical naturalism or historicism. These studies are among the richest in Husserl's corpus, yet they produced a number of paradoxes, most notably the 'paradox of human subjectivity' (Husserl 1954: 182/178): the subject is a being in the world—one entity among others—but is simultaneously the transcendental origin of that world, an 'absolute' to which the world is 'relative'.[1]

Husserl sought ways to mitigate such paradoxes. From the perspective of natural science, for instance, the subject—and so the paradox—can be made to disappear. As a natural entity, subjectivity appears as *psyche*—a 'stratum' of the 'animate organism'

---

[1] On the paradox of subjectivity, see Carr (1999). On the distinction between 'absolute' and 'relative' here, see Husserl (1950), pp. 80–4, 91–3/94–8, 109–12, and Boehm (1968).

studied by psychology, which accounts for it in terms of 'psychophysical conditionalities' and ultimately natural causality.[2] As it appears within the human sciences, however, the subject is *Geist* (mind, spirit), a *person*, the entity that expresses itself in the meaningful forms of language and culture, the understanding of which is precisely the concern of such sciences. Thus, unlike the psyche, the person remains both subject and object of the human sciences, and so the paradox becomes pressing: the person is an entity *in* the world, but seemingly also that whereby the world and everything in it gets its meaning. Thus it must somehow be *self*-constituting.

But Husserl believed that the person could not be self-constituting. For one thing, persons are natural beings; for another, they depend on traditions. Both nature and tradition belong to what Husserl calls the 'pre-given world'—that is, they are *presupposed* in the person's capacity to give meaning to the world—and so a transcendental grounding of the human sciences must provide an account of such pre-givenness. This demand shapes transcendental phenomenology as Husserl conceived it: namely, as the science of an 'absolute consciousness', prior to both psyche and person. Despite common opinion to the contrary, later phenomenologists such as Heidegger and Merleau-Ponty did not reject the project of transcendental phenomenology; rather, they denied that a phenomenology of *consciousness* was adequate to the task. How, then, did they manage to avoid the worries that led Husserl to the notion of 'absolute' consciousness in the first place? Partly it was by avoiding what I will call a 'naturalistic assumption' in Husserl's conception of the relation between consciousness and the person. Once this assumption is identified and bracketed, the idea that the person (*Geist*, mind) is the self-constituting transcendental subject ceases to appear paradoxical, and what is most valuable in transcendental phenomenology is preserved.

In this chapter I will attempt to extract the defensible core of Husserl's transcendental phenomenology by means of a twofold argument. On the positive side, I will argue (in Section 3) that Husserl's analysis of the person as an essentially practical, embodied subject *suffices*, in spite of his own assessment, as an account of the transcendentally constituting subject. On the negative side, I will argue (in Section 4) that Husserl's assessment that it does *not* suffice rests upon an illicit 'naturalistic' assumption that informs his identification of the person with the *human being*.[3] I will conclude (in Section 5) with some suggestions for how the topics of embodiment and action—and the attendant concept of 'nature'—might be approached by a transcendental phenomenology that dispenses with the naturalistic assumption. But first (in Section 2), the general character of a specifically *phenomenological* transcendental philosophy must be outlined.

---

[2] Husserl (1952), pp. 281–302/294–316, argues that a complete reduction of the psyche to nature is in principle impossible, but his argument runs into some problems (see Crowell 2010b).

[3] I adopt the term 'person' as a convenience, since in Husserl's texts it designates the site where the relevant distinctions between the transcendental and the empirical show up. For various reasons, however, it is not a particularly suitable term, which is why Heidegger resorted to the neologism *Dasein*. Though the present chapter will concern itself with Husserl in particular, the points at issue are, I believe, of broader relevance. They appear, for instance, in contemporary efforts to establish just what the term 'mind' ought to cover (embodied mind, extended mind), the question of whether phenomenal consciousness is 'intrinsically' intentional, and the relation between biology and consciousness. (See,

2 The two motivating strands of
transcendental phenomenology

Appreciating the argument to come depends on recognizing that transcendental phenomenology arises from two distinct intellectual strands: a *Geltungs*-theoretical (or normative) strand and an experience-theoretical (or psychological) strand. It is this combination that distinguishes it from other forms of transcendental philosophy, including Kant's and the neo-Kantian and analytic versions that proceed by way of construction and transcendental argumentation.[4] In Husserl's *Logical Investigations* (1900–1) the first strand set the terms of the problem—to clarify the nature of logical laws in such a way as to make their universal validity (*Geltung*) intelligible—while the second strand suggested the solution. Agreeing with neo-Kantians like Paul Natorp that logical validity cannot be explained through empirical psychology, Husserl nevertheless rejected the neo-Kantian claim that such validity is primitive. Even if it cannot be explained psychologically, the normativity of logical laws can be *clarified* by means of a 'descriptive psychology' that shows how such laws express what is essential to signifying acts (acts of judgement) as potential bearers of truth. Despite his critique of logical psychologism, then, Husserl made common cause with those who sought a basis for epistemology in conscious experience, and phenomenology was born of this marriage between *Geltungslogik* and psychology.

By 1913, when Husserl introduced his specifically transcendental version of phenomenology in the first volume of *Ideas* (Husserl 1950), he had recognized that the puzzling phenomenon of 'validity' is not limited to the *a priori* sciences of logic and mathematics. Indeed, it is co-extensive with experience of the world, with experience of 'transcendence', as such. Everyday experience in the 'natural attitude' takes the world for granted as an infinite horizon of real being, and this consciousness of real (or 'transcendent') being already contains the kind of validity claim that made *logical* objectivity difficult to explain empirically. To experience something as real is not merely to undergo some conscious content but to undergo it in a normative light; that is, to take it in as governed by certain rules or standards that conditionally establish the course of future experiences. To have the perceptual experience as of a red apple on the table, for instance, one must be responsive to the normative distinction between what *truly* is and what merely *appears* to be—to a validity claim inherent in the perception, a claim to a certain normative necessity. My actual perception is what it is only because it involves awareness that if

for instance, Clark 2008, Crane 2001, Strawson 2009, Siewert 1998, and Searle 1994, for a range of views. For a transcendental approach that contrasts in interesting ways with Husserl's, see Cassam 1997.) Unfortunately we will not be able to pursue these connections in detail here.

[4] On the distinctive character of transcendental phenomenology, see Mohanty (1985). On the relation to neo-Kantianism in particular, see Crowell (2001), Part I, 'Reconfiguring Transcendental Logic.'

the apple is real, further perceptions *must* occur in certain specific ways and not others. And as in the case of logical validity, any empirical account of this normative moment will beg the question: I cannot appeal to the actual course of psychological experience to account for a rule that establishes how such experience ought to go. Or again, to perceive something as an *apple* is to perceive it in light of what Husserl calls an 'essence', a norm that prescribes a further set of possible experiences that are appropriate to apples under these specific conditions and excludes others that are not.[5] Once Husserl had recognized this normative moment in all intentional experience, phenomenology became 'transcendental'; its task was to clarify how all 'transcendent objects' (all 'real unities') are 'constituted' as valid 'unities of meaning' for consciousness (Husserl 1950: 106/128).

But if transcendental phenomenology concerns the constitution of all transcendence, it can no longer be understood as psychology—'descriptive' or otherwise—since the very consciousness to which such psychology appeals, the psyche, is itself a transcendent entity, constituted by certain norms of validity. It is here that the experience-theoretical project of clarifying the *constitution* of transcendence demands the method of phenomenological *reduction*. Without providing a full account here,[6] it is necessary to say a few words on this topic if the tension between naturalism and transcendentalism in Husserl's thought is to be properly understood.

To begin with, it is misleading to speak of 'the' reduction, since there are at least three distinct aspects, whose independence from one another is a matter of some controversy: the *epoché*, the transcendental–phenomenological reduction, and the eidetic reduction. The *epoché* is an act of will whereby I set aside all commitments, or 'positings', with regard to some matter up for phenomenological analysis—for instance, my perception of an apple. In reflecting on that experience I 'bracket' the 'existence' of the apple; that is, I do not deny or doubt that the apple exists (or that the tree on which it hangs or the table on which it sits exists), but I 'make no use' of that fact. Instead, I engage in the reflective task of describing *how* it gives itself in my first-person experience of it—taking note, for instance, of the fact that it *presents itself as* existing. The point of the *epoché*, then, is primarily negative: it precludes me from appealing in my analysis to *any* third-person explanatory *theories* of the experience in question (for instance, causal-genetic ones), since any such theory necessarily posits the existence of both *explanans* and *explanandum*. The *epoché* expresses transcendental phenomenology's commitment to the analytic autonomy of first-person experience.

But the field of experience thus singled out is by no means devoid of complexity and structure, and the transcendental–phenomenological reduction highlights this fact. Here the notion of phenomenological 'constitution' gains its sense, for this reduction discloses the *necessary* connections between the way things appear and the subjectivity

---

[5] This point has been at the centre of recent debates over the nature of perceptual 'content'—in particular, the question of whether such content is 'conceptual' has largely to do with whether (and if so how) it involves a normative structure (see McDowell 1996 and more recently 2009, Peacocke 1998, Dreyfus 2007, and McDowell 2007).

[6] For a relatively clear discussion of the issues, see Mohanty (1997), pp. 9–11, *et pass.*

to which they appear. If, for instance, I reflect on my perception of this apple, I note that the apple is given as a whole but that only one side of it appears while others are occluded. Further, the apple is given as the same even as other sides of it come into view. But reflection also shows that the order and connection that defines the object of such experience necessarily makes reference to the subject whose experience it is. This side of the apple is currently appearing because *I* am seeing it from here; these other sides come to appear because *I* am now seeing it from another angle, and so on. In Husserlian terms, the object that appears, precisely in the various *ways* that it appears in experiences of various sorts, is called the 'noema', while the experiencings themselves in and through which these various self-showings become manifest are called 'noeses' (Husserl 1950: 179–88/211–21).[7] It is the task of the transcendental–phenomenological reduction to focus the analysis on the laws and structures informing these noetic–noematic correlations.[8]

In so doing, it reveals the 'constitution' of objects of experience. Given the *epoché*, constitution must be clearly distinguished from material *composition* and from causal *effectuation*. These are matters for empirical inquiry, whether everyday or scientific. Reflection on the noetic–noematic correlations within first-person experience, in contrast, analyzes the specific conditions that enable something to appear *as* an apple, or as a real thing, or as a cause, theory, baseball bat, person, or whatever. The central claim of Husserl's transcendental phenomenology—one that is endorsed in some version by all the major phenomenologists—is that constitution involves 'laws' that are neither logical nor natural, and that the meaning or experiential 'content' thus constituted is *prior* to any scientific theorizing, since the latter presupposes that its objects have been constituted as meaningful. Thus the reduction discloses a 'transcendental' field of being—that is, a field of meaning constitution in which beings of any sort can show themselves as what they are. But in doing so it also discloses a 'transcendental' *subjectivity* that cannot simply be identified with any constituted ('transcendent') entity, any natural or cultural being.

With that, we are returned to the relation between the *Geltungs*-theoretical and the experience-theoretical strands that define the transcendental phenomenogical concept of constitution. For while both are necessary to the concept, they can pull in different directions, thus opening a fissure within it.[9] On the one hand, the experience-theoretical

---

[7] The fact that Husserl acknowledges descriptive access to experiencings (or noeses) as such lines him up with those who, in recent debates, hold that mental processes, such as thinking, willing, and perceiving, each have a distinctive phenomenal character, not reducible to the character of what such thinking or willing is *of*. For the initial arguments in favour of such 'cognitive phenomenology', see Siewert (1998). For a glimpse at the contemporary debate, see Bayne and Montague (2012).

[8] The third aspect of the reduction—reduction to the *eidos* or 'essence' of the phenomenon in question—points to the fact that *transcendental* phenomenological analysis is not finally interested in what is *particular* to any given noetic–noematic correlation, but rather in what is *necessary* to its type. Though all of Husserl's analyses are governed by the eidetic reduction to 'essence', the difficulties associated with this notion are not germane to the present argument, and are hardly unique to transcendental phenomenology. Any philosophical analysis is concerned with 'essences' in this sense.

[9] Since both are necessary, I cannot accept Nam-In Lee's argument (2010) that they belong to different kinds of transcendental phenomenology: static and genetic.

strand is *motivated* by the normative one: validity and meaning cannot be accounted for without reference to a subject who is able to experience such claims, respond to the normative. But experience conceived as 'consciousness' can be investigated in ways that break altogether free from the problem of validity.[10] Thus, when Husserl is focused on the experience-theoretical strand he can write that

> the transcendentally 'absolute' which we have brought about by the reductions [*sc.* the correlation between noesis and noema] is, in truth, not what is ultimate; it is something which constitutes itself in a certain profound and completely peculiar sense of its own and which has its primal source in what is ultimately and truly absolute. (Husserl 1950: 163/193)

The truly absolute that Husserl is here talking about is 'phenomenological time'—an 'absolute' that is prior to *all* meaning and is at best *proto*-intentional (see Brough 1972). On the other hand, the *Geltungs*-theoretical strand is *grounded* in the experiential one: validity is to be clarified as an aspect of consciousness, the reduced correlation of noesis and noema. Yet an account of the constitution of meaning seems to require more than a phenomenology of consciousness. As Husserl acknowledges, even perceptual intentionality can be understood only in the context of practices, and so of embodied, social subjects whose constitutive life seems irreducible to noetic–noematic structures, concatenations of conscious acts or experiences.

If this potential fissure in the transcendental concept of constitution is allowed to open up, the paradox of subjectivity results. From the *Geltungs*-theoretical perspective, 'subjectivity' is a property of that entity in whose experience unities of meaning are constituted, and such an entity is necessarily practical, embodied, and social. From the experience-theoretical perspective, however, practical, embodied, and social subjectivity is the *person*—apparently a transcendent entity, part of the natural world and determined by a particular culture and history. If transcendental subjectivity must constitute *all* transcendence, then apparently it must be a subjectivity free of all transcendence, such as the absolute temporal flow of consciousness is supposed to be. But this clears up the paradox only if such subjectivity has the resources to constitute meaning—which, being pre-personal, it does not. Thus the fissure in the concept of transcendental constitution appears to force a choice between a paradoxically self-constituting person or an absolute consciousness that seems too anemic to constitute a world. By examining a related paradox—which Husserl calls the 'paradox of the pre-given world'—however, I will argue that the two strands can be reconciled. One need only reject a naturalistic assumption in Husserl's conception of the person that makes it *seem* as though personalistic self-constitution were impossible.

---

[10] This is especially the case when 'phenomenology' is simply *identified* with a description of the 'what it is like' aspect of experience. This seems to be how John Searle understands it in his debate with Hubert Dreyfus (see Searle 2000). The phrase was introduced in Thomas Nagel's classic article, 'What is it Like to be a Bat?' (Nagel 1974).

3 THE PARADOX OF THE PRE-GIVEN WORLD

To say that the world is 'pre-given' is to say that it is experienced as having already been there, in these and those ways, before I take up what is given to me to do. That is, the world is not just 'the given', or 'what is', but rather what is presupposed as being in these and those distinct ways in every experience that I, as engaged in this world, have. The pre-given world—or lifeworld (*Lebenswelt*)—is thus quite distinct from the logical idea of the world as 'everything that is the case', since everything that is the case is in no way experienced, let alone experienced as pre-given. The phenomenological task is to describe how 'world' shows itself in experience and to analyze its constitution. In carrying out part of this analysis in a text from 1931, Husserl describes an apparent paradox that seems to threaten the central thesis of transcendental phenomenology. The thesis holds that 'there is for us no other world than the one that gains its ontic meaning [*Seinssinn*] in us and from out of our own consciousness' (Husserl 2008: 444; all translations from this volume are my own), and the paradox concerns what is to be understood by 'us' and 'our own consciousness' here. Less colloquially, how must we understand the subject of the pre-given world?

Husserl begins with 'I in my being as ego'—that is, with I who am conscious 'of my existence [*Dasein*] as human being in the world'. Under the reduction, I am 'the ego of pure acts'—that is, I reflect on my experience in a purely first-person way, without assuming anything that goes beyond the descriptive content of my self-experience. But how is such an ego properly described? One straightforward suggestion would be to describe it as Husserl typically describes the person: namely, as a *practical* ego.[11] If we follow that route, then transcendental constitution will be modelled on action. Indeed, only four years earlier Heidegger had proposed that the transcendental subject be approached through a phenomenology of action. In *Sein und Zeit* (1927) he had sought to illuminate the phenomenon of 'world' by describing the entity which 'each of us is' in its 'everydayness' (Heidegger 1962: 36–7/H15–16). Heidegger argued that the norms that make a context of meaning possible and thus constitute a world are immanent to the practices in which 'everyday' Dasein is engaged. Husserl objected that Heidegger's phenomenology did not reach the transcendental level at all but remained a presupposition-laden philosophical anthropology.[12] He had many reasons for this view, but in this 1931 text he tries to support the claim with an argument: namely, that if we model constitution on practice, an infinite regress results.

In its simplest form the argument runs as follows. If the transcendental subject is practical, then constitution of meaning has the character of an action. Now 'every action

---

[11] See Husserl (1952), §50. 'In a very broad sense, we can also denote the personal or motivational attitude as the *practical* attitude' (Husserl 1952, pp. 189–90/199).

[12] For most of the materials pertaining to this matter, see Husserl (1997). For a critical discussion, see Crowell (2002b).

[*Handlung*] produces beings on the basis of what is already in being [*schon Seiendem*].' But given the thesis of transcendental constitution—namely that 'being as such is something acquired [*Erwerb*]'—this leads to 'an infinite regress' (Husserl 2008: 441). Transcendental constitution thus requires that there be a doing (*Tun*) that is not an acting:

> The being of the world for us is always already being with an ontic meaning [*Seinsinn*] that has been constituted through action; yet unless action is absurdly to be based on previous action *in infinitum*, it must originate from a constitution that is not yet an action. (Husserl 2008: 444)[13]

'How', Husserl asks, 'are we to clear up this paradox?'

In elaborating his argument against Heidegger's claim that *Dasein* is the transcendental subject, Husserl reveals his own reasons for holding that the *person* cannot be the transcendental subject.[14] It will thus be instructive to examine this regress—and the nature of the paradox to which it leads—more closely, since it shows just how *far* Husserl goes in linking *Geltungs*-theoretical constitution of meaning with practical subjectivity (thus testifying indirectly to the possibility of identifying the person with transcendental subjectivity), while also suggesting why his experience-theoretical solution to the paradox of the pre-given world no longer operates in the realm of transcendental constitution at all.

Acting involves two aspects, each of which yields a regress. First, 'to carry out acts is to busy oneself *with* something [*sich beschäftigen mit etwas*]'—for instance, Husserl mentions a 'hammer' (Husserl 2008: 438). When I use a hammer, according to Husserl, it holds (*gilt*) for me in a specific ontic modality (it is *real*) and it holds as something (it is *a hammer*). Not every busying myself with something is an action, however. The pencil I gnaw on as I drive the nail is not part of any action. Busying myself with something is *acting* only if a second aspect is present: I must be *trying* to do something with it ('Ich habe damit etwas vor'). As Husserl defines it, *vorhaben* means that 'prior to actual having' I am 'oriented toward a having which, however, is not already an actual having' (Husserl 2008: 439). Trying (*Streben, Wollen*) thus involves something 'had' in advance; I must have something definite in mind: to make a birdhouse, to draft environmental protection legislation. With the completion of the action, the 'having in advance'

---

[13] Husserl's language reminds one of Fichte's *Tathandlung*—a connection that has been explored by Gethmann (1974) and Kern (1964).

[14] The claim here is *not* that the person cannot be considered as a transcendentally constituting subject *at all*. Husserl employs the concept of a 'transcendental person' to denote precisely the constitutive activities of practical, embodied, social subjectivity as such. See, for instance, Husserl (2002), pp. 198–201. The point is that such subjectivity and its accomplishments are, for Husserl, made possible or constituted by—'founded' upon—a deeper, pre-personal stratum of transcendental subjectivity, namely, pure consciousness. From the point of view of the transcendental reduction, then, the idea of a 'transcendental person' still involves some 'positive' presuppositions; indeed, the naturalistic assumption we are tracking belongs among these, though Husserl himself does not recognize the *naturalistic* character of his understanding of the 'founded' character of the person. It is this that many later phenomenologists will reject.

becomes 'having itself' (*Selbsthabe*): the birdhouse is there, the bill is put to a vote. Action thus yields a 'lasting acquisition' (*bleibender Erwerb*). This lasting acquisition can then become the basis for further action: I can busy myself with the birdhouse under the *Vorhabe* of trying to make an environmentally friendly garden, which latter can in turn become a lasting acquisition in *Selbsthabe*, and so on.

This notion of lasting acquisition is the crux of Husserl's argument that viewing action as the model for transcendental constitution involves an infinite regress. Both in *that with which* it busies itself and in what it is *trying to do*, action presupposes something already constituted as a lasting acquisition. Yet in the present text—and arguably throughout his work—Husserl conceives action so broadly that it covers the entire sphere of the personal world. Not only is making or fabricating a case of acting; so too are perceiving, discoursing, and other forms of cognitive opinion-formation. Indeed, *all ontic meaning*, all 'being' (*Seiendes*) is, for Husserl, a lasting acquisition of acting.

Perceiving, for instance—'the simplest perceptual considering' of something—is a kind of action (Husserl 2008: 440). Whether it occurs within a more encompassing action (as when, in making the birdhouse, I move to get a better look at a nail that I notice might be bent), or is done for its own sake (as when I am curious to know what the inside of my computer monitor looks like), 'perceptual considering' is a kind of *trying*, 'an 'acting' ['handelndes'] fore-having... a striving toward the entity 'itself', toward the actualization of it itself in its perceptual selfhood' (Husserl 2008: 440). When perceptual considering is complete, a lasting acquisition has been established within the flux of my conscious life, an *opinion* to which I can return, something that remains mine 'even when I am asleep' (Husserl 2008: 441). I now know that the nail is bent, I 'have' *it*. But such *Selbsthabe* is possible only because I *had* it in my *Vorhabe*—that is, my recognition (*Kenntnis*) of this nail presupposes the familiarity (*Bekanntheit*) of nails as such. Perception is thus caught in the regress of action: perceiving is not simply opening one's eyes but is cognition as recognition; seeing is *trying* to see more or better. The perceptually pre-given world is thus always a lasting acquisition of action. But if perceptual meaning arises on the basis of previously acquired meaning, what sort of trying accounts for this prior meaning?

A regress also appears if we consider that *with which* acting busies itself. In order to make a birdhouse, I busy myself with a hammer; but this hammer has itself been made, and in that process the maker busied herself with wood and metal. These, in turn, are lasting acquisitions of certain processes of production, and so on. Now it might appear that this regress could be stopped at something that was not itself the lasting acquisition of an action—mere 'matter'—but from the phenomenological point of view this will not work. What action busies itself with is never just *something*; it is something *in particular*, something with a specific meaning. Invoking matter will not suffice, since the regress concerns the immanent meaning of the act itself, not the countless things that a third-person investigation could ascertain as being causally involved in acting. I cannot busy myself with mere matter. Were there such a thing it would do me no good in building my birdhouse. To do that I need a *hammer*, which must be constituted as such; and to make a hammer I need wood and metal, which must themselves be constituted as appropriate for the job.

Nor is it enough that there merely *be* such a thing; to use it I must be able to *recognize* it as wood, metal, a hammer. And as in the case of perception, such recognition is possible only if I have prior familiarity with things of that type. When I act, a 'framework of general-typical familiarities' is always pre-given, and without it I could grasp no particular thing as anything in particular. My acting—my fabricating, perceiving, and cognizing—adds to this framework by establishing lasting acquisitions of meaning. But how are we to understand its *origin*? As Husserl puts it: 'The difficulty does not lie in the fact that new things can be formed *in infinitum*; it is rather that the new always presupposes the already long-familiar, thus what has been acquired previously' (Husserl 2008: 444).

The issue, then, is this: if the person is transcendental subjectivity, meaning is constituted through action—through perceiving, fabricating, and cognizing—within a pre-given world whose meaning, in turn, derives from previous perceiving, fabricating, and cognizing. From the *Geltungs*-theoretical perspective this is not a problem: the pre-given world is *always already* a world where meaning has been established. Being is constituted, yet always on the basis of being; meaning and normativity are possible only where there is already meaning and normativity. But if from an experience-theoretical (genetic) perspective this regress is seen as a problem, then we must look for a pre-personal (pre-practical) subjectivity to preserve the thesis of transcendental constitution. The whole pre-given world seems to point back to an entirely different sort of subjective experience, to a 'pre-being and a doing that makes beings familiar in advance' (Husserl 2008: 444-5). The question for transcendental phenomenology thus becomes:

> [How can] an originary acquiring be made intelligible and be grasped with insight as necessary, in which 'thing' and 'fore-having' are not already worldly but rather arise purely out of sources of subjectivity—as the 'primal establishment of worldhood'? (Husserl 2008: 445)

In other words, if we are not simply to *posit* some 'first' meaning but are to retain the thesis that all meaning is constituted, then within the experience-theoretical perspective of a genetic phenomenology terms like *Erwerben*, *Sache*, and *Vorhaben* 'must change their meaning fundamentally':

> Acquiring would still refer to a doing, but it cannot be a willing-planning sort of doing, doing in the usual sense (one that actualizes fore-havings, purposes, represented and posited goals, etc.). Its material cannot be a thing, then, something that already is—if being itself is supposed to have the meaning of something acquired, something that gains the meaning 'in being' only through an originary acquiring. (Husserl 2008: 445)

According to Husserl, then, the regress argument shows that transcendental constitution cannot be understood on the model of *praxis*—*not* because practical constitution presupposes a pre-given *perceptual* world (the perceptual world *is* constituted practically), but because *praxis* cannot be self-constituting. And for this reason the person cannot be the transcendental subject.

However, Husserl's awkward appeal to 'pre-being', and to a transcendental subject who 'does', but does not 'act', should warn us of a possible problem in his conception.

Indeed, it is precisely here that the *Geltungs*-theoretical and the experience-theoretical strands of transcendental phenomenology are allowed to come apart, with the latter demanding a level of subjectivity that is both phenomenologically accessible in first-person experience and yet *prior to* the constitution of 'valid' meaning—a pure 'consciousness', the analysis of whose structure would provide the ultimate basis for personalistic constitution and so put a halt to the regress. But this, in turn, seems to land us in the terrain of a psychology of consciousness that is neither the exclusive province of—nor best carried out by—phenomenology.[15]

With this in mind, we should recall that from a *Geltungs*-theoretical perspective the regress poses no problem. Meaning is constituted on the basis of revisions of prior meaning; norms hold and are revised through our commitment to them as persons engaged practically in the world. But if the infinite regress is not *necessarily* a problem for transcendental phenomenology—that is, for one that stays within a practical, personalistic attitude—then what is it, exactly, that makes the concept of personalistic self-constitution appear paradoxical? In the following section I shall argue that the problem lies in a naturalistic assumption that distorts Husserl's reflections on the relation between the person and *consciousness*.

4 Diagnosing the appearance of paradox

Husserl identifies the personalistic attitude as the real 'natural' attitude, because it is not adopted on the basis of some particular cognitive or practical interest, as is (for example) the 'naturalistic' attitude of the natural scientist (Husserl 1952: 181–4/190–3). In the personalistic attitude I experience myself as embodied, as situated in a world in which there are others more or less like me, a world I did not create but upon which I can act and can engage communicatively with others, an historical world in which things are more or less familiar. The personalistic pre-given world is a world of *meaning*.

Phenomenological reflection shows that such meaning is constituted by 'apperceptions' (*Apperzeptionen*). This technical term designates the fact that in all perceiving (and by extension in any intentional experience) there is a system of co-intended or co-perceived ('apperceived') implications that specify which *possible* further experiences will cohere with my current and former perceptions and which will not. The phenomenon of apperception thus signals a normative order *within* first-person experience—one

---

[15] This is not to say that phenomenology has nothing to contribute to a psychology of consciousness. On the contrary, both in genetic and in cognitive terms there is a very productive symbiosis between phenomenological and empirical inquiries. See, for instance, Gallagher and Zahavi (2008), Noë (2004), Thompson (2007), Varela *et al.* (1991), and Petitot *et al.* (1999). The present point, however, concerns the question specific to *transcendental* phenomenology: how is *meaning* constituted? Here we touch on the relation between a transcendental philosophy carried out phenomenologically and a phenomenological *psychology*. The argument of this chapter is that they are distinct, though their relation cannot be treated here in detail.

that provides the thread (*Leitfaden*) that guides phenomenological analyses of meaning-constitution. What distinguishes transcendental phenomenology from other philosophical approaches is not that it recognizes this normative order in experience, but that it grounds it in *subjectivity*. In a text from 1916, Husserl spells this out: 'The ego of all objective apperceptions of different levels is from the outset a skilled-ego [*Vermögens-ich*], a subject of the "I can".' More specifically, 'every basic form of apperception corresponds to its own stratum of the skilled-ego' (Husserl 2008: 422–3). Thus we may identify a principle of all meaning constitution: no skill, no apperception.

To busy oneself with a hammer, for instance, is to apperceive certain intentional implications that prescribe the *successful* course of further experience with it, a prescription normatively grounded in what a hammer is *supposed* to be. This norm does not lie in the hammer itself, however. Rather, it is available only in an holistic context that includes both what I am trying to *do*—build a birdhouse—and what I am trying to *be* (a carpenter, not a creative artist). The skilled-ego is not merely one who is *able* to use a hammer appropriately; a robot could do that. Rather, it is one who can act *in light of* (or in recognition of) the norm that determines what 'appropriateness' means here. This attentiveness to the normative in experience operates at two distinct levels. First, there is the sort of skill that pertains to getting the *job* done right: it is because boards must be joined in just this way to make a good birdhouse that I am wielding the hammer in the way that I wield it and that its 'properties' (too heavy, too large for the nails, and so on) show up as they do. Second, there is the sort of skill that pertains to getting *myself* right, as it were: what it means to get the job done right (what I am *doing*) is determined by what I am trying to *be*. It is because I am trying to be a carpenter—trying to act in light of the norms of carpentry, trying to live up to them rather than, say, those of being a creative artist—that I experience the hammer as 'inappropriately' sized for the job. Were I trying to live up to the norms of being a creative artist, the very same heavy hammer and the very same resultant bent nails and split boards might be apperceived as perfectly appropriate.

Thus, if 'every basic form of apperception corresponds to its own stratum of the skilled-ego' (Husserl 2008: 423), this is because apperception ultimately depends on a kind of *self*-understanding in which I take responsibility for a normative framework (that of *being* a carpenter) that distinguishes my behaviour from mindless movement and from other things I might be doing. Such understanding, in turn, cannot be a matter of reflecting on myself or thematically noticing what I am doing or trying to be. It must already inform pre-reflective practical engagement—the very level at which the apperceptions in question show up. Understanding myself as a carpenter—trying to be one—constitutes me as one; acting thus involves a distinctive kind of *self-constitution*, and only thus does the prescriptive system of apperceptions necessary for the experience of meaning become available.[16]

How is such self-understanding to be described phenomenologically? Fatally, Husserl holds that it is *itself* a kind of apperception. He first distinguishes between 'the ego as sub-

---

[16] This sort of position is elaborated further in Haugeland (1998), Haugeland (2000), Crowell (2007), and Crowell (2010a).

ject of all affects, actions, apperceiving accomplishments, etc.' and 'the ego that itself becomes an apperceived object' *for* the ego in the first sense. Thus, for instance, when I am deeply absorbed in the work of carpentry I have not yet become an 'apperceived object' *for* myself, but I can *become* such an object—say, when I run into a problem I have never encountered and have to ask myself, as it were, what a carpenter should do in such a situation. However, after making this distinction Husserl goes on to suggest that 'in its various actions and in its apperceptions of objects, the ego constitutes itself in *originary apperception*, whether I attend to the ego *reflectively* or not' (Husserl 2008: 422; my emphasis). But given the principle, 'no skill, no apperception', this is puzzling. Thanks to the skills I exercise as a carpenter, my surroundings are apperceived in light of the norms of carpentry: as boards to be joined, as nails to be driven, and so on. But in exercising these skills *I* do not appear to *myself* as a carpenter, even pre-reflectively; I am nothing like an object for myself, with co-perceived or co-intended aspects that *result* from trying to be a carpenter. Understanding myself as a carpenter just *is* trying to be one, exercising the attendant normative sensitivities and skills. Self-understanding cannot be self-*apperception*, if apperception is something distinct from, and 'correlated' to, the exercise of my abilities.

Thus, either I can understand myself as a carpenter in the very act of trying to be one (which would amount to personalistic self-constitution without appeal to apperceptions); or there must be another capacity of my ego (another stratum of the *Vermögens-Ich*) which operates according to norms that allow an empirical (quasi-objective) apperception of myself *as* a carpenter to emerge. In the former case, the person would be the transcendental subject; in the latter the person would be a constituted *acquisition* of the transcendental subject, conceived as a more primitive level of conscious experience. But then we need an account of the capacity that enables such a transcendental subject to generate an apperception of itself as a person.

It is at this point that Husserl's account of self-apperception links up with our earlier discussion of the paradox of the pre-given world. For Husserl believes he can ground the apperception of myself as a carpenter (and personalistic self-apperception more generally) in my supposedly more primordial, *pre*-personal, experience of myself as a human *animal*, of whose natural being the person is a constituted modification, and whose 'skills', ultimately, are those of consciousness itself, a 'doing' that is not a 'willing-planning sort of doing' (Husserl 2008: 445). But before examining this suggestion we should recall that the thought that there *must be* a pre-personal level of constitution is not motivated by experience, but by an argument; and though arguments are fair game in phenomenology, they must be used with caution, since they may include phenomenologically inadmissable assumptions. Indeed, just such an assumption infects Husserl's thinking on this point, and it is shared, I would argue, by many current approaches to understanding the achievements of 'mind.'[17] The regress argument seems to compel a

---

[17] There are two types of approach I have in mind here, both of them reflecting the kind of naturalistic assumption that tacitly guides Husserl's view. The first—for example, Searle (1994)—holds that the mind (consciousness) is intrinsically intentional *and* that it is in some sense nothing but the brain. The second looks for the emergence of intentionality in the evolutionary explanation of the organism and its behaviour more generally. For some examples, see the essays in Walsh (2001).

distinction between the person and the transcendental subject only if one does not reflect on the person in a purely transcendental–phenomenological way, but instead approaches the relation between animality and personality armed with the naturalistic assumption that the former is *constitutionally* prior to the latter. This assumption seduces Husserl into disregarding the *epoché*'s strictures against importing theoretical constructions into transcendental phenomenology, as I will now try to show.

In a text from 1929, for instance, Husserl makes a series of what appear to be entirely uncontroversial claims. He begins with the idea that 'human being' names a 'regional unity' (Husserl 2008: 289)—roughly, an ontological category of entities. 'Personhood' is taken to be a constituted aspect of this unity. This becomes evident in the way Husserl describes the *death* of the human being. 'Every [real thing] has its way of being destroyed', a way that is predelineated by its ontological region (Husserl 2008: 288). Destruction of the person is 'spiritual death'; destruction of an animal is 'death of the organism'. The 'death of the human being', in turn, is 'organic and spiritual death in one' (Husserl 2008: 287). Thus, while it is possible that the person could suffer spiritual death without the death of any organism, it is not possible for the *organism* that constitutes the *human being* to die without the simultaneous spiritual death of the person. On this picture the person is inseparable from the human being, and being human involves a founding stratum of 'animality' (*Animalität*; Husserl 2008: 344). To explain the apperceptive constitution of the person, then, Husserl must turn to the 'pre-human, to the pre-personal in human existence [*menschlichen Dasein*]' (Husserl 2008: 391), since the subjectivity that accomplishes such constitution must be of the sort that persons share with other animals.

What is the 'skill' that allows pre-personal subjectivity to accomplish this? Husserl's answer again appears relatively uncontroversial. What links animal subjectivity with personal (or *geistig*) subjectivity is *embodiment*. In a text from 1926 he writes: 'To every body [*Leib*], including that of the animal, belongs an ego-centering and a universal structural form that circumscribes everything psychical, thanks to which the one and identical ego of this body lives in a multifarious ego-life'—a life that has 'the character of...ego-centred intentionality' (Husserl 2008: 274). 'Living' subjectivity in this sense has passive and affective moments, but it also has 'its "abilities", its habitualities, its lasting cognitions [*Kenntnisse*]...cognitive convictions, practical convictions (decisions), etc.; in short, it is in a primitive [*erster*] sense *personal* ego' (Husserl 2008: 274). For instance, Husserl holds that animal subjectivity constitutes species-relative 'environments', including analogues of those structures that characterize the human lifeworld: tradition, nature, sociality, and so on.[18] He further holds that these operations of animal subjectivity 'from instinctual sources' provide the human being with the 'basis for a life of will, for the development of will-subjects, i.e., persons, and for the development of personalistic communities of will' (Husserl 2008: 390). Though Husserl reminds us that in regard to animal sociality 'there can be no talk of...genuine willing and acting', he

---

[18] See, for instance, Husserl (2008), pp. 339, 344.

nevertheless holds that this 'living instinctivity and sociality' serves 'continually as the underlying basis' for personalistic achievements, 'insofar as those born into animality must first emerge into being persons' (Husserl 2008: 391). Thus, on the assumption that person and animal subjectivity are linked through the embodiment of the living, Husserl can address the paradox of the pre-given world by first constructing the animal subject as an impoverished version of the acting subject and then holding it to be foundational for the person.

This solution may seem obvious; certainly, the idea that human subjectivity must ultimately be understood in terms of animality in some sense is hardly unique to Husserl. Who could deny that infants are not persons at the outset; that they must be socialized into the practices and institutions that will become, for them, 'second nature'; that animals are social creatures, act purposively, and so on?[19] The only question is whether any of this is relevant from the point of view of *transcendental constitution*. If one limits one's genetic considerations to the emergence of the person from animal subjectivity one may be tempted to think that it is, but this is not the whole story about the pre-personal subjectivity that Husserl's response to the infinite regress requires. To hold that the person cannot be the transcendental subject is to commit oneself not merely to the relatively benign thesis that human subjectivity has analogues in the animal world; rather, it is to commit oneself to the thesis that pure consciousness is *sufficient* to constitute a world. How so?

The subjectivity that constitutes itself as a tiger differs from the one that constitutes itself as a human animal only in its particulars. At the relevant phenomenological level both are subjects as 'animate organisms'. Simplifying considerably we can say that, on the basis of different bodily abilities, the one constitutes what it is like to be a tiger while the other constitutes what it is like to be a human animal (Husserl 2008: 429–32). According to Husserl, however, 'animate organism' is *itself* an apperceived sense and thus a *contingent* form that the (transcendental) subject can take. For this reason there must be a further level of pre-personal subjectivity—a 'pre-animal' skilled-ego, so to speak—whose normatively structured abilities would be responsible for constituting its self-apperception as animate organism. Husserl describes such constitution in terms of the phenomenon of 'double sensation'. When I touch a ball, there is a rule-governed correlation between the sensed properties of the ball and the touch-sensations 'localized' in my hand. When I touch my arm, however, there is a *second* set of touch-sensations that I do *not* correlate with objective properties of my arm. 'If I *do* include them', Husserl writes, 'then it is not that the physical thing [my arm] is now richer [*sc.* in objective properties], but instead it *becomes Body [Leib]*' (Husserl 1952: 145/152). But a subjectivity that could in this way apperceive itself *contingently* as *animate organism* must possess an essential structure, or 'skill', not dependent on the body. Such a subjectivity is, according to Husserl, 'pure consciousness' in its pre-intentional temporal flow, a standing-streaming

---

[19] For a phenomenologically sensitive argument that such animal 'teleology' is the root of intentionality, see Okrent (2007). But most of those who argue in this way are not at all concerned with phenomenology. For a representative sampling of essays, see Walsh (2001).

'living present' of primal sense-impressions with their retentional and protentional modifications, primal noticings, passive associations, and so on. At this level alone, according to Husserl, do we reach an 'ability' that is genuinely self-constituting (thus putting an end to the regress), one that yields the necessary 'pre-being': a 'doing' that is not 'a willing-planning doing, doing in the usual sense' (Husserl 2008: 445).

But at this point the key demand of the experience-theoretical strand of transcendental phenomenology—the demand that constitutional analysis be grounded in first-person experience—must be abandoned. In a text from 1933, Husserl acknowledges this: 'Primal affection in primal passivity, the fields of sensation with their primal contrasts in primal temporalizing—Is this really more than an abstraction and reconstruction?' (Husserl 2008: 432). Such things, he continues, 'I have never experienced.' Yet he claims that in 'asking back into the structure of meaning-giving, the constitution of ontic meaning', in 'following up the intentional implications' of what is currently experienced, and in 'reconstructing what is implicit', the phenomenologist will be forced to posit what he here calls 'inactive constitution', a standing 'core' of 'the pre-egological' which is 'ultimately presupposed in all egological achievements' (Husserl 2008: 432–3). In other words: yes, this is an 'abstraction and reconstruction', but it is *justified* as *necessary*. How? Since we have no experience of such things, it must be on the basis of arguments such as the infinite regress we have been considering. But do such arguments really authorize these genetic conclusions, which in part involve genuine descriptions but in part do not?[20]

I do not believe so, but even if they motivate something *like* such conclusions—that is, even if they suggest that personalistic constitution rests upon conditions that it does not constitute—this does not mean that these are *constitutive* conditions. They may contribute no more to the transcendental analysis of how *meaning* is constituted than does digestion, conceived outside the reduction as a natural process. And if that is so, then in identifying the regress in personalistic constitution one also identifies the limits of the phenomenological doctrine of constitution itself. This may appear to limit phenomenology in a very crippling way; but as I will argue below, it does not. Rather, it brings within reach one of Husserl's most cherished goals: a clear demarcation between transcendental phenomenology and empirical science that allows for their mutual interaction, but without the paradox of subjectivity.

The key is to bracket the naturalistic assumption that seduces Husserl into thinking that the experience-theoretical strand in the concept of constitution provides a way out of the infinite regress. The problem lies not in the appeal to nature as such, but in the 'naturalistic' way that Husserl understands it—one that transgresses the *epoché* by importing

---

[20] Zahavi (2005), p. 65, for instance, explains how some aspects of Husserl's account of consciousness at this level—the structure of inner time-consciousness, the notion of primal self-affection—can be understood as 'an analysis of the (micro)structure of first-personal givenness.' But Zahavi appeals to aspects of Husserl's account that can be verified in phenomenological reflection, not the sort of genetic reconstructions that some believe to be *authorized* by such descriptions. On the use of constructions and transcendental arguments in genetic phenomenology, see Welton (2000) and Bruzina (2004). For some criticisms of this view, see Crowell (2002a).

'results' of third-person inquiry into transcendental phenomenology. When Husserl claims that the subject of the personalistic attitude is a 'human being' (*Mensch*), he believes that he is entitled to the idea that the sense, 'human being', carries with it reference to *natural kinds*—not merely in some culturally relative sense in which the pre-given world contains various familiar 'types' of creature, but in the strict sense of scientific *naturalism*. In this, again, Husserl is hardly alone. Such naturalism seems almost to be a criterion of philosophical respectability in our scientistic age. But the importation of this sort of third-person assumption into transcendental phenomenology is pernicious, because it makes it seem as though the pre-personal processes characteristic of consciousness conceived as a *natural function* could somehow be 'reconstructed', in the absence of first-person evidence, as *constitutive* abilities of transcendental subjectivity.

While the intentional implications of what is experienced do point back to various pre-personal processes of consciousness, they do not point back to *constitutive* processes in the *Geltungs*-theoretical sense. It is a naturalistic prejudice to hold that just because the person is conscious, its constitutive achievements are *transcendentally* grounded in what it shares with animals. Or, to put it another way, it is a naturalistic prejudice to think that, *as constituting*, the person is a stratum of the third-person natural kind, 'human being'. Rather, a fully consistent transcendental phenomenology will show how this supposedly founding level is *founded* upon the person—how my 'nature', my instinctual life, my animality, is constituted *as* pre-given in the way I take it up, answer for it, as a person. In the following section I will conclude by developing this point a little more fully.

5 Toward a transcendental naturalism

The problem with Husserl's genetic regress via the experience-theoretical strand of his transcendental phenomenology becomes most pressing not at the level of animality but at the point where constituting the *difference* between animate organism and the rest of reality requires a subjectivity in which the body (*Leib*) is not yet constituted. But if we abandon the naturalistic assumption that the person is founded on the human being conceived as a natural kind, then the body need not be seen as constituted at all. As transcendental subjectivity the person is not *contingently* embodied, and its embodiment belongs neither to nature as the object of natural science nor to nature as a dimension of the person's pre-given world. It is important to insist that the problem with Husserl's stance lies *not* in the idea of transcendental constitution but in his naturalistic assumption, for then we may appreciate the real phenomenological task posed by Husserl's texts: to develop a *transcendentally viable* concept of nature.[21]

---

[21] In contemporary philosophy, such a project is not at all limited to phenomenology. McDowell's notion of 'second nature' aims at something of the sort, and Joseph Rouse (2002) proposes specifically to 'reclaim' naturalism from positivistic notions of natural necessity that seems to rule out normativity. For an historical account of 'post-positivism in the study of science from Quine to Latour', see Zammito (2004).

If we bracket the naturalistic assumption that the person is founded on the human being considered as a natural kind, then the concept of *Leib* becomes systematically ambiguous.[22] On the one hand, *Leib* is that which incorporates, as it were, the person's ability to try—its skills and habitualities; its 'I can'—which opens up the practically normative space of apperception necessary for the constitution of meaning. Let us call this 'lived body'. On the other hand, *Leib* is the 'animate organism', the body that belongs to constituted nature as part of the pre-given world. Let us call this 'living body'.[23] Recognizing this ambiguity has implications for our understanding of *consciousness*, for while it is still possible to conceive consciousness as a distinct stratum of the *living* body—for instance, one can distinguish between the living body and the corpse by appeal to the presence or absence of consciousness as psyche—it is no longer possible to distinguish between *constituting* consciousness (*Vermögens-ich*) and the *lived* body. Thus, from the experience-theoretical perspective it is no longer possible to work back from personalistic, practical constitution to a supposedly deeper level of primal passivity and association at which the lived body itself is apperceptively constituted. Without the naturalistic assumption, the only transcendental question is how such pre-personal processes are constituted, *within* the personalistic attitude, *as* pre-personal, passive, and so on.

How do the pre-personal processes of consciousness show up in the personalistic attitude? One way is as objects of natural scientific investigation. Whether in psychoanalysis, neuroscience, psychology, or some other branch of natural science, pre-personal (and sub-personal) processes are constituted as objects by means of evolving epistemic practices and third-person theories. This 'naturalistic' nature is a region governed by causal law—one that does not strictly speaking 'appear' because its constitution presupposes a process of idealization that leaves the perceptual world behind (Husserl 1952: 86–8/91–2). Thus, bridging principles are required to link nature in this sense to the objects of ordinary experience. As phenomenologists we may critically reflect on the experiences from which scientific concepts are drawn, and we may work back and forth between empirical investigations and phenomenological reflection to refine such concepts and develop bridging principles. But without the naturalistic assumption we will not be able to hold that what such investigations uncover are *constitutive* conditions—conditions of possibility for the consciousness of *valid* unities of *meaning*.

But the 'naturalistic' nature of science can be approached phenomenologically only through the ordinary personalistic (intuitive or perceptual) experience of a pre-given world, which may include a concept of 'nature' as a region within it that contrasts with regions that are *not* nature: for example, 'culture' or 'artifice'. Drawing such a distinction

---

[22] This systematic ambiguity has been skillfully explored by Taipale (2014).

[23] Since Husserl does not take note of this ambiguity, the standard English translations of Husserl, which translate *Leib* simply as 'lived body', will also be insensitive to the points at issue here. One would have to translate *Leib* either as 'lived body' or as 'living body', depending on whether the context concerned embodied subjectivity as *constituting subject* or as part of 'nature' (either in the naturalistic or the lifeworld-cultural sense of 'nature').

rigorously is notoriously difficult, but in a text from 1928 Husserl attempts it by distinguishing between what is 'immediately' and what is only 'mediately' given: 'The universe of objects that are given as immediately experienceable by me (immediately demonstrable in original intuition) and must be so given is *nature*' (Husserl 2008: 30). It is not clear, however, that an ontological region is picked out this way.

Like Aristotle, Husserl wants to circumscribe a region of things that are pre-given in the sense of not arising through *praxis*, and it is tempting to define nature as that which can be *perceptually* given without any apperceptions that refer to cultural production. But there seem to be no such things. As we saw, perception is a practice whose aim is to grasp (or 'have') the 'thing itself'. Thus one might be tempted to say that natural things are those that can be successfully 'had' through sensible intuition *alone*. I can perceive a tattoo, for instance, but the tattoo 'itself' cannot be adequately given (or 'had') merely through the perceptual practice of looking at it from a variety of perspectives, since tattoos are constituted in part by the symbolic usages of particular cultures. In contrast, I might believe that a *tree* can be adequately given (or 'had') through the exclusively perceptual practice described above. But unless we move to the level of a naturalistic third-person theory, what counts as a tree—and so, whether this thing here actually *can* be adequately given in perception—can vary significantly from culture to culture. Thus, simplifying drastically, we might say that because of its *socially* constituted character, the 'nature' that belongs to the phenomenologically pre-given world is relative to *culture* in just the way that 'nature' as the object of natural science is relative to *theory*.

No matter how these questions sort themselves out, one thing is clear. As part of the pre-given world, nature is always normatively constituted within an horizon of valid meaning; it never presents itself as the correlate of pre-personal processes of consciousness. It is constituted *as* pre-given in what I do. The woods I walk through were there 'long before I was born'; I must 'find' the perfect wave, and in order to surf it successfully I must 'conform myself to *it*'; the wood I am trying to lay down as flooring is 'warped'. In a similar way, my *own* pre-given 'nature' (if we are to use this term for the pre-personal processes of embodied consciousness) is constituted *as* pre-given in my urge 'for ice-cream', my striving 'for a better world', my fear 'of stepping on a crack', my commitment 'to curbing my enthusiasm for irony', and the like. Constituted as *my* pre-given nature, pre-personal processes, associations, drives, urges, bodily conditions, and the like, are experienced as what I undergo; but what I undergo is always there meaningfully, in light of the stand I take toward it.[24] In no case can such 'nature' be *directly* equated with 'naturalistic' nature, and in every case it is there *as* something—that is, it is experienced in light of some norm-governed horizon.

What is the relation of the person to nature in this sense? For Husserl, the connection is found in the body as *Leib*. According to Husserl, the *Leib* appears both as a privileged centre of the environment—as 'organ' of my will—*and* as one animate organism among others,

---

[24] This view of the primary processes of first-person experience is akin to the notion of 'avowal' developed in Moran (2001).

though a 'remarkably imperfectly constituted' one, since 'it obstructs me in the perception of itself' (Husserl 1952: 158–60/166–7). Here again we encounter the systematic ambiguity in this concept. In the first instance, *Leib* is the *lived* body; in the second, the *living* body. What is 'remarkably poorly constituted' is not my lived body but my *living* body, which I can later describe as an 'animate organism'. The *lived* body does not appear as a thing in the world at all. Since Husserl does not recognize the ambiguity, he thinks that *Leib* as organ of my will *appears*, and can thus provide the basis for an 'apperceptive transfer' thanks to which I recognize other things in my world as 'animate organisms', thus constituting myself contingently as part of nature (Husserl 1963: 138–43/108–13). But if we suspend the naturalistic assumption and clearly disambiguate these notions, the *lived* body cannot be the basis for grasping the *living* body. The lived body cannot show up at all as an *object* in the world without losing the very characteristics that make it what it is.[25] Thus it cannot serve as the basis for an apperceptive transfer of sense to something that *does* show up in the world—an animal body.

To grasp myself as living body, as one animate organism among others, requires a constituted space of practices in which norms of the real, and its 'essential' regions, are already there. Another way to put this is that the sense, 'animate organism', will always be concretely expressed in terms of the loose 'types' that emerge from historically and culturally contingent personalistic practices. A consistent transcendental phenomenology must therefore hold that the person, as transcendental subject, constitutes the 'human being' as a denizen of pre-given 'nature', and in so doing constitutes something like an 'us' in contrast to other beings. Such grouping need not map onto conspecificity in the naturalistic sense: 'us' might include our totem animals, pets, or whatever. In no case, however, does a part of such constituted nature show itself as an *organ* of constitution—neither the body nor consciousness and its pre-personal associative processes. The lived body, the person, does not show up in nature in that sense at all; it shows up *only* under the reduction, in transcendental–phenomenological reflection on the *Geltungs*-theoretical constitution of meaning. Husserl's idea that the living body is part of nature—and that it is therefore constituted and relative—is thus correct; but this does not entail that the *person* is constituted by some pre-personal form of subjectivity. Thus, as Husserl rightly insisted (though for the wrong reasons), the paradox of a subjectivity that is part of the world but also constitutes the world is only apparent, since the subjectivity that constitutes the world is not *in* the world at all; it is, as Heidegger will say, being-in-the-world.

---

[25] This does *not* mean that it is not a 'worldly' subject in the transcendental sense: in the personalistic attitude the pre-given world is as apodictic as the 'I am'. Husserl acknowledged this in a series of texts penned between 1921 and 1937, in which he argued that for an ego conscious of a world, 'it is simply not *possible* to represent the world as non-existent, though it is possible to do so for every particular being in it (with the exception of its own being as human subject)' (Husserl 2008, p. 256). The latter caveat includes the *body*: Cartesian dualism is 'counter-sensical' (*widersinnig*), since I cannot represent my body as not existing without thereby losing the 'essentially human form' of my 'conscious life as a person' (Husserl 2008, p. 248). Of course, Husserl thinks that a further step is possible—from the personalistic/human level to the genuinely 'transcendental' level of 'pure consciousness' or 'immanence', where the world is no longer apodictic. But these texts are interesting for the way in which he questions whether this view might not merely be 'a leftover from the old psychology and its sensualistic empiricism' (Husserl 2008, p. 229).

References

Bayne, T. and Montague, M. (eds) (2012), *Cognitive Phenomenology* (Oxford: Oxford University Press).

Boehm, R. (1968), 'Das Absolute und die Realität', in R. Boehm, *Vom Gesichtspunkt der Phänomenologie, vol. I* (Den Haag: Martinus Nijhoff).

Brough, J. B. (1972), 'The Emergence of an Absolute Consciousness in Husserl's Early Writings on Time-Consciousness', *Man and World* 5/3: 298–326.

Bruzina, R. (2004), *Edmund Husserl and Eugen Fink: Beginnings and Ends in Phenomenology, 1928–1938* (New Haven: Yale University Press).

Carr, D. (1999), *The Paradox of Subjectivity: The Self in the Transcendental Tradition* (Oxford: Oxford University Press).

Cassam, Q. (1997), *Self and World* (Oxford: Oxford University Press).

Clark, A. (2008), *Supersizing the Mind: Embodiment, Action, and Cognitive Extension* (Oxford: Oxford University Press).

Crane, T. (2001), *Elements of Mind: An Introduction to the Philosophy of Mind* (Oxford: Oxford University Press).

Crowell, S. (2001), *Husserl, Heidegger, and the Space of Meaning: Paths Toward Transcendental Phenomenology* (Evanston: Northwestern University Press).

——(2002a), 'The Cartesianism of Phenomenology', *Continental Philosophy Review* 35/4: 433–54.

——(2002b), 'Does the Husserl/Heidegger Feud Rest on a Mistake? An Essay on Psychological and Transcendental Phenomenology', *Husserl Studies* 18/2: 123–40.

——(2010a), 'Heidegger on Practical Reasoning: Morality and Agency', in A. M. González and A. Vigo (eds), *Practical Rationality: Scope and Structures of Human Agency* (Hildesheim: Olms).

——(2010b), 'Husserl's Subjectivism: The "ganz einzigen 'Formen'" of Consciousness and the Philosophy of Mind', in C. Ierna, H. Jacobs and F. Mattens (eds), *Philosophy, Phenomenology, Sciences: Essays in Commemoration of Edmund Husserl* (Dordrecht: Springer).

Dreyfus, H. (2007), 'Return of the Myth of the Mental', *Inquiry* 50/4: 352–65.

Gallagher, S. and Zahavi, D. (2008), *The Phenomenological Mind: An Introduction to Philosophy of Mind and Cognitive Science* (London: Routledge).

Gethmann, C. F. (1974), *Verstehen und Auslegung. Das Methodenproblem in der Philosophie Martin Heideggers* (Bonn: Bouvier).

Haugeland, J. (1998), 'Truth and Rule-Following', in J. Haugeland, *Having Thought: Essays in the Metaphysics of Mind* (Cambridge, MA: Harvard University Press).

——(2000), 'Truth and Finitude: Heidegger's Transcendental Existentialism', in M. Wrathall and J. Malpas (eds.), *Heidegger, Authenticity, and Modernity. Essays in Honor of Hubert L. Dreyfus*, vol. I. (Cambridge, MA: The MIT Press).

Heidegger, M. (1962), *Being and Time*, tr. John Macquarrie and Edward Robinson (New York: Harper and Row).

Husserl, E. (1950), *Ideen zu einer reinen Phänomenologie und phänomenologischen Philosophie, Erstes Buch,* Husserliana III, ed. W. Biemel (Den Haag: Martinus Nijhoff); *Ideas Pertaining to a Pure Phenomenology and to a Phenomenological Philosophy, First Book,* tr. F. Kersten (The Hague: Martinus Nijhoff, 1983).

——(1952), *Ideen zu einer reinen Phänomenologie und phänomenologischen Philosophie, Zweites Buch,* Husserliana IV, ed. M. Biemel (Den Haag: Martinus Nijhoff); *Ideas Pertainting to a Pure Phenomenology and to a Phenomenological Philosophy, Second Book*, tr. R. Rojcewicz and A. Schuwer (Dordrecht: Kluwer, 1989).

Husserl, E. (1954), *Die Krisis der europäischen Wissenschaften und die transzendentale Phänomenologie*, Husserliana VI, ed. W. Biemel (Den Haag: Martinus Nijhoff); *The Crisis of European Sciences and Transcendental Phenomenology*, tr. D. Carr (Evanston: Northwestern University Press, 1970).

——(1963), *Cartesianische Meditationen und Pariser Vorträge* Husserlania I, ed. S. Strasser, (Den Haag: Martinus Nijhoff); *Cartesian Meditations: An Introduction to Phenomenology*, tr. D. Cairns (The Hague: Martinus Nijhoff, 1969).

——(1997), *Psychological and Transcendental Phenomenology and The Confrontation with Heidegger (1927–1931)*, ed. and tr. T. Sheehan and R. Palmer (Dordrecht: Kluwer).

——(2002), *Zur phänomenologischen Reduktion. Texte aus dem Nachlass (1926–1935)*, Husserliana XXXIV, ed. S. Luft (Dordrecht: Kluwer).

——(2008), *Die Lebenswelt: Auslegungen der vorgegebenen Welt und ihrer Konstitution. Texte aus dem Nachlass (1916–1937)*, Husserliana XXXIX, ed. R. Sowa (Dordrecht: Springer).

Kern, I. (1964), *Husserl und Kant. Eine Untersuchung über Husserls Verhältnis zu Kant und zum Neukantianismus* (Den Haag: Martinus Nijhoff).

Lee, N. (2010), 'Phenomenological Reflections on the Possibility of First Philosophy', *Husserl Studies* 26/2: 131–45.

McDowell, J. (1996), *Mind and World* (Cambridge: Harvard University Press).

——(2007), 'What Myth?', *Inquiry* 50/4: 338–51.

——(2009), 'Avoiding the Myth of the Given', in J. McDowell, *Having the World in View* (Cambridge, MA: Harvard University Press).

Mohanty, J. N. (1985), *The Possibility of Transcendental Philosophy* (The Hague: Martinus Nijhoff).

——(1997), *Phenomenology: Between Essentialism and Transcendental Philosophy* (Evanston: Northwestern University Press).

Moran, R. (2001), *Authority and Estrangement: An Essay on Self-Knowledge* (Princeton: Princeton University Press).

Nagel, T. (1974), 'What is it like to be a bat?', *The Philosophical Review* LXXXIII/4: 435–50.

Noë, A. (2004), *Action in Perception* (Cambridge, MA: The MIT Press).

Okrent, M. (2007), *Rational Animals. The Teleological Roots of Intentionality* (Athens: Ohio University Press).

Peacocke, C. (1998), 'Nonconceptual Content Defended', *Philosophy and Phenomenological Research* LVIII/2: 381–8.

Petitot, J., Varela, F. J., Pachoud, B., and Roy, J.-M. (eds) (1999), *Naturalizing Phenomenology: Issues in Contemporary Phenomenology and Cognitive Science* (Stanford: Stanford University Press).

Rouse, J. (2002), *How Scientific Practices Matter. Reclaiming Philosophical Naturalism* (Chicago: The University of Chicago Press).

Searle, J. (1994), *The Rediscovery of the Mind* (Cambridge, MA: MIT Press).

——(2000), 'The Limits of Phenomenology', in M. Wrathall and J. Malpas (eds), *Heidegger, Coping, and Cognitive Science: Essays in Honor of Hubert L. Dreyfus*, vol. 2 (Cambridge, MA: MIT Press).

Siewert, C. (1998), *The Significance of Consciousness* (Princeton: Princeton University Press).

Strawson, G. (2009), *Selves: An Essay in Revisionary Metaphysics* (Oxford: Oxford University Press).

Thompson, E. (2007), *Mind in Life: Biology, Phenomenology, and the Science of Mind* (Cambridge: Harvard University Press).

Taipale, J. (2014). *Phenomenology and Embodiment: Husserl and the Constitution of Subjectivity* (Evanston: Northwestern University Press).

Varela, F. J., Thompson, E., and Rosch, E., (eds) (1991), *The Embodied Mind: Cognitive Science and Human Experience* (Cambridge, MA: MIT Press).

Walsh, D. (ed.) (2001), *Naturalism, Evolution, and Mind*, Royal Institute of Philosophy Supplement to 'Philosophy' 49 (Cambridge: Cambridge University Press).

Welton, D. (2000), *The Other Husserl: The Horizons of Transcendental Phenomenology* (Bloomington: Indiana University Press).

Zahavi, D. (2005), *Subjectivity and Selfhood: Investigating the First-Person Perspective* (Cambridge, MA: MIT Press).

Zammito, J. (2004), *A Nice Derangement of Epistemes: Post-positivism in the Study of Science from Quine to Latour* (Chicago: University of Chicago Press).

CHAPTER 3

....

RESPECTING APPEARANCES: A PHENOMENOLOGICAL APPROACH TO CONSCIOUSNESS

....

CHARLES SIEWERT

1 THE CALL FOR CLARIFICATION

....

The explanation of consciousness is often seen as one of our greatest intellectual challenges. If so, we surely need to start from an adequate conception of just what is to be explained. And since the right way to understand talk about consciousness is notoriously unclear and disputed, this is no simple matter. This call for clarity arises not just from an interest in seeing consciousness explained, but from the desire to understand its place in our *knowledge* and in our *values*. So potentially, much is at stake. This task of clarification is a central concern of phenomenology as I interpret it here.

Carrying out this task in a way that will help us address such topics requires we enter into basic controversies about how consciousness applies to sense experience and thought. For suppose we purport to clarify the 'phenomenal' sense of 'consciousness' by saying that it has to do only with the 'qualities' of our sensations. This will have consequences for how we think consciousness figures in our knowledge. For it will then be hard to see how sense experience (or the phenomenal aspect of it at least) could be anything more than a *cause* of our judgements about what we find around us; it will seem unable to *legitimize* them, and to 'ground' knowledge in that sense. Against this, we might argue that sensory consciousness (the kind we adult humans have anyway) is *not* mere sensation, but has 'conceptual content' (and only because of this can legitimize belief). (This, roughly, is McDowell's (1994) argument against Davidson). But this conflicts also with the view that while experience indeed has a 'representational' or 'intentional' character (lacking in mere sensation), this is 'non-conceptual' in a way that distinguishes sensing from thinking.[1] Such disputes bear not just on how to understand perceptual knowledge, but on how we think consciousness may be explained. For some (such as Dretske 1995, and Tye 1995, 2000) see a specifically sensory form of representation as the key to a reductive naturalistic explanation of consciousness. And that theoretical strategy clashes not only with the McDowellian idea that perceptual experience is conceptually 'permeated', but with the view of others (such as myself, Siewert 2011b) who argue that conceptual thought is phenomenally conscious.

These complicated disagreements about the richness and reach of consciousness gain further significance when we consider the question of how we know our own minds. Given what we should say about sensory experience and thought, can we somehow transpose an account of perceptual knowledge of our bodies and surroundings into an account of how we know our own minds? Should we posit an 'inner' sense that provides us with such knowledge? And would this perhaps also yield a theory of consciousness (as advocated in Armstrong 1968, Carruthers 2000, 2004, and Lycan 2004)? On the other hand, if inner sense is rejected—as in Dretske (1995), Shoemaker (1994), Siewert (1998, 2011c), and Tye (2000)—what, if anything, can we make of the notion of *introspection* and the role of consciousness in it? Finally, how should we best contrast such self-knowledge with—and relate it to—our knowledge of *others* and theirs of us? The view we take of the content of experience will affect our conception of how we experience other people and how this relates to our thoughts about them—and thus will affect our answer to 'other minds' issues as well.

Just how we sort through all this will also impinge on questions about *value*. How does our conception of consciousness and its extent allow us to make sense of the ethical concern we have for the character of our own and others' conscious experience?[2] How does this affect our understanding of the role of empathy in moral life? And how, if at all, might our accounts of consciousness illuminate aesthetic experience, and the role of art in extending and shaping the range of experience we recognize? To answer such questions we need to better understand how to situate consciousness with respect to imagination, emotion, and desire.

These issues demand careful examination of the distinctions we need. And this calls for ways of thinking that are recognizably philosophical. In saying this, I do not intend to deny the pertinence of experimental research in psychology. I only want to say that no small part of the challenge before us concerns how best to describe and coherently organize what is already available to us prior to any new experiments and clinical studies—including what is available to us from the critical examination of personal experience. To take this seriously, we need not purport to engage in a *purely 'a priori'* inquiry—whatever that might mean. We do need to keep an open mind about the value of conceptual clarification and self-examination; to belittle this or deny its importance out of hand *would* be '*a priori*stic' in a deservedly pejorative sense.

---

[1] For debates on 'non-conceptual content', see Gunther (2002).

[2] In Siewert (1998), Chapter 9, I argue that consciousness in the phenomenal sense is strongly intrinsically valuable.

Here I will summarize a few aspects of my efforts to provide the philosophy I say is called for, focusing mainly on just three foundational concerns. These are: first, the character of a phenomenological approach; second, its use to clarify the notion of phenomenal consciousness (or 'phenomenality'); and finally, its application to questions about a specifically *sensory* phenomenality and its 'intentionality' or 'object-directedness'. Towards the end, however, I will briefly indicate some ways these ideas may be extended to engage a portion of the large issues to which I have alluded.

2 PHENOMENOLOGY IN WHAT SENSE?

In what sense is my approach phenomenological? Students of that part of the 'phenomenological tradition' that stretches from Brentano through Merleau-Ponty will see its influence in what I say. I am glad to acknowledge that influence, and do not claim any great originality for my approach or results. But determining just where my views coincide or conflict with those of classical phenomenologists would take me into involved exegetical and historical questions I must largely set aside here (save for a few remarks in footnotes and in my conclusion), so that I can focus on the issues themselves.[3] So let me start by briefly stating just what I take phenomenology to be. And that is this: *a sustained and unified effort to clarify our understanding of philosophically or theoretically relevant distinctions, with recourse to an underived and critical use of first-person reflection.*

To clarify your understanding of distinctions is to explain what you mean by a term or phrase. To do this you may offer positive examples—real and hypothetical—of what you are talking about, and contrast these with negative examples—cases where you take it the expression does or would not apply. This clarification can, but need not always, also involve statements of strongly necessary, or sufficient, or necessary-and-sufficient conditions. Does this then purport to be an analysis of 'our' concepts? The understanding which phenomenology seeks is, of course, rooted in ordinary, shareable applications of language that precede it. However, it does not primarily aim simply to reflect or analyze that prior usage, but to use it as a starting point to *create* an articulate understanding of terms that will serve us well in addressing questions that arise regarding what we had already been speaking of. And this may well involve drawing and sharpening distinctions that were not recognized before. Thus phenomenological clarification is not measured by strict faithfulness to some prior pattern of usage, or by how well it analyzes concepts previously in currency, but by the extent to which it can generate an understanding that has relevance for philosophical or theoretical issues—including those mentioned above.

---

[3] More detail about how I view the relationship of classical phenomenology and analytic philosophy of mind can be found in Siewert (2011c).

I have said that phenomenology involves the use of 'first-person reflection'. That means that it asks you to clarify your understanding by relying on a way of judging about your own attitudes, thought, and experience—and a type of warrant in so judging—distinctive of the *first-person* case, in consideration of real and hypothetical cases. This use is *critical* insofar as it regards such judgements as fallible but correctible through an indefinitely renewable process of making them coherent and explicit by questioning that draws out implications and exposes neglected distinctions. This proceeds on the basis of a warranted if defeasible presumption that one understands the terms in which one expresses the first-person judgements in question, which entails that one enjoys some competence in thus using them to state what is so. Phenomenology accordingly makes what I call an 'underived' use of first-person reflection. It does not assume that the warrant we have for first-person claims about experience is limited to what they can derive from the fact that granting them some sort of accuracy best explains 'third-person' observational data acquired *without* reliance on first-person reflection. I have no right to assume the warrant I have for speaking of my own experience is entirely derived from that which others would have for speaking of me.

Elsewhere (Siewert 2007a, 2007b, 2011a) I have defended my version of phenomenology as relatively theoretically neutral in methodologically desirable ways. Though I cannot now recapitulate those arguments, I should say this about limiting initial presuppositions. I ask us not only to be on guard against latent behaviourist epistemology, but to beware of overconfidence in our grasp of overworked terms of art such as 'qualia', 'representation', 'intentionality', and 'content', so often used to define the controversies in the philosophy of mind. That is not to say we can find—by contrast to such vocabulary— one that is purely presuppositionless, fit to serve as our special 'phenomenological language'. But we can try to start relatively close to the ground, by rooting our discussion in the use of language with which we need to assume some competence, if we are to develop any creditable understanding of the sort of jargon just mentioned. Accordingly, I seek to anchor my phenomenology in the use of homely terms such as 'experience', 'look', and 'feel'.

I have not identified phenomenology by reference to a special subject matter, and have left open just how we are to understand the 'first-person reflection' on which it relies. But that is as it initially should be; phenomenology cannot *start* with a positive account of its domain and rational basis, since these are issues it has to investigate. However, in anticipation I might say that phenomenology as I pursue it leads to a rich and broad conception of what we might call the 'field of appearances'. And for me, phenomenology is ultimately (as its etymology suggests) a rational account 'respecting' appearances in the sense that it is *about* them. But I also want my phenomenology to 'respect' these appearances in another sense: to see them as worthy of careful attention in their own right, and not just as a source of intellectual anxiety we must still, or as mere surface to be sloughed off on the way to the 'really real'.

3 A PHENOMENOLOGICAL CONCEPTION
OF CONSCIOUSNESS

I propose three distinct but mutually supportive ways of introducing the notion of phenomenal consciousness, designed to help us fairly address the issues in which it figures, drawing on (and hopefully improving on) suggestions already in circulation. Taken together, they make up my basic phenomenological conception of consciousness. So as to start from what is most likely to be common ground, I will focus on sensory cases.

I begin with what I call *the subjective experience conception*. One sometimes hears it said (in Block 2002, for instance) that anything that is *an experience* is conscious in the phenomenal sense. But we need to say more to specify the sense of 'experience' at issue. Consider: those who study the nervous systems of sea slugs speak of these creatures 'learning from experience'. And we may find ourselves saying that a sea slug 'experiences' an electric shock. Or even that, as a result, it 'experiences' a chemical change in its nervous system. And we might say that what it thus experiences are its experiences. There does seem to be some sense in which an animal like the sea slug can, fairly uncontroversially, be said to have 'experience'. But if this is uncontroversial, it seems that it is only because we are saying no more than that something *happens* to it that *affects* it in some way. An experience is just something it has 'been through' or undergone. And that is *not* all I understand by the notion of experience invoked in relation to (phenomenal) consciousness.

What *do* I understand by this? Notice there is a sense in which you can say you feel *pain*, an *itch*, or *pleasure*—and consider *what is felt* in each case to be none other than *the very feeling of it*. The pain you feel in your hand just *is* feeling pain, as the itch you feel in your back is a feeling, and the pleasure you feel holding a loved one in your arms is: none other than this very feeling of pleasure. Then, in each case, you *feel a feeling*—in the 'internal accusative' sense in which you may also be said to 'dance a dance'. At least you can so interpret true statements about what you feel. Furthermore, in these very cases you can also speak of *how a feeling feels to you*, and of *differences* in how feelings feel to you: how the pain feels to you differs from how the itch feels to you, how one pain or itch feels to you differs from how another does, and so on.

Now let us take such cases (in which one *feels a feeling*) to be *species* of the broader class: *experiencing an experience*. And let us now take how *feelings feel* to you to be species of *how you experience experiences*. We thus begin to recognize the sense of 'experience' that I wish to make evident. In this sense your experience *coincides* with your experiencing it (in the way the feeling felt coincides with feeling it), and an experience differs from others with respect to *how it is experienced by you* (as the feelings you feel differ with respect to *how they feel* to you).

The next step is to see how the relevant sense of 'experience' can extend well beyond the cases just invoked (where it is natural to speak of 'feelings' and of 'how they feel'). So, for example, there is a sense in which, normally, when you see something somehow coloured and shaped, its colour and shape *look* somehow to you. Now, we do not normally speak of *looking* as a kind of *feeling*, nor do we say there is a way something's looking red *feels* to us. But in the same sense in which you experience your feelings, you can *experience* something's looking to you as it does; in that sense *you experience its visual appearance*. Its looking to you as it does is thus an experience in the coincident sense. Further, you may speak of *differences* in *how you experience* something's looking to you as it does. So, for example, something may look blue and circular to you. And how you experience its looking blue and circular to you may change—say, as lighting, orientation, and focus of attention alter. We may also say, when this happens, *how* it looks coloured and shaped to you changes, as long as we recognize that this does not entail that something then *appears to you to change shape or colour*. In fact, during this change in how you experience the appearance of a certain shape and colour, it may nonetheless *appear or look the same* in shape and colour.

We will come back to this point (about phenomenal constancy) in connection with the 'objectuality' of sensory appearance. For the moment the crucial point is just this. In the same (internal accusative) sense in which you may experience a feeling, you may also experience something's looking to you somehow coloured and shaped. And just as we may speak of differences in *how your feeling feels* to you, so we may speak of differences in *how you experience something's looking blue and circular* to you. And we may take these latter also to determine differences in how something looks to you. But all this is compatible with saying: what looks blue and circular to you is not the *experience*, the *visual appearance* of colour and shape. For even as the experience *changes*, what looks blue and circular may also both *look* and *be constant* in colour and shape.[4]

Now return to our friend the sea slug. We can see that the concept of experience I have explained is not the same as that which unquestionably applies to this creature—where to experience something is merely to be affected by it. If in that sense, we can speak of *how the slug experienced the shock*, this would most plausibly mean: *how the shock affected the slug* (what it caused). But since here 'experiencing the shock' amounts to *being affected by* what is experienced (the shock), the experiencing does not *coincide* with the experience, as required by the phenomenal sense. Similar remarks would apply if we speak of the change to the slug's nervous system as something it 'experiences'. None of this, of course, is meant to assert or deny phenomenally conscious experience to the slug. That is not the issue. The point is just to distinguish the *phenomenal* sense of 'experience' from another, which is without question applicable to the slug—a sense in which to 'experience' something is just to be affected by it.[5]

I can now summarize my first way into the notion of phenomenality. A state of S is *phenomenally conscious* just in case it is an experience S experiences in the *coincident* sense, and differs from other experiences with respect to *how it is thus experienced*.

---

[4] My conception of the coincident sense of 'experience', and of phenomenal constancy as the preferred starting point for clarifying the idea that sense experience is intentional (hence my notion of 'objectual sensing' to be discussed below), are heavily indebted to my reading of Husserl (2001), Investigation V, Chapters 1 and 2.

[5] I wish to thank Anna Christina Soy Ribeiro and Dan Zahavi for discussion on these points.

Differences in how experiences are experienced are differences in their *phenomenal character*. And to experience experiences differing in phenomenal character is to have different *phenomenal features*. To this I would add, not just the aforementioned looking and feeling, but *sensory appearances generally*. Instances of something's *sounding, tasting, smelling*, or (tactually) *feeling* somehow to someone are phenomenal—provided they are experienced in this internal accusative sense. Whether experiences are *all* sensory in nature we leave undecided for now. This I call the 'subjective experience' conception of phenomenality, since it utilizes a conception of experience on which this is something that coincides with the subject's experience of it, and differs insofar as the subject experiences it differently.

Now let us look at the second conception of phenomenality—what I will call the *subjective contrast* conception. This aims to *make consciousness conspicuous by its absence*. We appeal to first-person reflection on real and hypothetical cases to contrast situations in which certain types of phenomenal states occur from otherwise similar situations in which they are absent. My point of departure is an interpretation of the condition known as 'blindsight'. Subjects suffering damage to the visual cortex deny seeing types of visual stimuli in circumstances where—pre-trauma—they would have affirmed it. All the same, some of them can still successfully identify the stimulus type, when 'forced' to select from a list of set options. One way to interpret this is to say that such subjects have 'blindsight' is to say that in *one* sense they *do see* the relevant stimulus, and in *another* they are *blind* to it (and their denials of seeing it are correct). We can interpret talk of an object *looking* somehow to someone so as to make sense of this. That is, we can grasp a specifically visual sense of 'look' in which no object *looks* any way at all to you in a lightless room, while we can interpret 'see' in such a way that you cannot be rightly said to *see* something that *looks* to you no way at all. Then we may further interpret this use of 'look' and 'see' so as to say that the blindsighter correctly denies *seeing* the stimulus; it does not *look* anyway to her. Nonetheless, she accurately reports on it because of the activity it triggers in what is left of her visual system. And that too we may call a kind of 'seeing'.

It would be enough for my purposes if this were merely an *intelligible hypothetical* case. But it is reasonable to believe that *actual* cases of blindsight are as I have described. However, we may refine our understanding by going on to consider forms of blindsight that are apparently merely hypothetical. We may conceive of the blindsighter being able to make 'blind' visual discriminatory judgements regarding at least some restricted range of stimulus types, not just in response to 'forced choices', but spontaneously, unprompted by some menu of options. Accordingly, we may conceive of a form of blindsight in which one thus discriminates shapes, position, orientation and movement of optically presented figures with no less accuracy and acuity than one would in cases where the stimuli *do* look somehow to the subject, though only very *blurrily*—in a way that would put one well within the territory of so-called 'legal blindness'.[6]

---

[6] This is the sort of case I describe in (Siewert 1998), Chapter 3, as 'spontaneous amblyopic blindsight'. It corresponds to what Block (2002) calls 'superblindsight'. Our expositions differ somewhat in their details, however, and mine does not utilize a contrast with what Block calls 'access consciousness'.

Further refinements are possible; but what I have said so far is enough to convey the basic strategy. Imagine being a blindsight subject as described, and contrast the case (a) where the stimulus looks to you no way at all, though you still spontaneously judge it to be there when it stimulates your visual receptors, with (b) the case where it does look to you somehow—albeit quite blurrily—so as to afford at best very low-acuity discriminations. Now we say that the sense of 'look' that allows you to intelligibly contrast (a) and (b) is a sense in which something's looking somehow to you is for it to *phenomenally* visually appear somehow to you. And its appearing to you this way constitutes a *phenomenally conscious* state. If adoption of a theory of mind would rationally commit you to denying the intelligibility of the sort of scenario just described—if it implied that once you rightly understood whatever consciousness we possess, you should find blindsight as (purportedly) just conceived ultimately *incoherent*—then that theory implicitly denies the reality of phenomenal consciousness.

Thus, on this 'subjective contrast' conception, phenomenality is that feature exemplified in cases of something's *looking* somehow to you, as it would not be in blindsight as just conceived—cases whose very reality would be denied in denying intelligibility of such blindsight. Such instances of its looking somehow to you are, necessarily, *phenomenally conscious visual states*. Building on this, we may define 'phenomenal *character*' as that subjectively discernible respect in which phenomenally conscious states, and *only* phenomenally conscious states may differ. Finally, for subjects to have different phenomenal *features* is for them to have states differing in phenomenal character.[7]

I intend this 'subjective contrast' conception to converge with the first 'subjective experience' conception. For what we are supposing the blindsighter to lack visually is a certain type of *experience* that is somehow *experienced by her* in the *coincident* sense: she does not experience a visual appearance of the stimulus. We may well also theorize that there are *some* visual, perhaps representational, states mediating stimulus and discriminatory response in blindsight judgement. But then we should want to recognize that the visual states postulated would not themselves be *experienced by the subject* in a sense in which her *experiencing* them would *coincide* with states experienced.

Now to introduce the third, 'what it is like' or 'subjective knowledge' conception of phenomenality. Recall that the term 'experience' was liable to be construed in a way that did not capture what we required. Similarly, while we may wish to say (with Block 2002) that what makes a state phenomenal is that there is 'something it is like' to be in it, we must recognize that we can speak of there being something it is like for someone to be in a state, even where its phenomenality cannot be assumed. For example, one may know or be curious about 'what it is like' for someone to be over seven feet tall, or have a conjoined twin, or walk on the moon. On the face of it, the 'something it is like' criterion of phenomenality embraces too much for it to ground our understanding of what consciousness, specifically, is supposed to be.

But as before, a few refinements will meet the difficulty. Consider how there may be 'something it is like' for one to have certain features only *non-essentially* or in a manner

---

[7] This is roughly the conception of consciousness I articulate in Siewert (1998), Chapter 3.

that is *derivative* from what it is like for one to have other features. This is relevant to helping us to sharpen the notion of phenomenality, inasmuch as those features that, by contrast, have this status (of there being 'something it is like' for one to have them) *essentially and non-derivatively* will be the *bona fide phenomenal* features—those whose instances constitute phenomenally conscious states.

To see how this would work, consider what it is like to walk on the moon. Plausibly, there is something it is like to walk on the moon, only because there is (for instance) a way it *feels* to one to walk on the moon (and there is something *that* is like for one). But then there will be something it is like to walk on the moon only accidentally or non-essentially, if lunar walking could possibly occur *without the feeling* (or other—such as visual—experiences). Moreover, suppose (for the sake of argument) that no lunar walking could occur without being *felt*. There might still only *derivatively* be something it is like for one to walk on the moon.

Let me explain this last point. What it is like to have some feature F 'entirely derives from' what it is like to have some other feature just when one could *know* what it is like to have F if and only if one knew what it is like to have some *other* (maybe highly complex) feature G, to which having F is inessential—and other necessary conditions obtained, which did not consist in knowledge of what it was like to have some feature. Plausibly, what it is like to moon walk is derivative in this sense. For one could know what that was like, just by knowing (for example) how it *felt* (plus knowing things like: that is the way it feels to walk on the moon). And it is reasonable to suppose one could (for example) *feel* that way without actually walking on the moon (some kind of virtual moonwalking, or walking on a planet similar to our moon might do).

By contrast, there is *essentially and non-derivatively* something that it is like to *feel* the way the moon-walkers feel. At least we will think so, if we think that one could not possibly feel this way, when there was just *nothing* that was like for one, and we can identify no further feature, to which feeling this way is inessential, such that what it was like feel to this way derived entirely from the presence of *that* feature.

So far, my exposition of this 'what it is like' conception has relied on this locution without attempting to explain it in other terms. But we can say something more about the relevant interpretation of this handy if puzzling phrase. To begin: there is something it is like to have some feature just when that feature is of a kind suited for one to claim or desire *knowledge* of what it is like to have it. And, I propose, knowledge of what it is like for one to have a feature is a knowledge of *what feature it is*, of a kind that requires either *having that feature oneself* or else *being able to imagine having it*. In that sense, it is a kind of knowledge whose possession demands that—as Nagel (1974) suggests—we 'take up the subject's point of view'. It is then, a 'subjective knowledge' of the feature in question. This is the sort of knowledge we want when we express a curiosity not only (for instance) about how some unfamiliar food tastes or colour looks, but when we wonder what it is like for someone to undergo a religious conversion, be falsely condemned to death, play virtuosic jazz saxophone, or grow up in a remote Amazonian tribe. The knowledge longed for (maybe futilely) is, I want to add, '*non-theoretical*' in this sense: here knowledge of *what the feature in question is* (for example, knowing what it is to be converted) does not require that one can give a theoretically satisfying *account or explanation* of what that feature consists in.

So, by this criterion, there can indeed be 'something that it is like' to have all kinds of features—phenomenal and non-phenomenal alike. But there is something it is like to have a non-phenomenal feature only when it is appropriately associated with some phenomenal feature; that is, with *some feature essentially and non-derivatively suited for one to claim or desire a non-theoretical subjective knowledge regarding what feature it is*. This, then, I offer as the 'subjective knowledge' (or 'what it is like') conception of phenomenality. A phenomenally conscious state—an experience—is just an instance of a phenomenal feature, so understood. And we may say that different phenomenal features differ phenomenally (their instances differ in phenomenal character), just when they differ in some way such that it is suitable for one to claim or desire a subjective, non-theoretical knowledge of what that difference is. I believe this conception coordinates well with the previous two. Phenomenal differences, understood as differences in 'what it is like' (as just interpreted), correspond to differences in *how an experience is experienced by a subject* in the coincident sense. And as for the 'subjective contrast' conception: whatever 'visual states' may mediate the blindsighter's retinal stimulation and her discriminatory judgement, there is nothing it is *essentially non-derivatively* like for her to be in just *those* states—thus they are not phenomenal. But there is, essentially and non-derivatively, something it is like for something to look chartreuse to you, for example.

The conception of phenomenality I have just summarized combines three ways of getting at phenomenal consciousness (*subjective experience, subjective contrast*, and *subjective ('what it's like') knowledge*), elaborating on each of these to yield distinct but mutually reinforcing accounts. The merit I claim for this threefold conception is that it coherently unifies and refines different, prominent, intuitively appealing ways of identifying the topic—phenomenal consciousness—in a manner that can prepare us to address the controversies that this arouses without making needless assumptions about their correct resolution.

Let me say a little to underscore this claim that I desirably avoid certain prejudicial assumptions. First, talk of 'experiencing an experience' may suggest to some that, in being experienced, the experience is itself 'represented'—or maybe 'self-representing'. But we have not taken this step. So far all we are saying is that the way you experience your experience simply *is* its phenomenal character. We have as yet given no reason to think that any inner representation of the experience is involved. Neither the subjective experience conception of phenomenality—nor I would add, the subjective contrast and subjective knowledge conceptions—by themselves take sides for or against 'self-representational', 'higher-order', or 'inner sense' theories of phenomenal consciousness.

Notice too that this initial conception leaves open questions about the *range* of phenomenal differences—whether they somehow incorporate differences in a subject's conceptual understanding, and whether they straddle some distinction between sense experience and conceptual thought, and just how they relate to the notion of intentional or representational 'content' generally. We have appealed to examples of sensory appearance to fix the sense of 'experience' we're after. But this does not immediately tell us whether phenomenal character is purely a matter of 'sensory qualia', or whether it is 'intentional' or 'representational', and if so whether it is 'conceptual' or 'non-conceptual'. Nor does it preclude believing that we also *experience* our own conceptual thought—and not merely sensory appearances and imagery—and that differences in how we experience our own thinking are inseparable from the exercise of our conceptual abilities. Finally, notice that, while I speak here of 'subjective experience', nothing in this conception implies that experience is something entirely 'internal' to the subject, exclusive of anything in the 'external world'. For all that has been said so far, experiences may or may not be entirely 'in the head', and it may or may not be that environmental entities are constituents of experience. Subjective experiences are experiences 'in the subject'. But equally, the experiencing subject may essentially be 'in the world'—an embodied agent at grips with its surroundings. Finally, note that nothing in this conception of consciousness directly forces our hand in disputes between physicalism and dualism. All this is (rightly) left open in our *initial* conception of phenomenality.

4 SENSORY APPEARANCE AND INTENTIONALITY

Of course, the relative neutrality of this threefold conception of consciousness will be methodologically beneficial, only if it helps us to justify answers to at least some of the questions initially left in suspense. So I now want to indicate how to put it to work, first addressing questions about the 'intentional' or 'representational' status of conscious sense experience and how it is related to our 'conceptual capacities'. This comes first, since I think we must deal with such questions in order to answer the others (for example, regarding the phenomenality of conceptual thought, and the nature of introspection).

The discussion so far not only offers us a way of understanding what it means to say that sensory appearances are phenomenal, it also affords us a way of focusing specifically on *sensory* appearances and questions about their phenomenal character. The 'subjective contrast' conception of consciousness makes *certain types* of conscious states conspicuous by their absence in blindsight. And those types are specifically *sensory* forms of appearance—in this case *visual*—marked by a use of the term 'look'. Analogous considerations could yield a similar result for other commonly recognized modalities. (So, for example, we could think of auditory appearances as what would be missing in hypothetically considered 'deaf-hearing'—in which you correctly judge as to the occurrence of sounds that did not *sound* anyhow to you). And then, using the subjective experience and 'what it is like' conceptions of phenomenality, we could inquire about the phenomenal character of these sensory appearances by asking about *how they are experienced* (in the coincident sense) or (equivalently) about *what it is like for us* (essentially and non-derivatively) for something to appear (look, sound, and so on) to us as it does.

Notice that this approach does not rely on introducing the notion of phenomenal sensory appearances (as have some) by *contrasting* the allegedly 'phenomenal' or 'phenomenological' use of 'appears-' talk ('look', 'sound', 'taste', and so on) with some supposedly distinct 'intentional' or 'epistemic' use. On the conception I have offered, 'That wine looks yellow to me' and 'It looks to me as if that wine is yellow' can both count as reports of 'phenomenal' looks.[8] It will not automatically cancel this if we say that the second also attributes to me an intentional or representational state of some sort. And my notion of phenomenal sensory appearance does not tie its expression to specific *grammatical forms* (so that, for instance, 'looks like' and 'looks as if' would not count as expressions for *phenomenal* appearings). All this is desirable in how it leaves open at the outset questions about the relation among sensory appearances, intentionality, and the exercise of conceptual abilities. I maintain it leaves these open, because when I say that the 'looks' in 'It looks to me as if that wine is yellow' counts as a phenomenal 'looks', I do not mean to assume that it cannot be somehow analyzed into two aspects: one a phenomenal 'non-intentional and purely qualitative' aspect, and one a separable *non*-phenomenal and 'intentional' or 'representational' aspect (perhaps a dispositional *belief* of some sort). That sort of issue is yet to be resolved.

To help us resolve it, we need to become clearer about what I will call 'objectual sensing'. I have already hinted at this notion. Commonly, when something *looks* somehow shaped to you (in the phenomenal sense operative in consideration of blindsight), *how you experience* the appearance of its shape varies (*what it is like* for it to look to you as it does changes). And so in *some* way how it *looks* to you changes, even while *it constantly appears the same shape* (it looks the same in shape) throughout. Moreover, in these situations, the *way* the experience of the shape-appearance varies is what determines it to be, discernibly to first-person reflection, the appearance of a constant shape. By discerning *how you experience* the disk's looking to you as it does (in other words, *what it is like* for it to look to you as it does) when it rotates, or when you shift your attention, you can tell that throughout it *looks circular*—and does *not* appear to 'morph'. In first-person reflection, you can also—by contrast—discern what it is like for something to look to you as it does (how your experience of its appearance alters), and thereby tell that sometimes something *does* appear to you to change shape; it does look differently shaped to you as you are looking at it. If we speak of this *looking*, this visual appearing, as a kind of *sensing*, we may redescribe this contrast as one between two conditions: (a) *how you sense* some feature of something changes (though you do *not sense it to change* in that respect), and (b) you do *sense something to change* in that very respect. Wherever there is such an (a) type constancy in *what* is sensed amid fluctuation in *how* it is sensed—where there is this form of *phenomenal sensory constancy*—I will speak of '*objectual sensing*'. Here, in sensing, something 'stands firm', 'thrown against the sensory flux'—an 'ob-ject'—so that *what is sensed* does not simply *coincide* with *how it is sensed*.

From a traditional empiricist perspective one might challenge my remarks, claiming that nothing ever really *phenomenally* looks constant in shape as orientation changes or attention wanders. It is only that some special ways of appearing to morph give rise to separable judgements about some stable object behind them, which are hypothesized as causes of the 'Protean' display—whereas *other* ways of appearing to morph do not.

---

[8] Here I borrow an example from (and contrast my position with) Maund (2003).

In response, I would first ask: just what *is* the difference in appearance that occasions the difference in judgement? The straightforward way to characterize it is this. In some cases something *appears or looks the same* (in shape or colour) throughout the change in manner of appearance, while in others it *appears to change* (shape or colour). But the 'Protean' view cannot accept this. And if it offers no clear alternative way to describe the difference in appearance, we should stick with the description that recognizes phenomenal constancy. Second, it is doubtful that the Protean view can account for the appearance of *depth*. For example, as the disk tilts towards the viewer, the Protean would have to say that the boundary appears to bend and stretch out horizontally in a certain way. But for the edge to appear in depth, and look, as it does, *now farther, now nearer*, it must appear rigid, unbending, as it approaches. If it apparently morphed by horizontally bending and stretching in the envisaged manner, it would not be *looking nearer*. And it is untenable to deny that we really do experience appearances of depth. Otherwise, how are we to describe the often quite vivid visual *illusions* of depth in two-dimensional images?

Finally, I would ask: if we do not admit the reality of phenomenal sensory constancy, how are we to make sense of what I will call the 'experience of disillusionment'? Consider a case where a flat surface appears protuberant, as it might if skilfully painted *trompe l'oeil* style. As you get a better look at what appears to you, the illusion vanishes, when what had appeared protuberant now appears flat, *though in the meantime it appeared unchanging in shape*. But there was disillusionment only if a conflict in appearance was resolved. And something can present conflicting appearances over time, only if what appears to have first the one shape, now the other, also appears unchanged in shape throughout. For otherwise, there is no *conflict* to be resolved, only an *appearance of change*. It seems you can deny apparent shape constancy here, while acknowledging that you can somehow correct illusory appearances of shape by getting a better look at something, only if you try to reconstruct this as proceeding by way of an inference—from the belief that some surface *appeared to flatten out*—to the belief that *it was actually flat all along*. But if those who experienced visual disillusionment would not avow this inference or its premise, we have no reason to attribute it to them, and there would, in any case, be no accounting for why, in these instances, something's appearing to *become* flat should give one a reason to think that it (or something else 'behind' it) was *already* flat.

All this, I argue, supports the phenomenology of 'objectual sensing' sketched above. This is significant because it furnishes the rudiments of sensory *intentionality*, and prepares us to consider questions about 'content' and 'conceptuality'. The general notion of intentionality ('mental reference to an object', 'object directedness') is admittedly vague. But an *objectual* sensing able to generate *conflicts in appearances* (hence *illusion* and *disillusion*) would seem to be sufficient for sensory *intentionality* on any reasonable construal. If this is right, then the idea that the phenomenal is specifically a domain of raw sensation, sense-data, or non-intentional qualia should be firmly rejected—and on *phenomenological* grounds.[9]

---

[9] I first made a version of this 'argument from disillusionment' against sense-data in Siewert (1998), Chapter 7. I further discuss issues concerning the experience of disillusion and perceptual constancy in Siewert (2006, 2012a, 2012b).

Should we worry that not just the occurrence of some stretch of experience, but the possession of certain *general abilities* is needed for having intentionality, even of the sensory sort? Then we may reasonably say that it is enough for this that an animal has the *sensorimotor skills* to reliably generate appearances of stable objects in its environment, and to resolve conflicts in appearance through their exercise. This is not to assume that the character of the sensory appearances we and other animals ordinarily experience can be divorced from the possession of such skills. But if it can be, we could then explicitly add them, to account for the intentionality of sense experience.[10]

Notice that *this* sort of 'intentionalism' about phenomenal character does not commit one to saying that it can be reductively explained in terms of representational content. For that matter, I have so far kept the very notion of representation at arm's length. The question of whether sense experience has 'conceptual' or 'non-conceptual content' is also still in suspense. The words 'content' and 'representation' are used repeatedly in the philosophy of mind. Just what they convey is not always so clear. But about 'content' I would now say this. We have spoken of how phenomenal sensory appearances are experienced, and we have recognized a distinction between *how they are experienced*, and how the *objects* of appearance both *appear* and *are*. And we have said that how the appearances are experienced suffices for objectual sensing, hence for intentionality. If the 'intentional content' of sense experience is regarded as that aspect of it in virtue of which it is objectual, in an intentional 'refers to an object' sense, then we can indeed conclude that *how we experience experiences*—what it is like for us to have them, their phenomenal character—constitutes a kind of 'intentional content'.

But does my phenomenology thus far support our regarding experiential content as 'representational'? And should we see it as 'conceptual'? Our answers depend, naturally, on what we think they would entail. We might think that wherever there is representation there is a 'vehicle' of representation—something (like symbols or pictures perhaps) that 'carries' the content. But we have as yet found no such symbol- or image-like vehicle separable from content in the phenomenology of sense experience. Also, it seems questionable that sensory experience is representational, if this assumes that the content of experience can be exhaustively captured somehow sententially or (quasi-) pictorially. If we consider cases where we 'experience visual disillusionment', it is hard to see how we could always distinguish appearances by the attribution of either sentential or (quasi-) pictorial content to them (I discuss this in Siewert 2005, pp. 282–4). To regard experience as representational in this sense may be to force onto it a kind of determinacy alien to its character.

One might, however, have in mind a *thinner* notion of representation, whose application is warranted by the phenomenology. So, given how you are experiencing (and

---

[10] I propose we understand sensory intentionality in terms of motor skills in Siewert (2012b), in criticizing what seems to me McDowell's (1994) overly intellectualist notion of what is needed for perceptual experience of spatial objects. In this article too I explain my interpretation of Merleau-Ponty (2003) in ways that indicate his influence on my proposal, and why I think a Merleau-Pontian perspective is, nonetheless, more compatible than it might seem with the belief that rationality 'permeates' our experience—even if this is not to be understood in quite the way that McDowell would understand it.

disposed to experience) visual appearances during a certain time, if there is then something with a certain shape in a certain location, the way it looks to you is accurate (and if not, then it is inaccurate). In this sense, having experience with a certain phenomenal character entails having experience with certain 'accuracy' or 'correctness' conditions.[11] And one might have a notion of 'representation' thin enough that this by itself is trivially sufficient for making it true that your experience 'represents' things as somehow shaped and situated.

Once we have these points sorted out, it remains to be determined whether phenomenal sensory content is 'conceptual'. This, of course, will again depend on how one interprets the claim at issue. If we think that having experience with a certain 'conceptual content' entails having certain conceptual (especially inferential) abilities essential to possessing certain concepts, then the claim is certainly questionable. We should not just assume that, for instance, if something looks shaped and situated in a certain way to S, then S 'possesses the concept' of that shape and position—where this involves having the ability to make appropriate voluntary inferences regarding shape and location. There is evidently no good reason why an animal could not enjoy objectual sensing of shape, size, movement, and location in the sense discussed, without having the correlative *inferential* capacities.

Still, even if that is right, it may be that *typically* the character of *adult human sensory* experience does also essentially involve inferential abilities tied to the possession of concepts with which its content would be characterized. But how might this be so? To look into this I suggest we start by considering what I will call 'recognitional appearances'. The capacity to *recognize* a sensed object as *of a given type* is presumably often at least a *part* of having a concept of that type. So if *what it is like* to recognize a sensed object as of a type involves the exercise of these recognitional capacities, and these are (rightly exercised) sufficient for some kind of concept possession, then ordinary phenomenal sensory experience will essentially involve having concepts.

The question is not whether there is something it is like for one to recognize types of object by their sensory appearance. Once we acknowledge that there may only *derivatively* be something it is like, we should not be reluctant to grant this much. What is the issue then? The key question is whether there is essentially and non-derivatively something it is like for something to sensorily *appear* (such as look, sound) *recognizable as of a given type*.

What I mean by 'appear recognizable' is this. One can experience visual appearances of similarities and differences among objects in a sense that require more than just seeing their spatial extent, colour, and location. So, for example, faced with the task of selecting which visible figures are not like others in some group, one may see where all the variously coloured objects in the group are, without yet seeing *which are alike and*

---

[11] I argue in Siewert (1998), Chapter 7, that since such 'assessments for accuracy' follow, once the character of one's experience and the condition of one's environment are given, even without the need for additional 'interpreting' conditions, visual phenomenal features should be regarded as *intentional* features.

which dissimilar, and in what respect. But then suppose that one notices or is struck by some similarity (say, in shape) among a subgroup. The respect in which they appear similar constitutes a type, and they then 'appear recognizable as of that type'. This is a 'recognitional' appearance. Here we might also consider examples of *ambiguous figures.* For example, a capital M might suddenly appear to you recognizable as a sigma turned on its side. Or we may reflect on cases where there is a *delay* in recognition. Consider, for example, the following sequence of characters: =):-)=. It may take you a moment to see it as a (sideways) picture of Abraham Lincoln (or of 'a guy with hat and a beard')— in my terms, for it to *look to you recognizable as* such a picture. One use of 'looks like' marks what I am pursuing here, as when we say: 'Now this looks to me like a sigma', 'Now that looks to me like a picture of Lincoln'. (These need not be interpreted as asserting a 'mere resemblance'.)[12]

Reflecting on such examples, and employing the conception of phenomenality sketched above, we are in a position to ask: is there only *derivatively* something that it is like to experience such recognitional appearances? That is, can we reduce what it is like to experience them to how we experience appearances that are *not* recognitional? Can we identify *non*-recognitional appearances of an object, so that what it like for us to experience them is just the same as what it is like for us to experience recognitional appearances?

Here is a way I propose to start assessing this. Consider a case of someone with severe visual form agnosia. We may suppose that things do not *look recognizable to her as of kinds*—even though she may see with normal visual acuity how things are distributed in space around her. Now consider the experience you have when something you see at first does not look recognizable to you as of a given kind, and then it does—and the change in what it is like for you to see that thing when this happens. These will include cases of recognition as just illustrated with figures and pictures. But you might also consider ordinary cases where—because of absentmindedness, or unusual orientation, or partial occlusion, or 'messy' surrounds—you *see* some F (a toothpaste tube, scissors handles, a pen) *before it looks recognizable to you as such*—and then it *does* so appear to you. Then ask yourself: if you now suppose what it is like for you when undergoing these changes were generally to become what it was like for the agnosiac to see things, would they *still* not look recognizable to her? In other words, can you sustain the supposition that she remains a visual form agnosiac, when you conceive of her becoming your visual

---

[12] So I intend 'appear recognizable as an F' to cover *both* cases in which one *successfully recognizes* an F, and cases in which one *mistakes* something for an F. There is a tricky question here about whether something could look to you recognizable as F even on an occasion in which neither condition obtained. I do not want to have to *assume* that it is strictly impossible that someone might visually attend to some F for a brief time in exactly the same way as one who does visually recognize it as an F, but without such recognition, and without there being *at that time* a phenomenal difference in their visual experience. But if that is admitted I would still count both as cases where something appears *recognizable* as an F—hence as 'recognitional appearances' in my terms. For *had* the experience of the non-recognizer occurred in the context of a general disposition to experience *other* such appearances, it *would have* constituted the exercise of a *bona fide* skill for recognition. I am indebted to Kevin Connolly for making me aware of this complication.

phenomenal twin? If not, then you should think what it is like to experience recognitional appearances is not generally reducible to what it is like to experience non-recognitional ones.

If we accept this result, then we may go on to ask what range of types admit of *phenomenally* differing recognitional appearances. Shall we include here, for example, 'looks like a *computer keyboard*', 'looks like a *pine tree*', 'looks like a *beckoning gesture*'? I believe we will not be able to justify an especially restrictive attitude about this, once we accept that if the agnosiac were to become generally phenomenally visually like us, she would be cured of her agnosia. I should make it clear, however, that I do not think this issue (or neighbouring ones) can be quickly resolved just by first-person reflection on the sort of examples just mentioned. We need to look in more detail at the forms of agnosia (and at relevant psychological research generally) together with greater clarification of the issues, and more detailed reflection on cases. I should also here make a little more explicit the relationship of my position on recognitional appearances to the question of whether 'high-level properties' (such as natural or artifactual kinds) are 'represented in visual experience' (as Siegel 2006 argues). I do not regard this as settled once we admit recognitional appearances of, for instance, pine trees and gloves. For I do not think we can move straightaway from 'It looks recognizable to me as a glove (or a pine tree)' to 'My visual experience *represents it to have* (or *attributes to it*) the property of being a glove (or a pine tree)'. For suppose that (by some unlikely twist) it turns out that what looked recognizable to me as a glove was actually fashioned for some *non-glove* purpose (which just happened to make it also perfectly *serviceable* as a glove). Or suppose the genetic background of a plant that looked recognizable to me as a pine kept it from being a genuine pine tree. It would not, I think, follow that the way it then *looked* to me, in virtue of the character of my visual experience, was *inaccurate*. Maybe we should just say: I only *falsely judged* it to be a glove (or pine tree) from its *accurate* 'glovey' (or 'piney') *appearance*. So these questions about 'representational content' remain open.[13] And there is still the additional matter of how the experience of recognitional appearances relates to conceptual abilities.[14]

So we may ask: is experiential content that is irreducibly recognitional 'fully conceptual'? For this we need to consider whether the kinds of recognitional appearances we acknowledge as phenomenal are detachable from having relevant *inferential* conceptual capacities. Again, the issue is complex. We should want to say that *some* phenomenal recognitional appearances can precede one's coming into the relevant inferential abilities. For example, one can recognize shapes before being able to make appropriate voluntary inferences regarding shapes, and can recognize beckoning or angry gestures before being able to make appropriate 'theory of mind' inferences. (Here, incidentally, we see where the phenomenology of perceptual experience feeds into discussion of 'other

[13] I am grateful to Casey O'Callaghan for discussion of these points.
[14] I regard Husserl's (2001) subtle though elusive and incomplete discussion of 'categorial intuition' in the Sixth Logical Investigation as a still valuable resource for exploring these difficult issues about the borderland between 'sensibility' and 'understanding'.

minds'). It seems that such recognitional experience must come before full concept possession, if we are to *acquire* the relevant concepts *through* experience. However, it might also be that some skills of sensory recognition could conceivably be learned only against the background of a lot of relevant inferential ability. Think, for example, of the visual recognitional skills of a medical technician or an art historian.

This suggests that it will be misguided to ask simply whether experiential content in general is not only intentional, but *conceptual* as well. For the phenomenology I have been sketching tends towards the conclusion that while the 'recognitional capacity' aspect of concept possession commonly helps constitute the phenomenal character of sensory appearance, its tie to the 'inferential capacity' aspect is looser—though also not completely detachable. So we can say that when sense experience of space is non-recognitional (as it can be), it has non-conceptual content. But there also will at least be the (proto-conceptual?) content of recognitional experience. And if the latter is *sometimes* inseparable from background inferential abilities, we might say there is 'conceptual content' in experience, in a sense. But in a normal longish course of experience there seems to be no way to cleanly segregate—either running throughout or intermittently present—some distinct 'layer' of purely non-conceptual content, or, say, just when some specific *fully* conceptual content is implied and when it is not. And if that is so, the notion of 'non-conceptual content' cannot do much to reveal to us what distinguishes the intentionality of sense experience.

All this still leaves the question of how (or whether) we are to include the occurrence of *thinking* (as distinct from sensing)—which *is* as 'fully conceptual' as we could wish— in the domain of the phenomenal. Thus we come to the issue sometimes discussed under the rubric of 'cognitive phenomenology'. Is phenomenality confined to sensory experience, or is occurrent non-sensory conceptual thought and understanding also phenomenal? Here again I can only briefly outline my response, which I discuss elsewhere (Siewert 1998, Chapter 8, 2011b) in detail. To some extent my approach to the question of phenomenal thought parallels my treatment of recognitional sensory appearances. The issue is not just whether there is 'something that it is like' to engage in conceptual (not merely imagistic) thinking. In first-person reflection we can recognize that, for example, we may read a given passage without following it, without an ongoing understanding of it; and then we re-read it *with* such an understanding of meaning—a sort of semantic understanding that involves full-blown concept possession. And what it is like to read with understanding differs from what it is like to read without it, in the sense of 'what it is like' previously explained. The question, then, is whether there is essentially and non-derivatively something it is like to enjoy some form of conceptual thought in these and other cases. I argue that we should address this question by asking whether we can identify some sensory appearances or imagery we could have in the absence of conceptual understanding, the experience of which we would judge to be phenomenally just the same as the experience in which understanding *does* occur. If we cannot, then (on the basis of this and additional considerations) we should include the sort of occurrent thought and understanding of which we are subjectively aware in our lives—and not just sensory appearances and imagery—within the realm of the phenomenal.

Similar arguments proceed from reflection on cases where understanding of an utterance is momentarily delayed, and on cases where understanding of an ambiguous phrase 'flips' or 'switches'. (There is something that it is like for us when we suddenly seem to 'get' what the speaker just meant, or when we suddenly reconstrue what she just said). An absence of suitable sensory differences that might rightly serve as the sole locus of phenomenality—differences utterly detachable from the relevant conceptual understanding—should bid us to acknowledge that our own occurrent thought and understanding is not to be excluded from the realm of authentically phenomenal experience. None of this entails that conceptual thought can occur in atomistic isolation, or in the complete absence of a capacity to give it sensible expression, or in some solipsistic 'de-worlded' soul or brain. It merely restores our cognitive lives to experience, from which recent philosophy has temporarily estranged them.

5   Applications

Although my account here has been (unavoidably) rather schematic, I hope to have said enough for us to see roughly how it connects with an array of philosophical issues. To start with, consider the issues of intentionality and content broached in the last section. Many of the controversies in this area have tended to pit those who defend the idea of 'non-intentional' or 'non-representational' sensory 'qualia' (or at least to non-representational differences among experiences) against proponents of 'representationalist' accounts that purport to explain phenomenal character in terms of some notion of content that does not presuppose it, hoping thereby to implement some physicalist or naturalizing program regarding the mind. The approach I indicated above suggests a different take on these issues. It starts from a phenomenological conception of consciousness illustrated by reference to sensory appearances (without necessarily being confined to them) understood in a way that neither affirms the existence of non-representational sensory qualities, nor appeals to notions of 'content' drawn from discussion of propositions (and 'propositional attitudes') and pictorial and quasi-pictorial forms of representation. I proceed to argue on phenomenological grounds that the character of sense experience makes it 'objectual' and susceptible to experiences of illusion and disillusion. If we therefore speak of phenomenal or experiential content as *intentional*, and of a kind of 'intentionalism' about consciousness, this is not on the basis of any conception of mental representation that furnishes a means to explain phenomenality in non-phenomenal terms. Recognition of this essential tie to intentionality can thus be severed from any reductionist project.

Further development of this phenomenology actually casts doubt on proposals for reducing consciousness to a sensory non-conceptual form of representation. Partly this is because it leads us to include occurrent conceptual thought and understanding in the phenomenal domain, and not confine it to the specifically sensory. It does, however, agree with some reductionist representational theories that the intentionality of perception can precede the exercise of robust, distinctively conceptual capacities. But it also leads us to find recognitional capacities that are integral to concept possession irreducibly manifest in the phenomenal character of much normal human perception. And as it is doubtful whether we can everywhere divorce these capacities from background inferential abilities, it is doubtful too whether we can generally isolate some layer of 'non-conceptual content' and restrict sense experience entirely to this.

My results not only help us in this way to evaluate strategies for explaining phenomenality; they also help us to understand the epistemic role of experience. For phenomenal sensing, being 'objectual', and capable of undoing the illusions to which it is vulnerable, makes it possible for thought to identify, with warrant, objects of predication. And being 'recognitional', it gives us warrant for these predications, since something's *appearing recognizable* as F gives one some warrant for thinking it *is* F.

This perspective also prepares us to examine 'higher-order' and self-representationalist strategies for explaining consciousness. I argue (in Siewert 2012a) that the sort of phenomenal constancy to be found at the first-order level (which there grounds the notion of objectual sensing) cannot be found at the second-order level (where the putative objects are states of one's own mind). And this speaks *against* the notion of 'inner sense' which some have associated with consciousness. This forms part of a larger case that we lack any basis (phenomenological or otherwise) for construing phenomenality as the mind's self-representation. Still, that is not to deny there is a distinctively 'introspective' form of attention to one's own experience involved in the warrant peculiar to knowledge of it. There is, and phenomenology demands it. But such attention is not some additional layer of quasi-sensory scrutiny, but a special (and only occasional) cognitive form of attention, parasitic on first-order 'looking outward'. And cognitively 'looking harder' at one's experience does not mean turning some gaze ever more firmly 'inward'. It involves attending indivisibly both to the world and one's experience of it, *while asking better, more probing questions about it*. This is, in fact, what I have been trying to do in the preceding phenomenological investigation.

Limitations of space prohibit further elaboration of these themes, and their extension to the questions about value raised at the beginning. But I hope that the foregoing conveys something of the feasibility of a contemporary phenomenological approach to consciousness. By taking seriously a critical use of first-person reflection, and striving to avoid precipitous theoretical commitments, we may gradually build up a conception of phenomenal consciousness—of experience—that restores to us an appreciation of its reach, its richness and its importance, one which can help us come to terms with fundamental philosophical problems including (but not limited to) those that concern the form its *explanation* might take, its role in *knowledge* (of ourselves, our surroundings, and others), and its place in our *values*.

It might seem that much about my approach differs little from that adopted (though perhaps less self-consciously) by many in mainstream 'analytic' philosophy of mind. So it may seem unwarranted to insist on the label 'phenomenological' for philosophy not more closely and explicitly identified with that of classic figures from the 'phenomenological tradition'—especially Husserl. But I am not especially worried about blurring the line between the philosophy of mind and traditional phenomenology. On the contrary, I think it could be a salutary corrective to distortions wrought by taking the 'continental/ analytic' distinction too seriously. However, I also am not reluctant to admit that the views I have outlined here have more in common with those found in phenomenologists such as Brentano, Husserl, and Merleau-Ponty than do those of the average 'analytic' philosopher. And this—as I have said—is no accident. Methodologically, this influence can be seen in my unabashed reliance on critical first-person reflection to identify and clarify crucial distinctions, while simultaneously striving to limit presuppositions. Substantially, it is evident in my broadly inclusive and happily realist view of consciousness, and my defence of an intentionalist conception of perception, grounded in the phenomenon of object constancy, and linked to an understanding of bodily skill. Finally, like the phenomenologists I have named, I believe philosophy developed along these lines—even though it advances no reductionist theory—can do much to further our understanding of the mind in positive ways.[15]

References

Armstrong, D. (1968), *A Materialist Theory of Mind* (London: Routledge).
Block, N. (2002), 'Concepts of consciousness', in D. J. Chalmers (ed.) (2002), *Philosophy of Mind: Classical and Contemporary Readings* (Oxford: Oxford University Press).
Carruthers P. (2000), *Phenomenal Consciousness* (Cambridge: Cambridge University Press).
—— (2004), 'Hop over For, Hot theory', in R. Gennaro (ed.) (2004), *Higher-Order Theories of Consciousness* (Philadelphia: John Benjamins Publishers).
Dretske, F. (1995), *Naturalizing the Mind* (Cambridge, MA: MIT Press).
Gunther, Y. (ed.) (2002), *Essays on Nonconceptual Content* (Cambridge, MA: MIT Press).
Husserl, E. (2001), *Logical Investigations*, tr. J. Findlay (London: Routledge).
Lycan, W. (2004), 'The superiority of Hop to Hot', in R. Gennaro (ed.) (2004), *Higher-Order Theories of Consciousness* (Philadelphia: John Benjamins Publishers).
Merleau-Ponty, M. (2003), *Phenomenology of Perception*, tr. C. Smith (London: Routledge).
Maund, B. (2003), *Perception* (Montreal: McGill-Queen's University Press).
McDowell, J. (1994), *Mind and World* (Cambridge, MA: Harvard University Press).
Nagel, T (1974), 'What is it like to be a bat?', *Philosophical Review* 4: 435–50.
Kriegel, U. (2009), *Subjective Consciousness: a Self-Representational Theory* (Oxford: Oxford University Press).
Rosenthal, David (2002), 'Explaining consciousness', in D. J. Chalmers (ed.) (2002), *Philosophy of Mind: Classical and Contemporary Readings* (Oxford: Oxford University Press).
Shoemaker, S. (1994), *The First-Person Perspective and Other Essays* (Cambridge: Cambridge University Press).
Siegel, S. (2006), 'Which properties are represented in perception?', in T. Gendler Szabo and J. Hawthorne (eds), *Perceptual Experience* (Oxford: Oxford University Press).
Siewert, C. (1998), *The Significance of Consciousness* (Princeton: Princeton University Press).

[15] I thank Dan Zahavi and an anonymous reviewer for comments that helped me to clarify how I view the relationship between my account and the phenomenological tradition.

—— (2005), 'Attention and sensorimotor intentionality', in Smith and Thomasson (2005).

—— (2006), 'Is the appearance of shape protean?', *Psyche* 12/3. (http://psyche.cs.monash.edu.au).

—— (2007a), 'In favor of (plain) phenomenology', *Phenomenology and the Cognitive Sciences: Special Issue on Dennett and Heterophenomenology* 6/1–2.

—— (2007b), 'Who's afraid of phenomenological disputes?', *Southern Journal of Philosophy* XLV/Supplement.

—— (2011a), 'Socratic introspection and the abundance of experience', in *Journal of Consciousness Studies*, Special issue on R. Hurlburt's and E. Schwitzgebel's *Describing Inner Experience? Proponent Meets Skeptic.*

—— (2011b), 'Phenomenal thought', in T. Bayne and M. Montague (eds), *Cognitive Phenomenology* (Oxford: Oxford University Press).

—— (2011c), 'Philosophy of mind', in S. Luft and S. Overgaard (eds.), *The Routledge Companion to Phenomenology* (London: Routledge Press).

—— (2012a), 'On the phenomenology of introspection', in D. Smithies and D. Stoljar (eds), *Introspection and Consciousness* (Oxford: Oxford University Press).

—— (2012b), 'Intellectualism, experience, and motor understanding'. in J. Schear (ed.), *Mind, Reason, and Being-in-the-World: the McDowell/Dreyfus Debate* (London: Routledge Press).

Smith, D. W. (2005), 'Consciousness with reflexive content', in Smith and Thomasson (2005).

—— and Thomasson, A. (eds) (2005), *Phenomenology and the Philosophy of Mind* (Oxford: Oxford University Press).

Tye, M. (1995), *Ten Problems of Consciousness* (Cambridge, MA: MIT Press).

—— (2000), *Consciousness, Color and Content* (Cambridge, MA: MIT Press).

CHAPTER 4

....

ON THE POSSIBILITY OF NATURALIZING PHENOMENOLOGY

....

SHAUN GALLAGHER

In this chapter I address two questions. First, can phenomenology be naturalized? Second, if so, how? There is some controversy about how to answer the first question, and there are different proposals in response to the second question.

One important clarification about these questions is called for at the very beginning. We should distinguish between two current senses of the term 'phenomenology'. On the one hand, some theorists use the term to refer to consciousness itself—specifically, the phenomenal aspects of experience, the 'what it is like' to experience something. The question of naturalizing phenomenology in this sense (that is, the question of naturalizing consciousness or the mind, addressed, for instance, by Dretske 1997) often tends to imply a reductionistic project that would ultimately explain consciousness in terms of physical processes. On the other hand, 'phenomenology' also refers to the philosophical tradition originating in Europe with Husserl. In this sense, the question of naturalizing phenomenology would ask about how this philosophical approach relates to natural science, and whether one can employ phenomenological methods in the service of psychology or cognitive science. In this paper I will use the term 'phenomenology', and understand the question, in this second sense. At the same time, responses to the question about naturalizing consciousness and the question about naturalizing phenomenology, in this second sense, are intertwined. On the one hand, if one thinks of philosophical phenomenology as essentially non-reductionistic with respect to consciousness, and of naturalism as always and completely reductionistic in this regard, then naturalizing phenomenology may appear difficult if not impossible. On the other hand, if one thinks that there can be a non-reductionist naturalism, then naturalizing phenomenology may appear a greater possibility.

1   CAN PHENOMENOLOGY BE NATURALIZED?

A natural scientific explanation of consciousness—for example, a psychological or neuroscientific explanation—accounts for the mind by invoking causality and empirical facts. The transcendental account, in contrast, attempts to say what makes it possible for the mind to be able to invoke something like causality in the first place. Husserl defined phenomenology within this broadly transcendental agenda, with some important differences from the Kantian idea of a transcendental deduction. Specifically, Husserl, in contrast to Kant's hypothetical–deductive method, viewed phenomenology as a way to put ourselves into a transcendental stance or attitude that provides non-empirical access to consciousness as a field of analysis, and allows us to see and describe how the mind (or consciousness) is structured.

Husserl was careful about how he defined phenomenology, and he distinguished it from a naturalistic enterprise for two reasons. First, he adopted a traditional concern about establishing a firm epistemological foundation for doing science. Like Descartes and Kant before him, he wanted to ensure that the basic categories employed by natural science were not thought to be the products of some merely contingent features of human psychology. Second, he wanted to define the limits of what science, or naturalism broadly construed, can tell us.

> Naturalism is a phenomenon consequent upon the discovery of nature…considered as a unity of spatiotemporal being subject to exact laws of nature. With the gradual realization of this idea in constantly new natural sciences that guarantee strict knowledge regarding many matters, naturalism proceeds to expand more and more…[T]he natural scientist has the tendency to look upon everything as nature, [just as] the humanistic scientist sees everything as 'spirit', as a historical creation. By the same token, both are inclined to falsify the sense of what cannot be seen in their way. Thus the naturalist, to consider him in particular, sees only nature, and primarily physical nature. Whatever is, is either itself physical, belonging to the unified totality of physical nature, or it is in fact psychical, but then merely as a variable dependent on the physical, at best a secondary 'parallel accompaniment'. Whatever is belongs to psychophysical nature, which is to say that it is univocally determined by rigid laws. (Husserl 1965: 79)

To be clear, Husserl was not opposed to natural scientific explanation. Indeed, he wanted to ensure that science and our knowledge of the laws of nature were firmly grounded. Rather, Husserl was opposed to scientism—the positivistic view that everything is fully explained by natural science. Specifically, he regarded the naturalizing of consciousness, including intentionality, but also the naturalizing of norms, and things like formal logic, mathematics, and ideal essences as wrong-headed. In his arguments against psychologism, in *Logical Investigations*, for instance, he shows that this extreme naturalism refutes itself by undermining any formal–logical principle or law of nature by reducing it to mere psycho-physical processes. Simply put, on the extreme version of naturalism, if our brain processes evolve over time (which they certainly do), then the laws of nature may be different in the future than they are now. A law of nature would accordingly be relative to the particular neurological or psychological constitution of the historically situated knowing subject. This is what Husserl wants to reject.

On Husserl's view, psychology, as a legitimate natural science, is one thing; phenomenology is something else. Psychology treats consciousness as belonging to natural human or animal organisms. In conducting their studies and experiments, however, psychologists already and unavoidably employ consciousness in the very obvious sense that they tend to be conscious when they conduct their studies. In taking natural, third-person perspectives on cognition and behaviour—that is, in conducting their specific research—psychologists are not concerned with a basic interrogation into the invariant structures that are constitutive of any consciousness whatsoever.

Consider, for example, the temporal structure of consciousness. According to phenomenology, this is something that permeates all experience—all cognitive processes including perception, memory, imagination, judgement, emotion, and so on—as well as all action. Although psychological science has long studied reaction times, timing in neuronal processing, the subjective experience of time passing, and phenomena such as time estimation, all such studies employ the notion of objective time and attempt to measure these phenomena, literally, by the clock. Even in studies of working memory, researchers raise questions that can be answered only in terms of objective time—how many units of information, or how much representational content can be held in consciousness for how long? Such questions define the nature of the psychological and neuroscientific investigation of such phenomena. Neither psychology nor neuroscience, however, asks about the temporal nature of experience *as experienced*. The phenomenological question is something like this: what must consciousness be like if the subject is able to experience the passage of time, to remember what just happened, and anticipate what is just about to happen, and perceive temporal objects such as melodies, sentences, horse races, or indeed, any object that endures or changes—including the various instruments used in psychological or neuroscientific experiments to measure time. This question marks the subject matter of Husserl's phenomenological analysis of time-consciousness in terms of a retentional/primal impressional/protentional structure. Without explicating the details of such an analysis here, one could suggest that psychology itself, from the time of William James' (1890) analysis of the specious present through recent attempts to study the neural correlates of temporal experience (such as Pöppel 1994), consistently misses the phenomenon of temporality in this sense of a temporal structure that characterizes experience at its most basic level. This is not meant as a criticism of psychology; rather, it is an attempt to point out that psychology, and naturalism more generally, do not aim at this kind of analysis, and do not take the transcendental attitude required for this analysis.

In one sense the transcendental investigation seems more basic; in another sense one might think that the neuroscientific investigation is equally basic. One could posit the neuroscientific question in this way: how must the brain function if it allows consciousness to have this retentional/primal impressional/protentional structure? The issue, however, is not about which type of investigation is more basic. It is rather that these are two different kinds of investigation that are not reducible to one another. Accordingly, phenomenologists maintain a strong distinction between phenomenology as a transcendental study, and psychology or neuroscience as a natural science. Precisely for these reasons, some phenomenologists argue that to naturalize phenomenology would be to do something other than phenomenology, or that even to speak of a naturalized phenomenology is absurd (Lawlor 2009, for instance). Phenomenology is defined as a transcendental discipline, conducted within a transcendental attitude. If one takes the naturalistic attitude, then one is not doing phenomenology. If one ignores Husserl's anti-naturalism and proposes to do phenomenology within the natural attitude, then that just is not phenomenology.

2 A BROADER CONCEPTION OF PHENOMENOLOGY

One response to this strict or narrow definition of phenomenology is to point out that phenomenological philosophy involves more than the pure description involved in the transcendental project. Viewing phenomenology in this broader way does not, however, 'contradict Husserl's entire conception of phenomenology' (Lawlor 2009, 2). Indeed, Husserl (1977) suggested the possibility of developing a phenomenological psychology. This project would differ from transcendental phenomenology but would still be a reflective investigation of intentional consciousness from the first-person perspective, while remaining within the natural attitude. The task of phenomenological psychology is to study consciousness, not as the transcendental foundation of the sciences and the condition of possibility for all meaning, but as a phenomenon in its own right. The idea that one can do phenomenology, or we might say *use* phenomenology, while remaining in the natural attitude signals a way of thinking of phenomenology that is quite different from Husserl's original project, which required phenomenological–transcendental reductions to escape the natural attitude. But such an approach is clearly consistent with a broader conception of phenomenology held by Husserl himself. Husserl certainly thought that the results of transcendental phenomenology should not be ignored by science, and the idea that they might inform the natural sciences is not inconsistent with the value of transcendental analysis. He suggested, quite clearly, that 'every analysis or theory of transcendental phenomenology—including... the theory of the transcendental constitution of an objective world—can be developed in the natural realm, by giving up the transcendental attitude' (Husserl 1970, §57).

Lawlor nonetheless worries that the naturalization project 'aims to swallow phenomenology up' (2009, 2). This rather dramatic way of putting it indicates a point carefully made by De Preester (2002): namely, that given the assumptions of cognitive science concerning issues like computationalism and representation, it seems that there is a basic opposition between phenomenology and cognitive science. Accordingly, if naturalization means that phenomenology simply adopts such assumptions, then phenomenology self-destructs. 'A naturalized phenomenology is no longer phenomenology' (De Preester 2002, 645). This would be the case, however, only if the question were precisely the one that Edelman (2002, 125) asks: 'Is a new phenomenology, which would completely eschew transcendentalism in favor of computational principles, possible?' The issue really goes the other way, however, as De Preester herself notes. That is, the introduction of phenomenology into cognitive science has critically challenged the basic assumptions of cognitive science, including computationalism, and indeed the very concepts of nature and naturalism, and has moved cognitive science towards a view that is more consistent with the views of Husserl and Merleau-Ponty on intentionality, intersubjectvity, action, and embodiment (see Gallagher and Varela 2003, Thompson 2007, Varela, Thompson, and Rosch 1991).

Beyond Husserl, others in the phenomenological tradition followed this same path, carrying phenomenology to broader application, and integrating the natural sciences of consciousness and behaviour into their considerations. Gurwitsch, Sartre, and Merleau-Ponty, for example, are philosophers who pursue what could be generally called phenomenological psychology. Gurwitsch appeals to Gestalt psychology, animal studies, and developmental psychology to support the proper phenomenological characterization of various experiences. For example, if we want to provide a phenomenological description of how we go about solving a problem in the real world, or how, in that context, a certain object can take on the meaning of a tool, we can benefit from something that Gestalt theorists have described very well: a perceptual reorganization involving the 'restructuring of the given situation, the regrouping of the facts of which it is composed' (Gurwitsch 2009, p. 246). It is only by attending to such reorganizations and reformations of *structures* that proper phenomenological accounts of such experiences can be developed. Gurwitsch further finds evidence in developmental studies that our primary perception of the world is an enactive and pragmatic one where things have their meaning in terms of how we can use them (Gurwitsch 2009, p. 250). Accordingly, a proper phenomenology of perception needs to take into consideration this full pragmatic meaning of perceptual experience.

In his phenomenological examination of the imagination Sartre draws from empirical psychology. He refers us to Flach's experiments on images associated with presented words, and offers a reinterpretation of Flach's experiments to work out distinctions between symbols and images (for example, 2004, p. 107ff). He considers the views of Binet and the Würzburg psychologists on the relation of image and thought, suggesting, in contrast to Binet, that the image has a sense and may play a role in thought (2004, p. 108). In *Being and Nothingness*, too, Sartre makes use of naturalistic psychological studies to inform his phenomenology.

Merleau-Ponty is well known for his integration of phenomenology, psychology, and neurology. In *Phenomenology of Perception*, for example, he makes extensive use of the experimental literature and case studies. In lecture courses at the Sorbonne in 1950–2 (under the title 'Human Sciences and Phenomenology') he discusses a 'convergence' of phenomenology and psychology, explicating various misunderstandings on both sides of this relationship (Merleau-Ponty 2010, p. 317). He takes Sartre's analysis of imagination as a good example of how phenomenological (eidetic) analysis can be integrated with psychology, and shows how eidetic (imaginative) variation works in a correlative way with scientific inductive procedures. Like Gurwitsch and Sartre, Merleau-Ponty appeals to psychology (Goldstein's distinction between centred and decentered behaviour, and Koffka's Gestalt psychology) as a possible guide for phenomenological insight, suggesting that 'the distinction between phenomenology and psychology must not be presented as a rigid distinction' (2010, p. 329)—without, of course, denying the distinction. Indeed, we can find in psychology itself (specifically, in Koffka's distinction between geographical and behavioural environments) a useful way not only to think of the difference between third-person naturalistic accounts, and first-person phenomenological accounts, but to understand why a full third-person (geographical) account (an account as if from nowhere) is impossible.

Following Gurwitsch, Merleau-Ponty rejects the constancy hypothesis (the idea that there is a point-to-point correspondence between stimulus and perception), not by offering an independent phenomenological analysis, but by citing experimental work within psychology itself (see Merleau-Ponty 2010, p. 347). Merleau-Ponty's conclusion is consistent, not only with earlier phenomenological distinctions in Heidegger between *Zuhandenheit* and *Vorhandenheit*, but also with more recent naturalistic distinctions, between pragmatic and semantic functions of perception (Jeannerod 1997). Accordingly, these distinctions are correlatively phenomenological *and* psychological, and they provide supporting evidence for enactive accounts of perception that draw from both phenomenology and natural science.

What we see in each of these cases is, to use Merleau-Ponty's term, a convergence of phenomenology and the natural sciences of psychology and/or neuroscience. This is more than a convergence of results. That is, the convergence is not simply that phenomenology and psychology have reached the same conclusions about specific topics. Indeed, in some cases, there is a critical distance between the view defended by phenomenology and the received view of psychological science. Rather, the convergence pertains to how phenomenology is put to use in the research fields of psychology and neuroscience. It is a convergence on a methodological plane. Moreover, the convergence does not signify a change in the definition of phenomenology. Nor is it a threat to transcendental phenomenology. The transcendental project remains as its own phenomenological project. What we find in Husserl's concept of a phenomenological psychology, however, and in the work of Gurwitsch, Sartre, and Merleau-Ponty, is a certain pragmatic application of phenomenological method. Accordingly, these theorists have already provided a positive response to the question of whether phenomenology can be naturalized.

3 HOW CAN PHENOMENOLOGY
BE NATURALIZED?

Turning now to the second question, addressing precisely *how* phenomenology can be naturalized, several answers have already been proposed in the recent literature. In this regard I will briefly summarize three general proposals without providing anything close to the full critical discussion that each one deserves. I will then turn to a more extended discussion of specific examples of where phenomenology has been playing a role in natural-science accounts of the mind.

(1) Formalizing phenomenology

One approach to naturalizing phenomenology, proposed by Roy *et al.* (1999), involves translating the results of phenomenological analysis into a formal language that is clearly understood by science: namely, mathematics. We could call this the CREA proposal, since it was proposed by an interdisciplinary group of researchers at the Centre de Recherche en Epistémologie Appliquée (CREA) in Paris: Jean Petitot (a mathematician), Jean-Michel Roy (a philosopher), Bernard Pachoud (a psychiatrist), and the late Francisco Varela (a neurobiologist). They write: 'It is our general contention . . . that phenomenological descriptions of any kind can only be naturalized, in the sense of being integrated into the general framework of natural sciences, if they can be mathematized. We see mathematization as a key instrument for naturalization . . .' (Roy *et al.* 1999, p. 42).

We can understand this proposal as building on the work of Eduard Marbach (1993), who suggested a formal symbolic language for phenomenology. One important question is whether it is possible for mathematics to capture the lived experience described by phenomenology. The description of lived experience, of course, already involves expressing the experience in language. It takes an additional step to formalize those verbal or written descriptions. This is a strategy that can be employed to clarify word-meaning and to facilitate scientific communication. As Marbach (1993, 2010) suggests, formalizing the language can improve the possibility of formulating intersubjectively shareable meanings. As in science, terminological problems are addressed through the use of formalized language systems like those found in mathematics. Marbach thus attempts to develop a formalized notation to express phenomenological findings, not just about the content of experience, but about its structure.

Husserl's analysis of episodic memory, for example, suggested that it involves the re-enactment of previous perceptions. He relies on the notion of 're-presentation' (*Vergegenwärtigung*); literally, 'to make something present again'. Whereas perception is an intentional reference to something present, and thus an activity of 'presentation', memory refers to something absent. Even intentional reference to something absent, however, requires a presentational activity where reference to that which is not present is made 'as if' it were given to me in perception (Marbach 1993, p. 61). The 'as if' is the re-presentational modification. Marbach, following Husserl's own proposals for formal notation,[1] attempts to make the structure of re-presentation clearer. Let '(PER)x' signify the act of perceiving some object, x. Remembering x involves (PER)x, not as an actual and occurent act of perception, but as a re-enactment of a past perception. To signify this in the notation, the parentheses become brackets: [PER]x. Furthermore, an element of belief (signified by **) distinguishes a re-enactment in memory from an imaginary enactment. In other words, in contrast to imagination, episodic memory involves a belief that in the past I actually did perceive x. Let 'p' signify that the perception of x is in the past rather than in the future (to differentiate it from expectation). Marbach thus attempts to capture the structure of an act of episodic memory in the following formulation: '(REP p**[PER])x'—a re-presentation of x by means of 'a perceiving of x bestowed with the belief of it having actually occurred in the past.'

Things become more complicated (see Marbach 2010), but the virtue of formulating a notation like this should be clear if it can show clearly the complexity of consciousness and the explication of that complexity provided by phenomenological reflection. In addition, with respect to these phenomenological insights concerning episodic memory, for example, a formal notation may also help to link up in a precise way with certain neuroscientific findings that indicate memory processes occurring in 'the same early sensory cortices where the firing patterns corresponding to perceptual representations once occurred' (Damasio 1994, p. 101). One could imagine a neuroscientific notation for just such processes correlating with the phenomenological notation for episodic memory. Such notational correlations could make very clear just where phenomenological analysis confirms and supports the neuroscientific model of memory (and reciprocally, where the neurological evidence supports the phenomenological description),[2] or precisely where there are differences.

The hypothesis that at some suitable level of abstraction the phenomenological and the neurological notations would turn out to be consistent leads directly to the CREA proposal made by Roy et al. (1999).[3] Mathematics is purportedly a formal and therefore neutral language with which we can set out results that are either first-person (the results of phenomenological reflections) or third-person (the results of natural science).

---

[1] See Husserl (2001), 5th Investigation, §39, and Husserl (2005), Text No. 14 (1911–1912), 363–77; Marbach (2010); Yoshimi (2007). Marbach (2010) also notes the connection with Frege's *Begriffsschrift*.

[2] Further support for the Husserlian view that memory involves the re-enactment of a previous perceptual experience is to be found in neurological differences involved in illusory versus veridical memory (see Schacter et al. 2006).

[3] We note that Husserl, himself a trained mathematician, viewed mathematical formulae as incapable of capturing phenomenological results. 'One cannot define in philosophy as in mathematics; any imitation of mathematical procedure in this respect is not only unfruitful but wrong, and has most injurious consequences' (Husserl 1976, p. 9). Roy et al. argue, however, that even if this was true of the mathematics of Husserl's time, the development of dynamic systems theory offers new possibilities in this regard (1999, p. 43). For some critical remarks, see Zahavi (2004).

Specifically, the CREA proposal suggests that a sufficiently complex mathematics—specifically, the mathematics of dynamic systems—can facilitate the translation of data from phenomenological and naturalistic realms. In Varela's (1996) specific proposal for a neurophenomenology we can see a good example of how phenomenology, experimental brain science, and dynamical systems theory can be integrated in a way that pushes cognitive science in a new direction.[4]

(2) Neurophenomenology

The aim of neurophenomenology is to incorporate phenomenological investigations of experience into neuroscientific research on consciousness. Neurophenomenology focuses especially on the temporal dynamics of conscious experience and brain activity (Lutz 2002, Lutz and Thompson 2003, Thompson, Lutz, and Cosmelli 2005). Varela formulates the 'working hypothesis' of neurophenomenology in the following way: 'Phenomenological accounts of the structure of experience and their counterparts in cognitive science relate to each other through reciprocal constraints' (Varela 1996, 343). By 'reciprocal constraints' he means that phenomenological analyses can help guide and shape the scientific investigation of consciousness, and that scientific findings can in turn help guide and shape phenomenological investigations. An important feature of this approach is that dynamic systems theory can mediate between phenomenology and neuroscience. Neurophenomenology thus comprises three main elements (see Fig. 1):

(1) Phenomenological accounts of the invariant categorical and structural features of lived experience.
(2) The use of formal dynamical approaches to model these structural invariants.
(3) Neurophysiological measurements of large-scale, integrative processes in the brain.

Reciprocal constraints means not only (i) that the subject is actively involved in generating and describing specific experiential invariants, and (ii) that the neuroscientist is guided by these first-person data in the analysis and interpretation of physiological data, but also (iii) that such phenomenologically enriched neuroscientific analyses provoke revisions and refinements of the phenomenological accounts, as well as facilitate the subject's becoming aware of previously inaccessible or phenomenally unavailable aspects of his or her mental life. Preliminary examples of this third step can be found in neurophenomenological studies of epilepsy (Le Van Quyen and Petitmengin 2002) and pain (Price, Barrell, and Rainville 2002).

Neurophenomenology aims to integrate the invariant structures of subjective experience with the real-time characterization of large-scale neural activity. This involves producing phenomenological accounts of real-time subjective experience that are

---

[4] Jean Petitot also provides good examples of this approach in his analyses of spatial perception (Petitot 1999, 2008), as does Varela (1999) in his dynamical analysis of time-consciousness.

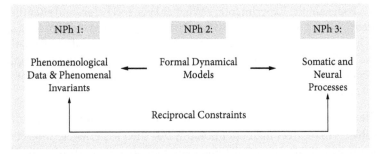

FIGURE 1. Neurophenomenology. (From Thompson 2007.)

sufficiently precise and complete to be both expressed in formal and predictive dynamical terms, and showing that such experiences are realized in specific neurodynamical properties of brain activity. Accordingly, neurophenomenology takes the framework of dynamic systems theory as important for characterizing the neural processes relevant to consciousness (see Le Van Quyen 2003). Such phenomenological, formal, and neurobiological descriptions of consciousness could provide a robust and predictive way to link reciprocally the experiential and neurophysiological domains.

The practice of neurophenomenology, in the laboratory, requires training subjects to employ phenomenological methods, including the *epoché*, and to deliver consistent and clear reports of their experience. Specifically, Varela (1996) identified three steps in phenomenological method:

(1) Suspending beliefs or theories about experience (the *epoche*).
(2) Turning to experience and gaining intimacy with it *(phenomenological reduction and focused description)*.
(3) Developing descriptions and using intersubjective validations *(intersubjective corroboration)*.

In effect, this follows standard phenomenological method in which we bracket opinions, beliefs, and theories about our experience, reflectively turn our attention to that experience to develop a detailed description, and produce a report that can be compared with other reports of the same sort of experience.

Many aspects of experience are not noticed immediately, but require multiple sessions. The repetition of the same task in an experimental setting allows for new contrasts to arise, and can help us to discover consistent categories and structural invariants in experience. The reduction can be either self-induced by subjects familiar with it, or guided by the experimenter through a set of open questions—questions not directed at opinions or theories, but at experience.

To train the subjects, open questions were asked to try to redirect their attention towards their own immediate mental processes before the recordings were taken ... For example: Experimenter: 'What did you feel before and after the image appeared?' Subject S1: 'I had a growing sense of expectation, but not for a specific object; however when the figure appeared, I had a feeling of confirmation, no surprise at all'; or subject S4: 'it was as if the image appeared in the periphery of my attention, but then my attention was suddenly swallowed up by the shape.' (Lutz *et al.* 2001)

In the context of experiments, questions posed immediately after the experimental task help the subjects to redirect their attention towards their experience. Subjects can be re-exposed to the stimuli until they find 'their own stable experiential invariants' to describe the specific elements of their experiences. These invariants can then become the defining elements that are used as analytic tools in further trials (for further theoretical and methodological discussion of this experiment, see Lutz 2002).

(3) Front-loaded phenomenology

Another closely related approach to integrating phenomenology and experimental cognitive science has been called 'front-loaded phenomenology' (Gallagher 2003, Gallagher and Brøsted Sørensen 2006). This approach is closely connected with neurophenomenology in the sense that front-loaded phenomenology can draw on the results of neurophenomenological experiments. At the same time the basic strategy of front-loaded phenomenology is integral to doing neurophenomenology properly. Rather than starting with the empirical results (as one would do in the formal mathematical approach) or with the training of subjects (as one would do in neurophenomenology), this approach starts with the experimental design. The idea is to incorporate phenomenological insights into the design of experiments: that is, to allow the insights developed in phenomenological analyses to inform the way experiments are set up. The phenomenological insights might be drawn from Husserlian transcendental investigations, or from neurophenomenological experiments, or from the more empirically oriented phenomenological analyses found, for example, in Merleau-Ponty (1962). To front-load phenomenology does not mean to presuppose or automatically accept the phenomenological results obtained by others. Rather, it involves testing those results and more generally a dialectical movement between previous insights gained in phenomenology and preliminary trials that will specify or extend these insights for purposes of the particular experiment or empirical investigation.

The idea that one can incorporate the insights of phenomenology into experimental protocols without training subjects in the method is not meant as a rejection of the neurophenomenological approach. As already indicated, neurophenomenological experimentation can be an important source of insights for front-loading. Front-loaded phenomenology, however, can address certain limitations involving training in neurophenomenological procedures. Specifically not every psychological experiment can be designed to allow for the training of subjects in phenomenological methods. In some cases one wants the subject to be naïve about what is being tested, for example. In other cases one might be testing subjects who are unable to follow phenomenological method (such as young children or pathological subjects). In such cases, it may still be possible to employ the front-loading technique.

Experimental design is always based on some concept or distinction. Most often such ideas come from previous experiments. If one traces these ideas back far enough, however, one finds that some of the concepts and distinctions are based on previously operationalized concepts that are themselves drawn from folk psychology, our everyday natural attitude, or varying philosophical traditions. In this regard there may be less control involved in experimental design than the experimenters believe; specific theories lurking in the background may already introduce certain biases that are shaping the kind of conclusions that can be drawn from the experiments. To the extent that the concepts and distinctions incorporated into the experiment are generated in careful phenomenological analyses, closer to experience and less influenced by established theoretical considerations, the scientist gains a certain degree of control that is otherwise missing.

A good example can be found in the much discussed experiments on free will conducted by Benjamin Libet (1985, Libet *et al.* 1985). In these experiments Libet appealed to philosophical concepts of mental causation and agency that can be traced back to Descartes: namely, the idea that free will is consistent with the conscious control of bodily movement. Haggard and Libet (2001), for example, frame the question in exactly this way, and refer us directly to the traditional question: 'How can a mental state (my conscious intention) initiate the neural events in the motor areas of the brain that lead to my body movement?' (p. 47). In more recent experiments, Tsakiris, Haggard, and colleagues (such as Tsakiris and Haggard 2005a, 2005b, Tsakiris, Prabhu, and Haggard 2005, Tsakiris *et al.* 2007a, 2007b), as well as others engaged in brain imaging experiments (such as Farrer and Frith 2002, Farrer *et al.* 2003) have adopted a more phenomenologically informed definition of agency—one that takes into consideration the effects that actions have on the environment (see Skewes 2011 for this history of this development). Specifically, they make reference to a phenomenological distinction between the sense of agency and the sense of ownership (Gallagher 2000), which motivates the experimenters to control for the sense of ownership when they want to focus on agency, and *vice versa.*

4 PHENOMENOLOGICAL INTERVENTIONS IN ONGOING DEBATES

To move beyond formal proposals for naturalizing phenomenology and to clarify how phenomenology is already contributing to a number of ongoing debates in the cognitive sciences, it will be helpful to provide a brief overview of several of these research areas.

(1) Embodiment and agency

In general, the ongoing development of the theory of embodied cognition in the cognitive sciences has been heavily influenced by the resources of phenomenology, with respect to issues in the areas of both artificial intelligence/robotics (Dreyfus 1973) and neuroscience (Varela, Thompson, and Rosch 1991, for instance). Recent works continue along this line and draw especially on the work of Merleau-Ponty (such as Gallagher 2005, Noë 2004). It would be impossible to summarize the vast array of issues involved in this research area in this short chapter. Accordingly, I will limit discussion here to a small corner of research on embodied cognition and action. The distinction between the sense of agency (SA) and sense of ownership (SO) is a good place to start—first, because it is a phenomenological distinction that has found its way into a significant number of experimental studies (as such, an example of front-loaded phenomenology), and second, because it has been reciprocally productive: that is, it has been productive not only for clarification of the science, but also for phenomenological analysis.

Numerous phenomenologists have indicated that there is a sense of 'mineness' or ipseity built into every experience. This is sometimes called the 'sense of ownership', where 'ownership' means not some external relation of *having* something (as in ownership of property), but signifies the intrinsic 'ownness' or mineness of experience—an aspect of the experience that makes it subjectively my experience. SO, as such, holds not only with regard to experiences of my body or my body parts—for example, when I reach and grasp something, the sense that it is my arm that is reaching and my hand that is grasping—but also in regard to my experiences of self-movement and action: this is, not only my arm, but also *my* action. SO also holds with respect to my thinking or stream of consciousness. It is directly tied to the phenomenological idea of pre-reflective self-awareness, that is, when we consciously think, or perceive, or act, we are pre-reflectively aware that we are doing so, and this pre-reflective awareness is something built into experience itself, part of the concurrent structure of any conscious process.

Pre-reflective self-awareness, however, also involves a sense of agency, which is conceptually distinct from SO: the pre-reflective experience that I am the one who is moving or undergoing an experience. SA can be defined as the pre-reflective experience that I am the one who is causing or generating a movement or action or thought process. This is a phenomenological distinction that can be easily understood in the experience of involuntary movement. If someone pushes me from behind, I experience the initial movement as something happening to me, as something that I am experiencing, and so have an experience of ownership for the movement. I do not claim that it is someone else who is moving, since I have an immediate sense that I am the one moving. At the same time, however, I can say that I have no experience of self-agency for this movement. I did not cause it; someone else pushed me. So in the case of involuntary movement (as well as in reflex movement), SA and SO come apart. In the case of voluntary action, on the other hand, SA and SO seem tightly fitted and indistinguishable in pre-reflective experience.

Neuropsychologists have found this distinction useful for clarifying their studies of agency and perceptual illusions: for example, the rubber hand illusion and whole body displacement. I will start with the studies of agency. One question which experimenters have tried to answer concerns the neural correlates for SA. Let us think again about involuntary movement. In the case of involuntary movement there is SO for the movement but no SA. The neuroscience suggests that awareness of my involuntary movement is generated in reafferent sensory feedback (visual and proprioceptive/kinaesthetic information that tells me that I am moving). In the case of involuntary movement there are no initial motor commands (no efferent signals). Thus, it seems possible that in both involuntary and voluntary movement SO is generated by sensory feedback, and that in the case of voluntary movement SA is generated by efferent signals. Tsakiris and Haggard (2005, Tsakiris 2005) review empirical evidence that supports this division of labour. As they put it:

> [...] the sense of agency involves a strong *efferent* component, because actions are centrally generated. The sense of ownership involves a strong *afferent* component, because the content of body awareness originates mostly by the plurality of multisensory peripheral signals. We do not normally experience the efferent and afferent components separately. Instead, we have a general awareness of our body that involves both components. (Tsakiris and Haggard 2005, 387)

On this view SA is conceived as generated in motor-control related brain processes. But this may not be the whole story, as Haggard himself points out, since 'actions seem to aim towards a goal, as if pulled teleologically from the intention through to the intended effect' (2005, 292). SA, in addition to being a sense of embodied movement, involves a sense of controlling events in the external world. Haggard accordingly distinguishes between 'urge' and 'effect'—the former associated with an experience generated in motor control processes, the latter associated with perceptual monitoring of what one actually accomplishes by the action. Both of these aspects—the *intentional aspect* (what gets accomplished, or fails to get accomplished, by the action) and the *motor (or efferent) aspect* (the sense that I am causing or controlling my bodily movement)—enter into SA. It seems clear that there is a confirmatory consistency between the neuroscience and the phenomenology. That is, phenomenologically one can make the same distinctions between SA taken as a sense of bodily control, and SA taken as a sense of controlling what one accomplishes in the world (Gallagher 2007).

In an fMRI experiment conducted by Farrer and Frith (2002), and designed to find the neural correlates of SA, subjects are asked to manipulate a joystick to drive a coloured circle moving on a screen to specific locations on the screen. In some instances the subject causes this movement, and in others the experimenter or computer causes it. The subject is asked to discriminate self-agency (when they feel they are in charge of the movement) and other-agency (when they feel the other person is in charge of the movement). Farrer and Frith, citing the distinction between SA and SO, associate SA with the intentional aspect of action: that is, whether I am having some kind of effect with respect to the goal or intentional task (or what happens on the screen). Accordingly, they claim that SO ('my hand is moving the joystick') remains constant while SA (based on the intentional aspect) changes. When subjects feel that they are not controlling the events on the screen, there is activation in the right inferior parietal cortex and supposedly no SA for the intentional aspect of the action. When the subject does have SA for the action on the screen, the anterior insula is activated bilaterally.

Although Farrer and Frith clearly think of SA as something tied to the intentional aspect of action and not to mere bodily movement or motor control, when it comes to *explaining why* the anterior insula should be involved in generating SA, they frame the explanation in terms of motor control.

> Why should the parietal lobe have a special role in attributing actions to others while the anterior insula is concerned with attributing actions to the self? The sense of agency (i.e., being aware of causing an action) occurs in the context of a body moving in time and space...There is evidence that both the inferior parietal lobe and the anterior insula are representations of the body...the anterior insula, in interaction with limbic structures, is also involved in the representation of body schema...(Farrer and Frith 2002, 601)

In all of these experiments the phenomenological distinctions are put to good use. Indeed, closer attention to the phenomenology of agency could help to clarify the distinction between the intentional aspect and the motor (efferent) aspect of agency—a distinction that can easily become lost in the neurological explanation. Phenomenologists can also suggest that there is more to SA than the pre-reflective elements delineated here. In actions that involve reflective deliberation or retrospective evaluation, these more reflective aspects of action, which may also bring into play social norms and forces that are not reducible to processes confined to individual brains, may enter into the experience of agency (Gallagher 2010). In this regard, phenomenology tends to support a non-reductionist approach to the naturalistic study of human agency.

The sense of ownership is also something that can be studied by experimental science. In the rubber hand illusion, you sit at a table with your left arm and hand placed under a cover (Botvinick and Cohen 1998). A rubber arm-hand is placed on the table in front of you, canonically positioned near your left hand. Your left hand undergoes passive tactile stimulation (such as a brushing of the fingers), and simultaneously you see the similar stimulation being made on the rubber hand. You almost immediately start to feel as if the rubber hand is your own, and you feel the stimulation as being in the rubber hand. SO—specifically, your sense of body ownership—extends into the rubber hand.

In the rubber hand illusion experiment, the subject is not allowed to move his real hand, and this controls for SA. The focus is on SO. But what happens if we introduce movement? Tsakiris and Haggard (2005) demonstrated that during the rubber hand illusion there is a 'proprioceptive drift' toward the rubber hand. That is, the passively stimulated finger (of one's real hand) was judged to be significantly closer to the location of the rubber hand than it really was. But this effect was localized only for the stimulated finger and not for the whole hand. Tsakiris and Haggard then hypothesized that a more holistic body (motor) schema, engaged when in action, and thereby involving SA, would contribute to a more coherent or holistic sense of embodiment. In a further experiment, subjects viewed video of their hands under two conditions: when the subject moves his own index finger, and when the subject's index finger is moved by the experimenter. In the first case of self-generated movement there is SA; in the second, passive movement and no SA. Tsakiris and Haggard show that while the proprioceptive drift in the passive movement is just for the one finger, the drift is for the whole hand in self-generated movement. They conclude: 'The active body is experienced as more coherent and unified than the passive body' (2005b; see Tsakiris, Schütz-Bosbach, and Gallagher 2007). Agency and the corresponding efferent signals involved modulate afferent feedback, and more generally bodily awareness, and thereby modulate the SO for one's actions. In the case of action, SO is integrated into the more holistic body-schematic processes of motor control, confirming suggestions made from a phenomenological perspective about how we experience bodily action (Gallagher 2005).

(2) Pathologies

The same distinction between SO and SA is useful in trying to make sense of a variety of pathologies. Here I will focus on schizophrenic symptoms of delusions of control and thought insertion. There are, however, clear applications of the concepts of SO and SA to various disorders, such as Anarchic Hand Syndrome and Somatoparaphrenia (see, for example, Gallagher and Væver 2004).

A schizophrenic patient may suffer from delusions of control, where he complains that someone else is controlling his bodily movement, or thought insertion, where he might claim that he is not the one who is thinking a particular thought, when in fact he is the one who is thinking the thought. Consider the following example of a schizophrenic's report: 'Thoughts are put into my mind like "Kill God". It's just like my mind working, but it isn't. They come from this chap, Chris. They're his thoughts' (from Frith 1992, p. 66). Frith offers an explanation of delusions of control and thought insertion in terms of a neurocognitive model in which normal self-monitoring breaks down. Frith (1992) appeals to the notions of efference copy and comparator mechanisms involved in motor control (Sperry 1950, Holst and Mittelstaedt 1950). Normally, a comparator mechanism operates as part of a non-conscious pre-motor or 'forward model' that compares efference copy of motor commands with motor intentions and allows for rapid, automatic error corrections (Wolpert et al. 2000, Frith et al. 2000). Putting this in terms of SA and SO, the proposal is that the forward comparator process, based on efference copy, normally anticipates the sensory feedback from movement and generates SA, while the sensory-feedback processes themselves generate SO. If the forward model fails, or efference copy is not properly generated, sensory feedback may still produce SO ('I am moving'), but SA will be compromised ('I am not causing the movement'), even if the actual movement matches the intended movement.

In the case of practiced voluntary action, SA and SO are indistinguishable; we noted, however, that they come apart in the case of involuntary action. In the case of delusions of control where the schizophrenic patient claims that he is not the agent of a particular action, SA is not present, but SO is still present, similar to the case of involuntary action. Indeed, this is necessarily so for the patient's report to make sense: '*my* body has engaged in an action; *my* body has been moved'—this is his complaint, that he is the one being moved, or being made to act, and that the action is not something he intended. SO is still intact for his body and for his movement, even as the sense of self-agency is not. This is precisely why he feels that this movement or action is *his* concern rather than someone else's; it is not happening to someone else, it is happening to him.

It turns out that schizophrenic patients who suffer from delusions of control do have problems with the forward, pre-action monitoring of movement, but not with motor control based on a comparison of intended movement and sensory feedback (Frith and Done 1988, Malenka *et al.* 1982). While motor control based on sensory feedback is thought to involve the cerebellum (Frith *et al.* 2000), problems with forward monitoring are consistent with studies of schizophrenia showing abnormal pre-movement brain potentials associated with supplementary motor, pre-motor, and pre-frontal cortexes (Singh *et al.* 1992). On this account, problems in precisely these brain areas may therefore result in the lack of SA, characteristic of these kinds of schizophrenic experiences (Hohwy 2004, Gold and Hohwy 2000, Mundale and Gallagher 2009).

Turning to the problem of thought insertion, Frith (1992) considers thinking to be a form of action, and attempts to apply the same motor control model in this realm. If this solution works to explain delusions of control, however, it is not clear that it can also explain thought insertion. Indeed, phenomenologists are in a good position to argue that this solution does not work for thought insertion. A number of phenomenological issues become obvious when one tries to apply the motor control model to thinking. First, while it is possible to talk about an intention to act in a certain way, it is problematic to talk about an intention to think, since such an intention would be itself a thinking, and an infinite regress threatens.

Second, it is not clear what role something like efference copy or a comparator would play in conscious thinking. In the case of visuomotor control, efference copy serves a pragmatic, executive function—it informs the visual and vestibular systems that the organism, rather than the world, is moving. Its purpose is to instruct the motor or sensory system to make important adjustments. Is there anything like this happening in the thinking process? One might think that efference copy functions to keep thoughts on track, checking 'that the thoughts you actually execute form coherent trains of thought' (Campbell 1999, 616). This proposal attributes a semantic function to a subpersonal, non-semantic mechanism when, simply put, we are already consciously aware of our thoughts and can keep track of them, and keep them on track, at a conscious level.

Third, there are a number of aspects of the experience of thought insertion that Frith's comparator model simply does not explain. Most obviously, and in a similar way to the proposed solution to delusions of control, it might be able to explain the lack of SA, but it fails to explain why the schizophrenic who experiences thought insertion attributes the thought to someone else. Let me conclude, however, by mentioning one other problem. If there is a comparator mechanism for thought, and it breaks down or is put out of operation, why do not all thoughts seem alien to the schizophrenic? When a particular thought seems inserted, there are other aspects of conscious experience that do not seem inserted. Either simultaneously with or immediately after the thought that seems inserted, there is the feeling that it is inserted. But this feeling does not itself feel inserted. That is, the subject, in recognizing a thought as inserted, does not claim that his recognition of this fact is also inserted. He is seemingly speaking in his own voice when he complains about the inserted thought. This is not just a phenomenological fact; it is a logical necessity. The subject's complaint that various thoughts are inserted depends on a necessary contrast between thoughts that seem inserted and those that do not seem inserted—and at a minimum, the thoughts that constitute the subject's complaint cannot seem inserted.

Just as the phenomenological distinction between SA and SO is able to clarify certain aspects of the schizophrenic's experience in cases of delusion of control and thought insertion, so also certain phenomenological considerations suggest that the same comparator model that might help to explain the breakdown of SA in delusions of control cannot provide an explanation of the breakdown of SA in thought insertion. These phenomenological interventions, accordingly, can contribute important insights that need to be taken into account in any neurocognitive account of these symptoms.

(3) Intersubjectivity

One other area of concern where phenomenology can make important contributions pertains to questions about intersubjectivity. There is a long history of discussion within phenomenology about intersubjectivity, but up until approximately ten years ago such phenomenological considerations were not brought to bear on the ongoing debate within philosophy of mind, psychology, and cognitive science concerning social cognition or theory of mind (ToM). A number of phenomenologists have now developed a critique of the standard approaches—'theory theory' (TT) and simulation theory (ST)—and have put forward alternative theories (Gallagher 2001, 2005, 2008, Gallagher and Hutto 2008, Ratcliffe 2006, Thompson 2001, Zahavi 2001).

The critique of TT and ST focuses on several claims made in these approaches: (1) that our normal everyday stance towards the other is a third-person observational one in which we attempt to explain and predict the other person's behaviour; (2) that such explanation and prediction depends on inferring or simulating ('mindreading') the other's mental states which are generally hidden from view; (3) that our ability to mindread is the result of some mechanism found in the individual mind or brain (a ToM mechanism or mirror neurons); and (4) that these mindreading processes are primary and pervasive, characterizing the majority of our everyday encounters. For those theories that make the mindreading processes (whether theoretical inferences or simulation routines) conscious or introspective (for example, Goldman 1995, 2006), phenomenology points out that there is simply no evidence of such processes in our everyday experiences, and that such processes are not primary and pervasive. Rather than third-person observation, our relations with others are better characterized in terms of second-person interaction where most of what we need for a pragmatic understanding of the other person are not hidden mental states, but embodied expressions that we can easily perceive on their faces, in their postures, movements, and gestures—none of which float around in thin air but are situated in social and pragmatic contexts. On the phenomenological view, *interaction*, rather than observation, constitutes our primary way of being with others, and social cognition is not reducible to some mechanism or set of processes found within the individual, since it involves the individual in dynamic processes with others and in an environment that is already social.

One important issue that continues to be a point of dispute between the standard approaches and phenomenological approaches concerns the relevance of phenomenology for understanding subpersonal processes that are, of course, non-conscious (Spaulding 2010). Can phenomenology tell us anything about mirror neuron activation, for example? In this regard, some defenders of the standard TT and ST approaches dismiss phenomenology as irrelevant.

The role of phenomenology is not to ascertain the nature of specific sub-personal processes, of course. It is possible, however, to look to phenomenology for part of the evidence about what might be going on at the level of subpersonal processes. Since phenomenology can help to specify the explanandum on the personal level—for example, whether we are attempting to explain something that involves conscious reflective processes, of an inferential or a simulative nature perhaps, or more pre-reflective bodily perceptual processes—it can provide clues about what might be happening at the subpersonal level, and perhaps contribute to our understanding of why correlated neuronal activations in frontal areas versus more primary perceptual-motor systems make sense. This corresponds, moreover, to a current scientific view of things. Thus, for example, Gallese (2001) claims that a phenomenology of empathy correlates with sub-personal simulation on a functionalist level, and with mirror neuron activation on a neurological level. That claim may be correct, or not. But even on a more methodological level pertaining to how the relevant experiments are done, if subjects are not in a specific personal-level situation (such as attending to the other's actions) there is no expectation that MNs will fire, or that low-level simulations will happen. Neuroscientists frequently appeal to personal-level practices and phenomenological experiences in setting up their experiments, and in many cases the only way to define the explanadum is in terms of phenomenology. Without phenomenology it is not clear that an analysis of mechanical sub-personal processes plus mindless behaviour can add up to anything like a full account of human social cognition.

5 CONCLUSION: COLLABORATION AND MUTUAL ENLIGHTENMENT

There are clearly multiple ways in which one can naturalize phenomenology, in the sense of integrating phenomenological data, methods, and insights into natural scientific experiments in cognitive science, including psychology and neuroscience, without engaging in naturalistic reductionism. I have not provided an exhaustive list of all possible ways. Practically speaking, one of the most straightforward and productive ways of providing opportunity for this kind of integration is for phenomenologists to work together with psychologists and neuroscientists. Just this kind of engagement may be what Dan Zahavi has in mind when he writes:

> To naturalize phenomenology might simply be a question of letting phenomenology engage in a fruitful exchange and collaboration with empirical science. Phenomenology does study phenomena that are part of nature and therefore also open to empirical investigation, and insofar as phenomenology concerns itself with such phenomena it should be informed by the best available scientific knowledge. (Zahavi 2010, p. 8)

It remains the case that phenomenology is an attempt to do justice to first- and second-person experiences, to explicate such experiences in terms of their meaning. As such, phenomenology does not directly address the questions of subpersonal mechanisms or causal factors. And yet phenomenology can offer some insight to the studies of consciousness and cognition, at the very least by providing personal-level *descriptions* of the explicandum for those studies. Furthermore, it is a matter of historical fact that phenomenology (in the works of Gurwitsch and Merleau-Ponty, for example) has always learned from disciplines such as psychopathology, neuropathology, developmental psychology, cognitive psychology, and neuroscience. The influence goes both ways, in a process of mutual enlightenment (Gallagher 1997).

Mutual enlightenment is a relatively mild way to put it, however. A more radical proposal would be to pursue what Merleau-Ponty called the 'truth of naturalism' and the idea that 'it would be necessary to define transcendental philosophy anew in such a way as to integrate with it the very phenomenon of the real' (1983, 224). The 'truth' of naturalism is not the naturalism which Husserl cautioned against, but a redefined non-reductionist naturalism that correlates with a redefined phenomenology.

REFERENCES

Botvinick, M. and Cohen, J. (1998), 'Rubber hands "feel" touch that eyes see', *Nature* 391: 756.

Campbell, J. (1999), 'Schizophrenia, the space of reasons and thinking as a motor process', *The Monist* 82/4: 609–25.

Damasio, A. R. (1994), *Descartes' Error: Emotion, Reason, and the Human Brain* (New York: Putnam Publishing).

De Preester, H. (2002), 'Naturalizing Husserlian phenomenology: An introduction', *Psychoanalytische Perspectieven* 20/4: 633–47.

Dretske, F. (1997), *Naturalizing the Mind* (Cambridge, MA: MIT Press).

Dreyfus, H. (1973), *What Computers Can't Do* (New York and Cambridge, MA: MIT Press).

Edelman, S. (2002), 'Constraints on the nature of the neural representation of the visual world', *Trends in Cognitive Sciences* 6: 125–31.

Farrer, C., Franck, N., Georgieff, N., Frith, C. D., Decety, J., and Jeannerod, M. (2003), 'Modulating the experience of agency: a positron emission tomography study', *NeuroImage* 18: 324–33.

Farrer, C. and Frith, C. D. (2002), 'Experiencing oneself vs. another person as being the cause of an action: the neural correlates of the experience of agency', *NeuroImage* 15: 596–603.

Frith, C. D. (1992), *The Cognitive Neuropsychology of Schizophrenia* (Hillsdale, NJ: Lawrence Erlbaum Associates).

—— and Blakemore, S., and Wolpert, D. (2000), 'Abnormalities in the awareness and control of action', *Philosophical Transactions of the Royal Society of London* 355: 1771–88.

—— and Done, D. J. (1988), 'Towards a neuropsychology of schizophrenia', *British Journal of Psychiatry* 153: 437–43.

Gallagher, S. (1997), 'Mutual enlightenment: Recent phenomenology in cognitive science', *Journal of Consciousness Studies* 4/3: 195–214.

—— (2000), 'Philosophical conceptions of the self: implications for cognitive science', *Trends in Cognitive Science* 4/1: 14–21.

—— (2001), 'The practice of mind: Theory, simulation or primary interaction?', *Journal of Consciousness Studies* 8/5–7: 83–108.

—— (2003), 'Phenomenology and experimental design', *Journal of Consciousness Studies* 10/9–10: 85–99.

—— (2005), *How the Body Shapes the Mind* (Oxford: Oxford University Press).

—— (2007), 'The natural philosophy of agency', *Philosophy Compass* 2/2: 347–57 (http://www.blackwell-synergy.com/doi/full/10.1111/j.1747-9991.2007.00067.x).

—— (2008), 'Inference or interaction: Social cognition without precursors', *Philosophical Explorations* 11/3: 163–73.

—— (2010), 'Multiple aspects in the sense of agency', *New Ideas in Psychology*. (http://dx.doi.org/10.1016/j.newideapsych.2010.03.003). Online publication April 2010.

—— and Brøsted Sørensen, J. (2006), 'Experimenting with phenomenology', *Consciousness and Cognition* 15/1: 119–34.

—— and Hutto, D. (2008), 'Understanding others through primary interaction and narrative practice', in J. Zlatev, T. Racine, C. Sinha and E. Itkonen (eds), *The Shared Mind: Perspectives on Intersubjectivity* (Amsterdam: John Benjamins), 17–38.

—— and Varela, F. (2003), 'Redrawing the map and resetting the time: Phenomenology and the cognitive sciences', *Canadian Journal of Philosophy* (Supplementary) 29: 93–132.

—— and Væver, M. (2004), 'Disorders of embodiment', in J. Radden (ed.), *The Philosophy of Psychiatry: A Companion* (Oxford: Oxford University Press), 118–32.

Gallese, V. (2001), 'The 'shared manifold' hypothesis: from mirror neurons to empathy', *Journal of Consciousness Studies* 8: 33–50.

Gold, I. and Hohwy, J. (2000), 'Rationality and schizophrenic delusion', in M. Coltheart, and M. Davies (eds.), *Pathologies of Belief* (Oxford: Blackwell Publishers), 145–65.

Goldman, A. I. (1995), 'Desire, intention and the simulation theory', in B. F. Malle, L. J. Moses, and D. A. Baldwin (eds), *Intentions and Intentionality: Foundations of Social Cognition* (Cambridge, MA: MIT Press), 207–24.

—— (2006), *Simulating Minds: The Philosophy, Psychology, and Neuroscience of Mindreading* (New York: Oxford University Press).

Gurwitsch, A. (2009), *Constitutive Phenomenology in Historical Perspective, The Collected Works of Aron Gurwitsch (1901–1973)*, Vol. I, tr. and ed. J. García-Gómez (Dordrecht: Springer).

Haggard, P. (2005), 'Conscious intention and motor cognition', *Trends in Cognitive Sciences* 9/6: 290–5.

—— and Libet, B. (2000), 'Conscious intention and brain activity', *Journal of Consciousness Studies* 8/11: 47–63.

Hohwy, J. (2004), 'Top-down and bottom-up in delusion formation', *Philosophy, Psychiatry and Psychology* 11: 65–70.

Holst E. von, and Mittelstaedt H. (1950), 'Das Reafferenzprinzip (Wechselwirkungen zwischen Zentralnervensystem und Peripherie)', *Naturwisenschaften* 37: 464–76.

Husserl, E. (1965), *Phenomenology and the Crisis of Philosophy*, tr. Q. Lauer (New York: Harper).

—— (1970), *Cartesian Meditations*, tr. D. Cairns (The Hague: Martinus Nijhoff).

—— (1976), *Ideen zu einer reinen Phänomenologie und phänomenologischen Philosophie I*, *Husserliana III/1–2* (The Hague: Martinus Nijhoff); tr. F. Kersten, *Ideas Pertaining to a Pure Phenomenology and to a Phenomenological Philosophy. First Book. General Introduction to a Pure Phenomenology* (The Hague: Martinus Nijhoff, 1982).

—— (1977), *Phenomenological Psychology*, tr. J. Scanlon (Hague: Martinus Nijhoff).

—— (2001), *Logical Investigations*, 3 vols., tr. J. N. Findlay (London: Routledge).

—— (2005), *Phantasy, Image Consciousness, and Memory (1898-1925)*. tr. J. B. Brough, Collected Works, Volume XI (Dordrecht: Springer).

James, W (1890), *Principles of Psychology* (New York: Dover, 1950).

Jeannerod, M. (1997), *The Cognitive Neuroscience of Action* (Oxford: Blackwell Publishers).

Lawlor, L. (2009), 'Becoming and Auto-Affection (Part II): Who are we?', Invited Lecture, ICNAP, 2009. http://www.icnap.org/meetings.htm (accessed 15 January 2011).

Le Van Quyen, M. (2003), 'Disentangling the dynamic core: A research program for neurodynamics at the large-scale', *Biological Research* 36: 67–88.

—— and Petitmengin, C. (2002), 'Neuronal dynamics and conscious experience: An example of reciprocal causation before epileptic seizures', *Phenomenology and the Cognitive Sciences* 1: 169–80.

Libet, B. (1985), 'Unconscious cerebral initiative and the role of conscious will in voluntary action', *Behavioral and Brain Sciences* 8: 529–66.

—— and Gleason, C. A., Wright, E. W., and Pearl, D. K. (1983), 'Time of conscious intention to act in relation to onset of cerebral activity (readiness potential): The unconscious initiation of a freely voluntary act', *Brain* 106: 623–42.

Lutz, A. (2002), 'Toward a neurophenomenology as an account of generative passages: A first empirical case study', *Phenomenology and the Cognitive Sciences* 1: 133–67.

—— and Lachaux, J.-P., Martinerie, J., and Varela, F. J. (2002), 'Guiding the study of brain dynamics using first-person data: Synchrony patterns correlate with on-going conscious states during a simple visual task', *Proceedings of the National Academy of Science USA* 99: 1586–91.

—— and Thompson, E. (2003), 'Neurophenomenology: Integrating lived experience into cognitive neuroscience', *Journal of Consciousness Studies* 10: 31–52.

Malenka R. C., Angel R. W., Hampton B., and Berger P. A. (1982), 'Impaired central error correcting behaviour in schizophrenia', *Arch Gen Psychiat* 39: 101–7.

Marbach, E. (1993), *Mental Representation and Consciousness: Towards a Phenomenological Theory of Representation and Reference* (Dordrecht: Kluwer Academic Publishers).

—— (2010), 'Towards a formalism for expressing structures of consciousness', in S. Gallagher and D. Schmicking (eds), *Handbook of Phenomenology and Cognitive Science* (Dordrecht: Springer).

Merleau-Ponty, M. (1962), *Phenomenology of Perception*, tr. C. Smith (London: Routledge and Kegan Paul).

—— (1983), *The Structure of Behavior*, tr. A.L. Fisher. Pittsburgh: Duquesne University Press.

—— (2010), *Child Psychology and Pedagogy: The Sorbonne Lectures 1949–1952*, tr T. Welsh (Evanston: Northewestern University Press).

Mundale, J. and Gallagher, S. (2009), 'Delusional experience', in J. Bickle (ed.), *Oxford Handbook of Philosophy and Neuroscience* (Oxford: Oxford University Press), 513–21.

Noë, A. (2004), *Action in Perception* (Cambridge, MA: MIT Press).

Petitot, J. (1999), 'Morphological eidetics for a phenomenology of perception', in J. Petitot, F. J. Varela, B. Pachoud, and J.-M. Roy (eds), *Naturalizing Phenomenology: Issues in Contemporary Phenomenology and Cognitive Science* (Stanford, CA: Stanford University Press), 330–71.

—— (2008), *Neurogéométrie de la vision: modèles mathématiques et physiques des architectures fonctionnelles* (Montreal: Presses internationales Polytechnique).

Pöppel, E. (1994), 'Temporal mechanisms in perception', *International Review of Neurobiology* 37: 185–202.

Price, D., Barrell, J., and Rainville, P. (2002), 'Integrating experiential–phenomenological methods and neuroscience to study neural mechanisms of pain and consciousness', *Consciousness and Cognition* 11: 593–608.

Ratcliffe, M. (2007), *Rethinking Commonsense Psychology: A Critique of Folk Psychology, Theory of Mind and Simulation* (Basingstoke: Palgrave Macmillan).

Roy, J.-M., Petitot, J., Pachoud, B. and Varela, F.J. (1999), 'Beyond the gap: An introduction to naturalizing phenomenology', in J. Petitot, F. J. Varela, B. Pachoud and J.-M. Roy (eds), *Naturalizing Phenomenology: Issues in Contemporary Phenomenology and Cognitive Science* (Stanford, CA: Stanford University Press), pp. 1–80.

Sartre, J.-P. (1956), *Being and Nothingness* (New York: Philosophical Library).

—— (2004), *The Imaginary: A Phenomenological Psychology of the Imagination*, tr. J. Webber (London: Routledge).

Schacter, D. L., Reiman, E., Curran, T., Yun, L. S., Bandy, D., McDermott, K. B., and Roediger, H. L. (1996), 'Neuroanatomical Correlates of Veridical and Illusory Recognition Memory: Evidence from Positron Emission Tomography', *Neuron* 17/2: 267–74.

Singh J. R., Knight, T., Rosenlicht, N., Kotun, J. M., Beckley, D. J., and Woods, D. L. (1992), 'Abnormal premovement brain potentials in schizophrenia', *Schizophrenia Research* 8: 31–41.

Skewes, J. C. (2011), *Agency: A Philosophical Context in Psychological Science*, PhD dissertation, Faculty of Humanities, Aarhus University.

Sperry R. W. (1950), 'Neural basis of the spontaneous optokinetic response produced by visual inversion', *J Comp Phys Psychology* 43: 482–9.

Thompson, E. (2007), *Mind in Life: Biology, Phenomenology, and the Sciences of Mind* (Cambridge, MA: Harvard University Press).

—— (2001), *Between Ourselves: Second Person Issues in the Study of Consciousness* (Exeter: Imprint Academic).

—— and Lutz, A., and Cosmelli, D. (2005), 'Neurophenomenology: An Introduction for Neurophilosophers', in A. Brook and K. Akins (eds), *Cognition and the Brain: The Philosophy and Neuroscience Movement* (New York and Cambridge: Cambridge University Press).

Tsakiris, M. (2005), 'On agency and body-ownership', Paper presented at Expérience Subjective Pré-Réflexive and Action (ESPRA) Conference, CREA, Paris. December 2005.

—— and Haggard, P. (2005), 'Experimenting with the acting self', *Cognitive Neuropsychology* 22/3–4: 387–407.

—— and Hesse M. D., Boy C., Haggard P., and Fink G. R. (2007), 'Neural signatures of body ownership: A sensory network for bodily self-consciousness', *Cerebral Cortex* 17: 2235–44.

—— and Schütz-Bosbach, S., and Gallagher, S. (2007), 'On agency and body-ownership: Phenomenological and neurocognitive reflections', *Consciousness and Cognition* 16/3: 645–60.

—— and Prabhu, G., and Haggard, P. (2006), 'Having a body versus moving your body: How agency structures body-ownership', *Consciousness and Cognition* 15/2: 423–32.

Varela, F. J. (1996), 'Neurophenomenology: A methodological remedy for the hard problem', *Journal of Consciousness Studies* 3/4: 330–49.

—— (1999), 'The specious present: A neurophenomenology of time consciousness', in J. Petitot, F. J. Varela, B. Pachoud, and J.-M. Roy (eds), *Naturalizing Phenomenology: Issues in Contemporary Phenomenology and Cognitive Science* (Stanford, CA: Stanford University Press), 266–314.

—— and Thompson, E., and Rosch, E. (1991), *The Embodied Mind* (Cambridge, MA: MIT Press).

Wolpert, D. M. and Ghahramani, Z. (2000), 'Computational principles of movement neuroscience', *Nature Neuroscience Supplement* 3: 1212–17.

Zahavi, D. (2001), 'Beyond empathy: Phenomenological approaches to intersubjectivity', *Journal of Consciousness Studies* 8/5–7: 151–67.

—— (2004), 'Phenomenology and the project of naturalization', *Phenomenology and the Cognitive Sciences* 3/4: 331–47.

—— (2010), 'Phenomenology and the problem of naturalization', in S. Gallagher and D. Schmicking (eds), *Handbook of Phenomenology and Cognitive Science* (Dordrecht: Springer).

CHAPTER 5

THE PHENOMENOLOGY OF LIFE: DESIRE AS THE BEING OF THE SUBJECT

RENAUD BARBARAS

1 THE LESSON OF THE *A PRIORI* OF CORRELATION

In the *Crisis of the European Sciences and Transcendental Phenomenology*, Husserl characterizes the task of phenomenology as the elaboration of the universal *a priori* of correlation between transcendent being and its subjective modes of givenness; in other words, between the world and consciousness. He writes: 'Every entity that is valid for me and every conceivable subject as existing in actuality is thus correlatively—and with essential necessity—an index of its systematic multiplicities', which means that 'no conceivable human being, no matter how different we imagine him to be, could ever experience a world in manners of givenness which differ from the incessantly mobile relativity we have delineated in general terms: that is, as a world pre-given to him in his conscious life and in community with fellow human beings' (Husserl 1970, p. 165). This means that the Being of the world itself always implies a reference to a consciousness, just as the reference to a world is included in the Being of all consciousness.

It is, however, necessary to examine the consequences of this discovery in terms of the status of the terms in relation—in terms of the Being of consciousness and the Being of the world. The *a priori* of correlation stipulates the relativity of the transcendent being to consciousness, that is, the dependence of its Being *vis-à-vis* its appearance. But, as soon as we start to talk about appearing, it becomes necessary to introduce a distinction between the being that appears and its appearance. If it is true that the Being (*être*) of the being (*étant*) consists in its appearing, then this appearance itself demands that the being not be confused with its appearance, that it remains withdrawn or somehow lacking in relation to its appearance, precisely so that it may appear. Suffice to say, what appears is always absent from its own appearing(s), since it is the subject of these appearings and thus remains concealed by its own appearances. The distance of what appears is transcendence itself, and it is as irreducible as it is ineluctable: it neither refers to a dimension situated beyond the appearance, nor is it the inverse of a possible proximity. Insofar as it is nothing other than its appearance, the being that appears cannot be grasped elsewhere than in its appearance—it is given only as its own depth and transcendence. Thus, affirming that the essence of the being consists in its appearing is also to say that a being must not be confused with its appearances, it always withdraws behind them. But it is also to insist that the appearances are nevertheless appearances *of* this being, such that the being reveals itself in them, and they lead back to it, even if it continuously slips away in this search. In short, the *a priori* of correlation leads us to characterize the being as what presents itself in its appearances only by being absent from them, as offering itself up to an exploration, in the face of which, it continuously steps back or withdraws. This is the fundamental situation that is captured in the doctrine of givenness by adumbration (*Abschattungslehre*).

This *a priori* of correlation is as binding at the level of the subject as it is in the sphere of the transcendent. It signifies that the essence of consciousness implies its relation to a transcendent, to the extent that a consciousness that is not in relation to what is other to it is not a consciousness: consciousness is as relative to the world as the world is relative to it. It is clearly this property—summarized by the concept of intentionality—that characterizes the essence of consciousness. But the *a priori* of correlation also has another consequence—one that immediately presents itself as a problem. Even if consciousness is that to which the world appears, it is also, as such, a being that belongs to the world. To put it another way, if the world is truly an all-encompassing reality—the totality of what is—it must necessarily contain consciousness, and the fact that consciousness is involved in the appearance of the world does not change this in the slightest. To the contrary, one must emphasize that consciousness can only make the world appear *because* it is, in a certain way, in the world; in other words, intentionality presupposes a deeper co-belonging between consciousness and world. A consciousness that was foreign to or outside of the world would not have the world in the two senses of the term: if it did not belong *to* the world, there would not be a world for it. Husserl's own findings left him with no choice but to recognize this: 'Thus, *on the one hand consciousness is said to be the absolute* in which everything transcendent and, therefore, ultimately the whole psychophysical world, becomes constituted; and on the other hand, consciousness is said to be a *subordinate real event within that world*. How can these statements be reconciled?' (Husserl 1983, p. 124). Put in these terms, the situation presents us with a considerable difficulty: how can the absolute, from which the world originates, also be an event that takes place within the world; how can the subject that we are also constitute itself as the psychophysical reality that it is?

Confronted with this problem, two attitudes are possible. We can hold firm to the duality of the absolute and the event—that is, of constitution and the intra-mundane—and conclude from it, as Husserl does, a mysterious self-constitution (of empirical consciousness by transcendental consciousness). Such an attitude as good as removes the transcendental subject from the correlation by making it an absolute, and thus insists on the duality of the transcendental and the empirical over and above their unity. This amounts to a definitive prohibition against thinking this unity, as it remains the work of the absolute—that is, of what forever remains foreign to this unity and takes its leave from it at the very moment when it founds it. In order for this to be realized (thinking the unity), the absolute must renounce its own absoluteness, it must pass into its other; in short, the transcendental must make itself empirical. But there is also another way. We can emphasize the consequences of correlation against the absoluteness of consciousness. In other words, we can put the symmetry of the relation of correlation to work against the Husserlian dissymmetry that wants to make the world relative to a consciousness that is itself not relative to the world. By taking this route, we affirm that if consciousness is in its essence consciousness of the world, it must necessarily also be a part of the world, which amounts to saying that the transcendentality of this consciousness envelops its empiricity, and that the belonging of consciousness to the world, far from being opposed to its constituting activity, conditions it. But insisting on this belonging to the world as an essential dimension of the subject is clearly to reject the distinction between the transcendental and the empirical—between the absolute and the event—in favour of a more originary dimension in relation to which Husserlian duality appears as derivative and already abstract. If we wish to take correlation seriously we must confront the necessity of uncovering a sense of subjective Being that is completely foreign to the split between the empirical and the transcendental—a sense of Being in relation to which the dimensions of belonging to the world and of the phenomenalization of the world appear as subordinate.

2 LIFE

The question is thus the following: how can we characterize the sense of the Being of the subject in such a manner that it is both, from the same view point, a part of the world and the condition of the world? Or, how can we think the subject of correlation in such a way that its intentionality does not exclude, but rather calls for its belonging to the world, in such a way that it does not make the world appear except by passing over into the world? Or, yet again, how can we think the subject in such a way that insofar as it phenomenalizes the world, it can only be conceived as belonging to the world? In fact, Husserl's characterization of transcendental consciousness shows us the way towards a response. Transcendental consciousness is constituted by lived-experiences (*vécus* or *Erlebnisse*); it is in and by them that it lives (*erlebt*) in the world. The experience through which the world appears refers back to *life*, insofar as this experience is quite simply the experience of living. Yet it is this same dimension of life that we find in the characterization of the empirical subject as a psychophysical reality. In effect, the question then becomes: how can we define the subject and its interworldly existence, how can we distinguish it from other beings other than by saying that it is alive? Of course, we could exploit the duality and claim that these two senses of life are also foreign to one another;

that we are dealing with the activity of a transcendental consciousness and its empirical realization. But in this case we would still have to justify the use of the same concept: life. It serves no purpose to say that in the case of the life (*erleben*) of transcendental consciousness we are using the concept 'life' in a metaphorical sense. We would then be left to explain and understand what, at the heart of this transcendental life, motivates our bringing in this metaphor in the first place.

Transcendental life must contain something living in order for us to be able to characterize it as life. In other words, there has to be a shared dimension between these otherwise apparently separated spheres, an original kinship from which the metaphor draws its force, an axis on which the communication between the two spheres takes place. It is thus more coherent and more productive to look to this kinship—more primordial than the split between constituting activity and psychophysical existence—for an indication of the sense of originary Being. In French, the term life signifies both 'being alive' and 'experiencing'; it is neutral *vis-à-vis* the distinction between an intransitive (*leben*) and a transitive (*erleben*) meaning of life. This life that is, indistinctly, existence in the world, and experience of the world corresponds to the sense of Being that we are looking for. It is situated ontologically prior to the partition between the empirical and the transcendental, and therefore blurs the boundary between the two. Living signifies an existence in the world that encompasses the appearance of the world; it is an experience of the world that implies its inscription in that which it experiences: At the heart of life, belonging to the world and the phenomenalization of the world are joined together.

If we properly interrogate the sense of the Being of the subject in light of the *a priori* of correlation, we are led into a dimension where subjective experience and belonging, a transitive activity and an intransitive existence, combine and meld into one another. This is the dimension of life. In this sense, having once again recovered its original project, phenomenology necessarily opens itself up onto a phenomenology of life. Comprehending the correlation and particularly the sense of the Being of the subject of correlation is inevitably to seek to characterize the life of the subject, the life by which the subject, situated within the world, is at the same time able to make the world appear. But if the recourse to life does in fact clarify the task of phenomenology in terms of its fundamental project, then conversely, it is also the case that phenomenology clarifies life insofar as it permits us to approach it without the prejudices of biology or the majority of philosophical approaches that take a biological understanding of life as their starting point. Approaching life from within a phenomenological framework, which life itself has allowed us to specify, is evidently a shift out of the natural attitude. As a result, it also demands that we give up referring to life as the property of a living organism—an approach which would situate life in the world with the same status as other beings. Bringing the problem of life into a phenomenological framework means that it must be approached as an originary or primordial dimension that is in an awkward position *vis-à-vis* the split between the empirical and the transcendental. This is because life is in some sense situated beyond the simple inscription in the world—since life always has experience of this world—but insofar as life encompasses an existence within the world it is nonetheless on this side of pure constitutive or transcendental activity. Simply put, life is transcendental activity itself as activity; that is, as entailing an act within the world.

From this we must already draw two conclusions. First of all, in liberating our approach to life from naturalist and realist prejudices, we separate the question of life from that of living. This allows us to think about living on the basis of its life, rather than on the basis of the category of beings *qua* living organisms. Thus it allows us to open the way (the path we will follow) towards thinking about life in a manner that is detached from the reference to living beings, and towards a more profound sense of life than the one suited to living beings. Second, if it is true that life is a sense of Being at the heart of which phenomenalizing the world and belonging to it are joined, then it goes without saying that the status of both is going to be profoundly modified in light of this original sense of Being: that is, life. If it was necessary to emphasize that the constituting subject cannot but belong to the world, in the same manner as all other beings, we must now add that, precisely as a constituting subject—that is, as a living subject—its belonging to the world can never merely indicate a simple inclusion, the occupying of a place within the world. It thus falls upon us to ask, in light of a more profound characterization of life, what the true meaning of 'belonging' in fact is—in what sense precisely is the subject *in* and *of* the world? In the same line it follows that the manner in which the subject makes the world appear cannot, within the framework of a phenomenology of life, be reconstructed in a satisfying manner solely on the basis of the play between immanent lived-experiences (*vécus immanents*). It is not even certain that the living subject is really the phenomenalizing subject, insofar as the life that inhabits him is perhaps not only its own, and comes from beyond itself.

3 Desire

What remains is to attempt to characterize this concept of life through which we have defined the subject of correlation. It is a life that runs deeper than the distinction between *leben* and *erleben* and that, to this end, does not belong to the world in the same manner as any other being, but is also not foreign to the world, in the sense that it would be were it an absolute consciousness. Taking the life of living beings into consideration put us on the right path. The life of a living being is attested to in the incessant movement through which it maintains the relation with its world. It is thus on the side of movement that we must search for the essence of life. In fact, it suffices to draw out the consequences of a negative characterization of life in order to confirm the validity of this proposition: the speculative constraints converge with the description here. If not *self-movement* within the world, what else could signify a mode of belonging to the world that is not conflated with a simple localization? How else could one be *of* the world without being situated somewhere within it? If movement is truly dependent on the world as a frame within which it unfurls itself, it is then also an active negation of all localization, and in this sense it remains irreducible to a simple inscription in the world. Movement is, without doubt, *of* the world, and yet it also escapes the world because it is nowhere *in* it. However, this response remains insufficient insofar as it exposes us to the same difficulty that led us to put life in the first place. We could in fact be tempted to place the split between the empirical and the transcendental at the heart of movement itself and affirm that if the living being accomplishes actual movements—its own displacements—there is a constitutive 'movement' that has nothing to do with such displacements and corresponds to the work of consciousness. But again, this position turns out to be unstable and thus only provisional because it leaves unexplained what justifies calling a transcendental activity that is completely foreign to the changing of place movement. A tension emerges between the restricted sense that we have accorded to movement—the changing of place—and the need that we feel to call upon a more extensive and 'metaphoric' use of the idea of movement, when we speak, for example, of a movement of ideas, a movement of sympathy, or a constitutive movement. What founds this propensity that the concept of movement has to proliferate and 'metaphorisize'? Along what axis, in the name of what secret kinship, does the passage from a simple displacement to all these activities that have nothing to do with spatiality operate? A closer examination reveals that it is ultimately life that founds this extensive usage of the concept of movement: we speak of movement everywhere that life emerges, no matter whether it is a question of our life as organisms or the life of ideas. Movement brings us back to life and the question is to know what this life consists of such that it can give rise to movements in the strict sense, but is not exhausted by them (and this is precisely why it can be attributed to what does not move at all).

In light of the analysis of phenomenological correlation, the characterization of life that defines the Being of the subject is subject to two constraints. First, this life is more than a simple movement but less than pure experience. It is, in some sense, an experience that is merged with an advance, or a movement that unveils its own object. What is proper to the object of this life *qua* movement is that its *sense* (in French, the word *sens* has a double meaning, indicating both sense and direction) is only given as *direction*; it assumes an originary status of sense, more primordial even than the split between signification and direction. Second, we have to remember the other pole of the correlation and emphasize that this life is the condition of the appearance of a being that is absent from what presents it; that is, the being that appears retreats behind the appearances in and through which it manifests itself. Thus, due precisely to its constitutive transcendence, which is nothing other than the transcendence of the world, the being offers itself up to an exploration that is, in principle, unending. And yet these two conditions are strongly correlated. It is because of its constitutive depth and opacity that the experience of the being is at the same time always an advance or moving towards. It is because it continuously slips away from the gaze that it is given as the end or goal of a movement. The active dimension of life, that distinguishes it from a simple lived-experience, responds to the excess of the being in relation to the realm of the object: it offers itself up as a weak directionality because it cannot be possessed in an intuition. Insofar as it responds to this double condition, living can only be characterized as *desire*. What is unique to desire is that it only experiences its object in advancing towards it; it does not become conscious of its object except through the momentum with which it approaches it; but it does so in such a way that what desire reaches exacerbates as much as appeases it. The objective and finite forms that desire is likely to meet reveal what it truly aims at as always lacking in these forms: desire never meets its object except in the mode of the object's own absence, and this is why nothing stops it. Everything occurs as if desire had no object, not in the sense of not desiring anything but rather because it is oriented towards that which transcends all objects; while we may say that it always aims at something, we must also add that nothing can fulfil it. This is why what fills it only serves to further hollow it out, and why it can only be effectuated as movement. Insofar as it appears in the world that it also makes appear, life must be characterized as a kind of movement; and insofar as the world is only given to life as what continuously and indefinitely withdraws behind its own appearance, this movement of life must be characterized as desire. To the non-positive excess of the world corresponds the insatiable advance of desire.

These initial conclusions call for two remarks. First, by bringing desire to the fore we set ourselves down the path of a phenomenology of affectivity. Thinking life as desire is to install affectivity at the very heart of life. More primordial than consciousness and movement, we find desire as the relation between the two other terms. Desire is to movement and to consciousness what living was to *leben* and *erleben*. Beneath all motion there lays an e-motion that is nothing other than desire itself, and it is in this emotion that the most originary sense of consciousness resides. This co-originarity of life and affect would seem to situate our approach in the same vicinity of that of Michel Henry, all the more so since Henry calls his approach a phenomenology of life. But such a *rapprochement* would be superficial, since, in truth, our approach here is completely at odds with Henry's. What characterizes desire is that it is only experienced in being affected by an other, which is also to say that it only comes about in actively carrying itself towards this other. Originary affection is hetero-affection, and this is why desire is not distinguishable from the movement that projects it towards the world: being-next-to-oneself (*être-auprès-de-soi*) demands an entrance into exteriority. We situate ourselves here resolutely on the side of ontological monism, tirelessly critiqued by Henry, and our approach even constitutes a form of radicalisation. To situate desire at the heart of the subject is to assert the idea that there is no appearance, including appearance of oneself to oneself, except in and through a distance that exceeds that distance manifested by a simple object. The subject can only make something appear insofar it is capable of relating to the transcendence of the world that hides itself, or better, slips away, in the appearance of the object. The correlation between desire and the world is the truth of the relation between consciousness and object. Thus, we discover at the heart of the subject an affective dimension—desire—that ek-statically projects the subject towards the world, so as to make it appear in conformity with its irreducible transcendence. Henry, to the contrary, refers movement back to a power that underpins it, and in turn refers this power to a more originary power, which is the power to posses itself, the power to auto-affect. He names this power, life. But this life that no lack can hollow out, that consists only in the self's distanceless embrace of itself, and that finally merges with complete immobility, is synonymous with death.

We must also underline that by placing desire at the heart of life we resolutely distance ourselves from the presuppositions of most other theories of life. As Hans Jonas has clearly shown, at least since antiquity philosophy and science have been prisoners of a 'universal ontology of death'—for which inert matter is the ontological norm, and in relation to which life appears as an inexplicable exception—to such an extent that philosophical thought has unceasingly tried to resituate the phenomenon of life within the laws that govern matter (Jonas 1966). From this perspective, life is approached from within the horizon of death—that is to say, as always threatened by the forces that will inevitably lead to its indistinction with matter and submission to its laws. Life is thus rendered as the negation of the negation that is death, a struggle against the forces that would restore its lack of distinction from inert matter. Life consists in maintaining life; life is survival, and its proper activity is thus that of need, through which the living being reconstitutes itself unendingly. The approach that I am developing here is radically opposed to this. In taking the phenomenological correlation as the point of departure we immediately neutralize the ontology of death, which always presupposes a naturalist perspective. Instead, we approach life on the basis of itself rather than on the basis of what negates it. In doing so, we ask what life *does*, in place of investigating what it struggles against. What we discover is that, insofar as life's work is the phenomenalization of the world, life is best characterized as desire rather than need. Expressed otherwise, in approaching life without presuppositions we discover both its profusion, which goes well beyond the requirement for self-conservation, and its reach, which exceeds that of need, because it plunges into the furthest depths of the world. Contrary to need, life does not assimilate substances, contrary to knowledge it does not intuit objects. It makes the transcendence of the world appear, and it advances towards it: this is why we characterize it as desire. It is thus on the express condition of engaging in a phenomenological approach that it becomes possible, as we have seen, to renew a universal ontology of life.

4 THE LACK OF BEING

Understanding life as the sense of the Being of the subject has led us to desire as its most profound determination, but as we have seen, a deeper consideration of desire has in fact revealed to us an even more profound sense of life. We have insisted, up to now, on the properly intentional dimension of desire, or rather on desire as original intentionality, as the hinge or pivot of the experience of movement. This approach, of course, presupposes a separation between the subject and the world. It is situated in the framework of a philosophy of correlation, understood as the relation between beings that are first of all ontological strangers to one another. But there is another dimension to desire—this time rather more ontological than phenomenological—which must also be taken into consideration. All desire is, at its core, a *desiring for the self* (*désir de soi*), in the sense that it proceeds out of an ontological lacuna or lack: it is oriented towards an other because its own Being resides in this other. Desire is not a form of knowing (*connaissance*) an object, but an attempt at self-realization. It is the search for the self in an other; a reconciliation of the self with itself, or an accomplishment of the self through the mediation of an other. Put otherwise, desire always refers to a form of alienation. If it is oriented towards an other with so much fervour, it is because it is in the other that desire's own Being resides. This is the most profound reason for insisting that, properly speaking, desire or desiring does not have an object: its object is nothing other than itself, or rather the Being of the desirer. Yet, insofar as desiring is characterized by a fundamental alienation—a lack of Being that prohibits it from ever fully being what it is and without which it would not even begin to desire, and hence, exist—desire as a search for the self in the other is condemned to a never-ending quest, the insatiability of which is the measure of the subject's self-privation. Thus, saying that the subject of correlation is desire is also to recognize that beyond the phenomenalizing relation between the subject and the world, which we had up to this point held fast to, there is a more profound *ontological kinship* between the subject and the world, a kinship that is in fact what motivates desire. If the subject advances towards the world, it is because the subject's own Being resides in the world. The subject's quest within the world must be understood, from this point of view, as an attempt to realize itself, to realize its own unity—its own selfhood—through the mediation of the world. It is essentially itself, its own Being, its own selfhood, that the subject aims at in the transcendence of the world; a transcendence, the irreducibility of which is the measure of the ontological fault line that separates the subject from itself. It is for this and no other reason that the subject's advance toward the world in desire is unceasing and relentless.

We also discover here a new, more profound sense of belonging. It is not inclusion—occupation of a space—nor is it dynamic inhabitation of the world; it is ontological kinship. What the essence of desire reveals is that the subject is made of the same stuff as the world. Underpinning their apparent distance, there is between them a profound ontological continuity. Before being *in* the world because it moves, the subject is *of* the world in the sense that it proceeds from it ontologically—in the sense that the Being of the subject resides in the world. *Nota bene*, it is precisely this point that marks our departure from the phenomenological framework and the entrance into an ontological one. We have passed over from the sphere of correlation between subject and world to the sphere that attests to their commonality of being. We have gone from the relation as such to its *Being*—that is, to the common ontological element that underpins and allows for this relation between subject and world in the first place. If consciousness can orient itself towards the world, it is essentially because it is made up of the world, because it belongs to it ontologically, and one of the merits of the determination of the subject through desire is precisely to make the ontological relation beneath the intentional one appear—or in other words, to make the commonality that subtends the quest appear. The subject can only relate itself to the world as such—make it appear—because its Being emerges from the world. Yet if the Being of the world permitted us, in the first place, to progress in the characterization of the Being of the subject, it is now the Being of the subject, in light of these ontological considerations, that permits us to grasp, in a more profound manner, the Being of the world. We have defined the subject as desire and, as a consequence, as movement, because an experience or affect always implies its proper realization in motor activity. The subject of correlation possesses an originarily dynamic sense. On the other hand, we have brought to light, thanks to the analysis of desire, the fact that it presupposes a rapport with Being, in such a manner that we must acknowledge an ontological kinship between the desiring and what is desired. This leads to the following conclusion: if the subject is well and truly movement, the world to which it belongs in an ontological sense must itself be conceived as a dynamic reality. The world that an essentially self-moving subject desires—that is, the world that it orients itself towards—can only itself exist as movement or becoming. The subject understood as movement implies a belonging to a world as a Space where its interaction unfolds. But the desire that this movement presupposes involves a still more profound sense of belonging to a world that is not an all encompassing *totality*, but rather, a *process*. This is exactly what Jan Patočka realized in several decisive texts and notably in an unpublished letter to Robert Campbell dated 20 March 1964: 'The becoming and movement that are at the origins of all of our experiences are themselves impossible without a more elementary and profound becoming that is, not movement in experience and in the world, but rather the becoming and movement of the world as such; ontological becoming.' This remark echoes a published text where Patočka refers to the world as φύσις (nature), which appears as its most primordial and profound determination: 'insofar as we move ourselves, insofar as we act, and in this "doing" we understand ourselves, along with the things, we become part of the φύσις, of the all encompassing world, of nature' (Patočka 1988: 107). Here the essence of the subject reveals a belonging in a much more radical sense: an insertion into the process of the world. While in the strict phenomenological framework of correlation, the subject is in a certain sense opposed to the world that it makes appear, and figures as a sort of ontological exception, in the ontological framework that we are developing here, the movement of the subject appears as inscribed in a more primordial and profound movement that it prolongs or pursues and in which the true subject is not other to the world itself.

5 THE ARCHI-MOVEMENT

The analysis of desire thus leads us to surpass correlation as such—between a subject that is oriented movement and a world that is given as the constitutive depth of the being—in favour of a more radical dimension: that of an ontological kinship as the true fundament of the relation between subject and world. Yet it is the subject *qua* essentially dynamic reality that reveals this dimension to us, and the subject, conceived as such, leads us towards a dynamic essence of the world itself. Only a movement can relate the subject and the world to one another: one and the other are the modalities or the movements of one sole primordial movement. Thus the dynamic phenomenology that sees in desire the essence of the subject leads to a dynamic that has a truly ontological scope. Expressed in other terms, beyond the subject and the world, beyond the life of the subject and the movements that take place within the world, there is an *archi-movement* of 'natural' (in the sense of φύσις) processes, in which both the emergence of the world and the activity of the subject that makes it appear participate. It is this archi-movement that makes the two poles of correlation possible, prior to their relation to one another, by giving them a common fabric. And it is this archi-movement that Patočka recognizes when he writes: 'Concept of movement as fundament—movement conceived not as the movement of an object, but as the work of φύσις (nature) prior to all objectification and subjectification—φύσις as essence that is an event, that becomes' (Patočka 1995: 269). The fundament is no longer to be found on the side of the being or its essence, but in the movement that, insofar as it founds the relation between the subject and its object, is no longer objective or subjective. This movement is the essence understood as event—that is, the advent itself of the essence—and hence also of the being, for which it is the essence. It is precisely for this reason that it is characterised as φύσις. To speak of φύσις here is not to reduce phenomenology to a philosophy of nature. To the contrary, it is to confer upon nature, in the Aristotelian sense of φύσις, a phenomenological scope. It is to see in the archi-movement that it follows the trajectory of the advent of the being, or otherwise put, its appearance. From there, what is *originarily there*, what truly *is*, and thus occupies the place reserved since Plato for the essence is no longer the essence but its happening itself: 'What is constantly present is not only the *eidos*, the form, but in the same way and in a manner even more fundamental, the progression from non-Being to Being, *metabole*, movement' (Patočka 1988: 133).

It remains, of course, to further characterize this movement. Insofar as our own phe-nomenalizing movement is inscribed within this archi-movement, and draws its power from it, we must also affirm that the archi-movement of φύσις is the movement of appearance or appearing itself. Saying that our movement finds itself inserted in that of φύσις, conceived as the process of nature's becoming, means also recognizing that things cannot appear to us except insofar as they appear first of all in themselves. It is only because things, so to speak, prepare themselves for our apprehension or sketch out this apprehension that we are capable of perceiving them. Thus we never carry out the least synthesis—what the Being for us of an object always finally consists in—if that synthesis is not already carried out in the things themselves, precisely under the form of a produc-tion of the object *qua* object—in short, of a determination: 'Sense of the identification: there is not identity because I synthesize, but I synthesize because I put my finger on an identity—the change, the processes, the transformation are themselves the identifications, are the material syntheses, and my subjective synthesis of identification is simply the grasp-ing and recognizing of this singular identity, of this interior liaison between things' (Patočka 1995: 32). Expressed otherwise, we have to take stock of the fact that it is *the world itself* that appears. We can, of course, understand this fact from within the static framework of correlation as the recognition that in each appearance it is the world in person that appears: that is, the world in itself as distinguished from its appearance. This is precisely what distinguishes phenomenology from all forms of realism or phenomenalism. But this formula also has a more profound meaning. It signifies that it is the world itself that is the subject or the source of its appearance, that this appearance is the work of the world rather than that of the subject. And it is precisely insofar as the world makes itself appear that it then becomes susceptible to the appearance of a subject. The movement through which we go towards the world in order to make it appear precedes itself under the form of a movement through which the world manifests itself and thus itself reaches out towards us so as to prepare itself for our apprehension of it.

And yet, what could this archi-movement signify if not the process by which the world emerges out of the night of indifferentiation—synonym of non-Being from a perspective where nothing is created, where everything is already there—in order to constitute itself as world: that is, as the multiplicity of being. More precisely, it is in making the beings in their identity—in their unity—happen that it makes their multiplicity happen and hence constitutes itself as the unity of this multiplicity. The birth of the world is the work of this unity twice over: the unity of mundane beings and the unity of the world that totalizes them. Thus the work of this archi-movement is well and truly an ontogenetic operation. It carries out a departure from the undifferentiated fundament by way of the constitution of beings as such, as unities. This archi-movement is the incessant passage of the world from fundament to multiplicity of beings by way of differentiation within the fundament. It is a process of constitution of beings through the individuation of the fundament. As Patočka says, 'there must be something like a movement through which the heart of the world constitutes its contingent content, and of which space-time-quality is a sediment' (Patočka 1995: 157). Naturally, this process of individuation never exhausts the power of the fundament, and therefore it continues in the world in the form of the movements that affect beings. Beings are never fully individuated, but always on the path to individuation; they are mixed with their own processes of individuation in which they attest their appearance in the world. On the other hand, what is given as form or the principle of unity for all being (space, time) is nothing other than the trace of the fundament that remains within all beings: the sediment of its indifferentiation within the multiple.

6 THE LIFE OF MANIFESTATION

One could legitimately ask how this ontogenetic process refers back to manifestation, how the constitution of its own content by the world belongs to the realm of appearance; in short, how this cosmology is still in fact part of a phenomenology. This question is, however, motivated by a certain idea of appearance, as pregnant as it is contestable, which is precisely the one that we are trying to overcome. Contesting that the process refers to appearing is to suppose that all appearing rests on the activity of a subject, that there is no appearance except as subjectivation. But the passage to ontology, made possible by the analysis of desire, shows us that, on the contrary, subjective appearance (appearance to a subject) is thinkable only insofar as it is preceded by the appearing of the world, in the sense that it is the work of this world, as becoming differentiating and unifying of the fundament. How does this becoming refer back to appearing? In truth, all appearance is a discovery and hence, in turn, always breaks off a process of recovery. But there are at least two manners of being recovered, and hence also of being discovered. On the one hand, discovery can involve the interposition of something; the discovery proceeds by way of the retreat of what had interposed; this is *unconcealment*. On the other hand, being recovered can mean indifferentiation with the environment, continuity with the surrounding; in this case the discovery signifies the circumscription of what is discovered, the tracing of a border *vis-à-vis* the surrounding, its differentiation from its environment; this is *delimitation*. Delimitation is truly the first sense of definition: defining is first of all tracing a border (*finis*). It is thus not surprising that the essence—that is, the form—is originarily an event, since it first of all has the sense of a delimitation that only a movement could perform. Insofar as it is the 'separator', the movement is the source of the form, the first operator of the definition. This is precisely what appearance, in its most originary sense, consists in: it is the delimitation and the determination of a being; individuation by separation; material synthesis. Patočka underlines this perfectly in a note:

> Each thing acquires its figure—is delimited—and becomes an individual in setting itself apart from others. This becoming traces the borders *vis-à-vis* something else; it is a process of definition, of putting into form…This defines—the appearance of the thing as its Being. The thing is not only 'in itself', but also in all the others; it is its relation of delimitation *vis-à-vis* the totality of what is. (Patočka 1995: 114)

We must thus admit that there are two degrees of manifestation: manifestation as delimitation that is effectuated by the world, or rather that is merged with the 'physical' process of the constitution of the world (in the double sense of the genitive); and manifestation as unconcealment that is carried out by the subject itself. This latter type of manifestation goes back over the trace of the former in order to apprehend the border for itself; that is, to re-comprehend the thing *as such*; it unconceals by putting to one side the world within which the frontier is traced.

We must remind ourselves that we have determined the sense of the subject as life. It is this life that, insofar as it is at its core desire, finally led us to the process of the world itself. The archi-movement appeared as a process of manifestation, first of the world by itself, then of the world by a being of the world. This leads to the conclusion that if our subjective phenomenalizing work is inscribed in a process of the world's own phenomenalizing work that it prolongs, and if on the other hand our subjective operation of unconcealment merges with the activity of life, we must then acknowledge that the archi-movement is also the movement of a life. There is a life of the world in the sense that is evoked by the Aristotelian understanding of φύσις, a life of things. As a process of phenomenalization, life finds itself detached from the reference to a single living thing and transferred to the world itself: it is insofar as we inscribe ourselves in the life of the world and recuperate it for ourselves that we are alive, or rather, that our existence accomplishes itself as living. Thus it is not because we are living creatures that we are capable of living. It is rather that we are living beings because we are traversed by a life that is, in the first instance, not our own but that of the world. Our *being alive* rests entirely on the power of phenomenalization that is originarily the power of the world. We have recovered here the 'universal ontology of life' that Hans Jonas showed to be definitively supplanted by classical ontology. As Canguilhem has stressed, against a certain form of vitalism, life cannot be an empire within an empire; life is the only empire. This means that if we recognize ourselves as living beings, the life of living creatures can no longer be opposed, as some sort of singular force, to the forces at work in inert matter. Taking note of our singularity as living beings only has meaning on the condition that we stop opposing it to other types of beings and recognize that this life emerges at the very heart of Being, and that all beings fall within its reign. Of course, the enormous challenge is to give some sense to this formula without falling back into a naive form of vitalism that would consist in thinking all things on the model of living beings—a vitalism that the later Jonas was not far from. The task is thus to found a universal ontology of life without renouncing the ontological split between subject and world, and without therefore attributing the mode of Being of the subject to all worldly beings. This becomes possible only on the condition that we do renounce the naive sense of life as the activity of an organism in favour of a more originary sense, which is the sense that I have tried to elaborate here. Life is, at its core, phenomenalization—that is, circumscription (individuation) of the being—and this circumscription is as much the work of the world (delimitation) as it is the subjective activity of unconcealment. On the basis of this sense of life it becomes possible to think its universality without compromising the singularity of the living beings that we are. Likewise, it becomes possible to reconcile the ontological kinship of the subject and the world, both of which, in their difference, reveal the archi-movement (or the archi-life) of manifestation. The two poles of the correlation correspond to two modalities of phenomenalization and ultimately refer us to two degrees of the accomplishment of archi-life. Finally, it is obvious that in this framework it is impossible to define the relationship between the subject and the world by way of constitution. The transcendant being is not constituted by the subject; it is rather the subjective life that is constituted by the life of the world, in the sense that the life of the subject prolongs and accomplishes the life of the world.

7 THE ARCHI-EVENT

This conclusion nonetheless raises a serious difficulty. We have demonstrated, thanks to a regressive approach and guided by the Being of the beings that we are, an archi-movement of appearance that we in turn showed to be a process of individuation and delimitation. And yet nothing in this movement calls for the emergence of the being that we are. It is impossible to traverse backward the path that led us to the archi-movement, to go back from the archi-movement to the acts by which we phenomenalize the world. Expressed otherwise, if it also refers to the process of the world, the individuation from which we emerge as subjects is not reducible to a simple circumscription within the world. In contrast to other beings we are capable of opposing ourselves to the world—that is, of making it appear; we recuperate for ourselves the process of phenomenalization initiated by the world. Thus all of this occurs as if the movement of the manifestation of the world were separated from itself at a point *in* the world in order to become the singular work of a being in the world. This is what led us to consider desire as a starting point. We have shown that as desire is always desire for its self it manifests an ontological kinship with what it desires: the world. But that is only half of the complete story. If the subject desires—that is, aspires to reconcile with its self through the mediation of the world—it is first and foremost because it is separated from itself. And, if desire is by definition inextinguishable, it is precisely because the separation of the subject from its self is radical, and this is also why the depth of the world, where the Being of the desiring subject lies, is irreducible. This comes down to the same thing as saying that desire is endless, that the subject radically lacks itself and that the transcendence of the world is unobjectifiable. Thus, desire is what joins the community and the scission of subject and world, and therefore, of subject and itself. Desire is both the subject's lack of self and its search for itself in the other, for the simple reason that it is fundamentally the loss of the self. Correlation brings these two dimensions together: the ontological kinship without which the relation between subject and world would not be possible, and the distance or separation without which the relation would not be necessary. The determination of the subject by desire rigorously corresponds to the phenomenological correlation. The passage by way of desire confirms that, in our individuation, there will be a separation and thus a loss. It is because the subject that we are has lost the world to which it ontologically belongs that the movement of phenomenalization, which the subject inherits from the world, suddenly reverses direction and returns in a certain fashion to its origin, becoming a movement of the unconcealment of the world. This occurs as if, through this singular individuation of the being that we are, the process of the phenomenalization of the world came to inhabit another subject and was affected by a sort of drift thanks to which the archi-movement of the world changes its status and its direction: it discovers its source in orienting itself towards it.

We can thus easily see the difficulty. If it is true that the subject takes up the archi-movement of the phenomenalization of the world under the form of a desire that is turned towards the world, then nothing in this archi-movement allows us to account for the loss that brings about the desire. Expressed otherwise, the individuation by separation that is the condition of the singularity of our desiring existence cannot be the work of the archi-movement. We understand, in light of this, that our existence is movement, but insofar as it presupposes a separation, we cannot explain the singularity of this movement. This separation, which is at its core nothing other than the birth of the subject, is like an inflexion or a drift within the archi-movement, like a movement that affects the archi-movement's movement. But what is a movement within a movement if not an *event*? Thus the scission from which the desire of the subject (the subject as desire) emerges refers back to an *archi-event* that affects the *archi-movement* itself: the archi-event of a separation at the heart of the phenomenalizing movement, through which the movement comes to exile itself in a singular being and thus longs to return to its origin. Subjectivity is precisely the unity of this loss and this longing: its being refers back to the event of a loss of its existence that takes the form of a longing. We must note that this separation truly corresponds to the advent of living being; the living being is born from life by a scission that affect life's fundamental process, in such a way that it is no longer life that refers to living as its determination, but rather living that refers back to life as a form of scission deep within its core, that is to say, fundamentally, as its negation.

As we have seen, this archi-event has no place within the ontological process; it affects the archi-life but does not belong to it. The archi-event evades the ontological frame that phenomenology demands: it is what we must presuppose to account for phenomenality, and thus it falls within the scope of *metaphysics*. At the same time, this archi-event is absolutely required to account for the distance that underpins the phenomenological correlation. In this sense, phenomenology includes the recourse to metaphysics as a necessary dimension: it encompasses a constitutive relation to its other. Three levels must thus be distinguished: the phenomenological level of *correlation* which opposes the subject as desire and the world; the ontological level of the phenomenalizing *archi-movement* as the foundation of the ontological kinship between subject and world; and finally the metaphysical level of the *archi-event* of separation as the condition of the emergence of the subject and hence correlation. As an incessant search for itself in the other, desire joins the essential ontological belonging to the world wherein its Being resides and the loss of this world. It is for this reason that phenomenology is consistent only insofar as it integrates the ontological sphere of the archi-movement and the metaphysical sphere of the archi-event. Insofar as *life* does indeed describe the sense of the Being of the subject of phenomenality and this life ultimately refers back to desire, we must conclude that the phenomenology of life calls, at once, for an ontology of the archi-movement and a metaphysics of the archi-event.

8 Exodus, exile, death

Two questions remain at the end of this long analysis. The account that I have given here is affected by a fundamental ambiguity owing to the fact that I have, from the beginning, characterized the subject(s) that we are through life, as though the two were simply indistinguishable. But if our subjectivity is life, we are not the only possessors of it. What about all the other living beings? The whole of my account here aims at founding the reciprocity between life and subjectivity as I have defined it—and it is in this sense that fundamentally it refers back to a phenomenology of life. All living is characterized by desire: it is traversed by a phenomenalization, as simple as it is, and possesses a world, as coarse as it is. In other words, all living beings are individuated by separa-tion—they are all affected by the archi-event of the scission—and this is the reason why all living being desire and possess a world. What, then, is the difference between the kind of living beings that we are and other living beings? Both draw upon the power of the archi-movement and are affected by the archi-event; however, while animals still keep the power of the archi-life and in doing so bear witness to it in a privileged manner, humans are closer to the archi-event, affected by its violence, which we attest more than any other living being. In this sense, if the animal is a cosmic creature, the human is, in turn, a metaphysical being. To express it in another way: if the archi-event is a principle of singular individuation within the phenomenalizing archi-movement of the archi-life—that is, the source of life as such—we must conclude that the human is the living being *par excellence*, whereas the animal is still only traversed by life. Thus the difference between animal and human is, so to speak, a difference in degree, since the resonance of the archi-movement and the depth of the separation (the archi-event) are not found, so to speak, in the same proportions in the two. Because the power of the Fundament remains in the animal within the separation, the desire of the animal is more *movement* than experience: its separation takes the form of an *exodus*. For humans, on the contrary, the power of the archi-movement is as though silenced by the separation, driven back by the violence of the archi-event, in such a manner that its desire is realized as lived-experi-ence (*vécu*) rather than as movement. The singular aptitude of humans to make the world appear before them is like the power of their powerlessness. For man, separation is *exile*.

The second difficulty concerns death. What place could death have in a philosophy for which our life—the life of living beings—emerges, by scission, from an archi-life that is originally the life of the world. Indeed, in a universal ontology (we should say phenome-nology) of life, death can have no special status, nor be of a rank, so to speak, equal to that of life. It follows from what has been said that life must not be thought of on the basis of its own negation, as the negation of that negation. From our perspective, life accepts no other but itself; there is nothing it could be foreign to insofar as it is synonymous to the archi-movement of appearance. In truth, 'Life' is the name given to the sense of Being: nothing that claims to be can stand outside life's embrace. The life of the living that we are and that corresponds to what we mean by the normal use of the word 'life' comes, for its part, from the archi-life of the world thanks to the archi-event of separation. Its death can thus be only its own: it is not so much the negation of life in this living as negation of the living that carries it—that is to say, a return to the universal archi-life, a regression towards the general regime of individuation. Death is ultimately the negation of the originary negation that is the archi-event, it is de-differentiation, and this is why, in the same man-ner as the archi-event of which death is the loss, it possesses a metaphysical status. If each of our singular lives is the negation of universal life, the loss of its productive power, our death can have sense only as the loss of this loss. Death is not the disappearance of life, but the end of desire.

Translated by Darian Meacham

References

Canguilhem, G. (2008), *Knowledge of Life*, tr. Stefanos Geroulanos and Daniela Ginsburg (New York: Fordham University Press).

Henry, M. (2000), *Incarnation* (Paris: Seuil).

Husserl, E. (1970), *The Crisis of the European Sciences and Transcendental Phenomenology, An Introduction to Phenomenological Philosophy*, tr. D. Carr (Evanston: Northwestern University Press).

—— (1983), *Ideas Pertaining to a Pure Phenomenology and to a Phenomenological Philosophy. First Book*, tr. F. Kersten (The Hague: Martinus Nijhoff).

Jonas, H. (1966), *The Phenomenon of Life: Toward a Philosophical Biology* (New York: Harper & Row).

Patočka, J. (1988), *Le monde naturel et le mouvement de l'existence humaine*, trad. E. Abrams (Dordrecht: Kluwer Academic Publishers).

—— (1995), *Papiers phénoménologiques*, trad. E. Abrams (Grenoble: Jérôme Million).

PART II

INTENTIONALITY, PERCEPTION, AND EMBODIMENT

CHAPTER 6

INTENTIONALITY WITHOUT REPRESENTATIONALISM

JOHN J. DRUMMOND

INTENTIONALITY is most broadly characterized as mind's directedness upon something. This broad characterization accords with our sense of the mind's 'openness to the world', as Tim Crane puts it (2006: 134), or of the mind's self-transcendence in apprehending the world, as a phenomenologist might put it. Such language captures the ordinary belief that one is directly and without mediation aware of worldly entities. By 'worldly entity' I mean not only existent things, states of affairs, properties, relations, and events, but also the kinds of things, such as possible objects, fictional objects, ideal objects, and so forth, the understanding of which is tied to our understanding of actual entities (cf. Crane 2001b: 337). This belief entails that the subject and the world stand, as it were, in a certain kind of relation that is not merely the relation of being *in* the world. The subject–world relation is a unique, dyadic relation of mind to world; the subject is subject *of* the world and can recognize itself as *in* the world only insofar as it is the intentional awareness *of* the world. Representationalism claims that mind is only *mediately* aware of worldly entities. The intentional relation, on this account, is triadic: mind, representation (or representational content), and world. This paper (1) considers the issues that motivate representationalist accounts, (2) discusses different versions of representationalism as responses to these issues, (3) offers a descriptive 'presentationalist' account that preserves the straightforward sense of the mind's openness to the world, and (4) responds to the motivating issues.

1 MOTIVATING REPRESENTATIONALISM

The view that mind is only mediately related to the world is motivated by two epistemological problems arising in the critique of perceptual experience. The first problem is perceptual illusion. If one defines an illusion as 'any perceptual situation in which a physical object is actually perceived, but in which that object perceptually appears other than it really is' (Smith 2002: 23), then, to the extent that the subject in the presence of red lighting sees the wall-as-pink, the perception is illusory. The illusory character of the perception can suggest that it is not directed upon the worldly, *white* wall at all, but rather some (pinkish) object other than the worldly thing.

The second problem is hallucination, and the conclusion is similar. On the (questionable) assumption that hallucinations are from the first-person perspective phenomenally indistinguishable from perceptions, and given, by hypothesis, that the object of the hallucination is no worldly thing, the object of the hallucination must be some kind of special, non-worldly object—something other than an ordinary, worldly thing to which the hallucinatory experience only apparently directs itself.

While these problems arise in the critique of perception, both can be generalized to other kinds of experience. The problem of illusion can be generalized as the problem of the conception-dependence of intentional relations (Smith and McIntyre 1984: 13–15). An object is invariably experienced *in a particular way* or *under a particular description* or *under a particular conception*. The generalized problem can then be stated as follows: insofar as one intends an existent worldly entity—say Sp—but under a false description—as Sq—the intentional object Sq must be distinct from the intended worldly entity Sp. For example, one might believe that Barack Obama is a Muslim when he is actually a Christian. The difference between the supposed state of affairs that is the object of the belief *that O is M* and the actual state of affairs *that O is C* motivates the claim that our belief is directed to an object ontologically distinct from the actual state of affairs.

The problem of hallucination can be generalized as the problem of the existence-independence of intentional relations (Smith and McIntyre 1984: 11–13). One can, for example, intend something that is logically impossible—say, a square circle—or one can imagine something that is empirically impossible—say, a golden mountain—or one can wish for something that is non-existent or even impossible. These experiences take an object, but the object we experience does not exist. The object, then, must once again be a special kind of object that is other than an actual entity. This is most clearly the case when the experience aims at what is logically impossible, but it is equally true when the experience aims at what is logically possible but non-existent. Whether the experience aims at the fanciful, such as the golden mountain, or an empirical impossibility—not having eaten that extra piece of pie at Thanksgiving dinner—or a non-existent empirical possibility—that I win the billion-dollar lottery—the experience seems aimed at an object that is no ordinary, worldly existent.

Both conception-dependence and existence-independence give rise to related issues in the philosophy of logic and language. These issues arise in 'intensional contexts' wherein the truth-value of a sentence cannot be determined by the extensions of its semantically significant parts. Intensional contexts typically involve modal operators or the attribution of mental events or propositional attitudes to a subject. In the context of a discussion of intentionality, our concern is primarily with contexts involving mental events and states.

The conception-dependence of intentional relations manifests itself as the failure of the logical principle of the substitutivity of identity (Smith and McIntyre 1984: 26). This principle states that for two expressions which are extensionally, but not logically, equivalent, the substitution of one expression for the other yields a proposition having the same truth-value as the original proposition. The principle fails in intensional contexts because the substitution of one expression for the other yields a proposition having a different truth value when the subject of the act is unaware of the extensional equivalence of the expressions. So, for example, from the fact that Jones believes that William Jefferson Clinton was impeached, it does not follow that Jones believes that the forty-second President of the United States was impeached when Jones is unaware of the fact that William Jefferson Clinton was the forty-second President of the United States.

The existence-independence of intentional relations manifests itself as the failure of existential generalization. While we can ordinarily infer from the fact that John Doe is a murderer (Mj) to the fact that there exists someone who is a murderer [$(\exists x)(Mx)$], such an inference fails in intensional contexts just in case either of two conditions is satisfied: (1) a singular term fails to refer to any existent entity (Smith and McIntyre 1984: 28–30), or (2) a singular term refers to a unique but indefinitely determined existent (Smith and McIntyre 1984: 30–1). To exemplify the first kind of failure we note that from the fact that Jones believes that Pegasus is a winged horse (Jones believes Hp) we cannot infer that there exists something such that Jones believes it is a winged horse [$(\exists x)$(Jones believes Hx)], and to exemplify the second kind of failure we note that from the fact that Jones believes that the best crime fiction writer of the century wrote a trilogy (Jones believes Tw) we cannot infer that Jones believes there exists some identifiable person who wrote a trilogy [$(\exists x)$(Jones believes Tx)].

We are dealing with a special kind of indeterminateness in the second failure of existential generalization: namely, intentions that are existentially indefinite. Quine's example (1961: 148) for illuminating the difference between *de dicto* and *de re* modalities is instructive. In a game in which no ties are permitted it is necessary that someone win, although it is not necessary that any particular player win. Hence, the *de dicto* modality $\square\,(\exists x)(x$ will win) is true, but the *de re* modality $(\exists x)\,\square\,(x$ will win) is false. In modal contexts, the difference is explained in terms of the placement of the quantifier relative to the modal operator. In intensional contexts, by contrast, the difference is explained by the distinction between existentially indefinite intentions and definite ones (Smith and McIntyre 1984: 32). Thus, if Jones believes that the best crime fiction writer of the century wrote a trilogy but does not know who the best crime fiction writer of the century is, we have a *de dicto* intention for which existential generalization fails. We cannot infer from 'Jones believes that the best crime fiction writer of the century wrote a trilogy' that '$(\exists x)$(Jones believes Tx),' since Jones cannot identify x. However, if Jones believes both that the best crime fiction writer of the century wrote a trilogy and that Stieg Larsson is the best crime fiction writer of the century, existential generalization is valid. We can infer that Jones believes that '$(\exists x)$(Jones believes Tx [namely, Stieg Larsson]),' even though Jones's intending 'Stieg Larsson' is indefinite in another respect. It is indefinite because Jones cannot intend all Larsson's features and attributes—all there is to know about Larsson (Smith and McIntyre 1984: 18–21). We might say that Jones's *de re* intending 'Stieg Larsson' is attributively indefinite but existentially definite, whereas Jones's *de dicto* intending 'the best crime fiction writer of the century', even though it intends a unique individual, is existentially indefinite because it fails properly to identify which uniquely existent individual is intended.

2 Representationalism

A number of positions can be developed in response to these issues. One might argue that the new type of object is a psychological entity—that it is, as it were, mind-contained. On this view there are at least two possibilities: (1) an indirect realism of the sort we find in Descartes and Locke in which the psychological entity represents (or fails to represent) the worldly thing, or (2) a subjective idealism in which the only objects for the mind are the psychological entities themselves and concatenations thereof—for example, Berkeleyan perceptions and their phenomenalist organization. Alternatively, one might argue, at least regarding perception, in favour of (3) a sense-datum theory, where the sense-datum is not a psychological entity—not mind-contained—and it might or might not be mind-independent (cf. Moore 1953 for the former and Robinson 2001 for the latter). On either account, however, the sense-datum is a new type of object to which a perception is directed.

Arguments for indirect realism, subjective idealism, and sense-datum theory all assume the 'phenomenal principle': 'If there sensibly appears to a subject to be something which possesses a particular sensible quality then there is something of which the subject is aware which does possess that sensible quality' (Robinson 2001: 32). This assumption can be generalized: if one is aware of something's instantiating F, then there is something of which one is aware that does instantiate F. Generalizing the principle in this way yields what we might call, with Smith and McIntyre (1984: 41), an object-theory of intentionality. Object-theories of intentionality conceive the intentional relation as an ordinary relation in which all the *relata* belonging to the relation must exist. Hence, insofar as the objects of illusions, mistaken conceptions, and experiences intending non-existent objects are not the ordinary, worldly thing, the intentional relation must exist (in all mental events and states, not only the problematic ones) between the mental event or state and a special kind of object, namely, the intentional (but not intended) object.

The generalized phenomenal principle underlying the object-theoretical approach to intentionality is controversial and open to challenge. One challenge arises immediately from our original sense of the mind's openness to the world. This challenge claims that object-theories of intentionality, insofar as they depend upon the generalized phenomenal principle and posit property-instantiating intentional objects distinct from worldly objects, imply that mental events and states apprehend the world, if they apprehend it at all, only indirectly and mediately. On all these views the mind is no longer conceived as directly and without mediation aware of ordinary worldly things and states of affairs. At best, the world is experienced behind a 'screen' or 'veil' of intentional objects, and we have no direct contact with it. At worst, all experience that purports to apprehend the world directly involves, as Mackie (1977: 35, 48–9) has put it in another context, a fundamental error (cf. Martin 2002: 421).

Mental events and states, on this view, purport to be directed upon mind-independent things and states of affairs. But in fact they are not, and to the extent that we believe that we apprehend a mind-independent world, we are systematically mistaken. If, by contrast, we take seriously our understanding that the mind is open to the world and that mind is in some kind of direct contact with the world, such object-theories and error-theories do not explain experience so much as explain it away on the basis of exceptional experiences. Unless there is an absolutely compelling reason to accept the generalized phenomenal principle over our belief in the mind's openness to the world, there is no reason to accept either an object-theory or error-theory view of intentionality—a point addressed by a second challenge.

This challenge claims that the intentional object need not instantiate the property of which one is aware but that it need only represent it (cf. Anscombe 1965: 62, 67; Searle 1983: 43). Hence we might recast the phenomenal principle as: if one is aware of something's instantiating F, then there is something proper to the awareness itself (an intentional content) that represents F. The intentional content represents the intended thing or state of affairs in the same sense of 'represents' that a speech act represents a thing or state of affairs (Searle 1983: 4, 12).

The intentional state, on Searle's view, combines a representational or intentional content and a psychological mode in a manner similar to the speech act's combining a propositional content and an illocutionary force (Searle 1983: 6). The similarity between speech acts and representational content means that we can understand intentionality in terms of a set of notions such as propositional content, direction of fit, and conditions of satisfaction. Searle characterizes his view as a 'non-ontological' approach to intentionality (Searle 1983: 16), since he is not concerned with bringing intentional events and states under an ontological category. He is instead concerned with bringing them, or rather their representational content, under appropriate logical categories. A belief, for example, 'is a propositional content in a certain psychological mode, its mode determines a mind-to-world direction of fit, and its propositional content determines a set of conditions of satisfaction' (Searle 1983: 15).

Searle's approach entails that an intentional object has no special ontological status. Indeed, the intentional object is, for Searle, 'just an object like any other' (Searle 1983: 16). The intentional object is just the intended, worldly entity—what the mental event or state is directed upon. To use Searle's example (1983: 16–17), 'if Bill admires President Carter, then the intentional object of his admiration is President Carter, the actual man and not some shadowy intermediate entity between Bill and the man.' The intentional object of the mental event or state might not exist, but even when it does not, the mental event or state is still characterized by a representational or intentional content in a psychological mode. The mental event or state has, in other words, an intrinsic intentional content by virtue of which it is directed to an intentional object which might or might not exist. But this, for Searle, is no more puzzling than linguistic expressions that fail to satisfy their conditions of satisfaction. There is no need to posit 'an intermediate Meinongian entity or intentional object' for mental events or states to be about. A mental event or state has an intentional content, but it is not *about* that content (Searle 1983: 17).

Other content-theories, however, take a more ontological approach to questions about representational or intentional content. Some views—for example, Føllesdal's (1969; 1990) and Smith and McIntyre's (1984)—construe intentional content as an intensional entity mediating the relation of the mental event or state to the world. Føllesdal, following Husserl's view in the first of the *Logical Investigations*, distinguishes the intentional and intended objects. The intentional object is an intensional entity, and not that to which the mental event or state is directed. Føllesdal argues that the intentional content intrinsic to a particular mental event or state intending an object in a determinate manner is the instantiation of a meaning-species (Føllesdal 1969: 684), or alternatively, the token of something like a Peircean type (Føllesdal 1990: 270–1). The intentional object, on this view, is the meaning-species or type.

Smith and McIntyre have the same general type of theory, but they differently distinguish the intentional object from the intended, worldly entity (Smith and McIntyre 1984: 80). The intentional object for them is again an intensional entity—a sense or mode of presentation of the object—and, again, not that to which the mental event or state is directed. The intentional object for them, however, is not a meaning-species or type. Following Husserl's *Ideas I*, they claim that the intentional object is instead an abstract particular (Smith and McIntyre 1984, 123). For Føllesdal, the mediation of the mental event or state's intentional relation to the intended, worldly thing is a result of that mental event or state's instantiation of a species. The species serves as a mediating entity, although not an intermediary, standing between the mental event or state and its object. For Smith and McIntyre, by contrast, the mental event or state *entertains* a sense, which sense *prescribes* an ordinary, worldly entity (Smith and McIntyre 1984: 143). Thereby is the intentional relation to the intended entity, if it exists, realized; but even when the intended entity does not exist, the intentional relation holds between the mental event or state and the abstract, particular, and intentional object.

For both Føllesdal and Smith and McIntyre, the directedness of the mental event or state is realized by virtue of the fact that the mental event or state has an intentional object (= intensional entity) that refers to a worldly thing or state of affairs. The referent of this intensional entity is the intended object of the mental event or state. The intensional entity or intentional object is a mind-dependent (but not mind-contained), non-physical (= abstract) entity that represents the intended thing, and in representing it, refers the mind to it.

Despite significant differences, Searle's, Føllesdal's, and Smith and McIntyre's views are similar in an important respect. In all cases the intentional content mediates the relation of the mind to the intended thing or state of affairs, which might or might not exist and which might or might not exist as conceived in that experience. These views differ from object-theories of intentionality that posit a special ontological kind—the intentional object—as the *target* of the mental event or state. For object-theories the relation to the intended object is neither direct nor unmediated. For content-theories the relation to the intended object is direct, although mediated. There is no intermediate entity that takes the place of the intended thing or state of affairs as the object of the mental event or state—nothing that 'stands in' for the intended, worldly entity as the object of the mental event or state. There is only an intensional content with particular logical (and, on some accounts, ontological) properties, and by virtue of that content the mental event or state is directed upon a worldly thing or state of affairs.

Crane (2001a; 2001b), who in some respects holds a view similar to Searle's, nevertheless, like Føllesdal and Smith and McIntyre, rejects the identification of the intentional object with the intended, worldly entity. Given that intentional objects are what mental events or states are about, and given that mental events or states can be about entities that do not exist, Searle's claim that intentional objects are ordinary existing entities is, on Crane's view, absurd, since that would entail that some ordinary existing entities do not exist (Crane 2001a: 14–15; 2001b: 337). Crane denies that we can articulate a *substantial* conception of an intentional object—a conception that identifies those general features or conditions that make something a particular kind of object, for example, a material object or an abstract object or an intentional object (Crane 2001a: 15; 2001b: 341). He claims that intentional objects have no nature of their own (Crane 2001a: 16; 2001b: 340, 342), and that we can have only a *schematic* conception of an intentional object (Crane 2001a: 15). A schematic conception does not require that all intentional objects need have some features in common or need satisfy some conditions in common. Instead, a schematic conception simply identifies the *role* of an intentional object as the object of a directed mental event or state. This makes sense of the claim that an intentional object can not-exist, for while all members of a substantial category of objects exist, this need not be true for instances of a schematic conception (Crane 2001a: 17). As long as the mental event or state has representational content, it will be directed to an intentional object whether or not that object exists. On Crane's view, however, this does not entail that an ordinary, substantially conceived, worldly entity does not exist.

Although Crane does not directly address Føllesdal's and Smith and McIntyre's views, his rejection of substantial conceptions of intentional objects entails the rejection of the identification of intentional objects with intensional entities. Furthermore, as Crane points out (2001a: 12, 21), the concepts of intentionality and intensionality are distinct and have distinct origins, and finally, when one thinks of one's cat, the intentional object of the mental event or state (what it is about) is one's cat, not an intension 'cat' (Crane 2001b: 341).

3 PRESENTATIONALISM

In this section I sketch as an alternative to representationalist accounts what I call a 'presentationalist' account of intentionality. I should note at the outset, however, that the point of the contrast between presentationalism and representationalism is not to claim that the representationalist cannot account for the distinction between presentation and representation. Searle (1983: 45–6), for example, thinks that perception is presentation but that perceptual presentation is a species of representation. Smith and McIntyre, following Husserl, distinguish empty and full intentions, and identify perception as the archetypical full intention or presentation (Smith and McIntyre 1984: 136–40). Neither of these accounts of presentation, however, fundamentally alters the characterization of the overall views as representationalist. On both views there is a representational (or intensional) content that mediates the relation of the mental event or state to the intended, worldly thing or state of affairs. The introduction of a mediating representational content—no matter how that content is characterized philosophically—conflicts with our common-sense view of the mind's openness to the world—the view, that is, that the world is directly present to mind without the presence of mediators. The 'content' of experience on the presentationalist view is what the experience is about, what it is directed to, its intended object just as it appears in and to the experience itself.

Moreover, the representationalist views do not adequately address the ontological and epistemological problems that underlie representationalism. Perceptual illusions, for example, have sensory contents; indeed, this is crucial to something's being a *perceptual* illusion. Hallucinations appear to have sensory content, which is why they seem to many to be indistinguishable from perception. To the extent that illusion and hallucination are perception-like with regard to intentional content, the content-theories of intentionality do not adequately address the problems that initially motivated the development of representationalism.

We can illustrate this point by considering Borromini's striking example of a *perspettivo*—a perceptual illusion based on perspective—in the Palazzo Spada in Rome. After entering the palace you look left through a double set of French doors on either side of a library and see a courtyard with a long arcade and a walkway lined by the columns supporting the arcade. The walkway, which appears to be more than forty yards in length, leads to a statue that appears life-sized. In fact, however, the arcade is fewer than nine yards long, and the statue measures just less than two feet high. What makes the illusion work is threefold: (1) the columns lining and supporting the arcade diminish in size; (2) the floor rises as the ceiling lowers; and (3) all other visual cues are removed by limiting the device of looking through the library to see the arcade without seeing anything else in the courtyard. But nothing in the representational content can distinguish the presumed perception from the illusion. Even were I to know that the scene is illusory, the representational content would be identical to that of the presumed perception. The illusion is revealed only when one is taken to the other side of the library, where one can more fully engage the body in exploring the arcade, the statue, and their features, and where one can see the arcade and the statue spatially contextualized by the rest of the courtyard surrounding them. Examples of this sort point toward an account of intentionality that extends beyond the momentary mental event or state and its representational content, and they provide motives for a different way of thinking about the distinction between presentation and representation.

My claim—to invert Searle's formulation—is that intentionality is presentational and that representation (in many different senses, for example, memory and imagination) is a species of presentation. Moreover, my claim is that our mental events or states have intentional content by virtue of the intrinsic and fundamental intentionality of the mental event or state; they have intentional content by virtue of being directed upon worldly entities (in the expansive sense stated earlier) and apprehending them in their significance. Entities—not *simpliciter* but in their significance for us—are the intentional content of mental events and states. Content-theories reverse this relation, claiming that the mental event or state is intentional by virtue of having or entertaining a content (psychological, intensional, or semantic) that refers to an object and that can be specified only in 'objective' terms; their intentionality is derived, in other words, from the referentiality of their content.

The presentational account (cf. also Bernet 1990; Gurwitsch 1967; Holmes 1975; Langsdorf 1984; Sokolowski 1984; Zahavi 2003) draws no ontological distinction between the intentional object and the worldly, intended thing or state of affairs. The intentional object just is the intended thing or state of affairs but precisely as it is intended. We can put the matter this way: our ordinary experience focuses its attention on worldly *things* and *states of affairs* in their significance for us. This intended, worldly thing or state of affairs with its significance is the *object* of our experience. When we reflect on our experience, however, to ask, say, whether the perceptual appearance is veridical or the judgement true, our attention subtly shifts its focus. At such times we focus not straightforwardly on the worldly *thing* or *state of affairs* in its significance for us but on the *significance* the thing or state of affairs has for us. On this view, the significance of the entity in question, its sense—what others are calling the representational content—belongs neither to the mental event or state itself as an intrinsic part, nor to some 'logical' domain divorced from the ontological. Rather, sense belongs to the entities that are the objects of our experience. We speak of things 'making sense' to us and of 'my sense of a thing' or 'my making sense of things'. But the 'my' in the latter expressions merely refers to the first-personal character of our experience of things having sense, and our *making* sense refers to the subject's synthetic performances and achievements— the perceiving and articulating activities we undertake in relation to the object—in drawing out or disclosing that sense.

On this score, therefore, I disagree with Searle's and Crane's distinction between the intentional object and intentional content where the intentional content is thought to be an intrinsic part of the mental event or state. There is no content other than the sense that attaches to the intended object and that is disclosed and elucidated by a subject. Of course, in all cases—perceptions, judgements, beliefs, emotions, evaluations, desires, and so forth—that sense necessarily involves a relation to the subject and to the subject's history, interests, cares, and commitments. We should not, however, infer from the fact that the sense of the intended thing is *relative to* the subject of the experience in which the object is intended to the conclusion that the sense *belongs to* the intending experience itself (as a property or part). Hence, while Crane uses the language of presentation, saying, for example, that 'in an intentional state, something is presented to the mind'

(Crane 2001a: 28), 'presentation' for him refers to the intentional content of the mental event or state. On the view presented here, 'presentation' refers to the object's presenting itself to the subject in a particular manner—a manner that depends upon the interests, attitudes, concerns, cares, and commitments of the subject, as well as subjective performances and synthetic achievements. The presentational content is an aspect of the object rather than an intrinsic part of the mental event or state.

Similarly, *contra* Føllesdal and Smith and McIntyre, there is no ontological distinction between two entities; there is instead an attitudinal difference introduced by our adoption of a reflective stance, a shift that brings about a focus on the sense of the intended object. The intended object reflected upon as having precisely this sense for the subject(s) of the mental event(s) or state(s) just is the intentional object. Crane echoes this view, but to a different end, when he says: 'The idea of an intentional object is a phenomenological idea… It is an idea which emerges in the process of reflecting on what mental life is like' (Crane 2001a: 17).

The intentional object on the presentational view is neither a mediating entity ontologically distinct from the intended object nor an intentional content that is a property or feature inherent to the mental event or state. There is no introduction of a third *relatum* into the intentional relation between the mental event or state and its intended object. The intentional relation remains dyadic. This is not to deny that experiences can be directed to non-existent objects—a fact that leads some to question whether intentionality is best considered a relation at all (cf. Zahavi 2003: 20).

Indeed, Crane is one who denies that intentionality is necessarily a relation. He articulates a trilemma (Crane 2001a: 23):

(1) All thoughts are relations between thinkers and the things which they are about.
(2) Relations entail the existence of their *relata*.
(3) Some thoughts are about things which do not exist.

While any two of these propositions can be true at the same time, it is impossible for all three to be true together. Crane takes (3) to be obviously true, and while he considers arguments against (2) he rejects them. He does not admit the existence of non-existent entities, and insists that relations obtain among entities. Although he admits that some intentional objects do not exist, he claims, as we have seen, that intentional objects appeal to a schematic conception of an object. An intentional object is whatever is designated in response to the question: what is that mental event or state about? An intentional object is not a real entity of the sort that is a *relatum* in a relation. To say that an intentional object does not exist is simply to say that the answer to the question has no referent (Crane 2001a: 25). On this basis Crane concludes that 'not all thoughts are relations between thinkers and the thing they are about' (Crane 2001a: 26), or, to put the matter another way, 'intentional states cannot, in general, be relations to their objects' (Crane 2004: 225).

We might, however, understand the expression 'in general' in two ways. Crane's way is to understand it as saying something about a general truth inferred from individual cases; hence, we cannot generalize to all cases from those where intentional objects do exist and a relation exists between the thinker and the worldly entity that is the object of her thought. The second way is to understand the 'in general' as meaning 'as a whole'. On this understanding we might say that intentionality 'as a whole' is a relation between mind and world. Every mental event or state 'hooks onto the world,' even though some mental events or states are directed at a particular object that does not exist. I believe this is the sense of mind we find in Crane's view that 'a minded creature is *one which has a world*' (Crane 2001a: 4). My claim is that the primary predication of intentionality is to mind 'as a whole' rather than to particular mental events or states (cf. Drummond 1990, 1992, 2003). Mind as such is intentional. Mind as such transcends itself towards the world and relates itself to the existent world, and every instance of 'minding' the world participates in this relation, albeit, as we shall see, in different ways.

Focusing attention on the general relation helps to focus presentationalism's response to the problems of perceptual illusion and hallucination that motivate representationalism. This response involves three important considerations: (1) the environmental factors in which the perceptual relation to the world occurs; (2) the temporal and horizonal character of perceptual experience; and (3) what has come to be called the 'enactive' character of perceiving (Noë 2004: 2)—a reference to the bodily activities that Husserl had identified as early as 1907 as central to generating the flow of appearances characteristic of perception (Husserl 1973; 1997). The first consideration arises from the fact that the sensory appearance of a perceived thing can change without any real change in either the perceptual intention or the perceived thing. For example, the identical perceived thing presents itself in a flow of varying appearances. The wall presents itself as having a constant colour even when the lampshade causes parts of the wall to appear to be different shades of colour. The thing changes its appearance in changing illumination (as when daylight fades), or in a modification of the perceptual medium (as when a fog rolls in), or when there is a real change in the perceptual organ as a result, say, of disease or injury, or when the perceiver's psychic state changes, say, from a cheerful to a melancholic state. These medial and subjective factors condition the object's appearances and our sense of the worldly thing. The system of such psychophysical conditions is, in general, a necessary constituent of the perceptual correlation. The perceptual appearance, illusory or veridical, is the perceived thing precisely as it appears under present psychophysical conditions.

There are, however, certain conditions, such as seeing in daylight, that establish themselves as 'normal' (Husserl 1952: 58–65; 1989: 63–70). The combination of these normal conditions with others, such as being the proper distance from an object, establish themselves as 'optimal' conditions, and these conditions are always relative to the particular interests that motivate the perceiver in her inspection of the object (Husserl 1973: 127–9; 1997: 106–7). The non-veridicality of an appearance, its illusory or misleading character, is the result of variance from these normal conditions and optimal conditions (Husserl 1952: 61; 1989: 66). A distorted shape results from seeing the object from the wrong perspective; improper illumination brings about non-veridical colour-appearances, and so forth. The illusory character of these perceptions results from the failure to satisfy normal or optimal conditions.

This leads to the second consideration relevant to the presentationalist account's addressing the problems motivating representationalism: namely, the temporal and horizonal character of experience. The anomalous appearances of the sort discussed in the previous paragraph are overcome by the establishment of a temporally extended perceptual experience that 'corrects' the anomalous appearance. Such corrections can occur within the same continuous perceptual experience or on the basis of other perceptions by the same sense. If, however, the organ is permanently damaged or some other permanent anomaly exists, the correction occurs on the basis of perceptions by other senses or at the level of intersubjective encounters of the object (Husserl 1952: 67, 82; 1989: 72, 87).

By way of example, consider a visual perception. The visual perception of a three-dimensional material thing in space apprehends the object from a certain perspective. I see, for example, the front of the house. But in seeing the front of the house I do not see merely the front. I see the *house* from the front. The perceptual sense of the object includes the sense that the house is three-dimensional; that it has other sides and a back; that the other sides are coloured, most likely, the same colour as the front; and so on. These other sides and aspects of the house are not directly given in the way the front is given. They are given as the 'inner horizons' of the appearance (Husserl 1963: 82; 1970b: 44)—a pointing beyond what is directly seen to other parts of the intended thing. What is given horizonally can also be directly seen in a temporally extended perception in which the perceiver moves her body so as to see other sides or aspects of the object. This perspective leads to an analysis of the dynamic character of our intentional experience, the on-going revisions of our intention within the temporal extension of the experience, and the satisfaction or disappointment—and subsequent modification—of this intention in subsequent phases of an unfolding experience or in different experiences. At the same time, the appearance's 'outer horizons' present other objects in the background and spatial surroundings of the appearing thing. The outer horizons turn our attention to the worldly context in which the thing exists. The worldly thing intended in the perception is, then, the identical object presented in the directly appearing side and its horizons, whether or not the flow of appearances is actualized.

Let us examine this in a little more detail. Any perceptual phase within a concrete, temporally extended perception entails an entire perceptual system by virtue of the structure belonging to it—a structure that accounts for the temporality of experience. This structure is a complex of empty and full intentions such that any single perceptual phase (1) presents (*gegenwärtigt*) the directly sensed side or aspect of the object, (2) re-presents (*vergegenwärtigt*; that is, makes present again to mind) previously experienced and retained sides of the object as well as previous experiences of the same or similar objects, and (3) also makes present to mind (*vergegenwärtigt*) yet to appear and expected sides and aspects of the object (Husserl 1966: 80–3; 1991: 84–8; cf. Brough 1972, 1991). (1) presents the direct appearance of the object in a filled, sensuous, partial intention, whereas (2) and (3) incorporate in empty, partial intentions the unseen sides and aspects of the object, thereby making perceptually, but not sensuously, present the unseen sides of the perceived thing. The view that the present perceptual phase intends unseen sides or aspects of the object does not entail that this making present is accomplished through memorial or imaginative presentations. If the front of the house is presented sensuously in a perceptual phase and the unseen sides of the house are made present in memorial or imaginative phases, the concrete perception would no longer have its proper unity as a perceptual experience. In brief, there would no longer be a perception of the whole house but only of its front (Husserl 1973: 49–50, 55; 1997: 42–3, 47).

This structure is intimately bound up with the temporality and horizonality of intentional experience. It is this structure that allows the subject to recognize her own experience as a temporal flow, for it introduces the distinction between elapsed experiential phases, the directly presenting experiential phase, and experiential phases yet to come. At the same time, this structure allows the presentation of the horizons in which the momentary, direct appearance is situated. The momentary phase of experience, as it were, 'adds' to what is now directly present what has elapsed such that the sense of the object as previously experienced contributes to my present sense of the object, and the two together shape my expectations about how the experience will continue to unfold. This structure makes the perception the perception of the identical object and not merely its side. At the same time, the object is given against a background of other objects, and elapsed experiences contribute to our perceptual grasp of this background as well as to the shaping of our expectations about changes in the background as the perception of the object upon which the perceiver is focused unfolds in time.

The third consideration relevant to the presentationalist account's addressing the problems motivating representationalism is the 'enactive' character of perception. Our bodily movements in which we move the sense organs in relation to the object generate the flow of appearances showing different sides or aspects of the perceived object. We approach the house to see features of its trim in greater detail; we turn our head to a noise or cup our ear to collect the sound of a voice; we bend over the oven and use our hand to draw the aromas of the cooking food toward our nose. Consider again the visual perception of the house. I walk around the house in order to see its other sides. Starting with a view of the front of the house, it is expected, as was the case in past perceptions of houses, that as I walk around the house I shall see in succession the side of the house, its rear, and its other side. There is a correlation between the ordered progression of bodily movements I undertake and the ordered progression of sensuous appearances presenting the sides of the house. The awareness of the house as a spatially individuated, identical object is necessarily mediated by the movements of the body, for it is only through such activity that the manifold of appearances in and through which one and the same object is given as identical is generated (Husserl 1973: 170; 1997: 143–4; Drummond 1979: 19–32).

Most significantly, these bodily activities bring about the awareness of an object, its bodily enclosedness, and its own position in space (Drummond 1979: 37–41). In general, as we approach an object it occupies a larger portion of our visual field, and as we retreat from it it occupies a smaller part of the visual field; these changes in the object's appearance indicate that the object has its own fixed position in space. As we walk around an object, part of the appearance first presenting an object disappears from one side of the visual field and is replaced by another part that previously had been its neighbour, while a new part enters the visual field from the other side. Such phenomenal ordering in the changing appearances—along with ordered phenomenal changes in the outer horizon of the object—indicate the presence of an identical object throughout the flow of appearances. While I have focused on visual perception here, there are analogous examples for other senses and for higher-order experiences. The identically intended object is what reveals itself in systematic alterations from one presentation to the next. There is an ordered and continuous series of changes that underlies the sense of an identical object or state of affairs. In our straightforward experiencing of objects, this identity is an identity in and through time, in and through apparent change, in and through real change, in and through relations (for example, spatial or causal relations) with other objects, and in and through various valuations, uses, and so forth.

In summary, then, the introduction of a mediating representational content—no matter how that content is characterized philosophically—conflicts with our common-sense view of the mind's openness to the world as a dyadic, not triadic, relation. Like representationalism, presentationalism holds that the relation between mental events or states is direct but mediated. The two accounts differ radically, however, in their views of the nature of the mediation involved in the mind's intentional directedness to the world. On the representationalist view, the mediation of the intentional relation is a function of something attaching itself to the mental event or state as its content or of some 'third' thing (an abstract species or an abstract particular) mediating the mental event or state's relation to its intended, worldly entity. On the presentational view, by contrast, it is not the intentional *relation* that is mediated by some content by virtue of which the mental event or state is intentional. The mental event or state is intentional—directed upon worldly entities—originally and in its own right. It is instead the *sense* of the object as presented in the momentary experiential phase that is mediated by the causal relations between our environment and our bodies, by our bodily activities in perceiving, and by the sense of worldly entities as apprehended in previous experiences and as handed down to us by others in the cultural communities in which we live and by the traditions which inform those communities.

4 PRESENTATIONALISM'S RESPONSE TO THE MOTIVATING PROBLEMS

Let us now reconsider the problems of illusion and hallucination and the generalized issues of conception-dependence and existence-independence in the light of presentationalism's account of intentionality. The ingredients of the response to these problems have already been laid out. The psychophysical conditions necessarily involved in the perceptual relation between subject and object affect the appearance of the object to the perceiver. Our acquired sense of the normal and optimal conditions for perception, our acquired sense of how to move the body so as best to realize those conditions, and our experience of the object in the past, all work to 'correct' our illusory perception in the course of the experience itself. I learn the effects of changed illumination (coloured or fluorescent lighting, for example), 'automatically' adjust my perceptual sense of the object to adjust for any abnormality in the perceptual medium or my sense organ, and thereby correct what considered by itself is an illusory appearance. The object perceived is existent, but it is—at least in the particular sensuous appearance—perceived incorrectly. It is in the unfolding inner horizons of the perception as I bring about the normal or optimal conditions for perceiving that the possibility for the correction of my perception lies. Moreover, in at least some cases—most cases for the mature perceiver—the occurrent sense of the inner horizons of the object—specifically, of its possible appearances in other, more normal, more optimal conditions—allows me, as it were, to look right through the illusion and see the object as it really is (Drummond 1990: 226).

A similar case obtains with respect to judgements involving conception-dependence but made under a misconception. Consider, for example, the judgement 'Barack Obama is a Muslim.' This judgement intends a non-existent state of affairs. The person about whom I judge, however, does exist, and he is actually a person with religious convictions and allegiances. But the actually existent state of affairs—namely, that Barack Obama is a Christian—is other than the judgement supposes. To put the matter another way, the conception of Obama-as-Muslim underlying the false judgement intends Obama as determined in a particular manner, one that does not truthfully grasp Obama, although (1) it is directed to an actually existent Obama, and (2) Obama is truthfully determined in another manner. The judgemental intention still directs itself to the actual world and to an actual existent therein. Moreover, such false judgements directed to existent objects but non-existent states of affairs do reveal something about the sense of the existent object to which they are directed. If I claim, for example, that Obama is a Muslin and somebody corrects me, saying 'No, he is not a Muslim; he is a Christian', the sense that Obama is only charged with being a Muslim but is not actually Muslim and that he is instead a Christian makes an important contribution to my sense of Obama beyond his simply being a Christian. To take a different kind of example, consider the false judgement 'Dan is arrogant.' The correcting claim, 'He is not arrogant; he is just shy', illuminates how we are to understand Dan. The shyness-that-can-be-mistaken-for-arrogance is a feature of Dan that reveals more than the sense of shyness alone. The resolution of problems regarding illusion and conception-dependence rests, in summary, on understanding concrete intentional reference to a worldly thing or state of affairs as mediated by the manifold of experiential phases—the horizons of the experience—presenting both possible (even false) and actual determinations of the intended object.

Consider now the case of hallucination and existence-independent intentions. Suppose I (unknowingly) see a mirage. I see water ahead on the road, and form the judgement 'There is water ahead on the road'. The perception intends a non-existent puddle, and the judgement intends a non-existent state of affairs, but now the thing about which I purportedly judge, the water, is also non-existent. In this example, my recognition that the judgement is incorrect depends upon my recognition that the perception of water is non-veridical or—better—that there is in fact no perception of water at all. The latter recognition depends upon my awareness that as I approach what I (mis)take to be water, the water disappears from view. In an ordinary perception, however, we would expect the activity of approaching the object to motivate an enlargement of the perceived thing's appearance in the visual field. The disappearance of the water motivates instead the recognition that the perception is not genuinely a perception of water at all but is hallucinatory. It is facts such as these that make the indistinguishability thesis contestable. People experience hallucinations differently from how they experience perceptions, but the decisive factor is not a question of a difference in presentational or representational content. The decisive factor is what happens in response to bodily movements over time, what happens with regard to verification by other sense-systems, and what happens at the level of intersubjective verification. As Merleau-Ponty has pointed out (1962: 33–45), the mere fact that we can even ask the question about hallucination indicates that we have an experiential way of distinguishing hallucinations from perceptions.

Moreover, in at least some cases we intend non-existent or even impossible objects knowing they are non-existent as, for example, in hoping for world peace, or in wishing I had not had that extra piece of pie at Thanksgiving dinner, or in promising to build a new house for a spouse. In all such cases where a non-existent worldly thing or state of affairs is intended, the subject's attention and intention are directed in part to the actual world—say, to the road and its conditions, or to the world and its political condition, or to what might have been better had it happened, or to what will be realized in the future—and although reference fails in certain respects (for example, to the water), it does not in others (for example, to the road).

The problems of conception-dependence and existence-independence involve special cases of horizonal reference. Reference to an actuality is achieved by virtue of the fact that the objectivity as (wrongly) intended in the present experience has horizonal references to both the inner and outer horizons of the object. The objectivity as presented contains horizonal references both to other views or presentations of the same objectivity (the inner horizon) and to other objects in the various fields (spatial, temporal, causal, and contextual) in which the experienced thing or state of affairs is situated (the outer horizon). Thus, 'Obama as Muslim'—the sense upon which the judgement 'Obama is a Muslim' is founded—has as its inner horizon other possible and actual presentations of the actually existent Obama, and thereby reference to an actual existent is achieved. Similarly, the seen water has within its outer horizon the road upon which the water appears. The complex perceptual sense 'water-on-the-road' underlying the judgement that there is water on the road is composed of presentations of different things comprised by the intended state of affairs—things including both the water and the road, the latter of which is actual. Thereby is reference to an actuality achieved in the apparently objectless intention—an actuality, however, which is other than the thematically intended thing and which is apprehended in a manner other than it actually exists.

In yet other cases, the object which is intended might be posited as a fictional object—for example, Pegasus—or an ideal object—say the triangle—whose actuality cannot be given in a perceptual act but must be imaginatively or ideally presented. But the imaginative presentation presupposes perceptual presentations which the imaginative presentation modifies or from which the imaginative presentation draws its materials. The fictional object has its sense both in this relation to and contrast with the actual world. The fictional object presents a non-actualized possibility for the world, and in, say, the case of didactic literature, a possibility whose realization in the real world is recommended. The ideal presentation, too, is possible only insofar as we can construct a progression of actual and imagined cases of, say, a figure, a progression that approaches an ideal of exactness in, for example, the reproduction of angular or length relationships. The ideal presentation, in other words, has its foundation in the experience of the actual and imaginative variations thereof. It is posited as the ideal, limit case of the ordered progression of such presentations toward the limit. As such, however, it belongs to a different dimension—namely, the ideal—but once again its new ontological dimension depends for its sense upon the contrast with the real. It *is* ideal only in its union and contrast with that series of actualities and possibilities in the real world rather than in a fundamental separation from the real (Drummond 1995: 34–41).

Finally, let us turn to the issue of intensional contexts and the failures of substitutivity of identity and existential generalization. The reason for the failure of substitutivity of identity is that the propositions in question are not genuinely about the facts believed but are about the believing of the facts, and the substitution of one expression for the other within the statement of what is believed yields a proposition about a distinct act of believing. When we consider intensional contexts, we must be cognizant of the fact that we attend to the intentional object—the intended thing just as intended—rather than the intended thing *simpliciter*. While there is no ontological distinction between the intended and intentional objects, the manner of considering them differs. In dealing not with the intended object *simpliciter* but the intended object just as intended, we attend to the sense the object has for us. The substitution, then, in intensional contexts is the substitution of one sense (rather than, as it were, the referent) for another sense. This is why in intensional contexts we cannot substitute non-equivalent expressions referring to the same state of affairs. The non-equivalence of the original and substitute senses render the principle of the substitutivity of identity inapplicable. We are no longer dealing with identicals; the sense-objects are, by hypothesis, non-equivalent and therefore not identical.

The situation regarding the failure in intensional contexts of the principle of existential generalization is similar. Such failures occur, as we have seen, when a singular term refers to a non-existent thing or state of affairs or to a unique but existentially indefinite object. Since, however, the intensional context is such that we are dealing with the object just as intended in the mental event or state defining the intensional context rather than the intended object *simpliciter*, applying rules of inference (existential generalization and existential instantiation) that properly apply to existent entities *simpliciter* cannot yield valid inferences over senses.

In closing, I have not attempted to offer a knock-down argument against representationalism. I have instead attempted to identify the problems that motivate representational views and to indicate how representational theories of intentionality, in both their object-theoretical and content-theoretical forms, do not address these problems fully. In particular, they do not provide adequate grounds for distinguishing non-veridical or hallucinatory experience from veridical ones, and they do not adequately account for how we *know* an intentional experience is objectless or mistaken. Moreover, both object-theories and content-theories are unfaithful to our basic understanding of the mind's 'openness to the world' as a dyadic relation, although content-theories, especially those of the Searle and Crane variant, better capture that understanding. By contrast, the presentational view of intentionality is more capable of addressing the motivating problems and of preserving our sense of the mind's openness to the world. These advantages of the presentational view provide reasons for accepting it over representationalist views.

References

Bernet, R. (1990), 'Husserls Begriff des Noema', in S. IJsseling (ed.), *Husserl-Forschung und Husserl-Ausgabe* (Dordrecht: Kluwer Academic Publishers), pp. 61–80.

Brough, J. (1972), 'The Emergence of an Absolute Consciousness in Husserl's Early Writings on Time-Consciousness', *Man and World* 5: 298–326.

—— (1991), 'Translator's Introduction', in Husserl 1991.

Crane, T. (2001a), *Elements of Mind* (Oxford: Oxford University Press).

—— (2001b), 'Intentional Objects', *Ratio* 14: 336–49.

—— (2004), 'Summary of Elements of Mind and Replies to Critics', *Croatian Journal of Philosophy* 4: 223–40.

—— (2006), 'Is There a Perceptual Relation', in T. S. Gendler and J. Hawthorne (eds), *Perceptual Experience* (Oxford:Oxford University Press), pp. 126–46.

Drummond, J. J. (1979), 'On Seeing a Material Thing in Space: The Role of Kinaesthesis in Visual Perception', *Philosophy and Phenomenological Research* 40: 19–32.

—— (1990), *Husserlian Intentionality and Non-Foundational Realism: Noema and Object* (Dordrecht: Kluwer Academic Publishers).

—— (1992), 'De–ontologizing the Noema: An Abstract Consideration', in J. J. Drummond and L. Embree (eds), *Phenomenology of the Noema* (Dordrecht: Kluwer Academic Publishers), pp. 89–109.

—— (1995), 'Synthesis, Identity, and the A Priori', *Recherches husserliennes* 4: 27–51.

—— (2003), 'The Structure of Intentionality', in D. Welton (ed.), *The New Husserl* (Bloomington: Indiana University Press), 65–92.

Føllesdal, D. (1969), 'Husserl's Notion of Noema', *The Journal of Philosophy* 66: 680–87.

—— (1990), 'Noema and Meaning in Husserl', *Philosophy and Phenomenological Research* 50 (Supplement): 263–71.

Gurwitsch, A. (1967), 'Husserl's Theory of Intentionality in Historical Perspective', in E. N. Lee and M. Mandelbaum (ed.), *Phenomenology and Existentialism* (Baltimore: The Johns Hopkins University Press, 1967), 24–57.

Holmes, R. (1975), 'An Explication of Husserl's Theory of the Noema', *Research in Phenomenology* 5: 143–53.

Husserl, E. (1952), *Ideen zu einer reinen Phänomenologie und phänomenologischen Philosophie: Zweites Buch* (The Hague: Martinus Nijhoff).

—— (1963), *Cartesianische Meditationen und Pariser Vorträge* (The Hague: Martinus Nijhoff).

—— (1966), *Zur Phänomenologie des inneren Zeitbewusstseins (1891–1917)* (The Hague: Martinus Nijhoff).

—— (1970a), *Logical Investigations*, tr. J. N. Findlay (London: Routledge and Kegan Paul).

—— (1970b), *Cartesian Meditations*, tr. D. Cairns (The Hague: Martinus Nijhoff).

—— (1973), *Ding und Raum: Vorlesungen 1907* (The Hague: Martinus Nijhoff).

—— (1984), *Logische Untersuchungen II/1: Untersuchungen zur Phänomenologie und Theorie der Erkenntnis* (The Hague: Martinus Nijhoff).

—— (1989), *Ideas Pertaining to a Pure Phenomenology and to a Phenomenological Philosophy*, tr. R. Rojcewicz and A. Schuwer (Dordrecht: Kluwer Academic Publishers).

—— (1991), *On the Phenomenology of the Consciousness of Internal Time (1893–1917)*, tr. J. Brough (Dordrecht: Kluwer Academic Publishers).

—— (1997), *Thing and Space: Lectures of 1907*, tr. R. Rojcewicz (Dordrecht: Kluwer Academic Publishers).

Langsdorf, L. (1984), 'The Noema as Intentional Entity: A Critique of Føllesdal', *The Review of Metaphysics* 37: 757–84.

Mackie, J. L. (1977), *Ethics: Inventing Right and Wrong* (London: Penguin).

Martin, M. G. F. (2002), 'The Transparency of Experience', *Mind and Language* 17: 376–425.

Merleau-Ponty, M. (1962), *Phenomenology of Perception*, tr. C. Smith (New York: Humanities Press).

Moore, G. E. (1953), *Some Main Problems of Philosophy* (London: George, Allen and Unwin).

Noë, A. (2004), *Action in Perception* (Cambridge, Mass.: The MIT Press).

Quine, W. V. O. (1961), 'Reference and Modality', in *From a Logical Point of View* (New York: Harper and Row), 139–59.

Robinson, H. (2001), *Perception* (London: Routledge).

Searle, J. (1983), *Intentionality* (Cambridge: Cambridge University Press).

Smith, A. D. (2002), *The Problem of Perception* (Cambridge, MA: Harvard University Press).

Smith, D. W. and McIntyre, R. (1984), *Husserl and Intentionality: A Study of Mind, Meaning, and Language* (Dordrecht: Reidel).

Sokolowski, R. (1984), 'Intentional Analysis and the Noema', *Dialectica* 38: 113–29.

Zahavi, D. (2003), *Husserl's Phenomenology* (Stanford: Stanford University Press).

CHAPTER 7

···

PERCEPTION, CONTEXT, AND DIRECT REALISM

···

DAVID WOODRUFF SMITH

1 INTRODUCTION: PHENOMENOLOGY AND PERCEPTION

···

Our concern is the phenomenology of perception, especially the role of content and context in the intentionality of perception.[1]

What we seek is a detailed account of the structure of perceptual experience and its intentional relation to its objects, considering how these tie into the contextual spatio-temporal–causal relation between a perceptual experience and its environment, in accord with the indexical content of perceptual experience. In the background are important results of Husserl and Merleau-Ponty, along with more recent issues in philosophy of mind, perception, and consciousness. But here I shall concentrate exclusively on the phenomena themselves.

I will assume a core conception of phenomenology as a discipline, then move to a preparatory account of perception in context. Then we are off the races, looking to basic features of perception and how they figure in the phenomenology and ontology of perception.

Basically, phenomenology is the study of conscious experience as lived from the first-person perspective. Consciousness is characteristically *intentional*, or directed toward some

---

[1] The present account of perception extends and amplifies results in Smith (1989), which tie into views on indexical intentionality in perception, consciousness, and reference addressed in Smith (1981), (1982), (1984), (1986), and (2004). Background approaches to phenomenology and its role in philosophy of mind including perception theory are addressed in Smith and McIntyre (1982), Smith and Thomasson (2005), and Smith (2007). Some ties to recent work on perception and consciousness will be cited along the way; Siegel (2010) is especially pertinent. I thank Chad Kidd for many discussions of issues in contemporary philosophy of perception, with a nod to Kidd (2011). And I thank Johannes Brandl and an anonymous referee for comments on the penultimate draft of this essay.

object: a consciousness *of* or *about* something. The *content* of an experience embodies the way the object is 'intended'—presented, represented, given—in the experience. The *object* of an experience, if such exists, is distinct from the experience and its content. The object is whatever is prescribed by the content of the experience: as we often say in today's parlance, whatever *satisfies* the content. Thus, we characterize or delimit the content of an experience by specifying the *conditions of satisfaction* of the content in the experience.[2] In the case of perception, the role of the *context* of perception is crucial, and that will be a point of focus in what follows. The context of a particular perception involves the relation between the subject and object of perception: that is, the actual relation within the surrounding world. We focus on veridical perception, allowing for illusion and hallucination in due course. That is, we begin with the normal case where a person sees (hears, touches, and so on) something appropriately present in her immediate environs, something that affects her senses, something of which she is perceptually conscious as in her immediate presence.

Addressing intentionality in perception, we distinguish the *intentional character* of an experience from the *intentional relation* between the experience and its object (if such exists). Its intentional character is the character the experience has in virtue of having a certain content—and so being a consciousness *as if* of a presented object. Its intentional relation, by contrast, is the relation the experience has to its object in virtue of its content—where the object actually exists and satisfies the content in the experience on the relevant occasion.[3]

In veridical perception the intentional relation between the visual experience and its object—its being an experience *of* that object—involves a *causal* relation between the experience and the object. That causal relation is part of the relevant context of perception and is implicitly invoked in the content of experience, as I *experience* the visual impact of the object I am seeing (compare touching). However, the intentional relation is distinct in kind—categorially distinct—from the causal relation. For the causal relation holds in virtue of light-waves interacting with neuronal processes, whereas the intentional relation holds in virtue of the object satisfying the content in the experience. The light's affecting my optic system is one thing; my visual experience being a veridical *presentation* of the object (partly in virtue of that causal impact) is quite another.[4]

A few points of terminology are needed, since philosophers in different traditions and eras have used similar terms differently. The term 'phenomenology' is traditionally used for the discipline that studies consciousness, and so on. A more recent use, in analytic philosophy of mind, speaks of the 'phenomenology' of an experience, meaning the

---

[2] Contemporary intentionality theory characterizes the intentional force of the content of an experience in terms of conditions of truth/veridicality, satisfaction, or accuracy. Compare Smith and McIntyre (1982) on 'truth-conditions', Searle (1983) on 'satisfaction conditions', Siegel (2010) on 'accuracy conditions', noting the evolution of this perspective on content.

[3] This distinction between intentional *character* and intentional *relation*, crucial to the structure of perception, is detailed in Smith (1989).

[4] The role of context in content-satisfaction, including the implicit sense of causation in perception, is a recurrent theme in Smith (1989), Chapters I, IV–VI. Compare Searle (1983), Chapter 4, and Siegel (2010), Chapter 5, on the role of causation in visual content.

phenomenological character of the experience itself, and especially the character of *what it is like* to have such an experience. I will stay with the discipline: phenomenology studies the structure of conscious experience, its phenomenological structure, including its sensuous character, its intentional character, and where veridical its intentional relation to the object perceived, which involves its contextual relation to the object before the subject on the occasion of perception.

Philosophers also speak of the 'phenomenal' character of an experience, meaning the character of what-it-is-like to have the experience, if you will, the way the experience 'appears' in consciousness. This notion will appear later in our story below. Specifically, 'qualia' are the phenomenally appearing colours (shapes, sounds, and so on) that we experience in perception: more precisely, the phenomenal *appearances* of the colours (shapes, sounds, and so on) that we perceive in objects around us (the status of these things being subject to debate)...but phenomenal character is not limited to sensuous character involved with sensuous qualia.

The term 'content' has moved around in recent analytic philosophy of mind. Some philosophers address internal or 'narrow' content, while others pursue external or 'wide' content.[5] If 'content' means *what* is experienced, well, that is ambiguous between the object of experience and the way the object is experienced. I will use 'content' for that aspect of an experience that embodies the way the object is presented, the mode-of-presentation, in the experience. And I will use 'object' for the object itself, the external object toward which the experience is directed. This usage follows the established usage in traditional phenomenology.[6] I find it misleading to co-opt the term 'content' for the perceived object itself, as some 'externalist' and 'relationalist' views do.

Even the terms 'representation' and 'intentionality' have been modified in recent philosophy of mind, especially philosophy of perception.[7] 'Representation' traditionally means the way in which, say, an experience 'represents' its object. 'Intentionality' traditionally means the property wherein an act-of-consciousness is directed toward—is a consciousness (as if) of or about—some object: that is, the act's property of 'representing' its object (if such exists). We should note that in some quarters in philosophy of mind, the terms 'representation' and 'intentionality' are loaded with the naturalist assumption that, somehow, intentionality consists in a physical relation between a mental brain state and the object it 'represents'. I shall keep the traditional use of these terms, which is not committed to physicalist reduction. After we have a clear story of how consciousness,

---

[5] Many variations on this distinction have been employed. The most relevant source of using 'content' to include the *object* of reference (and perception) stems from David Kaplan's logic of demonstratives: see Kaplan (1989). On Kaplan's model of demonstrative reference *vis-à-vis* Husserl's model of demonstrative reference in relation to perception, see Smith (1982), and compare Beyer (2004).

[6] The classical distinction among act, content, and object—refined notably in Husserl—is detailed in Smith and McIntyre (1982). Husserl called content 'sense', *Sinn*—a conception akin to Gottlob Frege's famous logical notion of *Sinn*. Siegel (2010) works with a notion of 'rich' internal content while addressing external conditions.

[7] Compare Strawson (2005) on uses and abuses of key terms regarding intentionality and experience, including how these terms are 'looking-glassed'!

intentionality, and representation work (here, in the case of perception), we can subsequently look into how these phenomena are realized by—founded or 'supervenient' on—neural processes in causal contexts. Here, however, our task is analysis of consciousness and intentionality in perception: the phenomenology and ontology thereof, opening into further theory about their neural underpinnings.

2 Perception and perceptual experience: intentional relation versus intentional character

Perception is among our most familiar activities in dealing with things around us. In the normal course of events, perception is always interdependent with action. Accordingly, when philosophers focus on perception, we are in fact abstracting perception from its normal situation where the *unit of activity* is perception-and-action in interaction with what is perceived.[8]

I see a yellow tennis ball arcing and spinning toward me as I pivot and dance into a position where I swing my racquet upward and into the ball, hopefully sending it back from whence it came. What am I doing? Seeing-and-hitting the ball. I cannot hit it unless I am actively visually tracking it; and I cannot see it unless I move my eyes and head and torso and feet so that I can track its flight into my oncoming racquet face.

Even a simpler perception, in a possibly simpler life form, follows this pattern of perception-and-action or action-and-perception. As the wily rat smells that deliciously fromageous scent, it (she, he) is actively sniffing the cheese, pointing its active snout about, with alert nostrils, while its feet scurry selectively in the vicinity of oh-so-many odours. (The beauty of the rat, my neuroscientist colleague once observed, is that it is but two neurons from world to cortex! The rat remembers and distinguishes nearly every smell it smells. And the scent-most-pungent ties directly to the cheese-most-edible.)

The point is not that perception is really a species of bodily action or behaviour. It is that perception normally occurs within a unit of activity that includes both perception and action in interaction with the perceived. There is a concrete situational whole within which perception is a proper part, a dependent part. We *abstract* that perception-part when we focus on perception in philosophical theory.

To see the point, let us adapt the broadly Husserlian ontology of parts-and-wholes, distinguishing dependent and independent parts.[9] Take my bicycle. The frame is an

---

[8] This structure of embodied perception is appraised in Husserl (1989) and amplified in Merleau-Ponty (2003). In Noë (2004), perception and action are simply merged, ontologically, as 'enactive perception', so that perception becomes a species of action. I hold, instead, that perception and action are, normally, distinct *dependent parts* of a structured unit of conscious intentional activity.

[9] Compare the notion of dependent or 'abstract[ed]' part, or 'moment', detailed in Husserl (2001): see the Third of the *Logical Investigations*. Such 'moments' are sometimes called 'tropes' today.

independent part of the bicycle: it can exist apart from the bike as a whole (if damaged, it can be replaced by a similar frame). But the particularized cyan colour *in* my bike's frame (an instance of the 'universal' colour cyan) is a *dependent part* of the frame: that cyan cannot exist apart from that frame (as Aristotle said of 'accidents' in a 'substance'). Now, the point here is that the whole *perceptual situation* includes some three dependent parts: my visual *experience* presenting the tennis ball, my volitional-bodily *action* of turning head and eyes toward the ball, and the *causal process* wherein light from the ball affects my eyes so as to produce my visual experience. In the normal perceptual situation these three processes are interdependent: none can exist apart from the whole in that structure; each is a *dependent part* of the perceptual situation. My perceptual experience depends on my action in looking toward the ball, and on the way the ball affects my eyes.

Within the *context* of perception, in the normal course of events, there is then a complex relationship between perceiver and perceived. Perception involves a *causal relation* between subject and object, as the tennis ball reflects yellow light into my eyes, or as the mellowing cheese sends complex molecules into the rat's nose. Furthermore, perception involves an *intentional relation* between the perceiver's experience and the object perceived, as the content of perception on that concrete occasion is in fact satisfied by the relevant object in the context of perception—namely, the tennis ball being before my eyes, or the cheese before the rat's nose.

Again, we philosophers abstract from the unit of activity that is perception proper (itself a dependent part of the subject's activity of perception-*cum*-action). Within the context of perception, we note two importantly distinct types of relation between perceiver and perceived: the causal relation, and the intentional relation. The causal relation is defined by the physiological interaction of light and optic sensors, or by chemical decomposition and olfactory sensors. By contrast, the intentional relation is defined by the way the perceived object satisfies the content of the perceptual consciousness (registered in the perceiver's brain, we know, but that feature we have abstracted away from).

Each of these two relationships is a dependent part of the *whole perceptual situation*. Two types of relation are instanced in the situation; each concrete relationship is a concrete, dependent part of the whole situation. The causal relationship is one part of the situation. The intentional relationship is another part of the same situation. In philosophical theory we abstract each from the whole, focusing on relevant features of each.

And again, we philosophers abstract from these two relationships something else: the *perceptual experience*, the act of perceptual consciousness. My experience of seeing the ball, or the rat's experience of smelling the fromage, is distinct from the object perceived, the speeding ball itself, or the fragrant cheese itself. Here we speak in the first person. (By a bit of empathy we may speak of the rat's experience of smelling the fromage, distinguishing the experience itself from the cheese and its glorious chemistry.) My visual experience stands in a concrete *causal* relation to the moving tennis ball. Further, my visual experience stands in a concrete *intentional* relation to the arcing ball. My experience itself is distinct from the tennis ball. The ball is here before me, impressing my eyes, but my experience is part of my stream of consciousness, whereas the ball is part of the stream of particles, formed from rubber and wool and air, hanging together in flight.

My stream of consciousness occurs in the spatiotemporal world of nature. As I move and look about, light stimulates the optic nerves in my two eyes, my brain goes to work, and a certain pattern of neural activity ensues in the visual cortex of my brain. My experience of seeing the tomato on the sill depends or supervenes on this complex neural activity within my environment.[10]

We thus abstract my visual experience itself from this complex worldly situation. We abstract my act of consciousness from its intentional relationship with the ball itself. Also, notice, we abstract my experience from its causal relationship with the same ball. We need not remark that philosophy has long struggled with the ontology of mind, body, causation, and consciousness. The traditional problems may look different when we observe the way we are abstracting these distinct parts of the worldly situation: my conscious experience, its content, its involvement in the larger context of perception. Frequently we distinguish 'internal', subjective features of perception from 'external', objective, especially causal, features of perception. From our current perspective we should see these different aspects of perception as *bona fide* parts—dependent parts, called 'tropes' or 'moments'—of perception and indeed of perception-*cum*-action. Our concern here, in any event, is to appraise these distinguishable parts of the phenomenon of perception.

Is perception, then, a *relation* or an *experience*? Yes. That is: both. That is: the whole phenomenon of perception-*cum*-action is a complex situation comprising distinguishable parts that include a 'pure' act of perceptual consciousness, experienced or enacted by a perceiving subject, occurring in an intentional relation to the object of perception (a content-involving relation), and in a causal relation to that same object (a physiology-involving relation).

As long observed, the normal structure of perception may involve break-down situations. Some perceptual experiences arise from deviant or unusual causal circumstances, where there is no such object in the environment: namely, in hallucination. Some perceptual experiences present objects as appearing different from what they are: namely, in illusion. In these cases, normal perception is disrupted. It is an empirical matter just how the disruptions unfold. The philosophy of perception seeks to order these different cases. And the phenomenology of perception addresses, first, the structure of familiar perceptual *experiences*, featuring their contents and what these contents present or prescribe in ordinary circumstances. Against that background, the phenomenology of perception may then also interrogate the structures of perceptual experiences where, despite what our experience tells us, the object perceived is either non-existent or is different from what it appears to be.

---

[10] The structure of the stream of consciousness and the experience of embodied perception of things in space-time are analyzed in detail in Husserl (1991; 1997 and 1989). It is from this complex structure that we abstract simplified experiences of perception, in effect 'toy' perceptions.

We shall focus on simple cases of visual experience in paradigmatic contexts. With those results in place we may proceed to more unusual cases or perception, but those issues must largely await a different occasion of discussion.

Bear in mind the idioms that I will employ here. 'Phenomenology' means the discipline that studies conscious experience: here perception. 'Phenomenal' means the character of what it is like to experience a certain form of consciousness: here a perceptual experience. 'Content' means *what* we experience just *as experienced*: here, not the object perceived, but the way it is perceived—its mode-of-presentation in perception. Crucially, we shall distinguish sensory or sensuous content from the richer 'meaning' in perceptual experience, presenting objects or events with various properties including sensuous qualities. We should let the terminology become clearer as we proceed in our account of various aspects of perception.

What then could be more familiar than a simple case of visual perception in a garden-variety activity such as picking a tomato and putting it on the window sill to ripen, now just *seeing* it there?

3 SEEING RED: SENSIBLE QUALITIES VERSUS THEIR PHENOMENAL APPEARANCES

Since at least the early empiricists, from Locke, Berkeley, and Hume in the eighteenth century to A. J. Ayer and others in the twentieth century, the philosophy of perception has been concerned with sensory impressions of colour and shape. These issues are back on the table with recent writings on 'qualia', often seeking to externalize or naturalize colour perception. Let us return to the phenomenology proper.

I am looking at a tomato, ripening on the window sill. I see red. More precisely, I see the glistening red of the hemispherical top of the tomato. The red looks different as the light shifts. The sun is shining on the red tomato. As I am looking to see how ripe the tomato looks, a cloud passes, and the light shifts in intensity and in hue. Suddenly, even as I look on, the red of the tomato looks less intensely red, a darker red, just a hint of blue now in the red, and not so smooth and glistening a red but a slightly textured red—I can almost feel the skin of the tomato with its not-quite-smooth texture, its texture felt as it were in its red. Yet it is *the same red* I see, the red in the tomato. And it looks like the same red, indicating ripeness, even as its *appearance* shifts in the new light.

This shifting appearance of the colour of an object is familiar in our everyday, *Lebenswelt* experience. What we observe—in phenomenological reflection on our perceptual experience—is the difference between the *sensible quality* of the object, its red, and the *sensous appearance* of that quality, its *phenomenal* appearance. The quality itself is part of the *object* of my perception. The appearance of that quality, however, is part of my *visual experience* of the object—part of what it is like to have the experience.

In describing the experience I should like this talk of *parts* to have a familiar and intuitive ring. But we may also press the ontology of parts, in a way that helps our analysis.
Thus, the colour quality itself is a dependent part, a 'moment' or 'trope', of the object, the
tomato. This trope, the tomato's concrete redness, is an instance of a certain shareable
property, the ideal shade of red an instance of which is literally part of this tomato.
Meanwhile, the appearance of red, this appear*ing* of red, is a dependent part, a moment
or trope, of my visual experience, my seeing the red tomato. That trope, the concrete
appearance-of-red in my experience, carries an ideal type of visual sensation—a type of
sensation, not a type of tomato-skin. Noting the ontology of this concrete red in the
tomato helps us keep track of where we are: in the tomato, or in my consciousness.

We must distinguish thus between sensible qualities, *in an object*, and sensuous
appearances of those qualities, *in a visual experience*. For, to one and the same *quality*
there correspond a variety of possible *appearances* of that quality. The quality itself is a
part of a concrete object, the tomato itself, its skin; by contrast, the sensuous appearance
is part of the experience of the object with that quality. (As is well known, Husserl distinguished a sensible quality from its 'appearance', or *Erscheinung*, in its varying 'adumbrations', or *Abschattungen*, literally shadings (see Husserl 1983: §§40–1, cf. 42–3)).

In terms I prefer, the quality itself is part of the *object* of consciousness, whereas the
sensuous appearance of the quality is part of what is presented by the *content* of the
experience, the content of consciousness in seeing the object. Here we distinguish content from ideal types or species (more on content anon!). Then, the *content* of my visual
experience includes a distinctive *sensuous* content <red>. But that content <red> in my
experience also presents or represents the red in the tomato: it is a meaningful intentional content, a conceptual as well as sensuous content. This sensuous-intentional content <red>, I would urge, is part of what are now called the 'qualia' in perception. And,
observing the distinction at hand, we emphasize that sensuous or sensuous-conceptual
qualia are part of the sensory experience, not part of its object.

Philosophers today speak of 'qualia' as aspects of 'what it is like', say, to see red. This
'qualitative character' or 'phenomenal character' in a visual experience is treated in various ways, in light of different theoretical commitments (notably, concerning how sensation arises from the etiology of sensory stimulation but also how sensation 'appears'
phenomenally in conscious experience). Suffice it for now to say, in phenomenological
analysis, that the phenomenal character of seeing red, with the sensuous-conceptual
content <red>, is part of the visual experience, not part of its object.[11]

Take another case. There is a dove sitting on the railing (a China spotted dove, if you
know the species). Apart from a few blackish spots, its body and wings are a soft grey, a hint
of brown in the grey (words fail here, but you know what it looks like if you have seen this
bird). The dove's grey is a fuzzy grey. You can almost feel the soft feathery feel of its grey.

---

[11] In terms I find most relevant here, qualitative or phenomenal characters are treated as central to
consciousness (see Kriegel and Williford 2006; Janzen 2008; and Kriegel 2009), putting aside for now
what is deemed more fundamental in consciousness (as between phenomenal character and self-
representational character).

Perhaps there is some synesthesia here, the visual appearance of the grey drawing in a bit of the tactile feel of the bird's coat. In any event, I see the grey of the dove, and the grey appears as a soft, fuzzy grey, a particular hue appearing in the morning sunlight. Again, we distinguish the grey itself, in the bird, from the visual appearance of the grey: the warm, soft, fuzzy grey, as it so appears in the early sunlight. Clearly, the colour in the bird's feathery coat is one thing, and the visual appearance of that quality in my experience is another.

(Maurice Merleau-Ponty noted how different a colour looks in different objects, noting the woolly red of a carpet, in contrast to the oversimplified empiricist account of visual appearance, or sense data.[12])

Modern science tells a rich story of light (in energy packets called quanta), its absorption and reflection by a physical object, the transmission of light (even in units called information) between an object and the nervous system of a human organism. The physics and physiology will condition my experience of seeing the colour-in-an-object in a certain lighting. However the physical processes go, my experience has a certain phenomenological character. Even in everyday life, and in light of our physical science, we know there is a difference between what the tomato or dove itself is—including its chromatic manifestation—and how my experience presents it. Our concern in phenomenology is to discern the character of my *conscious experience* in seeing the object, my experience as if of that object with its sensible colour.

Turn now to shape. The top of my coffee mug is circular, but from an angle it looks elliptical. More precisely, when I see the circular mug-top, it presents an elliptical appearance, in my visual experience of the mug. Yet the mug-top *looks* circular to me. That is, my visual experience presents a circular mug-top, a mug with a circular top, but a top that 'looks' elliptical from my perspective if I attend to its appearance. Again, we must distinguish the visible *shape* from its visual *appearance*. As I move to pick up the mug, my perspective changes, and its top presents a shifting appearance; as I look down from above, its appearance is now circular. Notice how flexible is this talk of what it 'looks like'. The top looks like a circular top as seen from a particular perspective. Indeed, I must shift my attention from the appearing shape to its perspectival appearance, if the shape is to look elliptical rather than circular. This shift is perfectly familiar. Yet we must observe that the *appearance* of a shape is not normally our focus; we are usually just looking at the mug, which looks circular even from an angle as I tilt it, careful not to spill the coffee.

In everyday life it takes some effort to 'see' the appearance of a colour or shape, rather than the quality itself, in the object seen. However, even subtle shifts in the appearance of an object's colour or shape gain the attention of a photographer or a painter.

Famously, the impressionist painter Claude Monet put on canvas the very difference we are noting, between an array of colour itself and its changing *appearance* under different lighting. Monet painted the same cathedral, in Rouen, from the same spatial perspective in a series of paintings that present the cathedral—its colour, but also its texture—under different lighting conditions, at different times of day and in different seasons. As the quality of light changes, the visual appearance of the subtle colouration

---

[12] See Merleau-Ponty (2003).

of the front of the cathedral changes, as does the appearance of rough stone of its facade. The painter's eye focuses on the appearance, capturing in oil on canvas the appearance itself. When we view the series of paintings in a museum, we readily appreciate the difference in appearance. Monet demonstrates for us the *phenomenology* of his visual experience in seeing the same cathedral with the same pattern of colouration presenting different visual *appearances* in different lighting. When we view the paintings, unless we are looking for his technique, we do not see a certain patch of colour in the oil dabbed on a certain canvas at a certain spot (in the museum's lighting!). Rather, in the painting we see the cathedral *as its colouration appears* in the lighting captured in that painting.

Whatever else we say about the phenomenological structure or content of a visual experience, we distinguish the object perceived, its colour (shape, and so on), and the varying appearances of that colour in that object. The sensible quality itself is part of the *object* of perception, while the sensuous *appearance* of the quality is part of the visual experience, part of the sensuous-intentional *content* of the experience. Thus, the colour of the tomato I see is visually presented not merely as red, but as red *as appearing* in the morning sunlight (as opposed to the differently hued light in the afternoon storm); and the shape of the top of the coffee mug I see is presented not merely as circular, but as circular *as appearing* from this angle.

Some contemporary theorists seem in effect to place sensuous appearances or 'qualia' in the physical object itself, as units of physical 'information' transmittable to our sensory organs.[13] By my lights, such efforts obscure the distinction between an experience and its substrate, the conditions giving rise to the experience as experienced.[14] At any rate, any would-be physicalist model of perception—articulating neural activity in the visual cortex of the brain—will still need to make the distinction between an objective colour and its subjective appearance, or it will simply fail to account for the phenomenological structure of perception realized in the visual cortex. And our concern here is that phenomenological structure.

4 SEEING 'THIS' OBJECT ACTUALLY NOW HERE BEFORE ME: SENSUOUS INTUITIONAL PRESENCE

Perceptual experience is not only *sensuous*. It is paradigmatically *intentional*, a perception *of* something.[15]

Despite the ubiquity of seeing colours, seeing shapes, feeling shapes, hearing sounds, and so on, our perceptual experience is always much richer. Already in the above exam-

---

[13] A seminal version of this approach is Fred Dretske's information-theoretic model of perception and cognition: see especially Dretske (1995) addressing consciousness in perception. Compare Tye (2000).

[14] This distinction is elaborated in several essays in Smith (2004).

[15] Husserl's theory of intentionality in Husserl (1983) is recurrently focused on perceptual experience. Compare Føllesdal (1982) on the Husserlian theory of perception.

ples we find that perceptual consciousness presents one with *objects*, objects bearing more than sensible properties that appear sensuously in certain ways. Indeed, perception presents one with *particular* objects, particular objects *in one's presence* in perception. Let us reflect on this character of everyday perceptual experience.

Bear in mind the distinction between the *intentional character* of a visual experience of an object and the successful *intentional relation* between the experience and the object (in veridical perception).

When I see this tomato, I see—I am visually presented with—not just a pattern of sensible qualities sensuously appearing in certain ways, a certain round spread of red. No, I see a *red round object*, its red appearing a certain way in the sunlight, its slightly lopsided spherical shape appearing a certain way from my perspective, its texture appearing a certain way in the light. Indeed, I see *this tomato*, red and round, sitting on the window sill, glistening in the morning light. In my visual experience this object is given as a tomato, a fruit, plucked and ripening, a kind of physical thing whose botanic traits are implicit in my so taking it. And such a thing, I take it, is far more than a bundle of sensible qualities, or even a bundle of botanical as well as sensible properties. What I see, *as I see it*, is an object, bearing certain properties: an individual object with such properties, including *inter alia* sensible properties each with a certain sensuous visual appearance. I see a 'red, roundish tomato ripening on the sill'.

Furthermore, in seeing this tomato, I see—I am visually presented with—a *particular* object. I am presented with not just 'a' tomato, 'some' tomato, red and round and ripening. No, I am presented with 'this' tomato, *this particular* tomato, *right here visually before me now*, affecting my eyes.[16]

Suppose you are trying to trick me by a slight of hand, moving that tomato around in your right hand and a second tomato around in your left hand. As you slide the second tomato into the place of the first, I am not fooled; 'this' tomato is the one I see moving around, the particular tomato I saw at the beginning of the trick, having kept my eyes on it all along. Now, suppose you succeed in tricking me, announcing that, *voila!*, what I take to be 'this' tomato is actually the other tomato. You have placed two little stickers on the bottoms of the two tomatoes. Though the two tomatoes look indistinguishable to me, one sticker says '1' and the other says '2'. The '1'-sticker is on the bottom of the first tomato, 'this' tomato that I see at the outset. When you effect the slight of hand, turning over the tomato I now see, so as to reveal the '2'-sticker, I realize the difference. At first I see 'this' particular tomato, and then you substitute for it a second, unbeknownst to me, thanks to your fast hands. But then I realize that my initial perception of 'this' object

---

[16] The demonstrative structure or content of perception is explored in Smith (1989), also in other works noted above. My account thereof is influenced by Husserl's view of demonstratives-and-perception in Husserl (2001), Hintikka's notion of 'demonstrative' or 'perceptual' individuation in Hintikka (1969), and Kaplan's notion of the 'character' of a demonstrative pronoun in Kaplan (1989) (Kaplan's view tracing to around 1970). A rather different view of 'demonstrative identification', whence demonstrative content, in perception develops from Evans (1982). My own account of an essentially indexical *phenomenological content* or *sense* in perception is laid out below, following Smith (1989). The sense of particularity (as opposed to persisting identity) is emphasized in Montague (2010) and Kidd (2011).

presented me with the one tomato, and not—here is the point—the other tomato, the second tomato! In other words, we emphasize, the *content* of my original perception presented a particular object: the content of my original perception, presenting its particular tomato, would be satisfied by the '1' tomato but not by the '2' tomato! So, in my experience of 'this' tomato, I am presented with an object with a sense of its particularity, its individuality, a sense of its identity—if you will, its 'this'-ness. (That is, *haecceitas* in the Latin: the ontological point has been appreciated already in medieval times, though we are here emphasizing the *perceived* particularity or 'thisness' of the object.)

And, moreover, not only do I see 'this' particular tomato. I see—I am visually presented with—'this' particular tomato *present to me on this occasion*. That is, I see this tomato 'actually now here before me' on this occasion. Part of my visual experience is this object's being presented *as in my presence*, that is, as 'actually now here before me': this object 'itself' is presented as *visually before me*, located now here before me, before my eyes, and affecting my eyes on this occasion.

The tomato's presence before me is indeed visually impressed on me. I *feel* its presence, as it were. If I pick up the tomato I *feel* it between my fingers, right here in my hand, physically present to me. I immediately sense its presence, as it presses itself against my fingers. And where I see the tomato, right here before me, I also *feel* its presence, its visual presence, as it reflects light into my eyes. It is as if the tomato is pressing light into my eyes, even as the tomato is pressing its surface into my fingers when I grasp it. In seeing it, I experience this tomato as 'bodily' present to me, right here 'in person' (*leibhaftig*, in Husserl's idiom).

We are here describing, in impressionistic terms, a certain sense of causal contact with the tomato. In my visual experience I 'feel' the presence of the tomato itself, as light streams from the tomato into my eyes. If you will: I see—I am visually presented with—this particular tomato actually now here visually before me: that is, causally stimulating my eyes on this occasion. That is, in seeing this tomato, I so take it as affecting me, causally affecting my eyes.

Gathering together these several features of phenomenological structure, we craft this *phenomenological description* of my visual experience:

> I see this red, round, ripe tomato actually now here visually before me affecting my eyes.

In this form of phenomenological description we articulate distinctive features of *content* in my experience (using angled brackets to 'quote' these items of content):

(i)   <this>, presenting a particular object in visual presence to me;
(ii) <red>, presenting a certain colour as it appears visually in this lighting;
(iii) <round>, presenting a certain shape as it appears visually from this perspective;
(iv) <ripe>, presenting a certain botanic state;
(iv) <tomato>, presenting a certain sort of fruit;
(v)   <actually now here visually before me affecting my eyes>, presenting a spatiotemporal and causal relation of the object to me on the occasion of my experience, that is, wherein the object itself I experience as *present to me*, to my eyes, to my experiencing body.

In a traditional idiom, from Kant to Bolzano to Husserl, perception is a form of *intuition* (*Anschauung*). The phenomenological analysis above explicates this form of awareness: a direct (indexical) awareness of a particular object sensuously present to me on the occasion of perception: that is, a veridical intentional relation to this object actually now here visually before me.

Here we characterize the way the object itself is given in my visual experience: its *mode of presentation* in my consciousness, whence the *intentional character* of the experience. The way the object is so presented defines the *content* of the experience. Importantly, the content <this> presents that *particular* object in a certain *contextual relation* to my experience, that is, its being actually now here visually before me affecting my eyes—its being so present to me, its presence so felt by me—on the occasion of perception. The *intentional relation* of the experience to the object is achieved by virtue of the overall content of the experience, and the content <this> plays a central role—to which we now turn.

To be a little more precise as to content in the conscious visual experience: the content <actually now here visually before me affecting my eyes> is *implicit* in the content <this> in the visual experience.[17] These elements of content belong in the 'horizon' of the experience. The object presented is implicitly given as actually now here visually before me affecting my eyes; but these aspects of perception are not explicitly given in the experience (except under unusual circumstances, say, where I am unsure if 'this tomato' is perhaps an illusion). And of course those aspects of perception are not in the focus of attention (again, unless something in the occasion spurs my wonder what doth confront me, say, as Hamlet wonders about the ghost of his father appearing visually before him).

5 INDEXICAL AWARENESS VIA INDEXICAL CONTENT: THE DUAL ROLE OF CONTEXT IN PERCEPTION

I see 'this' object. The content of my perception is, in part, an *indexical* content, as the content <this> 'indicates' a particular object visually before me affecting my eyes on the occasion of perception. We ascribe this feature of perceptual content with the demonstrative pronoun 'this'. The point is not that the word 'this' is running through my mind as I see a particular object before me, as if in a silent soliloquy. ('Oh, dear self, tis 'this' I see before me!', as if raising my proprioceptive index finger within the purview of my mind's eye while thinking the word 'this'.) No, we use the demonstrative to express the *form of visual experience* itself: the visual content in the experience, not the word. Indexical

---

[17] A guiding theme in Smith (1989) is the implicit interdependence among a 'circle' of indexical or 'acquainting' senses: <this>, <now>, <here>, <me>, and others. Each has its intentional force within this circle of implicit presupposition, whereby the one cannot 'intend' what it does unless the others intend as they do.

terms include 'this', 'I', 'now', 'here', and so on, all keyed to the context of utterance. We assume that such terms express essentially indexical forms of *content*, as displayed in our phenomenological description above.

How does the indexical perceptual content <this> work? Basically, it prescribes a particular object in the subject's presence on the occasion of perception—that is, playing an 'indicating' role *in the actual context* of perception. Typically, as in my seeing 'this' tomato, the content <this> prescribes the object appropriately located before me and affecting my eyes on the occasion of perception. Again, my visual experience bears the content <this> (along with other content), and my experience is intentionally related to the existing tomato if and only if that tomato satisfies the content <this> in my experience. This is to remind us of the difference and connection between the *intentional character* (*cum* content) of my visual experience and the *intentional relation* between me or my experience and its object in the context of perception.

Do not think of the content <this> as a bare pointer (as sometimes assumed). Rather, think of <this> as visually indicating a particular object *within* a visual field: as on the Gestalt model of a figure seen against or within a background. Generally, an indexical content—<this>, <now>, <here>, <I>—prescribes the relevant item (object, time, location, self) within a relevant circumstance or context. The satisfaction-conditions for that content in an experience in that context, then, spell out the appropriate structure or context within which the item is so prescribed.[18] Bear in mind that the intentional force of the content <this> in a visual experience is not a matter of mere sensuous appearance, or what 'this' *looks* like: the point of 'looks' talk is to abstract away from the rich intentional content of visual experience so as to focus only, rather as a painter might, only on the array of colours sensuously appearing.

Thus, in the assumed indexical-content model, context plays two roles in perception. On the one hand, in veridical perception there is a *contextual*—partly causal—relation between subject and object. On the other hand, in veridical perception the *indexical content* in the perceptual experience is satisfied, in part, by virtue of the object's standing in that contextual relation to the subject.

In more formal terms, the 'semantics' of perception—and specifically of the indexical content <this> in visual perception—we may map out as follows:

> A visual experience E by subject S in context K is *intentionally related* to the object O in the context K if and only if the content <this> in S's experience E in context K is *satisfied* by object O in context K,

where:

> The content <this> in subject S's visual experience E in context K *prescribes*, or is *satisfied* by, object O in context K if and only if in context K object O is actually before subject S and affecting S's eyes at that time and place in K—that is, so that light from O is causally affecting S's visual system so as to produce S's visual experience E.

---

[18] This model of indexical contents and their appeal to appropriate contexts is detailed in Smith (1989) for the 'acquainting' senses <this>, <now>, <here>, <I>, and <she> or <he>.

Following the form of truth-definitional semantics, we frame these *satisfaction-conditions* for the content <this>. The notion of satisfaction-conditions or truth-conditions is now familiar in philosophy of mind, and I have long used the form above in characterizing the intentional force of indexical content in intentional experience.[19]

It is by virtue of the *content* in an intentional experience that the experience is directed as it is. Accordingly, by virtue of the content <this> my experience of seeing 'this tomato' is directed toward the particular tomato actually now here before me and affecting my eyes *in the context* of this perception. The ontology of contents is not our focus here, yet we note that the content <this> can be shared by other visual experiences on different occasions, and so it takes effect only where realized in a concrete circumstance of perception. Thus, the content <this> can 'mean' this particular tomato actually now here before me only where the content is realized in *my* visual experience *in the present context*. We might treat this content as an ideal meaning entity, along the lines of Bolzano, Husserl, and Frege. But, however the ontology of contents runs, the visual demonstrative content <this> goes to work only where realized in a particular visual experience in a particular context of perception.

What is crucial, then, in the satisfaction-conditions for an *indexical* content is the way the *content* appeals to the actual *context* of experience. In the case at hand, I am standing in the kitchen gazing at a tomato on the window sill. We assume this situation is actual, not a figment of my hallucinating brain. So there is a physical space wherein I am standing before the window and the tomato is sitting on the window's sill: the object is actually now here before me. Morning light is reflecting from the tomato into my eyes, the light falling within the red range of the optical spectrum. In this circumstance I am having a visual experience with a certain content, realized in the visual cortex of my brain. This complex relationship we assume is actual—that is, occurring on the occasion of perception. *In that context* the content <this> *in my visual experience* is satisfied by the tomato on the sill. That object satisfies that content in that experience in that context: because, as prescribed, the tomato on the sill plays the appropriate role in relation to me and to my visual experience.

It should be emphasized that, on this indexical-content model, 'satisfaction' is not a matter of the object of perception matching a description specifying various properties, nor of the object resembling an internal image (forming a complex sense-datum?). The condition of satisfaction for the indexical content <this> is rather a matter of the *intuitional contact* between the object and the perceptual experience, between subject and object in perceptual consciousness. Yet this contact is not simply a causal relation

---

[19] The present formulation of satisfaction-conditions for indexical contents follows the style introduced in Smith (1989). Here I try to emphasize further the phenomenology of the forms of experience carrying such contents. The experience of causation in visual experience is not a matter of the object's 'looking' like it is affecting my eyes, as (say) it looks like that man is pushing his stalled car to the roadside. Normally, the *sense* of causation is implicit in seeing an object, yet carries sensuous support, as Husserl would say. Compare the varied accounts of causal circumstance in the content of visual experience according to Searle (1983: Chapter 4), and Siegel (2010: Chapter 5).

between object and experience. Rather, the contact consists in a consciously experienced contact — again, the experience of the object's being sensuously 'given' as actually 'bodily present'.[20]

This model of indexical content offers a perspective on the issues of 'internalism' and 'externalism' in perception.[21] The internalist view says the intentional content of an experience determines the object of consciousness—that is all. The externalist view says the external context of perception determines the object of perception—that is all. In light of our reflections above, both of these views are incorrect. The strict internalist view leaves out the external context. Indeed, the twin-tomatoes experiment shows that content alone, restricted to the subject's consciousness, does not settle which tomato is the correct object of perception. Yet the strict externalist view leaves out, well, consciousness: it leaves out the way the object is *experienced*, namely, as 'actually now here before me'. Indeed, content plays no role in the strict externalist model. So what should we say?

The answer follows the satisfaction conditions for the content <this> in a visual experience. The content *in* the experience *in* the context of perception prescribes or (inversely) is satisfied by the *object* of perception *in* that context—and so the content effects the *intentional relation* of the visual experience to the object perceived. Clearly, the satisfaction of an indexical content in an experience involves both internal and external elements in perception. Content-*cum*-context forms, as it were, the *medium* of the intentional relation. And then it is misleading to ask whether content 'determines' object (per internalism) or instead object 'determines' or 'individuates' content (per exernalism).

6 Perception, veridical or hallucinatory or illusory or otherwise defective: 'disjunctivism' notwithstanding

Recall now our opening account of perception *vis-à-vis* perceptual experience, and fold in our account of indexical awareness.

On the indexical-content model, the distinction between veridical and hallucinatory perception follows naturally. Perception is veridical when the content of the visual experience is 'true' to the world, that is, satisfied in the context of perception. Perception is hallucinatory when the content is not satisfied because there is no object actually visually present to the subject in the context of the perceptual experience. ('Is this a dagger

---

[20] Pun intended. An intuitive characterization of such 'intuition', of the object's being itself 'given' in perceptual intuition, is that in Hintikka (1995).

[21] Compare Beyer (2004) on Husserl's account of indexicality. Husserl's view incorporates both internalist and externalist elements.

I see before me?' There is nothing there at all: there is no actual contextual relation between me and an optically-stimulating dagger.)

To be sure, there is a sharp difference in *ontological* structure between veridical and hallucinatory perception. And there are often differences in *phenomenological* structure between hallucinatory and veridical perception (say, where the hallucinator feels that the appearing object is not real). But the difference in ontological structure concerns *parts* of the *whole* perceptual situation. The perceptual experience itself, we held, is a proper *dependent part* of the perceptual situation. This part has content, which may or may not be satisfied. Where the content is not satisfied because there is no actual object *in contextual relation* to the perceptual experience, the perceptual situation is different. There is a breakdown in the normal structure: that is hallucination, the experience being hallucinatory. However, the normal situation is that of veridical perception, as appraised above.

This account of difference in ontological (and often phenomenological) structure in the perceptual situation does not, however, entail a form of 'disjunctivism'. In perception theory *disjunctivism* holds that perception is *either* veridical *or* hallucinatory *or* illusory, *and so on*, and that there are wholly disjoint *types* or natural kinds of perception, namely, veridical and hallucinatory and illusory, amd so on.[22] On our account above, however, there is one overall typical structure of perception: a structure involving perceptual experience, phenomenological content, intentional relation, contextual relation, *and so on*. When things go wrong, the situation remains a situation of perception—just as much as your body remains a human organism even if an organ goes awry.

In the normal perceptual situation, my visual experience engages and is engaged by things in the context of perception. And that connection is definitive of perceptual *intuition*.

7 DIRECT AWARENESS IN PERCEPTION OF AN OBJECT: CONTEXTUAL INTENTIONALITY AS DEFINING 'INTUITION'

Perception, we feel, places us in *direct contact* with things in our environment. In seeing the tomato, for example, I have a *direct awareness* of the thing itself in my immediate environs. Again, in grasping, touching, the tomato, all the more *direct* is my awareness of the tomato itself, as I experience grasping it. Again, as Husserl was fond of saying, in perception the object 'itself' is 'bodily present' or present 'in person' (*leibhaftig*).[23] How should we explicate this phenomenon? In what sense does perception afford such a 'direct' awareness of something?

---

[22] Disjunctivism is surveyed in Soteriou (2009). Compare Mulligan (1995) on Husserl's theory of perception, looking toward disjunctivist forms.

[23] This *leibhaftig* character is a running theme in Husserl (1989).

One issue concerns the proper object of perception. On the neo-empiricist sense-datum theory of perception, what I see is not the tomato itself, but a *sense datum*: simply a red, round patch. That sense datum in turn represents the tomato, insofar as light from the tomato produces in my mind the sense datum (adding a point from the causal theory of perception). This is to assume a realism about the tomato (more on 'direct realism' in a moment). The sense datum itself would form a sensuous appearance, but that red–round appearance is cast in the role of *object* of perception—rather than an element of content. On the sense-datum model, then, there is a *veil of appearance* that stands between my visual experience and the external object, the tomato itself. This view fails to make the crucial distinctions we have drawn among the perceived object itself, its sensible qualities, the diverse sensuous appearances of those qualities, and—more generally—the distinction between the (external) object and the (internal) content of an experience.

A neo-phenomenalist phenomenological theory of perception holds that the proper object of perception is not the external physical object itself, but the 'phenomenal' content presenting that object (if such an object actually exists). This content may be imbued with conceptual content like <organic heirloom red tomato>, richer than <red, round>. Or the content may involve a demonstrative content <this>. In any case, the neo-phenomenalist view holds that this perceptual content—'the object *as* perceived'—is, strictly speaking, what I see, the object of perception, when I see this tomato. On that view, again, there is a veil of appearance, or perceptual 'phenomenon', that stands between my visual experience and the tomato itself (if indeed there is such a thing). What I see is not the tomato itself, but a phenomenologically rich 'appearance' of the tomato: the tomato-as-it-appears in my visual experience. That phenomenon represents the tomato itself—if such object exists beyond my experience. Crudely put, the problem with this theory is that it fails to put content and object in their proper places in the *intentional relation* of perception. My consciousness does not reach the object itself, but only the appearance, which is something else entirely. Hence, on that view, perception does not afford a direct awareness of the object. Yet, in fact, we *experience* perception as a direct awareness!

On our unfolding theory of perception, then, in seeing the tomato I have a *direct* visual awareness of the tomato itself. My visual experience has a complex content, <this red, round, ripe tomato actually now here visually before me, affecting my eyes>, a part of which is the sensuous-appearance content <red, round>. But that 'sense-datum' or sensuous 'appearance' (if such terms apply) is a proper part of the *content* of the experience; it is not the object of perception, but part of the *way* the object is presented. The awareness, or intentionality, achieved in my visual experience is direct in the sense that the experience reaches out and touches the object itself, not something like a sense datum, or even a much richer perceptual content, or indeed a fulsome phenomenological content (like a Husserlian perceptual 'noema' informed by sensation or sensuous 'hyle'; see Husserl 1983: §84 on *hyle cum noesis*, and §§88ff on *noema*).

A further aspect of 'direct' awareness is the *sense of presence* in perception. The visual indexical content <this> carries the implicit sense-of-presence <actually now here before me and affecting my eyes>. If this content in my visual experience is satisfied, in the actual context of my perception, then the object itself is *present* to me in seeing it: that is, the object itself is actually here before me on this occasion. Perception is accordingly a form of *intuition*, or direct cognition (*cognitio intuitiva*, in Ockham's medieval idiom; *Anschauung*, in the idiom of Husserl, Bolzano, and Kant). In touch, in grasping the tomato I feel the object itself in my presence; similarly, in vision, in seeing the tomato, I see the object itself in my presence.

Perception thus affords a *direct awareness* of an object in the sense that, first, the external object is itself the *object* of perception (the tomato itself, not some representative content), and, second, the object is *actually present* to the subject and *experienced as actually present* in the context of perception (if the content is satisfied and the perception is veridical). Indeed, on the present theory the indexical content <this> in the visual experience semantically prescribes this direct connection with the object. So (as noted) the object of perception is not specified by a descriptive content that appeals to a bundle of properties unique to the object (being a tomato, being quite ripe, being quite round, and so on). Rather, the indexical *content* in a perceptual experience intentionally appeals to the *context* of perception.

8 Direct realism in perception of an object: no veil of appearances

Direct realism in perception follows from this account of direct awareness in perception.

In perception theory *naïve realism* says the object perceived is a *real* object, existing outside perceptual consciousness, say, the tomato I see rather than some intermediary, sensuous, red-tomato-ish *appearance*. That is, I see—I am visually–intentionally related to—the object *itself*: just as our naïve, everyday experience declares. Then *direct realism* says both that the object perceived is *real* (the tomato, external to consciousness) and that it is perceived *directly*, that is, without going through some sensory appearance that is the immediate object of perception—such as a sense datum or a phenomenal appearance or even a sensuous-conceptual tomato-appearance.[24]

The additional wrinkle, in the present theory, is that the direct relation in perception—the relation of subject or act to object in perception—is effected through an *indexical content* that appeals to the *context* of perception. Perception is 'direct' because, in the case at hand, the indexical content in my visual experience links me (intentionally) to the tomato directly 'present' to me on the occasion of perception. To say that perception is a 'direct' intentional relation to the tomato, then, is not to say there is no content involved in the relation: the point is that the tomato is *directly present* to me in the perception, just as prescribed by the indexical content in my visual experience.

---

[24] Hirst (1959) surveys issues of naïve and direct realism *vis-à-vis* representative and sense-datum models of perception—a useful retrospective in the hey-day of sense-datum theories.

Of course, a purely causal or functional theory of perception will find perception to be a direct *causal* relation between a real external object and the perceiver's neural system—'direct' meaning a relevantly direct causal road from object to visual cortex (no smoke or mirrors). However, on the present theory, that causal relation is not the same thing as the direct *intentional* relation between the experience and its object. And what we want to account for is an intentional relation of 'direct' awareness between act and object in perception—effected through the appropriate content.

So the 'direct' intentional relation in perception is not without content. According to the theory at hand: first, the content is not what is perceived (the proper object of perception—that is, the tomato, its skin, its redness, and so on); and second, the content is (in part) an indexical content, whose satisfaction involves the subject's direct contextual relation to the object of perception.

In Husserlian jargon, 'intuition' is just such a 'direct' consciousness of an object: an awareness of an object 'bodily present' to the subject on the occasion of veridical perception. In the present model we take perception to be 'direct' insofar as the indexical content in the visual experience prescribes, or is satisfied by, the object in the presence of the subject—that is, within the actual context of perception.

9 CONSCIOUSLY SEEING SOMETHING: 'TRANSPARENCY' NOTWITHSTANDING

An experience of consciously seeing something is much richer in phenomenological structure than a bare presentation of a particular object with qualities. In the case at hand, the object is presented as 'this red, round, ripening tomato'. Yet the experience involves more than a free-floating apparition of 'this red... tomato'. In the first place, the experience is one of *seeing* 'this tomato'—rather than touching or contemplating or desiring such. Further, the experience is enacted *by me*, from the first-person perspective: with the character whereby *I* see 'this red... tomato', and indeed *I now here* see 'this red... tomato'. Moreover, I *consciously* see such—as opposed to blind-sightedly see such. Thus, the object-presentation of 'this red... tomato' is modified by several further characters, so that the intentional experience has the character whereby 'consciously I now here see this red... tomato'.

Accordingly, we may divide the overall phenomenological structure of an intentional experience into two formally distinct parts called the 'mode' and 'modality' of presentation.[25] The *mode of presentation* of the object includes the way the object is

---

[25] The distinction is developed in Smith 1986, 1989, 2004, and 2006. This distinction can be seen in part as amplifying Husserl's distinction between the noematic *Sinn* of an act and the thetic character(s) of the act: see Smith 2007 on Husserl's distinction. Many philosophers assume that every intentional mental act has a form like <S believes that p>. That assumption misses most of the 'modal' structure of experience, while wrongly pressing all object-presentation into a propositional form.

presented or represented: say, as 'this red, ripening tomato'—noting sensuous, extra-sensuous, and demonstrative elements of content. This object-presenting content is further modified by the *modality of presentation*, which includes the way the experience is executed, as opposed to the way the object is depicted. 'Modal' characters of the experience include, if you will, its unfolding visually, attentively, first-personally—and consciously.

Specifically, following the *modal model* of consciousness recounted elsewhere,[26] the full phenomenological structure of the featured experience carries the complex content:

<consciously I now here see this...tomato...>

or more fully (on a certain analysis):

<Phenomenally in this very experience I now here see this red, round, ripening tomato on the sill>

The mode-of-presentation <this red, round, ripening tomato on the sill> characterizes how the object is presented, while the modality-of-presentation <Phenomenally in this very experience I now here see> characterizes how the *act* of consciousness itself is executed. In particular, the content <phenomenally in this very experience> characterizes the form of *inner awareness* of the experience itself. On the modal model, this form of awareness renders the perception *conscious*, as opposed to an act of blindsight.[27]

Now, as it happens, the structure of such inner awareness is at stake in current perception theory. A popular thesis nowadays holds that perception is 'transparent' (as Fred Dretske, Michael Tye, and others say) or 'diaphanous' (as G. E. Moore said a century ago).[28] The claim is that perceptual consciousness is *transparent* or *diaphanous* in that introspection shows, in the case at hand, that in seeing the tomato I am *aware* of the tomato and its redness (and some other properties), but I am never aware of my *seeing* it, my visual *consciousness of* the tomato. I can become aware of that consciousness later, in recollection or reflection, but in the very act of seeing the tomato (it is held) I am only aware of the tomato and its redness, *and so on*. What shall we make of this phenomenological claim?

Well, as Sartre explicitly held, consciousness-of-some-object is 'translucent' (= transparent) yet it is *ipso facto* also a 'pre-reflective' consciousness-of-that-consciousness.[29] That view is part of what motivated the modal model I myself have worked with. Indeed, from the preceding phenomenology of perception we should clearly see that we are *aware* of more than the tomato and its redness, its roundness, and its resting on the sill. Normally, my attention is focused on the tomato (as I am about to render it part of a salad). My attention may even be narrowly focused at one moment on the redness of the tomato (indicating it is ripe enough for the salad). But my visual field also includes the

---

[26]   See details in Smith 1986, 1989, 2004, 2006.

[27]   Inner awareness is given a somewise different analysis in Kriegel 2009. See Kriegel and Williford 2006 for contrasting approaches to such awareness.

[28]   The 'transparency' thesis is dissected in Stoljar (2004), addressing its roots in G. E. Moore. Compare, notably, Dretske (1995) and Martin (1997).

[29]   See Sartre 1956: 9–17.

visible *background* of the tomato, featuring the window sill, the coffee mug nearby, and so on. These things are presented outside the centre of my current visual field and outside the focus of my current attention. Yet I am aware of them in seeing the tomato: *peripherally*, in the periphery of my visual field; and *inattentively*, in the horizon or background of my consciousness. Furthermore, *in seeing the tomato* I am also aware of my *seeing* it—sometimes in quite different ways: peripherally, attentively or inattentively, and reflexively.[30] As Sartre noted (to vary his example), if I were asked, 'What were you just looking at over there, what did you just *see*?', I would immediately reply, 'This tomato'—'This red, round, ripening tomato on the sill'. My attention is focused on the tomato, but I am peripherally and inattentively aware of the sill, the coffee mug, the fluttering wings of the hummingbird just outside the window. Moreover, in the normal course of events I am *aware* of my visual experience in seeing the tomato. That *inner awareness* is not something extra that I do; it is a *proper part* of the familiar form of everyday perceptual experience—the form of phenomenal, reflexive awareness of my transpiring visual consciousness, where 'phenomenally in this very experience I now here see...'[31]

It is simply not true, then, that all I am aware of in seeing the tomato, typically, is the tomato—and/or its red-round-ness. The transparency claim is inaccurate to the phenomenology of my everyday experience in seeing the tomato. That claim simply fails to recognize the complexity of such a familiar type of experience. There seems to be a problem too with the appeal to 'introspection'. Phenomenological reflection is richer than the oversimplified understanding of introspection on which the transparency claim relies. (Just look inside and note what you see? Well, *reflection* on my seeing-this-red-round-tomato leads into the formulation of satisfaction conditions as pursued above!) Indeed, the several features of 'modal' content, distinguished or factored in the modal model of consciousness, are simply overlooked in the transparency claim.

To put the point bluntly, there is more to my visual experience than the free-floating *sensuous appearance* of 'red' or of 'red, round tomato', or even of '*this* red, round, ripening tomato on the window sill'. There may be cases where my *attention* really is completely focused on the tomato itself: say, as I focus intently on its red-round-ness, which I am trying to capture on canvas in a still-life painting. But even then it is not as if I am completely *unaware* that I am *seeing* the tomato. In any event, in the more typical form of everyday tomato-seeing, there is considerably more structure in the content of my visual experience, and inner awareness of visual experience is a characteristic feature of those forms of everyday perception.

My *inner* awareness of my seeing this tomato does not, by the way, preclude my perception being a direct visual 'intuition' of the thing itself. Quite the contrary, my inner awareness *leads me in reflection* to characterize direct perception in the indexical-content model pursued above.

---

[30] The distinctions among peripheral, inattentive, and inner awareness of experience are drawn in Ford and Smith (2006).

[31] Lay (2010) develops an analysis of a specific form of *temporally* peripheral awareness of one's passing experience—an analysis that extends Husserl's account of temporal 'background'; awareness in 'inner time-consciousness'.

REFERENCES

Beyer, C. (2004), 'Edmund Husserl', in *The Stanford Encyclopedia of Philosophy*, ed. Edward N. Zalta (2004 edition). http://plato.stanford.edu/entries/husserl/.

Dretske, F. (1995), *Naturalizing the Mind* (Cambridge, MA: MIT Press).

Evans, G. (1982), *The Varieties of Reference*, ed. J. McDowell (Oxford and New York: Oxford University Press).

Føllesdal, D. (1982), 'Husserl's Theory of Perception', in Hubert L. Dreyfus (ed.), *Husserl, Intentionality, and Cognitive Science* (Cambridge, MA: MIT Press), pp. 93–6.

Ford, J. and Smith, D. W. (2006), 'Consciousness, Self, and Attention', in U. Kriegel, and K. Williford (eds) (2006), *Self-Representational Approaches to Consciousness* (Cambridge, MA: MIT Press), pp. 353–77.

Hintikka, J. (1969), 'On the Logic of Perception', in Hintikka, J., *Models for Modalities* (Dordrecht: D. Reidel Publishing Company; New York: Springer), pp. 151–83.

—— (1995), 'The Phenomenological Dimension', in B. Smith and D. W. Smith (eds), *The Cambridge Companion to Husserl* (Cambridge and New York: Cambridge University Press), pp. 78–105.

Hirst, R. J. (1959), *The Problems of Perception* (London: George Allen and Unwin; New York: The Macmillan Company).

Husserl, E. (1970/2001), *Logical Investigations*, vols. 1 and 2, tr. J. N. Findlay and D. Moran (ed.) (London and New York: Routledge). (German original, first edition, 1900–1; second edition, 1913, 1920. English translation, first edition, 1970.)

—— (1991), *On the Phenomenology of the Consciousness of Internal Time (1893-1917)*, tr. J. B. Brough (Dordrecht and Boston: Kluwer Academic Publishers; New York: Springer).

—— (1997), *Thing and Space: Lectures of 1907*, tr. and ed. R. Rojcewicz (Dordrecht and Boston: Kluwer Academic Publishers; New York: Springer).

—— (1983), *Ideas pertaining to a Pure Phenomenology and a Phenomenological Philosophy, First Book: General Introduction to Pure Phenomenology*, tr. F. Kersten (Dordrecht and Boston: Kluwer Academic Publishers; now New York: Springer.) (German original 1913).

—— (1989), *Ideas pertaining to a Pure Phenomenology and to a Phenomenological Philosophy, Second Book: Studies in the Phenomenology of Constitution*, tr. R. Rojcewicz and A. Schuwer (Dordrecht and Boston: Kluwer Academic Publishers; New York: Springer). (Original manuscript dating from 1912, posthumously published in German in 1952.)

Janzen, G. (2008), *The Reflexive Nature of Consciousness* (Amsterdam and Philadelphia: John Benjamins Publishing Company).

Kaplan, D. (1989), 'Demonstratives: An Essay on the Semantics, Logic, Metaphysics, and Epistemology of Demonstratives and Other Indexicals' and 'Afterthoughts', in J. Almog, J. Perry, and H. Wettstein (eds), *Themes from Kaplan* (Oxford and New York: Oxford University Press), pp. 481–614.

Kidd, C. (2011), *Seeing Particulars* (Doctoral dissertation, University of California, Irvine).

Kriegel, U. (2009), *Subjective Consciousness: A Self-Representational Theory* (Oxford and New York: Oxford University Press).

—— and Williford, K. (eds) (2006), *Self-Representational Approaches to Consciousness* (Cambridge, MA: MIT Press).

Lay, C. (2010), *Time to Account for Consciousness* (Doctoral dissertation, University of California, Irvine).

Martin, M. G. F. (1997), 'The Transparency of Experience', *Mind and Language* 17/4: 376–425.

Merleau-Ponty, M. (2003), *Phenomenology of Perception*, tr. C. Smith (London and New York: Routledge). (First English edition, 1962; French original, 1945).

Montague, M. (2010), 'The Phenomenology of Particularity', in T. Bayne, and M. Montague (eds), *Cognitive Phenomenology* (Oxford and New York: Oxford University Press).

Mulligan, K. (1995), 'Perception', in B. Smith, and D. W. Smith (eds), *The Cambridge Companion to Husserl* (Cambridge and New York: Cambridge University Press), 168–238.

Noë, A. (2004), *Action in Perception* (Cambridge, MA: MIT Press).

Sartre, J.-P. (1956), *Being and Nothingness*, tr. H. E. Barnes (New York: Washington Square Press; French original, 1943).

Searle, J. R. (1983), *Intentionality: An Essay in the Philosophy of Mind* (Cambridge and New York: Cambridge University Press).

Siegel, S. (2010), *The Contents of Visual Experience* (Oxford and New York: Oxford University Press).

Smith, D. W. (1981), 'Indexical Sense and Reference', *Synthese* 49/1: 100–27.

—— (1982), 'Husserl on Demonstrative Reference and Perception', in H. L. Dreyfus (ed.), *Husserl, Intentionality, and Cognitive Science* (Cambridge, MA: MIT Press), pp. 193–213.

—— (1984), 'Content and Context of Perception', *Synthese* 61: 61–87.

—— (1986), 'The Ins and Outs of Perception', *Philosophical Studies* 49: 187–211.

—— (1989), *The Circle of Acquaintance: Perception, Consciousness, and Empathy* (Dordrecht and Boston: Kluwer Academic Publishers; New York: Springer).

—— (2004), *Mind World: Essays in Phenomenology and Ontology* (Cambridge and New York: Cambridge University Press), 'Return to Consciousness', pp. 76–121.

—— (2006), 'Consciousness with Reflexive Content', in D. W. Smith and A. L. Thomasson (eds) (2005), *Phenomenology and Philosophy of Mind* (Oxford and New York: Oxford University Press), pp. 94–114.

—— (2007), *Husserl* (London and New York: Routledge).

—— and McIntyre, R. (1982), *Husserl and Intentionality: A Study of Mind, Meaning, and Language* (Dordrecht and Boston: D. Reidel Publishing Company; New York: Springer).

—— and Thomasson, A. L., (eds) (2005), *Phenomenology and Philosophy of Mind* (Oxford and New York: Oxford University Press).

Soteriou, M. (2009), 'The Disjunctive Theory of Perception', in E. N. Zalta (ed.), *The Stanford Encyclopedia of Philosophy*, 2009 edition (online).

Stoljar, D. (2004), 'The Argument from Diaphonaousness', *Canadian Journal of Philosophy* 30: 341–90.

Strawson, G. (2005), 'Intentionality and Experience: Terminological Preliminaries', in D. W. Smith, and A. L. Thomasson (eds), *Phenomenology and Philosophy of Mind* (Oxford and New York: Oxford University Press), pp. 41–66.

Tye, M. (2000), *Colour, Content and Consciousness* (Cambridge, MA: MIT Press).

....

CHAPTER 8

COLOURS AND SOUNDS: THE FIELD OF VISUAL AND AUDITORY CONSCIOUSNESS

....

JUNICHI MURATA

1 INTRODUCTION: CONSCIOUSNESS AS A FIELD

....

Perception plays a central role in our everyday experience.

According to Husserl, perceptual experience is considered to be the ultimate source of the 'general thesis' of the world, in which we always live and have various experiences (Husserl 1982: 82). Perceptual experience is regarded as a 'primal experience' (*Urerfahrung*), in which all physical things are originally self-given and from which 'all other experiences derive a major part of the grounding force' (Husserl 1982: 82).

Perceptual experience is, in this sense, a basic mode of our 'being in the world' and a 'place' where various objects are given in their original ways of appearance.

The phenomenological analysis of perception is characterized by its efforts to describe and explicate various features of this perceptual 'being in the world', without presupposing the traditional dualistic conceptual framework, such as subject and object, mind and body, or consciousness and world. Through these efforts, various factors, such as adumbration, horizontal structure, passive synthesis, or kinesthesis and embodiment, have been focused on, but one of the most conspicuous characteristics, which is commonly related to these factors, is the 'spatial' character of the perceptual 'being in the world'.

We can find these circumstances in phenomenological analyses of almost every phenomenological philosopher in some way or other, but it is Aron Gurwitsch who most clearly emphasizes this 'spatial' character of perceptual consciousness.

What Gurwitsch accomplished in his major work, *The Field of Consciousness*, was the task of clarifying the field structure of consciousness on the basis of a psychological and phenomenological analysis of perceptual experience. Combining Husserl's phenomenology with the Berlin school of Gestalt theory and W. James' analysis of consciousness, he proposed his well-known triadic structure of the field of consciousness, which consists of *theme*, *thematic field*, and *margin* (Gurwitsch 1964).

One of the most significant implications of his field theory is the thesis that consciousness has not only a temporal structure, but always has a certain organizational structure or Gestalt-coherence and, in this sense, a *spatial* structure. Whatever unity the perceptual experience accomplishes emerges 'autochthonously' from its spatial structure or the 'organization in consciousness', and the unity is not imposed on it from outside (Gurwitsch 1964: 30ff.; Embree 2010: 418).

Some might think that it is too strong or too one-sided to claim that Gurwitsch's concept of field can be understood above all in a spatial sense. Surely Gurwitsch applies this concept not only to perceptual experiences, in which objects appear in a spatial perspective, but also applies it to various conscious experiences, such as thinking, remembering, or imagining, in which the triadic field structure cannot be understood in a spatial sense in the strict sense of the term (Gurwitsch 1964: 318ff.).

In spite of these circumstances, when Gurwitsch attempts to explicate various factors related to field structure, he always goes back to examples of perceptual experiences, in which themes are experienced in a certain spatial perspective. It is clear that the original meaning of field structure comes from the spatial relation of various factors: for example, a figure and ground relation of visual perceptions, or a spatial character of things on which attention is focused, or a marginal domain, which is co-present but irrelevant to and hidden from a thematic field. Without spatial meaning, the concept of field could not be understood, just as in the case of the concept of gestalt in Gestalt theories.

What I would like to concentrate on in this paper is to clarify this implication of the spatiality of the concept of the field of consciousness, especially when we consider sensible qualities such as colours and sounds.

In his major work it seems that Gurwitsch did not present many concrete discussions concerning colours and sounds. Gurwitsch himself admits that his field theory remains a formal theory of organization and lacks any specification of content (Gurwitsch 1964: 10; 50). Indeed, when he analyses a field structure of perceptual experience he seldom enters into detailed analysis of colours and sounds. On the other hand, we must be careful to notice that he sometimes develops extremely interesting discussions about sensible qualities.

What I would like to do is to find and develop various insights implicated in his work concerning colours and sounds, and discover what characteristics we can identify in the field structure of perceptual consciousness.

The main question is therefore the following. What can we learn for the phenomenology of perception when we focus our attention on the colours and sounds that play an important role in constituting our field of perceptual consciousness?

To tackle this question, first, I will go back to Husserl and his fundamental concept of adumbration, which plays a central role in his philosophy of perception, and explicate the implications of Husserl's insight focusing on the phenomena of colours and sounds. Second, I attempt to take up James J. Gibson's ecological approach to confirm and develop further the Husserlian phenomenological view of colours and sounds. What I try to draw out through these discussions is the thesis that colours and sounds have essentially a certain spatiality and are intrinsically multi-dimensional. In the third and last part I will deal with three topics, which are discussed in the contemporary philosophy of colours and sounds in order to make my thesis of the multi-dimensionality of colours and sounds more persuasive.

Through these discussions, I hope, it will become clear that the field of our consciousness not only has a one-dimensional formal structure, but also shows a multi-dimensional structure that implicates various depths corresponding to various kinds of colours and sounds.

2 ADUMBRATION: IDENTITY AND MANIFOLD

One of the most characteristic concepts in the Husserlian phenomenology of perception is 'adumbration' (*Abschattung*).

The concept is well known, but let me nevertheless recapitulate it and confirm the meaning and the scope of the central thesis of the Husserlian phenomenology of perception and start our discussions on the basis of it.

Every object of perception appears through various aspects, corresponding to the situation of the environment and the perceiver. The object perceived under a certain aspect always presents itself as having other hidden aspects, which would appear in other situations. Especially as the way of appearances of objects is essentially correlated with the way the perceivers realize their bodily movements, the perceptual consciousness includes not only a cognitive consciousness of 'I perceive', but also a practical and kinesthetic consciousness of 'I can'. These are the essential characteristics of the intentional structure of perceptual experiences.

In one part of *Ideen 1*, Husserl explains the adumbration structure in the following way:

> Like the perceived thing as a whole, whatever parts, sides, or moments accrue to it necessarily, and always for the same reasons, transcends the perception regardless of whether the particular property be called a primary or secondary quality. The colour of the seen physical thing is, of essential necessity, not a really inherent moment of the consciousness of colour; it appears, but while it is appearing the appearance can and *must*, in the case of a legitimating experience, be continuously changing. *The same* colour appears 'in' continuous multiplicities of colour *adumbrations*. Something similar is true of every sensuous quality and also of every spatial shape. (Husserl 1982: 87)

In this citation we can find various interesting points which are important for clarifying the ontological status of colours and sounds.

(1) Identity and manifold

First, Husserl emphasizes the essential connection between the identity of an object of perception and the multiplicity of ways of appearance. The identities of objects of perception can and must realize themselves in and through various appearances. It is not *in spite of* changing appearances but rather *because of* changing appearances that the identical object can be experienced. Without changing the multiplicity of appearances it is impossible to perceive an identical object in perceptual experiences. In one sense, Husserl here reverses the orthodox and traditional conceptual order of identity and multiplicity. Identity without multiplicity is impossible.

(2) Spatiality of colours and sounds

Second, this point is especially important in the case of sensible qualities such as colours and sounds. It is sometimes conceived in the following way: as sensible qualities are experienced in different ways corresponding to the changing situations of environments and perceivers, their ontological status is relative, unstable, and subjective in contrast to spatial and physical qualities, which are intrinsic to things themselves. However, this kind of differentiation cannot be retained in the adumbration structure. According to Husserl, as far as perceptual appearances are concerned, there is no fundamental difference between so-called primary and secondary qualities. Colours and sounds, as well as shapes and sizes, adumbrate themselves in a similar way, and we can find no fundamental ontological difference between them.

On the other hand we must be careful, because in the above citation Husserl characterizes sensible qualities as parts, sides, or moments of things. In this context Husserl does not talk about colours *per se* but about the colours of the seen physical objects, and indicates the essential connection of sensible qualities to their bearers.

Husserl did not explicate any further the phenomenological implications of this connection between colours and their bearers. It was David Katz who explicated it with his well-known differentiation of various modes of colour appearances (Katz 1935).

According to Katz, colours are always realized in some particular spatial mode: for example, surface colour, film colour, volume colour, luminous colour, and so on. Above all, the distinction between surface colour and film colour is important in this context.

A typical example of surface colour is the mode of appearance of the surface of everyday objects. It is characterized by a way of appearance that is localized at a determinate distance from the viewer and offers also a visual resistance to it. In contrast, the character of film colour is indefinite with regard to distance. It displays itself in an essentially frontally parallel orientation, but one feels that one can penetrate more or less into it. A typical example of it is the colour of the sky or the mode of appearance of the colour of a surface as seen through a small hole (Katz 1935: 7ff.).

Considering this distinction, it is clear that what Husserl refers to as colours in the above citation is a surface colour and not a film colour. A surface colour appears in and through a variety of different appearances, especially corresponding to changes of illumination, but maintains its identity. In contrast, a film colour cannot realize this kind of adumbration structure. In the case of a film colour, if the appearance changes, the colour itself changes correspondingly. For example, if the appearance of the colour of the sky changes from blue to red in the evening, we see the colour of the sky itself changing.

What about the case of sounds? In a paragraph near the above citation, where he explains the adumbration structure, Husserl uses the example of the sound of a violin, which we hear differently at various locations in a concert hall, and confirms that hearing sounds also has an adumbration structure (Husserl 1982: 96). In such an example, Husserl does not indicate that only the sound belonging to and emitted from a definite sound source can adumbrate itself. However, if we consider the above citation, in which sensible qualities are restricted to the parts or moments of things, I think we can assume that in the case of hearing the sound of a violin the essential connection to the sound sources is implicitly presupposed. In this case, however, he does not further explicate the phenomenological implication of this connection of sounds to their sources.

In this context we can find in Gurwitsch's book an interesting explication on characteristics of sounds. Gurwitsch writes the following:

> We may assume, hearing the sound, that we have no other experience, especially no visual experience, of the source of the sound. This situation occurs rather frequently. Still, the sound itself functions as an experience of its source. Apart from the apprehension of musical notes in the specific musical attitude, auditory data are not experienced as 'pure' self-contained qualities, entirely disconnected and severed from the objects by which they are emitted. Normally, and as a rule, auditory data, sounds and noises alike, are experienced as referring to their sources. (Gurwitsch 1964: 230)

In this citation Gurwitsch clearly differentiates between two modes of hearing. One is a mode of hearing in which we hear sounds in a normal everyday attitude and sounds are experienced as being emitted from certain sources. The other is a mode of hearing in which we hear sounds in a specific musical attitude and sounds—that is, musical notes are experienced as being detached from their sources. Perhaps it would be questionable if we can really hear sounds as purely self-contained and detached from any sources. As Husserl's example of hearing the sound of a violin indicates, we usually hear sounds in some spatial orientation, even in a concert hall.

In this sense, I think we should not overemphasize the difference between the two modes of hearing. But, in any way, the difference could be interpreted as a difference concerning the mode of spatial appearance just as in the case of the difference between surface and film colour, and we could use this distinction to restrict the kind of sounds that adumbrate themselves, in the same way as in the case of colours. Considering this restriction we should say that only sounds heard in an everyday attitude can retain their identity in and through various changes of appearances. Without this relation to sound sources, if the appearance of a sound changes we hear that the sound itself changes. One important point is that the difference between two modes of hearing does not originate from some subjective interpretation or volitional choice, but is found in the auditory data themselves.

(3) Ontological implications

Third, this differentiation between modes of appearances of colours and sounds has an important implication for the question of how to think about the ontological status of colours and sounds.

On the one hand, in the way appearances of colours and sounds correspond to the situation of the environment and perceiver, they have essentially a relational character. Husserl emphasizes the ontological meaning of this relational character, saying that even the omnipotent God cannot but perceive the object through 'adumbrations' (Husserl 1982: §43). The character of adumbration is not originated from the finiteness of a human perceptual capacity, but it constitutes the ontological meaning of objects of perceptions themselves. In this sense, the phenomenological theory of colours and sounds can be regarded as a kind of *relationalism*.

On the other hand, this relationalism does not exclude the fact that the perceived colours and sounds are seen as being located in an objective environment and are characterized as qualities of physical objects. It is rather the relational adumbration structure that makes it possible for colours and sounds to be perceived as being transcendent and out there in the world. In this sense this relationalism does not contradict a common-sense realism, but it gives a 'transcendental' condition of the possibility of the common-sense realism of colours and sounds.

We must add one point here. As we have seen above, not every colour or not every sound is regarded as a property of physical objects, but only surface colours and sounds heard in an everyday attitude are regarded as properties of physical objects. That means, although we can claim the realist view of colours and sounds with the help of phenomenological analysis, the realist view can be retained only in the cases of definite modes of colours and sounds. Without considering the difference between the spatial modes and restricting the scope of the concepts, questions concerning the ontological status of colours and sounds are meaningless. We must ask first what kind of colour and what kind of sound we are discussing. We cannot simply ask a question about whether colours are properties of physical objects or subjective sensations, or other kinds of being. There are no colours and no sounds as such, but various kinds of colours and various kinds of sounds. Emphasizing this variety of kinds of colours and sounds, I would like to call this characteristic *multi-dimensionality of colours and sounds*.

I think this multi-dimensionality thesis shows typically an important difference between phenomenological ontology and traditional ontology. In a traditional ontological analysis, some ontological framework, such as subjective and objective being or psychic and physical being, is presupposed, and on the basis of this framework ontological questions are posed. Under this kind of presupposition we ask, for example, a question of whether colours are subjective or objective beings. But when we pose an ontological question in this way, the role of phenomenology is restricted from the outset and the efforts to find an answer cannot but have a reductionist tendency or sometimes even an eliminativist tendency. Against these tendencies, the phenomenological ontology is characterized by the fact that a meaningful ontological claim can be made only on the basis of a phenomenological analysis of concrete phenomena. The ontological status of colours and sounds cannot be determined independently of the differentiation of modes of appearances found out in the phenomenological analysis but rather is 'constituted' by it.

In the next section I consider James. J. Gibson's ecological approach to perceptual experiences, in order to show that the multi-dimensional view is not only brought about from investigations in a philosophical armchair but is also supported by scientific empirical investigations.

3 ECOLOGICAL APPROACH: PERCEPTION OF INVARIANTS

(1) Perception as information pick-up

It is not clear whether and to what extent Gibson's ecological view was influenced by Husserl or Merleau-Ponty, but it is clear that Gibson's view was influenced by a phenomenological approach as well as Gestalt theory, because Gibson himself referred to works of D. Katz and K. Koffka in several places.

What is conspicuous in the Gibsonian approach is its fundamental criticism of the traditional approach to perception, which seems to be still dominant in orthodox psychology and cognitive sciences.

According to the traditional view, perceptual cognitions are constituted of two stages: the first stage is the reception of some input in some sense organ (formation of retinal images, for example, in the case of vision), and the second stage is the process of interpreting the inputs with various theoretical hypotheses to reach a cognition of objects (process of information processing which occurs mainly in the brain).

From this view it is important to identify what is received as inputs, and researchers prepare various experimental situations in which sensory stimuli are measured and controlled precisely. According to Gibson, 'vision is studied by first requiring the subject to fixate a point and then exposing momentarily a stimulus or a pattern of stimuli around the fixation point' (Gibson 1979: 1). Gibson calls this kind of vision 'snapshot vision'. In this approach, the snapshot vision made possible in laboratories is regarded to be a typical case of perception.

Against this approach, Gibson proposes an ecological approach, in which natural and everyday perceptions are regarded as a typical case. In everyday perceptions, perceivers interact with objects in various ways in everyday situations. Only in the process of inter-action between perceivers and objects is perception made possible. In this case, perception and action, as well as object perception and self-perception, are inseparably related (Gibson 1979: 203ff., 303).

In this ecological approach, traditional concepts such as stimulus and sensation must be radically transformed.

A stimulus is no more understood as a momentary picture such as a retinal image that is given momentarily but rather as 'information' picked up through various exploratory actions of perceivers. The function of sensation is also reinterpreted as a function of the 'perceptual system', which picks up information through interactions with objects (Gibson 1966; Gibson 1979: 238ff.).

It is not easy to understand the Gibsonian concept of information, but Gibson refers to it as an invariant structure through various changes of the relation between a per-ceiver, an environment, and an object.

Just like Husserl, Gibson emphasizes the necessity of changes and variations to obtain information on the invariant structure that corresponds to the characteristics of objects. Picking up information on an invariant structure is made possible only through various changes of perspective structures and other factors. Gibson explains this seemingly par-adoxical situation by citing the following folk wisdom: 'The more it changes, the more it is the same' (Gibson 1979: 73).

(2) An ecological optics

What is most conspicuous in the ecological approach is to focus on the important func-tion of the medium for the realization of perceptual experiences. Invariant structures are to be found in the medium, but the way the medium functions is different in each perceptual modality. In the case of visual perception, the medium is filled with illumi-nations and is called an 'illumination field'. In the case of auditory perception, the medium is filled with the vibrations of various sound waves and is called a 'vibration field' (Gibson 1966: 11f.).

In the illumination field, various lights are reflected from surfaces in the environment and constitute a stable structure that corresponds to each surface structure of the envi-ronment and is called 'ambient light' (Gibson 1966: 186ff.; Gibson 1979: 65ff.). It is the task of the ecological optics to clarify this structure of ambient lights and make a clear distinction between ambient light and radiant light. From a purely physical view, this difference has no meaning, as there is no difference when they are seen as physical energy. But, from an ecological view, the difference is decisive (Gibson 1979: 50ff.).

First, as this distinction corresponds to the distinction between luminous bodies and illuminated bodies, it corresponds to the distinction between luminous colours and sur-face colours. Whether the perceived object is a fire that shows a luminous colour or a surface of some solid thing that shows a surface colour is a decisive problem for us to survive in an environment.

Second, what is more important is that only the ambient lights that fill the empty space of the medium are essentially correlated to the surface colours and make the adumbration structure possible. That means we can pick up invariant structures through changes of ambient lights and see the same colour even if the illumination changes. In contrast, we see the colour of a luminous object differently if the radiant light emitted from it changes.

In this way, the information that can specify the character of the surface colour is implicated already in the structure of the ambient light. The fact that a colour is a surface colour is not the result of the interpretation of perceivers or merely the fact of appearance, but is a basic fact of optics—at least the fact of *ecological* optics (Gibson 1966: 214f.; Gibson 1979: 86f.). From an ecological point of view, the question of whether or not a seen colour is a surface colour is regarded as the most important and basic factor with regard to colour perception.

(3) An ecological acoustics

The situation of ecological acoustics is not very different. The information corresponding to the objects of auditory perception is considered to be implicated in the structure of the vibration field. For example, the structure of a wave front corresponds to the direction of a sound source, and the structure of a wave train corresponds to the characteristics of a sound source (Gibson 1966: 79ff.). Gibson did not explicate the structure of a vibration field in detail, but several attempts have been made to follow him.

For example, William Gaver attempts to classify three basic sorts of sound, which corresponds to three kinds of sound-producing events: that is, events involving vibrating objects (for example, the sound of a door closing), events involving aerodynamics (the sound of a balloon exploding), and events involving liquids (the sound of water dropping into a pool). According to Gaver, 'Although participants often misinterpreted the sources of sounds they heard, no mistakes crossed these categories: Nobody confused the sounds made by vibrating solids, for instance, with those made by water' (Gaver 1993: 22).

Attempts made with ecological optics and ecological acoustics still remain in a hypothetical status. However, at least they can be considered to be attempts, which support the phenomenological view we confirmed in the previous section. The multi-dimensionality of colours and sounds is not only a philosophical thesis, but it can also be regarded as a kind of research program of empirical investigations.

In this way, the ecological approach to perception could be regarded as an attempt to undertake empirical research corresponding to the phenomenological insight of perception. Ecological and phenomenological approaches can cooperate to clarify the structure of perception and perceptual phenomena such as colours and sounds. I would like to call this cooperative approach *ecological phenomenology*.

Perhaps the concept of 'ecological phenomenology' sounds a little unfamiliar, but as to the philosophical direction suggested by this concept it is not as exceptional as it seems. For example, in the so called *enactive* approach of Alva Noë (Noë 2004) and Evan

Thompson (Thompson 1995) we can find a similar direction in which a phenomenological approach is combined with an ecological one. In particular, Thompson's philosophical investigations on colour based on comparative studies of colour vision are explicitly related to the ecological view of Gibson and the phenomenological view of Merleau-Ponty. Thompson clearly criticizes two main streams of philosophical views of colour vision—computational objectivism and neurophysiological subjectivism—and proposes an alternative relational view, in which a perceptual content is regarded as relational in the sense that it is jointly constituted by a perceiver and its environment. What I have attempted to formulate here is to develop a similar relational and ecological view, focusing on the multidimensional character of colour and sound phenomena.

In the following last section I take up important problems discussed in the contemporary philosophy of colours and sounds and confirm how the viewpoint of ecological phenomenology can contribute to clarifying them.

4 Multi-dimensionality of colours and sounds

If you open standard textbooks on the science of colour, you always find the explanation that colours are constituted of three basic factors: hue, brightness, and saturation. These three factors constitute three dimensions, with which a so-called 'colour space' is formed, in which every colour is given its proper position. The difference among the spatial modes of appearances, such as surface colour, film colour, and so on, is characterized as factors that are added afterwards to these basic factors. If we take this standard view seriously, it seems as if we could fully identify colours without referring to spatiality. However, as every colour shows itself in some spatial mode in our perception, a colour without any spatial mode would be a colour that cannot be perceived.

Surely we can use the three basic factors to classify and identify various colours that are realized in some spatial mode. The tendency to identify colours with these factors has been strengthened by the development of colourimetric thinking in our contemporary science-based cultural world (Mausfeld 2010: 141). However, it does not mean that there is a colour that is constituted only of three factors. If we think it is possible, it would be a typical case of falling into 'the fallacy of misplaced concreteness' (Whitehead), which means that what is in fact the result of abstraction is confused with something that is most basic and concrete.

The situation is not very different in the case of the science of sounds. In the case of sounds, pitch, timbre, and loudness are regarded as the three basic factors that constitute the essential core of any sound. In this view, the relation to sound sources and its spatial properties is considered to be extrinsic to the basic factors.

In this way, in the standard view of colours and sounds, the thesis of multi-dimensionality is not fully recognized. This is not only true in the case of sciences but also in the case of philosophy. This disregard of multi-dimensionality sometimes brings a decisive deficit into philosophical discussions. In the following, I take up three topics, in which we can find a typical case of this disregard.

(1) Spatiality of sounds

First, I would like to take up Peter Strawson's thesis of the non-spatiality of sounds, which is one of the most popular topics in the contemporary philosophy of sounds (Strawson 1964: 59ff.).

Strawson attempted to demonstrate that sounds are intrinsically non-spatial by using an interesting thought experiment. In his thought experiment, Strawson delineated a certain possible world, in which people have only auditory experiences and these auditory experiences include nothing related to other sensory modalities. This possible world, therefore, can be regarded as a purely auditory world, and in it there are only pure sounds.

Strawson fully acknowledges that in our usual experiences we can acquire spatial information only through hearing sounds, as hearing sounds is inseparably related to other modalities, at least related to modalities such as tactual and kinaesthetic modalities, from which we can get spatial information. However, according to Strawson, if these factors are excluded and only purely auditory experiences remain, we can have no spatial information.

Strawson writes, as follows:

> Sounds of course have temporal relation to each other, and may vary in character in certain ways: in loudness, pitch and timbre. But they have no intrinsic spatial characteristics: such expressions as 'to the left of,' 'spatially above,' 'nearer,' 'farther' have no intrinsically auditory significance...A purely auditory concept of space, on the other hand, is an impossibility. (Strawson 1959: 65f.)

It is interesting that in his thought experiment Strawson attempted to construct a quasi-spatial order in a purely auditory world. He assumes that there is a 'master sound' in this purely auditory world and this master sound is always heard but changes its pitch in correlation with the appearance of various other sounds. If each sound heard at each time is combined with the state of the pitch of the master sound, we could regard each state of pitch as a kind of 'location' of the sound in the auditory world, and the values of the pitch could be regarded as constituting a quasi-spatial order. But, according to Strawson, it remains only a *quasi*-spatial order and cannot be regarded as a spatial order in the usual sense.

Strawson's attempt is interesting, but it also contains a decisive deficit. First, his description premises that we could easily imagine a purely auditory world, in which we can hear relatively distinctive sounds. However, if we try, we immediately notice that it is not easy to imagine such a world, because in our everyday situation every clear sound is heard as being emitted from some source and as having some spatial meaning.

Perhaps, having the experience of some peculiar sounds ringing in one's ears is an example, in which we cannot attribute a clear spatial location to sounds. Or, if we are in a room which is filled with loud sounds and we cannot recognize where the sound sources are located, we would have such an experience. However, even if we admit there are cases in which we would experience sounds without definite locations, the sounds we hear in such cases are very unclear and indistinctive, and sometimes chaotic.

In the first section we have seen, with the help of the indication of Gurwitsch, that there is a possibility of hearing sounds as self-contained and detached from sound sources. But this is a possibility only when we adopt a specific attitude—the musical attitude—and it does not entail the possibility that there might be a world in which only pure sounds exist.

In fact, when Strawson explains the characteristics of his 'master sound', he compares it to the sounds emitted from a broken radio. He says that it is like 'the persistent whistle, of varying pitch, which, in a wireless set in need of repair, sometimes accompanies the programs we listen to' (Strawson 1964: 76). This explanation clearly shows that even in cases in which we think we can imagine a non-spatial sound we need to connect images of non-spatial sounds to some sound sources, explicitly or implicitly, in order to make it understandable. In this way, it is questionable if Strawson's world is really a world of non-spatial sounds.

Second, perhaps the difficulty of imagining the world of non-spatial sounds comes from the limited capacity of the imagination of philosophers, and there remains a possibility that in reality there is an example of non-spatial sounds. Indeed, in cases of patients with brain damage, for example, we sometimes find unimaginable pathological cases, which surpass the philosophers' imagination by far.

In the case of visual perception, for example, it has become known that in a brain there are two different pathways, which can function independently. The first pathway deals with the cognition of the localization of objects (where system), and the other deals with the function of the identification of objects (what system). This dual-system theory of vision is supported by pathological cases: in one case, a patient can recognize what an object is but cannot find where it is and cannot control her action toward it (visual ataxia), and in another case a patient can perform actions related to various objects, but she cannot answer the question of what the objects are (visual agnosia) (Goodale and Milner 2004).

Recently, it has become clear that a similar situation can be found in the case of audition. There is a case of a patient who can recognize what an object is but cannot find where it is (spatial deaf) and a patient who can find where an object is but cannot recognize what it is (auditory agnosia) (Casati and Dokic 2009: 107; Clarke et al. 2002). Perhaps this way of describing the present research situation is an oversimplification. But, in any case, there is a physiological theory, according to which it is logically possible that one experiences sounds without spatial information.

In spite of this possibility of thinking of a world of non-spatial sounds, we must point out that it does not mean that such an auditory experience of sounds is a form of pure and basic hearing, and that it constitutes a basic level of every kind of hearing. Even if we admit that there is such a case of experiencing non-spatial sounds, we must be careful not to forget that it is only one kind of experience—indeed, an exceptional and pathological kind of experience—and it is far from being the purest kind of auditory experience. If one regards the exceptional case as a basic and pure case, it would be nothing but falling into a 'fallacy of misplaced concreteness'.

(2) Constancy of colour

One of the characteristics of surface colour is its essential connection to illumination. In fact, when we see some surface colour we always see it in and through some illumination, which we simultaneously notice in some sense. This essential relation between surface colour and illumination plays an important role in understanding the familiar phenomenon of colour constancy.

One of the conspicuous characteristics of colour vision in our everyday lives is that they show a remarkable constancy over a wide range of illumination changes. If the colours perceived on the surfaces of things change corresponding to changes in the composition of reflected lights that reach our eyes, we cannot attribute a definite and stable colour to the surface of things. In this sense, colour constancy, as well as size and shape constancy, plays a central role in our visual lives, but the explanation of this phenomenon still remains a major task for the science of vision.

One of the reasons for the difficulty in understanding colour constancy is that constancy is not perfect. Colour constancy, just as in the case of size and shape constancy, does not mean that the appearances of an object do not change and continue to be the same.

For example, when we see some object in sunlight at first and then in shadow, we see that the colour does not change (successive constancy). At the same time, we notice that the illumination changes and the appearance of the colour changes. We see the sameness of the colour and the changes of its appearances at the same time. This is exactly the structure of perception we identified with the help of the Husserlian concept of adumbration. In this sense, we can interpret that Husserl's analysis of adumbration is a general theory of constancy phenomenon, which we experience in everyday perception.

In addition, we have also confirmed that an understanding of the multi-dimensionality of colours is necessary to understand the adumbration structure of colours appropriately. This implies that the concept of multi-dimensionality would also help to understand colour constancy appropriately.

Now, to understand the role of the multi-dimensionality of colours in the case of colour constancy, I would like to take up the analysis proposed by Jonathan Cohen (Cohen 2009: 53ff.).

Cohen uses a photograph of a coffee cup on a table. The coffee cup is located partially in direct sunlight and partially in shadow (simultaneous constancy). According to Cohen, the regions of the coffee cup (and the table) that are in sunlight are perceptually distinguishable by the subject from the (qualitatively identical) contiguous regions of the coffee cup (and the table) that are in shadow, so we can say that there is a perceptual variation in respect of colour.

On the one hand, subjects judge that adjacent regions have one colour rather than two. On the other hand, it is meaningful to say that subjects will judge that the two regions are not alike in colour.

On the basis of these interpretations of the phenomenon, Cohen describes the problem in the following way:

> So it looks as if the neutral thing to say is that subjects in colour constancy experiments actually make two different judgements: they judge not only that the two regions of interest are (in some sense) alike in colour, and also that the two regions are (in some sense) not alike in colour. (Cohen 2009: 55)

Probably the immediate critical response to this way of grasping the example would be to say that the two judgements of the subject cannot be accepted in the same way. That means, we can claim that the subject does not judge that two regions are not alike in colour in spite of the perceptual variation. However, according to Cohen, this kind of response does not solve the problem but only raises another problem, namely the problem of answering the question of what colour it is that the subject judges to be alike. There are two possible answers: one is the colour of the region in sunlight, and the other is the colour of the region in shadow. However, neither answer would be persuasive because the two regions clearly appear not to share it.

In the face of this difficulty, Cohen proposes an answer in which a counterfactual condition has a decisive role. He proposes that if the subject judges that two regions share a same colour, it does not mean that two regions share one of the occurrently manifesting colours, but it means that they share a colour that is not occurrently manifesting: 'That is, the subject judges that, although the sunlit region looks different (in respect of colour) from the region in shadow, the two regions would look the same (in respect of colour) were they both viewed under sunlight' (Cohen 2009: 56). In this way he finds a counterfactual judgement at the core of the phenomena of colour constancy.

In one sense Cohen points out an important character of colour constancy in showing that the occurrently manifesting perceived colours are not seen as constant and no manifesting colour can be recognized as a veridical colour of the object. Husserl already clearly pointed out that no appearance has a privileged status in respect of validity in the adumbration structure (Husserl 1982: 96).

On the other hand, Cohen's way of grasping the problem of colour constancy is a typical case of the disregard of the multi-dimensionality of colours. Indeed, while the colour of the coffee cup perceived in sunlight is a surface colour, the colour of the coffee cup perceived in shadow is the colour of the casted shadow. The colour of the shadow cast does not show itself in the spatial mode of surface colour but in the spatial mode of film colour (Gibson 1966: 213), so we cannot simply compare the two colours. They are not merely different colours, but different *kinds* of colour.

This difference in the kind of colours corresponds to the difference in illuminations. We experience not only two different kinds of colour, but also two different kinds of illumination. One is illumination that illuminates one part of the coffee cup and the other is illumination that cast a shadow on the other part of the coffee cup. The two parts of the coffee cup appear in different 'perspectives of illumination' (Katz 1935: 79f., 95)—or in other words, in a different 'depth' that is made by different kinds of illumination.

If we take a photograph of the object, the difference between the surface colour and the colour of the casted shadow (film colour) is diminished, and correspondingly, the difference of illumination—that is, the difference of 'depth' constituted by illumination is diminished as well. Colours perceived on photographs and colours perceived in our usual situations are different kinds of colour.

In spite of these circumstances, if we regard colours on a photograph as a typical case of colours we see and on the basis of which we interpret the phenomena of colour constancy, it is again an example of the fallacy of misplaced concreteness.

From these considerations I hope it has become clear that to understand the phenomena of colour constancy it is necessary to confirm the inevitability of the change of colour appearances and the role of illumination. If we consider these points seriously we can immediately understand the reason why the orthodox computationalist view of colour constancy is destined to fail. According to the orthodox view, colour constancy is explained by the recovery process that eliminates the effect of illuminations and picks out the surface reflectance of objects on the basis of given data. In this view, the role of illumination is totally neglected, and constancy is interpreted as an unchanged identity. Against this one-sided view we must emphasize that changes of colour appearances according to the changes of illumination play an important ecological role in our everyday life, as we can notice a range of important environmental properties, such as weather conditions and time of day (Thompson 1995: 102, 196f.; Jameson and Hurvich 1997: 178).

(3) Quality or event?

Until now I have thematized mainly the similar structures of colours and sounds, but have not focused on their differences. At least, as far as fundamental characteristics, such as adumbration and multi-dimensionality, are concerned, we have no reason to emphasize differences rather than similarities from a viewpoint of ecological phenomenology.

Traditionally, although there have been endless disputes concerning the ontological status of colours and sounds, there has been a common understanding that they are similarly regarded as sensible qualities.

However, in the recent philosophy of sounds, the question of whether colours and sounds can be regarded as qualities of objects has become one of the important problems. On the basis of the temporal character of sounds, some philosophers propose the *event theory* of sounds, claiming that sounds must be regarded as events and not qualities of things, and emphasize the uniqueness of sounds in contrast to other sensible qualities.

Even among philosophers who make claims for the event theory of sounds, there seem to be subtle or fundamental differences (Nudds and O'Callaghan 2009), but what is interesting in our context is the question of whether we can deal with colours and sounds in a similar way. If not, we need to fundamentally revise our phenomenological and ecological view concerning the ontology of colours and sounds.

In the following final part, when considering the question of if colours and sounds can and must be regarded as being fundamentally different in respect of their ontological status, I will take up discussions of Casey O'Callaghan, who emphasizes their ontological difference.

One of the discussions O'Callaghan presents is as follows:

> In short, sounds have durations. A sound has a beginning, a middle, and an end. But not only do sounds continue through time, sounds also survive changes to their properties across time. A pitch shift is not the end of a sound. Unlike the way that a wall loses one colour and gains another when it is painted, an object does not lose its sound and gains an entirely new one when it goes from being low-pitched to being high-pitched, as with an ambulance siren's wail. A sound can have a low-pitched part and a high-pitched part, and this is not just a matter of some source's being low-pitched at one time and high pitched at another. Rather, a distinct particular survives the change. (O'Callaghan 2007: 22)

O'Callaghan proposes an interesting and unique claim that sounds are not the properties of some objects but rather are particular individuals, which have various properties. I think the claim that sounds are particular individuals has certain validity. In some cases, sounds, in comparison to colours, show themselves as being relatively independent from their sources. For example, Gurwitsch points out an interesting example of hearing a human voice. Even when we find out that the sound is produced by a phonograph, 'the sound continues to present itself in immediate experience as coming from a human voice' (Gurwitsch 1964: 233). This is an interesting point that might be discussed further, as it can be interpreted as an example that shows a peculiar spatial character of recorded sounds. But I would like here to focus on the problem of whether the reasons referred to in the citation are sufficient for demonstrating the fundamental difference between colours and sounds.

Surely, as the citation indicates, when a new colour is painted on a wall we will probably admit that the colour of the wall itself changes. In contrast, there are cases in which a sound survives the changes to its properties, as in the case of an ambulance siren, and we say that we hear the same sound of siren for a certain duration.

However, is the difference O'Callaghan mentions so decisive that we can draw an ontological conclusion from it? I think the comparison seems to be rather arbitrary, as we must take into consideration that there are various kinds of colour and various kinds of sound.

First, think of the possible case of the warning light of an ambulance, which changes its brightness together with the change of pitch of the siren. Do we see, in such a case, that the light loses its bright red colour and gains a new dark red colour? I think the answer is ambiguous. But, at least if we consider the luminous colour of a warning light instead of the surface colour of a wall, the difference between sounds and colours is not so obvious. On the other hand, if the sound of the siren changes not only its pitch but also timbre and other characteristics, it is not clear if we hear a continuous identical sound. For example, if one part is constituted of a melody of some music and the other part is constituted of the sound of the siren, I think it is difficult to say that the sound does not change. In this way, the difference between the two cases O'Callaghan describes as contrastive seems to be rather arbitrary and not so persuasive.

Second, there are not only sounds that are heard as being clearly emitted from some definite object, but also sounds that come from a main city road or highway and are heard constantly in our everyday lives. This kind of sound constitutes the background of our auditory life and is used by blind people to identify their positions when they navigate in a city. In this case, a background sound plays a similar role to what Strawson attributed to the master sound in his imaginative auditory world. But, this time the background sound helps people to perceive not a quasi-spatial order but a real spatial order (Sasaki 2001).

In addition, it is not a rare experience for us to investigate the content of a thing by tapping it and hearing the sound emitted from it. For example, when we buy a watermelon, we tap it and listen to the sound coming from it to conclude if it is sufficiently ripe. This is a typical way of 'giving a voice to a mute object' (Ihde 2007: 67).

There are people (DAKENSHI) in Japan who earn their living by tapping a large number of cans in order to investigate whether or nor their contents are defective. In such a case, hearing the sound means nothing more than investigating to find out if the contents are defective or not. The situation is not very different from the situation in which we investigate it by seeing the colour of the content (Oukura 2001). This means that there is a case in which we hear a sound that informs us about the properties of things, just as seeing the colour shows us the properties of things.

Third, when we consider some kind of event, which we experience in multiple modalities, the difference between colours and sounds seems to be all the more superficial. Take the example of the perception of a fire. When we encounter an event of something burning, we see the luminous colour, hear the sound of burning, feel the heat of the fire, smell the odour of burning, and so on. The way of perceiving is very different corresponding to the different sense modalities, but what is perceived through these different modalities can be considered to be the same object: namely, a fire.

J. Gibson characterizes this circumstance as 'the partial equivalence of perceptual systems' and describes it as follows:

> Consider a fire—that is, a terrestrial event with flames and fuel. It is a source of four kinds of stimulation, since it gives off sound, odour, heat, and light. It crackles, smokes, radiates in the infrared band, and radiates or reflects in the visible band. Accordingly it provides information for the ears, the nose, the skin, and the eyes. The crackling sound, the smoky odour, the projected heat, and the projected dance of the coloured flames all specify the same event, and each alone specifies the event. One can hear it, smell it, feel it, and see it, or get any combination of these detections, and thereby perceive a fire. Vision provides the most detailed information, with unique colours, shapes, textures, and transformations, but any one of the others will also serve. For this event, the four kinds of stimulus information and the four perceptual systems are *equivalent*. (Gibson 1966: 54)

Surely in the case of a fire, the object is an event whose temporal character is conspicuous and it is relatively easy to find a similar structure in different modalities. In this sense we cannot generalize this case without any restriction. And even in this case we cannot neglect differences between the perceptual modalities. As Gibson himself indicates, the kinds of information and the degree of detail in the information are different, corresponding to each modality. However, what we perceive through different modalities remains the same.

If we take these cases into consideration I think we need not overemphasize differences among perceptual modalities, especially between colours and sounds. This confirmation provides us with an interesting insight into a unity of our experiences.

The concept of multi-dimensionality makes us notice the remarkable diversity of the world of colours and sounds. There are not only different colours and different sounds, but also different kinds of colour and different kinds of sound, which open up various spatialities and dimensions. On the other hand, this multi-dimensionality makes us notice the equivalence of different senses, or at least partial equivalence, as Gibson indicated. Although we experience objects through a variety of different ways, our experiences are not divided into pieces. Rather, because of this diversity and because of the multiplicity of dimensions, our experiential world is unified at least in a partial way.

5 Conclusion

What can we learn for the phenomenology of perception when we focus our attention on colours and sounds that play an important role in constituting our field of perceptual consciousness? This is the original question with which I began this article.

We have surveyed a variety of phenomena concerning colours and sounds. But, I hope one point has become clear. Colours and sounds do not only fill the formal structure of the field of consciousness, they exhibit the diversity and multiple dimensionality of the field of consciousness. We do not live in a one-dimensional world but in a multi-dimensional world that implicates various depths corresponding to various kinds of colours and sounds. It is not the case that there is a common formal field structure, which is filled with a variety of sensible qualities. Rather, there are a variety of field structures corresponding to various qualities, and through this diversity the 'unity' of a world emerges.

It is important to notice that the diversity and multi-dimensionality does not contradict the unity of our experiences and the unity of our world. Husserl expressed this insight with his well-known concept of adumbration. Gibson expressed it with the phrase 'The more it changes, the more it is the same'. And perhaps Gurwitsch implicitly indicated it with his concept of organizational unity that is 'autochthonously' realized in the field of consciousness.

In any case, this seemingly paradoxical structure of perception is a remarkable riddle, which continues to attract and motivate every phenomenologist to investigate the perceptual world endlessly.

REFERENCES

Casati, R. and Dokic, J. (2009), 'Some variety of spatial hearing', in M. Nudds and C. O'Callaghan (eds), *Sounds and Perception: New Philosophical Essays* (Oxford: Oxford University Press), pp. 97–110.

Clarke, S., Bellmann Thiran, A., Maeder, P., Vernet, O., Regli, L., Cuisenaire, O., and Thiran, J. P. (2002), 'What and where in human audition: Selective deficits following focal hemispheric lesions', *Experimental Brain Research* 147: 8–15.

Cohen, J. (2009), *The Red and the Real: An Essay on Color Ontology* (Oxford: Oxford University Press).

Embree, L. (2010), 'Editorial Introduction', in R. Zaner and L. Embree (eds), *The Collected Works of Aron Gurwitsch (1901–1973), Volume 3, The Field of Consciousness: Phenomenology of Theme, Thematic Field, and Marginal Consciousness* (Dordrecht: Springer), pp. 413–45.

Gaver, W. (1993), 'What in the world do we hear?: An ecological approach to auditory event perception', *Ecological Psychology* 5/1: 1–29.

Gibson, J. J. (1966), *The Senses Considered as Perceptual Systems* (Boston: Houghton Mifflin Company).

—— (1979), *The Ecological Approach to Visual Perception* (Boston: Houghton Mifflin Company).

Goodale, M., and Milner, A. D. (2004), *Sight Unseen: An Exploration of Conscious and Unconscious Vision* (Oxford: Oxford University Press).

Gurwitsch, A. (1964), *The Field of Consciousness*, (Pittsburgh: Duquesne University Press).

Husserl, E. (1982), *Ideas Pertaining to a Pure Phenomenology and a Phenomenological Philosophy*, First Book, tr. F. Kersten (The Hague: M. Nijhoff).

Ihde, D. (2007), *Listening and Voice: Phenomenology of sound*, Second Edition (Albany: SUNY Press).

Jameson, D. and Hurvich, L. M. (1997), 'Essay Concerning Color constancy', in A. Byrne and D. R. Hilbert (eds) *Readings on Color, Volume 2: The Science of Color* (Cambridge, MA, and London: MIT Press), pp. 177–98.

Katz, D. (1935), *The World of Colour*, tr. R. B. MacLeod and C. W. Fox (London: Kegan Paul; reprinted by Routledge, 2002).

Mausfeld, R. (2010), 'Color within an internalist framework: The role of 'color' in the structure of the perceptual system', in J. Cohen and M. Matthen (ed.), *Color Ontology and Color Science* (Cambridge, MA: MIT Press).

Noë, A. (2004), *Action in Perception* (Cambridge, MA, and London: MIT Press).

Nudds, M., and O'Callaghan, C., (eds) (2009), *Sounds and Perception: New Philosophical Essays* (Oxford: Oxford University Press).

O'Callaghan, C. (2007), *Sounds: A Philosophical Theory* (Oxford: Oxford University Press).

Oukura, M. (2001), 'The skill of DAKENSHI', in M. Sasaki and H. Mishima (eds), *Affordance and Action* (in Japanese) (Tokyo: Kaneko Shobou), pp. 162–96.

Sasaki, M. (2001), 'Navigation and Occlusion', in M. Sasaki and H. Mishima (eds), *Affordance and Action* (in Japanese) (Tokyo: Kaneko Shobou), pp. 85–130.

Strawson, P. (1964), *Individuals: An Essay in Descriptive Metaphysics*, University Paperbacks (London: Methuen).

Thompson, E. (1995), *Colour Vision: A Study in Cognitive Science and the Philosophy of Perception* (London and New York: Routledge).

CHAPTER 9

···

BODILY INTENTIONALITY, AFFECTIVITY, AND BASIC AFFECTS

···

DONN WELTON

> It is not I who play
> it is the music
> the music plays itself
> is played
> plays me
> small part of an innumerable
> unnumberable orchestra.
> I am flung from note to note
> impaled on melody
> my wings are caught on throbbing filaments of light.
>
> Madeline L'Engle (2005: 37)

THE concepts of affects and affectivity are simultaneously two of the most promising and the most confused ideas under current discussion. They are *confused* because they tend to become *fused* and then taken as equivalent to inner feelings or, alternatively, emotions. Yet they are *promising* because, to put it negatively, they stand at the intersection where the modern notions of mind and body collide and prove themselves untenable, and, to put it positively, they open up a different account of the motivational structure of action and, with it, an internal connection between intentional and bodily structures.

One of the reasons why the notion of affectivity and the complementary concept of engagement are so difficult for phenomenological analysis is that they are resistant to a direct reflective account and can be approached only by moving through the surface structure of intentionality to the deep structure making it possible. This paper begins by taking that path. Without moving to the deep structure, the notions of affectivity and engagement will inevitably get misplaced. I am forced to assume that this path is somewhat familiar as I can offer only the barest of sketches, with little argumentation, and will have to move much more quickly than I should.

1 THE INTENTIONAL STRUCTURE OF ACTION AND INVOLVEMENT

A phenomenological analysis of intentionality argues that any perceptual *object* (x) is given one-sidedly in and through its *profiles*, its *facets* (f), and furthermore, is always given *as* something, as configured by its qualitative determinations or 'senses' (y). 'The given' here is complex due to its *as-structure*:

(1) f/x-as-y

The presence of profiles, to carry this further, entails *perspectives*, and the presence of determinations entails *discriminations*. There is one (s) *to* whom or *for* whom significant objects are present in and through a set of cognitive acts[1] that *perceive* or, more broadly, *present* (p) the object. The as-structure, then, does not stand alone but entails a *for-structure* and, thus, acts that *strive* toward an *optimal* or *normative* presentation of the f/x-as-y (see Kelly 2010).

(2) s/p-of-f/x-as-y

Profiles do not refer to but open upon or point to yet others.[2] The movement from profile to profile—and, thereby, for the progressive appearance of the object as a whole in and through its profiles—is controlled by the actual and virtual sense(s) of the object. This implies that each node in a web of senses is internally related to the others, that its 'content' is dependent upon ties of similarity, contrast and opposition to yet other senses. To reframe this in terms of experiential acts, which should be understood as what Husserl would call noetic achievements or enactments (*Leistungen*), the senses constitutive of manifest perceptual objects are themselves constituted by different *schemata* of perceptual discrimination—a type of accomplishment quite different from conceptual sorting. Yet this also implies that a perceptual event is situated in something larger than itself, that it is rooted in multiple webs without which its content would lack sufficient identity and difference to be discriminatory. Husserl characterizes the *being* of such webs as *horizonal*.

---

[1] 'Cognitive acts' is a placeholder until the next paragraph.
[2] The meaning-reference dyad works for speech but not perception.

What this analysis suggests, then, is yet a deeper dimension of intentionality. The treatment of intentionality as involving horizons carries in its wake an extension of the basic structure of s/p-of-f/x-as-y. In addition to the as-structure (f/x is always f/x-as-y) and the for-structure (f/x-as-y is always f/x-as-y-for-s) intentional objects and, by extension, the acts of perceiving intentional objects are always situated in the *world*. The world, transcendentally characterized, is the space of significance.[3] Intentionality has an *in-structure* and it is twofold. Each manifest object is always in the world; each f/x-as-y is always f/x-as-y-in-w. Yet we have already seen that f/x-as-y is necessarily situated in s/p-of-f/x-as-y. By implication, not only the object but also the entire event is organized by the in-structure: each s/p-of-f/x-as-y is always

(3)   [s/p-of-f/x-as-y]-in-w

The introduction of the world into our account of intentionality must be understood correctly. The fact that f/x-as-y is always situated *within* a world is made possible by the fact that the whole structure of s/p-of-f/x-as-y is itself *in* the world. Tracing the situational character of what is given *to* consciousness leads us to the horizonal character *of* consciousness. We just saw how the in-structure expands our notion of intentionality and situates it within horizons. I now want to suggest that it also enlarges our understanding of the nature of perceptual acts by situating them in the realm of *action*.

Studies of acts in contrast to action carry the weight of many traditional accounts because action is generally treated as bodily movement expressive of or 'motivated' by intentional acts. The effect of this is to relegate action to a supporting role, i.e., to allow action to be contained by an analysis of consciousness. Heidegger's displacement of consciousness by a structural analysis of Dasein certainly had the effect of recentering action and making consciousness secondary, almost incidental. But the difference between regional or what he called 'ontic' analysis, to which he relegated accounts of the body, and ontological analysis, as well as his framing of the latter as transcendental,[4] meant that his structural account of action *cannot* have specific reference to the body. Ironically, with the eclipse of consciousness as a primary focus of his phenomenology, the living human body was lost as well.

Some analytic accounts fare worse. It is not the requirements of a transcendental account, which do continue to pose interesting issues, but rather the boundaries of a Cartesian field of discourse that keep the players running for one goal or the other, for either reducing consciousness materially or functionally to the body, or for a certain autonomy to first person descriptions of conscious life in which the body, impenetrable

---

[3] For a discussion of this see Welton 2003.

[4] 'Every disclosure of being as the *transcendens* is *transcendental* knowledge. *Phenomenological truth* (*disclosedness of being*) is *veritas transcendentalis*.' All the concepts of his fundamental ontology, 'all fundamental existentials,' posses 'transcendental 'universality'.'' (Heidegger 1928: 38, 200/34, 185). On the relationship between transcendental analysis and an analysis of the body see note 20 below.

from this perspective, has nothing to offer to its phenomenal structure. Here the irony doubled: in the very process of rejecting the Cartesian solution, it nevertheless accepted its operative framework; in accepting its framework, much of current philosophy of mind loses the possibility of a richer account of the body and affectivity that would have taken it outside of that framework.

Except for brains in vats and philosophers in chairs, perceptual acts are internally connected to getting about in the world. Seeing a stick as a sword is only possible for ones who engage in fighting and who take it as such while they march off to battle, be it real or imaginary. And this entails that acts that are specimens of presenting are not just ways of 'taking' but also ways of 'taking up' objects. Before perceptual acts are representing, and well before they are cases of conceptual sorting, they are tethered to ways of handling or coming to grips with materials at hand. With the in-structure now in play, perceptual acts are controlled by *acting upon* and *acting toward*. As such, they are always integrated into *actions*, even if that action is nothing more than sitting still.

Yet not all action is guided or directed by *prior* intentional acts, which is how actions are frequently treated, even in the phenomenological literature. To be sure, we often do find what can be called *intention-of-action*. I decide to have my favorite lunch and set about fixing my usual recipe of sardines, blue cheese and sour milk in my blender. I will call this type of action *scripted*. My prior intention guides my action, with a conceptual matrix determining the focus of my action and even the act of seeing. In intention-of-action vision is invested with an epistemic interest in which seeing is tied to looking-for and looking-for is guided by propositional content.

By contrast, *intention-in-action* does not require a prior intention, for the intention is formed in and by the action itself. In the heat of a game the action of picking up and throwing a baseball itself constitutes the intention to throw it. Or consider spontaneously reaching out and flipping the wall switch as you enter a room. Doing so forms the intention to turn on the light. The chipped blade of the jackplane has me reaching for the smoothing plane next to its vacated slot in the tool cabinet without a moment's hesitation and without a prior well-formed intention. An *unscripted* action does depend upon a preconscious acquaintance with our ability to move and take up the objects with which we are involved, as well as upon a task and, more broadly, upon a practice organizing the chain of actions. But treating its 'intentional content' as a conceptually formed belief is a product of reflecting upon the action after the fact. It assumes that unscripted action is regulated by rules and then conflates acting according to a rule with acting by or following a rule, taking the rule, which is *post hoc*, as *propter hoc*.

This type of action, of course, is not blind and there is a type of vision or, more generally, perception that is embedded in and controlled by the intention-in-action. Here the 'sight' of the ball, the switch or the plane utilizes different schemata of discrimination and discernment internally tied to possible ways of engaging the object. There is a co-dependency between the place and the manifest features of the object, on the one hand, and the way we act in relation to it, on the other. Caught in the rain while hiking the Long Trail, for example, we first see what is before us as a place of shelter into which we can scurry and only subsequently as a hole in the side of a cliff. After leaving the bat, the ball is seen as catchable or not by the fielder and, so framed, as a solid, round object. J. J. Gibson, using Kurt Lewin's notion of 'affordances' (*Aufforderungscharakte*; see Gibson 1986: 138), captures phenomena like this and allows us to see that with intention-in-action the content of the embedded perceptual act is not defined by a core of 'physical' features to which the action adds 'practical' properties. Rather, having a tacit familiarity with possible bodily schemata of action is a setting condition for perceptual acts to apprehend the sort of basic features that they do. With the onset of rain the action is drawn to or, better, *inclined toward* the cave, which is manifest as what 'affords' shelter and invites us to scurry inside it. Here perceptual content, action and world are interlocked and frame the intention in play.[5] In turn, the perception (p-of) in play is one that *discerns* the usability of the object as it facilitates the ongoing course of action.

In treating action we need, then, to distinguish between at least these two types of intentional structures:

(4) i-in-a [s/p-of-f/x-as-y]-in-w
(5) i-of-a [s/p-of-f/x-as-y]-in-w

While intention-in-action and intention-of-action are the two poles establishing the limits of any concrete action,[6] they are asymmetrical, with intention-in-action being developmentally and systematically more basic. It requires nothing of language and the huge edifice of conceptual thinking to crawl about in the world or run for cover.[7]

The concept of intention-in-action allows us to enrich our initial characterization of the in-structure. We often perceive what, at first, may be indistinct but, as it emerges from its cover and catches our attention, what then takes on a certain significance, a certain as-structure sustained by a certain for-structure. Here the act is in a *receptive* mode.[8] By contrast, the in-structure accounts for how those objects that are experienced fit into

---

[5] Heidegger characterizes such objects as 'ready-to-hand' (*Zuhandenes*) and this type of vision 'circumspection' (*Umsicht*), but fails in *Being and Time* to root his analysis in either a rich account of consciousness or a robust theory of action. See 1928, §15; 1996, §15.

[6] A richer definition of intentionality with the full range of the in-structure in play, I am suggesting, must tether it to action and speak of both intention-in-action and intention-of-action, of both unscripted and scripted action. A particular concrete intentional action, in fact, might be situated between two limits: (a) the first where a deliberate intention alone defines and directs the action and where the content of the embedded act guiding the action is propositional, and (b) the second where the action alone delimits the intention and where even the imbedded act achieves non-propositional discriminations controlled by schemes of action. In the latter case our actions are drawn toward objects whose actual and virtual features are determined by what matters for action. This is central to our account as it allows us to get at a notion of action that does not treat it as the effect of active intentions and decisions.

[7] The relationship between training and coping is complex but even when an action involves training, it ceases being constitutive once the action becomes habitual and fluid. On this and related matters see the recent controversy between Dreyfus and McDowell (Dreyfus 2005, McDowell 2007, and Dreyfus 2007).

[8] The tendency in Husserl is to restrict the notion of affectivity to the domain of perception and to understand it as 'an allure exercised on consciousness [*bewußtseinsmäßigen Reiz*], a peculiar pull that an object given to consciousness exercises on the ego.' (Husserl 1966: 148/196). By contrast, we are interested in affectivity not as the most basic receptive mode of the *for*-structure but as what co-determines the *in*-structure.

that horizon that frames our existence as a whole, how they do not just catch our attention but also *take hold* of us. The sense of the emerging object itself is always situated in a space of significance to which we are open and from which we live. This openness, a function of our involvement in situations, we will call *affectivity*.[9] We are not just *receptive* beings, capable of registering what appears to us, we are also *responsive* beings capable of caring about what appears. Affectivity means that we are constituted in such a way that things and situations *matter* to us.[10]

Situations that matter, however, are also situations with which we are occupied. Acting upon a particular object that matters to us presupposes that our being in situations is one of *engagement*. Affectivity and engagement are 'equiprimordial' (*gleichursprünglich*) moments of our being-in. What we are calling the in-structure, then, is sustained by *in-volvement*.[11] To get at this from the side of the object, the interrelationship of objects within the world is predicated upon the in-volvement of us as acting agents in the world. This takes us back to the issue at hand: the primary mode of in-volvement is intention-in-action. In turn, the *dynamics* of intention-in-action are constituted by affectivity and engagement.

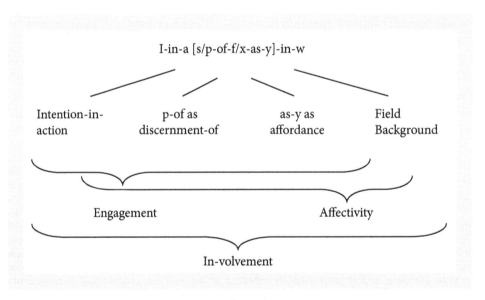

The scope of in-volvement.

[9] Heidegger attempts to capture this with his notion of this *Befindlichkeit* (see Heidegger 1928: §29). But Heidegger does not have what we have found, namely the sense in which Dasein is 'flesh' and rooted in a 'felt' rapport with others and the world. See note 21 for further detail on this issue.

[10] Crowell also argues this point (see Crowell 2005: 100).

[11] In discussing involvement (*Bewandtnis*) Heidegger restricts it to 'the to-be of beings in the world.' Even though 'the totality of involvements' tracks back to Dasein, he uses the term mainly to characterize the ready-to-hand as a whole and not the being-in of Dasein, which he describes in terms of affectivity

With the notion of intention-in-action in hand we are now in a position to under-write our very provisional sketch of intentionality: non-epistemic perceptual intention-ality is internally connected to intention-in-action, which, for its part, is rooted in the interplay of affectivity and engagement. This yields a richer understanding of the in-structure. As undergirded by affectivity, the world is *background*, the dark horizon *from* which object-complexes emerge that solicit actions directed toward them. As sustained by engagement, the world is the *field* of *possible* actions that articulate and transform significant objects inviting our dealings with them. With affectivity, our being becomes being-in; with engagement our being-in becomes a being-beyond.

You will, no doubt, be puzzled by the fact that we have been able to introduce the notion of affectivity without so much as mentioning a single affect. Only a batty philoso-pher, of course, would attempt this. This account is still formal for yet another reason: it lacks any consideration of the *motivational* structure accounting for the dynamics of intention-in-action. I will look to the internal connection between basic affects to get at the *emergence* of affectivity in the next section, holding off a fuller discussion of motiva-tion and the interplay of affectivity and engagement until the third section.

2 BASIC AFFECTS AND THE EMERGENCE OF AFFECTIVITY

In receptivity, as we have described it, we often find a certain dissonance or disruption within the field of experience. A sudden intrusion, a partially concealed shape, or a con-fusing presentation beckons, catches our attention and invites exploration. With the noetic mode of the perceiver being receptive, the emerging object coming into an 'opti-mal' present controls the perceptual experience. With its 'primordial vivacity', what Husserl calls 'affective force' is in play (Husserl 1966: 169/218).We have also seen that objects correlated to particular actions are often manifest in terms of their affordances, a set of features that invite us to use them. Introducing this more 'pragmatic' characteri-zation of features stands the modern approach since Hobbes and Descartes on its head, for now the use-features of objects gain primacy over the physical features it took as experientially basic. But even this pragmatic approach runs the risk of missing an entire dimension of the constitution of salient objects and, thereby, the noetic conditions making it possible. Things matter not just because they intrude and not just because they fit into a practical project or problem that requires their use and invests them with relevance. Things in situations also matter because they give us pleasure or cause us pain, provide gratification or drive us to frustration, capture our heart or tear it to

(*Befindlichkeit*) and understanding (*Verstehen*). Our contrast is not between affectivity and understanding but affectivity and engagement, treating both as co-dependent modes of involvement that characterize the in-structure of embodied existence as a whole. See Heidegger 1928: 83–5, 134–40, 142–6/77–80, 126–31, 134–9.

shreds. Objects can exercise not just a pull upon our attention or an invitation to take them in hand, but they can also quicken a *longing* or, perhaps, *revulsion*. Indeed, our actions are as much controlled by these features as they are by affordances. Here the disruption is not 'conceptual' and not (yet) 'emotional', but properly affective, for it traffics in the *alluring* or *repelling* powers of objects, be they present or absent, and in bodily *tendencies* calling us to action. Even before what we normally think of as experiential acts and even before emotions, there is a level of what I will call basic affects.[12] It has received scant attention in the philosophical literature. But just what are they and how can they be described?

If all emotions are understood as act modalities (loving, hating, and so on) correlated to specific thetic qualities of objects (the beloved, the hated, and so on), basic affects, as I will use the term, belong to a realm subtending what we usually identify as intentional acts. Basic affects, I will suggest, consist of *needs, wants,* and *desires.* They function more like the setting conditions for intentional acts than one of them. At the same time, they cannot be reduced to bodily sensations as they, in some sense, involve appraisal. With them values arise (Fridja 2000: 63). Their primary function is to provide the 'motivational loop' controlling intentions-in-action. They are fundamental to any dynamic account of action, and their efficacy, I hope to show, is due to the sense in which they are both intentional and bodily in nature. In unpacking them we will, of course, have to tidy up the usual way we use these terms.

Basic *needs* generally arise because the homeostasis of various bodily systems has been disturbed and we are sent into the environment looking for what will restore balance. Hunger and thirst are the clearest examples. But this also includes such states as sleep deprivation, feeling hot or cold, the felt effects of hormonal or vitamin imbalance, gasping for air, and feeling bound.[13] At their onset at least, needs function as 'non-deliberative' motives for action and seem to be both different from and more basic in structure than emotions. To be sure, they can quickly link up with emotions. Not finding food can make one angry, envious, or resentful. But the feeling of hunger seems to be more like the underpinning for a variety of possible emotions rather than one of them, more like a driving force for action rather than a well-formed act.

Basic needs, I would suggest, also extend to a global felt longing for warmth and security. Think of Harlow's famous experiments in which a hungry infant monkey quickly moves after a few minutes from the bare wire-mesh mother with the nursing bottle to the one with a warm fluffy blanket without food, clinging to the second for as many as eighteen hours.[14] What in everyday language gets called affection is the most basic of the different types of loves: we can live without friendship and even eros, but the frustration or absence of affection leads to a complete breakdown even in

---

[12] This essay will not attempt to bridge its account of affects and affectivity to the emotions, a task that will have to wait for another time.

[13] See Craig 2008. His term for needs is 'homeostatic emotion' but I suggest that needs are not intentional acts and thus cannot be viewed as emotions.

[14] For a video of this see Harlow 2010a.

some of the infant monkeys (Harlow 2010b). This is not a crisis of emotions but of biosocial needs.

Keeping in mind that we are dealing with sensible experience before the introduction of reflection and certainly before the onset of discourse and rational motives, we can extend our account further. Once needs are refocused on secondary or related objects that come to provide satisfaction, and such objects are integrated into daily living, biologically based requirements give way to preferentially articulated demands. As satisfaction becomes gratification and gratification leads to habits, needs become *wants*. Water fulfils a basic need; Smutty Nose ale does not. As much as we love tea or coffee, we forget that our first taste of it as children was bitter. It is an acquired taste. The risk with wants, of course, is that they can spiral out of control. Wants growing out of needs can themselves become needs and our ale drinker gets trapped in addiction. Longing for or demanding objects of gratification arises out of and often overrides yearning for objects satisfying bio-based needs. The difference between needs and wants can be seen clearly with objects that we need but do not necessarily want– for example, the infamous cod liver oil that is an excellent source of Omega-3 but tastes horrible and sends children running for cover.

Wanting brings contributions of its own to the process. When it comes to need, the materials needed are grasped only according to their most general typology, only according to their use in satisfying hunger, quenching thirst, meeting nutritional requirements, giving secure warmth, each of which are rooted in the bio-neural demands of the body. The element of choice is missing or restricted, the range of things limited. But as we move beyond biological necessity, things manifest themselves in terms of their potential response to a range of human preferences. Objects gain a life of their own due to the felt values they acquire through the appropriations we make of them.

Needing and wanting are organized egocentrically and teleologically. Both are rooted in what is not had, in lack, and both are always longing-for or longing-toward. What gives the object seen or touched its *salience* is the fact that it fits into a circuit of needs or wants. In the case of needs, the deeper lying sociobiological requirements of the body determine salience. The biophysical requirements for nutrition, for example, work causally to configure a range of objects that will match the need. In the case of wants, self-projected demands and self-generated habits are in control. With wants a certain focused cultivation of tastes comes into play. For both, the relevance of objects is controlled entirely by an economy of satisfaction and gratification. As a result, needs and then wants involve a kind of circumspective seeing in which 'felt' values are as much a part of objects as is their utility. If the notion of affordances is to account for the type of features that are uncovered in the course of engaged perception, the sort always in play in intentions-in-action, it must be expanded to include not just use-values but also affective values. Because the appetites, with varying qualities and intensity, are always in place, the perceptual achievements embedded in needing and wanting keeps the focus on what the object *yields*.

There is a crucial difference between needing and wanting, on the one hand, and *desiring*, on the other. Desire[15] is directed not toward f/x-as-y but toward the *enjoyment* of f/x-as-y. Desire, then, effects a twofold shift: (a) we move from the object *having* a feature (y) giving it salience to the *being* of the object-complex as a whole; and (b) the being of the object-complex is unfolded by the *enjoyment* we have of it. To say that desire is directed to the enjoyment of f/x-being-y is to realize that a basic shift in the configuration of the perceptual content has taken place, a certain shift from focusing on the object in terms of its felt utility to attending to a felt 'good' to be enjoyed. The *integrity* of the *subsisting* object-complex comes into view. With it, the *existence* of the one so engaged is uncovered as well. Levinas puts this well: 'Things come to representation from a background from which they emerge and to which they return in the enjoyment we have of them' (Levinas 1969: 130).

In that desire is controlled by enjoyment and enjoyment is neither an act nor an object but regulates whole intentional events, enjoyment gives sensible acts of presenting objects and sensuous acts of needing or wanting objects their affective underpinnings. With enjoyment in play, the interplay of needing and wanting is sustained by desire— that is, enjoyment *modulates* needs and wants. The enjoyment anchoring needs and wants should be understood not as some buried, inner feeling but as what characterizes the in-structure as a field of sensuous involvement. In desire we are connected to objects in terms of the way they fit into our being-in-the-world. Affectivity as a whole emerges as enjoyment.

Perhaps the reason why the proverbial *object* of desire is so elusive, then, is that it is not an object at all. And perhaps the reason why *desire* is so intangible is that its focus is not on the objects of needs and wants but on the enjoyment that allows them to stand apart from other things and to matter for our existence.

What makes desire so hard to capture is that the everyday language of feelings seems to constantly shift, often treating desire as a synonym for want and, sometimes, need. To want x is just to desire x. But the contrast in play between the of-structure and the in-structure enables us, once we emphasize the felt quality of each, to distinguish wanting f/x as y and desiring the enjoyment of f/x as y. Compared to needing and wanting which are directly focused on objects in terms of their salient features, desire is oblique. When the object is absent, desiring moves toward or longs for the enjoyment missing from needing and wanting; when present, needing and wanting find not just satisfaction but also resolution in the enjoyment of what they have. Enjoyment as the focus of desire *frames* the acts of needing and wanting. The enjoyment of f/x *being* y becomes the 'horizon' in which particular acts of needing and wanting take place.

These contrasts work best, however, when the 'object' with which we are involved is a significant person. To see this we must set aside yet another covert assumption: namely, that we are first related to objects that we then interpret as persons as we imbue them

---

[15] What we are calling needs, wants and desires are sometimes amalgamated and labeled desire, which is much closer to what we have described as wants (as can involve greed or lust). Still, there is the recognition that they involve 'impulses to act' and are not quite emotions (see Fridja 2000: 63).

with affective or emotive features. There is strong research showing that the opposite is the case.[16] The felt presence of the other rather than his or her physical features is primary. Infants need not only food, not only warmth, but also the tender embrace of a caregiver. The breast (or its surrogate) is the source from which the infant derives not just a quelling of its hunger but also the satisfaction of its biosocial need to be held. With long-term satisfaction, with consistent holding and caring, and with the face of the other gradually coming into focus, need develops into desire. An atmosphere of enjoyment arises, resulting in a bond of basic trust.[17]

Yet, tragically, the opposite is also possible. Enjoyment, while global, is not the only mode of affectivity and stands opposed to another. The child can be neglected and even rejected. Even if fed, the absence of a caring face and love produces anxiety and a sense of basic fault develops, as object-relations theory has argued. Dread rules in place of enjoyment, and this is often strong enough to turn what is needed into what is refused, what is wanted into what is repulsive.

The notion of desire now allows us to return to our preliminary contrast between receptivity and responsivity. Objects of perception, be they familiar or foreign, quicken needing or wanting only as they exercise an *allure*, be it positive or negative, to which we respond. Yet the intentional acts of needing and wanting, we are suggesting, rest upon an affective qualification of the intentional event as a whole in which s/p-of-f/x-as-y is modulated by desire. It is due to enjoyment or its dreadful opposite, revulsion and dreading harm, that receptivity becomes responsivity. Only with the interplay of need, want, and desire does the sensible become the *sensuous* and anchor motivation.

To be sure, the object experienced may be indistinct or intrusive. But more often we undergo not the sudden invasion of the unexpected, as in our first account of receptivity, but the sustained anticipation of an object drawing us to it, often distracting us for days on end. It is precisely because it appears to us even in its absence as alluring or loved or, in more tempestuous times, as repulsive or hated, that our attention is held in chains, denying us any escape. Once objects are inserted into the circuit of desires and enjoyment, a well-organized set of protentions comes into play and surrounds them. We become infatuated.

This story, of course, becomes much more complicated when we resituate actions in a field of discourse. A reflective element seeps in and intentions-in-action bleed into intentions-of-action. Giving expression to wants, wishes, hopes and requests introduces motives of varying complexity that function less like descriptions and more like explanations of feelings. 'I need a happy meal', says the child, and we realize that nothing else will do. In this case of needing f/x-as-y, (a) what is desired is a certain state-of-affairs upon which the subject is reflecting, (b) the content of what she desires is propositionally

[16] For a general account of the theory of mind debate from a phenomenological perspective, see Gallagher and Zahavi 2008: Chapter 8. For a detailed analysis of imitation see Gallagher 2005: Chapter 3.

[17] Famously for Erikson, the opposition between trust and mistrust constitutes the very first stage of his epigenetic account of the development of personal identity. Basic trust is 'the cornerstone of a vital personality' (Erikson 1968: 97).

configured, and (c) the motives for wanting are 'rational'—that is, explained by reasons that she or I can articulate. They can also become complex: we discover that it is not just a familiar meal that has quelled hunger before, but the plastic toy at the bottom of the box that is in play, thereby transposing needing into wanting. The introduction of various reasons and explanations in everyday language can also overwhelm the contrast we are making between needs, wants, and desires. If by motivation we mean 'rationally' motivated, then many other things come into play besides enjoyment or abhorrence. I can want to own a red 1964 Porsche not because I am drawn to them or they exercise an allure on me or even that I would enjoy one, but simply because I know that I will get a good rate of return when I sell it in five years or because I have an obligation to keep my word to my rich aunt, who set aside part of my inheritance for this purpose. In this essay, however, we will keep intention-of-action at arm's length and will stay focused on unencumbered affects, turning now to their role in motivating intentions-in-action, as we have yet to do them justice.

3 MOTIVATION AND ACTION

The account of basic affects offered so far is abstract as it fails to account for the way in which they are *necessarily* tied to actions. I am suggesting that intentions-in-action in particular are rooted in basic affects. But this requires us to flesh out our preliminary typology of basic affects with a fuller account of their internal structure and their role in motivation, an issue that we have skirted until now. I will begin with needs and wants, taking up the difficult notion of desires in a moment.

Give a particular task, as we have seen above, an everyday object exhibits features that *invite* use within a field of action. The interconnected web of actual and virtual profiles controlled by the sense(s) of the intentional object, however, must be understood not simply in terms of resolving a problem but also in terms of affects, not just in terms of means–ends *indications*, but also in terms of *felt solicitations*. Objects of use invite because they solicit and they solicit because they are useful. That circular exchange is rooted not just in the way objects of use respond to the task at hand but also in the way the qualities (the as-y) of such things fulfil felt needs and wants. What draws unscripted actions, then, are felt qualities of objects, and what responds to and then modifies the affective features of objects are actions resolving needs and wants. Without the affective component, unscripted actions lack motivation, eventually becoming routine movements; without 'taking them to hand' affective objects lose their powers, eventually sinking into oblivion. Put plates of mashed potatoes in front of satiated students and they will grow cold; deny hungry students any access to mashed potatoes or replace them with something else and they will eventually lose interest in them.

This way of approaching the issue of motivation begins to refine our understanding of basic affects. A plate of potatoes can draw our attention because its sensible features cross a certain perceptual threshold and grab our attention, because a certain figure stands out from a ground, triggering the tilting of the head or the turning of the eyes. But to understand the power of potatoes to attract and to call our hands to take up a fork requires us to go beyond this and situate them within a dialectic of basic affects. To ask how an object not only draws but also solicits is to query how an unscripted action directed to that object is *internally* motivated. Our wager here is that affective objects arise not because of a prior appraisal involving conceptual evaluations.

Though this might be true of rationally defined emotions, relying on prior appraisal to account for this level of affective involvement always runs the risk of begging the question: an object is emotionally salient because it is valued as emotionally salient. But what motivates the valuing? In the case of scripted actions, the answer is simply that (a) we have a prior history with the object, (b) I go off looking for the object I already love, and (c) the prior valuing of it as loved entails that the presence of the object is sufficient to experience it as loved. But while unscripted action does have (a) in play, an action is guided not by a pre-appraised object, but by my needs, wants and desires. Objects draw, then, because our previous 'felt' involvement with them establishes kinetic values giving them the enticing or repelling powers they have. We should be careful here. Felt values are not added to a preexisting perceptual core or, in better accounts, to a set of use-values. Nor are values, at this level, 'interpretations' of what is otherwise devoid of them. Viewed concretely, what has priority is the entire 'fleshy' object located in the nexus of our affective engagement. These are the primary terms of what we are calling the *appraisal circuit* motivating intention-in-action. But we must add something more to the analysis thus far. To get at the special motivational structure of intention-in-actions, and then its difference from the conceptually configured motives of intention-of-action, we must integrate our analysis of needs and wants into an account of desire and pay special attention to how desire is constitutive of the general shape of such actions.

If it is the gradual emergence of a profile that *invites* the perception of an object, and if it is the 'useful' qualities of the object responding to needs and wants that *solicits* taking up such an object in actions, it is the enjoyment of the being of the sensuous object as situated in an intentional event as a whole that *entices* our engagement with it.[18] It is not the qualities of f/x-as-y soliciting but the *being* of f/x-as-y enticing that frames our deepest involvement with it. But this needs to be understood dynamically: the transformation of indication into solicitation is itself controlled by enticement.

I awaken on a cool morning, with my hand resting on the shoulder of the love of my life. In the enjoyment of her presence in these few moments, my hand slowly begins to stroke her arm and gradually moves up to her shoulder and then neck, none of which I am directly looking at, but all of which invite my embrace. My enjoyment of the being of this very special person engages a particular scheme of sensuous differentiation: my

[18] Again, we are taking ordinary language to school and stipulating definitions. All I offer as an excuse for using 'enticement' for this last stage of enjoyment is its probable etymological derivation from the old French *enticier*, which has a base meaning of 'to set on fire.' Even here it is not the intensity but the sense in which it consumes the whole that is in view. Solicitation, by contrast, is more focused on a particular feature.

hands are drawn to her shoulder, neck, and face, not the pillow or the water glass on the nightstand. They come into play not so much as 'moments' or 'parts' but as 'powers' soliciting the movement of my hand. With enjoyment in play, it is not their *sensible* but their *sensuous* existence that qualifies their presence—that is, the 'physical' qualities of an object are secondary to its 'fleshly' qualities. As we are lost in the enjoyment of what we desire, the physical features of an object function more like after-effects surrounding an affective core than the reverse. The 'substance' of an object of desire is its feel. It is this that invites, entices, and sometime seduces, and it is this that situates and controls the qualities and values discriminated. Undergirded by enjoyment, this feel gives the neck or the breasts the particular vitality that constitutes them and invites tender embrace. The dialectic of need, want and enjoyment is one of the triads, perhaps the most basic, that accounts for the sensuous attunement of circumspective perception and, thereby, for the motivational structure of basic actions.

The interplay of desire and enjoyment is deeper and broader in scope than the elementary cycles of need and satiation, and of want and gratification. The object with its allure kindles desire, yet it does so only with a view toward its enjoyment. At the same time, enjoyment carries the memory of desire and is manifest as desire's fulfillment.[19]

Is enjoyment the only hyper-mode that can frame in-volvement? Heidegger, for example, privileges *Angst*. But this may be due to taking understanding (*Verstand*) and not engagement as equiprimordial with affectivity (*Befindlichkeit*; Heidegger 1928: §31) and, for methodological reasons, to suspending any consideration of either as bodily in nature.[20] The outcome of this suspension is not neutral, as it results in suppressing what we are calling intention-in-action. We take the dyad of enjoyment and revulsion to be basic to action. To the extent that cognition in general is either a form of or rooted in action, to that extent enjoyment and revulsion are basic to intentional life in general and, thus, form the background to any other 'global' stances (*Einstellung*) that might come into play. However this is decided, we have the key to the sense in which experiential events as a whole are laden with pathos. With this we are pressing beyond the more pragmatically defined concepts of the in-structure that are now prevalent in phenomenological thinking. Enjoyment should be understood, first and foremost, not as some buried, inner feeling, but as what characterizes the in-structure as a field of sensuous involvement.

---

[19] See Levinas 1969: 113 for a fuller treatment of enjoyment and memory.

[20] Heidegger denies that Dasein is in the world in the sense in which 'a material body [*Körperding*], a human body [*Menschenleib*] is in something objectively present' (1928: 54/50), a claim that Husserl, too, would deny. But the key issue is that he also considers the notion of lived body (*Leib*) to be an empirical matter and thus irrelevant to an analysis 'of *the kind of being* of this being that we ourselves are' (1928: 50/46). This is clearly seen in §§23 and 24 of *Being and Time* where he, being fully aware of Husserl's manuscript now published as *Ideas II* (Husserl 1952), offers a full account of spatiality that circumvents the notion of 'corporeality [*Leiblichkeit*]', i.e., it is not the lived body that generates lived space but the directionality of Dasein that provides orientation to it (Heidegger 1928: 108/101).

4 THE STRUCTURE OF BASIC AFFECTS

We are finally in a position to suggest a typology of basic affects. Rather than two facets of basic affects functioning as motives—a felt urge impelling and an anticipated feature drawing the action—we discover three, each more complex than first suggested. Needs and wants consist of (a) a 'lived-through' *feeling* that impels the action as a whole, giving the affect its *efficacy*, (b) a whole body *motor tendency* that inclines the particular action 'animated' by that feeling to move in one way and not another, giving the affect its *shape*, and (c) a soliciting 'feel' to the object—something we, following others, would describe as the *valence* of the object—giving the affect a telos whose *kinetic values* reflexively draw the action as a whole and give the affect its *direction*. We need to dwell on this for a few moments since cognitive theories tend to reduce affects to the first and use proposition-ally articulated beliefs in place of the rest, an approach we reject.

While the feeling component of the affect accounts for the impetus behind intention-in-action, that impetus has a behavioral tendency that is constitutive of the general style of that action. So close is the relationship between feeling and tendency that often a sin-gle term characterizes the first in terms of the second, as in the case of repulsion, which etymologically means 'driven back', or attraction, which means 'draw near'. Behavioral tendencies are not an effect of feelings nor are they simply regulated by them. They are *constitutive* and thus internal to the nature of affects. Affects, however, have a third com-ponent and are internally triangulated: the feeling would lose its quality and the behav-ioral tendency lack direction without the valences of the object, accounting for its ability to allure. All three, not just the first, are inherent in the affect and provide the motiva-tional matrix undergirding specific actions upon the object. Various particular actions of drawing-near in contrast to withdrawing, for example, do vary according to the dif-ferent configurations of objects and the possibilities of their use, but they are pre-struc-tured by a certain lack 'impelling' the actions and a certain general 'style' of movement, both of which are internally regulated by the 'over-there' values of the object.

The tri-dependency between a qualitatively discernable feeling, the form of behavio-ral direction, and the valence of an object accounts for the peculiar intentionality organ-izing basic affects.[21]

A basic affect, then, is not just a 'raw feel', whose being, in the words of Berkeley, is exhausted by its being perceived, as might be the case with non-intentional feelings such

---

[21] For an effort to do justice to affects within the scope of an appraisal theory of emotional valences, see Prinz 2004. For an important attempt to develop a notion of affective intentionality and use it as the primary point of access to the emotions, see Slaby 2008. Colombetti and Thompson 2007 add much to the discussion of an embodiment theory of emotions by tackling the other side of the divide, by offering an embodied approach to cognition to complement the reevaluation of the body in the constitution of affects. Our account attempts to reach deeper ground than these efforts by focusing on the triadic structure of basic affects and the way they motivate intentions-in-action. It would take another study, though, to argue that they configure the field in which something like basic emotions arise.

as pangs or startles. Rather, a basic affect consists of an archetypical behavioral scheme, a felt quality to the goal toward which the action is directed, and a qualitatively distinguishable urge.[22]

The inclusion of behavioural direction allows us to characterize our basic affects as *drives*[23]; the presence of feeling as well as the valences of the object further qualifies them as *sensuous*. The qualitative differentiation of drives into needs and wants, as well as their ability to account for motivation, is possible only because of the interdependency between these three aspects: without contrasting behavioral tendencies, the feelings as felt would tend to fuse, and the valences would lose their connection to certain types of actions; without feelings the tendencies would cease to configure actions and the valences would cease to solicit; without valences feelings tending in a certain direction would wander aimlessly. We should be careful here: neither felt urges nor valences alone motivate behavioral directions. Rather, the three work together to motivate actions. Together they ground the appraisal loop that is constitutive of intentions-in-action.[24]

We are attempting to account for the motivational structure of unscripted actions that are directed to salient objects or persons. Let me suggest the following contrasts,

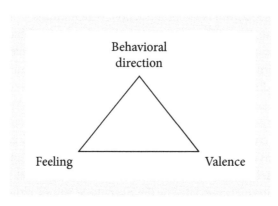

Internal structure of affects.

---

[22] James (1884), as is well known, insisted that emotions consisted of patterns of physiological autonomic responses and their feedback (Frijda 2000: 65). He misconstrued the bodily states as particular sensations and not the way the body as a whole feels. He also had difficulty handling the intentionality that is a part of emotions (see Pickard 2003: 94–5). Even if we correct for these mistakes, basic affects are different from emotions in three ways: (a) their status as feelings is tied to certain styles of bodily action and not just whole bodily states; (b) what gives the feeling 'intrinsic' direction is not understanding the reason for the state one is in (ibid.: 96) but rather certain lacks rooted in the body; and (c) the motives for action are drives that establish the motivational field in which objects acquire their affective valences.

[23] The notion of drives is all but missing from recent discussions of emotions. It does not even appear in the index of Lewis and Haviland-Jones (2000). For an important effort to rehabilitate the concept see Bernet (2005) and (2007).

[24] For speculation on whether needs, wants and desires form a distinct natural kind, called 'reflexive affects', rooted in lower regions of the brain stem see Panksepp 2000: 142–3.

struggling with the fact that everyday language is not as fine-grained as the structures we are after. To flesh out our account thus far, the basic types of affects are each triadically structured with the moments of each type being dyadically organized.

5 The dynamics of affectivity and engagement

The rhythm of feelings is essentially bodily in nature, with their cycle of imbalance, swelling demand, intake and resolution. I am also sure that the inclusion of behavioral forms as part of affects has not been lost on you. Behavioral tendencies do not take place 'in' a body but are inherently *bodily* in nature. As we turn to affects to account for the motivation of the action as a whole, we discover that they already contain an implicit schematization of bodily movements. The body is not secondary to the affect, added either to account for its cause or its implementation. Rather, the tendency to move in one way and not another—structured by such schemata as near-far, coming-leaving, front-behind, in-around, and so on—is inherent in the being of the affect. Affects involve, as a consequence, a certain 'spatialization' of consciousness. As our reaching-for arises with our feeling of need, the felt intensity of need is itself shaped by our ability to reach-for and the anticipation of the pleasure or pain that awaits us. The closer 'to hand' supper is, the hungrier one becomes. Not the feeling alone but the feeling and behavioral direction, reflexively guided by the valence of the meal, induce the particular

Affect	Feelings	Behavioural tendencies[25]	Valences
Need	Satisfaction or dissatisfaction	Reach-for and push-away	Pleasant and painful
	Security or insecurity	Clinging and fleeing	Warm and cold
Want	Gratification or disaffection	Attraction ('draw near') and rejection ('throw back')	Attractive and unattractive
Desire	Enjoyment or revulsion	Embracing ('arm around') and repelling ('driven back')	Enjoyable and revolting

Internal structure of affects.

[25] For simplicity's sake, I restrict the account of directions to the upper body.

action of picking up the fork. The feeling functioning as a motive in an intention-in-action is always a schematized feeling. The interplay of urge, motor tendency and valence, we are suggesting, constitutes an *affective appraisal circuit* motivating intentions-in-action.[26]

This account might correct one tendency we find in phenomenological accounts of the body. They rely almost exclusively on proprioception to provide a 'felt' sense of the body in action. Of course, we need to distinguish between proprioceptive information and proprioceptive awareness, as Gallagher does (2005: 46–7, 75–6) but Husserl does not. The former controls the movements of the body but is non-conscious. The latter does give us a felt sense of the actual position and movements of the body in various actions, itself a source of our direct awareness of the body. But proprioceptive awareness is neither intentional in structure nor does it *motivate* bodily actions. An awareness attending the position and movements of the body, while necessary to the functioning of a body schema, is different in kind from an affective drive motivating those movements. The awareness of the body we have in motivating affects is explicit and more complex: the quality of the drive is a 'global' bodily urge that includes felt behavioral tendencies of the acting body of which we are proprioceptively aware.[27] The lived body is flesh.

We have focused on the notion of intention-in-action from the side of basic affects, using it to account for the motivation of such actions. This now allows us to return to the 'transcendental' contrast between engagement and affectivity organizing the in-structure and glimpse two different ways in which the rich *dynamic* interrelationship between basic affects and intention-in-action can unfold.

Tracing the arrows clockwise along the inside loops, starting from the action box, gives us a depiction of engagement; counterclockwise along the outside loop, starting from valenced affordances, tracks the movement of affectivity. Each is designed as a feed-forward loop with feedback. The internal dynamics of the appraisal loop accounts for the complementary 'directions' of affectivity and engagement at play in the action loop.

The affectivity circuit usually starts with what is not yet a profile coming to prominence out of a dark background. A gradual process of discrimination enters in which

---

[26] It is also 'behind' every p-of-f/x-as-y, even when p is an emotion. But this requires a separate treatment. As developed thus far, the account of affects is still 'static', i.e., basically concerned with the structure of intention-in-action 'on the way' toward its goal. A dynamic account would (a) enlarge the account by discussing what happens when it reaches its goal, and (b) describe the development of both needs and values over time. In particular, it could handle the way in which valences have a 'history', i.e., the way in which the cycles of 'awaiting' and 'finding' establish the valences of different sorts of objects. Only at the end of this paper do I nod in this direction.

[27] We are leaving open the question as to whether need, want, and desire incorporate the body with the same compass and to the same degree. Desire, we have already suggested, is focused on the enjoyment of f/x being y, itself a global feeling; as such it correlates to embracing (or revulsion) and thereby brings our entire bodily relationship to the fore. Need, at the other extreme, is often acute and focused, perhaps the most visceral. It is schematized by tendencies to particular action. Perhaps the way that feelings of need bring the body to the fore is what is preserved by want and desire. If want and desire can be seen as transformations of need with part of its motivational structure preserved in the higher types, then the bodily 'feel' of needs continues in them.

we are not just awakened to the object but also, in varying degrees, attracted to it. The power of the object to solicit depends upon a past history of how it fitted into an economy of bodily needs and wants (bodily drives in the chart). Its use-sense has valences derived from patterns in which past affective drives were 'fulfilled' by the object. But in this case these drives are not what call for the object, but the object with its valenced affordances is what brings them forth. Not just the temporal contrasts between retained and present and between present and protended, but especially the spatial dyads of here-there, over-under, left-right, and so on, schematize the drive and are essential to it. Because its valences are internally connected to certain behavioral tendencies that call forth appropriate body schemata, the sensuous object motivates action, giving it direction and a goal. We can speak here of local-to-global motivation. The cigarette on the

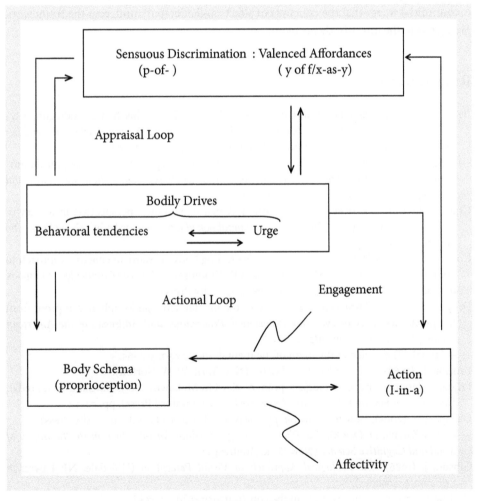

Appraisal and action.

table proves irresistible. We are enticed, and our hand reaches for it precisely because it has us in its grip.

The circuit of engagement, by contrast, is initiated by a bodily drive *seeking* resolution. The hungry hiker sets out looking for food that promises satisfaction and for a cave that affords her shelter from the cold, pounding rain. The action is often a modification of a previous action or part of a chain of actions and takes its bearing from them. Here it is not the affordance, with valences configured by an affect, that solicits the action but rather the action, responding to a felt lack, that motivates behavioral tendencies, which allow certain valenced objects to stand out. Here global-to-local motivation is in play.

Let me conclude by returning to the beginning. Could it be that placing affects, with their behavioral tendencies, in the center of intentions-in-action and viewing intentions-in-action as inherently bodily also entails that at least these sorts of intentions have not only a temporal but also an internal spatial organization and, perhaps, that what is called consciousness has a certain 'extension' to it? If so, then we have at least made good on our initial wager that the concepts of affects and affectivity undercut the framework giving rise to the mind-body problem.

References

Bernet, R. (2005), 'Trieb, Lust und Unlust. Versuch einer philosophischen Grundlegung psychoanalytischer Begriffe', in U. Kadi, and G. Unterthurner (eds), *Sinn macht Unbewusstes: Unbewusstes macht Sinn* (Würzburg: Königshausen & Neumann), pp. 102–18.

—— (2007), 'Drive: A psychoanalytical or metaphysical concept? On the philosophical foundation of the pleasure principle', in P. Birmingham, and J. Risser (eds), *Refiguring Continental Philosophy*, SPEP Supplement 2007: 107–18.

Craig, A. (2008), 'Interoception and emotion: A neuroanatomical perspective', in M. Lewis, J. Haviland-Jones, and L. F. Barrett, (eds), *Handbook of Emotions* (3rd edn.) (New York: The Guildford Press), pp. 272–88.

Colombetti, G. and Thompson, E. (2007), 'The feeling body: Toward an enactive approach to emotion', in D. Zelazo, M. Moscovitch, and E. Thompson (eds), *The Cambridge Handbook of Consciousness* (Cambridge: Cambridge University Press).

Dreyfus, H. (2005), 'Overcoming the myth of the mental: How philosophers can profit from the phenomenology of everyday experience', *Proceedings and Addresses of the American Philosophical Association* 79/2: 47–65.

—— (2007), 'The return of the myth of the mental', *Inquiry* 50: 352–65.

Erikson, E. (1968), *Identity: Youth and Crisis* (New York: W. W. Norton).

Frijda, N. (2000), 'The psychologists' point of view', in M. Lewis, and J. Haviland-Jones (eds), *Handbook of Emotions* (2nd edn.) (New York: The Guildford Press), pp. 59–74.

Gallagher, S. (2005), *How the Body Shapes the Mind* (Oxford: Oxford University Press).

—— and Zahavi, D. (2008), *The Phenomenological Mind: An Introduction to Philosophy of Mind and Cognitive Science* (New York: Routledge).

Gibson, J. (1986), *The Ecological Approach to Visual Perception* (Hillsdale, NJ: Lawrence Erlbaum Associates).

Harlow, H. (2010a), http://www.youtube.com/watch?v=KlfOecrr6kI.

—— (2010b), http://www.youtube.com/watch?v=rQBnNvyaNPY&feature=related.

Heidegger, M. (1928), *Sein und Zeit* (Tübingen: Niemeyer); tr. J. Stambaugh, *Being and Time* (Albany: State University of New York Press, 1996).

Husserl, E. (1952), *Ideen zu einer reinen Phänomenologie und phänomenologischen Philosophie*, Band 2, *Phänomenologische Untersuchungen zur Konstitution*, M. Biemel (ed.), *Husserliana* IV (The Hague: Martinus Nijhoff); tr. R. Rojcewicz, and A. Schuwer, *Ideas Pertaining to a Pure Phenomenology and to a Phenomenological Philosophy*, Book Two, *Studies in the Phenomenology of Constitution, Collected Works*, 3 (Dordrecht: Kluwer Academic Publishers, 1989).

—— (1966), *Analysen zur passiven Synthesis: Aus Vorlesungs- und Forschungsmanuskripten 1918–1926*, M. Fleischer (ed.), *Husserliana*, XI (The Hague: Martinus Nijhoff); tr. A. Steinbock (ed.), *Analyses Concerning Passive and Active Synthesis: Lectures on Transcendental Logic* (Dordrecht: Kluwer Academic Publishers, 2001).

James, W. (1884), 'What is an emotion?', *Mind* 9: 188–205.

Kelly, S. (unpublished manuscript), 'The Normative Nature of Perceptual Experience', lecture at the APA-Chicago, 18 March 2010.

L'Engle, M. (2005), *The Ordering of Love* (Colorado Springs: Water Brook Press).

Lewis, M., and Haviland-Jones, J. (eds) (2000), *Handbook of Emotions* (2nd edn.) (New York: The Guildford Press).

Levinas, E. (1969), *Totality and Infinity: An Essay On Ontology*, tr. Lingis, A. (Pittsburgh: Duquesne University Press).

McDowell, J. (2007), 'What myth?', *Inquiry* 50: 338–51.

Panksepp, J. (2000), 'Emotions as natural kinds within the mammalian brain', in M. Lewis and J. Haviland-Jones (eds), *Handbook of Emotions* (2nd edn.) (New York: The Guildford Press), pp. 137–56.

Pickard, H. (2003), 'Emotions and the problem of other minds', in A. Hatzimoysis (ed.), *Philosophy and the Emotions* (Cambridge: Cambridge University Press), pp. 87–103.

Prinz, J. (2004), *Gut Reactions: A Perceptual Theory of Emotion* (Oxford: Oxford University Press).

Slaby, J. (2008), 'Affective intentionality and the feeling body', *Phenomenology and the Cognitive Sciences* 7: 429–44.

Welton, D. (2003), 'World as horizon', in D. Welton (ed.), *The New Husserl: A Critical Reader* (Bloomington: Indiana University Press), pp. 223–32.

CHAPTER 10

THOUGHT IN ACTION

KOMARINE ROMDENH-ROMLUC

A distinction can be drawn between our actions—the things we do—and those things that merely happen to us. The traditional view holds that actions are essentially brought about and guided by the agent's intentions. They can be distinguished from happenings on this basis. Intentions are mental states that bring about and guide action by represent-ing its performance.[1] There are two versions of the traditional model. The Simple View holds that every action is brought about by an intention that represents the performance of that very action—thus an act of φ-ing is brought about by the intention, 'I intend to φ'. The Single Phenomenon View, in contrast, allows that an act of φ-ing may also be brought about by an intention(s) that represents the performance of a different, but relevant action(s), such as the components of φ-ing.[2] Both versions of the traditional account hold that intentions must bring about movement in a non-deviant way for it count as action.

The traditional model still dominates the philosophy of action, but there is increasing dissatisfaction with it. Whilst it is undoubtedly true that intentions play *some* role in at least some actions, the claim that they are *essential* in every case is problematic. There are many cases of action that cannot be accommodated by this model—see, for example, the cases discussed by Dreyfus (1991, 1999, 2000, 2002, and 2005a), Pollard (2006), and Romdenh-Romluc (in press). Empirical evidence concerning the way our brains func-tion also gives us reason to doubt that intentions play the kind of role in action envisaged by the traditional account—see, for example, Romdenh-Romluc (2011), and Jacobson (unpublished manuscript). For these and other reasons an increasing number of theo-rists are turning to the work of Merleau-Ponty, who offers us an alternative account of

---

[1] On this conception, intentions are independent of the bodily movements they cause, and the very same bodily movement can be either an action or a happening depending on whether or not it is caused in the appropriate way by an intention. An alternative conception holds that there are no agency-neutral bodily movements. Certain bodily movements are intrinsically actions. Theorists who take this view often conceive of intentions, not as independent causes of action, but as inseparable components of those bodily movements that count as actions. See, for example, O'Shaughnessy (1980). Space prevents me from discussing this possibility here.

[2] Bratman (1984) introduces this distinction.

action. On his view, mental states, such as intentions, are not necessary for action. Instead, the agent's bodily skills play an essential and central role in agency.

An important figure in the recent debate is Hubert Dreyfus. In a series of papers he provides an elegant elucidation and defence of Merleau-Ponty's view that brought it to the attention of theorists working in a number of different disciplines, and which opened up new ways to understand agency.[3] However, as many writers—such as Romdenh-Romluc (2007), Berendzen (2010), and Mooney (unpublished manuscript)—have pointed out, there is a central problem with Dreyfus's account: he places too little importance on the role of thought in human action. His account is thus problematic—both as a reading of Merleau-Ponty (whose view at least provides the resources for understanding thought's role in agency) and as a model of action in its own right. Those who want to endorse the Merleau-Pontyian account as an alternative to the traditional model of action must find some way of remedying this lack. The present paper takes up the challenge and offers a proposal for understanding the role of thought in action.

1 MERLEAU-PONTY, BODILY SKILLS, AND ACTION

In this section I will present those features of Merleau-Ponty's model that Dreyfus elucidates. I take there to be broad agreement that his reading accurately captures these aspects of Merleau-Ponty's view. It also lays the groundwork for an alternative to the traditional model of agency.

Merleau-Ponty's view of action is inextricably linked with a theory of perception that is inspired by Gestalt psychology. Its fundamental claim is that the perceiver is presented with the world in terms of its value for her behaviour. Rather than simply seeing, for example, a chair in front of her as an object with a particular shape, size, colour, and spatial location, the perceiver sees it as within reach and as offering an opportunity to sit down. These are not judgements that the perceiver makes about the chair on the basis of her perceptual experience; she immediately perceives it in these terms. Dreyfus (2005a) draws our attention to an important distinction that we should bear in mind here. The distinction is between Gibson's (1977) term 'affordances' and the Merleau-Pontyian notion of a 'solicitation'.[4] There is dispute over the exact nature of affordances, but for Gibson, at least, an affordance is a possibility for action offered by an environment of a certain sort to a particular kind of creature. The possibilities for action that an environment affords a creature depends on the physical structure of that creature, its motor capacities, the nature of the environment, and how the creature is situated with respect to that environment. A gap in a fence affords escape to a mouse chased by a cat—but not a cat chased by a dog—due to the size and shape of the gap, the size and shape of the mouse, and its ability to leap through the gap. The gap affords escape by running in *this*

---

[3] See, for example, Dreyfus (1991, 1999, 2000, 2002, 2005a, 2005b, 2007).
[4] See Merleau-Ponty (1962, 1964).

direction—but not *that* one—due to the relative locations of the mouse and the gap. Affordances are subject-relative insofar as they are indexed to the physical structure and capacities of particular creatures, but they are also real features of the world. There is a fact of the matter about whether or not the gap in my fence affords escape to a pursued mouse. Furthermore, an environment will afford certain actions to a particular creature, independently of whether she actually perceives those affordances. The notion of a solicitation differs in that it is a perceptual notion, which concerns how affordances are experienced. Merleau-Ponty argues that a creature perceives her environment as drawing her to perform certain actions. These felt 'pulls' are solicitations. Merleau-Ponty holds that the solicitations differ in their 'urgency'—that is, the strength with which they draw the agent to act. The urgency with which the agent is solicited will depend on what might roughly be called the salience of the affordance for the agent. She will experience those affordances that are most salient for her as soliciting her most strongly. Less salient affordances will solicit her more weakly. She may not be solicited at all by those affordances that lack salience for her altogether.

Merleau-Ponty holds that the agent's behaviour can be immediately drawn forth and controlled by the solicitations of her environment. The agent is solicited to act in a certain way, and immediately responds by performing the relevant action. She does not need to form a conceptual representation of the action, such as an intention. Her behaviour will be drawn forth by the most urgent solicitations.[5]

The ability to experience the world as soliciting her and respond accordingly is made possible by the agent's motor skills—what Merleau-Ponty calls 'habits' (1962: 143). One acquires such skills through practice. (We can see here why he calls them 'habits', since one's habits just are those things one does repeatedly.) Practice is the body's becoming familiar with the activity in question. Initially, the movements will feel awkward and alien. One's attempts to perform them will be clumsy and lacking in fluidity. Engaging in the activity will be more difficult. As one practices, the movements start to feel familiar and 'natural'. One is able to perform them more smoothly and with more grace. Performing the movements becomes easier. Initially, for example, it will feel very odd to sit on a bicycle. The bodily movements required to move the pedals, grip the handlebars, reach the brakes, and so on will feel awkward, and I will only manage to do them with difficulty, if at all. However, as I continue to practice, these things will start to feel familiar. My body will become used to the position required to hold the bars and reach the brakes and pedals. The movements will become easier for me to perform. To acquire a motor skill, the body has to—as Merleau-Ponty puts it—'catch the movement' (1962: 142). This is vividly illustrated by an experience, which is not uncommon when learning a new skill. First, one tries to φ but fails miserably. The next day, one tries again, not

---

[5] It might be supposed that the view of actions as brought about and guided by the solicitations of the agent's environment is compatible with the claim that such actions involve an intention-in-action (Searle 1983). Dreyfus (1991, 1999) argues against this possibility. I do not have space to consider this here.

expecting things to be any different. But despite one's expectations, one finds one can φ, as if by magic. One's body has suddenly grasped what to do.

The body's familiarity with an activity is not only manifest in the relatively smooth grace with which one can perform the relevant bodily movements. It is also manifest in the perception of appropriate parts of the world as soliciting those movements. To exercise any motor skill, one must be in an appropriate part of the world. To walk my dog, for example, I must be in an environment that contains my dog, his leash, and space for walking. I cannot exercise my dog-walking skills if I am alone in the park. Furthermore, one must know which particular movements are required to φ effectively (there may be an indeterminate number of movements that will satisfy this requirement). To walk my dog up a hill, I must know which particular bodily movements are required to propel myself up the incline, whilst holding my dog's leash to prevent him from chasing sheep. It follows that being skilled at φ-ing essentially involves the ability to both pick out those places where one can φ, and to select the movements required to do so successfully in that particular place. The more skilled one is, the better one will be at selecting more or less appropriate places to φ, and the movements that make for successful φ-ing. Merleau-Ponty holds that these capacities are manifest in perception. One experiences appropriate parts of the world as soliciting one to perform particular movements that together constitute an instance of φ-ing. Thus I see the hill as soliciting me to perform the movements required to propel myself up it and control my dog. Once I possess a skill, I can perceive what to do, and respond to these solicitations by acting, without the need to conceptually represent the performance of the action.[6]

2 Dreyfus, expertise, and thought in action

Theorists are broadly in agreement over the components of the account presented so far. But it is incomplete as it stands. It needs to be developed to encompass the role of thought in action. In this section, I explain how Dreyfus develops this account.

Dreyfus takes certain instances of expertise in sport as his paradigm cases. Whilst not many of us are sporting experts, we are all experts at some set of everyday motor skills required in the course of living, such as opening doors, scratching itches, writing letters, driving cars, riding bicycles, making tea, and so forth (Dreyfus 2007). Dreyfus tends to assume that the exercise of *all* motor skills can be assimilated to the particular instances of sporting expertise that he takes as paradigmatic. The examples he has in mind are

---

[6] Merleau-Ponty allows that in certain unusual cases, the perceptual and the motor components of a skill can come apart, so that an agent may perceive opportunities to perform actions that she cannot perform. He analyses phantom limb cases in this way—the phantom limb comes about because one experiences the world as soliciting one to perform actions with a limb that one does not possess. In this case, the agent possesses a defective motor skill (Merleau-Ponty 1962: 81–2).

those that are sometimes described as 'acting in the flow'. The agent is completely focused on what she is doing. Her actions flow smoothly, and she is playing extremely well—to the best of her ability. Importantly, if the agent begins to *think* about what she is doing, the 'flow' is disrupted. There are many examples of this phenomenon. Cricketer Ken Barrington describes his experience of playing cricket like this: 'When you're playing well you don't think about *anything* and run-making comes naturally. When you're out of form you're conscious of needing to do things right, so you have to think first and act second. To make runs under those conditions is mighty difficult' (Barrington 1968: 97f). Dreyfus calls acting in flow, 'absorbed coping'. He uses Merleau-Ponty's account to explain how action is achieved in these cases. He takes the fact that thought disrupts flow to show that these actions cannot be satisfactorily understood as bodily movements that are brought about by conceptual representations of action, such as intentions. Instead, the player's skill consists in the capacity to perceive what to do—which takes the form of solicitations—and respond to those solicitations by acting. Dreyfus then uses these cases to conclude that being an expert at anything—and, remember, we are all experts at the skills we use in living our daily lives—involves being able to act smoothly, successfully, and without thinking about what one is doing. In all cases, thought—where this is understood as conceptual representation—gets in the way of an optimal execution of the action.

Dreyfus does not deny that thought plays *some* role in an agent's behaviour. His understanding of its role in action is based on his assumption that the 'acting-in-flow' cases are paradigmatic. First, he allows that thought is sometimes instrumental in the learning process whereby an agent acquires the expertise to 'act in flow'. Prior to acquiring the skill, the agent cannot perceive the world as soliciting her to exercise it. Her first attempts at gaining the skill cannot, therefore, be brought about by the way she perceives her environment. Instead, the agent's behaviour will be brought about by thought. This is not to say that thought is *always* involved in skill acquisition—we learn some skills by copying other people. Neonates have the capacity to imitate others. But a newborn baby is not yet capable of conceptual thought. It is thus plausible to think that the ability to copy what someone else is doing is a hardwired, perceptual capacity that does not necessarily require the formation of conceptual representations of movement. In (at least some) cases where an agent—such as a very young child—learns a skill by copying someone else, it therefore seems that no thought is involved.[7] Nevertheless, there *are* cases where an agent learns a new skill by thinking about what she is doing. Dreyfus (2002) describes these instances of skill acquisition in the following terms. First, the agent learns a set of explicit rules, stating what she should do. She engages in practice by following these rules. The agent conceptually represents what is prescribed by the rule, and these conceptual representations initiate and guide her first attempts. As she continues to practice, the agent comes to perceive appropriate parts of the world as soliciting the movements required by her activity. The perceived solicitations draw forth her

---

[7] Copying someone else may *sometimes* require one to think about what one is doing.

actions, so that she needs fewer and fewer conceptual representations to guide her behaviour. Once she has become an expert, she can dispense with the conceptual representations altogether. Her behaviour is entirely controlled by a perceptual 'grasp' of what is required by her situation, which is constituted by the solicited requirements for action she experiences.

The second way in which thought may play a role in action on Dreyfus's account is in cases where the seamless flow of perceptually-driven action breaks down (2000: 300–1). The flow of action can break down for a number of different reasons. In some cases, the world will behave unexpectedly—the door handle may come off in my hand as I attempt to open the door. In other cases, 'the situation is so unusual that no immediate response is called forth. Or several responses are solicited with equal pull' (Dreyfus 2005a: 57). There are, no doubt, many other ways in which action may be, to a greater or lesser degree, thwarted, and the flow of coping disrupted. Dreyfus contends that in at least some cases where the seamless flow of successful action is disrupted, thought must take over. When I find the door handle in my hand, my actions no longer flow smoothly from my perceived surroundings. I must stop and think about how to open the door in order to progress through it. I may, for example, see a gap in between the door and the frame, and reason that it is wide enough for me to grasp the door with my fingers and pull it open. These thoughts about how to proceed bring about my next action of pulling the door open in the way described. Once I am through the door, the smooth flow of coping can recommence. Similarly, when I find myself in an unusual situation, or one where I am solicited equally by conflicting affordances, my actions no longer smoothly flow from my perceptual situation. I must think about what to do.

Finally, Dreyfus allows that thought will play a role in bringing about action in cases where the activity in question involves problem-solving that must take account of future possibilities (Dreyfus and Wakefield 1991: 264–5). An example is activity that results from practical deliberation. In these cases, the agent decides what to do by considering the various options and their future outcomes. Dreyfus and Wakefield point out that these future possibilities cannot feature as perceptible elements of the agent's current situation. Instead, she must represent them in thought. The agent's consideration of the options available to her allows her to come to a decision, and so form an intention, which she then acts upon.[8]

Dreyfus claims that where thought is involved in action, its role is merely to trigger absorbed coping. He writes: '...the brain correlate of an act of volition would put the system into a specific attractor landscape [the hypothesized brain correlate of absorbed coping]. After that, the brain correlate of the volition would no longer be causally active, but would, as it were, be thrown away as the dynamics of the attractor landscape took over as the brain correlate of the agent's movements' (Dreyfus 1999: 8). He makes much the same point a little later, when he writes: 'Merleau-Ponty would contend that the

---

[8] Dreyfus and Wakefield also allow that thought is involved in activity that is very complex. But they offer no indication of the sort of activity that is at stake here. Moreover, this possibility seems to drop out of the picture in Dreyfus's later work.

intention in action is only an occasional cause that merely initiates the absorbed coping that carries out the action' (Dreyfus 1999: 10).

Dreyfus does not explain how thought initiates absorbed coping. However, he could do so by appealing to salience. We saw earlier that the agent experiences those affordances that are most salient as soliciting her most strongly. Those that are less salient solicit her more weakly. Those that are not salient may not solicit her at all. On Merleau-Ponty's account, the agent's behaviour is drawn forth by the most urgent solicitations. No doubt there are a number of different factors that contribute to salience. But one such factor is the agent's current task. What the agent is currently doing makes certain opportunities for action—those that are relevant to her current task—salient for her. These opportunities will then solicit her more urgently, and so play a greater role in drawing forth her behaviour. In many cases, the agent takes on a task by forming an intention to do so. Dreyfus could thus offer the following account of how thought triggers absorbed coping: the agent's formation of an intention changes the salience of the opportunities offered to her by her environment. Once the pattern of salience has been altered by the intention, the agent's perception of her surroundings as soliciting her to act in various ways controls her activity. The intention has no further role to play in bringing about the agent's behaviour.

3 PROBLEMS FOR DREYFUS

Dreyfus's account is important and contains some valuable insights. But as an account of human action, his view is inadequate. The basic problem is that by taking the acting-in-flow cases as paradigmatic, he both misrepresents the role that thought plays in human action, and the extent to which human activity involves thought.

Dreyfus's assumption that everyday action should be assimilated to expert acting-in-flow leads him to conceive of thought's role—on those occasions when it is involved in action—as triggering absorbed coping. On this view, there are phases of smooth expert coping, where the agent seamlessly and unthinkingly responds to her perceived environment, punctuated by episodes of thought that initiate further phases of absorbed coping. Crucially, thought and perception do not control action simultaneously.

The first thing to note is that Dreyfus's conception of thought's role as merely initiating absorbed coping means that his account of thought's role in action fails on its own terms. Consider his account of skill acquisition, which is central to his model of agency. According to Dreyfus, the novice begins by conceptually representing rules, which she uses to guide her behaviour. As she progresses, she comes to see the world as soliciting the required actions, and she no longer needs to think about every aspect of her behaviour. Eventually, if all goes well, she becomes an expert and need not think about her behaviour at all. However, at some point, the agent will be reasonably proficient, but not yet an expert. She is skilled enough to perceive certain opportunities for action, but she must still think about what she is doing to act successfully. In other words, there will be certain requirements for action that she is not yet skilled enough to perceive and must represent in thought. Moreover, these conceptually represented requirements will play an ongoing role in guiding actions. In such a case, her behaviour is *simultaneously* controlled by both thought and perception. Before I can climb, for example, the fissures and cracks in the rock-face are not presented to me as hand-holds and foot-holds. I do not perceive them as affording me passage up the rock-face. My first attempts at climbing are controlled by conceptual representations of what I should do. Through practice, I gradually acquire the perceptual and motor capacities that together comprise the skill. At a certain stage in learning, I can perceive larger fissures as handholds, but my instructor must still tell me which smaller cracks will take my weight. My progress up the rock-face is guided by both the perception of certain cracks as soliciting me to use them as handholds, and the conceptual representation of the smaller fissures in the rock as capable of supporting my body. Since Dreyfus's model does not allow us to make sense of thought playing an ongoing role in guiding action, he cannot accommodate these cases.

The problem is further reinforced once it is recognized that by taking acting-in-flow cases as paradigmatic, Dreyfus misconstrues the phenomenology of human action. Thought plays a far greater role in our behaviour than he allows. His conception of thought as merely initiating phases of absorbed coping means that he cannot satisfactorily account for much of it. First, Dreyfus is wrong in thinking that *all* skills follow the pattern of acquisition he outlines, where—if all goes well—one progresses from a beginner who must think about what she is doing to an expert who can rely solely on perception to control her behaviour. There are some cases where even the master must routinely think about what she is doing to exercise her skill to the very best of her ability. Furthermore, the role of thought in these cases is not to initiate absorbed coping after the flow is disrupted. Instead, thought plays an ongoing role in guiding action, like it does in the case of the proficient climber. A skilled surgeon, for example, must think about the surgery she is performing in order to carry it out properly. She will perceive more of what has to be done than the novice. But she can never rely solely on these perceived requirements to perform the surgery in the way implied by Dreyfus's account. Conceptually represented requirements for action must continuously guide her behaviour.[9]

Second, as Dreyfus acknowledges, human beings often engage in practical reasoning. We weigh up our various reasons for action, and come to a decision about what to do, which we then act upon. There would be no point in deliberating if we could not act on the decisions we reached. Whilst it would be false to think that *all* our actions are the result of conscious deliberation, we must recognize that *many* of them are. Dreyfus conceives of the deliberation as initiating an episode of absorbed coping. However, it seems that in many cases this description is inaccurate, and instead the practical reasoning is integrated with the flow of action. Consider this example. I got up this morning and

---

[9] Gallagher (2009) also notes in passing, the way that thought can enter into the expert exercise of motor skills.

wondered whether to drink tea or coffee. I thought about the fact that I really like coffee, but am trying to imbibe less caffeine. I reluctantly decided to have tea, and so I made a cup. I then pottered around the kitchen and tried to decide what to eat for breakfast. I thought about making some porridge, but then realized there was not enough time. I decided to eat cereals instead, and poured some into a bowl. It would surely be wrong to describe this case as small episodes of absorbed coping, punctuated by stretches of practical reasoning that restart the smooth, unthinking flow. Instead, as Mooney points out, these thoughts—the conceptual representations that play a role in guiding my action in a case like this—should be thought of as part of my flow of behaviour. His example from academic life beautifully illustrates this point:

> As I approach Newman House to hear a paper, I realize that I am daydreaming and dawdling and had better take longer strides, and later on again I decide to run. The conference room has tightly bunched chairs and a creaky floorboard near the door. It is a lot harder to sneak in late and find a free chair without making a commotion. Should accelerating into a run not be enough, I have a contingency plan of how to regain my breath, tiptoe around the floorboard and squat on the ground. It will be as if I were there from the beginning, and free from the disapproving stares of others. (Unpublished manuscript, pp. 26–7)

Mooney calls the thoughts that feature in the flow of everyday action 'little reflections'. In such cases, the agent's thought plays an ongoing role in controlling her activity, which cannot be properly captured by Dreyfus's conception of thought as triggering episodes of absorbed coping.

4 THOUGHT AND ACTION: A MERLEAU-PONTYIAN PROPOSAL

A Merleau-Pontyian account of thought's role in action must accommodate it within his basic framework. For him, action has the following structure. The agent 'grasps' the possibilities for action afforded by her surroundings. Her 'understanding' of what she can do in that particular environment initiates and controls her behaviour. The agent's 'grasp' of these possibilities is manifest in perception of her environment as soliciting her in various ways. There is no need for the agent to conceptually represent the action to be performed. Action is made possible by the agent's possession of motor skills. I propose that there are two central ways that thought can enter into this picture.

First, thought can have an ongoing effect on the way the agent perceives her environment. There are different ways that thought can do this. One thing thought does is affect the salience of different action possibilities. We saw above that the agent experiences solicitations as varying in their 'urgency' or attractive power. Certain possibilities for action solicit her more strongly than others, demanding that she take them up. Other possibilities solicit her more weakly, merely suggesting themselves as things she could do. The agent's actions are drawn forth by the solicitations with the greatest attractive power. The urgency with which an affordance solicits the agent depends on its salience. Thought contributes to the salience of a possibility for action. Different types of thought can make a contribution. We have already seen that an important factor in determining salience is the agent's current task. Those opportunities for action that are relevant to what she is currently doing are salient for her, and will solicit her more strongly. My goal of baking a cake will make those action possibilities that are relevant to this task—such as flour-buying, bowl-cleaning, sugar-weighing, and so on—salient for me, and they will solicit me accordingly. In many cases the agent takes on a task by intending or deciding to do so. Thus the agent's intentions/decisions affect the way she perceives the world. But intentions are not the only sort of thought that can affect salience. The agent's desires will also make certain possibilities for action more salient, and thus stand out as more attractive than others. My intense desire for lasagne makes the Italian eatery salient as a lasagne-procuring opportunity. I thus experience the restaurant as soliciting me strongly. The saliency of affordances will be affected by the agent's beliefs. My belief that a notorious prisoner has escaped makes dark alleys appear more threatening. I am more inclined to notice them as places that a dangerous convict might hide. The opportunity to avoid them thus becomes more salient for me, and I experience them as soliciting me to give them a wide berth. The way the agent imagines her surroundings can also affect the salience of affordances, and so the strength with which they solicit her. I imagine a werewolf lurking in the woods outside my house. I know there are no such things as werewolves, so there cannot be one there. Nevertheless, my imaginings affect how I perceive the entrance to the woods—it becomes salient for me as to-be-avoided. In each of these cases, the agent's thoughts affect the way that she perceives her environment—they play a role in determining which affordances are salient for her, and so which solicit her most strongly. Notice, moreover, that it seems implausible to suppose that the thought only plays a momentary role in patterning the salience of affordances. I must, for example, *continually* imagine the lurking werewolf for the entrance to the woods to stand out as salient for me as to-be-avoided. The persistence of the imagining sustains the salience of this affordance. Since the agent's actions will be drawn forth by the solicitations with the strongest attractive power, this is one way that thought can play an ongoing role in the guidance of action.[10]

The second central way that thought can play an ongoing role in bringing about action is by adding to the agent's grasp of the possibilities afforded by her environment. The agent can conceptually represent more possibilities for action than those she currently perceives. In these cases, the way the agent conceptually represents her environment, together with her perception of it as soliciting certain actions, jointly bring about and

---

[10] It is also worth noting that thought can affect perception in another way: the agent's conceptual capacities can play a role in shaping her powers of perceptual discrimination, which in turn affects the way she is solicited by her environment. See, for example, Gumperz and Levinson (1997), Bowerman and Choi (2001), and Roberson *et al.* (2000). This fact belies Dreyfus's (2005a, 2005b) claim that coping does not involve our conceptual capacities.

control her behaviour. For example, I develop diabetes and must avoid sugary food. I go to the buffet table and see a cake. I know I must not eat cakes, and so I conceptually represent the cake as not-to-be-eaten. At the same time, I experience the fruit salad as soliciting me to eat it. This composite apprehension of my environment, which combines a conceptually represented affordance (avoid cake) and a perceived solicitation (eat fruit salad), brings about my behaviour of fruit salad-eating.

At this point one might wonder how to make sense of the idea that a conceptually represented possibility for action can bring about behaviour on Merleau-Ponty's account. A key component of his view is that the agent's motor skills make it possible for her to discriminate possibilities for action and to respond accordingly. A Merleau-Pontyian model of thought's role in human behaviour should show how the ability to act in response to a conceptually represented opportunity for action is also made possible by the agent's motor skills. Merleau-Ponty himself offers such an account. It centres on a capacity he calls 'the power to reckon with the possible' (1962: 109). Merleau-Ponty reveals this capacity to us through his discussion of the case of Schneider—a veteran with a rather odd set of disabilities resulting from a brain injury he incurred during World War I. Merleau-Ponty argues that Schneider's disabilities stem from a deficit in his power to reckon with the possible. It will be useful to focus on one particular feature of his case here. Schneider is unable to recognize a house he has visited many times unless he is actually going there. If Schneider simply passes the house on his way elsewhere, it does not appear familiar to him (Merleau-Ponty 1962: 134—5). Things are, of course, very different for a normal human agent (one with no injury or damage to the brain or nervous system), who *will* recognize a house she has often visited, even when she is going somewhere else.

I have suggested elsewhere that Merleau-Ponty can be read as holding that Schneider's problem results from an inability to access his motor skills in the normal way.[11] Consider what is involved in perceiving something—a place or object—as familiar, on Merleau-Ponty's account. One perceives something as familiar when one has acquired the skill or habit of interacting with it. For example, it is by practising, and so gaining the skill of playing the saxophone that the instrument comes to feel familiar in my hands. Initially, its size and weight, and the finger positions needed to play it, feel odd and uncomfortable. Gaining the skill partly involves these things coming to feel natural and familiar. Similarly, the city where I live was once a strange place to me. I did not know how to orient myself in it and find the various shops, cinemas, markets, and so forth. As I spent my days moving around it, I came to know the city. Through my repeated interactions with it, I developed a skill of navigating the city. I came to perceive certain roads as offering passage to particular places, and certain places as affording certain possibilities for my actions, such as buying bread, visiting a friend, walking in the park. The city became familiar to me. To perceive something as familiar is thus to perceive it as requiring (or being appropriate for) certain habitual forms of interaction. It is to be solicited by that

---

[11] See Romdenh-Romluc (2007) for a detailed argument in favour of this interpretation of Merleau-Ponty.

place or thing. To be solicited to perform a certain action is to exercise the same skill used in performing that action. To perceive something as familiar is therefore to exercise one's skills of interacting with it. Schneider has visited the house he does not always recognize many times; he habitually interacts with the house. His habit allows him to recognize the house—its familiar appearance is itself an exercise of this habit. The reason that Schneider cannot always recognize the house is because his skill of interacting with it is not always available to him. He cannot access this skill when he is doing something else. Schneider's case is thus different from that of the normal human agent, who will recognize a house she has visited many times, even if she merely passes it on her way elsewhere. The normal human agent is able to perceive the house as familiar, no matter what she is doing, because her skill of interacting with it is always available to her.

This peculiar feature of Schneider's case illustrates what Merleau-Ponty takes to be a more general fact about him. Schneider can only access a certain subset of his motor skills or habits: those that are relevant to what he is actually doing. To put matters another way, Schneider's current task and actual environment make certain skills available to him, which he can then use in perception and action. The skills made available are those required to carry out those elements of his current task that he can complete in his actual environment. In contrast, the motor skills and habits of the normal human agent are constantly available to her. It is this constant availability of the agent's motor skills that Merleau-Ponty calls 'the power to reckon with the possible' (1962: 109).

How does this power enable the agent to act in response to a conceptually represented possibility for action? To understand this we need to consider Merleau-Ponty's account of perception in a little more detail. For him, perception does not involve passively receiving data from the world. Instead, the agent is active in perception. As we have seen, she does not simply perceive the objective features of her environment, she perceives it in terms of its significance for her actions, and what is salient for her. Merleau-Ponty holds that the agent 'summons' solicitations from the world. In so doing, she 'projects' a situation around herself—one that calls for a certain mode of action (Merleau-Ponty 1962: 136). On this picture, the content of perception is partly determined by the nature of perceived things, but also shaped by the perceiver herself. We can see from this description that the perceptual component of a motor skill is the ability to appropriately invest one's environment with bodily significance. For example, my skill at snowboarding comprises the capacity to summon the invitation to snowboard from the snowy mountain slopes. In so doing, I project a snowboarding situation around me—one that calls for snowboarding actions. I do so appropriately insofar as I can actually snowboard in my present environment, and so the solicitations I experience correspond to real possibilities for action that it affords me. Merleau-Ponty holds that the capacity to project a situation around oneself, which is part and parcel of possessing a motor skill, is not confined to perception. It is also involved in imagination. He writes: 'To say that I imagine Peter is to say that I bring about the pseudo-presence of Peter by putting into operation the "Peter-behaviour-pattern"' (1962: 181). In this passage, Merleau-Ponty suggests that imagining one's friend Peter involves exercising the bodily skills one usually uses to interact with him. These 'Peter-skills' comprise two elements: a perceptual component

(I perceive him as lovable, familiar, and so on), and a motor component (I behave in certain friendly ways towards Peter). Imagining Peter involves exercising Peter-skills when he is absent, summoning up the demands he would make on me if he were here. Thus I bring about Peter's 'pseudo-presence'. Merleau-Ponty holds that the same operation is used to invest a conceptual representation with bodily significance—that is, to imbue it with value for one's actions.[12]

We can gain a better grip on the phenomenon that Merleau-Ponty has in mind here by thinking about the following example. Annette knows that her great-grandfather was a miner. She knows of the long hours he spent deep underground, the cramped conditions in which he worked, the ever-present danger of explosions. One day, however, Annette is out walking when she falls down a pothole. She has to make her way along a narrow tunnel to an opening further down the hill where she can escape into the sunlight. The experience of being trapped below the surface, in cramped, claustrophobic conditions, gives Annette a new insight into her great-grandfather's life. She does not learn any new facts about his existence. But she now has a different appreciation of what it was like to work down the mine. For Merleau-Ponty, Annette has gained a bodily understanding of her grandfather's life and the demands for action that his situation would have made upon him. The conceptual representation of his existence that constitutes her knowledge of his life has taken on a bodily significance. Annette's bodily grasp of her great-grandfather's situation is an exercise of her motor skills, including those required to move through the pothole to free herself after she is trapped. Investing a conceptual representation with bodily significance involves the body's grasping the action possibilities afforded by the represented state of affairs. Where the subject conceptually represents her own environment, this allows the representation to function like a perceived affordance and solicit action.

It is worth noting that thought's role in action is very different on this model to the role it plays on the traditional account. On the traditional view, intentions are necessary for action, and whilst intentions may be informed by the agent's desires and beliefs, it is only intentions that can directly bring about action. In contrast, the Merleau-Pontyian model allows a much wider range of thoughts to play a direct role in bringing about action, and it is not necessary for the agent to form an intention to act. As we have seen, action can be brought about by intentions, desires, beliefs, imaginings, and so on. Moreover, the thoughts that bring about action on the traditional view represent the action to be performed. However, according to the Merleau-Pontyian account, they may *sometimes* represent the action to be performed, but they need not do so. Instead, there will be cases where the thoughts that control action represent the agent's environment, like in the example above where I conceptually represent the cake as not-to-be-eaten. The traditional view takes thought to have sole responsibility for producing action. Perception plays a role in guiding actions, but it does so by providing sensory input for thought, which then produces action as its

---

[12] See, for example, Merleau-Ponty's remarks on moral situations (Merleau-Ponty 1962: 112).

output.[13] On the Merleau-Pontyian account, however, thought never has sole responsibility for producing action. The agent's behaviour is always also controlled by her perceived environment. Thus the Merleau-Pontyian model does not conceive of thought as a 'middleman', standing between perception and action.

My proposed model offers a nice analysis of the cases that cause problems for Dreyfus's account. The basic difficulty his view faces is that his conception of thought as merely triggering episodes of absorbed coping means that he cannot explain cases where thought plays an ongoing role in action.

I presented four examples. The first is the agent who is learning to climb. Before she has acquired the skill, she cannot perceive the rock-face as soliciting her to climb it. Her initial attempts to climb will be brought about by conceptual representations specifying what she should do. Through practice, the agent gains the perceptual and motor capacities involved in climbing, and is thus able to perceive the fissures and cracks in the rock as places she can grip with her hands, or stand on with her feet. At some point in this process, the agent will be sufficiently skilled to perceive some requirements for action, but she will still need to think about what she is doing. Moreover, the conceptually represented requirements for action will be continuously involved in guiding her actions. On my account, the agent perceives her environment as soliciting her to perform certain actions. She can 'add' further affordances to her perceived environment by conceptually representing action requirements that she does not perceive. These represented affordances then function like solicitations, playing a role in controlling the agent's actions. This is what the agent does when she first learns to climb. She represents a certain fissure in the rock as a handhold. Her representation functions like a solicitation. It is part of the pattern of solicitations—both perceived and represented—that together make up her apprehension of her world. The perceived solicitations, together with the conceptual representation of the fissure as a handhold, draw her to act. As the agent practices, she comes to see appropriate cracks in the rock as handholds, and no longer needs to conceptually represent them as such to climb up the rock-face. It is possible that the expert climber need not think about what she is doing at all—her actions are entirely controlled by perceived solicitations. However, it may be that even the expert climber must think about some aspects of her behaviour to exercise her skill effectively. This is so in the second case examined above—that of the skilled surgeon. She is an expert in her field, but must always think about what she is doing to exercise her skill effectively. In a case like this, the agent must always conceptually represent certain requirements for action; she cannot come to perceive everything she must do, no matter how skilled she is. As in the previous case, the represented requirements for action form part of the agent's apprehended environment, together with the perceived solicitations. This composite apprehension of her environment draws forth and guides her behaviour.

The third and fourth cases were examples of what Mooney calls 'little reflections'. These are thoughts about what one is doing, which play a role in one's doing of it, and which

---

[13] Hurley (2001) calls the view that perception functions as input for a system that produces action as its output, with thought in the middle, 'the classical sandwich model'.

should be thought of as part of the flow of behaviour. In the third case, I potter around my kitchen deciding whether to make tea or coffee, decide to make tea, and so make a cup. I then wonder what to eat for breakfast, decide to eat cereals, and so pour myself a bowl. In the fourth case, Mooney realizes he is late for a lecture at Newman House, and so quickens his pace, before later breaking into a run. Before he arrives, he thinks about the tightly packed chairs and squeaky floorboard, working out how to enter the room with as little noise as possible. His plan controls his actions as he arrives in the room. These cases may involve representing requirements for action that go beyond the way the agent perceives the world. Perhaps Mooney has not avoided the squeaky floorboard in Newman House a sufficient number of times for it to solicit him to avoid it. In this case, his representation of it as squeaky—and so to-be-avoided—adds extra significance for his actions. His action of stepping over it when he enters the room is drawn forth and guided by both perceptual solicitations and the represented requirement that he avoid the rogue floorboard. But it may be that in both cases, the agent's thoughts do not add requirements that go beyond those perceived. Instead, thought may play a role in controlling action by affecting the salience of the solicitations. My decision to make a cup of tea makes tea-making solicitations more salient for me than coffee-making ones. I will be more strongly solicited to make tea than coffee, and I will thus make a cup of tea. Similarly, Mooney may often avoid the squeaky floorboard, and thus be solicited to avoid it. However, his thought that he really must avoid it so that he makes as little disturbance as possible, makes the solicitation very salient for him, and so it solicits him very strongly. Importantly, it seems that the thought that makes the affordance salient cannot be discarded once it has served its role of highlighting the affordance. Instead, the affordance only remains salient for the agent as long as the thought is in play. If, e.g., Mooney stops thinking about avoiding the squeaky floorboard, he is likely to step on it as he enters the room. The absence of the thought means that avoiding the squeaky floorboard is no longer salient for him, and the floorboard no longer urgently solicits him to avoid it.

Finally, I must explain how the acting-in-flow cases can be accommodated on my account. I have criticized Dreyfus for taking these cases to be paradigmatic of human action. As we have seen, this leads him to a distorted view of the phenomenology of our behaviour. Thought plays a different, and much greater role in our actions than he allows. Nevertheless, it is clear that the acting-in-flow cases are real phenomena that must be accommodated. I must explain why thinking about what one is doing interferes with action in these cases for my proposal to be satisfactory. I can accommodate these cases in the following way. In certain circumstances, the exercise of certain skills is best controlled by perception. Sporting skills are a typical example.[14] There are a number of

---

[14] Perception is not always the best way to control one's expert exercise of a sporting skill. Berendzen (2010) rightly draws attention to the phenomenon of coaching, which requires the agent to think about what she is doing. Dreyfus (2007) claims that in such activity, the expert regresses to a prior level of proficiency. I agree with Berendzen (2010) that this is unsatisfactory, since coaching is surely an essential part of skilled sporting activity. The top experts are those who can make use of coaching to hone their skills. They are superior to players who cannot adapt their skills to incorporate new techniques and strategies. Thus it is only certain instances of exercising (some) sporting skills that are best controlled by perception.

reasons why this is so. One factor is the speed at which one must act. A familiar fact from everyday experience is that we can sometimes act more quickly than we can think. I catch the mug that falls out of the cupboard before I have time to form any intention to do so. Likewise, I have already swerved to avoid a squirrel in the road before I have time to remember that this is dangerous and could cause an accident. Thus, for those activities where skilful engagement in them requires the agent to act quickly, there will be insufficient time for the agent to think about what she must do. Instead, action must be accomplished in some other way. On the Merleau-Pontyian account, it will be driven by perception. It is also plausible to suppose that we can perceive more finely-grained action requirements than those we can conceptually represent. I can see exactly how far, and in which direction, I must move my leg to kick the ball. It is not clear that I even possess concepts that would allow me to conceptually represent this fact. Of course, I could use a perceptual-demonstrative, and form a representation with the content, 'I must move my leg like *this* to kick the ball' (where the content of 'this' is determined by my perception of how I must kick the ball). But in this case, the relevant information about the action requirement is specified perceptually. Thus the conceptual representation adds nothing further to the action requirements the agent perceives. It is therefore redundant for the control of action; the perceived solicitation is sufficient. There are, no doubt, further reasons why the exercise of certain skills on certain occasions is best controlled by perception, rather than conceptually represented requirements for action.

The cases of acting-in-flow that Dreyfus cites will be instances where the exercise of the skill is best driven by perception. Thought disrupts the flow of action in the following way. When the agent starts to think about what she is doing, she conceptually represents requirements for action. These will be inferior for the control of action to the requirements she perceives—that is, the solicitations. But these conceptually represented requirements will form part of a composite apprehension of her environment, which includes the perceptual solicitations. This composite 'grasp' of her surroundings and the possibilities of action they afford will draw forth and guide her behaviour. Since it incorporates the inferior, conceptually represented action requirements, the resulting behaviour will be less successful than if those conceptual representations were absent. This is why thinking about what one is doing in these cases adversely affects one's doing of it.

5 CONCLUSION

Merleau-Ponty offers an alternative to the traditional view of action as essentially brought about by the agent's intentions. Dreyfus has done much important work in elucidating Merleau-Ponty's view and bringing it to the attention of contemporary theorists. However, Dreyfus conceives of thought as merely triggering absorbed coping, which is entirely guided by the agent's perceptions. Consequently, he cannot explain how the agent's thoughts can play an ongoing role in guiding her behaviour. Dreyfus's view should thus be rejected, both as an interpretation of Merleau-Ponty, and as an account of action in its own right. Whilst Merleau-Ponty does not address the issue of thought-driven action in any detail, his account provides the resources to accommodate this form of behaviour. In this paper, I offer a Merleau-Pontyian proposal for explaining the role of thought in bringing about action.

On my proposal, the agent's behaviour is initiated and controlled by her apprehension of her environment. The agent apprehends her surroundings in terms of the action possibilities they afford her. These are ordered in terms of their salience, with the most salient possibilities soliciting her most strongly. The agent's thoughts are one of the factors that affect the salience of the action opportunities available to the agent. The most salient action possibilities—those with the strongest 'attractive power'—are those that draw forth action. The agent's apprehension of her environment comprises both her perceptions and her conceptual representations of it. The agent may conceptually represent her environment as having properties that go beyond those she perceives. It is the agent's motor skills or habits that make action possible. A motor skill has two interrelated components: a motor aspect (the ability to perform the relevant bodily movements), and a perceptual aspect (the ability to perceive appropriate parts of the world as soliciting those bodily movements). The perceptual component of a motor skill is effectively the power to invest one's surroundings with significance for one's actions. In perception, this involves summoning solicitations from the world. But the same capacity can also be used to imbue conceptual representations with significance for one's behaviour, so that one has a bodily grasp of the action possibilities afforded by the represented state of affairs. This allows the conceptual representation to function like a perceived affordance, drawing forth one's actions.

My proposal explains how thought and perception can combine to simultaneously control action. Indeed, it is doubtful that there are any forms of human action where thought plays *no* role. Even where the agent is not actually thinking about what she is doing, her standing beliefs, desires, intentions and so on will partly determine the strength of the solicitations that draw her to act. It follows that thought plays a far more important role in human behaviour than Dreyfus recognizes.

REFERENCES

Barrington, K. (1968), *Playing it Straight* (London: Stanley Paul).

Berendzen, J. (2010), 'Coping without foundations: on Dreyfus' use of Merleau-Ponty', *International Journal of Philosophical Studies*, 18/5: 629–49.

Bowerman, M., and Choi, S. (2001), 'Shaping meanings for language: Universal and language specific in the acquisition of spatial semantic categories', in M. Bowerman and S. Levinson (eds), *Language Acquisition and Conceptual Development* (Cambridge: Cambridge University Press), pp. 475–511.

Bratman, M. (1984), 'Two faces of intention', *The Philosophical Review*, XCII/3: 375–405.

Dreyfus, H. (1999), 'The primacy of phenomenology over logical analysis: A critique of Searle', *Philosophical Topics*, 27/2: 3–24.

—— (2000), 'A Merleau-Pontyian critique of Husserl's and Searle's representationalist accounts of action', *Proceedings of the Aristotelian Society*, 100/3: 287–302.

Dreyfus, H. (2002), 'Intelligence without representation: Merleau-Ponty's critique of mental representation and the relevance of phenomenology to scientific explanation', *Phenomenology and the Cognitive Sciences*, 1/4: 367–83.

—— (2005a), 'Overcoming the myth of the mental: How philosophers can profit from the phenomenology of everyday expertise', *Proceedings and Addresses of the American Philosophical Association*, 79/2: 47–65.

—— (2005b), 'Response to McDowell', *Inquiry* 50/4: 371–7.

—— (2007), 'The return of the myth of the mental', *Inquiry*, 50/4: 352–65.

—— and Wakefield, J. (1991), 'Intentionality and the phenomenology of action', in E. Lepore and R. Van Gulick (eds) *John Searle and His Critics* (Oxford: Blackwell), pp. 259–70.

Gallagher, S. (2009), 'Review of *Reading Merleau-Ponty: On Phenomenology of Perception*, edited by Thomas Baldwin. London and New York: Routledge, 2007', *Mind* 118/472: 1105–11.

Gibson, J. J. (1977), 'The theory of affordances', in R. Shaw and J. Bransford (eds), *Perceiving, Acting, and Knowing: Toward an Ecological Psychology* (Hillsdale, NJ: Erlbaum), pp. 67–82.

Gumperz, J. J., Levinson, S. C. (1997), 'Rethinking linguistic relativity', *Current Anthropology*, 32: 612–23.

Hurley, S. (2001), 'Perception and action: Alternative views', *Synthese* 129/1: 3–40.

Jacobson, A. J. (unpublished manuscript), 'Implicit bias and moral blameworthiness'.

Merleau-Ponty, M. (1962), *Phenomenology of Perception*, tr. C. Smith (London: Routledge).

—— (1964) 'Indirect language and the voices of silence', in M. Merleau-Ponty, *Signs*, tr. R. McCleary (Evanston: Northwestern University Press), pp. 39–83.

Mooney, T. (unpublished manuscript), 'Reflection as work ongoing: On developing human perception in Merleau-Ponty'.

O'Shaughnessy, B. (1980), *The Will: A Dual Aspect Theory* (two vols.) (Cambridge: Cambridge University Press).

Pollard, B. (2006), 'Explaining actions with habits', *American Philosophical Quarterly*, 43/1: 57–69.

Roberson, D., Davidoff, J., and Shapiro, L. (2000), 'Colour categories are not universal: Replications and new evidence from a Stone-Age culture', *Journal of Experimental Psychology: General*, 129: 369–98.

—— (2002), 'Squaring the circle: The cultural relativity of good shape', *Journal of Cognition and Culture*, 2: 29–53.

Romdenh-Romluc, K. (2007), 'Merleau-Ponty and the power to reckon with the possible', in T. Baldwin (ed.) *Reading Merleau-Ponty* (London: Routledge), pp. 44–58.

—— (2011), 'Embodied cognition and agency', *Proceedings of the Aristotelian Society*, 111/1: 79–95.

—— (in press), 'Habits and attention', in R. Jensen and D. Moran (eds), *The Phenomenology of Embodied Subjectivity* (Dordrecht: Springer).

CHAPTER 11

....

SEX, GENDER, AND EMBODIMENT

....

SARA HEINÄMAA

THE concept of gender is an integral part of contemporary social and human sciences (see, for example, Haig 2004). It covers wide areas of theoretical discourse on communality and intersubjectivity, both empirical studies of human relations and philosophical debates on humanity. *Gender* is used in the analysis, interpretation, and explanation of all essential types of human interaction: social, cultural, historical, economic, political, educational, and religious.

In its explanatory uses the concept has its origin in the anthropological and psychological theories of the 1950s and in the interpretations and applications that early women's studies gave to these theories in the 1960s and 1970s. Since then the concept has been subjected to many forms of critique and has undergone several transformations. Nevertheless, gender discourse has retained its basic theoretical parameters and its central position in human and social sciences. As such, it structures our investigations into the relations between women and men, and between human beings in general.

The aim of this paper is to offer an alternative to this dominant articulation of human existence on the basis of classical phenomenology. I will argue that Husserl's phenomenological inquiries into the structures of embodiment offer a very different starting point for the investigation of sexual difference than the ideas of gender and sex. Whereas gender theories aim at explaining observed differences between men's and women's behaviours, dispositions, accomplishments, and positions by the interplay of social, cultural, and biological forces, phenomenology studies how the sense of sexual difference is established in personal and interpersonal experiences in the first place. It does not offer any empirical theory of human development nor any theory of historical construction. Instead of theorizing it inquires into the meaning foundations of all discourses on men and women, males and females, and masculinity and femininity: biological, psychological, anthropological, historical, and sociological.

Moreover, I will argue that the current debates on the validity of the sex/gender distinction are naïve in the sense that they do not clarify the experiential foundations of the two contrasted objectivities: sex and gender. The aim of the paper is thus to demonstrate the critical philosophical potential of the phenomenological understanding of human beings as bodily-expressive wholes in contrast to the dualistic discourses on gendered roles and sexed bodies.

The paper consists of two major parts. The first part (Sections 1–4) offers a set of systematic and historical clarifications of the conceptual distinction between *gender* and *sex*. The aim is to get clear about the senses in which these concepts are used in contemporary social and human sciences. The latter part (Sections 5–6) shows how the phenomenological account of human embodiment differs from the dominant paradigm of sex-gender interaction. It argues that the female and male bodies which are thematized, theorized, and explained by the biosciences, and distinguished from gendered roles and gendered performances in the social sciences, are themselves results of complicated processes of objectification which rest in their sense on two fundamental types of experiencing bodies: living bodies as instruments for intending material things and living bodies as expressions in communicative interaction with others. This does not mean that the human body would be a mere social construct or cultural artifact. Even if the bioscientific articulation of the human body is an outcome of complicated scientific practices of objectivization and idealization, the body itself is fundamentally a prescientific object that is co-given to us in action and communication and is not something that we make, fabricate, or invent.

1 Two IDEAS OF GENDER: SUBSTANTIAL AND CRITERIAL DEFINITIONS

The current theoretical uses of the concepts of sex and gender, and the conceptual distinction between them, brings together two ideas which are logically distinct but historically conflated (see Heinämaa 1997).

First, sex, and gender are understood and defined by the distinction between *bodily* features and *mental-behavioural* features. In this usage 'sex' refers to the somatic and physiological characteristics of men and women—that is, to the genetic, anatomic, gonadal, hormonal, cerebral, and/or neural aspects of their bodies. 'Gender', on the other hand, refers to the mental-behavioural characteristics of men and women and to their emotional, intellectual, and cognitive capacities and dispositions. Thus, the claim that women are verbally more competent then men would according to this definition be a claim about gender differences; and the claim that women's hormonal balance varies in a cyclic fashion would be a claim about sex. The argument that the hormonal changes in women's bodies engender variations in their cognitive performances would be a claim about a causal relation between sex features and gender characteristics.

I call this the *substantial use* of the concepts *sex* and *gender*; and correspondingly, when the sex/gender distinction is made by reference to the distinction between the bodily and the mental, or the somatic and the psychic-behavioural, I call it the *substantial sex/gender distinction.* Lisa Tuttle's definition in *Encyclopedia of Feminism* gives a good example of this way of understanding the concepts:

> Gender: Whereas sex refers to the *biological, anatomical* differences between male and female, gender refers to the *emotional and psychological* aspects which a given culture expects to coincide with *physical maleness and femaleness.*[1] (Tuttle 1986: 123, my emphasis)

Another example is presented in Anthony Gidden's *Sociology*:

> Sex refers to the *physical* characteristics *of the body*; gender concerns socially learned forms of *behaviour*. (Giddens 2009, my emphasis)

The most common hypotheses of *psychological* gender differences concern motor, perceptual, spatial, verbal, mathematical, and logical skills. Men in general are assumed to manifest well-developed capacities of large-scale spatial articulation, manipulation, and transformation of spatial objects, and/or formal reasoning, whereas women are claimed to perform universally better in verbal, perceptual, and/or fine motor tasks (see, for example, Kimura 1999). The most often discussed supposedly universal differences in *behaviour* include aggressive, assertive, dominating, authoritative, and regulating conduct in men, and empathic, supportive, and caring comportment in women.[2]

The other main way of using the terms 'sex' and 'gender' depends on the distinction between features that are given by nature and features that are determined by social and cultural factors. This way of making the distinction does not include any reference to the contrast between the mental and the bodily; the features of men and women are distinguished and classified solely on the basis of their causal origin or genesis. I call this the *criterial use* of the terms, and the corresponding distinction I call the *criterial sex/gender distinction.* A typical example is found in another feminist encyclopedia:

> Gender: a culturally-shaped group of attributes and behaviours given to the female or the male. (Humm 1990: 84)

In this usage, 'gender' refers to any differences between men and women—be they mental, behavioural, or somatic—which have their origin in society or culture—that is, in social practices, norms, and traditions. Correspondingly, 'sex', and the related terms 'male' and 'female', refer to properties which are determined purely biologically without any social or cultural conditioning. Thus, on the criterial understanding, it is the causal origin of a characteristic that determines whether it is to be classified as a sex or a gender feature. For example, if the observed differences in men's and women's brains (for example, Kimura 1993) would turn out to be results from different treatment, experience, and training, then these bodily differences would be called 'gender differences' according to the criterial understanding of the terms. On the other hand, if it were to be established that the differences in men's and women's motor or verbal performances have a genetic

---

[1] See Fausto-Sterling: 'the term *gender*...necessarily excludes biology' (Fausto-Sterling 2000: 21).
[2] For critiques of such assimilations, see Section 4 below.

ground (for example, Watson and Kimura 1991; for a contrary argument, see Young 1990), then these differences would be sex differences.

The criterial understanding of the terms 'sex' and 'gender' is not restricted to feminist theory but extends to vast areas of social and human sciences as well as to medical discourses on human affairs. A recent example is provided by the World Health Organization webpage:

> Gender refers to the *socially constructed* roles, behaviours, activities, and attributes that a particular society considers appropriate for men and women. (WHO, my emphasis; see Ryan 2007).

Many different sets of theoretical concepts are used in the description and explanation of the process in which biologically determined sex turns into socially significant gender.

One group of concepts comes from theories of learning: gender is understood as the adopted way of construing and executing sex characteristics. Some learning-theoretical concepts are mentalistic and some are behaviouristic; some have positive connotations, some negative, and some are neutral: gender is claimed to result from conditioning, reinforcement, encouragement, discouragement, imitation, discipline, and/or coercion.

Another influential group of ideas is derived from the psychoanalytical theories of Sigmund Freud, Jacques Lacan, Melanie Klein, and Donald W. Winnicott. Here gender is understood as resulting from the imaginary identifications typical of the mirror stage of infant development or from the object-relation dynamics of early childhood. These are not processes of learning but processes of primary individuation and development of selfhood. Theories derived from or inspired by psychoanalysis imply that gender identification is a primordial formation and deeply integrated with the structures of selfhood, individuality, and autonomy. They also suggests a very different set of practices for any attempt to change or transform gender characteristics than do learning theories: rather than referring to education or enculturation by school, media, and other social agents, these theories focus on the dual relations and early interactions between newborns and their caretakers (for example, Mead 1950; Chodorow 1978).

Many feminist theories resort to the concepts of *matter* and *form* to illustrate the processes in which sex turns into gender: sexed bodies are characterized as the physical stuff or material substance, which the social machinery as a whole shapes or molds into gendered persons. Early childhood relations, training in nurseries and schools, models of the media, working life, and leisure activities are all studied as stages of a large scale 'production of gender'. Gayle Rubin's characterization is exemplary and has been very influential in all areas of women's studies. For her, gender is 'a set of arrangements by which the biological raw material of human sex and procreation is shaped by human, social intervention' (Rubin 1975: 165; see Grosz 1994: 55).[3]

---

[3] Anne Fausto-Sterling introduces the Aristotelian metaphors of clay, carving, and sculpting to make sense of the idea of gender-construction: while 'bodies provide the raw material, without a human cultural setting the clay could not be molded into recognizable psychic form' (Fausto-Sterling 2000: 23).

2 Conceptual clarifications

As said, the substantial and criterial usages are often conflated in gender discourse: gender is associated with the mental *and* with the social, and sex is linked to the bodily *and* to the natural. For systematic and historical purposes it is important to distinguish these two uses, since their implications differ in crucial respects, and the combinatory usage is not the only usage that we find in the history of modern life-sciences, biosciences, and human-social sciences. On the contrary, the combinatory usage is a relatively recent phenomenon.

In the following I will offer an analysis on the implications of the substantial and criterial usages of the sex/gender distinction and a short overview of the history of the distinction. We will see that even if the two ways of defining and understanding the sex/gender distinction differ in crucial aspects, they share some common starting points which can been questioned by radical critical inquiries into our experiential and conceptual possibilities. After these clarifications I will sketch a phenomenological alternative to the sex/gender framework, and argue that it involves broader and philosophically more adequate insights than theories of biological sexes and sociocultural genders.

The first thing to notice is that whereas the substantial definition specifies the content of the two categories *sex* and *gender*, the criterial usage leaves the content of each category for empirical and critical inquiries to decide. More precisely, the criterial usage does not directly specify which personal attributes or types of personal attributes belong to the category of sex and which to the category of gender. If it turns out, for example, that some hormonal or cerebral differences between men and women result from complex long-lasting interactions between biological and cultural–social factors, then these differences, which by definition are sex differences according to the substantial understanding, would be classified as gender differences according to the criterial understanding. In short, the two ways of classifying sex and gender characteristics mark them out on a different basis, and thus their categories may not correspond or coincide.

Insofar as the two definitions are conflated, the assumption is that *only* behavioural and mental differences between men and women have their origin in culture and society. In other words, bodily differences (differences in body shape, structure, and physical constitution) are supposed to be largely independent of sociocultural factors. Nancy Chodorow's influential characterization of gender personalities serves as an example here:

> Girls and boys develop different *relational capacities* and *senses of self* as a result of growing up in a family in which women mother. These *gender personalities* are reinforced by differences in identification processes of boys and girls that also result from women's mothering. (Chodorow 1978: 173, my emphasis)

The main idea in Anthony Gidden's definition of gender is the same:

> Gender: Social expectations about behaviour regarded as appropriate for the members of each sex. Gender does not refer to the *physical* attributes[4] in terms of which men and women differ, but to *socially formed* traits of masculinity and femininity.[5] (Giddens 2009, my italics)

Gender qualities are here defined by two independent factors: firstly they are sorted out as non-bodily—mental, psychological, or behavioural—qualities, and secondly as those qualities that originate in social interaction. Hence, two theoretical options are rejected by definition: the extreme bio-determinist hypothesis according to which most, if not all, observed differences between men and women have purely biological origins (for example, Kimura 1993, 1999), and the radical constructivist idea according to which most, if not all, of these differences result from cultural and social arrangements (for example, Devor 1989; Fausto-Sterling 1992, 2000, 2003).

Second, the substantial and the criterial senses of the sex/gender distinction relate to two very different groups of classical conceptual distinctions. The substantial definition refers back to the distinctions soma/psyche, body/mind, and physical/mental, whereas the criterial definition associates with the distinctions natural/cultural, permanent/changing, natural/artificial, given/made, and real/fictitious (see Gatens 1991; Jay 1991; Fausto-Sterling 1992; Grosz 1994; Fausto-Sterling 2000: 3–5). According to the first set of associations, sex is the bodily setting of a gendered soul; according to the latter, sex is the raw matter that nature provides for the cultural production of gendered artifacts, constructs, and fabrications.[6]

The next section illuminates the short history of the sex/gender distinction with the purpose of making sense of its ambiguous and equivocal character. The exercise has two advantages: first it shows how the conceptual distinction between the substantial and the criterial sex/gender distinction became historically possible; and second, it also allows us to study the common presumptions about human existence that both uses share.

---

[4] The term 'physical' is multiply equivocal and covers several related senses which can be distinguished analytically. 'Physical attributes' can refer to (i) attributes studied in the *medical sciences*, (ii) natural material attributes given through *sense-perception*, (iii) attributes discovered by *natural scientific* methods, or finally (iv) *bodily* or *corporeal* attributes. Thus, Gidden's definition of gender could in principle be read as simply operating with the contrast between natural and cultural and not restricting gender construction to mental or psychological features. However, if we keep in mind his definition of sex quoted above ('sex refers to the physical characteristics of the body') then his understanding of gender seems to involve both the idea of culture and the idea of the mental.

[5] See David Halperin's characterization of sexual orientation: 'sexuality is not a *somatic fact*, it is a *cultural effect*' (Halperin 1993: 416, my italics).

[6] For the metaphors of production and machinery in gender research and bio-sciences, see Birke 1999.

3 Historical backgrounds

Before the 1950s the terms 'gender' and 'sex' were often used interchangeably and synonymously in reference to men and women and to human males and females. The terminology was fluent, and not yet theoretically nor conceptually fixed.[7]

The theoretical concept of gender was introduced in the 1950s in Anglophone psychomedical discourse concerning the behavioural differences between men and women. It was erected on the new classifications of human types which developed in the nineteenth century with the progress of the biosciences and medicine.

Studies in the history the life sciences show that toward the end of the nineteenth century a new dimorphic conception of sex (male versus female) replaced the old polymorphic conception (for example, Dreger 1998, Laquer 1990). This change involved several ideas. The first new idea was that the organic and functional sex-features given in perception correspond uniformly with unobservable mechanisms and components disclosed by the developing medical sciences and biosciences. Thus, the external and internal sex organs of women (for example, the vagina and the womb) and the female reproductive functions (for example, menstruation and lactation) were connected, step by step, to a network of chromosomal, genetic, hormonal, and cerebral factors. Correspondingly, observable male organs and functions (for example, the penis and ejaculation) were connected to a different set of unobservable components. Second, the newly-discovered *imperceptibles* were taken as *causally responsible* for the observable differences. Female hormones and chromosomal structures were identified as the ultimate causes of female genitals, gonads, and functions, and correspondingly with the male structures. Third, the idea was that sex characteristics are mutually exclusory.

---

[7] The terms 'sex' and 'gender' have been used interchangeably in English language sources from the fourteenth century for referring to the characteristics that differentiate between men and women. Beginning in the 1960s, 'gender' became more and more used as an euphemism for 'sex': since it lacked connotations to sexual intercourse and copulation and sexual activities more generally, it allowed a general discourse on men and women, their differences, similarities, and relations (OED). The theoretical usage of 'gender', discussed in this paper, should not be confused with this rhetoric usage, even if both uses have common historical roots.

The term 'gender' also has the special linguistic usage: it differentiates between three (or two) grammatical kinds of substantives (and pronouns). The phenomenon of grammatical or syntactic gender characterizes all Indo-European languages, but it is named differently in different languages (not always by a word that has roots in the Latin 'genus'). Moreover, there is variation in the number of the syntactical categories thus named: German language, for example, has three grammatical genders, but the Romanic languages only have two. There are languages and families of languages that do not have anything equivalent to grammatical gender (for example, the Finno-Ugrian languages Estonian and Finnish). In *Female and Male* (1950), Margaret Mead underlines the methodological importance of this linguistic fact: 'We know by sad experience how difficult it is for those who have been reared within one civilization ever to get outside its categories, to imagine, for instance, what a language could be like that had thirteen genders. Oh, yes, one says, masculine, feminine, and neuter—and what in the world are the other ten' (Mead 1950: 35; see Chiland 2003: 6–7).

Individuals that combined male and female body features, organs, functions, or structures were considered medically abnormal or biologically deformed.

The dimorphic model is so commonplace to us now that it is hard for us to imagine any other way of conceiving sex and discussing it. However, a series of studies in the history of sex-concepts show that prior to twentieth-century maleness and femaleness were not conceptualized as mutually exclusive features. Individuals with mixed or ambiguous genitals and gonads were considered exceptional but not medically or physiologically abnormal. Similarly, women with male bodily features, such as a beard, and men with female bodily features, such as breasts, were considered as normal variations of human embodiment (Dreger 1998).

The theoretical concept of gender was established on the foundation of the new dimorphic idea of sex. The main discourses in which it was introduced were psychodynamic and psychological studies on intersexed individuals.[8] The first principled distinction between sex and gender was made by the psychologists John Money and his colleagues, who in the 1950s studied the mental development and the behaviour patterns of precocious and intersexed children.[9]

Money's main aim was to explain observed variations in the emotional and intellectual development of these individuals by reference to social and cultural factors. In his early studies with Joan G. Hampson he argued that the somatic condition of sexual precocity does not correlate with any aspects of psychological maturity—intellectual, emotional, or linguistic. Hampson and Money presented an alternative hypothesis, according to which psychological maturity is a result of several factors, some of which are somatic and genetic, but many of which include social and cultural interaction.[10]

---

[8] Starting already in 1930s, comparative studies in anthropology disclosed a wide variation in the social roles and forms of conduct of men and women of different cultures. Margaret Mead studied the behavioural patterns of men and women in New Guinean tribes, and demonstrated that these patterns vary greatly: men in one tribe conducted themselves in ways which were considered natural and proper to females in another tribe, and conversely. Moreover, Mead argued that the behavioural patterns of modern Western cultures are very similar to the patterns identified in one of such tribes. However, Mead did not introduce the term 'gender' as a theoretical or analytical concept, but used the terms 'sex', 'style of behaviour', 'constitutional type', 'role', and 'temperament' (Mead 1950).

[9] John Money worked in an interdisciplinary group of psychologists and physicists at the pediatric endocrinology clinic of the Johns Hopkins Hospital.

[10] Money and Hampson used the concept of life experience to account for the individual variations that were reported, observed, tested, and measured in the development of the children under study. They argued that 'psychosexual maturation is determined by various life experiences encountered and transacted, and is not predetermined as some sort of automatic or instinctual product of the bodily achievement of sexual maturation' (Hampson and Money 1955: 16).

The most well-known case of Money is the case of David Reimer, who was born male (on the basis of chromosomal and genital-gonadal criteria) but reassigned and raised as female after an unsuccessful cauterization that destroyed his penis when he was nine months old. Reimer was subjected to several surgical and hormonal treatments for the creation of female genitals. He was renamed and educated as a girl under the supervision and counselling of Money. After several years of counselling, Money reported the reassignment as successful, and used it to argue that gender is not biologically determined. Raimer, however, changed his sex back to male at the age of fifteen, was operated again, and lived as man (Diamond and Sigmundson 1997). He challenged Money's judgement in public, and wanted to make his case well-known in order to warn about superficial and arbitrary classifications and mistreatments. His case is discussed in the literature under the title 'the John-Joan case'; see, for example, Butler 2004.

In another paper, Money introduced the term 'gender role' to describe and explain how individual children adjust their outlooks, bearing, and behaviour in order to compensate for the disparity between their bodily development and the social expectations and standards of normality:

> The term 'gender role' is used to signify all those things that a person says or does to disclose himself or herself as having the status of boy or man, girl or woman, respectively. It includes, but is not restricted to, sexuality in the sense of eroticism. (Money 1955; see 1994)

Money's idea of behavioural gender roles was adopted by the psychoanalyst and psychiatrist Robert Stoller and applied in the analysis of the transvestism and transsexualism (Stoller 1964).[11] Stoller put forward the argument that transvestism and transsexualism are behavioural and mental conditions which are not determined by the biological constitution of the individuals but involve crucial sociocultural determinants—most importantly, the dynamism of the early mother–child relationship. Stoller titled his work *Sex and Gender: The Development of Masculinity and Femininity* (1968). He defined 'male sex' and 'female sex' as two exclusionary sets of interrelated organic, anatomical, and biological characteristics, and 'masculine gender' and 'feminine gender' as two sets of behaviour and mental properties: feelings, thoughts, fantasies, self-identifications, roles, and ways of posturing, gesturing, and moving. I quote a rather long paragraph to make clear how the terms were delineated in this early study:

> Thus, with few exceptions, there are two sexes, male and female. To determine sex, one has to assay the following physical conditions: chromosomes, external genitalia, internal genitalia (e.g., uterus, prostate), gonads, hormonal states, and secondary sex characteristics. (It seems likely that in the future another criterion will be added: brain system). One's sex then is determined by an algebraic sum of these qualities, and, as is obvious, most of the people fall under one of the two separate bell curves... Gender is a term that has psychological and cultural rather than biological connotations. If the proper terms of sex are 'male' and 'female', then the corresponding terms for gender are 'masculine' and 'feminine'; these latter being quite independent of (biological) sex/ (Stoller 1974: 9; see 1964: 220–1)

Money's and Stoller's ways of using the concepts *sex* and *gender* were primarily substantial, dependent on the distinction between the physical–bodily and the mental, but their arguments about gender development introduced the idea of sociocultural origin and conditioning which later became the core idea of the criterial usage and understanding of the term 'gender'.

Many Anglophone feminists of the 1960s and 1970s adopted and developed further this explanatory strategy. Prominent theorists such as Kate Millett (1969), Germaine Greer (1970), Ann Oakley (1972), and Nancy Chodorow (1978) applied Stoller's sex/gender framework in their analysis of the relationships between women and men. They

---

[11] For a critical discussion of the Moneyan paradigm, see Chiland 2003: 4–10, 14–18, 81.

referred directly to Stoller's work and used his conceptual distinctions to argue that the dominance of men and the subordination of women are not hard-wired in the biology of the human species. Like Money and Stoller, the early feminists argued that most behavioural patterns result from complex causal interaction between biological and social factors, such as the early mother–child interaction,[12] training and education, and the stereotypes distributed by the media. Consequently, social arrangements are largely responsible for women's subordinate position, and conversely this subordination can be terminated by transforming social practices.

It is important to notice that with the concepts of sex and gender, the feminists of the 1960s and 1970s adopted the explanatory framework of Money and Stoller: the term 'gender' was first fixed substantially to refer to mental and behavioural features, and it was then *argued* that gender, thus defined, is a product of sociocultural forces (for example, Millett 1970: 26–33; Greer 1972: 12–22; Oakley 1972: 16). Two crucial factors of this explanatory framework are the idea of a biological basis of sexual differences and the causal paradigm of explanation.

First, the presumption was that all human beings are naturally divided into two categories of bodily beings: male beings and female beings. The question was why and how male beings typically develop into masculine beings and female to feminine beings. The assumption that the categories of male and female reflect natural kinds, and are not themselves socially influenced, was not problematized.

Second, the process of becoming gendered was understood causally in these early feminist treatises: masculinity and femininity were described as the combined effect of social, cultural, and biological causes. So, although Money, Stoller, and their feminist successors questioned the assumption that mental and behavioural differences are determined by biological ones, they did not question the adequacy of the causalistic framework as such but reinstated and remodelled it in their own accounts of the establishment of gender. To be sure, they theorized a great variety of different sorts of causes, psychological, social, and biological, but the main element of causal explanation in the Humean sense prevailed: the idea that the objects that operate as causes in explanations can and must be identified independently of objects that operate as effects, and conversely.

Metaphors of production and construction proved useful and powerful in these early critical accounts of sexual differentation. Sexed bodies were understood as natural resources that the patriarchal society uses for making gender products for its stability and preservation. In this discourse, one did not *become* a woman, as Simone de Beauvoir argued in *The Second Sex* (1991: 295), one was *made* a woman (for example, Millett 1969: 32; Greer 1970: 17ff.).

---

[12] The most common version of Freudian psychoanalysis that was, and is, used in these arguments was the so-called *object relations theory*, which is one form of psychodynamic theories and was developed in the 1940s and 1950s by British psychoanalysts Donald Fairbairn, Melanie Klein, Donald W. Winnicott, and others.

4 THREE CRITIQUES OF THE SEX/GENDER DISTINCTION

Starting in the 1970s and 1980s, this understanding of how women and men are made has been problematized in several different ways. Especially, three central arguments should be kept in mind.

First, the validity of the substantial concept of *gender* is questioned by theorists who emphasize differences in the ethnic identities, sexual orientations, or historical settings of human individuals. These critical attacks are launched against the idea of gender as a uniform category. The argument is that women and men do not fall into two separate and internally unified groups on the basis of their behavioural or psychological qualities. Their forms of conduct, experiences, dispositions, and capacities vary greatly according to ethnic and religious setting, sexual orientation, and historical period.

Moreover, theorists of race and sexuality maintain that psychological and behavioural differences among women and differences among men are equally prevalent and fundamental as the differences between the sexes. Thus, they contend that the analytic concepts of gender, race, and class are mutually informing (e.g. Hooks 1981; 1990; Collins 1990; 2005).

Second, also the adequacy and validity of the substantial concept of *sex* has been questioned—that is, the idea of dimorphism of the human organism. This attack comes from two different but interrelated directions.

As we have already seen, historians of science have demonstrated that the dimorphic concept of sex is a relatively recent formation, dating back to the nineteenth century. Moreover, these investigations suggest that the sense and validity of the concept of sex is limited and restricted by the specific interests that dominated the development of the behavioural sciences at the turn of the century: organization of large-scale population surveys, mathematization of psychological and social studies, and progress in biomedical technologies (for example, Herd 1996; Dreger 1998).[13]

Also feminist biologists have questioned the substantial concept of sex. These critiques attack the presumed correspondences between the genetic, hormonal, and neural structures associated with genital and gonadal sex. Moreover, the division male/female has proved fuzzy on all levels of investigation. Anne Fausto-Sterling summarizes this line of argument by stating: 'There is non either/or. Rather there are shades of differences' (Fausto-Sterling 2000: 3). In light of such critiques it seems that the sex characteristics of human individuals vary greatly, and on all levels, and that pure maleness and pure femaleness are two extremes on a rich and multilayered continuum.[14]

---

[13] Many of these arguments are influenced by Foucault's genealogical–historical methods.

[14] Based on this, some theorists have suggested that the concept *sex* should be taken as a cluster concept in Putnam's sense or as a family resemblance concept in Wittgenstein's sense (Wittgenstein 2003: 77–88, 145–52; Putnam 1979: 52ff.). Stone (2007), for example, argues that instead of looking for necessary and sufficient conditions for the usage of *male* and *female*, we should acknowledge that both concepts cover a variety of different phenomena which are connected only by partial and sporadic links.

Together, historical and biological inquiries suggest that the dimorphic notion of sex is prescriptive and constructive[15]: rather than neutrally describing the factual condition of human bodies, it directs and motivates individual and collective decisions and actions that make human bodies adjust to the dualistic categories (for example, Eder 2010).

Third, a more radical line of critique is presented by Judith Butler in *Gender Trouble* (1990). Influenced by the Foucault's theory of epistemic regimes and discursive constitution of objects,[16] Butler argues that sex and gender are both 'discursive effects' that lack all grounds and referents outside our conceptual systems (Butler 1990: 6–8; 1993: 29). This would mean that both individual sex characteristics and sex identity as the supposedly underlying base for gender production are cultural formations. Moreover, Butler claims that the idea of a natural basis of sex is itself part of the ideology which construes and molds human bodies: 'gender is also the discursive/cultural means by which "sexed nature" or "a natural sex" is produced and established as "prediscursive", prior to culture, a politically neutral surface *on which* culture acts' (Butler 1990: 7, see 73–4).

As a result of these new developments in gender and women's studies, the sexed body is no longer conceived as a natural given but is theorized as a result of sociocultural conditions. However, this idea can be—and has been—formulated in several different ways, and these formulations are not themselves innocent but carry with them assumptions concerning the sense of the body and the nature of human embodiment.

The new insight is often expressed using the criterial concept of gender and the related metaphors of production and construction. Butler, for example, states that 'gender ought not to be conceived merely as the cultural inscription of meaning on a pre-given sex', but 'must also designate the very apparatus of production whereby the sexes themselves are established' (Butler 1990: 7). Similarly, Thomas Laquer resorts to the criterial concept of gender when summarizing the results of his studies in the history of biosciences: 'some of the so-called sex differences in biological and sociological research turn out to be gender differences after all' (Laquer 1990: 13).

It is crucial to notice that although these kinds of formulations reject the idea of pre-given sex—male or female—free of all cultural and social influences and determinants, they retain the two basic explanatory parameters of the dominant sex/gender theories: (i) the idea of a biological–organic substratum, and (ii) the paradigm of causal explanation.

The concepts of production, construction, machinery, and apparatus bring with them the idea of a *raw material*—that is, the biological organism, that is prior to and independent of the process of 'sexing' human bodies; in other words, molding them into

---

[15] Two main ideas must be distinguished here: (i) construction in the concrete sense of surgical manipulation of genitals or medical manipulation of hormonal balance, and (ii) construction in the abstract sense of formation of beliefs, values, and theories that concern human bodies and affect our handing of them (see Haslanger 2003).

[16] Butler (1990, 1993) draws from several different sources. The main framework of her critique of the sex/gender distinction is Nietzschean–Foucaultian, but this methodological ground is enriched and complicated by pragmatistic, deconstructivistic, psychoanalytical, and semiotic–semantic arguments.

females and males, women and men. The new hypothesis is that even females and males are results of sociocultural forces. This implies that there must be something that precedes theses constructs and passes as their raw material: an organism that is free of the dichotomous categories and norms of the culture.

So, even though the line between the naturally given and the culturally produced is drawn in a new way within the stock of human qualities, it is still there, with the traditional epistemological and ontological assumptions about the primacy and independency of the natural.[17]

The concepts of production, construction, mechanism, and apparatus also suggest a certain understanding of the interaction between the biological body and the normative and signifying practices of the culture. It suggests that the interaction between them is essentially *causal or functional*: the organic material (genes, hormones, gonads, genitals, brains, organisms) and the machinery of sex/gender are conceived as two separate systems that can be identified and described independently (see Birke 1989: 88–91; see also Merleau-Ponty 1964: 38–46/20–6).[18]

So, when the sex/gender distinction is rejected by arguing that even sex is a sociocultural product, part of the 'logic' of the distinction remains: the logic of raw materials and formative forces, causes and effects, and facts and fabrications.

Husserlian phenomenology offers a philosophical alternative to this way of understanding human bodies. Instead of substituting social explanations for biological ones, or mixing both to theorize sociobiological interaction, it demonstrates that the explanatory framework of causes and effects on the whole is inadequate for the analysis of the plurality of our bodily existence and sexual difference as a dimension of this existence.

5 The many senses of the body

While studying the experiential grounds of spatiality and thinghood, Husserl developed a rich set of conceptual distinctions between different senses of the living body.[19] The French phenomenologists, Lévinas, Sartre, Merleau-Ponty, and Beauvoir, complemented

---

[17] This is why Butler, who in her account of sex and gender wants to get rid of all nature/culture distinctions, needs to elaborate on her claim. She adds that the production of sex is a process which generates even its own materials (Butler 1990: 37–8, 73–7; see 1993: 29). This elaboration is just another way of stating that the process in question should not be conceived as a process of production in the usual and proper sense of the word. In effect, *Gender Trouble* aims at demonstrating that becoming sexed—male/female—must be conceptualized in another way: as repetitive *action* and citational *performance* (Butler 1990: 136–9, 144–5, see 1993: 9–11, 107–9).

[18] In *Bodies that Matter*, Butler explicitly rejects this implication of her earlier formulations by writing: 'construction is neither a single act nor a causal process initiated by a subject and culminating in a set of fixed effects' (1993: 10). In order to make sense of her Foucaultian notion of intentional but non-subjectivistic sex-construction (see Foucault 1976: 118–25/90–5), she introduces the concepts of sedimentation, repetition, reiteration, variation, and flesh, which have their origin in phenomenological and post-phenomenological accounts of sense and signification.

[19] For an explication of Husserl's originative analyses of embodiment, see Heinämaa 2011.

these studies with analyses of affective and erotic relations. Lévinas inquiries focused on the phenomena of fecundity and generativity but he also developed an influential account of caress and its dynamism. Sartre studied the constitution of human subjectivity and embodiment in interpersonal relations, and analysed our attempts to overcome our fundamental indeterminacy in self-deception or bad faith and in relations of love, desire, hate, indifference, and sadism–masochism. Merleau-Ponty related the phenomena of sexuality and sexual desire to the fundamental processes of motility, sensibility, and affectivity; and Beauvoir introduced the problematics of sexual hierarchization and ambivalence.[20]

Thanks to this groundwork, contemporary phenomenology contains a powerful toolkit for the examination of the various aspects of human embodiment. In this framework, sexual difference is disclosed not as one unified structure or as a simple opposition, but as a multiplicity of different and interrelated phenomena. To be sure, sexual difference is a bodily difference, though its bodiliness is not one formation but involves several components and layers: sensibility, motility, thinghood, materiality, perceptibility, affectivity, and expressivity.

The traditional oppositions of mind/body and culture/nature can be avoided, since all phenomena—mental and bodily, cultural and natural—are studied under their subjective *and* objective aspects and under the *correlation* between the subjective and the objective. Instead of two separate realms or layers of reality, the mental–cultural and the material–natural, we discover a variety of phenomena with intentional as well as sensible determinants: The human body is not just grasped as a material thing or a bio-mechanism, but is also understood as our fundamental way of relating to the material world and all worldly objects. The human mind is not a self-enclosed pure spirit but is necessarily expressed in bodily gestures and corporeally related to other 'embodied minds' or 'minded bodies'. Nature is not just an object of the physical sciences but is also the common field for all perceiving, moving, and acting bodies. And culture is not merely a system of varying significations and cumulative productions but more fundamentally a form of generative life grounded in the consciousness of mortality (for example, Husserl 1988: 140–2, 180–2).

Unlike the traditional concepts of mind and body, the phenomenological concepts of consciousness and objectivity are mutually implicatory: intentional consciousness is always consciousness *of something*, and the intended objectivity is always valid *for someone*. This means that all bodily phenomena involve both subjective and objective factors. By differentiating between their types and forms, we can disclose several aspects and layers of human embodiment.

First, when human and animal bodies are studied by the experimental and mathematical methods of modern natural sciences—in medicine, physiology, and zoology

---

[20] This discourse has influenced contemporary theory of sexual difference also through Lacan's critical discussion of Sartre (for example, Lacan 1973) and through the works of the so-called French feminists—most importantly, Irigaray and Kristeva (see Heinämaa 2010). For the Husserlian starting points of feminist phenomenology, see Heinämaa and Rodemeyer 2010.

for example—they are thematized as *complicated mechanisms*. They appear as individuals of biological species, as biochemical structures, or as information systems. The causal–functional concepts are necessary for the natural scientific articulation of bodies, but they do not exhaust the senses of human embodiment (Husserl 1952: 159–60/167–8, 181–4/190–4; see Sartre 1943: 349–52/409–13; Merleau-Ponty 1945: 82–105/67–89, 173–9/148–53; 1964: 38–46/20–6). Several other senses are essential to and central in our conscious lives.

In everyday practical contexts, our own bodies and the bodies of others appear to us primarily as *instruments* for the manipulation of material things. I throw the ball in the air and the dog catches it with its mouth; the child reaches for a cup and I hand it over to her. At the same time, our bodies are given to us as our ultimate means for using other tools; and this is also how other living bodies appear to us in everyday practices. The sailor manipulates the lines with his fingers in order to manoeuvre the sails and to propel the boat; the surgeon presses the scalpel on the skin of the patient in order to cut it open and to obtain access to the damaged inner tissues (see Husserl 1952: 152/159–60, 203–5/214–15, 234–6/246–7; 1954: 108–11/106–9, 219–22/215–19). Therfore, we can characterize our bodies as second-order tools or as *meta-instruments* (Sartre 1943: 362–5/425–7, 380/446–7; see Heidegger 1927: 67–70/95–100, Merleau-Ponty 1945: 271–2/235).²¹ Or alternatively we can also say that the living bodies incorporate instruments and thus extend their active and habitual reach of the world (Merleau-Ponty 1945: 90–1/106–7, 166–72/142–7; 1963: 59/138).

We can also manipulate our own bodies, and use tools for this. When we cut our own skin with a knife, for example, in order to remove a thorn or a piece of glass, one part of our body functions as a tool and the other part is intended as mere flesh or fleshy matter (see Husserl 1952: 154–6/162–3, 160–1/167–8). This type of thingly self-objectification is not restricted to situations of injury. In *Being and Nothingness*, Sartre studies social contexts which motivate similar acts of self-objectification. He gives the example of a young woman who tries to avoid the advances of a male companion by neglecting the erotic significations of his words.²² When the admirer dares her physical rejection and touches her hand, the woman changes her relation to her own body in a complex way in order to

---

²¹ Also, animal bodies are meta-instruments. Chimpanzees, for example, use straws to catch ants and worms, and octopods are able to open jars with their tentacles. However, within the framework of classical phenomenology, animal instrumentality proves to be severly limited in its temporal horizons: animal practices and animal tools are essentially bound to the present, since animals do not experience themselves as members of generations and chains of generations. Humans share their instruments with their predecessors and successors, and operate in an open infinity of such co-users, but animal instrumentality is bound to the present and shared—at best—merely with contemporaries (for example, Husserl 1973a: 181, 224–5; 1988: 97–100).

²² Sartre studies this example while developing his influential theory of bad faith or self-deception as a necessary structure of human existence. In the same context he also discusses the case of a frigid woman and that of a homosexual man. Several feminist commentators have problematized Sartre's use of examples and argued that they betray an androcentric or 'heterosexist' bias (for example, Le Dœuff 1989: 74–82/60–8; Barnes 1999; Hoagland 1999).

delimit the erotic senses involved in the situation. Instead of identifying with her hand, she distances from it and acts as if the hand would be just another thing lying on the table:

> To leave the hand there is to consent herself to flirt, to engage herself. To withdraw is to break the restless and unstable harmony which gives the hour its charm… the young woman leaves her hand there, but she *does not acknowledge* that she leaves it… the hand rests inert between the warm hands of her companion—neither consenting nor resisting—a thing. (Sartre 1943: 90/97, translation modified; see Merleau-Ponty 1945: 271/321)

Sartre's description also highlights the fact that in communicative contexts, instrumental articulations make way for expressive intentionality, and accordingly human bodies are given to us as *meaningful gestures* (see Merleau-Ponty 1945: 176–7/151). The caressing hand of the lover does not appear as an instrument for the manipulation of physical things but is given as an expression of his desire. It is exactly this expressive phenomenon that allows us to understand the absentminded and inattentive behaviour of the woman, her disinclination to respond to the touching by the habitual gestures of withdrawal or approach.[23]

Erotic situations in general frame human bodies as expressions of desire, passion, and pleasure. The face, the hands, the genitals, and the whole body of the desiring person indicate the presence of his or her passion and express or manifest its particular form. The ecstatic face is not given to us as a goal or a means to a goal, but appears as a manifestation of delight or *jouissance* which grows with each turn in the expressive exchange (see Lévinas 1947: 77–83/84–90; 1961: 264–5/262–3; Irigaray 1984: 27–39/21–33, 173–99/185–217). If we characterize emotional expressions as means that serve well-defined and predetermined ends, then we subject the phenomenon to inadequate concepts and neglect its specific structure and dynamism (see Merleau-Ponty 1945: 215–8/184–7, 229–30/196–7).

Finally, Sartre's case-study shows that instrumental intentionality may combine with the affective and erotic intentionality. However, by themselves, practical acts are not able to establish affective salience and sense which is a necessary component of all erotic life. For this, other types of act are needed—those of valuing and desiring—and these are established on feelings and intersubjective reciprocal drives.[24]

In the light of phenomenological analysis of embodiment, the concepts of sex are not sufficient for the philosophical theory of sexual difference, since they only capture

---

[23] Simone de Beauvoir argues in *The Second Sex* that this type 'indecision' or ambivalence between withdrawal and consent, repulsion, and attraction is characteristic of feminine desire in general: 'we should regard as originally given this type of call, at the same time urgent and frightening, which is woman's desire: it is the indissoluble synthesis of attraction and repulsion that characterizes it' (Beauvoir 1993: 92/81). Beauvoir also argues that instrumental intentionality dominates masculine desire, whereas feminine desire is affective in a more comprehensive way (for example, 1991: 147/393, 181–2/416).

[24] For drive intentionality, see Bernet 1996; Depraz 2001; Bernet 2006; Smith 2010.

bodies as components of causal–functional nexuses and thus overlook rich areas of experience in which bodies appear as motivational, intentional, and expressive. These latter types of relation are not reducible to causal relations, because their relata—the motivating and the motivated, the intended and the intending, and the expressed and the expressive—are mutually dependent and are not separable or changeable parts of a fixed whole (see Merleau-Ponty 1945: 184–94/158–66).[25] Human bodies are not just nodes in nexuses of causal–functional relations but are also expressive units tied to other expressive units by internal relations of sense, motivation, and communication. By definition, the bio-scientific concept of organic sex do not capture such bodily relations.

There is no use in adding gender as system of significance on the top of a body defined by purely causal–mechanical terms. Such an addition may present the body as invested with cultural significations and meanings, but it does not help us to capture the sense-*forming* aspects of embodiment or the body as a *source* of meaning. More precisely, the sex/gender distinction articulates womanhood and manhood[26] as two different types of psycho/physical reality—femininity/femaleness and masculinity/maleness—but it does not contribute to a philosophical understanding of the experiential foundations of these two-layered realities.

Husserl's phenomenology of embodiment provides a philosophical analysis of the psycho-physical articulation of human embodiment, its grounds, and its limits. At the same time it offers a set of alternative concepts for the thematization and analysis of human sexuality and sexual differentiation, concepts of expression and motivation and their components.

In addition to these conceptual advantages, Husserlian phenomenology also includes a strong argument which questions the ontological primacy of the biomechanical understanding of the living body and demonstrates its dependency on practical and expressive bodies. I have explicated this argument in previous works (Heinämaa 2003, 2011), and will not enter into the details of it here. For the purposes of this paper it suffices to point out that Husserl's argument questions the internal coherence of the physicalistic and the biologistic positions. He argues that the physicalist and the biologist, while defending

---

[25] The concepts of intentionality and motivational relations offer an alternative to contemporary depbates on the explanation of human action which are still largely predominated by the Humean analysis of causation. Motivating factors differ from Humean causes in that they necessarily *appear to* the motivated agents and, conversely, the motivated agenst are necessarily *directed at* them, so there is a mutual dependency between the relata. Husserl explains the one part of this mutual dependency as follows: 'what I do not "know", what does not stand over against me in my lived experiences… does not motivate me, not even unconsciously; (Husserl 1952: 231/243, see 186–7/195–6, 216/228). Motivational relations can be called 'motivational causality' or intentional or spiritual causality (Husserl 1952: 215–6/227, see 229/241, 233–4/244–5, 260–1/273, 381–2/390–1), but its structures are different from those of Humean causality, and comparable instead to Aristotelian causes and their contemporary formulations.

[26] At the same time, the sex/gender paradigm incites us to analyze other personality types as combinations of the psychological factors of femininity and masculinity and the physical factors of femaleness and maleness: lesbian women are characterized as masculine females and homosexual men as feminine males, and hermaprodites are understood as male–females or female–males.

their reductive materialistic ontology, are necessarily engaged in scientific practices of communication which presuppose the reality of the very objectivities, practical and expressive, which their own philosophies deny or theorize as mere epiphenomena.[27]

Even if one could not accept this argument about the constitution of the sense of reality, Husserl's conceptual distinctions between the different senses of embodiment remain crucial for all philosophies of sexual difference. An adequate account of this difference must not confuse the multiple senses in which we intend living bodies: as mechanical systems, as practical instruments, and as communicative means, or slide from one meaning to the other without an explicit account of their relations.

There is one final advantage in the phenomenological paradigm: it helps to distinguish between different senses in which we can speak about the components of human bodies. The next and final section of the paper is dedicated to this aspect of embodiment. It offers an overview of the phenomenological description and analysis of the different kinds of body parts that are thematized in the discourses on sex and gender. We will discover that the sexual body is not just a collection or system of sexual or reproductive organs, but is also a stylistic unity which consists of dynamic moments of relating to worldly realities. The phenomenology of sexual styles and sexually grounded forms of motivation offers conceptual tools for those theories of action which question the abstracting notion of a genderless agent, but it also opens a way out from the Butlerian impasse.[28]

6 THE DIVERSITY OF BODY PARTS

I argued above that the concept of sex is grounded on the idea of causal–functional connections and is ill-suited for the analysis of motivational and expressive relations. However, the concept also lacks precision and distinctions in another respect: it lumps together bodily components that are experientially very different in both their subjective and their objective aspects.

---

[27] Husserl discusses the physicalistic position under his critique of naturalism. His concepts of naturalism and the naturalistic attitude are meta-ontological concepts; they cover a number of different physicalistic positions that today are distinguished on the basis of methodological differences or differences in explanatory strategies. Most importantly, Husserl's concept of naturalism includes both reductionist physicalistic positions (for example, supervenience theories) and non-reductionsitic physicalistic positions (for example, property-physicalism and emergentism), since all these positions share the assumption that *all that there is* is physical or composed out of physical parts (see Crane 2000).

[28] By 'the Butlerian impasse' I mean the conclusion that Butler draws in *Gender Trouble* which conflates the political concepts of agency and action with those of deviation and abnormality: 'In a sense, all signification takes place within the orbit of the compulsion to repeat; "agency", then, is to be located within the possibility of a variation of that repetition...it is only within the practices of repetitive signifying that a subversion of identity becomes possible. The junction to be a given gender produces *necessary failures*, a variety of incoherent configurations that in their multiplicity exceed and defy the injunction by which they are generated' (Butler 1990: 145, my emphasis).

On the one hand, *sex* includes genital organs and reproductive functions. These are perceptible objects and processes—that is, objects given to us in straightforward experience. On the other hand, *sex* also refers to imperceptible and non-experienceable organic components, such as hormones, genes, and chromosomes, which cannot be perceived or experienced by anyone but can only be grasped in theoretical thinking and by natural scientific methods. Definitions and characterizations of sex treat these very different types of 'organs' as comparable and equal components of one bodily whole, despite crucial differences in their forms of givenness.

Moreover, phenomenological analysis shows that our *perceivable organs* are not all given to us in the same way.

First, our inner and outer organs appear to us differently and by different means. We can see and touch our external sex organs—the penis, the clitoris, the breasts—without mediation, but we need tools in order to see (visualize) our inner organs—the vagina or the testis. In this respect, the forms of givenness characteristic of internal genitalia are comparable to those of our abdominal organs and our brains, but there is also a crucial experiential difference: we do not feel the positions or movements of our liver or our brains, whereas we do feel the positions and movements of our inner sex organs. In other words, the inner organs are given to us not merely by the mediation of tools or other bodies, but also directly by introception, and/or proprioception.[29]

Also, different types of *inner gentalia* can be distinguished on the basis of their givenness. The vagina is 'hidden' in the body in a different way than is the testis; it resides in a folding of flesh, not inside 'a bag of skin'. This means that the vagina is accessible to touch and directly touchable, and as such can be compared to the mouth. Accordingly, different means are needed for the visualization of these two types of internal genitalia: in order to see the testis one needs to cut the skin, but in order to see the vagina one can use a mirror.[30] These experiential differences are crucial for our sense of the human body as an incomplete whole which can open itself to the environment and close itself from it—and do this in several different ways.

Second, our *external genitalia* are constantly given to us in a double way: we can perceive them but we can also feel their relative positions and movements and thus do not need to resort to sense-perception in order to 'know' where they are. I do not have to look at my breasts or touch them in order to 'know' how they are positioned and orientated in space; they are permanently known to me in a similar proprioceptive immediacy

---

[29] The vagina, the womb, and the ovaries, for example, are given in first-person experience by their involuntary movements, and by a variety of feelings (of pain and pleasure). These sensations are intensified in the experience of childbirth, but they belong, in 'milder' forms, to the normal cycles of experiential life.

[30] For the lived topography of the feminine body, see Irigaray 1974; 1984; Young 1989: 160–209; Gahlings 2006: 145–244; Heinämaa forthcoming.

as the positions of my hands, my feet, and my head. This is so obvious to us that the statement may sound trivial or ridiculous, or philosophically insignificant, but pathological experiences help to clarify the significance of proprioception and kinaesthesia for our possibilities of experiencing worldly objects and the world as a field of possible actions: we may loose the kinaesthetic and proprioceptive sensation of our organs, as well as our ability to feel pleasure and pain, and studies of such conditions show that the sensory and affective dimensions of our bodies shape our worldly relations in comprehensive or global ways (for example, Gallagher and Cole 1998; Gallagher 2005: 45–55; Gallagher and Zahavi 2008: 143–7).

The erotic zones of our bodies do not contribute to the thingly objectification of the world but they have an important role in our axiological lives, in the constitution of values. Merleau-Ponty's influential analyses of the case of Schneider, a First World War invalid, show that the when the body loses its affective and erotic intentionality, the whole environing world appears in a strange mode of inertia or neutrality:

> Faces are for him neither attractive nor repulsive, and people appear to him in one light or another only insofar as he has direct dealings with them, and according to the attitude they adopt toward him, and the attention and solicitude which they bestow to him. Sun and rain are neither gay nor sad; his humour is determined by elementary organic functions only, and the world is emotionally neutral.[31] (Merleau-Ponty 1945: 184/157)

Finally, the sex/gender paradigm is preoccupied with organs and organic functions. As we have seen, the focus is on genitals and their bio-scientific correlates. In lived experience, however, men and women are not always or even predominantly given to us as possessors of genitals or identified as such. Rather, they are distinguished in most circumstances by their ways of moving and bodily comporting towards the environment. As such they appear as two different modifications or variations of human movement and comportment, and as such differ from the other main variations of living movement, the animal and the infantile (see Husserl 1954: 190–1/187–8; 1988: 458–9/172–3; 1973b).

All living beings move in a way crucially different from the ways in which mere material things move in space; they all are capable of spontaneous, responsive, and motivated motions. Women and men, or feminine and masculine subjects, manifest two different forms of spontaneity and responsiveness. These dynamic forms cannot be characterized by the traditional concepts of substance or organism, but the phenomenological concepts of style, variation, and modification provide the basic framework for a description:

> A woman passing by...is a certain manner of being flesh which is given entirely in her walk or even in the simple shock of her heel on the ground—as the tension of

---

[31] Since Merleau-Ponty, phenomenologists have also studied how psychic disorders, such as depression and schizophrenia, manifest in bodily experiences in general and in sexual and erotic experiences in particular.

the bow is present in each fiber of wood—a very noticeable variation of the norm of walking, looking, touching, and speaking that I possess in my self-awareness because I am incarnate.[32] (Merleau-Ponty 1960: 67–8/54; see 1945: 183/156; Husserl 1952: 270–1/282–4)

The phenomenological concepts of style offer the possibility of formulating the question of sexual identity and difference in a new way. We do not need to restrict ourselves to explaining such identities and differences by empirical realities or theoretical objects of different sorts: hormones, genes, stimulus response-systems, social roles, or historical facts. More fundamentally, we can understand sexual difference, using intentional and temporal concepts, as a difference between two styles of intentional life—that is, as a difference in ways of intending realities and idealities, and being motivated by experiences and experienceable objects.[33] As stylistic characteristics of persons, 'manhood' and 'womanhood' are not anchored on any particular activities or objects, but are given as two different ways of relating to objectivity, acting on objects and being affected by them.

Understood in this way, sexual difference is not a difference between two substances but is a difference between two modes or modalities of relating. Accordingly, the question of sexual identity is not a question of 'what' but of 'how'.

Moreover, the concepts of style are not unificatory or oppositional but articulate the idea that human existence includes a multitude of varitations and unlimited possibilities of diversification. The distinction between a manly style and a womanly style of intentional experiencing does not imply that these two styles would be exclusive or incompatible. Rather, the distinction entails that human existence unfolds in two principal gestalts with two intentional histories and prehistories. These may develop in parallel but can also unravel and entagle (see Merleau-Ponty 1945: 249/215, 277/240).[34]

On this account, the concepts of man and woman are fundamentally similar to the concept of the human being which is defined not by realities or actualities, but by possibilities of action and passion. We find the idea first explicated by Simone de Beauvoir in *The Second Sex* but its roots are much deeper in the tradition and point back to Husserl's characterization of the human being as essentially a possibility-being (for example, Husserl 1988). Beauvoir writes:

It is often assumed that mere physiology can answer to the following questions: Is the success of the individual equally possible for both sexes? Which sex has a more important role in [the life of] the species? But the first problem does not at all come

---

[32] On Judith Butler's critique of Merleau-Ponty's phenomenology of sexuality and the limits of this critique, see Heinämaa 1996.

[33] See Waldenfels 1997: 63.

[34] The phenomenological tradition includes several competing accounts of the origin and continuity of the sexual duality, from Edith Stein's and Max Scheler's essentialist positions to the anti-essentialist views of Beauvoir, Sartre, and Merleau-Ponty. See, for example, Scheler 1955a; 1955b; Stein 2004; Beauvoir 1993: 37–77/37–69; Merleau-Ponty 1945: 180–202/154–73, 194–5/88–9; Sartre 1943: 83–102/89–112, 422–39/497–517; Stein 2000.

up in the same way for women and for other [animal] females, because animals constitute fixed species which can be described statically... whereas humanity is endlessly in becoming. Certain materialist savants assumed that they can pose the question in a purely static manner. Their thinking was dominated by the theory of psycho-physical parallelism, and so they tried to compare the organisms of women and men mathematically, and imagined that such measurements would directly define the functional capacities of the sexes... As for the present study, I categorically reject the notion of psycho-physical parallelism, for it is a doctrine whose foundations have long since been thoroughly undermined. I refer to it merely because it still haunts many minds in spite of its philosophical and scientific bankruptcy... It is only in a human perspective that we can study the female and the male of the human species. But the human being, by definition, is a being who is not given, who makes himself what he is... Woman is not a fixed reality, but a becoming. She should be compared with man in her becoming, that is to say, her *possibilities* should be defined. (Beauvoir 1993: 71–3/66)

7 CONCLUSION

I have argued that the concepts of sex and gender, widely used in contemporary human, social, and life sciences, are not univocal but include two different senses which stem from traditional discourses of human beings as psycho-physical compounds and products of natural and cultural forces. I differentiated between the substantial usage and the criterial usage, and argued that these are historically and logically distinct, but often conflated in contemporary discourses of the relations between men and women. The first part of the paper also offered an overview of the the most common forms of critique launched against the sex/gender paradigm. We saw that the distinction is questioned on the grounds of historical and conceptual as well as bio-scientific studies.

In the second part of the paper I presented a phenomenological alternative to the sex/gender discourse, basing on Husserl's inquiries into the different senses of human embodiment. I distinguished between three primary senses of the body that structure our experiencing of the world and thinking about it: the body as a mechanism, the body as an instrument, and the body as an expression. I argued that an adequate philosophy of sexual difference must take all these senses into account and must offer a coherent and comprehensive account of their mutual relations.

In the light of my explication of the concepts of *sex* and *gender*, the sex/gender paradigm cannot provide a basis for the philosophy of sexual difference. These concepts have a rightful place in positive scientific analyses of human conduct and human biology, but they cannot provide a sufficient ground for the philosophical discourse on the multiple and complex experiential relations between men and women and on their relevance to the process of sense-formation.

Finally, I claimed that Husserlian phenomenology of the body, supplemented by the findings of the French phenomenologists, provides a rich and solid conceptual and methodological foundation for such a philosophy. This task has already been taken up by a number of contemporary thinkers, but the work is far from being completed and is still in a dynamic phase of development.

References

Barnes, H. E. (1999), 'Sartre and feminism', in J. S. Murphy (ed.), *Feminist Interpretations of Jean-Paul Sartre* (Pennsylvania: The Pennsylvania University Press), pp. 22–44.

Beauvoir, S. (1991), *Le deuxième sexe II: l'expérience vécue* (Paris: Gallimard, (1949); tr. and ed. H. M. Parshley, *The Second Sex* (Harmondsworth: Penguin, 1987).

——— (1993), *Le deuxième sexe I: les faits et les mythes* (Paris: Gallimard, (1949); tr. and ed. H. M. Parshley, *The Second Sex* (Harmondsworth: Penguin, 1987).

Bernet, R. (1996), 'The unconscious between representations and drive: Freud, Husserl, and Schopenhauer', in J. J. Drummond and J. G. Hart (eds), *The Truthful and the Good: Essays in Honor of Robert Sokolowski* (Dordrecht, London, Boston: Kluwer Academic Publishers), pp. 81–95.

——— (2006), 'Zur Phänomenologie von Trieb und Lust bei Husserl', in D. Lohmar and D. Fonfara (eds), *Interdisziplinäre Perspektiven der Phänomenologie: Neue Felder der Kooperation: Cognitive Science, Neurowissenschaften, Psychologie, Soziologie, Politikwissenschaft und Religionswissenschaft* (Dordrect: Springer), pp. 38–53.

Birke, L. (1986), *Women, Feminism, and Biology: The Feminist Challenge* (Brighton: Harvester University Press).

——— (1999), *Feminism and the Biological Body* (Edinburgh: Edinburgh University Press).

Butler, J. (1990), *Gender Trouble: Feminism and the Subversion of Identity* (New York, London: Routledge).

——— (1993), *Bodies that Matter: On the Discursive Limits of 'Sex'* (New York and London: Routledge).

——— (2004), *Undoing Gender* (London and New York: Routledge).

Chiland, C. (2003), *Transsexualism: Illusion and Reality*, tr. Philip Slotkin (London, New York: Continuum, 1997).

Chodorow, N. (1978), *The Reproduction of Mothering: Psychoanalysis and the Sociology of Gender* (Berkeley and London: University of California Press).

Collins, P. H. (1990), *Black Feminist Thought: Knowledge, Consciousness and the Politics of Empowerment* (London: Routledge).

——— (2005), *Black Sexual Politics: African Americans, Gender and the New Racism* (New York: Routledge).

Crane, T. (2000), 'Dualism, monism, physicalism', *Mind & Society* 1/2: 73–85.

Depraz, N. (1994), 'Temporalité et affection dans les manuscrits tardifs sur la temporalité (1929–1935)', *Alter* 2: 63–86.

Devor, H. (1989), *Gender Blending: Confronting the Limits of Duality* (Bloomington and Indianapolis: Indiana University Press).

Diamond, M. and Sigmundson, K. H. (1997), 'Sex reassignment at birth: A long term view and clinical implications', *Archives of Pediatrics and Adolescent Medicine* 151: 298–304.

Dreger, A. (1998), *Hermaphrodites and the Medical Invention of Sex* (Cambridge, MA: Harvard University Press).

Eder, S. (2010), 'The volatility of sex: Intersexuality, gender and the clinical practice in the 1950s', *Gender and History* 22/3: 697–707.

Fausto-Sterling, A. (1992), *Myths of Gender: Biological Theories about Men and Women* (New York: Basic Books).

—— (2000), *Sexing the Body: Gender Politics and the Construction of Sexuality* (New York: Basic Books).

—— (2003), 'The problem with sex/gender and nature/nurture', in S. J. Williams, L. Birke, and G. A. Bendelow (eds), *Debating Biology: Sociological Reflections on Health, Medicine and Society* (London and New York: Routledge).

Foucault, M. (1976), *Historie de la sexualité 1: La volonté de savoir*, Paris: Gallimard; tr. Robert Hurley, *History of Sexuality, Volume I: An Introduction* (Harmondsworth: Penguin Books, 1984).

Gahlings, U. (2006), *Phänomenologie der Weiblichen Leiberfahrung* (Freiburg and München: Karl Alber).

Gallagher, S. (2005), *How the Body Shapes the Mind* (Oxford and New York: Oxford University Press).

—— and Cole, J. (1998), 'Body image and body scheme', D. Welton (ed.), *Body and Flesh: A Philosophical Reader* (Massachusetts and Oxford: Blackwell).

—— and Zahavi, D. (2008), *The Phenomenological Mind: Introduction to Philosophy of Mind and Cognitive Science* (New York: Routledge).

Gatens, M. (1991), 'A critique of the sex/gender distinction', in S. Gunew (ed.), *A Reader in Feminist Knowledge*(London and New York: Routledge).

Giddens, A. (2009), *Sociology*, 6th edn. (Cambridge: Polity Press), http://www.polity.co.uk/giddens5/students/glossary/s-z.asp#s.

Greer, G. (1970), *The Female Eunuch* (New York: Bantam Books).

Grosz, E. (1994), *Volatile Bodies: Toward a Corporeal Feminism* (Bloomington and Indianapolis: Indiana University Press).

Haig, D. (2004), 'The inexorable rise of gender and the decline of sex: Social change in academic titles, 1945–2001', *Archives of Sexual Behavior* 33/2: 87–96.

Halperin, D. M. (1993), 'Is there a history of sexuality?', in H. Abelove, M. A. Barale and D. M. Halperin (eds), *The Lesbian and Gay Reader* (New York: Routledge).

Hampson, J. G. and Money, J. (1955), 'Idiopathic Sexual Precocity in the female', *Psychosomatic Medicine* XVII/1: 16–35.

Haslanger, S. (2003), 'Social construction: The "debunking" project', in F. F. Smith (ed.), *Socializing Metaphysics: The Nature of Social Reality* (Lanham, Boulder, New York, and Oxford: Rowman & Littlefield).

Heidegger, M. (1927), *Sein und Zeit* (Tübingen: Max Niemeyer); tr. John Macquarrie and Edward Robinson, *Being and Time* (Oxford: Blackwell, 1992).

Heinämaa, S. (1997), 'Women: nature, product, style? Rethinking the foundations of feminist philosophy of science', in L. Hankison Nelson and J. Nelson (eds), *Feminism, Science, and the Philosophy of Science* (Dordrecht: Kluwer Academic Publishers), pp. 289–308.

—— (2003), *Toward a Phenomenology of Sexual Difference: Husserl, Merleau-Ponty, Beauvoir* (Lanham, Boulder, New York, and Oxford: Rowman & Littlefield).

—— (2010), 'Cixous, Kristeva and Le Dœuff: Three "French feminists" ', in A. Schrift (ed.), *History of Continental Philosophy, Volume 6: Poststructuralism and Critical Theory: The Return of the Master Thinkers* (Durham: Acumen), pp. 259–85.

Heinämaa, S. (forthcoming), 'Beauvoir and Husserl: An unorthodox approach to *The Second Sex*', in S. Mussett and W. Wilkerson (eds), *Beauvoir Engages the History of Philosophy* (New York: SUNY).

―― (2011), 'Body', in S. Luft and S. Overgaard (eds), *The Routledge Companion to Phenomenology* (London: Routledge, pp. 222–32).

―― and Rodemeyer, L. (2010), 'Introduction', *Continental Philosophy Review*, 43, no. 11: 1–11. Special Issue: *Feminist Phenomenologies*, S. Heinämaa and L. Rodemeyer (eds).

Herd, G. (ed.) (1996), *Third Sex, Third Gender: Beyond Sexual Dimorphism in Culture and History* (New York and Cambridge, MA: Zone Books).

Hoagland, S. L. (1999), 'Existential freedom and political change', in J. S. Murphy (ed.), *Feminist Interpretations of Jean-Paul Sartre* (Pennsylvania: Pennsylvania University Press), pp. 149–74.

hooks, b. (1981), *Ain't I a Woman: Black Women and Feminism* (Boston, MA: South End Press).

―― (1990), *Yearning: Race, Gender, and Cultural Politics* (Boston, MA: South End Press).

Humm, M. (1990), *The Dictionary of Feminist Theory* (Columbus: Ohio State University).

Husserl, E. (1952), *Ideen zu einer reinen Phänomenologie und phänomenologischen Philosophie, Zweites Buch: Phänomenologische Untersuchungen zur Konstitution*, Husserliana IV, M. Bimel (ed.) (The Hague: Martinus Nijhoff); tr. R. Rojcewicz and A. Schuwer, *Ideas Pertaining to a Pure Phenomenology and to a Phenomenological Philosophy, Second Book: Studies in the Phenomenological Constitution* (Dordrecht, Boston, and London: Kluwer Academic Publishers, 1993).

―― (1954), *Die Krisis der europäischen Wissenschaften und die transzendentale Phänomenologie: Eine Einleitung in die phänomenologischen Philosophie*, Husserliana VI, W. Biemel (ed.) (The Hague: Martinus Nijhoff); tr. D. Carr, *The Crisis of European Sciences and Transcendental Phenomenology: An Introduction to Phenomenological Philosophy* (Evanston: Northwestern University Press, 1988).

―― (1973a), *Zur Phänomenologie der Intersubjektivität, Texte aus dem Nachlass, Zweiter Teil (1921–1928)*, Husserliana XIV, I. Kern (ed.) (The Hague: Martinus Nijhoff).

―― (1973b), *Zur Phänomenologie der Intersubjektivität: Texte aus dem Nachlass, Dritter Teil (1929–1935)*, Husserliana XV, I. Kern (ed.) (The Hague: Martinus Nijhoff).

―― (1988), *Aufsätze und Vorträge (1922–1937)*, Husserliana XXVII, Th. Nenon and H. R. Sepp (eds.) (The Hague: Kluwer Academic Publishers).

Irigaray, L. (1974), *Speculum, de l'autre femme* (Paris: Minuit); tr. G. C. Gill, *Speculum of the Other Woman* (Ithaca and New York: Cornell University Press, 1986).

―― (1984), *Éthique la différence sexuelle* (Paris: Minuit); tr. C. Burke and G. C. Gill, *An Ethics of Sexual Difference* (Ithaca: Cornell University Press, 1993).

Jay, N. (1991), 'Gender and dichotomy', in S. Gunew (ed.), *A Reader in Feminist Knowledge* (London and New York: Routledge).

Kimura, D. (1993), 'Sex differences in brain organization', in *Neuromotor Mechanisms in Human Communication* (Oxford: Oxford University Press).

―― (1999), *Sex and Cognition* (Cambridge, MA: MIT Press).

Lacan, J. (1973), *Le séminaire, tome 11: Les quatre concepts fondamentaux de la psychanalyse, 1964*, J.-A. Miller (ed.) (Paris: Seuil); tr. Alan Sheridan, *The Four Fundamental Concepts of Psycho-Analysis* (London: Penguin, 1994).

Laquer, Th. (1990), *Making Sex: Body and Sex from the Greeks to Freud* (Cambridge, MA: Harvard University Press).

Le Dœuff, M. (1989), *L'étude et le rouet: des femmes, de la philosophie, etc.* (Paris: Seuil); tr. T. Selous, *Hipparchia's Choise: An Essay Concerning Women, Philosophy, Etc.* (New York: Columbia University Press, 2007).

Lévinas, E. (1947), *Le temps et l'autre* (Paris: Quadrige/PUF); tr. R. A. Cohen, *Time and Other* (Pittsburgh: Duquesne University Press, 1987).

——— (1961), *Totalité et infini: essai sur l'extériorité* (Paris: Kluwer Academic Publishers); tr. A. Lingis, *Totality and Infinity: An Essay on Exteriority* (Pittsburgh: Duquesne University Press, 1969).

Mead, M. (1950), *Male and Female: A Study of the Sexes in a Changing World* (Harmondsworth: Penguin).

Merleau-Ponty, M. (1945), *Phénoménologie de la perception* (Paris: Gallimard); tr. C. Smith, *Phenomenology of Perception* (New York: Routledge & Kegan Paul, 1995).

——— (1960), *Signes* (Paris: Gallimard); tr. R. C. McCleary, *Signs* (Evanston: Northwestern University Press, 1964).

——— (1963), *L'Œil et l'esprit* (Paris: Gallimard); tr. C. Dallery, 'The Eye and the mind,' in *The Primacy of Perception*, J. E. Edie (ed.) (Evanston: Northwestern University Press, 1964), 159–190.

——— (1964), *Le visible et l'invisible*, C. Lefort (ed.) (Paris: Gallimard); tr. A. Lingis, *The Visible and the Invisible* (Evanston: Northwestern University Press, 1975).

Millett, K. (1969), *Sexual Politics* (New York: Ballantine Books).

Money, J. (1955), 'Hermaphroditism, gender and precocity in hyperadrenocorticism: Psychological findings', *Bulletin of the Johns Hopkins Hospital* 96: 253–64.

——— (1994), 'The concept of gender identity disorder in childhood and adolescence after 39 years', *Journal of Sex and Marital Therapy* 20: 163–77.

Oakley, A. (1972), *Sex, Gender and Society* (London: Temple Smith).

Putnam, H. (1979), *Mind, Language, and Reality, Philosophical Papers 2*, (Cambridge: Cambridge University Press).

Rubin, G. (1975), 'The traffic in women: Notes on the 'political economy' of sex', in R. Reiter (ed.), *Toward an Anthropology of Women* (New York: Monthly Review Press).

Ryan, B. (2007), 'Sex and gender', in *Blackwell Encyclopedia of Sociology Online*, http://www.sociologyencyclopedia.com/subscriber/uid=671/tocnode?id=g9781405124331_chunk_g978140512433125_ss1-81&authstatuscode=202.

Sartre, J.-P. (1943), *L'être et le néant: essai d'ontologie phénoménologique* (Paris: Gallimard); tr. H. E. Barnes, *Being and Nothingness: A Phenomenological Essay on Ontology* (New York: Washington Square Press, 1956).

Scheler, M. (1955a), 'Zur Idee des Menschen', in *Gesammelte Werke, Band 3: Vom Umsturz der Werte, Abhandlungen und Aufsätze* (Bern: Francke Verlag).

——— (1955b), 'Zum Sinn der Frauenbewegung', in *Gesammelte Werke, Band 3: Vom Umsturz der Werte, Abhandlungen und Aufsätze* (Bern: Francke Verlag).

Stein, E. (2000), *Die Frau: Fragestellungen und Reflexionen, Edith Stein Gesamtausgabe 13*, M. A. Neyer OCD (ed.) (Freiburg, Basel, and Wien: Herder); tr. F. M. Oben, *Essays on Woman, The Collected Works of Edith Stein II*, second revised edition (Washington: ICS Publications, 1996).

——— (2004), *Der Aufbau der menschlichen Person: Vorlesung zur philosophischen Anthropologie, Edith Stein Gesamtausgabe 8*, C. M. Wulf. (ed.) (Freiburg, Basel, and Wien: Herder).

Stoller, R. (1964), 'A contribution to the study of gender identity', *International Journal of Psychoanalysis* 45/4: 220–6.

———(1968), *Sex and Gender: The Development of Femininity and Masculinity* (London: Maresfield Reprints).

Stone, A. (2007), *An Introduction to Feminist Philosophy* (Cambridge: Polity Press).

Waldenfels, B. (1997), 'Fremdenheit des anderen Geschlechts', in S. Stoller and H. Vetter (eds), *Phänomenologie und Geschlechterdifferenz* (WUV-Universitätsverlag).

Watson, N. V. and Kimura, D. (1991), 'Non-trivial sex differences in throwing and intercepting: Relation to psychometrically-defined spatial functions', *Personality and Individual Differences* 12/5: 375–85.

Wittgenstein, L. (2003), *The Blue and the Brown Books: Preliminary Studies for the 'Philosophical Investigations,'* (Oxford: Blackwell, 1958).

World Health Organisation, http://www.who.int/topics/gender/en/.

Young, I. M. (1990), *Throwing Like a Girl and Other Essays in Feminist Philosophy and Social Theory* (Bloomington and Indiana: Indiana University Press).

CHAPTER 12

··

AT THE EDGES OF MY BODY

··

EDWARD S. CASEY

EDGES are rarely studied by philosophers, yet they are a permanent and pervasive part of human experience of every kind. In phenomenology they have figured most prominently as *horizons*—both 'external' and 'internal' in Husserl's distinction. External edges encircle a given physical thing; internal edges serve as adumbrational edges that foreshadow what lies on so far concealed sides of such a thing (Husserl 1986: 31–9, 149–52, 360–1). Beyond these two kinds of horizon—neither of which is to be confused with the vast horizon that rings around a landscape as its 'outermost edge'—there are edges of many particular sorts: rims and margins, borders and boundaries, brinks and precipices.

In my contribution to this volume I shall focus on the edges of the lived body. These are aspects of bodily selfhood that have been notably neglected in previous studies, whether within phenomenology or in other disciplines. My purpose is not to claim that these edges are emblematic of edges in general, but rather that they are a formative factor in the constitution and experience of the human body. In their constituent status they are in a class with such otherwise different edges as those of the perceived or imagined earth and the inner edges that structure the human psyche from within. In all three cases we have to do with edges that are deeply ingredient in that of which they are the edges; they figure as structural parameters. We cannot perceive or imagine the earth except as ending in a single vast edge (such as the far horizon at sea, where the water meets the sky), and the human psyche is especially prone to splitting as we know from inner turmoil: such states are constituted by unwonted and often painful edges that act to dissociate spontaneous acts of mind. In other words, edges outline the most encompassing phenomena in the experience of the planet we inhabit, as well as dividing us from within. In terms of scale and scope, bodily edges are located between these two extremes—one enormous in extent, and the other intangible and invisible. Situated on the near side of the earth's extremities, yet beyond the inner edges of the mind, the edges of our lived body act to mediate between these outermost and innermost edges—and many others. Their fate is to be always between—not just between earth and mind, but between my body and that of others as well as between myself as a self-regulating organism and the environment in which I am ensconced. In each of these situations, however differently, they constitute boundaries composed of interactive edges.

But what is it for a lived body to have edges? What kinds of edges are these?

1

The edge of my body? The phrase rings awkwardly. It is less awkward to speak of the body as having its own 'contour' or 'shape'. These latter terms make perfect sense in such concrete contexts as health or cosmetics, where issues of precise body outline are specifically at stake—especially when we find ourselves guided by a certain cultural norm such as gender. This norm, taken as something to which we aspire, is an instance of what is more properly called a 'limit', given that it is imposed rather than chosen and is subject to metric determination (for example, 'the perfect bust'). I may adopt this norm by my own volition, but the norm itself is a cultural ideal that I take over from others (peers, cultural stereotypes, film stars, and so on). I can attempt to approximate to this ideal, but I cannot create it myself; at the most, I can attempt to 'shape' my body to fit what the ideal or norm dictates. This I do by such means as diet, exercise, close-fitting clothes, and so on. To my chagrin, I often discover that I can alter my bodily shape with only scant success. My body is not a perfectly pliable material that I can sculpt, or re-sculpt, at will. Short of radical cosmetic surgery, I find that my body clings stubbornly to its usual form—give or take a few pounds. Nowhere near as mercurial as my mind, my body is also not subject to reconfiguration in the manner of an ordinary physical object which I create or manipulate for instrumental ends.

In contrast with its shape or contour, my body's edge is not merely recalcitrant to reshaping, but it remains what it is no matter what efforts I make to reconfigure it: it stays the same even as the exact form of my body may change. It is *my edge*, the outermost part of my body—inalienably so, in a way that cannot be altered, much less determined, by a cultural ideal or norm toward which I strive. It belongs to me and is one of the major ways by which I define myself—indeed, by which I exist. This is not to say that it does not change. It certainly does, especially as I grow up and age. But at each stage of my life it clings to me as indisputably *mine*, whatever may be the influences to which I am subject and despite the changing interpretations I may give to my bodily configuration. In addition to being able to claim it as unique (as 'mine') and as slow to change, what is such an edge? How is it to be described?

If we cannot answer these last questions readily, this is not just because the phrase 'my body's edge' is an awkward locution in English: this linguistic fact points to the difficulty of defining or describing the body's edge—in contrast, say, with its skin, which can be given a determinate physical description. Whenever we attempt to spell out what such an edge is, we find ourselves stalled: not only do we not know what it is, we do not even know *where* it is. As for the first perplexity ('what it is'), it does not seem to fit most of the common categories of edge: it is neither a separate margin, nor is it a strict rim, which connotes a fixed and often rigid edge *around* a physical object or place (a can or a canyon). It is like a boundary insofar as this term is taken to mean a porous edge that permits flow or traffic across it in more than one direction. It is closest to being a threshold, given that it is *through* my body's edge that I gain access to much of my surrounding world.[1] Concerning the second perplexity—that of its proper location ('where it is')—a moment's reflection indicates that my body's edge is not found in any precise corner or part of space. To point to the body's edge would be an act of referring without any definite referent. We cannot say *just where* it is located. Its locus is as indefinite as is a halo or a nimbus: it eludes my pointing finger, which cannot literally *touch* it as it can touch my skin. For it is not *there*—not in any customary sense of physical being-there. It is not some*thing* to which I can point, yet *it is there*, somewhere around me yet also part of me. In the case of one's own bodily edge, the paradigm of 'simple location' (in Whitehead's term) misleads us: this paradigm, stemming from early modern models of space and time, requires that location be determined at a definite point in a homogeneous spatial or temporal field—as with a location on earth that is designated by so many degrees of latitude and longitude.

Does this mean that my body's edge is to be grouped with such other nebulous phenomena as auras or silhouettes? I think not. As the term has been employed in the last century in the West, *aura* refers to a discharge of energy rays or vibrations emitted by the human body that is invisible to the naked eye yet can be detected in certain photographic or infrared images. It is a hybrid term, partly spiritual and partly scientific, in which the manifest image is held to demonstrate the existence of a psychical or parapsychological emanation. A *silhouette*, in contrast, is a projected image of my bodily edges construed as providing one continuous outline, at a certain moment in time and as conveyed by a certain lighting arrangement. It captures the *Gestalt* of my bodily edge at that moment and in that artificially generated condition. But my silhouette reduces my three-dimensional body to a two-dimensional image. Also reduced are such other qualitative aspects of my lived body as its exact colouration, felt flesh features (smooth, tawny, rugged), as well as subtle aspects of gender identity, a sense of my unique personal character and certain marks of age, and so on. A silhouette can be telling for purposes of sheer identification, and yet it does not provide anything like a complete picture of my bodily edge as I feel it from within.[2] It is a caricature of my lived body that is offered by the stark projection of its physical outline.

---

[1] In a larger study of edges of which this essay is an outgrowth, I propose that 'edge' is a genus of which border and boundary, rim and threshold—and several other instances—are the effective species. For instance, a boundary is a porous edge—one that permits two-way motion across it—whereas a border is an impermeable edge. A threshold is an edge that leads to, or ushers in, another contiguous space.

[2] It is the telling aspect of the silhouette that allows it to be employed by Jean-Luc Nancy in his discerning descriptions of our being-with-others, of whom we catch glimpses rather than steady perceptions: ' "People" are silhouettes that are both imprecise and singularized, faint outlines of voices, patterns of comportments, sketches of affects' (Nancy 2000: 7; see also Nancy, 1997: 53). But in these instances, 'silhouette' is being used metaphorically, by extension—not in the strict sense I invoke above.

Another model for understanding my bodily edge is found in its *profile*. A profile is something like a part-silhouette, since it is typically confined to the head or face. But 'profile' has two expanded senses. When we speak of a person's 'profile' we often mean that person's professional image—her persona, or her public reputation as supported by such things as a job description, honorary titles, and so on. This kind of profile belongs more to others than to myself (it is recognized primarily by these others), though its roots lie in my own accomplishments. In relation to it, my bodily edge is more or less indifferent. Another expanded sense is darker in connotation: 'racial profiling'. In this case I am singled out by others on the basis of my race or ethnicity or, more exactly, my appearing to look like those of a presumed racial or ethnic stock. Here the publicly construed aspect of myself may count for more than my consciously pursued professional profile and may have little to do with anything that I, personally, contribute to the type I am taken to exemplify. This type, moreover, is more of a stereotype than anything revealing of my deeper identity or being. Hence the ease with which racial profiling allows for stopping and arresting anyone suspected of illegality—for example, failure to possess a license or car registration or proper citizenship papers. Here my stereotypical profile plays into the hands of those who have a bias against others of a different race, ethnicity, or economic class. Neither of these two basic senses of profile is equivalent to my body's edge; indeed, each is reductive of it. The convolutions and complexities of this edge are suspended in an effort to simplify the way I present myself, or am perceived, in public life—flattening it out for the sake of ease of identification or recognition.

Figure is a fourth candidate for construing bodily edge. In one sense, figure is virtually synonymous with bodily outline or shape. This first, quite physical sense is at stake when we say that someone 'has a good figure', even if the parameters of this figure are often socially determined by norms of beauty that are current in a given culture: the admired female figure of Rubens' day is quite different from the almost anorexic extremes of contemporary Western culture as it is mediated through advertising. But we also speak of 'cutting quite a figure'—where this means being conspicuous in certain social or political settings. Once again, this usage trades on a very public sense of the self: myself as noticed by others. In a further extension, we speak of 'figure/ground', where 'figure' is no longer a separate and free-standing shape or the basis of an exclusively public image. 'Figure' in this sense has meaning only in relation to the perceived ground from which it arises, and is inseparable from it. As such, it is neither strictly private nor wholly public, but, as an inherently perceived particular, somewhere in between: neither one nor the other exclusively, yet having aspects of both (a given perception is always *my* perception; yet its content can be perceived by others in principle). Curiously, the same is true of the edges of my body: I can see (most of) them, and others can see them all. Thus my bodily edges possess an intermediate status: they manifest a figure that is shared by myself and others, albeit partially. It remains, however, that my bodily edge cannot be reduced to the perceived figure constituted by my body.

If my body's edge is not an aura or silhouette, profile or figure, then what is it? Where are we to find it?

2

To begin to answer these questions, let us consider two significant clues. First, my bodily edge is in fact plural: it is felt and perceived as my bodily *edges*. It does not possess a single, definitive, or final edge. Second, my bodily edges are not projected—as are, in varying measures, silhouettes, profile, and figure—but instead belong to me in a wholly singular way: they are *part of me*, an integral part of my own body as lived. As such, they do not belong to public space in the manner of the alternatives just discussed. As situated in such space, these alternatives lend themselves to public consumption, whether this takes the form of commercial or sexual exploitation, professional self-promotion, or bare recognizability by others. We might say that these four parameters present my bodily being as *turned out*—turned out from me toward others—whereas my bodily edges are ineluctably *turned in*: turned back in toward myself, tucked into my own body, inhering in it. These edges accrue to me and are indwelling in me—even as their outer surfaces (most notably, stretches of my skin) are exposed to the surrounding world, being open to the gaze of others, whether as appreciated or as reviled.

Concretely considered, this immanence of the edges of my body is felt as a burden when I am physically tired, or as ecstatically exceeded in orgasmic and other extraordinary experiences. Most of the time, however, I feel these edges as belonging to the outer flanks of my personal self, as providing the covering for the core of this self. They are sensed as stemming *from me* as its source and subject, while at the same time situated *on me*. This from/me and on/me dyad is an expression of the bivalent being of bodily edges, contrasting with other dyads such as private/public and felt/perceived. The from/on bivalency is constituent of who I am, is one with me, and is not situated outside or alongside me; it is part of my personal identity, my self-system.

Bodily edges are primarily experienced by me *from up close*. This happens continually during the waking day as well as through the night. Throughout, I catch glimpses of my own somatic edges. Sometimes I have occasion to gaze or stare at them, as in a mirror or when I am trying to apply a salve to a part of my skin that is experiencing pain. Otherwise, I know my bodily outer self only intermittently: in one glance and then another, in a discontinuous series of momentary lookings. Instead of my whole body, I see this forearm, that knee, that foot. I see body parts and thus their distinctive edges.[3] It is as if I were witnessing a 'fragmented body' (*corps morcellé*) in Lacan's term for the circumstance of the infant in the period before the mirror stage. But I also experience my body as one whole—from within, as it were. The fragmentation is not altogether radical but co-exists with a distinctive sense of my bodily integrity: I sense my own body as one body.

Despite the partiality of the up-close perception of my bodily state, it is definitive in its own way. I can trust it. I am, after all, grasping *my own bodily self* through its edges,

---

[3] Even in the mirror I see only one side of my body at a time—though I can then see several parts of this side at once, more than I usually see by unassisted glances cast directly at my own body.

however discontinuously. The edges I take in are certainly my own. They are not some-one else's: of this I am sure unless I am in a state of depersonalization.[4] As sure as know-ing that my thoughts are mine. Which is not to say that I know my body in its entirety, any more than all of my mind: parts of both remain concealed. But the parts I do see, or cognize in thought, I *know to be mine*. Such knowledge is definitive in its very partial-ity—that is to say, certain within the bounds of this very truncation.

Bodily edges realize this paradigm of definitive but incomplete self-knowledge in a very particular way: namely, that such edges are *parts of parts*. They are intrinsic features of my body regarded as a coherent collection of body parts—especially those I know from up close but, ultimately, all parts that are seen from a certain distance (if not by myself, then by others). Every such part has its own characteristic edges, ranging from the comparatively angular edges of my elbows and knees to the smooth and bulbous edges of my stomach or buttocks. Such edges, even if perceptible from without, I know from within as accruing to my own body parts, integral parts of these parts. I say 'inte-gral' to convey the way that such edges belong, intrinsically, to the parts themselves, rather than being imposed upon them as are items of clothing. The latter have their own separate edges, which are designed to 'fit' (closely or loosely) the edges of specific bodily parts such as the chest, the hips, the thighs.

3

At stake here is a special tension, which can be stated as the Antinomy of Corporeal Edges:

> *Thesis*: edges of any kind, including those belonging to my body, are parts in their own right. They are parts of a thing—primarily those outer parts where that thing terminates. Beyond them, there is nothing more of the thing in question: no sub-stance, no body. They are also parts of parts of a thing but with the special twist that such edges exist where a given part departs from and complicates its own thingly basis. It follows that the edge of any given particular body part is that portion or phase of the part where the body's flesh comes to a more or less abrupt end.[5]

---

[4] I am not able here to discuss pathological states in which bodily edges are radically distorted—for example, extreme self-alienation as in heautoscopy (seeing my own body as if from outside it) or the sensed detachment of my own body parts (as in certain kinds of schizophrenic self-perception). My model is based on the perception of my intact body as experienced by myself from within and felt to be my own singular body.

[5] A reviewer asks if bodily edges cannot be considered as the place where the body *starts*. I regard this as a valid alternative formulation of the same attribute: namely, that the edge of something is where it terminates; but it can terminate in two fashions: *ad quem*, toward which the body moves or tends; or *a quo*, from which it begins. I emphasize the former insofar as the more salient characteristic of edges lies in their capacity of delineating a thing (or event), beyond which this thing or event is no longer present or perceptible. But the latter is at stake when we think of this thing or event as giving rising to another thing or event.

Antithesis: yet, for all this, a part, including the edge of a body part, remains an integral *part of* the body part. It does so as felt and perceived, for it is demonstrably *there*— there with my body, where 'with' does not mean alongside (which would imply that it is detachable) but *right at*, just there, on a hand or thigh, finger or toe. As the edge of that body part, it is itself a part, belonging to the body part—even if it is, at the same time, the phase where that part vanishes from view or disappears from touch.

In this antinomy, which combines disruption with coherence, we witness another expression of the bivalence of bodily edges. On the one hand, such edges are situated where my skin comes to an end—and thus the whole flesh of the body part in which this skin inheres.[6] On the other hand, they belong to that same skin—and in this capacity they count as parts on their own account.

Although we here confront two very different aspects of the edges of my body parts, aspects that seem to look like Janus in two opposite directions, they prove to be compatible with each other—just as are space and time, freedom and causality in Kant's First and Second Antinomies: that is, once the antinomical terms are adequately understood. They complement each other, one being or having what the other lacks. Just as a part has to give out somewhere to be a part *of* something—though not of something infinite in extent: which can have no external edge—so it also has to inhere *in* some whole, organic or artificial, to which that same part belongs. To say that a bodily edge is a part of a part is to say no less. Yet such a part is not subordinate to the whole to which it belongs. As Aristotle remarks, 'we should take that which applies to the part and apply it to the living body as a whole' (Aristotle 1986: 412b). But it also goes the other way around: from the whole to the part. As Rilke says of a sculpted hand by Rodin: this hand 'has the power to give any part of [its] vibrating surface the independence of the whole' (Rilke 1986: 17–18).[7]

4

Each of the bodily edges on which I have focused so far is a case of what I earlier referred to as 'external edges': they are edges that give the distinctive configuration of something. In particular, these are edges where a body part comes to a shape by which we commonly identify something.[8] At the same time, however, bodily parts also possess *internal* edges.

---

[6] I am here taking 'skin' to be the cover or integument for 'flesh', construed as a term for felt body mass—a mass composed of adipose and muscle, ligaments and sinews. The edges of body parts are most directly attached to skin; but given that skin is contiguous with flesh, such edges are at the same time outer parts of this same subtending flesh. All three—flesh, skin, and edge—together compose the body part, which also, at a deeper level, contains bone and cartilage.

[7] Aristotle anticipates the two-way relation between part and whole by distinguishing 'the part in the whole' from 'the whole [as] in the parts' (Aristotle 1983: 210a 16–17). Gary Snyder puts it in this intriguing way: 'To know the spirit of a place is to realize that you are a part of a part and that the whole is made of parts, each of which is whole. You start with the part you are whole in' (Snyder 1990: 41).

[8] Auras and profiles and silhouettes are also external edges; but they are detachable from the bodily edges on which they depend and which they reflect.

These latter can be considered 'in-lines' rather than 'out-lines'. They come in two forms: the inner edges of bodily organs, normally not felt except in acute illness or certain forms of physical distress; and the edges constituted by creases and folds, scars and wrinkles. Though less useful for purposes of recognition, such internal bodily edges are subject to the same kind of analysis I have given of other body-part edges. For they too are places where human tissue, whether that of skin or that belonging to an internal organ, comes to a particular edge. We can say that they are the involutions of body parts, either as folds or cuts in the skin or as internal body organs.[9] They inhere—literally—in a body part even as they are parts on their own. Although they are not as graphically displayed as are external edges, they too are bivalent presences insofar as they are parts of parts.

The internal and external edges of bodily parts are not only glimpsed in the course of ongoing experience—seen as visual markings of various kinds—but they also provide a *grip* for our hands: we can touch them and sometimes hold onto them. This latter is especially true of external edges. Just as the lacing on a football furnishes an edge for holding the ball as we prepare to throw it, so we make use of such naturally given external bodily edges as are furnished by wrists, elbows, knees, and ankles—for example, in assuming certain postures in yoga. In particular, these fleshly edges give tangible purchase to our efforts to manipulate our body in certain contexts. They are analogous to the way that instruments and tools present features like handles for varied uses. In Heidegger's apt term, they are 'ready-to-hand' items of equipment in practical contexts. Due in large measure to its organically proffered edges, our own body is *zuhanden* for our own employment. Not only *are* we our own body—as Merleau-Ponty insists: 'I am not just in front of my body, I am in it, or rather I am it' (Merleau-Ponty 2012: 151)—but we deploy it in certain specific ways, regarding it as an instrument for the realization of diverse purposes: exercise of various sorts, skilfull movements, and many other manoeuvres. Whenever we do so, edges (most typically, external edges) are in play.

It is useful to compare bodily edges in their instrumental being with two other kinds of edge: rims and psychical edges. Rims, as I have mentioned, are comparatively rigid edges; they tend to be fixed in size and shape, since they are the rims of material things that are themselves comparatively unchanging whether these be tin cans or the Grand Canyon. As if to underline their rigidity, artificially produced rims are often reinforced in various ways—for example, by being constructed of extra layers of metal or being raised up. In the case of natural rims, they are composed of relatively dense or compacted matter—whether earth or stones—or else they would erode and lose their status as edges. In these various respects, rims contrast with bodily edges, which are comparatively soft and pliable. Fleshly edges are notably mobile, changing in contour in keeping with bodily movement such as walking or flexing one's biceps; only in deep sleep or a coma—finally, in death—does my body lose its mobility as well as its pliability (as is signified in speaking of *rigor mortis*).

---

[9] I cannot here treat Artaud's notion of a 'body without organs', as this has been adopted by Deleuze and Guattari, who argue that it signifies a body that has no intrinsic organismic unity.

Psychical edges are even more flexible than bodily edges. With the exception of schizoid states, they are remarkably fluent, as is signified by the strong temptation to regard them as belonging to streams or flows. Such edges flow into each other so subtly as often to make distinctions between them difficult to draw: it is not always possible to tell where one thought starts and another ends. It is as if their whole being were consumed in continual connection-making (for example, memories with each other, new ideas interconnecting with older ones)—whereas rims, by their very nature, set things apart: sometimes physical substances from each other (such as the kernels of corn contained in a metal can), sometimes one part of a landscape from another. Bodily edges are less separative than rims, but they do serve to distinguish one part of the body from another, such as those of the neck regarded as a part located between the head and torso. Whereas the neck both distinguishes and links, and the rim on the can of corn strictly separates, psychical edges are connective through and through: their primary being is that of *xunos*, Heraclitus's word for 'linkage' or 'tie'. If they are closer to bodily edges in this respect, this is not surprising, given the intimate bond between Psyche and Soma which their very existence reflects.

Despite their affinity with psychical edges, somatic edges constitute a class of their own. This essay aims to show that they are not a mere subclass of another edge-type but possess structures and functions of their own, rendering them unique in the world of edges. This is so despite the tendency to pass them over—to take them for granted and to bypass their significance in favour of more salient edge-types such as brinks or margins. Also, such edges tend to be subordinated to the actions of the mobile body. It is as if the edges of my body dissolve in such actions, disappearing in the continuously unfolding drama of manifest behavior—even though they are indispensable to the enactment of the drama itself.

5

Let us now take up two situations so far neglected in my treatment of bodily edges: the interaction of these edges with one another in the case of my own body, and the interaction of my bodily edges with those of other bodies. Since these situations are both quite complex, I shall restrict my discussion to one particular instance of each: touching myself and touching others. I leave aside other interactions that represent the merging of edges such as occur in eating or bleeding.[10]

(a) *touching myself*: by this basic action, I mean not only touching myself with my hands but the touching that occurs between two or more of my own bodily parts when

---

[10] I owe these last examples to the aforementioned reviewer, who also suggested the importance of the edges of internal organs. A more complete typology of bodily edges would have to consider these additional instances, along with numerous others. The present essay is meant as a first foray in the topic, not a fully comprehensive treatment.

they are contiguous, as when one leg crosses over the other or my upper arm touches my chest while I am walking. Either way, we have to do with an event in which one part of my flesh is in contact with another part of the same flesh: thus a flesh-on-flesh, edge-to-edge relation. Although we rarely attend to this phenomenon as such, it belongs to having the kind of multiply jointed and limbed bodies human beings (and other vertebrates) possess. For the most part, this happens spontaneously, without premeditation—indeed, every time we change our bodily position. Sometimes it arises from an act of exploration of edges; at other times, it is unintended and ongoing—as when I casually cross my hands. In the latter case, a momentary equilibrium of edges arises in which their interaction is not actively sought but is instead undergone in the course of experience.

A question arises just here: in self-touching, do we create or discover a *common edge*? Not so if this means a third edge beyond those of the (at least) two body parts that are touching. To think so raises the prospect of an indefinite positing of edges (positing an edge that subtends two edges that touch, then having to posit a new edge for the intersection of the first posited edge and the original two edges, and so on): in short, a version of Aristotle's 'third man' critique of Platonic Forms. At the very least, this is an instance of the futility of 'multiplying entities beyond necessity'. In fact, we have to do merely with a conjoining of co-existing and conterminous edges. This is complex in its own right, but it does not require the *ad hoc* positing of an extra edge. The issue is that of understanding what we are doing when one body part touches another. What is going on here?

To begin with, there is a *felt reciprocity* of self-touching. The hand or leg or arm that touches another part of the same body is *touched in turn*: touched back, as it were. The touching and the touching-back occur in the same moment: '*im selben Augenblick*' in a phrase of Husserl's that was meant to apply to the instant in which intended meaning is expressed by way of signs (see Husserl 2008, section 8; see also Derrida 1973). But the moment of self-touching, unlike that of self-expression, is notably thick—as thick as flesh itself. Even if this moment arises quickly (as when one body part brushes up against another), touching oneself requires a certain density of duration. For we have to do with a self-generated dyad of touching/being touched that takes its own time to happen. Unlike Plato's indefinite dyad of same and other, this binary is quite definite in character; for it consists in two (or more) body parts that enter into carnal reciprocity simultaneously and by means of the body's own external edges as the outermost parts of one's own flesh—in short, a same–same relation.

Merleau-Ponty adds to this analysis the fact that even if touching and being touched are the 'reverse' of each other—that is, if one can be considered the counterpart of the other, and their roles can be reversed—they never merge entirely: 'they do not coincide in the body: the touching is never exactly the touched' (Merleau-Ponty 1968: 254).[11] This

---

[11] On 'the reverse' as 'the other side' or 'the other dimensionality' (see Merleau-Ponty 1968: 254). Merleau-Ponty adds: 'This does not mean that they [touched and touching] coincide "in the mind" or at the level of "consciousness"' (ibid.). If anything, there is an 'untouchable' at stake here that has no exact bodily correlate—an untouchable that is the equivalent of the 'invisible' in the visual sphere (see Merleau-Ponty 1968: 254–6).

essential non-coincidence is what allows for the act of touching to take the initiative and for the touched to be the recipient—all this within a 'spread' or 'hiatus', that amounts not only to a durational moment but also to a non-negotiable difference.[12] This difference, however, is not equivalent to the distinction between sheer (voluntary) activity and abject (involuntary) passivity. Rather than any such strict oppositional difference, there is a drawing together of two sides of the same situation in and through a difference of modality within one and the same flesh (where 'initiating' and 'receiving' are regarded as modalities of one and the same lived body).

When one hand touches another that is, in turn, touching a thing alongside the body, we have a circumstance in which the touched hand becomes like the thing that it is touching—or more exactly, in which it has to assume one of two roles: to continue to touch the outside object or to relinquish its primary function of doing this in order to becomes the touched hand of one's own body:

> My left hand is always on the verge of touching my right hand touching the things, but I never reach coincidence; the coincidence eclipses at the moment of realization, and one of two things always occurs: either my right hand really passes over to the rank of touched, but then its hold on the world is interrupted; or it retains its hold on the world, but then I do not really touch *it*.[13] (Merleau-Ponty 1968: 147–8; his italics)

Here is a curious asymmetry at the heart of the touched/touching dyad—another exemplar of their non-coincidence. If my two hands form a 'circle' (as Merleau-Ponty adds), it is a circle differently centred in each case.[14]

Touching oneself is thus a complex and subtle process in which simplistic models of subjects in contact with objects fail to capture what is happening. What does happen is a process in which one and the same whole body manages to complicate its immediate life by turning around upon its own flesh rather than reaching out to objects around it. When the latter occurs, my effort to touch myself is distracted: my bodily intentionality exceeds my own body and extends to the thing touched. But when I do touch myself, I effect a momentary suspension of the environing world in order to concentrate on a part of my own body—a part that is being touched by another part. This is not a circumstance of *partes extra partes* (in the Cartesian phrase that applies to the relations between objects in the external world) but of *partes intra partes*: parts of one body feeling other parts of the same body—my own body, animated by a continuously self-generated intentionality. All of this happens thanks to an interplay of bodily edges, without which my body could not make contact with its own flesh at those determinate places where touching is felt to occur.

---

[12] 'If there is always a "shift", a "spread", between them… this hiatus between my right hand touched and the left hand touching…' (Merleau-Ponty 1968: 148). What guarantees that this 'hinge' (ibid.) stays open and operative is 'the total being of my body…the massive flesh' (ibid.).

[13] See also this statement: '…when my right hand touches my left hand while it is palpating the things…the "touching subject" passes over to the rank of the touched, descends into the things, such that the touch is formed in the midst of the world and as it were in the things' (Merleau-Ponty 1968: 133–4).

[14] 'There is a circle of the touched and the touching, the touched takes hold of the touching' (Merleau-Ponty 1968: 143).

(b) *touching another's body*. Just as in touching myself, there is no simple opposition between activity and passivity—instead, there is 'indivision' between these two modalities[15]—so when I touch you, neither of us is the sheer agent or the abject patient of the interaction. We are intertangled in such a way as to draw each of us into a special self/other bonding that has no exact equivalent in the rest of human experience. Nor are we exactly equal partners either; the matter is more complex than any model of sheer co-operation allows. If the interaction is not altogether one way (such as from active to passive, myself to yourself), it is also not two-way either (as if we were paired equals). Instead, things happen with an asymmetrical reciprocity that involves a certain overlap of bodily intentionalities: an overlap that is another expression of the non-coincidence emphasized by Merleau-Ponty—except that this time I cannot claim that I know what I touch from within: I know it as alien skin, as another's flesh. I touch it; it is flesh; yet it is not *my* flesh; it is the flesh *of someone else*—another bodily being.[16]

Let us consider two cases in point.

(i) *Erotic intertouching*. In an erotic experience of mutually attracted adults, a touched–touching dyad is generated that is like the number 2 raised to the second power: two concurrent pleasures, each intensifying and intensified by the other.[17] Let us take the caress as emblematic of this experience. Whether I or someone else initiates it, in caressing I derive pleasure from touching my partner and in being touched back by this same partner. I enter into an interplay of engaged reciprocity between myself as toucher-and-touched and the other as touched-and-toucher in turn. But this interaction, no matter how intense, is rarely strictly symmetrical. Rather than dialectical, it is an analectical process of shared enlivenment in which erotically enmeshed bodies play a game of continual catch-up: if I lead with a certain caress, the other is implicitly invited to follow up in some fashion; yet that same other can decline my offer and initiate a new round of quite different caresses. Both the leading and the catching-up (which are inter-personal avatars of the initiating/receiving modalization) involve an interplay of my body with another's body, and *vice versa*—the two bodies intertwining at their fleshly edges. For it is through the outer edges of flesh that the caress is accomplished, whether

---

[15] 'The flesh of the world (the "quale") is indivision of this sensible Being that I am and all the rest which feels itself (*se sent*) in me, pleasure-reality indivision' (Merleau-Ponty 1968: 255). What is true for the flesh of the world is also true for my bodily flesh. But indivision is compatible with distinguishability.

[16] 'If my left hand can touch my right hand while it palpates the tangibles, can touch it touching, can turn its palpation back upon it, why, when touching the hand of another, would I not touch in it the same power to espouse the things that I have touched in my own?' (Merleau-Ponty 1968: 141). The short answer is that only in my own case do I touch from 'within my landscape'; my two hands 'open upon one sole world' (ibid.). My hands, after all, 'are the hands of one same body' that has 'to do with one sole tangible' (ibid.). I cannot assume the position of the other; I cannot approach the world through *her hands*, which open onto *her world*: a world that may overlap with mine but that is never strictly coincidental with it.

[17] Recall Freud's observation that in sexual intercourse four adults are implicated, due to the lingering traces of the Oedipus complex.

these edges belong to the hand or breast, the lips or the leg, the forearm or the penis. These need not be the edges of the same bodily organ or body part in each of the two partners. Distinctively different edges of diverse bodily parts often conspire in the caress—say, those of the hand with those of the vagina. In each case, erotic contact is realized through the edges of living flesh—edges that vary in felt consistency and texture, indeed in their basic identity as determined by their locus in a given bodily part. Only something possessing the definiteness of an edge can accomplish this intimate interaction: edges bring the fleshly surfaces of bodies to bear on each other in erotically exciting ways.

These intercalated edges complicate the fleshly experience of the erotic partners—sometimes to their mutual delight, sometimes to the frustration or outright revulsion of one party or the other. Despite their differential character and difference in exact bodily location, they are synchronized through bodily movements that bring them into felt proximity. These are movements of my body and of the other that can be so closely coordinated that they can seem to become one movement of one body in which two otherwise distinct bodies are fused. At other times, they fall into divergent bodily trajectories.

Synchronization does not mean strict simultaneity. It should be conceived instead as a temporal convergence, an overlap in time, in which any divergence of bodily motions reconverges soon after. Although very close convergence can certainly be achieved—for example, in mimetic stroking or in 'mutual orgasm'—strict coincidence is by no means necessary to the enjoyment of erotic experience, any more than in self-touching. This is because there are many ways for the erotic intertouching of bodies to occur, some of which are quite familiar to the participants through certain habitual patterns but others of which are exploratory and invented on the spot. An interbraiding of known with not previously known touchings ensues—with many variations in between. Subtending the diversity of touchings is a shared erotic interest, which need not be the very same in each party for intense bonding to occur: *same* does not here mean *identical*. (The same dialectic of same-with-different obtains at other levels of the encounter such as occur when affection or love between the primary parties is at stake—levels that complicate and intensify the sensual excitement of interlaced edges.)

(ii) *Non-erotic interaction.* Less intensely intimate are the many ways by which bodily edges mingle when among friends or members of a family or other group. Very often, these interactions take the form of 'light touches'. In a handshake, for example, two people reach out to each other in a gesture of greeting. The surfaces of their hands interact in ways that are at once physically involved—each person literally 'grips' the other—and yet are tempered by being customary and transitory. Discontinuous surfaces of one person's hand are in touch with comparable surfaces of the other's hand—for example, their palm and fingers. (This indicates that the handshake is in principle reversible, for in it 'I can feel myself touched as well and at the same time as touching' (Merleau-Ponty 1968: 142).[18]) If the aim of many erotic gestures is to intensify and maximize skin contact, this is now no longer the case: only selected surfaces and their edges are here at stake. Much

---

[18] Merleau-Ponty is discussing the handshake in this passage.

the same is true of the embrace on parting, except that now entire arms and upper backs and cheeks momentarily interlock.[19]

Many gestures of touching among familiars are less mutual and less ritualized than handshakes or embraces: the touch on the shoulder, patting on the back, light stroking of the other's hair. In this domain are many expressions of affection or emotion, some of which are frequently repeated and others of which arise in the moment. These contrast with others that are enacted only within the bounds of a certain particular family or circle of friends: these latter are comparable to closed rituals in contrast to the open rituals of the handshake or mutual embrace in public space. If the intention of erotic gestures is to arouse the other and to facilitate sexual engagement with that other, the main aim of gestures of touching among one's family and friends is to recognize others and to reassure them of our continuing affection and trust—in other words, to reinforce a shared historicity and often to indicate a certain special interpersonal connection.

We may infer from these brief remarks that in erotic and non-erotic relationships with others alike, *it is primarily edges that interact*—and through them, *surfaces*. Across surfaces in turn, *whole bodies* are in touch with each other; and by means of these bodies, entire persons with multiple and dense psychical, characterological, and social dimensions. Experiences of touching bring persons to bear on each other through inter-involved bodily gestures, and this mutual bearing—the fulcrum of interpersonal connection, as it were—is effected first of all through the corporeal edges that convey greetings and partings, as well as affectionate (and aggressive) feelings. Thanks to their inter-articulated forms of crossing and tracing, such edges serve as effective vehicles of communication among people. The more or less continuous and subtle structure of these edges (a structure that reflects the disposition of bodily parts and organs) enables them to convey messages between people at a sub-vocal and pre-linguistic level. For this reason, bodily edges are a privileged medium of 'body language', thus capable of bringing about a deep level of empathic understanding between people—without a word of verbal language having to be spoken. This phenomenon exemplifies the general affinity between edges and signs—an affinity at play in the fact that the visible structure of written letters is traced by inscribed edges.

What is special about bodily edges at this level, then, is their ability to act as levers of intervention with ourselves and others—their weight-bearing powers, as it were—as well as their proclivity for semiotic employment.

---

[19] In this paragraph, 'surface' is more fully recognized than elsewhere in this chapter. In fact, surface is an indispensable substructure of edge, its tacit ally: surface provides the very plane of presentation whose terminations *are* its edges. These edges are the areas with sufficient structure or shape to allow a given surface to be brought to bear on another surface, whether one's own or another's. This is especially the case with the lived body, whose overall surface (normally designated as the 'skin') is in effect a continuous edge of the body mass and, conversely, whose effective edges assume the form of surfaces. A full treatment of the intimate and complex relationship between edges and surfaces is beyond the scope of this essay (see the insightful discussion of the perception of surfaces in Gibson 1986: 22–36, 170–81; consult my own treatment in Casey 2007: 47–8, 140–2, 274, 369–74).

Despite the crispness of bodily edges that lends itself to focused intentional engagements with myself and others, my bodily edges are altogether organic: they arise from, and continue to reflect, my actually living body. They remain creatures of its flesh. Compared to many other edges, they possess a unique vibrancy and responsivity, a felt consistency along with a decisive malleability of modes, shapes, and contours. For all their pliability, however, they realize in my body a familiar pattern—a configuration that I take to be the *Gestalt* of my own bodily being as witnessed from the outside, but that is at the same time felt from the inside.[20]

6

Edges of a bodily sort, we can say, come double-edged. In one respect, edges are angular and disjointed (like certain consonants); in another, they are curved and rounded-off, not unlike vowels. This is the primary way in which such edges occur in a given lived body: as fully organic, fleshly, and smooth. Yet some bodily edges are comparatively rigid, graphic, and cursive if not discursive: almost on the verge of writing, as we indicate when we speak of 'written in the flesh'. (Tattoos literalize this potentiality by inscribing words or pictograms on the physical skin.)

Such two-sidedness is also found elsewhere in the edge-world—for instance, in the doublet of border and boundary: these, too, are bivalent in comparable ways. They share with the two aspects of bodily edges just identified the fact that one and the same edge can be characterized by one descriptive term in certain contexts (say, as a delineated 'border', or as a distinct body-sign) and by another in other contexts (for example, as a porous 'boundary' or as the phasing-out of rounded flesh). This parallel is all the more remarkable in that borders and boundaries are most characteristically found in the landscape world—such as in international borders and the open boundaries of wilderness—while rounded versus angular bodily edges obtain for my own flesh as the two major ways for it to be, and to have, edges.

Despite such substantive differences in locus, these two basic edge-dyads (curvaceous/angular; border/boundary) can be encompassed in a more comprehensive bipolar model of edges in which one pole favours precision of form (as with edges like borders and crisp bodily edges), while the other gives preference to what is intrinsically indeterminate (such as boundaries and rounded bodily surfaces). With such a generic model we rise to a new level of bivalency—one that obtains not only for bodily and landscape edges, but that includes under its aegis a variety of other sorts of edge: rims and margins, thresholds and brinks, and doubtless many more.

---

[20] The other's body, if I know it well, also has a familiar pattern of edges as seen from without; but I cannot claim to know just how this pattern feels from within the other's sensibility, no matter how much he or she may attempt to describe this pattern to me.

7

In the case of bodily edges there is a particular basis for binary descriptions: the complexity and density of the lived body itself. Human flesh refuses to allow just one edge structure to prevail, but instead acts to engender any number of edge specificities. At work here is the body's 'genius for ambiguity' in Merleau-Ponty's telling phrase. This ambiguity is both intensive (that is, possessed from deep within the resources of the body itself) and extensive (able, with such resources, to range broadly over many experiences and situations). Acting to order the many edge variations to which the lived body gives rise are such paired structures as inside and outside, bodily members (arms, legs), the fact of having two eyes, touch and sight (themselves related to the inside/outside distinction)—as well as semiotic capacities and organismic substructures that also tend to fall into pairs (for example, the hand as gesturing in meaningful ways, the face as expressive through its grimaces and smiles).

Inside/outside is an especially significant binary edge structure, and is altogether central to edges that inhere in bodies. This is evident from evolutionary processes, which favour an intact and self-regulating bodily organism relating to its immediate environment. Even in the pre-biotic world that precedes evolution proper, the role of boundaries (such as selectively porous edges) is of paramount importance. Without boundaries that are self-generated and that maintain ambient complexes, life could not have arisen in the first place. These boundaries—initially physical only—come to constitute permeable cellular membranes across which matter and energy are selectively received by primitive organisms. In the case of highly evolved animals like human beings, their skin acts to mediate their interaction with the biological and social environments in which they dwell. If it is true that in this development 'the (self-)generation of an inside is ontologically prior in the dichotomy in–out' (Moreno and Barandiaran 2004), this is only because the inside of prebiotic phenomena as well as of primitive and advanced organisms has itself created or induced the boundaries on which they as well as their immediate interactive surroundings come to depend. These self-maintained boundaries, whether considered from the inside out, or from outside in, are essential edges in the evolution of life on earth.[21]

In higher primates the conjoining of semioticity and organicity is especially prominent—above all in human beings, in whom it attains its farthest reaches. In the case of creatures capable of emitting signals encoded broadly enough to include gestures, meaningful vocalizations, and written signs, the role of bodily edges is especially instrumental. These edges act as the hinges or pivots of communicative and expressive utterances, fig-

---

[21] I am indebted to the same reviewer for asking me to address the origins of bodily edges construed as boundaries as well as for the reference to the article by Moreno and Barandiaran cited above as well as to other essays such as Varela, Maturana, and Uribe (1974).

uring as the junctures where certain parts of the lived body are able to articulate and convey messages and thoughts that are meant for other human beings and not just for oneself. These semiotically charged parts are the critical purveyors of messages that are intended to influence other members of the species by letting them know just what we think or want, particularly as it bears upon our relationship with them. The edges of these intermeshed parts constitute a rich matrix of communicative possibilities, sketching the direction of intended actions and the content of closely held thoughts. They act to specify these actions and thoughts—literally to express them, so as to bring them into a shared public domain, however locally specified this space is in a given communicative circumstance.

The pervasive bivalency of edges to which I am here pointing is nothing metaphysical (in contrast with, say, Spinozian attributes of Thought and Extension), nor is it epistemological (as with Kant's distinction between intuitions and concepts). Rather, the bivalency is continuous with my lived body, immanent in it as a dual potentiality; as such, it is experienced by the speaker or actor herself rather than being posited strictly for reasons of system or knowledge. Nor is the bivalency an exclusive one, forcing us to choose between one member of a pertinent dyad rather than the other. For *my body as I live it can go both ways*: thus it can live from its own means, but it can also express itself to others. These alternatives need not be sequential: they often occur at once, co-enacted—as is, in fact, the usual case. I live out my bodily life even as I send signs to others through the expressively toned edges of my lived body construed as the messengers of my feelings and thoughts: starting with my lips and fingers as they articulate thoughts but also by means of other body parts (for example, the shoulder shrug). These edges are where I and others meet in meaningful ways, being the crossroads of communication.

This is not to claim that understanding between myself and others is transparent or straightforward. Any meaning conveyed by the corporeal semiosis of bodily edges comes shrouded in shadows of uncertainty. Interpretation is required at all times. Nor is meaning expressed or grasped once and for all; we are in a circumstance of ambiguity and of continual change of semiotic sense: an ambiguity and change that are themselves compounded in turn. Still, for all the complications and convolutions to which it is subject in corporeal expressivity, meaning comes to be transmitted and to be understood, however imperfectly, by those for whom I intend it when I wish to communicate with them.

Far from being self-contained, then, my bodily edges enter into the arc that extends from myself to others, and back again. In certain circumstances—when I am bottled up within myself, or the other refuses to listen to me—the arc is interrupted: the gamut between myself and others becomes a gauntlet. That the transmission occurs at all is remarkable; but whether the context of such transmission is erotism or affection—or the conveyance of abstract thought—it certainly does occur. Without it, we would be abjectly self-isolated, caught up within our own internal drama, stewing in our own corporeal and cognitive juices. Even when we are thus caught up, however, we never lose altogether the capacity to signal to others our intentions and thoughts through the expressive edges of our lived bodies.[22]

With this last set of remarks we see how bodily edges, even though experienced in uniquely intimate ways by those who possess them in first person, enter the domain of intersubjective life. They manifest one's own feeling or thought to others (who are called upon to interpret them), and they solicit concrete bodily actions on the part of these same others—who in turn express to us their subjectively sensed interests and tendencies through their own bodily edges. The circle of touching and the touched here expands to include the more capacious circle of semiotic expressivity; but it does so only insofar as the bodily edges of myself and and those of others act as indispensable intermediaries, as partners in an always imperfect but always ongoing communicative nexus.

8

Throughout this excursion into being at the edges of our bodies, we have found ourselves engaged with *mereology*, the study of parts of any kind, whether those of physical substances, geometrical figures, or bodies. Peculiar to bodily parts is not just their co-inherence in a given lived body but their capacity for making meaning that arises from movements of that body. For the edges of certain bodily parts have a unique potential to become meaningful in basic acts of communication with others: the flickering of my eyelids, the disposition of your hands. These parts reach out in social situations to connect with others by way of content expressed: they act to im-part this content. The very idea of bodily parts, like that of the edges that delimit them, cannot be confined to the isolated, single bodies they help to compose. At this level the choice is not restricted to that between internal and external parts. Now we must add another option: that of *partes inter partes*. Thanks to the intertwining of their respective edges, the parts of my body interlace with yours, both literally (in the circumstance of intercorporeal touching) and by way of making meaning together.

Beyond mereology we have also been practicing eschatology, given that bodily edges can be considered the end-points, the last stages of any of these same parts (*eschata* signifies 'last'). Even if much starts from edges, more often than not they are where things end—where they come to final states or stages. More generally, how the edges of things

---

[22] Those disabled by stroke or in other extreme conditions still manage to convey to those who look after them what they have in mind. The potentiality of interhuman communication continues to exist: witness the situation portrayed in the film *The Diving Bell and the Butterfly*, in which the protagonist manages to dictate an entire book solely with movements of his eyelids—yet another bodily edge that bristles with semiotic possibilities. My remarks in this last section are meant merely to sketch out the direction of a possible semiotics of bodily edges; the hard work remains to be done on another occasion.

relate to the parts of which they are composed (as well as to the whole that includes them) indicates where the mereological intersects with the eschatological. Edges are the link for these otherwise disparate enterprises, furnishing the effective hinge around which they turn. Limenology, the systematic study of edges, provides the concrete context in which mereology and eschatology find common ground. In and through edges, part and end meet.

This conclusion rejoins an opening point in this essay: bodily edges act as the mediatrix between the edges of the perceived earth (the farthest horizons) and those of the inner psyche (our most interior parts). Bodily edges link these extremities of edge: in such edges, *les extrêmes se touchent*. The edges of my body—and yours—are where what is way out in lived space and what is innermost in psychic space connect, just as in their midst, parts link up with ends. Bodily edges provide the conjunctures for many things in experienced life-worlds: for outlying landscapes with indwelling psyches, for lived bodies themselves, and for these bodies in meaningful communication with the bodies of others.

References

Aristotle (1986), *Aristotle: De Anima*, tr. H. Lawson-Tancred (London: Penguin).

—— (1983), *Physics: Books III and IV*, tr. E. Hussey (Oxford: Clarendon Press).

Casey, E. S. (2007), *The World at a Glance* (Bloomington: Indiana University Press).

Derrida, J. (1973), *Speech and Phenomena*, tr. D. Allison (Evanston: Northwestern University Press).

Gibson, J. J. (1986), *The Ecological Approach to Visual Perception* (Hillsdale, N.J.: Erlbaum).

Husserl, E. (1986), *Experience and Judgment*, tr. and ed. J. S. Churchill, K. Ameriks, and L. Landgrebe (Evanston: Northwestern University Press).

—— (2001), *Logical Investigations*, tr. and ed. J. Findlay and D. Moran (London: Routledge).

Merleau-Ponty, M. (1968), *The Visible and the Invisible*, tr. A. Lingis (Evanston: Northwestern University Press).

—— (2012), *Phenomenology of Perception*, tr. D. Landes (London: Routledge).

Moreno, A. and Barandiaran, X. (2004), 'A naturalized account of the inside–outside dichotomy', *Philosophica* 73: 11–26.

Nancy, J.-L. (2000), *Being Singular Plural*, tr. R. D. Richardson and A. E. O'Byrne (Stanford: Stanford University Press).

—— (1997), *The Muses*, tr. P. Kamuf (Stanford: Stanford University Press).

Rilke, R. M. (1986), *Rodin and Other Prose Pieces* (Salem House: Salem).

Snyder, G. (1990), *The Practice of the Wild* (Washington: Shoemaker and Hoard).

Varela, F. J., Maturana, H., and Uribe, R. (1974), 'Autopoiesis: The organization of living systems, its characterization and a model', *BioSystems* 5: 187–196.

PART III

SELF AND CONSCIOUSNESS

CHAPTER 13

ACTION AND SELFHOOD: A NARRATIVE INTERPRETATION

LÁSZLÓ TENGELYI

IN the original Greek, the word *drama* is marked by a fruitful ambiguity: its literal meaning is 'action', but it also designates a narrative that is staged in a theatre. This ambiguity is fruitful, because it reminds us of the remarkable fact that action lends itself to narration. Indeed, action is not just an event in the world, but it is also the germ of a story that can be expressed in a narrative.

In a well-known passage from his *Poetics*, Aristotle says: "Ἔστιν [...] τῆς [...] πράξεως ὁ μῦθος ἡ μίμησις᾽ (Aristotle 1934: 1450 a 3). Since no use is made of the idea of μίμησις ('imitation') in the following considerations, for our purposes, we can summarize this proposition in English as follows: 'The expression of action is a fable' or even 'a plot'. Aristotle especially has in mind a fable or a plot that is staged in a theatre. However, in his eyes, epic poetry is by no means opposed to drama; rather, in the *Poetics* he treats these artistic forms as species of the same kind: namely, διηγηματικὴ ποίησις—that is, 'narrative poetry'. But what, precisely, does Aristotle mean here by a 'fable' or a 'plot' (μῦθος)? He defines this term as a σύνθεσις or σύστασις τῶν πραγμάτων—that is, as a 'combination of the incidents, or of the things done in the story' (Aristotle 1934: 1450 a 3, 1450 a 14 and *passim*; see Aristotle 1952). The point of this definition is that action cannot be emplotted in a narrative without being inserted into a more encompassing whole, in which its consequences unfold and become perceptible.

In what follows I shall take this idea as a clue to a particular interpretation of action, which is appropriately characterized as 'narrative', because it looks at action in the perspective of its emplotment in a story to be told. From this point of view, action considered in its totality will prove to be a mixture of activity and passivity. Indeed, our actions are not only that which we perform but also that which *happens to us*. In other words, at times the narratives in which our actions find their place make them intelligible as events that have happened to us rather than as initiatives we have taken. Therefore, a 'combination of the incidents' of a story includes not only the initiatives that are taken intentionally, but also the consequences that supervene on these initiatives without having been, in their turn, properly intended or intended at all. It is a highly significant fact that the meaning or sense of an action does not remain unaffected by its unintended consequences, which therefore cannot be considered as merely external events, but must rather be acknowledged as subsequently revealed shreds of meaning that belong to the original deed. They adhere once and for all to this deed, modifying, in hindsight, its original meaning as well as its real significance. Since the unintended consequences of an action withdraw themselves from the control of the agent and happen to him unexpectedly, the agent goes through them more or less passively. Therefore, the 'agent' reveals himself or herself to be, at the same time, a 'patient' (in the original sense of this Latin word).

This intertwinement of action and passion in the combination of the things done in our life suggests that we cannot content ourselves with the simple definition of action as one event among other events in the world. In light of this fact, then, our first task will consist in taking a closer look at and, hopefully, offering a convincing critique of the kind of arguments adduced in favour of such a simple definition. This task will require that we enter into a debate with the analytic theory of action, especially the version developed by Donald Davidson (Section 1). Our second task, then, will be to complete or correct this definition by emphasizing the experience the agent gains of his or her action by undergoing its unintended consequences. Relying upon Paul Ricœur, but also making use of some of Maurice Merleau-Ponty's and Marc Richir's ideas, we shall engage in an inquiry that may be properly designated as a phenomenology of action (Section 2). The unfolding consequences of an action do not leave the agent's self untouched. Our third task, therefore, is to propose a narrative understanding of the agent's self. In order to arrive at an appropriate interpretation of this kind we have to reassess what may be described as the 'theory of narrative identity' (Section 3). It will be easy to show that this theory is unable to account for a dimension of self-constitution that belongs to the passive sphere and is related to affectivity rather than to self-reflective awareness (Section 4). However, it does not follow from this criticism that the idea of a narrative understanding of selfhood is entirely pointless. On the contrary, within its proper limits this idea is quite pertinent and fruitful. However, in its usual versions the narrative view of selfhood provides a too unified and monolithic representation of life-history, discarding or smoothing down the radical turns that often emerge in personal histories. Since, however, it does not reduce action to an isolated act, but grasps it in its relation with its—intended and unintended—consequences, it deserves to be refined in such a way as to account more adequately for the unexpected and unforeseeable changes in life-history. Such an attempt to refine the narrative understanding of selfhood will be made in the concluding part of the present paper (Sections 5 and 6).

1 FROM ACTION TO ITS AGENT

Disregarding the realm of the divine, one can say that only human beings are capable of performing actions. Action is not just different from natural events; it is also different from animal behaviour. But what precisely constitutes this difference? A traditional answer to this question identifies *intentionality* as the distinctive feature of action.

However, this answer raises a serious difficulty. For it is common knowledge that an intentional action can be described in different ways and that it does not remain intentional in all of the descriptions that apply to it. Saying that the future king Oedipus responds to an offense by killing a haughty stranger at the crossroads certainly does not amount to saying that the future king Oedipus commits patricide, and yet, in Sophocles, the two propositions describe one and the same action. However, it is only in the first description that this action can be considered intentional, whereas the second description frames the action in terms of one of its unintended consequences. Thus, the fact that an action does not remain an intentional piece of behaviour in all of the descriptions that truly apply to it rules out the claim that intentional actions constitute a univocally determined class of events in the world.[1]

This does not mean, of course, that intentional actions are not public events. The analytic theory of action that was developed in the wake of Wittgenstein's later philosophy at the end of the 1950s and in the early 1960s clearly demonstrated that the intentionality of action was inseparably bound up with some publicly established criteria. One of the arguments adduced in support of this view was that an agent could designate the intention of an action as his or her *reason* to act. Furthermore, from the fact that the initiator of an intentional action necessarily tries to realize his or her intention, it can be deduced that every intentional action is characterized by a *teleological* structure: an action serves as a means to achieve an aim, and the aim in question is none other than the realization of the agent's intention. As a consequence of this approach to intentionality, intentional action can be distinguished from all other events in the world by the fact that, in contrast with natural processes, as well as with animal behaviour, it requires a *teleological explanation.*

In the initial phase of the analytic theory of action, teleological explanation was strictly opposed to all causal explanations. Philosophers such as A. I. Melden (1961), Stuart Hampshire (1959), and Elisabeth Anscombe (1959) adopted the strategy of distinguishing reasons from causes. They considered 'actions' and 'reasons' on the one hand, and 'events' and 'causes' on the other, as pertaining to two different, or even heterogeneous, 'language

---

[1] The impossibility of considering intentional actions as a univocally determined class of events in the world is related to the *intensionality* of the linguistic expressions we use to attribute to somebody an intention to act; see Davidson 2001: 46. It is the expression 'semantic opacity, or intentionality' (with a 't') which is to be found in the passage, but 'intentionality' is used here in a semantical sense, in which it can be replaced by the more appropriate term 'intensionality' (with an 's').

games' (in the sense given this term by the later Wittgenstein). This conception also gave rise to an impulse to revive the Aristotelian doctrine of the 'practical syllogism' (Anscombe 1959: 57–74). In this epoch, then, the attempt of G. H. von Wright (1971) to put forward a theory capable of uniting teleological explanation with causal explanation was a notable exception. In retrospect, we may find the propensity to oppose reasons and causes to each other in such a strict manner all the more surprising since the category of 'wanting' or desire, as Ricœur rightly points out, 'offers itself as a mixed category, whose appositeness is missed as soon as, for logical reasons, one casts motive on the side of the reason for acting' (Ricœur 1990: 83/65).

Indeed, desire constitutes at once a *meaning* and a *force*. Consequently, it belongs just as well to the realm of physical energy that drives action as it does to the sphere in which actions are justified by reasons. That is why desire is never only a *reason* to act but also a *motive* or even a *driving force* of action. Therefore, it is not surprising that as early as the first half of the 1960s the strict opposition between reasons and causes—as well as that between actions and events—was placed in question.

Donald Davidson first expressed his doubts about this double opposition in 1963 in his famous essay, 'Actions, Reasons, and Causes'. In this essay he maintains that, as a matter of fact, an intention *is* a reason to act, but a reason to act is by no means *opposed* to a cause of action; rather, the agent's reason to act is *the very cause of his or her action*. In order to confirm this thesis, Davidson makes it clear that the upsurge of a desire to perform a specific action—or, more generally, the emergence of an attitude that is favourable to the performance of this action—is a natural event that is causally responsible for the action in question. Assuredly, this approach to reasons and causes involves the revision of certain aspects of the modern concept of causality. First of all, according to Davidson, it is a mistake to suppose that a causal explanation is necessarily based on a law (Davidson 2001: 17). In reality there are also causal explanations that are related to singular events without specifying any general law. Furthermore, he argues that we have to reconsider the widespread conviction that observation and induction are necessary to establish a causal relationship (ibid.: 18). Davidson rejects this belief and this allows him to maintain that we do not need to rely on observation or induction to know our own intentions (see Anscombe 1959: 13–15), and so, correlatively, the absence of such evidence does not constitute a significant obstacle to his thesis that an agent's intention is the very *cause* of his or her action (Davidson 2001: 18).

These reflections mark the first step on the road that leads Davidson to the conclusion that actions can be defined simply as events among other events in the world. Davidson opts for this road, it is important to note, because he aims to define action in a manner that is relevant to ontology; that is, he strives for a definition that clarifies precisely which entities must be presupposed if our language about actions is to be meaningful. In ontology, as in several other areas, Davidson remains a follower of Quine: he commits himself to the formula according to which '[t]o be is to be the value of a bound variable' (Quine 1994: 15). This approach to ontology relegates the decision regarding the existence of beings to the logical semantics of our linguistic expressions (especially the linguistic expressions deployed in our scientific theories). Thus, Davidson asks which entities must be presupposed in order that our propositions about actions may be true and the inferences we draw from them may be valid. And his answer to this question is that actions are *events* among other events in the world. He argues that an inquiry into intentional action compels us to supplement the substance-ontology underlying the logical semantics of first-order predicate logic. For individual substances as bearers of predicates are not sufficient to account for all of the particularities of the language of actions; for this purpose, it is equally necessary to admit of individual *events* as irreducible entities. Intentional actions, then, belong to this category of entities.

However, the difficulty encountered above re-emerges here: it is not clear whether intentional actions constitute a univocally determined class of events in the world, because intentionality is dependent on the descriptions that, in each case, happen to have been chosen for the characterization of these actions. And yet Davidson finds a way out of this difficulty by considering some mistakes committed in intentional actions. To understand precisely what he means by 'mistakes' here, a glance at a couple of his examples will be sufficient:

1. If a navy officer wants to scuttle the ship *Tirpitz* with a torpedo, but, by mistake, he hits the ship *Bismarck*, then he obviously did not scuttle the *Bismarck* on purpose; yet he remains the originator of the unintentionally performed deed.
2. In his mother's chamber, Hamlet intentionally kills the man hiding behind the tapestry; however, he does so without knowing that this man is Polonius; yet he remains the originator of the unintentionally performed deed.

These examples are designed to show that the agent is not only the initiator of his intentional actions, but also remains the originator of their unintended consequences. Since these consequences can be used to redescribe the original action and to give it, thereby, an entirely new shape, this observation carries with it a particular weight: it follows from it that *the agent remains the originator of his unintentionally performed actions.* Consequently, the relationship between an action and its agent can be expressed as follows: *the agent is the originator of all actions that can be ascribed to him under at least one description in which what he does is understood to be intentional.*[2]

The insight into this relationship allows us to consider, if not our *intentional* actions, at least our actions *as such* as events among other events in the world. For we have now come to understand that the relationship between an action and its agent does not depend on the description that, in each case, happens to have been chosen for its characterization. It is true that a piece of behaviour cannot be regarded as an action if there is *no* description under which it could be ascribed to a human being as intentional. But if there is only a *single* description under which an action can be ascribed to a particular agent as intentional, this action does not cease to be the action of this agent under other descriptions either, provided that they rightly apply to it. And this is the case regardless of whether, among these descriptions, there are some in which the action in question

---

[2] As Davidson puts it, 'a man is the agent of an act if what he does can be described under an aspect that makes it intentional'; see Davidson 2001: 46.

cannot be understood as intentional. Consequently, if it is true that an event cannot be ascribed to a particular agent as his or her action without there being at least *one* description in which this agent intentionally gives rise to it, it is no less true that once this condition is fulfilled, the action in question remains the action of this agent in *all* of the descriptions that rightly apply to it, including those in which the action ceases to be intentional.[3] Therefore, although we cannot do so with intentional actions as such, we are in a position to define the actions justly ascribed to a particular agent as a determinate class of events among other events in the world (Davidson 2001: 46ff).

This claim—that actions are justly ascribed to their agents even in descriptions in which they are not intentional—is less innocent than it may initially appear. For it follows from this fact that the initiator of an intentional action is just as well the originator of the unintended consequences of this action. That is why the relation between an intentional action and its unintended consequences must be distinguished from any relation between a natural event and its causal effects. For, as Davidson himself points out, 'each consequence presents us with a deed; an agent causes what his actions cause' (ibid.: 53).[4] This formula indicates that each new description of an action is a *re-description of the original action*. The causal effects of natural events do not enter into the meaning or the sense of the original event. The case is different with the unintended consequences of an action: they do enter into the meaning or the sense of the original action. The eruption of a volcano remains what it is, regardless of the more or less devastating effects brought about by it. Under certain circumstances, however, an act of revenge taken against a haughty stranger at the crossroads is not just an act of retribution, but it even takes on the sense or the meaning of a *patricide*. The difference between the two cases clearly shows that we are far from interpreting the consequences of actions in the same way as the causal effects of natural events (Davidson 2001: 54ff).

We can perhaps make the significance of this observation even clearer if we also take into account the temporal gap that sometimes separates the unintended consequences of an action from the original action. Undoubtedly, even the consequences of an action that emerge considerably later than the original action enter into the sense or meaning of this action. Just one example: we can say that Fichte founded German idealism by

---

[3] Here we should be mindful of the difference between an expression that we use to *describe* an action and the expression that we employ to *ascribe* this action to a particular agent. It is only in certain descriptions that an action is intentional; however, regardless of the way in which it is described, the action is ascribed once and for all to its agent. It follows from this that even if the *criterion* of action is intensional in the semantic sense of the word, the expression with which we ascribe an action to its agent is purely extensional; see Davidson 2001: 46ff. Once more, Davidson uses the word 'intentional' (with a 't'), but he adds that here this term is taken in the 'semantical sense' of the word. In this sense, also the perhaps more appropriate term 'intensional' (with an 's') could have been used.

[4] What Davidson describes here is, in the analytic theory of action, often designated, with a term coined by Joel Feinberg, as an *accordion effect*; see Feinberg 1965: 146: 'This well-known feature of our language, whereby a man's action can be described as narrowly or broadly as we please, I propose to call the "accordion effect", because an act, like the folding musical instrument, can be squeezed down to a minimum or else stretched out. He turned the key, he opened the door, he startled Smith, he killed Smith—all of these are things we might say that Jones did with one identical set of bodily movements.'

appropriating the philosophy of Kant in a quite special way in the first half of the 1790s, although it is only subsequently, in a perspective opened up by Schelling and Hegel, that the notion of German idealism could be connected with the activity of the early Fichte. From this observation we may draw some consequences that remain alien to the Davidsonian ontology of action. It is clear that, in a manner quite distinct from natural events, the sense or meaning of an action is far from being established once and for all; on the contrary, it remains unstable, unsettled, and subject to alteration. The alteration of meaning we have in mind has nothing to do with any progress of knowledge; it results solely from the unfolding of the—often unintended—consequences of the original action. Among these consequences there are some that only manifest themselves after a temporal shift of half a century or even more. Fichte's act of founding a current of thought that was to lose its original significance in the second half of the nineteenth century is a fact that may be employed in a subsequent redescription of an action performed in the 1790s.

Faced with these particularities of the events that we call actions, we may even be tempted to have recourse to the Kantian expression that action 'does not recognize any temporal difference' (see Kant 1913: 99). However, we must resist this temptation. Even if our reflections clearly show that we cannot content ourselves with defining action merely as an event among other events in the world, we must not put our confidence into the speculative notion of a noumenal freedom that 'does not recognize any temporal difference'. We must be cautious with this formula, since we have not yet succeeded in determining the nature of the relationship between an intentional action and its unintended consequences. Whatever approach we adopt to studying this relationship, one thing seems to be clear from the outset: it is not solely from the point of view of an external spectator that the relation between an action and its unintended consequences is established, because these consequences *happen* to the agent. In other words, they are something that the agent *undergoes*. Thus, they belong to the very *experience* the agent gains of his or her own action. From this it follows that in action, considered in its totality or, to put it in Aristotle's terms, as a 'combination of incidents', that which is actively done comes to be intertwined with that which is passively undergone. Consequently, it is only from the agent's point of view that the relation between the original action and its unintended consequences becomes properly perceptible. For, unlike natural causality, this relation does not simply connect different events in the world; rather, it links the entire chain of events with the agent as well. That is why the relation between an original action and its unintended consequences can be described as an *experienced* or, more generally, *experiential* relation. It is, indeed, the experience gained—or to be gained—by the agent of the consequences of his or her action that establishes this relation. Consequently, this relation is not so much observed by a spectator from the outside, as rather established by the agent from within: it is established by the very fact that the agent *relates* first-personally to the consequences of his or her action.

As an experienced or experiential relation the 'combination of incidents' mentioned by Aristotle does not belong to a world of *impersonal* events—to a world of events as impersonal as natural processes are. Ricœur makes this point by claiming that the particularity of an action is necessarily lost sight of if we raise the questions of 'what' and 'why' and fail to ask the question of 'who' (Ricœur 1990: 78ff and *passim*). However, if the relation between the original action and its unintended consequences is understood as an experienced or experiential relation that cannot be severed from the perspective of the agent, the question of 'who' re-emerges in all its significance. This question requires, in particular, an investigation into the *selfhood* of the agent. One cannot avoid asking himself or herself whether or not one remains *oneself*, if one is confronted with the unintended consequences of one's own actions. As Ricœur clearly sees, this new question urges us to pass on from the analytic theory of action to a 'phenomenological hermeneutics of acting human being' (Ricœur: 352), as well as to a 'hermeneutic phenomenology of the self' (ibid.: 106ff and 135ff).

Moreover, we might add that we shall also need a phenomenological approach in order to shed light on the meaning or sense of an action, which is characterized by a particular dynamism, since, as we have seen, it is never settled once and for all but remains constantly in formation. If we take seriously the task of deciding, to put it in Davidson's terms, 'what makes a bit of biography an action' (Davidson 2001: 44), we shall have to pass over from a Davidsonian ontology of impersonal events to a phenomenology of experience in the life-world. Here we may take inspiration from the phenomenology of *spontaneous sense-formation* that has been elaborated by Maurice Merleau-Ponty and especially by Marc Richir. Only such a phenomenology is capable of determining in what sense a 'combination of incidents' constitutes an experienced or experiential relation.

2 FROM THE EXPERIENCE OF ACTION TO THE STORY TO BE TOLD ABOUT IT

What is it, then, that 'makes a bit of biography an action'? Our considerations led us, first, to answer this question by pointing out the intentionality of action. Later, focusing on the relation between an action and its agent, we came to modify our first answer. We have made clear that action is not just an intentional piece of human behaviour but is rather a bit of my biography that I ascribe to myself when I consider myself as the initiator of the action. From this perspective, action as a whole is seen as a mixture of activity and passivity, and it turns out to be a 'combination of incidents' rather than a single act. This observation now leads us to a third answer to Davidson's question: what makes a bit of biography an action is nothing else than the *pattern of plot* it suggests. Accordingly, we may say that *a bit of biography is an action if—and only if—it contains in itself the germ of a story to be told about an initiative taken by the agent, as well as about the consequences— and especially the unintended consequences—of this initiative.*

That action gives rise to a story to be recounted, that it is, moreover, in search of a narrative, which alone can make it intelligible, is a fact that has been incessantly rehearsed since Hannah Arendt first pointed it out in *The Human Condition*. Yet, it is seldom added that it is the agent's experience of his or her action that supplies the missing link in the connection between acting and recounting (see Tengelyi 2004: chapter 1, section II. 3: 'Experience, action, and narration'). Grasped only in a *single* description, action is certainly *designated*, but it is not yet *narrated*. It is not claimed here that action as a piece of intentional behaviour cannot be understood without a story told about it. Every correct description of an action is based on an understanding of it as a piece of intentional behaviour. Here however, an holistic view of action is adopted, according to which a single description never exhausts the content of a deed. The plot of a story to be told about an action results necessarily from a connection between two or more different descriptions of it. What is properly claimed here is that it is precisely the articulated relation between the different descriptions of one and the same action that provides this action with a specifically narrative intelligibility. That is why it will be useful to examine the different kinds of this relation.

We shall begin with a look at the connection between different descriptions of one and the same action that is related to *practices*. A profession, a game, a science, or an art is just as well a practice as gardening in one's own estate or gossiping among neighbours. Practices are habits or customs that are often tied to certain institutions without coinciding with them. As Alasdair MacIntyre says: 'Chess, physics, and medicine are practices, whereas chess clubs, laboratories, universities, and hospitals are institutions' (MacIntyre 1985: 194). It can easily be seen that a practice always connects some different descriptions of one and the same action or activity. For instance, a professor of philosophy (i) presents a university lecture on the rise of Greek metaphysics, (ii) he sets forth his views on the relationship between Plato and Aristotle, (iii) he gives a course on the history of philosophy, (iv) he prepares his students for an examination, and (v) he insists on the standards of his profession. It is the very job of a professor of philosophy that connects these different descriptions of one and the same activity. The relation between the five descriptions is, of course, not of a logical or analytical character; it is, on the contrary, clearly of an empirical or synthetic nature. However, it is hardly dependent on the will of the agent; rather, it is given with the very job of being a philosophy professor, as it is understood in our days at almost all universities in the world. Yet the activity in question is intentional in all of the five different descriptions. It is obviously the internal coherence of a practice that assures the intentionality of action in all of these descriptions. One could say that a practice always rests on a systematic and, to some extent, impersonal articulation of certain intentions to act.

The actions performed in the framework of different practices are, of course, not impossible to narrate, but they seldom deserve the attention of a story-teller. For, at least in principle, the transparent structure of a practice that holds together the different descriptions of one and the same action does not often give rise to any surprises. However, the second kind of connection between different descriptions of one and the same action, which we shall consider in the next few paragraphs, is a rich source of stories to be narrated. The connection I have in mind here is the relation between an action and its unintended consequences.

Hegel was not the first to see that 'an action may have implications which transcend the intention and consciousness of the agent' and that the act often 'reacts upon the individual who performed it', moreover, it 'recoils upon him and destroys him' (Hegel 1994: 89; 1975c: 75). It is as early as Greek tragedy that these observations had been expressed for the first time. If we recall how, in the *Iliad*, Achilles' wrath leads, ultimately, to the death of his friend Patroclus, we come to see that, precisely in this respect, epic is not essentially different from tragedy. Aristotle, who, in the *Poetics*, has not only drama but also epic in mind, coins the very terms that are appropriate to express the tragic dimension of action hinted at by Hegel in the passage just quoted. I mean the terms περιπέτεια (reversal or turn) and ἀναγνώρισις (recognition, experience). In the *Poetics*, different kinds of recognition are enumerated; there are some among them that go without a turn or reversal. But Aristotle insists that the most significant kind of recognition is necessarily tied up with a turn or reversal, as it is exemplified by Sophocles' drama, *Oedipus Rex*. Since every action is apt to generate some unintended consequences and to give rise, thereby, to a sudden turn in the course of events, every action carries with it at least the possibility of an unforeseeable reversal, which happens unexpectedly to the agent. Consequently, the notion of περιπέτεια, as well as that of ἀναγνώρισις, is pertinent to every action, even if, in many cases, nothing but a tendency corresponds to these notions. Of course, it would be sinister to set every action in a tragic light. But this does not alter the fact that every agent takes at least the *risk* of experiencing some unforeseeable and unexpected turns that result from his or her action. Therefore, it is by no means a mere accident that the original meaning of the Greek word *drama* is not restricted to narratives staged in the theatre, but it is related to action as well.

Undoubtedly, the network of practices, with which our life-world is permeated, protects us against the radical turns that our actions are apt to take. Practices insert actions into the frameworks of certain forms of activity that have been elaborated by and permeated with long-lived traditions. That is why they are able to keep these forms of activity at a distance from the unpredictable paths that constitute personal histories.

It is clear from the outset, however, that this process of depersonalization is necessarily bound to come to an end. For even when he or she is entangled in a network of different practices, an agent necessarily remains the originator of his or her actions. And this fact connects the different actions in his or her life, even if they do not belong to one and the same practice. Such transversal relations preserve the traces of an *experiential way* through the life-world, which is characteristic of personal history. Such an experiential way can, however, never be entirely immune to the unintended consequences of actions. That is why action, as we may put it by converting the Davidsonian phrase, *remains always a bit of biography*.

The relationship between action and biography, life-history, or personal history has been explored by what we may designate as the 'theory of narrative identity'. In order to develop a narrative view of the agent's self, it is necessary to examine this theory.

3 LIFE-HISTORY AND SELFHOOD: THE THEORY OF NARRATIVE IDENTITY

The narrative interpretation of selfhood was initiated by Hannah Arendt. In *The Human Condition* she argues that in speech and action, people manifest who they are. She adds that actions, embedded as they are in the interrelations of human affairs, give rise to histories that shed more light on the self of the agent than the intentions he or she tries to realize.

Another thinker putting forward an early version of the narrative interpretation of self-identity is Wilhelm Schapp. Schapp, a former pupil of Edmund Husserl's, relies upon the experiences he gained as a professional attorney. An attorney usually encounters a culprit through an indictment, which necessarily takes the shape of stories. Schapp generalizes this experience by claiming that history represents the person: *Die Geschichte steht für den Mann* (Schapp 1976: 103). According to him, a person is entangled—*verstrickt*—in histories. Schapp adds that these histories can never be completely told, because every history that is expressly narrated points back to a *Vorgeschichte*, a 'prehistory', that remains in the background. Narratives expressly told about one's life are, so to speak, only 'continuations' of the histories oneself is involved in and is defined by.

In the 1980s these initiatives were picked up and elaborated by such excellent thinkers as Alasdair MacIntyre, Paul Ricœur, David Carr, Charles Taylor, and others. MacIntyre refers mainly to Hannah Arendt, drawing, to some extent, also upon the literary critic Barbara Hardy (Hardy 1968: 5–14; see Hardy 1975, especially Chapter 2); Ricœur, on the contrary, knows Wilhelm Schapp as well. To some extent, David Carr and Charles Taylor rely on both MacIntyre and Ricœur.

The theory of narrative identity put forward by these authors is based on the thesis that selfhood, which is to be distinguished from the substantial identity—or the self-sameness—of the things in the world, can be equated with the story of one's life. As Ricœur puts it: 'We consider life to be identical with the story or the stories we tell about it.'[5] In opposition to a philosophy of life, the theory of narrative identity characterizes life, instead of using the language of urge and drive, in terms of a recountable—and partly always already recounted—history.

A problematic aspect of the narrative approach to personal identity may be seen in the danger of reducing life and selfhood to fictional constructions. Telling stories on one's own life can easily be interpreted as an attempt to *construct* a meaningful life-history and, so to speak, to *invent* an appropriate selfhood. Even Ricœur seems to give support to such an interpretation of his position by saying that a life-history is 'an unstable mixture of fabulation and lively experience' (Ricœur 1990: 191).

---

[5] Ricœur 1988: 300: 'Nous égalons la vie à l'histoire ou aux histoires que nous racontons à son propos.'

Yet it is clear that such a constructivist interpretation of the theory of narrative identity is, ultimately, nothing but a misinterpretation. Ricœur leaves no doubt about the proper meaning of his theory. He says: 'Our life...appears to us as the field of a constructive activity, borrowed from narrative understanding', but he immediately adds that, by this narrative understanding, 'we attempt to *discover* and not simply impose from outside the narrative identity which constitutes us' (Ricœur 1991: 32).[6] However, the idea of a *discovery* of our narrative identity by telling stories about our lives clearly implies that our selfhood is somehow given before it comes to be specified and determined by narratives. Otherwise, it could not be *discovered* but only *invented* or *constructed*. However, it is by no means clear how a *narrative* view of the self could account for the constitution of a *pre*-narrative self-identity. There is no exaggeration in saying that this is a fundamental difficulty with which the proponents of the theory of narrative identity find themselves confronted.

The attempt to surmount this fundamental difficulty gives rise to heterogeneous currents that divide the adherents of the theory of narrative identity into different camps.

MacIntyre is committed to the assumption that life is an *enacted narrative*. He says: 'What I have called a history [of a life] is an enacted dramatic narrative in which the characters are also the authors' (see MacIntyre 1985: 215; see 211ff). MacIntyre opposes this thesis to Hayden White and Louis O. Mink, who emphasized the distance between narrative and reality. It is Mink who formulated the famous thesis: '*Stories are not lived but told*'. MacIntyre's reply to Mink runs as follows: '*Stories are lived before they are told*'.[7]

Ricœur, on the contrary, rejects the idea of an enacted narrative and envisages an 'application' of narrative to life (Ricœur 1990: 191). By 'application' he means a *redescription* of life by narratives, and even its *refiguration* by narrative structures. Here, however, the question arises of how, in such and such an episode of life, a story can be anchored and how it can find, in such and such an episode of life, structures to which it applies. Ricœur replies to this question by asserting that action—and even life as a whole—is something like a 'virtual story', 'a story in its beginnings' or 'in its germ', an 'inchoate' story, which is, so to speak, in search of a narrative (Ricœur 1983: 114). The idea of a hermeneutical circle makes it possible for him to bridge the gap between virtual or inchoate stories and literary narratives. However, it remains unclear how virtual or inchoate stories are constituted in action and in life, and, as Ricœur also admits, even in the unconscious, as it is studied by psychoanalysis.

This failure motivates Carr to define the relationship between life and narrative yet in another way. He takes Husserl's return to the life-world as a model of his approach. He distinguishes between stories told in the life-world and narratives elaborated in literature, trying to show that, in the life-world, the self-constitution of the individual, as well as that of human communities, rests already on recounted stories before an application of literary narratives to life takes place.[8] However, this approach results in a conception

---

[6] The emphasis is mine.

[7] See, on the genesis of the theory of narrative identity, Carr 1986: 7–17, 65–72.

[8] Carr 1991: 210: '...il est possible de concevoir la constitution de soi comme une narration de soi.' On Carr's relationship with Ricœur, see Carr 1991: 212–14.

that reminds us of MacIntyre's enacted narratives. Indeed, Carr envisages 'a mode of existence that is already narrative', and he determines the being of man and of human communities as a 'narrative existence' or as a 'recounted being'.[9]

Taylor employs the theory of narrative identity mainly to elucidate the structure of moral argumentation. He shows that a moral argument can only be convincing if it indicates a possible transition from one position to another, adding that in this field no transition can be considered as possible that cannot be lived through, or, in terms borrowed from Ernst Tugendhat, that does not take an 'experiential way' (*Erfahrungsweg*) (see Tugendhat 1979: 275). That is why, according to Taylor, this type of argument has its source in narrated life-histories (Taylor 1989: 72). Although this theory of moral argumentation is clearly committed to a narrative view of the self, it does not make it necessary to decide how precisely a narrative is related to life and reality.

In the past two decades, several studies were dedicated to the narrative approach to personal identity (these studies include Bruner 1990; Kerby 1991; Schechtman 1996; Schechtman 2011; Kraus 1996; Thomä 1998; Tengelyi 1998; 2004; Eakin 1999; Ochs and Capps 2001). They contributed to clarify the strength and the weaknesses of this approach. Also, some global criticisms were formulated (Blattner 2000: 187–201; Strawson 2004: 428–542, reprinted in Strawson 2005: 63–86; Strawson 2007: 85–115; Strawson 2009; Strawson 2011: 253–78. and discussed (Battersby 2006: 27–44; Schechtman 2007: 155–78; Römer (2011: 235–58)). As a result of such debates, the limits of a narrative interpretation of selfhood have now become more clearly visible than in earlier times.

From a phenomenological point of view, such limits have been pointed out especially by Dan Zahavi (Zahavi 2007: 179–201; Zahavi 2011: 316–35). He rightly puts the accent on the basic phenomenological insight, according to which there is no self without a 'pre-reflective self-intimacy' and a 'consciously experienced "mineness"' (Zahavi 2007; 186). It is clear that this pre-reflective experience of the self necessarily precedes storytelling. Therefore, narratives cannot be taken to constitute it.

It may be added that in the primitive sense of the word, selfhood is certainly assured on a passive and affective plane.

4 Pre-narrative Self-constitution in the Passive Sphere

That selfhood is related to passivity and affectivity is an observation that has played a central role in the phenomenological tradition from Edmund Husserl to Michel Henry and Emmanuel Levinas. However, it originally goes back to David Hume, who insisted

---

[9] Carr 1991: 206: 'existence narrative'; 212: 'existence racontée'; 214: 'un mode d'existence qui est déjà narratif'.

that 'we must distinguish betwixt personal identity, as it regards our thought or imagination, and as it regards our passions or the concern we take in ourselves' (Hume 1969: 301). Whereas he rejects the idea of personal identity in the first sense, he endorses it in the second. The importance of this distinction consists in showing, for the first time, that selfhood does not result from an act of reflection on oneself; it rather rests on the basis of an affectivity that is originally entirely passive.

Husserl picks up Hume's insight without, however, adopting Hume's sceptical attitude towards reflective self-awareness. On the one hand he takes it for granted that passivity is the very basis of all active accomplishments of the ego, while he emphasizes that passive processes lend themselves to be continued by active accomplishments on the other.

This twofold or double-sided relationship between passivity and activity is typical of Husserl's analysis of self-constitution. Although Hume's description of the self as a bundle of perceptions plays a fundamental role in Husserl's *Logical Investigations*, it would be abandoned as early as the *Ideas pertaining to a Pure Phenomenology and Phenomenological Philosophy*. Husserl came to understand that Hume was committed to a *reductive* interpretation of the self. Indeed, Hume considered one's idea of one's own self as illusory, and attempted to find out what lay *behind* this illusion—that is, what was, *properly speaking* or *in reality*, involved in one's idea of one's own self. Husserl, opposing and extending Hume's position, tries to elucidate and to articulate the *actual meaning* of one's talk of one's self, without reducing this meaning to anything that is *not intended* in it. This anti-reductionist attitude of the phenomenological approach to the self explains why, in his return to passivity, Husserl never neglects one's active reflection upon oneself. In the *Analyses on Passive Synthesis* we are told: 'A self... can be given... only in its relation with the active ego, it can only be "present" for this ego as something that is at its disposal, as something that remains always reidentifiable. And that we speak of a constituted self already in the passive sphere is only because the conditions for a free disposability are already predelineated in this sphere' (Husserl 1966: 203). By 'conditions for a free disposability of the self for the active ego', Husserl presumably means the *recollections* that play, not only according to John Locke but also according to himself, a pre-eminent role in the constitution of the self. However, insofar as they are awakened by actual perceptions or by accidental reminiscences, recollections still belong to the passive sphere, even if, once emerged, they are at the disposal of the ego, which then is able to submit them to an active elaboration.

Yet the idea of a passive self-constitution serves as a necessary corrective of all conceptions of the self that are based solely on the assumption of a reflective self-awareness. This idea makes it clear what we mean when we say that in an active search for the self, this self is not *invented*, but it is, in the full sense of the word, *discovered*. What is discovered is a passively constituted self. In this context it is important to know that not only Sartre but already Husserl spoke of a 'transcendence' of the self.[10] In the *Analyses on Passive Synthesis* he says: 'It is in the immanence of the primordial present that

---

[10] Used in its phenomenological sense, this expression refers to what transcends subjectivity (and, of course, not to what transcends the world of experience).

experiences of recollection emerge, but what they make once again present (*vergegen-wärtigen*), namely the past, is transcendent with respect to actual experience and to everything that belong to what is constituted as present' (Husserl 1966: 204). Husserl has, above all, the transcendence of one's own past in mind, and this not only insofar as this past consists of a certain amount of objective facts, but also insofar as this past was experienced and lived through consciously. (That is why, in the German original, the transcendence of one's own *Bewusstseinsvergangenheit* is mentioned). Everything one thought, felt, and did, everything one experienced and lived through, has become irrevocable. That is why one's owns conscious past constitutes 'a realm of real being that remains constantly identical with itself' (Husserl 1966: 207). Husserl describes this realm as 'a persistent and remaining in-itself (*Ansich*)' (ibid.), as an 'in-itself of the stream of consciousness' (ibid.: 208). What happened cannot be transmuted into what did not happen. Therefore, the self can never leave its own conscious past entirely behind itself. From this it follows that '...the self is transcendent in an original and good sense...' (ibid.: 204).

This transcendence of the self imposes a restrictive condition on the constitution of the self by narration. A narrative cannot adequately express a life-history if it does not account for the facts preserved in one's own memory. In opposition to fantasy, recollection supposes the existence of its object; it is, consequently, a positional act, and as such it necessarily remains in touch with reality. There is no conscious past—and therefore no life-history—without this adherence to reality. However, the relationship with reality that is characteristic of recollection is by no means constituted by story-telling; on the contrary, it precedes narration. In other words, the adherence to reality that marks the re-memoration of one's own conscious past is constituted in the passive sphere. Of course, Husserl clearly sees that, sometimes, recollection makes mistakes, and thereby gives rise to erroneous views of the past. But according to him, the mistakes of memory arise either from the fact that a recollection comes to be covered up by another one, or from the fact that two recollections merge and fuse. Both processes presuppose, however, some recollections that have their truth content. Recollection is certainly not infallible, but even in its errors it remains in touch with reality. Husserl expresses this insight by applying a principle of Herbartian provenance to memory. He says: 'So much illusion, so much being—which is only covered up and falsified thereby' (Husserl 1987: 105; 1999: 103). From this the following conclusion is drawn, limiting the validity of the theories of narrative identity outlined above: telling stories on one's own life can only contribute to the constitution of one's own self, if it preserves the adherence of recollection to reality.

Thus, Husserl maintains that in the passive sphere a self is constituted preceding active reflection. According to him, it is this passively constituted self that manifests itself in the internal, pre-reflective consciousness that accompanies intentional acts without being itself a separate act. Like Brentano, who assumes that such an internal consciousness necessarily takes the shape of a feeling (Brentano 1973: vol. 1, 203–18), Husserl describes the internal and pre-reflective consciousness of time as a sensation that is generally mixed up with feelings. In the *Analyses on Passive Synthesis* we are expressly told that feelings 'are originally united to data of sense' (Husserl 1966: 150, lines

31–2). This remark makes it evident that Husserl links passivity in the self-manifestation of the self with affectivity. In the phenomenological tradition this line of thought has been developed further by thinkers such as Michel Henry and Emmanuel Levinas (see Tengelyi 2009a: 401–14).

However, even if reflective self-awareness is preceded and founded by a self-constitution in the passive sphere, the theory of narrative identity may be right in maintaining that, in the full sense of the word, selfhood can hardly be given without being reflected upon. The constitution of selfhood is certainly a multi-layered process. The strength of the narrative approach to self-identity consists precisely in showing how the layer of reflective self-awareness is articulated by the stories about one's life.

Yet the existing versions of this approach seem to me to favour a too unified and too homogeneous type of personal history, disregarding the widespread experience that unexpected and unforeseeable turns may emerge in life. That is why some proponents of the theory of narrative identity are so indulgent with the tendency of biographical narratives to foster a more or less arbitrary selection between the different shreds of meaning that penetrate actions, as far as they are experienced by their agents. In what follows I will try to refine the narrative view of selfhood in order to account for the possibility of radical turns in life-history. First of all I shall dedicate myself to the question of how the freedom of action is to be revised in light of the observation that we are only 'co-originators' of the unintended consequences of our deeds. Secondly, picking up a term used by Ricœur, I shall characterize the agent's self as a 'decentred' self.

5 FREEDOM AS A PARTIAL CAUSALITY OF ACTION

There is an idea tied up with the narrative interpretation of personal identity that deserves special attention: the idea of *accountability*. As MacIntyre rightly says, we designate by the term 'action' an event for which *we can be held to account* (MacIntyre 1985: 209). To account for one's action is, in the first place, to give an account of one's *reasons* for acting. But the most exact and most convincing enumeration of these reasons can ultimately turn out to be insufficient, because the agent may be required to account also for the unintended consequences of his or her action. It is on this point that the agent finds himself or herself constrained to have recourse to the narrative intelligibility of the 'combination of the incidents' of his or her action.

From these considerations we can draw out an important consequence concerning the relation between acting and recounting: the reason why actions are narrated in stories is a double one—namely that, on the one hand, actions have a tendency to withdraw themselves from the control of the agent by generating unintended and unforeseeable consequences, and that on the other hand they remain nevertheless imputable to the agent. This latter fact—that the agent is supposed to be able to account for his or her action without, however, being in a position to control the unintended consequences of this action—may be described as the *fundamental dilemma of the freedom of action*. The stories told about actions are nurtured by this dilemma. They lend it a certain fertility or fruitfulness, without, however, being able to resolve it. Relying upon Ricœur, we may evoke here a *re-description* or even a *re-figuration* of actions by narratives.

But how can we conceive of the freedom of action if we consider it from a narrative point of view? I shall take two steps to answer this question. The first step leads us to a rather speculative conception that we stumble upon in Schelling's *Philosophy of Art*. In this work, Greek tragedy is characterized by an equilibrium between freedom and necessity (Schelling 1860: 699). In order to illustrate this conception, Schelling refers to Sophocles' drama *Oedipus Rex*. He says that Oedipus was afflicted by 'the greatest possible misfortune', which consists in 'becoming guilty by fatality, without any real fault' (ibid.: 695). Yet he adds that Oedipus was ready to 'assume voluntarily the punishment even for this fatal guilt' (ibid.: 697) in order to 'manifest, at the very moment of losing his freedom, precisely this freedom' (ibid.) and to re-establish, in this way, the disturbed equilibrium between freedom and necessity or fatality. From the point of view of historical research, this interpretation of Oedipus' tragedy cannot be designated as satisfying, since it attributes to Sophocles, anachronistically, an idea of freedom that must have been unknown to him. However, considered from a philosophical point of view it represents a serious attempt to resolve the fundamental dilemma of the freedom of action. Schelling's main idea is that freedom recuperates the unintended consequences of its actions from necessity (or fate) by assuming the responsibility for them. But it is not difficult to recognize the speculative character of this idea. Schelling himself describes the fact that Oedipus becomes 'guilty by fatality, without any real fault' purely and simply as a 'misfortune', thereby withdrawing it from the realm of freedom. He even designates it in contradictory terms by evoking the notion of an 'inevitable crime' (*unvermeidliches Verbrechen*) (Schelling 1860: 697). It is only in the modality of 'as if' that the agent can account for such a crime. Literally, the idea of an equilibrium between freedom and necessity or fatality does not seem to apply to a freedom of action that can be attributed to a finite being.

That is why it is necessary to take another step towards a possible resolution of the fundamental dilemma of the freedom of action. We may follow Ricœur, who relies here upon Aristotle (Ricœur 1990: 115ff). In the *Nicomachaen Ethics*, Aristotle analyses a particular consequence of action that is related to the formation of 'character' (ἕξις) in the agent. The formation of character is a consequence of action that is, to some extent, withdrawn from the agent's control: as we are told in the *Nicomachaen Ethics*, 'though we control the beginning of our states of character the gradual progress is not obvious' (Aristotle 1959: III 8, 1114 b 32–1115 a 1; see also Aristotle 1925). Yet Aristotle adds 'we are ourselves somehow co-originators [συναίτιοι] of our character'.[11] Taking inspiration

---

[11] Ibid.: 1114 b 23; W. D. Ross translates this passage, less literally, as 'we are ourselves somehow partly responsible for our states of character.'

from these thoughts and transferring them from the states of character to actions, we may say that we are initiators or originators of our intentional actions, but, as far as their unintended consequences are concerned, we have to content ourselves with being their *co-originators*. Since every action can give rise to some unintended consequences, it follows from this that we can attribute to ourselves only a *partial causality* of our actions (Ricœur 1990: 115). According to Aristotle, nothing more than such a partial causality is required for the imputability of action. This causality obliges us, indeed, to give an account of our actions and to assume responsibility for them, since it follows from it that we control at least their beginnings; it is 'in our power… to act in this way or not in this way' (Aristotle 1959: III 5, 1115 a 2–3). Yet the very idea of a partial causality indicates that another kind of causality is also involved in our actions, and that this latter causality is, to a large extent, beyond our control. That is why acting implies that we *become the accomplices of a reality that ultimately cannot be fully mastered.*

The reason why the notion of a noumenal freedom, in the Kantian sense of the word, has to be rejected is precisely its inability to account for this complicity with reality. The narrative view of action makes visible a self who is not just a bearer of free initiatives and who therefore cannot be considered as self-centred. As Ricœur clearly sees, the complicity with reality entails a 'decentred self' (Ricœur 1990: 357), which is strictly opposed to the self-centred, self-controlled, and self-assured ego of modern philosophy.

6 THE DECENTRED SELF OF THE AGENT

By presenting the combination of the incidents in the things done, narratives present our actions in their intertwinement with the causal mechanisms of the world. At the same time, they decide the question of '*who*' (Ricœur 1990: 76) by representing the agent not only as the originator of certain initiatives, but also as the decentred co-originator of the unintended consequences that supervene on these initiatives. These can be considered the most important contributions, yielded by a narrative interpretation of action, to the characterization of the freedom of action and of the selfhood of the agent.

At first glance, the narrative view of the agent's self seems to share a basic conviction with Hegel: *one's actions show who one is*. However, the same conviction is interpreted differently in the two cases. Hegel says in his *Encyclopaedia of the Philosophical Sciences* (§140): 'As a man is outwardly, that is to say in his actions (not of course in his merely bodily outwardness), so is he inwardly: and if his virtue, morality, etc. are only inwardly his—that is if they exist only in his intentions and sentiments, and his outward acts are not identical with them—the one half is as hollow and empty as the other' (Hegel 1975a: 139; 1975b: 197). This proposition does not just settle a fact, but launches an attack; its polemical thrust is directed against Kant's and Fichte's ethics. It is in the heat of this polemic that Hegel adopts the view that the interiority of a human being finds a complete expression in the exteriority of his or her deeds. The narrative interpretation of the agent's self is by no means constrained to share this—presumably exaggerated—opinion.

For it takes for granted that action is characterized by an internal difference between an intended deed and its unintended consequences. However, this difference entails a corresponding split between the interiority and the exteriority of the self. That is why a decentred self reveals itself to be marked by an internal conflict or discord. The split between interiority and exteriority is an inexhaustible source of discontent, because the self cannot act without having recourse to the causal mechanisms of the world which, however, in their turn are always prone to conjure up some unintended consequences of the intended actions.

However, the decentred self exhibits not only a split between interiority and exteriority, but shows also a rift between its being-for-itself and its being-for-others. This topic was dealt with extensively by Jean-Paul Sartre. However, in *Being and Nothingness* Sartre relied on a rather conflict-laden model of objectification and reification of one's consciousness by the Other's. The universal validity of this model was rightly placed into question by Maurice Merleau-Ponty. Let us remind ourselves of a not only acute but also highly pertinent remark of Merleau-Ponty's in his criticism of Sartre's conception of the Other: 'For the other to be truly the other, it does not suffice and it is not necessary that he be a scourge' (Merleau-Ponty 1964: 114/82). Therefore, a narrative interpretation of the self has the task of elucidating the difference between the self's being-for-itself and its being-for others without relying on Sartre's controversial model of objectification and reification. It is, however, not difficult to show that nobody can tell the story of his or her life without taking into account some stories told by others. One comes, in a sense, 'too late' to tell the first stories of one's own life; for example, it is others who tell how one came to life and lived through one's own early childhood. This situation does not necessarily lead to any conflict between one's being-for-oneself and one's being-for-others. But if such a conflict is by no means inevitable, it is nowhere excluded either. Since one's own life-history is inextricably intertwined with the life-histories of others, one never acquires an uncontroversial and privileged access to one's own life-history. In many cases the same episodes of life are differently told by different narrators. This divergence arises in most cases from the fact that these episodes are not only differently told and thus interpreted by different narrators, but that they are differently lived through and experienced by them. This is, however, precisely the reason why the crack between the self's being-for-itself and its being-for-others is, in a certain sense, irremediable.

Perhaps even a third type of breach can be discovered in the inner structure of a decentred self as well. I mean the 'line of break' between what *is* and what *is not* recountable. It is not without reason that Levinas comes to speak of what cannot be narrated (*l'inénarrable*) (see Levinas 1990: 258/166). He has the encounter with the Other in view, from which a task arises for the *I*. Levinas describes this encounter as a drama that *will always already have taken place*, whenever the *I* will respond to an appeal or claim of the Other. The future perfect tense used in this proposition refers to an immemorial past that, in its Levinasian 'diachrony', withdraws itself from retention and recollection, as well as from narration. By the analysis of diachrony, Levinas makes clear how the attitude of acting is separated from the attitude of story-telling. Narration necessarily presupposes a dramatic dimension of action, in which the agent finds himself or herself confronted with a task whose origin remains for him or her a mystery. Story-telling is by nature related to such a dramatic dimension in life without, however, being able to constitute it. What in this dimension happens can be narrated; but it cannot be narrated how this dimension itself is constituted. Therefore, a line of break between what can and what cannot be narrated belongs necessarily to every life-history.

If, however, there is necessarily an area in the self which cannot be narrated, can then a narrative provide access to the self at all? Is it not, just as necessarily, doomed to failure? In the concluding part of my reflections, I want to face this objection. It seems to me that this doubt about the viability of a narrative approach to the self can be eliminated: I am convinced that narratives are able to provide access even to a decentred self. For narration is not only capable of telling what is recountable; it is just as well capable of indicating what is not literally recountable. Literature seems to have precisely the task of telling what can be told in order to make perceptible, or even palpable, what cannot be told. In this respect it is a fact of fundamental significance that Levinas never accepted Wittgenstein's constraint on philosophy to remain silent with regard to the 'unsayable'. Therefore, by his remark on what cannot be narrated, Levinas could not have meant that a whole dimension of the self, being unsayable, should be abandoned to silence. For, contrary to Wittgenstein, he insisted that the task of philosophy consisted precisely in an 'indiscretion with regard to the unsayable' (Levinas 1990: 19/7). Could we not say, in the spirit of this quotation, that at least *one* way towards what cannot be narrated leads precisely through the narration of what can be narrated?[12]

References

Anscombe, G. E. M. (1959), *Intention* (Oxford: Basil Blackwell).

Aristotle (1925), *Nicomachean Ethics*, tr. and ed. W. D. Ross, *The Works of Aristotle Translated into English*, vol. IX (Oxford: Oxford University Press).

———— (1934), *Poetica*, A. Gudeman (ed.) (Berlin and Leipzig: W. de Gruyter).

———— (1952), *De poetica*, tr. I. Bywater, W. D. Ross (ed.), *The Works of Aristotle Translated into English*, vol. XI (Oxford: Clarendon Press).

———— (1959), *Eth. Nic.*, I. Bywater (ed.) (Oxford: Oxford University Press).

Battersby, J. L. (2006), 'Narrativity, self, and self-representation', *Narrative* 14/1: 27–44.

Blattner, W. D. (2000), 'Life is not literature', in J. B. Brough, and L. Embree (eds), *The Many Faces of Time* (Dordrecht, Boston, and London: Kluwer Academic Publishers), pp. 187–201.

Brentano, F. (1973), *Psychologie vom empirischen Standpunkt*, 3 vols. (Hamburg: Meiner).

Bruner, J. (1990), *Acts of Meaning* (Cambridge, MA: Harvard University Press).

Carr, D. (1991), 'Épistémologie et ontologie du récit', in J. Greisch, and R. Kearney (eds), *Paul Ricœur. Les métamorphoses de la raison herméneutique* (Paris: Cerf), pp. 205–214.

[12] An earlier German version of some parts of the present text can be found in my paper 'Narratives Handlungsverständnis' (Tengelyi 2007; French version: 2009b).

—— (1986), *Time, Narrative, and History* (Bloomington: Indiana University Press).

Davidson, D. (2001), *Essays on Actions and Events* (Oxford: Clarendon Press).

Eakin, J. P. (1999), *How our Lives Become Stories* (Ithaca: Cornell University Press).

Feinberg, J. (1965), 'Action and Responsibility', in M. Black, *Philosophy in America* (Ithaca: Cornell University Press), pp. 134–60.

Hampshire, S. (1959), *Thought and Action* (London: Chatto and Windus).

Hardy, B. (1968), 'Towards a Poetics of Fiction. An Approach through Narrative', *Novel* 2: 5–14.

—— (1975), Tellers and listeners: The narrative imagination (London: Athlone Press).

Hegel, G. W. F. (1975a), *Enzyklopädie der philosophischen Wissenschaften im Grundrisse (1830)*, F. Nicolin and O. Pöggeler (eds) (Berlin: Akademie-Verlag).

—— (1975b), *Hegel's Logic*, part 1 of the *Encyclopedia of the Philosophical Sciences*, tr. W. Wallace (Oxford: Clarendon Press).

—— (1975c), *Lectures on the Philosophy of History, Introduction: Reason in History*, tr. H. B. Nisbet (Cambridge: Cambridge University Press).

—— (1994), *Vorlesungen über die Philosophie der Geschichte, Band I: Die Vernunft in der Geschichte*, J. Hoffmeister (ed.) (Hamburg: Felix Meiner Verlag).

Hume, D. (1969), *A Treatise of Human Nature*, E. C. Mossner (ed.) (London: Penguin Books).

Husserl, E. (1966), *Analysen zur passiven Synthesis*, in *Husserliana*, vol. XI, M. Fleischer (ed.) (The Hague: Martinus Nijhoff).

—— (1987), *Cartesianische Meditationen*, E. Ströker (ed.) (Hamburg: Meiner Verlag).

—— (1999), *Cartesian Meditations. An Introduction to Phenomenology*, tr. by D. Cairns (Dordrecht, Boston, and London: Kluwer Academic Publishers).

Hutto, D. D. (ed.) (2007), *Narrative and Understanding Persons* (Cambridge: Cambridge University Press).

Kant, I. (1913), *Kritik der praktischen Vernunft*, Akademie-Ausgabe, vol. V (Berlin: G. Reimer Verlag).

Kerby, A. P. (1991), *Narrative and the Self* (Bloomington: Indiana University Press).

Kraus, W. (2000), *Das erzählte Selbst. Die narrative Konstruktion von Identität in der Spätmoderne* (Herbolzheim: Centaurus Verlag).

Levinas, E. (1990), *Autrement qu'être ou au-delà de l'essence*, Édition 'Livre de poche' (Dordrecht, Boston, and London: Kluwer Academic Publishers); tr. A. Lingis, *Otherwise than Being or Beyond Essence* (The Hague, Boston, and London: Martinus Nijhoff, 1981).

MacIntyre, A. (1985), *After Virtue: A Study in Moral Theory* (London: Duckworth).

Melden, A. I. (1961), *Free Action* (London: Routledge and Kegan Paul).

Merleau-Ponty, M. (1964), *Le visible et l'invisible* (Paris: Gallimard); tr. A. Lingis, *The Visible and the Invisible*, tr. A. Lingis (Evanston: Northwestern University Press, 1968).

Ochs, E., and Capps, L. (2001) *Living Narrative: Creating Life in Everyday Storytelling* (Cambridge, MA: Harvard University Press).

Quine, W. V. O. (1994), 'On what there is', in: *From a Logical Point of View. Logico-Philosophical Essays* (Cambridge, MA: Harvard University Press).

Ricœur, P. (1983), *Temps et récit*, vol. 1 (Paris: Seuil).

—— (1988), 'L'identité narrative', *Esprit* 7–8: 295–304.

—— (1990), *Soi-même comme un autre* (Paris: Seuil); tr. K. Blamey, *Oneself as Another* (Chicago: University of Chicago Press, 1992).

—— (1991), 'Life in Quest of Narrative', in D. Wood (ed.), *On Paul Ricœur. Narrative and Interpretation* (London and New York: Routledge), pp. 20–33.

Römer, I. (2011), 'Narrativität als philosophischer Begriff. Zu Funktionen und Grenzen eines Paradigmas', in M. Aumüller (ed.), *Narrativität als Begriff. Analysen and Anwendungsbeispiele zwischen philologischer und anthropologischer Orientierung* (Berlin/Boston: de Gruyter 2012).

Schapp, W. (1976,), *In Geschichten verstrickt* (Wiesbaden: B. Heymann).

Schechtman, M. (1996), *The Constitution of Selves* (Ithaca: Cornell University Press).

—— (2007), 'Stories, lives, and basic survival: A refinement and defense of the narrative view', in D. D. Hutto (ed.), pp. 155–78.

—— (2011), 'The Narrative Self', in S. Gallagher (ed.). *The Oxford Handbook of the Self* (Oxford: Oxford University Press), pp. 394–416.

Schelling, F. W. J. (1860), *Philosophie der Kunst (1802/03)*, in K. F. A. Schelling (ed.), *Sämmtliche Werke* (Stuttgart and Augsburg: Cotta).

Strawson, G. (2004), 'Against narrativity', *Ratio* 17: 428–542; reprinted in: G. Strawson (ed.) (2005), *The Self?* (Oxford: Basil Blackwell), pp. 63–86.

Strawson, G. (ed.) (2005), *The Self?* (Oxford: Basil Blackwell).

—— (2007), 'Episodic ethics', in D. D. Hutto (ed.), *Narrative and Understanding Persons* (Cambridge: Cambridge University Press), pp. 85–115.

—— (2009), *Selves: An Essay in Revisionary Metaphysics* (Oxford: Claredon Press).

—— (2011), 'The Minimal Subject', in S. Gallagher (ed.), *The Oxford Handbook of the Self* (Oxford: Oxford University Press), pp. 253–78.

Taylor, C. (1989), *Sources of the Self: The Making of the Modern Identity* (Cambridge: Cambridge University Press).

Tengelyi, L. (1998), *Der Zwitterbegriff Lebensgeschichte* (München: Wilhelm Fink Verlag).

—— (2004), *The Wild Region of Life-History* (Evanston: Northwestern University Press).

—— (2007), 'Narratives Handlungsverständnis', in K. Joisten (ed.), *Narrative Ethik. Das Gute und das Böse erzählen* (Berlin: Akademie-Verlag), pp. 61–73.

—— (2009a), 'Selfhood, passivity, and affectivity in Henry and Levinas', *International Journal of Philosophical Studies* 17/3: 401–14.

—— (2009b), 'Une interprétation narrative de l'action', in P. Kerszberg, A. Mazzù, and A. Schnell (eds.), *L'œuvre du phénomène. Mélanges de philosophie offerts à Marc Richir* (Bruxelles: Ousia), pp. 197–214.

Thomä, D. (1998), *Erzähle dich selbst. Lebensgeschichte als philosophisches Problem* (Frankfurt am Main: Suhrkamp).

Tugendhat, E. (1979), *Selbstbewußtsein und Selbstbestimmung* (Frankfurt am Main: Suhrkamp).

van Inwagen, P. (2005), 'The incredulous stare articulated', in G. Strawson (ed.), *The Self?* (Oxford: Basil Blackwell), pp. 111–24.

von Wright, G. H. (1971), *Explanation and Understanding* (Ithaca: Cornell University Press).

Zahavi, D. (2007), 'Self and Other: The limits of narrative understanding', in D. D. Hutto, (ed.), *Narrative and Understanding Persons* (Cambridge: Cambridge University Press), pp. 179–201.

—— (2011), 'Unity of Consciousness and the Problem of Self', S. Gallagher (ed.), *The Oxford Handbook of the Self* (Oxford: Oxford University Press), pp. 316–35.

CHAPTER 14

SELF-CONSCIOUSNESS AND WORLD-CONSCIOUSNESS

DOROTHÉE LEGRAND

1 SUBJECT AND OBJECT

The familiar experience of recognizing one's image in a mirror involves at least a double experience of oneself: one experiences oneself as an experiencing *subject*, the one who is looking from 'here' over 'there' where one concurrently experiences oneself as an *object* of visual experience, as the body which is looked at. Phenomenology has significantly contributed to the characterization of the subject and object of experience as being irreducible to each other. The subject is what the object is not. In particular, the object is understood phenomenologically as what is aimed at by the intentional act of consciousness. The object is characterized as transcending not only its contingent appearances but also the experiencing subject: the object is not experienced as exclusively here and now for me but as *before* me—always already there and over there at an experiential 'distance' from me-as-subject. This experiential 'distance' is not equivalent to the metric distance between objects but rather concerns the phenomenological distinction between subjects and objects of experience. Metric distance can be nullified when for example an object sits on the top of another one; experiential 'distance', conversely, is irreducible in the sense that experiencing an object is experiencing transcendence *vis-à-vis* oneself-as-subject of such experience. As far as self-consciousness is concerned, one may recognize oneself in one's image reflected in a mirror over there, thereby experiencing oneself as a (transcending) bodily *object*. Conversely, experiencing oneself specifically as *subject*—in a phenomenological sense—involves experiencing oneself as holding one's own experiences (for example, as being the one who is perceiving now the image of a body being reflected in a mirror) and this does not involve experiencing oneself as transcendent *vis-à-vis* oneself-as-subject. It is notably in this sense that subject and object are irreducible to each other: only the latter transcends the former. As expressed straightforwardly by Zahavi: 'For x to be an object for y is for x to be in possession of a certain transcendence *vis-à-vis* y, but it is strictly impossible for an experience to possess such a transcendence *vis-à-vis* itself' (Zahavi 2006: 7).

In this framework it has been stated that 'self-consciousness and object-consciousness are mutually exclusive modes of consciousness' and that consciousness of oneself-as-subject 'cannot be a question of a subject-object relation' (Zahavi 2006: 7). Arguably, Zahavi intends to express here that consciousness of oneself-as-subject cannot be reduced to consciousness of oneself-as-object. Nonetheless, while one may remain faithful to the phenomenological conceptualization of the subject as what an object is not, one may ask the following question: does experiencing oneself-as-subject of experience involve experiencing transcendence? More precisely: does one experience oneself-as-subject by experiencing object(s) as transcendent *vis-à-vis* oneself-as-subject? A positive answer to this question would support the idea that consciousness of oneself-as-subject and consciousness of objects are irreducible to each other but are constitutively interrelated to each other rather than being mutually exclusive, as well as it would support the idea that a subject-object relation is involved in consciousness of oneself-as-subject. It is this proposition that the present contribution explores. In that aim, I will first consider the view (held by Henry) according to which consciousness of oneself-as-subject fundamentally involves non-intentional self-affection versus world-directed intentionality. In a more integrative account (proposed by Zahavi), consciousness of oneself-as-subject and of the world involve two conscious gestures (subjectivity and intentionality) integrated into a single conscious moment. In this view, consciousness of the self-as-subject is both pre-reflective (non-self-objectifying) and reflexive (aiming at itself). I will propose that consciousness of the self-as-subject may involve neither reflectivity nor reflexivity, if it is not self-objectifying while not aiming at itself but at something other than itself—namely, the world. Such self-conscious mode of being open to one's world will be described as composed of two complementary orientations: centrifugally reaching-out (of oneself) and centripetally being-indicated-by (the world). The former notion will be elaborated on by referring to von Uexküll's treatment of the notion of Umwelt, and the latter to Gibson's account of self-environment co-perception. In a concluding section I will apply the proposed conception of consciousness of the self-as-subject to the special case of bodily self-consciousness, the body being the paradigmatic manner of being conscious of oneself as open to one's world.

2 INTENTIONALITY AND CONSCIOUSNESS OF ONESELF-AS-SUBJECT

Elaborating on the phenomenological distinction between subject and object, it has been argued that consciousness of oneself-as-subject is intrinsic to one's experience and that in this sense it is not intentional. Radicalizing this line of thought, Henry (1995) defends a *non-intentional* phenomenology. He underlines that any intentional act must differ from its intentional object. On the one hand, an intentional object is by definition incapable of appearing by itself: for an object to appear, it must be targeted by an intentional act which differs from the object. On the other hand, the intentional act is such that it is oriented towards something other than itself. The intentional act 'turns away from itself in such a radical and violent manner that it is entirely oriented toward other than itself, toward the outside' (Henry 1995: 386). The consequence of this is that intentionality does not make the intentional act appear to itself: only its object appears.

Given that intentionality is never and can never be its own object (Henry 1995: 390), another conscious gesture is needed for the intentional act to appear to itself. Henry argues that the apparition of the intentional act to itself is operated thanks to a self-affection which is heterogeneous relative to intentionality (Henry 1995: 392): self-affection appears on its own, and relies neither on intentionality nor on the world (Henry 1995: 393; Henry 1963: 279/226–7). Self-affection occurs when one is maintained close to oneself, not when one goes beyond oneself, nor when one manifests oneself in the world. Henry argues that self-affection is the only way to be conscious of one's consciousness: when occulted by intentional objects, the concrete life of human beings is missed, reduced to exteriority, left to an objectivism cancelling out its subjectivity to the benefit of a rational knowledge of the material universe (Henry 1995: 394).

In this view, any experience is characterized by a duality, an 'ontological dualism' between subjectivity and that which transcends it, between 'pure interiority' and 'pure exteriority' (Zahavi 1999: 114). Nonetheless, as underlined by Zahavi, 'Henry acknowledges that absolute subjectivity does transcend itself toward the world', as it corresponds to a 'self-revelation of the very act of transcendence' (Zahavi 1999: 114). In Henry's view it is indeed clear that no hetero-manifestation would be possible without self-manifestation. However, his analyses 'never take the interplay between self-manifestation and hetero-manifestation into sufficient consideration' (Zahavi 1999: 114). In particular, self-manifestation is conceived of as being 'self-sufficient, nonecstatic, irrelational' (Zahavi 1999: 115) but, Zahavi asks, 'how can [such subjectivity] simultaneously be directed intentionally toward something different from itself' (Zahavi 1999: 115)? This question is related to the one that is of relevance in the present context: can self-manifestation be coherently conceived of as a 'moment' of hetero-manifestation? In the terms chosen here: can consciousness of oneself-as-subject be given *by* consciousness of objects?

Intending to clarify the interplay between consciousness of the self-as-subject and world-consciousness, Zahavi distinguishes two options:

> … either it is claimed that it is in our confrontation with that which we are not that we are self-aware, or it is claimed that it is by being confronted with that which we are not that we gain self-awareness. Needless to say, there is a subtle but decisive difference between claiming that my subjectivity is revealed to me in its exploration of the world and claiming that I am conscious of myself via the world. (Zahavi 1999: 134)

Against the idea that consciousness of the self-as-subject would involve a conscious gesture or mode of givenness that comes after the conscious gesture or mode of givenness responsible for world-consciousness, Zahavi proposes that those two conscious gestures are contemporary and compose a single act of consciousness. In this sense it is not *via* some already acquired consciousness of the world that consciousness of oneself-as-subject would unfold secondarily. In this 'one-level' view of consciousness, subject and object come at once. 'The self-consciousness that is present the moment I consciously experience something', Zahavi argues, 'does not involve an additional mental state, but is rather to be understood as an intrinsic feature of the primary experience' (Zahavi 2005: 20). According to this view, any single act of consciousness is thus characterized by two modes of given-ness: intentionality by which the conscious subject transcends himself towards objects in the world, and subjectivity by which the subject is conscious of himself-as-subject. These two modes of givenness are intermingled into a single act of consciousness as 'two facets of one and the same act' (Merleau-Ponty 1945: 237–8) and in this sense, 'consciousness of the world is not based on self-consciousness: they are strictly contemporary' (Merleau-Ponty 1945: 344–5). To rephrase the contrast underlined above: subjectivity comes *together with* intentionality but subjectivity is not given *by* intentionality. Therefore, and importantly, this 'one-level' view of consciousness can be described as being *dual* in the sense that intentionality and subjectivity must be distinguished from each other even if they are not separable from each other (Zahavi 2005: 67).

This 'one-level' view, one may argue, is not the only way out of the problematic conceptualization of self-consciousness as being secondary to world-consciousness. Indeed, it could be defended (as here) that consciousness of the self-as-subject does not involve any other conscious gesture than world-directed intentionality, the latter giving at once the self as its subject and the world as its object, thereby avoiding the problems of prioritizing either the world or the self. In this sense, it would be *by* being conscious of the world that one would be conscious of oneself as the subject of one's world-directed experience.

With the 'one-level' view, Zahavi notably intends to characterize a form of self-consciousness that does not involve the 'distance' characteristic of reflectivity in which one's self-consciousness is divided between consciousness of oneself as subject of reflection and consciousness of oneself as object of reflection. Rather, the form of self-consciousness tackled by the 'one-level' view is both *pre-reflective* and *reflexive* (Legrand 2007c). That such self-consciousness is *pre-reflective* means here that one does not take oneself as an object of consciousness. Being non-self-objectifying in this sense, pre-reflective self-consciousness is a form of consciousness of oneself-as-*subject*. That such self-consciousness is *reflexive* here means that it does not aim at anything else than itself. In this sense, reflexivity is non-intentional: it is *not* intentionality turned inward (see also Mohanty 1985: 83–4). But does *pre-reflective* self-consciousness have to be *reflexive*? Can self-consciousness avoid self-objectification if consciousness of oneself-as-subject is given by consciousness of objects one is not? Is there a way of being conscious of oneself-as-*subject* by being conscious of what one is not, an intentional *object*, without turning the subject into an object? To address these questions it is warranted to consider again the phenomenological characterization of object and subject that has been sketched in the introduction.

3 AT A DISTANCE FROM THE OBJECT

It has been stated above that object and subject are irreducible to each other, notably in that the former transcends the latter, thereby being experienced at a 'distance' from the latter. This view should not be conflated with another one according to which perception involves a mode of aiming at objects without tension, without 'distance' (Benoist 2009: 19, 87) between what is aimed at and what is actually given (Benoist 2009: 51): in perception, intentionality constitutes objecthood (Benoist 2009: 35), as one's experience aims at the perceived object itself (Benoist 2009: 87), not at sensations or affections (Benoist 2009: 35). Reports of schizophrenic patients may illustrate this point relevantly. Indeed, when typical perception of objects is perturbed, the subject may experience mere appearances of objects, this being associated with derealization: the perceived world seems unreal because perception has lost its objectifying quality: 'Things are no longer the way they used to be. They are strange, as if they only were silhouettes' (Parnas *et al.* 2005: 248) reports a schizophrenic patient. In a sense, objects are here experienced at a 'distance' from themselves while it is not typically the case.

This view—according to which the appearance of the perceived object is typically experienced at no 'distance' from the object itself—is consistent with the different view—stated above—according to which the object is experienced at a 'distance' from the subject. The point involved in this latter consideration is indeed that, as the object experienced in perception is given in its objecthood, it transcends the experience one has of it contingently, thereby transcending the perceiving subject as well.

Because there is no 'distance' in perception between what is aimed at and what is given—the perceived object—Benoist resists the conception of intentionality that would equate it with desire—in its dynamic or economical sense, not its affective sense (Benoist 2009: 18). As desire-like, intentionality would involve a tension towards what is currently missing, a tension which may be fulfilled by the execution of an act of perceptual consciousness. This conception, Benoist argues, conflicts with the characterization of perception as unfolding the full-fledged presence of the perceived object (Benoist 2009: 32). Now, considering the 'distance' that is involved in perception between the object and the subject—rather than the typical lack of 'distance' between an object and its appearance—may lead to reconsider the desire-likeness of intentionality.

Barbaras (2008a) indeed describes subject-object 'distance' in terms of desire. This leads him to characterize subjecthood as constitutively involving an aspiration towards what the subject is not: intentional objects. Here, the relevance of the notion of desire comes from its contrast with the notion of need. As the fulfilment of needs allows self-preservation, it would lead to a conceptualization of subjecthood as primarily involving the maintaining of the constancy of a pre-constituted internal milieu, the conservation or restoration of a self-constituted subject. The notion of desire, by contrast, allows characterizing the subject as constitutively and incessantly reaching out towards what he is not, as the satisfaction of desire fuels the desire itself and unavoidably fails to nullify the 'distance' between the subject and the object he desires, thereby keeping the former oriented towards the latter. In this view, subjecthood does not involve the depreciative tension of needs towards 'more', 'better', or 'else' but is rather constituted through a never-fully-achieved self-realization through an incessant reaching-out-towards-what-one-is-not.

4 DISTANCE, CLOSENESS, AND OPENNESS OF THE SUBJECT

As stated above, the *subject*, by contrast with objects, is experienced at no 'distance' from himself. It should be clear that stating this is not to say that all together self-consciousness involves no distance whatsoever. Rather, there is an irreducible 'distance' between one's consciousness of oneself-as-subject and one's consciousness of oneself-as-object. In particular, as identified by Lacan (1949) and further commented upon by Merleau-Ponty (1951), recognizing one's image in a mirror transforms the subject, who can now acknowledge that there can be a spectator of himself: contrasting with the body as 'a strongly felt but confused reality... the collection of confusedly felt impulses' (Merleau-Ponty 1951: 136), the recognition of the specular body as one's own brings together with it the possibility of an ideal image of oneself, image which would 'henceforth be either explicitly posited or simply implied by everything I see at each minute' (Merleau-Ponty 1951: 136).

   What matters for the point at stake here is the experiential split that is involved in the recognition of oneself in one's specular image: 'at the same time that the image of oneself makes possible the knowledge of oneself, it makes possible a sort of alienation' (Merleau-Ponty 1951: 136). This 'alienation' does not involve the vanity of some excessive fascination for one's physical appearance. Rather, it involves the fact that 'inevitably there is conflict between the *me* as I feel myself and the *me* as I see myself' (Merleau-Ponty 1951: 137). Experiencing oneself notably involves a 'distance' between what is given 'here'—oneself-as-subject—and 'there'—oneself-as-object. By introducing such 'distance', the objectification of oneself occurring with the identification due to mirror self-recognition—'the transformation that takes place in the subject when he assumes an image' (Lacan 1949: 2)—would introduce a negation of the purity of one's subjecthood, a 'negation of its absolute' (O'Neill 1986: 202, quoting Henri Ey). Points of controversy notably concern whether the transformation that occurs through the identification with one's specular image can be achieved via other routes, whether the lived body prior to the mirror stage is a 'body in bits and pieces' (*corps morcelé*), or whether the body is first lived as a synesthetic whole which is notably sensitive to the rejecting or caring behavior of others (O'Neill 1986: 209). These different scenarios are nonetheless united by the idea that experiencing oneself as such involves experiencing a 'distance' between oneself-as-subject and oneself-as-object. It would be a mistake, however, to conceive of this 'distance' taking place within oneself as involving a gap between what one is and what one ought to be(come). Rather, it is a 'distance' between different irreducible dimensions of oneself.

Over and above such 'distance' between oneself-as-subject and oneself-as-object, is there any 'distance' within subjecthood itself? An answer to this question is suggested by reports of schizophrenic patients. Indeed, what can be symptomatically described as 'distorted first-person experience' may be expressed by patients as follows: 'I have had "slightly strange experiences of a lacking relation between myself and what I am thinking"' (Parnas *et al.* 2005: 245); 'My own "I", as a point of perspective, feels as if it had shifted a few centimetres backwards' (Parnas *et al.* 2005: 246). Such reports suggest a 'distance' within one's subjecthood. Its atypicality, however, points to its typical counterpart: the 'closeness' of the subject to himself. This 'closeness' does not correspond to any metric 'nearness' between an object and another. Moreover, and crucially, one's 'closeness' to oneself should not be conflated with any 'closedness' of oneself. To express it with Heidegger:

> ...human existing...is certainly not a self-contained object. Instead, this way of existing consists of...capacities for receiving-perceiving what it encounters and what addresses it. (Heidegger 1987: 2–3/3–4)
>
> Our being here is essentially a being with beings which we ourselves are not...[Being-at] is fundamentally different from...for instance, the shoes we put in front of our room door. Of course, we can say that the shoes are at the door. Here, this 'being-at' means the spatial juxtaposition of two things. In contrast, the 'being-at' of our being here with things has the fundamental characteristic of being-open-for [Offenstehen für] that which comes to presence [das Anwesende] where it is. (Heidegger 1987: 93–4/72–3)

Related to this conceptualization of 'openness' characteristic of subjects (versus objects), what follows from the previous discussion is that the subject experiences objects by reaching *out*, transcending himself in the intentional experience of the world out there, beyond the subject himself. But what does such 'openness' of the subject imply for one's consciousness of oneself-as-subject? Does experiencing the world as transcending the subject allow *experiencing* oneself-as-subject *by* this experiential act of 'reaching out'?

5 SELF-CONSCIOUSNESS AND OPENNESS

That the subject is 'open' notably means that the subject may not only be related to objects secondarily and contingently, but also primarily and constitutively (Heidegger 1927: 224/157). This view involves reconsidering the notion of intentionality itself in order to adequately conceive of consciousness of the self-as-subject as an intentional act, without reducing the subject to an intentional object. What is at stake here is the idea that 'the co-disclosure of the self belongs to intentionality' (Heidegger 1927: 225/158). Such co-disclosure is not the correlated disclosures of two objects, an object in the world and oneself-as-object. Rather, such 'unveiling of the self' (Heidegger 1927: 225/158) by the intentional act involves conceptualizing intentionality *itself* as twofold: it does not only correspond to a 'directing-toward', it does not only deliver an experience of the intentional object. Rather, it is also a 'mode of primary self-disclosure' (Heidegger 1927: 226/159). For that to be the case, intentionality itself has to give intentional objects as well as the intentional subject. In this framework, if consciousness of the self-as-subject involves a form of reflection/reflexion, it is not in any introspective sense:

> ... we must not take [reflection] to mean what is commonly meant by it—the ego bent around backward and staring at itself—but an interconnection such as is manifested in the optical meaning of the term 'reflection'. To reflect means, in the optical context, to break at something, to radiate back from there, to show itself in a reflection from something... (Heidegger 1927: 226/159)

In other terms, it is by consciously engaging ourselves in the world that we are conscious of ourselves-as-subjects: the objects we are conscious of 'reflect' to us that we are ourselves intentional subjects—that is, subjects of intentional consciousness. The claim that is made here (and which—I think—is not made in the 'one-level' view of consciousness described above) is that, at a primary level, consciousness of oneself-as-subject is given by *nothing else* than the subject's non-reflexive relation to otherness (Barbaras 2008a: 13). (Note that this view can be related to Sartre's view, as developed below.) Not only subjectivity and intentionality are contemporary—as the one-level view also defends—but in the view proposed here subjectivity is nothing else than a dimension of intentionality. In this view, the subject is 'never anything like a subjective inner sphere' (Heidegger 1927: 241/170). Rather, consciousness of oneself-as-subject proceeds by a 'detour' through one's consciousness of the outer world, but there is in fact no shorter way towards oneself-as-subject (Barbaras 2008a: 111). One is conscious of oneself-as-subject not *despite* the fact that one is intentionally oriented towards the outer world—as Henry would conceive of it—and not merely together with intentionality—as Zahavi wants it—but *thanks* to one's intentional orientation. A form of consciousness of oneself-as-subject may be—as the 'one-level' view of self-consciousness wants it—both pre-reflective (non-objectifying) and reflexive (non-intentional) but this does not prevent the subject to be also indicated to himself as subject, neither reflectively nor reflexively, by the very act of intentional consciousness that he performs.

In fact, it seems to follow directly from the characterization of consciousness as intentional that the transcendent object and the self-transcending subject are experienced relatively to each other. It is because the subject experiences himself as transcending himself towards the world, and as being transcended by objects he aims at, that the latter are experienced as transcendent *vis-à-vis* the intentional experience and its subject. The subject of intentional consciousness is intentional and experiences himself as such, not as an intentional object but as an intentional subject.

This view presents the advantage of clarifying that, as the intentional subject and object are given at once, there is no need for any further explanation of how they would be related to each other. In other terms, this proposal gets around Zahavi's worry about Henry's view, concerning how a self-sufficient, non-ecstatic, irrelational form of subjectivity could as well transcend itself to experience what it is not: the world (Zahavi 1999: 115).

Moreover, the proposed view allows capturing an essential dimension of pre-reflective self-consciousness—which both Henry's and Zahavi's view account for as well: it is non-objectifying, thereby giving oneself-as-*subject*, specifically. The crucial point here is that the subject would be given by its intentional act, but not as its intentional target. It is because the subject is indicated to himself by reaching out towards *what he is not* that it is neither a present object, nor an absent one; rather, it is present specifically as subject.

By the same token—that is, precisely because it is indicated by its intentional experience of objects in the world—it specifically experiences itself as a bodily subject who is embedded in the world. Such 'embeddedness' can be specified as being composed of two conscious 'gestures' pointing in opposite directions: centrifugal reaching-out and centripetal being-indicated-by. As expressed by Heidegger and Sartre respectively:

> Da-sein has a mode of being in which it is brought before itself and it is disclosed to itself in its throwness. (Heidegger 1927: 181/169)
>
> Disclosedness in general belongs essentially to the constitution of being of Da-sein... Throwness belongs to the constitution of being of Da-sein as a constituent of its disclosedness. In throwness the fact is revealed that Da-sein, as my Da-sein and this Da-sein, is always in a definite world and together with a definite range of definite innerworldly beings. (Heidegger 1927: 221/203)
>
> ... my being-in-the-world, by the sole fact that it realizes a world, causes itself to be indicated to itself as a being-in-the-midst-of-the-world by the world which it realizes. (Sartre 1943: 357/318)
>
> ... everything indicates [the given which I am] to me, every transcendent outlines it in a sort of hollow by its very transcendence without my ever being able to turn back on that which it indicates since I am the being indicated. (Sartre 1943: 366/327)

These quotes are meant to capture that Heidegger insists on a 'thrown-projecting' (1927: 181/170) 'subject' characterized by a centrifugal dynamic while Sartre points at the complementary aspect: the subject characterized by a centripetal dynamic as a 'center of reference which things indicate' (Sartre 1943: 359/320). Beyond their opposite directions, these dynamics would correspond to two aspects of the same act of consciousness, as two sides of the same coin, in the sense that the subject would be centripetally indicated to himself by the objects towards which he centrifugally reaches out.

6 CENTRIFUGALLY REACHING-OUT AND CENTRIPETALLY BEING-INDICATED-BY

To grasp the implication of differentiating between centrifugally reaching-out and centripetally being-indicated-by, it is worth comparing two authors who have strongly impacted research in biology and psychology: namely, Jacob Von Uexküll (1992) and

James J. Gibson (1979). While they are often associated with each other, underlining their differences seems more fruitful here than focusing on what they might have agreed upon.

As Kant places the subject at the center of its epistemic universe, Uexküll introduces the notion of subject in biology and places it at the centre of its natural world (Stjernfelt 2007). Such subject is perfectly adjusted to its milieu, its 'Umwelt'. The possibility of a subject fitting with 'completeness' (Uexküll 1992: 324) to its objects is rooted in the view that properties of objects are nothing but 'exteriorization of the subject'. Such 'subject's manifestations' (Uexküll 1992: 383) are operated thanks to a functional cycle linking the receptors of an organism to its effectors. Perception is thus conceived of neither as a passive reception nor as a grasping of information that would objectively characterize things in the world. Rather, perceived properties of objects are *projected* by the actions of the perceiving subject on elements of its surrounding milieu. Following this line of thought, Uexküll reaches the conclusion that 'each subject lives in a world composed of subjective realities alone...even the *Umwelten* themselves represent only subjective realities' (Uexküll 1992: 383). It is interesting to note that, on the one hand, Uexküll participates to the naturalization of the transcendental subject by rooting the phenomenal world (appearances) to a sensorimotor reflexive circle, while on the other hand he acknowledges that 'we know nothing so far of the extent to which the subject's own body enter into his Umwelt' (1992: 383). In other terms, elaborating on the biologist's framework, it could be said that in this analysis, intentionality may be based on a primordial reflexivity at the functional level, while neither such functional reflexivity nor the constitution of a phenomenal world necessarily involve self-perception/self-consciousness.

A very different picture is drawn by J. J. Gibson (1979), who completely reverses the terms of the problem, as he defends the view according to which, even without any reflexive process, self-perception is necessarily coupled with world-perception. Crucially, this coupling is *constitutive* (versus contingent). Perception indeed emerges from a 'perceptual system' (Gibson 1979: 183) which integrates both the whole body of the perceiver and its surrounding environment. Unorthodoxly, according to this systemic view of perception, one does not see the environment with the eyes but with 'the eyes-in-the-head-on-the-body-resting-on-the-ground' (Gibson 1979: 205). Detaching the perceiving body from the perceived environment would thus amount to a destruction of the perceptual system which, by the same token, would lead perception of both oneself and one's environment to vanish. Three forms of self-environment co-perception are differentiated from each other in Gibson's theory.

First, 'subjective objects' (Gibson 1979: 120), like the nose and the limbs of the observing subject, temporarily conceal portions of the environment 'in a way that is unique to that animal'. Because this information cannot be shared by other observers, it is 'propriospecific as distinguished from exterospecific, meaning that it specifies the self as distinguished from the environment' (Gibson 1979: 111). Here, self-related information leads the subject to miss environment-related information. 'Occluding edges' (Gibson 1979: 114) delimiting the boundaries of the visible environment are specific of the 'visual ego' (Gibson 1979: 208) and *appear* as such: the 'blind region' (behind one's head, for example) 'is blind only for exteroception, not for proprioception. It looks *like oneself*' (Gibson 1979: 208). In this first type of self-environment co-perception, '*two sources of information* coexist... When a man sees the world, he sees his nose at the same time; or rather, the world and his nose are both specified and his awareness can shift. Which of the two he notices depends on his attitude' (Gibson 1979: 116). The important point here is that Gibson insists on the fact that there must be *two* sets of information, which differ from each other in terms of content (oneself versus environment), while they are systematically joint to each other, as one provides the limit of the other.

The case is fundamentally different with the second form of self-environment co-perception that would be given by *one and a single flow of information*, information which is *about* the environment while its *concerns* the subject *by the same token*: 'The moving self and the unmoving world are reciprocal aspects of the same perception' (Gibson 1979: 123). A primary and reliable sense of one's locomotion is given by the processing of information depicting the outer environment (the structure of the visual array) rather than by the processing of information about the state of the perceiving body itself (states of muscles and joints). The former, Gibson argues, 'yields the only reliable information about displacement. The classical sense of movement is not trustworthy, for a fish in a stream and a bird in a wind have to exercise their muscles and joints strenuously merely to stay in the same place' (Gibson 1979: 125). What is important for the issue at stake here is that a single act of intentional consciousness can be conceived of as indicating not only the intended object but also, and by the same token, the intending subject.

Gibson identifies a third way in which the bodily subject is intermingled with its environment. By making up the notion of *affordance* (Gibson 1979: 127), Gibson indeed meant to capture that, for example, terrestrial surfaces are 'climb-on-able or fall-off-able or get-underneath-able or bump-into-able relative to the animal' (Gibson 1979: 128). This notion of affordance is notoriously ambiguous. On the one hand, affordances 'have to be measured relative to the animal. They are unique to that animal. They are not just abstract physical properties. They have unity relative to the posture and behaviour of the animal being considered' (Gibson 1979: 127). In other terms, 'affordances are properties taken with reference to the observer' (Gibson 1979: 143). On the other hand, 'An important fact about the affordances of the environment is that they are in a sense objective, real, and physical' (Gibson 1979: 129). Since affordances are defined as observer-relative, it might be difficult to understand that according to Gibson, 'the observer may or may not perceive or attend to the affordance, according to his needs, but the affordance, being invariant, is always there to be perceived. An affordance is not bestowed upon an object by a need of an observer and his act of perceiving it. The object offers what it does because it is what it is' (Gibson 1979: 139). The fact that an affordance is 'neither an objective property nor a subjective property; or it is both if you like' (Gibson 1979: 129) may be best captured by the statement that 'positive and negative affordances are properties of things taken with reference to an observer but not properties of the experiences of the observer... they are not feelings of pleasure or pain added to neutral perceptions' (Gibson 1979: 137). What matters here is that affordances are not intrinsic to a given subject or a given subject's perception of the environment, while at the same time perception of the environment is never 'neutral', never detached from its relevance for the perceiver. Affordances are not so ephemeral that they would vanish as soon as the perceiver loses consciousness. Rather, they are picked-up by the perceiver *because of what objects are*. Here it is the objective structure of the world itself that involves a way of processing information about intentional objects which indicates the bodily subject without requiring the perceiver itself to be taken as an object.

Sartre expresses this point most clearly:

> …orientation is a constitutive structure of the thing… If the inkwell hides a portion of the table from me, this does not stem from the nature of my senses but from the nature of the inkwell and of light. If the object gets smaller when moving away, we must not explain this by some kind of illusion in the observer but by the strictly external laws of perspective. Thus by these objective laws a strictly objective center of reference is defined. For example, in a perspective scheme the eye is the point toward which all the objective lines converge. Thus the perceptive field refers to a center objectively defined by that reference and located in the very field which is oriented around it. (1943: 356–7/317)

Gibson somehow exports this thought in the field of psychology and allows conceiving of the world as intrinsically structured, without the need of a structuring observer. This conception thus contrasts sharply with the account advocated by Uexküll, recalled above, and according to which the subject is an absolute 'here' projecting a unique and private world. All together, the work of the two authors may be fruitfully combined with each other, keeping in mind their differences, to better understand the way (consciousness of) oneself-as-subject and (consciousness of) the world constitutively relate to each other and the way 'centrifugally reaching-out' and 'centripetally being-indicated-by' participate jointly in this co-constitution.

7 BODY AND WORLD

The conception of the subject as being 'open' and of consciousness of oneself-as-subject as being given by intentionality may be exploited in order to consider how the *bodily* subject is given as such in one's experience. Indeed, if, as argued for here, consciousness of oneself-as-subject is given by world-consciousness, consciousness of oneself as a bodily subject is a privileged dimension of it, as the body figures as one element of the world that the subject identifies with.

A clear-cut dissociation between the body as lived subjectively and the body as living has been drawn by Henry, who differentiates the corporeal thing (*le corps chosique*) which is lived in its exteriority as a thing like any other thing, the organic body (*le corps organique*), which is both resisting and obeying our effort, and the original body (*le corps originaire*). The latter belongs to the absolutely immanent sphere of subjectivity—that is, it is the transcendental subject who embodies the power of experiencing the world. According to Henry, the fact that a subject has a body is not contingent (Henry 1965: 2), since the very nature of the body is subjective: '...our body is originally neither a biological body, nor a living body, nor a human body, it belongs to a radically different ontological region which is the one of absolute subjectivity' (Henry 1965: 11). This ontology defines the 'real body, and not only the idea of the body' as a 'subjective being' (Henry 1965: 78), advocating a 'rigorous dissociation' between, on the one hand, the subjective body felt as one's own (as oneself) and, on the other hand, the body characterized as a muscular mass (1965: 90).

Since this view deprives the 'subjective body' from its materiality—that is, since it dissociates the living and the lived body—the subject can here be considered as bodily only in a metaphorical sense (Barbaras 2008a: 9). In fact, in a radical inversion, Henry defines the body as what is traditionally opposed to it—that is, immanent subjectivity—thereby running against the literal conception of the body as involving some exteriority (Barbaras 2008a: 35). Yet the exteriority of the body is at least attested by the simple fact that bodily experience can be *expressed*. This is notably evidenced in the fact that we experience others not only in their physicality but also in their subjectivity. This possible expression of the 'subjective body' would contradict Henry's dualism (Barbaras 2008a: 36): 'If I attribute a carnal meaning to others or to my face, it is because *something within exteriority urges me to do that*...But this amounts to saying *that there is a mode of presence of living interiority within exteriority*, which directly conflicts with the division of appearing that Henry establishes' (Barbaras, 2008b: 7). In other terms, the subjective body cannot be only characterized by a form of immanent self-affection. On this basis, the question addressed above in general terms arises here in the particular case of bodily self-consciousness: can one's body-as-subject be experienced by one's externally oriented (intentional) conscious act?

An answer to this question that is classical in phenomenology is: No. As commented upon by Leder, 'insofar as I perceive through [my body, the body-as-subject-of-perception] necessarily recedes from the perceptual field it discloses' (1990: 14), 'my being-in-the-world depends upon my body's self-effacing transitivity' (1990: 15). As repeatedly described in phenomenology, the eye-as-subject is not itself seen. Leder generalizes this point to all perceptual organs which, he argues, are not perceived in the very field they themselves disclose. Strictly speaking, this point 'only' refers to the fact that a perceiving organ does not perceive itself. As such, however, this description does not allow the further generalization according to which the body as a whole is self-effacing in any world-directed experience. This more radical claim is what Leder intends to capture as he claims that 'the body conceals itself precisely in the act of revealing what is Other' (Leder 1990: 22). This 'primordial absence' (Leder 1990: 22) of the body, however, is not warranted, and Leder himself acknowledges it as he declares that the absence of the body 'is not equivalent to a simple void, a mere lack of being...[the body] is thus never fully eradicated from the experiential world' (Leder 1990: 22).

This point can be exemplified by the experience of one's bodily weight. Husserl mentions weight as a property of the corporeal thing, by contrast with the lived body. One of the differences between a thing and a subject's body is that the former has weight, while the latter *senses* that it has a weight: '...lifting a thing I experience its weight, but at the same time I have sensations, related to the weight, located in my lived body' (Husserl 1952: 146/153). In this sense, like touching, weighting is a 'reflexive process' (Welton 1999: 45): it indicates the touching/weighting subject to itself. Importantly, according to Husserl, this reflexive process—this form of consciousness of oneself as touching/weighting—involves the localization of touch/weight on/in one's body. The body is here the 'bearer of localized sensations' (Husserl 1952: 144/152).

These considerations, however, do not reach the target set here—that is, the characterization of the bodily *subject* as weighted. Indeed, for Husserl, the body is experienced as the 'bearer of localized sensations' when it is itself taken as an *object* of attention. However, such identification of one's body as the bearer of one's bodily sensations cannot ground consciousness of the bodily subject (Legrand 2007a), but is rather grounded on the body experienced as 'our general means of having a world' (Merleau-Ponty 1945: 171/146]). If this is correct, more needs to be said about the experience of the bodily *subject*.

In the case of body-weight, what follows from the conception of consciousness of oneself-as-subject as 'open' described above is that I may experience the weight of my body by experiencing surfaces as affording support or not: for example, I experience my bodily weight as I experience the snow sinking under it (Sartre 1943: 627/583). More generally, the weight of one's body is indicated by the objects it weighs on. This way of experiencing the materiality of one's body does not involve taking one's body as an intentional object. Rather, the body is lived as the weighted subject of the experience of a given surface as hard or soft, solid enough for supporting one's weight or not.

Likewise, both the density of one's body and the effort performed by the bodily subject would be experienced due to the resistance of matter to penetrability (Maine de Biran 1852/1952: 73): the effort is felt in its product—that is, the resistance, be it the resistance to movement of one's own body or the resistance of objects one intends to move with one's body (Maine de Biran 1852/1952: 121–2). Effort is thus here conceived of as a relation between a subject of wilful movement and an obstacle to this subjective will. This characterization is interestingly radicalized by Sartre who argues that 'we never have any sensation of our effort...We perceive the resistance of things. What I perceive when I want to lift this glass to my mouth is not my effort but the heaviness of the glass—that is, its resistance to entering into an instrumental complex which I have made appear in the world' (1943: 364/324). Importantly for the point at stake, one here does not experience one's body by taking it as an intentional object, but by experiencing the 'coefficient of adversity' in objects (1943: 364/324).

Experiencing bodily weight and effort are not the only ways of experiencing one's body as subject by experiencing the world. Another example of consciousness of one's body as a subject embedded in the world may be extracted from Henry's novel: '...as he closes his eyes and gives himself up to the immense force that supports him, the new element makes itself be felt at each point of his body, there is no part of his being which does not feel it and is not touched by it, the fullness to which he confides himself envelops him entirely' (Henry 1976: 36). Here, Henry describes a man immersed in the ocean. The way water itself is experienced involves one's feeling of one's bodily immersion. More generally, feeling one's body is pervasive in one's experience of the world. Paradigmatically, the way one experiences objects by touching them involves necessarily the experience of one's touching body. More subtly, seeing forward involves being aware that one does not see behind one's head, and thus involves, albeit implicitly, to experience oneself as being a voluminous body located and oriented in space (Legrand 2011).

These experiences can be interpreted as involving a form of self-affection different from and necessary for consciousness of the world—as the one-level view would have it—or they can be interpreted as involving an experience of objects in the world as indicating the experiencing subject, within the flow of intentionality itself—as the present view would defend. Either way, it remains that none of these bodily experiences of the world involve any form of inspection of the body itself. Paradigmatically, when immersed in water, one does not scrutinize one's body; when trying to find one's key thanks to a tactile exploration of the content of one's pocket, one does not focus on how one's fingers feel; when turning one's head to cross a street safely, one does not experience explicitly the limitation of one's visual field of perception. In other terms, none of these experiences rely on any form of explicit exploration of one's body-as-object. Nonetheless, in all of these scenarios, and pervasively, one's body-as-subject is experienced pre-reflectively (Legrand 2007a, 2007b). Moreover, as argued for here, one's body-as-subject would not be experienced by reflexivity but by the subject's intentional act of consciousness.

Experiencing oneself as a bodily subject in such a way involves a fundamental form of self-consciousness in which 'I am conscious of my body via the world' (Merleau-Ponty 1945: 97/82) and in which the body is experienced in its 'transparency' (Legrand 2006, 2005). To capture what is meant here by 'transparency', consider the way a window is (literally) experienced as transparent: not invisible, it appears as that through which something other trans-appears (Heidegger 1955). Quite similarly, the body is notably (and metaphorically) experienced as 'transparent': not strictly speaking as that through which objects in the world trans-appear, but more precisely as that which frames and anchors the subject's experiences to its bodily perspective (Legrand 2007b, 2011). For example, the viewer's body is experienced in the fact that 'the woman who is crossing the street appears smaller than the man who is sitting on the sidewalk in front of the café' (Sartre 1943, 357/318): their size is relative to and indicates the viewer's own—transparent—bodily location. As this example illustrates, the body experienced as transparent is not itself taken as a perceptual object that would mediate or obstruct one's experience of the world—the edges of one's nose occluding one's field of view are not transparent in this sense. The 'transparent' body is indicated to itself by the world it reaches. 'In this sense my body is everywhere in the world...My body is co-extensive with the world, spread across all things' (Sartre 1943: 357/318]).

8 CONCLUSION

While the subject is what is the object is not, consciousness of oneself-as-subject may be characterized as a form of consciousness of objects. Specifically, consciousness of the self-as-subject does not arise when the subject figures among its intentional objects of experience but rather pervasively arises when the subject experiences himself by experiencing any intentional object whatsoever. Such consciousness of oneself-as-subject avoids any self-objectification and in this sense it is non-reflective. Moreover, it has been described as involving a mode of givenness that aims at nothing else than oneself-as-subject, and in this sense it would be reflexive. Here, I considered the possibility of conceiving of consciousness of oneself-as-subject as being neither reflective nor reflexive. That it is not reflective is a prerequisite for it to concern oneself-as-subject rather than oneself-as-object; that it is not reflexive means here that it is intentional in the sense that it is oriented towards what the subject is not: the intentional object. Conceived of as such, consciousness of oneself-as-subject would involve two dynamics, both characterizing the constitutive 'openness' of the subject to the world he experiences: the subject would be centripetally indicated to himself by the objects towards which he centrifugally reaches out. Such opposite but complementary dynamics are particularly suited to characterize consciousness of oneself as a bodily subject embedded in a material world.

REFERENCES

Barbaras, R. (2008a), *Introduction à une phénoménologie de la vie* (Paris: Vrin).
—— (2008b), 'Life, Movement and Desire', *Research in Phenomenology* 38: 3–17.
Benoist, J. (2009), *Sens et sensibilité: L'intentionalité en contexte* (Paris: Cerf).
Gibson, J. J. (1979), *The Ecological Approach to Visual Perception* (Boston: Houghton Mifflin).
Heidegger, M. (1927), *Sein und Zeit* (Tübingen: Max Niemeyer); tr. J. Stambaugh, *Being and Time* (Albany: SUNY, 1996).
—— (1955), 'Uber die Sixtina', in *Aus der Erfahrung des Denkens 1910–1976* (Frankfurt am Main, 1983), 119–21; tr. Ph. Lacoue-Labarthe, 'Sur la Madone Sixtine', *Poésie* 81(1997).
—— (1987), *Zollikoner Seminare, Protokolle-Gespräche-Briefe Herausgegeben von Medard Boss* (Frankfurt am Main: Klostermann); tr. F. Mayr and R. Askay, M. Boss (ed.), *Zollikon seminars: protocols, conversations, letters* (Evanston: Northwestern University Press, 2001)].
Henry, M. (1963), *L'essence de la manifestation* (Paris: PUF); tr. G. J. Etzkorn, *The Essence Of Manifestation*. (The Hague: Nijhoff, 1973)
—— (1965), *Philosophie et phénoménologie du corps: Essai sur l'ontologie Biranienne* (Paris: Presse Universitaire de France).
—— (1976), *L'amour les yeux fermés* (Paris: Gallimard).
—— (1995), 'Phénoménologie non intentionnelle: une tâche de la phénoménologie à venir', in D. Janicaud (ed.), *L'Intentionnalité en question. Entre phénoménologie et recherches cognitives* (Paris: Vrin), pp. 383–97.

Husserl, E. (1952), *Ideen zu einer reinen Phänomenologie und phänomenologischen Philosophie, Zweites Buch: Phänomenologische Untersuchungen zur Konstitution*, Husserliana IV, M. Bimel (ed.) (The Hague: Martinus Nijhoff); tr. R. Rojcewicz and A. Schuwer, *Ideas Pertaining to a Pure Phenomenology and to a Phenomenological Philosophy, Second Book: Studies in the Phenomenological Constitution* (Dordrecht, Boston, London: Kluwer Academic Publishers Academic Publishers, 1993).

Lacan, J. (1949), *Écrits* (Paris: Seuil), 93–100.

Leder, D. (1990), *The Absent Body* (Chicago: University of Chicago Press).

Legrand, D. (2005), 'Transparently oneself. A commentary on Metzinger, *Being No One*'. PSYCHE 11/5.

—— (2006), 'The bodily self. The sensori-motor roots of pre-reflexive self-consciousness', *Phenomenology and the Cognitive Sciences* 5: 89–118.

—— (2007a), 'Pre-reflective self-as-subject from experiential and empirical perspectives', *Consciousness and Cognition* 16/3: 583–99.

—— (2007b), 'Pre-reflective self-consciousness: on being bodily in the world', *Janus Head, Special Issue: The Situated Body* 9/1: 493–519.

—— (2007c), 'Subjectivity and the body: Introducing basic forms of self-consciousness', *Consciousness and Cognition* 16/3: 577–82.

—— (2011), 'Phenomenological dimensions of bodily self-consciousness', in S. Gallagher (ed.) *Oxford Handbook of the Self* (Oxford: Oxford University Press), pp. 204–27.

Maine de Biran, P. (1852/1952), *Sur la décomposition de la pensée* (Paris: PUF).

Merleau-Ponty, M. (1945), *Phénoménologie de la perception* (Paris: Éditions Gallimard); *Phenomenology of Perception* (London: Routledge and Kegan Paul, 1962).

—— (1951), *Les Relations avec autrui chez l'enfant*. Centre de Documentation Universitaire. In Merleau-Ponty (1988), *Merleau-Ponty à la Sorbonne. Résumé de cours 1949 1952* (Grenoble: Éditions Cynara).

Mohanty, J. N. (1985), *The Possibility of Transcendental Philosophy* (Dordrecht: Martinus Nijhoff).

O'Neill, J. (1986), 'The specular body: Merleau-Ponty and Lacan on infant self and other', *Synthese* 66/2: 201–17.

Marnas J., Moeller P., Kircher T., Thalbitzer J., Jansson L., Handest P., and Zahavi D. (2005), 'EASE-scale: Examination of Anomalous Self-Experience', *Psychopathology* 38/5: 236–58.

Sartre, J-P. (1943), *L'être et le néant* (Paris: Tel Gallimard); tr. H. E. Barnes, *Being and Nothingness* (New York: Philosophical Library, 1956).

Stjernfelt, F. (2007), 'A natural symphony? von Uexkull's Bedeutungslehre and its actuality', in *Diagrammatology: An Investigation on the Borderlines of Phenomenology, Ontology, and Semiotics* (Dordrecht: Springer), pp. 225–40.

Uexküll, von, J. (1992), 'A stroll through the worlds of animals and men: A picture book of invisible worlds', *Semiotica*, 89/4: 319–91.

Welton, D. (1999), 'Soft, smooth hands: Husserl's phenomenology of the lived-body', in D. Welton (ed.), *The Body: Classic and Contemporary Readings* (Oxford: Blackwell), pp. 38–56.

Zahavi, D. (1999), *Self-Awareness and Alterity: A Phenomenological Investigation* (Evanston: Northwestern University Press).

—— (2005), *Subjectivity and selfhood: Investigating the First-Person Perspective* (Cambridge, MA: MIT Press).

—— (2006), 'Two takes on a one-level account of consciousness', *Psyche* 12/2: 1–9.

CHAPTER 15

SELF, CONSCIOUSNESS, AND SHAME

DAN ZAHAVI

On many standard readings, shame is an emotion that targets and involves the self in its totality. In shame, the self is affected by a global devaluation: it feels defective, objectionable, condemned. The basic question I wish to raise and discuss is the following: What does the fact that we feel shame tell us about the nature of self? Does shame testify to the presence of a self-concept, a (failed) self-ideal, and a capacity for critical self-assessment, or does it rather, as some have suggested, point to the fact that the self is in part socially constructed (Calhoun 2004: 145)? Should shame primarily be classified as a self-conscious emotion, or is it rather a distinct social emotion?

1 SHAME AND SELF-CONSCIOUSNESS

Emotion research has spent much time investigating what Ekman called the 'basic six': joy, fear, sadness, surprise, anger, and disgust (Ekman 2003). Allegedly, these emotions emerge early in human development, they have a biological basis, a characteristic facial expression, and are culturally universal. It is fairly obvious, however, that these basic or primary emotions do not exhaust the richness of our emotional life. Think merely of more complex emotions such as embarrassment, envy, shame, guilt, pride, jealousy, remorse, or gratitude. According to Michael Lewis, one useful way of classifying the different emotions is by operating with a distinction between self-conscious and non-self-conscious emotions. Whereas primary emotions do not involve self-consciousness, the more complex emotions do (Lewis 2007: 136). Indeed, on Lewis's account the latter group of emotions involves elaborate cognitive processes, they all come about through self-reflection, and they all involve and require a concept of self. Thus, a developmental requirement for experiencing such emotions is that the child is in possession of a self-concept or a self-representation, which according to Lewis only happens from around 18 months of age.

Lewis goes on to distinguish two groups of self-conscious emotions. Both groups involve self-exposure and objective self-consciousness—that is, self-reflection. But whereas the first involves non-evaluative exposure, the second involves both self-exposure and evaluation. The first group emerges around 18 months and includes emotions such as embarrassment and envy. The second group emerges around 36 months. It includes shame and guilt, and requires the ability to appropriate and internalize standards, rule and goals, and to evaluate and compare one's behaviour *vis-à-vis* such standards (Lewis 2007: 135).

Lewis ends up defining shame as an intense negative emotion that is elicited when one experiences failure relative to a standard, feels responsible for the failure, and believes that the failure reflects a damaged self. Whereas Lewis considers the issue of public failure to be relevant to the emotion of embarrassment, he denies its relevance when it comes to emotions such as shame, guilt, and pride (Lewis 1998: 127).

A very different account of shame can be found in the work of Rom Harré. Briefly put, Harré has argued that whereas shame is occasioned by the realization that others have become aware that what one has been doing has been a moral infraction, embarrassment is occasioned by the realization that others have become aware that what one has been doing has been a breach of convention and the code of manners (Harré 1990: 199).

I find both of these proposals problematic. Although we might readily agree that embarrassment is less shattering and painful than shame, that it is more obviously related to awkward social exposure (due to an open fly button, a loud stomach noise, inappropriate clothing, and so on) than to the violation of important personal values, Harré's definitions and neat distinction are unsatisfactory. Not only does he place too much emphasis on the presence of an actual audience—as if one cannot feel ashamed when being alone, as if one only feels shameful because one has been found out—his sharp distinction between moral infraction and breach of convention is also questionable. Although one can be ashamed of moral infractions, one can certainly also be ashamed of things that have nothing to do with ethics. Indeed, shame does not have to be brought about by something one wilfully does. One can feel ashamed of a physical disability or of one's parentage or skin colour. Thus, rather than linking shame and embarrassment to an infraction of moral values and social conventions respectively (an attempt that also flies in the face of the fact that the same event can be felt as either shameful or embarrassing by different people), I think a more plausible demarcation criterion is one that links shame, but not embarrassment, to a global decrease of self-esteem or self-respect. Embarrassment does not shade into shame until one's discomfort over exposure is joined by a negative self-assessment (see Miller 1985: 39). This would also match well with an observation by Galen Strawson: whereas past embarrassments can easily furnish funny stories to tell about oneself, past shames and humiliations do so rarely if at all (Strawson 1994).[1]

---

[1] As Strawson has subsequently pointed out, childhood shames might be some of the rare exceptions. Might we not in retrospect find it amusing that various trifles could back then be felt as shameful? I suspect, however, that the ability to feel amusement about such past shames is conditional upon us no longer identifying as strongly with our past self.

As for Lewis's account, I have various problems with his general understanding of consciousness and self-consciousness which in my view relies on a contentious higher-order representational theory of consciousness (Zahavi 2010), but my main concern for now is Lewis's downplaying of the social dimension of shame. Consider the title of Lewis's book: *Shame: The Exposed Self*. This is how Lewis explains the subtitle:

> The subtitle of this book is *The Exposed Self*. What is an exposed self and to whom is it exposed? The self is exposed to itself, that is, we are capable of viewing ourselves. A self capable of self-reflection is unique to humans. (Lewis 1992: 36)

In short, Lewis defines the exposure in question as one of being exposed to oneself. That is, when he talks of the exposed self he is referring to our capacity for self-reflection. Compare by contrast the following remark by Darwin: 'It is not the simple act of reflecting on our own appearance, but the thinking what others think of us, which excites a blush' (Darwin 1872/1965: 325). One problem with a definition of shame like Lewis's that focuses exclusively on an individual's own negative self-assessment is that it becomes difficult to differentiate shame from other negative self-evaluations, such as self-disappointment or self-criticism. Another problem with this highlighting of our visibility to ourselves is that it arguably fails to do justice to those undeniably social forms of shame which are induced by a deflation and devaluation of our public appearance and social self-identity, by the exposure of a discrepancy between who we claim to be and how we are perceived by others. In short, we need an account of shame that can also explain why personal flaws that are recognized and tolerated in privacy as minor shortcomings are felt as shameful the moment they are publicly exposed.

But my criticisms of Lewis and Harré seem to point in opposite directions. I blame Harré for exaggerating the need for an actual audience, and Lewis for downplaying the importance of sociality. How do these criticisms go together? Let us move onwards and consider some alternative views on shame found in phenomenology.

2 VARIETIES OF SHAME

In the third part of *L'être et le néant* Sartre argues that shame, rather than merely being a self-reflective emotion, an emotion involving negative self-evaluation, is an emotion that reveals our relationality, our being-for-others.

According to Sartre, shame is a form of intentional consciousness. It is a shameful apprehension of something, and this something happens to be myself. I am ashamed of what I am, and to that extent shame also exemplifies a self-relation. As Sartre points out, however, shame is not primarily and originally a phenomenon of reflection. I can reflect upon my failings and as a result feel shame, just as I might reflect upon my feeling of shame, but I can feel shame prior to engaging in reflection. Shame is, as he puts it, 'an immediate shudder which runs through me from head to foot without any discursive preparation' (Sartre 2003: 246). Indeed, and more significantly, in its primary form shame is not a feeling I can simply elicit on my own through reflection; rather shame is shame of oneself before the other (Sartre 2003: 246, 312). It presupposes the intervention of the other, not merely because the other is the one before whom I feel ashamed, but also and more significantly because the other is the one that constitutes that of which I am ashamed. That is, the self of which I am ashamed, my public persona if you will, did not exist prior to my encounter with the other. It is brought about by this encounter. Thus although shame exemplifies a self-relation, we are on Sartre's account dealing with an essentially mediated form of self-relation—one where the other is the mediator between me and myself.

To feel shame is—if ever so fleetingly—to accept the other's evaluation; it is to identify with the object that the other looks at and judges. In being ashamed I accept and acknowledge the judgement of the other. I *am* the way the other sees me, and I am nothing but that (Sartre 2003: 246, 287). The other's gaze confers a truth upon me that I do not control, and over which I am—in that moment—powerless. Sartre's central claim is consequently that for shame to occur there must be a relationship between self and other where the self cares about the other's evaluation. Moreover, according to Sartre, it makes no difference whether the evaluation of the other is positive or not, since it is the very objectification that is shame-inducing. As he writes:

> Pure shame is not a feeling of being this or that guilty object but in general of being *an* object; that is, of *recognizing myself* in this degraded, fixed and dependent being which I am for the Other. Shame is the feeling of an *original fall*, not because of the fact that I may have committed this or that particular fault but simply that I have 'fallen' into the world in the midst of things and that I need the mediation of the Other in order to be what I am. (Sartre 2003: 312)

Although Sartre's analysis of shame is the most well-known phenomenological account, his analysis is neither the first nor the most extensive phenomenological one.[2] In 1933 Erwin Straus published a short but suggestive article entitled 'Die Scham als historiologisches Problem' in the *Schweizer Archiv für Neurologie und Psychiatrie*, and already, twenty years earlier, Max Scheler had written a long essay entitled 'Scham und Schamgefühl'. One reason for looking at Straus and Scheler is that they both add to, as well as challenge, Sartre's analysis. Moreover, in the last few years Scheler's account has received something of a revival, and has been assessed positively in recent books by, for instance, Nussbaum (2006: 174) and Deonna, Rodogni, and Teroni (2011: 151).

One commonality between Straus and Scheler is that they both emphasize the need for a differentiation between various types of shame. They both argue against the view that shame is a negative and repressive emotion *per se*, one we should aim to remove from our lives (see Schneider 1987), and they would consequently disagree with Tangney and Dearing's general characterization of shame as an 'extremely painful and ugly feeling that has a negative impact on interpersonal behaviour' (2002: 3). Straus, for his part,

---

[2] Although there are many insights to be found in Sartre's analysis of intersubjectivity, there is certainly also a good deal to disagree with. This would include Sartre's excessively negative assessment and characterization of our encounter with others (see Zahavi 2002).

distinguishes between a protective form of shame which involves sensitivity to and respect for boundaries of intimacy, and a concealing form of shame which is more concerned with maintaining social prestige. As he points out, although language might not provide us with different terms for the two forms of shame, it does offer us different terms for the privation of the two forms: namely, the terms 'shamelessness' (*Schamlosigkeit*) and 'unabashedness' (*Unverschämtheit*) (Straus 1933: 341, 343; see Vallelonga 1976: 56, 59). To exemplify what Straus might have in mind when talking of the protective form of shame, consider the situation in which you feel ashamed as a result of having intimate details about your life revealed publicly. You might feel ashamed even if the audience does not react critically, but simply as a result of the exposure itself. Addressing the same phenomenon, Bollnow links shame to the desire to protect the most private and intimate core of ourselves from the violation that public scrutiny might cause (Bollnow 2009: 67, 91).

As for Scheler, he not only thinks the feeling of shame can in some instances be pleasurable, but more importantly, he considers a sensitivity to and capacity for shame ethically valuable and links it to the emergence of conscience: it is, as he points out, no coincidence that *Genesis* explicitly relates shame to knowledge of good and evil (Scheler 1957: 142). Scheler's first point, regarding the pleasurable quality of shame, is connected to a distinction he makes that matches the one made by Straus. Scheler distinguishes the anticipating and protecting shame of the blushing virgin, which, on his view, is characterized by lovely warmth,[3] from the extremely painful experience of repenting shame (*Schamreue*), a burning shame that is backward-looking and full of piercing sharpness and self-hatred (Scheler 1957: 140). As for the second point, Scheler emphasizes that when we are ashamed of something, the shame reaction must be seen in the light of a normative commitment that existed prior to the situation about which one is ashamed (Scheler 1957: 100). The feeling of shame occurs precisely because of the discrepancy between the values one endorses and the actual situation. Indeed, shame anxiety—the fear of shaming situations—might be considered a guardian of dignity. It puts us on guard against undignified behaviour which would place us (and others) in shaming situations.[4] As Plato already pointed out in the *Laws*, shame is what will prevent man from doing what is dishonourable (Plato 1961: 647a). Indeed, the very notion of shamelessness suggests that the possession of a sense of shame is a moral virtue. Rather than being inherently debilitating, shame might in short also play a constructive role in moral development.[5] In addition, Scheler argues that the occurrence of shame testifies to the

---

[3] One wonders whether a more appropriate English term for this would be 'bashfulness'.

[4] The following example might illustrate this. You are on a train and looking for the restroom. When you find it and enter, you discover that it is already occupied and used by an elderly woman who must have forgotten to lock the door. If you possess a developed sense of shame you will not only retreat immediately, but also search for another restroom in order to spare the woman the experience of re-encountering you when she exits.

[5] But even if shame anxiety can play a role in the process of socialization by promoting social conformity—just think, for instance, of the teenager who carefully selects his clothing in order to avoid being shamed by his peers—it can obviously also be debilitating by killing initiative. If I do not do anything, I do not risk potential shameful exposure. Likewise, it is hard to see anything positive in the so-called 'toxic shame' felt by some sexually abused children.

presence of a certain self-respect and self-esteem; it is only because one expects oneself to have worth that this expectation can be disappointed and give rise to shame (Scheler 1957: 141; see Taylor 1985: 80–1, Nussbaum 2006: 184).

Scheler would agree with the idea that shame is an essentially self-involving emotion, but he explicitly rejects the claim that shame is essentially a social emotion—one that by necessity involves others. Rather, he argues that there is a self-directed form of shame which is just as fundamental as the shame one can feel in the presence of others, and he argues that the central feature of shame is that it points to the clash or discrepancy between our higher spiritual values on the one hand and our animal nature and bodily needs on the other (Scheler 1957: 68, 78). This is also why Scheler claims that shame is a distinctly human emotion—one that neither God nor animals could have. It is, in his view, a fundamental human emotion—one characterizing *conditio humana* (Scheler 1957: 67, 91).

More recently, Nussbaum has argued that shame concerns the tension between our aspirations and ideals on the one hand, and our awareness of our finitude and helplessness on the other. Shame is an emotional response to the uncovering and display of our weakness, our defects and imperfections (Nussbaum 2006: 173). As Nussbaum remarks, the Greek term for genitalia, *aidoia*, is related to the term for shame, *aidos* (Nussbaum 2006: 182). One might add that the German term for shame, *Scham*, also refers to the genitals, as does the Danish term for labia, *skamlæber*, which literally means 'lips of shame'. One reason why nakedness has traditionally been associated with shame, one reason why we seek to cover our sexual organs, is, on Scheler's view, precisely because they are symbols of animality, mortality, and neediness (Scheler 1957: 75). By comparison, Sartre argued that modesty and the fear of being surprised in a state of nakedness are symbolic manifestations of original shame. The body symbolizes our defenceless state as objects. To put on clothes is to attempt to hide one's object-state; it is to claim the right of seeing without being seen—that is, to be a pure subject (Sartre 2003: 312). It is, in any case, hardly insignificant that shame has frequently been associated with nakedness and that the etymology of the word 'shame' can be traced back to the pre-Teutonic term for cover.

Nussbaum has suggested—partly influenced by psychoanalysis—that shame is on the scene before we become aware of what is normal within a particular social value system, and that it is most fundamentally an awareness of inadequacy, finitude, and helplessness that precedes any particular learning of social standards, although societies obviously have room to shape the experience of shame differently, by teaching different views of what is an appropriate occasion for shame (Nussbaum 2006: 173, 185). She also argues that whereas embarrassment is always social and contextual—it typically records unease about one's social presentation and deals with a feature of one's social situation which is often short-lived and not closely connected to important personal values—this is not the case for shame, which concerns matters that lie deep, and which can occur regardless of whether or not the world is looking (Nussbaum 2006: 204–5). But although Nussbaum denies that shame in general requires the presence of an audience, she does acknowledge that the earliest forms of shame do require and involve a dyadic relationship between infant and caretaker (Nussbaum 2006: 185, 191).

3 OTHERS IN MIND

At this point we need to become more clear about what role others play. To claim that shame only occurs in situations where a discrediting fact about oneself is exposed to others is not convincing. One can certainly feel shame when alone—that is, shame does not require an actual observer or audience. One may also feel ashamed of something even if one can be certain that it will forever remain secret. But does that mean that the reference to others is inessential, and that an account of shame can dispense with the social dimension? Let us not be too hasty. Let us consider some alleged cases of non-social shame.

1. You have a congenital facial disfigurement, and you feel shame when you see yourself in the mirror.
2. You have done something you believe should not be done (or failed to do something, you believe ought to be done). In such a situation you might indeed feel ashamed afterwards. You might feel guilty about the specific deed in question, but you might also feel ashamed of simply being the kind of person who could do (or fail to do) such a thing.[6]
3. You feel ashamed of who you have become when compared to who you were—that is, you feel ashamed of not living up to your capacities, of having betrayed your potential.
4. You have made a firm decision not to touch alcohol again; but in a moment of weakness you indulge your urge and begin a drinking binge that eventually leaves you senseless. When you emerge from your stupor you feel ashamed of your lack of self-control, of your surrender to what you consider base instincts.
5. You are together with a group of peers. They start to discuss a political issue and quickly a racist consensus emerges that you strongly disagree with. However, shame anxiety prevents you from expressing your dissenting opinion in order not to be ridiculed or ostracized. Afterwards, however, when alone, you are deeply ashamed of your cowardly attitude.

These examples certainly demonstrate that the feeling of shame does not require the presence of an actual observer. But what about an imagined other? In many cases where the shame-experiencing subject is physically alone and not in the presence of others, he or she will have internalized the perspective of the others, he or she will have others in mind, to use Rochat's phrase (Rochat 2009). The distinctive feeling tone of the shame-experience frequently includes the conviction that others would not have done or been like that. To fail at a task that nobody else is able to succeed at, and that nobody expects you to succeed at, is less likely to result in an experience of shame. The imagined other

---

[6] To insist that shame and guilt must be distinguished is, of course, not to deny that they can often occur together.

might consequently not only figure as a critical observer, but also as a point of contrast or comparison. Consider, as a case in point, the first example. Although the disfigured person who feels shame when looking in the mirror is alone, I think a natural interpretation would be that the feeling of shame is connected to the fact that the person experiences the disfigurement as a stigma, as something that excludes him or her from normality.

Objections to this line of reasoning, however, can be found in various recent publications by Deonna and Teroni. They insist that we ought to distinguish more carefully between different definitions of what a social emotion amounts to. Is the claim that 1) the object of shame is specifically social—its object being either somebody else or our own social standing—or is the claim 2) that the values involved in shame are acquired through contact with others, or 3) that shame always requires taking an outside perspective on ourselves, or 4) that shame always takes place in a social context? Deonna and Teroni basically reject all these proposals. It is on their view quite implausible to claim that there is always an actual or imagined audience when we feel shame, nor is it on their view correct to claim that shame is always connected to a perceived threat to our social standing or with the management of our social image (Deonna and Teroni 2011; Deonna and Teroni 2009: 39). Although this might indeed be the case when it comes to what they term 'superficial' shame, what they call 'deep' shame is something we feel as a result of personal failure quite regardless of the evaluation by others—for instance, when reflecting on our own morally repugnant behaviour (Deonna and Teroni 2011: 201). Deonna and Teroni next concede that the values involved in shame might be socially acquired, but they argue that this would hardly be sufficient to warrant the claim that shame is an essential social emotion, since the acquisition of values involved in other non-social emotions is equally social (Deonna and Teroni 2011: 195). Finally, Deonna and Teroni take up the issue of perspective change. It is, as they write, impossible to be ashamed of what one is wholly immersed in. In that sense, shame does involve the critical perspective of an evaluator. But they deny that the evaluator has to be another, or that the shift in perspective has to be motivated by others. Rather, and here they come quite close to Lewis's view, the shift of perspective is merely a question of a shift from an unreflective doer to a reflective evaluator (Deonna and Teroni 2011: 203).

What is, then, their positive proposal? In their view, shame involves a negative evaluative stance towards oneself. It is motivated by an awareness of a conflict between a value one is committed to, and a (dis)value exemplified by what one is ashamed of (Deonna and Teroni 2011: 206). More specifically, they propose the following definition of shame: 'Shame is the subject's awareness that the way he is or acts is so much at odds with the values he cares to exemplify that it appears to disqualify him from his very commitment to the value, that is he perceives himself as unable to exemplify it even at a minimal level' (Deonna and Teroni 2009: 46).

How should we assess these various objections and non-social definitions? Deonna and Teroni are very concerned with coming up with a definition of shame that covers all possible cases. To some extent this is, of course, a perfectly respectable endeavour, but such a focus also runs the risk of presenting us with a too undifferentiated picture of the emotion. It may offer us a definition that blinds us to important distinctions. I doubt anybody would deny that shame is a multifaceted phenomenon, but as we have already seen some would go further and insist on the need for a distinction between different irreducible forms of shame, such as disgrace shame and discretion shame, concealing shame and protective shame, moral shame and non-moral shame, or bodily shame (*Leibesscham*) and psychical shame (*Seelenscham*), to mention just a few of the available candidates (see, for instance, Ausubel 1955: 382; Bollnow 2009: 55–7; Smith *et al.* 2002: 157). Furthermore, we should not forget that shame belongs to a family of interrelated emotions. Indeed, the argument has been made that the word 'shame' once covered much of the ground now parcelled out between 'embarrassment' and 'humiliation' (Strawson 1994). It is not difficult to come up with examples where the demarcation gets somewhat fuzzy. The fact that the same event can be felt as humiliating or shameful or embarrassing by different people does not make things easier.

Given this situation I will refrain from the bold but perhaps also overly ambitious task of offering a clear-cut definition of shame—one that specifies its necessary and sufficient features. My goal in the following will be somewhat more modest. Rather than attempting to disprove that there are non-social types of shame, my claim is that there are other, and arguably more prototypical, forms of shame that cannot adequately be understood in non-social terms, and that an attempt to provide a non-social definition of shame is consequently bound to miss something quite significant.[7] Consider for a start—and in the following my main focus will be on disgrace shame—the following five examples:

1. When writing your latest article you make extensive use of passages found in an essay by a little known and recently deceased scholar. After your article has been published you participate in a public meeting where you are suddenly accused of plagiarism. You emphatically deny it, but the accuser—your departmental nemesis—produces incontrovertible proof.

2. You are ridiculed by your peers when you show up at a high-school party in out-of-fashion clothes.

3. You apply for a position and have told your friends that you are sure to get it, but after the job interview, and while in the company of your friends, you are informed by the hiring committee that you simply are not qualified for the job.

4. You have been having a row with your unruly 5-year old daughter, and you finally lose your patience and slap her. Right away you experience guilt, but then you suddenly realize that the principal of the kindergarten has been observing the whole scene.

---

[7] In addition, there is obviously also the problem of whether the definition provided by Deonna and Teroni, which mainly targets highly elaborate, self-directed judgemental forms of shame, really hits the mark. On the one hand, it seems to be so cognitively demanding that it would rule out anything like infantile shame. By contrast, Scheler would claim that shame is present in early form from birth onwards (1957: 107), and similar views can be found in many psychoanalytical accounts (see Broucek 1991; Nathanson 1994). On the other hand, the case could be made that shame is less about one's failure to exemplify a self-relevant value than it is about exemplifying a self-relevant defect—that is, what is shame-inducing is not the distance from ideal self but the closeness to undesired self (Lindsay-Hartz *et al.* 1995, 277; Gilbert 1998, 19).

5. You have started a new romantic relationship. After a while, in a moment of intimacy, you reveal your sexual preferences. Your disclosure is met by your partner's
incredulous stare.

If we consider these five examples—and to avoid any misunderstandings I should
emphasize that they are not autobiographical—how plausible is it to claim that others
are quite accidental to the emotion in question and that the very same experience of
shame could have occurred in a private setting?[8] I do not find such a suggestion plausible at all. Again, I am not denying that we can sit in judgement on ourselves and as a
result come to feel shame, but I think that this kind of repenting, self-reflective shame,
with its accompanying feeling of self-disappointment, self-misery or even self-loathing
has a somewhat different phenomenology than the intense feeling of shame which one
can experience in the presence of others.[9] In the latter case there is a heightened feeling
of exposure and vulnerability, and an accompanying wish to hide and disappear, to
become invisible, to sink into the ground. There is also a characteristic narrowing of
focus. You cannot carefully attend to details in the environment while being subjected to
that kind of shame. Rather, the world recedes and the self stands revealed. The behavioural manifestation of shame—slumped posture, downward head movement, and
gaze-avoidance—also emphasizes the centripetality of the emotion. The experience of
shame is an experience of self, but it is one that is thrust upon us. We are in the spotlight
whether we want it or not. It is one that overwhelms us and which is initially almost
impossible to avoid, escape, or control. As Nietzsche puts it in *Daybreak*:

---

[8] The same obviously holds true for something like vicarious shame. Consider the following example.
You are walking on the street with a friend of yours, who is black. You encounter your father, who hails
your friend with a racial slur. You might experience shame as a result, and it might take different forms.
You might feel shame *with* your friend, or feel shame *for* your father (see Scheler 1957: 81). That is, you
might sympathize with and share your friend's feeling of shame, or you might simply feel ashamed of
your father (who ought to be ashamed). These rather different cases of vicarious shame raise complicated
questions regarding the role of identification and its involvement in, for instance, honour killings, which
I cannot pursue further here. It is, in any case, noteworthy that the *Oxford English Dictionary* in defining
shame specifically includes a reference to those situations where shame arises from the consciousness of
something dishonouring, ridiculous, or indecorous in the conduct of those others whose honour or
disgrace one regards as one's own.

[9] In an intriguing study, participants were asked to read hypothetical accounts of an event that
could have happened to a person like themselves. They were told to try to imagine what the central
person in the account would be thinking and feeling. Then, after reading the accounts, participants
were asked to complete a set of items designed to measure their sense of this person's experience. In
one test, the different accounts involved a protagonist who committed a moral transgression, and the
story then varied according to three conditions (privacy, implicit and explicit public exposure). In
the first condition the transgression took place in privacy. In the second condition the transgressor
either saw or was reminded of someone who would have disapproved of the transgression, and in the
final condition the transgression was actually witnessed by another. The findings showed unequivocally
that explicit public exposure intensified the experience of shame when compared to the privacy
condition. If the transgression involved a violation of personal standards, the feeling of shame was
also significantly higher in the implicit exposure condition when compared to the privacy condition
(Smith *et al.* 2002).

> The feeling 'I am the mid-point of the world!' arises very strongly if one is suddenly overcome with shame; one then stands there as though confused in the midst of a surging sea and feels dazzled as though by a great eye which gazes upon us and through us from all sides. (Nietzsche 1997: 166)

This kind of shame also disrupts the normal temporal flow. Whereas repenting, self-reflective shame is backward-looking and past-oriented, and whereas shame anxiety—which in any case might be more of a disposition than an occurrent feeling—is by and large anticipatory and future-oriented, the acute experience of shame on which I am currently focusing might best be characterized in terms of a 'frozen now' (see Karlsson and Sjöberg 2009: 353). The future is lost, and the subject is fixed on the present moment. As Sartre writes, in shame, I experience myself as trapped in facticity, as being irremediably what I am (rather than as someone with future possibilities), as defence-lessly illuminated by an absolute light (with no protective privacy) (Sartre 2003: 286, 312). In his analysis of the different ontological dimensions of the body, Sartre further argues that the gaze of the other disrupts my control of the situation (Sartre 2003: 289). Rather than simply existing bodily, rather than simply being absorbed in my various projects, and interacting confidently with the environment, I become painfully aware of my body's facticity and being-there. I become aware that my body is something on which others' points of view bear. This is why Sartre speaks of my body as something that escapes me on all sides and as a perpetual 'outside' of my most intimate 'inside' (Sartre 2003: 375). Whereas guilt is primarily focused on the negative effects on others and includes a wish to undo the deed and might motivate reparative actions, the acute feeling of shame does not leave room for the exploration of future possibilities of redemption.

Taylor has at one point argued that shame (in contrast to embarrassment) involves an absolute sense of degradation, and not just one that is relative to a specific observer or audience. Whereas one might feel embarrassed *vis-à-vis* specific others—that is, whereas embarrassment might be relative to specific others, and whereas one might seek comfort for this embarrassment and even joke about it with friends and confederates—the experience of shame is different. Not only is shame difficult to communicate,[10] but we lack the inclination to let others in on it (in order to obtain their sympathy and consolation). Moreover, although shame might be induced by our encounter with a specific other, we are not merely shamed *vis-à-vis* him or her. Our relationship to everybody is affected. Shame is to that extent a far more alienating and isolating experience than embarrass-ment. But instead of seeing this as evidence for the fact that others play no significant role—which would be Taylor's interpretation—I find it more plausible to claim that shame, rather than simply involving a global decrease of self-esteem and self-confidence, also affects and alters our interaction and connection with others.

---

[10] Based on her clinical experience, Miller recounts how the speech of a person who attempts to talk about shame might at first be fragmented as a struggle takes place between the impulse to disclose and the impulse to conceal (Miller 1985: 36).

4 Standards and evaluations

As Aristotle pointed out in the *Rhetoric*, the people we feel shame before are those whose opinion of us matters to us (Aristotle 1984: 1384a25). Indeed, it is rarely the case that the identity of the audience is irrelevant. Not only might it make a difference whether the witness is a close family member, somebody who is part of your social network, or a total stranger (especially if the person in question does not know who you are either), but hierarchy and social status can also play a role. A sub-par performance in public will be experienced as more shameful if noticed by somebody with more rather than less social status than you. Compare, for instance, the situation where a pianist makes mistakes when practising a piece alone, with the situation where he makes mistakes at a public recital with the composer in attendance. However, as Landweer has observed, not only might the status and authority of the witness make a difference to the intensity of the experience of shame. If the witness expects and values your competence, and if she is sufficiently qualified to be able to notice your failure, her presence can also change the character and intensity of the shame, even if she might be less competent and have a lower social status than yourself (Landweer 1999: 94).

As already mentioned, Sartre argued that shame in the first instance is shame of oneself before the other, and that this involves an acceptance of the other's evaluation (Sartre 2003: 246, 287). This highlighting of the entailed acceptance matches well with an observation made by Karlsson and Sjöberg: namely, that that which is revealed in shame, although highly undesirable, is nevertheless experienced as familiar, as something that discloses the truth about oneself (2009: 350). Such claims have, however, been disputed by various authors, who by contrast have stressed the *heteronomous* character of shame. Deigh, for instance, has argued that we must 'admit cases of shame felt in response to another's criticism or ridicule in which the subjects do not accept the other person's judgement of them and so do not make the same judgement of themselves' (Deigh 1983: 233; see Wollheim 1999: 152). Calhoun has even argued that it is a mark of moral maturity to feel ashamed before those with whom one shares a moral practice, even when one disagrees with their moral criticisms (Calhoun 2004: 129). By arguing in this manner, Calhoun criticizes those who claim that 'mature agents only feel shame in *their own eyes*, and only for falling short of their own, autonomously set standards' (Calhoun 2004: 129).

I am not sure such use of the terms 'autonomous' and 'heteronomous' is really clarifying. When siding with Sartre, and when arguing that one only feels shame if one accepts the involved evaluation, I am obviously not suggesting that one only feels shame when falling short of one's own autonomously set standards. The relevant question is not whether the standards are set autonomously in the sense of being set completely independently of others—to quote Walsh, 'it is naive to suppose that human beings act in total isolation from their fellows, or to think that they bring virgin minds to their actions, minds which in no sense bear the impress of their associations with other men' (Walsh 1970: 8)—but whether the feeling of shame entails an endorsement of those standards, regardless of their origin. To put it differently, the point of disagreement is not over whether others might impose certain external standards on the subject—this is hardly disputed by anyone—but whether the subject needs to endorse the evaluation in order to feel shame. Now, Calhoun further argues that any strategy that roots 'the power to shame in the agent's endorsement of the shamer's evaluations will have trouble capturing shame's distinctively social character' (2004: 135), since it ultimately reduces 'the other before whom we feel shame to a mirror of ourselves' (2004: 129). But why should we accept this reasoning? Might an internalization of the other's evaluation not involve the acceptance of new standards? If so, it is hardly a question of making the other a mirror image of oneself, but rather of oneself responding to the other.

We need, however, to distinguish more carefully between the other's evaluation and the underlying value. Consider the following example. When giving mouth-to-mouth respiration to a girl after you have saved her from drowning, you are accused by passersby of taking advantage of the girl. Since you have a clear conscience, you do not accept the evaluation, but you do share the underlying value: that it is wrong to sexually exploit a defenceless girl. According to Castelfranchi and Poggi you will in this case feel ashamed in the eyes of others, without feeling ashamed before yourself (1990: 238). Is this suggestion convincing? Does it really make sense to speak of cases of shame where one is ashamed in the eyes of others, but not in one's own? It is obviously possible that others can think one ought to be ashamed when one is not, but that is not what Castelfranchi and Poggi have in mind. Rather, and to repeat, they think that one might feel shame without feeling it in one's own eyes. I am somewhat sceptical about this proposal. I think it would be more correct to interpret the case in question as a case involving embarrassment rather than shame. Why? Because I think shame in contrast to embarrassment is linked to a global decrease of self-esteem, and I do not think the situation in question—where one does not share the other's evaluation and know it to be false—would occasion such a decrease. Perhaps some might object to this assessment and insist that the situation described by Castelfranchi and Poggi could be shame-inducing. I agree that under some circumstances it could indeed, but even then it would not support their interpretation, since the feeling of shame would still be conditional upon the acceptance of the others' evaluation. How could that possibly be the case? Well, what if you were struck by the girls' beauty during your attempt to resuscitate her, and felt attracted by her, and even had the fleeting thought that her lips were voluptuous. Had that been the case, I think one might possibly feel ashamed by the accusation of the passers-by. It would sow a doubt in one's own mind: was there perhaps, after all, an illicit element of arousal involved? To make the case for this interpretation, consider a slight variation of the story. In order to save the woman, you had to risk your own life, since you are a very poor swimmer. After struggling to bring her in safety, and after commencing the attempt to resuscitate her, passers-by accuse you of attempting to exploit the situation in order to steal her valuables. In this case, the accusation is so far-fetched that it is very unlikely to be accepted by the accused, and as a result I find it quite implausible to claim that it would be shame-inducing. If anything, a more likely reaction would be strong indignation.

But are there not, some might insist, situations where one might feel ashamed even if one rejects the relevant standards and disagree with the evaluation? Consider the relation between shame and humiliation. Humiliation (or shaming) usually involves a temporary alteration of status—one is put in a lowered or degraded position—rather than a more enduring change of identity. Moreover, it usually comes about not because you yourself are doing anything, but because somebody else is doing something to you. In that sense it usually requires a foreign agent, one with power over you. To humiliate someone is to assert and exert a particular insidious form of control over the person in question, since one seeks to manipulate the person's self-esteem and self-assessment. In fact—and this is the central point—the person who feels humiliated might often have difficulties keeping his identity uncontaminated by the humiliated status. He might feel soiled and burdened with an unwanted identity, and might even begin to blame himself and feel responsible for the status. In such cases, shame will also follow (Miller 1985: 44). This, I think, might be part of the reason why people who have been sexually abused might feel shame, though they are obviously the victims and not the perpetrators. In some cases, however, humiliation and shame can come apart. In some cultures it might be humiliating to be treated as an equal by a person of lower status, but although you might feel humiliated by this, it does not entail that you accept the evaluation. It does not lead to the global decrease of self-esteem which I take to be a necessary feature of shame. Whereas people believe (in some cases quite wrongly, of course) that their shame is deserved and justified, they do not necessarily believe they deserve their humiliation. This is also why humiliation frequently involves a focus on the harmful and unfair other, and why it might be accompanied by a desire for revenge (Gilbert 1998).

I have repeatedly emphasized the link between shame and a decrease of self-esteem. But that link has also been questioned and challenged. It has been argued that the two can be dissociated and that it is possible to have a decrease of self-esteem without feeling ashamed (but perhaps merely mildly self-disappointed), just as it is possible to feel shame without experiencing any loss of self-esteem (Deigh 1983).

In voicing this objection, Deigh is primarily objecting to Rawls' characterization of shame as an emotion that one feels upon the loss of self-esteem (Deigh 1983: 225). How does Rawls analyse this loss of self-esteem? According to Deigh, he characterizes it as a question of failing to achieve a goal or an ideal that is integral to one's self-conception. More specifically, on this approach one experiences self-esteem if one regards one's aims and ideals as worthy and believes that one is well suited to pursue them. One loses self-esteem if one's favourable self-assessment is overturned and supplanted by an unfavourable one (Deigh 1983: 226, 229). But as Deigh then proceeds to point out, not only might some simply feel self-disappointment under such circumstances, but developmental evidence also suggests that children can feel shame before they have a well-defined self-conception that is centred around the pursuit of certain stable aims and before they are able to measure themselves against standards of what is necessary to achieve such aims (Deigh 1983: 232–4). And if this is so, a decrease of self-esteem cannot be essential to shame. Deigh continues by criticizing Rawls for failing to consider the possibility that the opinion of others might be internally related to shame, and suggests that shame is more often 'a response to the evident deprecatory opinion others have of one than an emotion aroused upon judgement that one's aims are shoddy or that one is deficient in talent or ability necessary to achieve them' (Deigh 1983: 233, 238).[11]

The reason Deigh objects to the proposed link between shame and a decrease of self-esteem is consequently because, on his view, it fails to consider the interpersonal dimension of the emotion. His proposal is instead to link shame to a threat to one's self-worth, since there are aspects central to one's identity which contribute to one's sense of worth independently of one's own achievements (Deigh 1983: 241).

As I see it, the main issue here is one of terminology. Deigh introduces a distinction between one's sense of worth and one's self-esteem, and follows Rawls in defining the latter in terms of achievements. But if one abandons such a narrow definition and basically uses 'sense of worth' and 'self-esteem' synonymously, while at the same time giving up the idea that a decrease in self-esteem is *sufficient* for shame, the objection seems to lose its force.

5 CONCLUSION

Let me conclude by returning to the questions with which I began. What does the fact that we feel shame tell us about the nature of self? What kind of self is affected in shame?

In a number of previous publications I have sought to articulate and defend the notion of an experiential core self, and have argued that such a notion can already be found in phenomenologists such as Husserl, Sartre, and Henry (see Zahavi 1999, 2003, 2005, 2009, 2011). More specifically, I have proposed that one can link a basic sense of self to the first-personal character of experiential life. When I taste a strawberry, remember the birth of my oldest son, or think about climate change, all of these experiences present me with different intentional objects. These objects are there *for me* in different experiential modes of givenness (as tasted, recollected, contemplated, and so on). This *for-me-ness* or *mineness*, which seems inescapably required by the experiential presence of intentional objects, and which is the feature that really makes it appropriate to speak of the subjectivity of experience, is obviously not a quality like green, sweet, or hard. It does not refer to a specific experiential content—that is, to a specific *what*. Rather, it refers to the distinct manner or *how* of experience—to the first-personal character of experience—and in the past I have argued that this constitutes a primitive form of selfhood. An important feature of this notion of self is that the self, rather than being conceived as an ineffable transcendental precondition that stands beyond the stream of experiences, or as a social construct that evolves through time, is seen as an integral but pre-social dimension of our experiential life.

---

[11] It is not entirely clear to me whether Deigh's interpretation does justice to Rawls' theory. Not only does Rawls operate with a distinction between natural shame and moral shame (Rawls 1972: 444), but he also explicitly writes that the latter involves our relation to others (Rawls 1972: 446).

The analysis of shame can illustrate the limitations of the just outlined notion of self. Shame testifies to our exposure, vulnerability, and visibility, and is importantly linked to such issues as concealment and disclosure, sociality and alienation, separation and interdependence, difference and connectedness. The shamed self is not the experiential core self. Or to put it more precisely, a self that can be shamed is a more complex (and complicated) self than the minimalist experiential self.[12]

Perhaps a reference to Mead might clarify matters. Mead is usually categorized as a defender of a social constructivist approach to the self. On his view, we are selves not by individual right but in virtue of our relation to one another. However, in *Mind, Self and Society*, Mead concedes that one could talk of a single self if one identified the self with a certain feeling-consciousness, and that previous thinkers such as James had sought to find the basis of self in reflexive affective experiences—that is, in experiences involving self-feeling. Mead even writes that there is a certain element of truth in this, but then denies that it is the whole story (Mead 1962: 164, 169, 173). For Mead, the problem of selfhood is fundamentally the problem of how an individual can get experientially outside himself in such a way as to become an object to himself. Thus, for Mead, to be a self is ultimately more a question of becoming an object than of being a subject. In his view, one can only become an object to oneself in an indirect manner: namely, by adopting the attitudes of others on oneself, and this is something that can only happen within a social environment (Mead 1962: 138).

If one compares Mead and Sartre there are, of course, some marked differences between the two. Whereas Mead distinguishes sharply between consciousness and self-consciousness, and even claims that we prior to the rise of self-consciousness experience our own feelings and sensations as parts of our environment rather than as our own (Mead 1962: 171), Sartre argues that our experiential life is characterized by a primitive form of self-consciousness from the very start. Despite this important difference, however, both of them highlight the extent to which certain forms of self-experience are constitutively dependent upon others.

Contrary to those who claim that 'what is distinctive of shame is the presence of a specific kind of *intrapersonal* evaluation, an evaluative perspective the subject takes upon himself' (Deonna, Rodogno, Teroni 2011: 135), I do not think one can capture the acute experience of shame simply by focusing on the fact that the shamed subject is thrown back upon itself. As Seidler points out—and I think this constitutes an essential insight—

---

[12] According to Deonna and Teroni, we need to operate with a distinction between superficial and deep shame (2011, 201), and only the former concerns our social identity. Their very choice of terms suggests that the core of our being, our real identity, is pre-social or asocial, whereas the social dimension of our identity is only skin-deep, a mere matter of appearance. In arguing like this they are getting very close to a view espoused by Kierkegaard in the following passage: 'Everyone who when before himself is not more ashamed than he is before all others will, if he is placed in a difficult position and is sorely tried in life, end up becoming a slave of people in one way or another. What is it to be more ashamed before others than before oneself but to be more ashamed of seeming than of being?' (Kierkegaard 1993: 53). Although I would agree that there is a core dimension of our selfhood that is pre-social (Zahavi 2009), I do not think that dimension, which on my terms is what should be called the experiential self, is or could be the subject of deep shame.

'Das Schamsubjekt ist *"ganz bei sich"* und gleichzeitig *"außer sich"*' (Seidler 2001: 25–6). This, I think, is also Sartre's basic idea. More generally speaking, Sartre takes shame to involve an existential alienation. I would agree with this—at least if one understands it as amounting to a decisive change of perspective on self. In some cases the alienating power is a different subject, and Sartre's description of our pre-reflective feeling of shame when confronted with the evaluating gaze of the other is an example of this. In other cases, the feeling of shame occurs when we sit in judgement on ourselves. But in this case as well, there is a form of exposure and self-alienation, a kind of self-observation and self-distancing. To put it differently, in the company of others the experience of shame can occur pre-reflectively, since the alien perspective is co-present. When alone, the experience of shame will take a more reflective form, since the alien perspective has to be provided through a form of reflective self-distancing.

I would consequently maintain that shame contains a significant and irreducible element of 'alterity'. This is obvious in those cases where the experience of shame arises as a reaction to the evaluation of others, but even past-oriented self-reflective shame and future-oriented shame anxiety contain this aspect—although both lack some of the characteristic phenomenology of the acute form of shame. This is so not only because of the self-distancing and doubling of perspectives involved, but also because others influence the development and formation of our own standards. To that extent, the evaluating perspectives of others may play a role in the structure of the emotion even if they are not factually present or explicitly imagined (Landweer 1999: 57, 67). Moreover, even if one could argue that the kind of shame you might feel when failing to meet your own standards is not socially mediated in any direct fashion (it is not as if you only feel shameful because you are losing face or that other people's evaluations are always part of what shame us) there is still the question concerning the relation between *intra*personal and *inter*personal shame. I have rejected the claim that the latter can be reduced to or explained on the basis of the former. In fact, although I cannot substantiate the claim in any detail in this chapter, I find it far more plausible to claim that intrapersonal shame is subsequent to (and conditioned by) interpersonal shame. Is it not by first being attentive to and sensitive to the attention and evaluation—that is, perspective of the other—that we gain the ability to internalize that perspective? Is it not by adopting the perspective of the other that we can gain sufficient self-distance to permit a critical self-evaluation? This would be the view not only of a number of developmental psychologists, but also of, say, philosophers such as Mead and Sartre. As the latter writes, 'although certain complex forms derived from shame can appear on the reflective plane, shame is not originally a phenomenon of reflection. In fact, no matter what results one can obtain in solitude by the religious *practice* of shame, it is in its primary structure shame *before somebody*' (Sartre 2003: 245).

There is much more to be said about shame. A more adequate understanding of this complex phenomenon would also require extensive analysis of, for instance, its developmental trajectory (how early does it emerge, how much does infantile shame—if it exists—resemble adult shame, what role does it play in adolescence, and so on), and cultural specificity (to what extent do the shame-inducing situations, the very experience of shame and the available coping strategies vary from culture to culture). But these are not topics I can pursue further on this occasion. In conclusion, let me just state that I think the preceding discussion has shown that it is questionable whether the self-relation we find in shame is as self-contained and inward-directed as Lewis and Deonna and Teroni claim. I think that prototypical forms of shame provide vivid examples of other-mediated forms of self-experience. More specifically, I think shame—and other forms of 'self-other-conscious emotions', to use Reddy's insightful term (Reddy 2008: 145)—can teach us something important about how our experience of and adaptation of the other's attitude towards ourselves contribute to the development and constitution of self.[13]

References

Aristotle (1984), *The Complete Works of Aristotle Vol. 2* (Princeton: Princeton University Press).

Bollnow, O. F. (2009), *Die Ehrfurcht: Wesen und Wandel der Tugenden*. Schriften Band II (Würzburg: Königshausen and Neumann).

Broucek, F. J. (1991). *Shame and the Self* (New York: Guilford Press).

Calhoun, C. (2004), 'An apology for moral shame', *Journal of Political Philosophy*, 12/2: 127–46.

Castelfranchi, C. and Poggi, I. (1990), 'Blushing as a discourse: Was Darwin wrong?', in W. R. Crozier, W. R. (ed.) *Shyness and Embarrassment: Perspectives from social psychology* (Cambridge: Cambridge University Press), pp. 230–51.

Darwin, C. (1872/1965), *The Expression of the Emotions in Man and Animals* (Chicago: University of Chicago Press).

Deigh, J. (1983), 'Shame and self-esteem: A critique', *Ethics* 93/2: 225–45.

Deonna, J. A., and Teroni, F. (2009), 'The self of shame', in M. Salmela and V. Mayer (eds.), *Emotions, Ethics, and Authenticity* (Amsterdam: John Benjamins), pp. 33–50.

—— (2011), 'Is shame a social emotion?', in A. Konzelman-Ziv, K. Lehrer, and H. Schmid (eds), *Self Evaluation: Affective and Social Grounds of Intentionality* (Dordrecht: Springer), pp. 193–212.

—— and Rodogno, R. (2011), *In Defense of Shame* (New York: Oxford University Press).

Ekman, P. (2003), *Emotions Revealed: Understanding Faces and Feelings* (London: Weidenfeld and Nicolson).

Gilbert, P. (1998), 'What is shame? Some core issues and controversies,' in P. Gilbert and B. Andrews (eds), *Shame: Interpersonal Behavior, Psychopathology, and Culture* (New York: Oxford University Press), pp. 3–38.

Harré, R. (1990), 'Embarrasssment: A conceptual analysis', in W. R. Crozier (eds), *Shyness and Embarrassment: Perspectives from Social Psychology* (Cambridge: Cambridge University Press), pp. 181–204.

Karlsson, G. and Sjöberg, L. G. (2009), 'The experiences of guilt and shame: A phenomeno-logical–psychological study', *Human Studies*, 32/3: 335–55.

---

[13] Thanks are due to Galen Strawson and especially Fabrice Teroni for helpful comments on an earlier version of this text.

Kierkegaard, S. (1993). *Upbuilding Discourses in Various Spirits*, tr. Howard V. Hong and Edna H. Hong (Princeton: Princeton University Press).

Landweer, H. (1999), *Scham und Macht: Phänomenologische Untersuchungen zur Sozialität eines Gefühls* (Tübingen: Mohr Siebeck).

Lewis, M. (1992), *Shame: The Exposed Self* (New York: The Free Press).

—— (1998), 'Shame and stigma,' in Gilbert, P. and Andrews, B. (eds), *Shame Interpersonal Behavior, Psychopathology, and Culture* (New York: Oxford University Press), pp. 126–40.

—— (2007), 'Self-conscious emotional development,' in J. L. Tracy, R. W. Robins, and J. P. Tangney (eds), *The Self-Conscious Emotions: Theory and Research* (New York: Guildford Press), pp. 134–49.

Lindsay-Hartz, J., de Rivera, J., and Mascolo, M. F. (1995), 'Differentiating guilt and shame and their effects on motivations,' in J. P. Tangney and K. W. Fischer (eds), *Self-Conscious Emotions: The Psychology of Shame, Guilt, Embarrassment and Pride* (New York: Guildford Press), pp. 274–300.

Mead, G. H. (1962), *Mind, Self and Society: From the Standpoint of a Social Behaviorist* (Chicago: University of Chicago Press).

Miller, S. (1985), *The Shame Experience* (London: The Analytic Press).

Nathanson, D. L. (1994). *Shame and Pride: Affect, Sex and the Birth of Self* (New York: W. W. Norton and Co).

Nietzsche, F. W. (1997), *Daybreak: Thoughts on the Prejudices of Morality* (Cambridge: Cambridge University Press).

Nussbaum, M. C. (2006), *Hiding from Humanity: Disgust, Shame and the Law* (Princeton: Princeton University Press).

Plato (1961), *The Collected Dialogues of Plato* (Princeton: Princeton University Press).

Rawls, J. (1972), *A Theory of Justice* (Oxford: Clarendon Press).

Reddy, V. (2008), *How Infants Know Minds* (Cambridge, Mass: Harvard University Press).

Rochat, P. (2009), *Others in Mind: Social Origins of Self-Consciousness* (Cambridge: Cambridge University Press).

Sartre, J.-P. (2003), *Being and Nothingness: An Essay in Phenomenological Ontology*, tr. Hazel E. Barnes, revised edn. (London and New York: Routledge).

Scheler, M. (1957), *Schriften aus dem Nachlass. Band I: Zur Ethik und Erkenntnislehre* (Bern and München: Francke Verlag).

Schneider, C. D. (1987), 'A mature sense of shame', in D. L. Nathanson (eds.), *The Many Faces of Shame* (New York: Guilford Press), pp. 194–213.

Seidler, G. H. (2001), *Der Blick des Anderen: Eine Analyse der Scham* (Stuttgart: Klett-Cotta).

Smith, R. H., Webster, J. M., and Eyre, H. L. (2002), 'The role of public exposure in moral and non-moral shame and guilt', *Journal of Personality and Social Psychology*, 83/1: 138–159.

Straus, E.W. (1933), 'Die Scham als historiologisches Problem', *Schweizer Archiv für Neurologie und Psychiatrie* 31/2: 339–43.

Strawson, G. (1994), 'Don't tread on me', *London Review of Books* 16/19: 11–12.

Tangney, J. P. and Dearing, R. L. (2002), *Shame and Guilt* (New York: The Guilford Press).

Taylor, G. (1985), *Pride, Shame, and Guilt Emotions of Self-Assessment* (Oxford: Clarendon Press).

Vallelonga, D. (1976), 'Straus on shame', *Journal of the Phenomenological Psychology*, 7/1: 55–69.

Walsh, W. (1970), 'Pride, shame and responsibility', *The Philosophical Quarterly*, 20/78: 1–13.

Wollheim, R. (1999), *On the Emotions* (New Haven and London: Yale University Press).

Zahavi, D. (1999), *Self-Awareness and Alterity: A Phenomenological Investigation* (Evanston: Northwestern University Press).

—— (2002), 'Intersubjectivity in Sartre's *Being and Nothingness*', *Alter* 10, 265–81.

—— (2003), 'Phenomenology of self', in T. Kircher and A. David (eds), *The Self in Neuroscience and Psychiatry* (Cambridge: Cambridge University Press), pp. 56–75.

—— (2005), *Subjectivity and Selfhood: Investigating the First-Person Perspective* (Cambridge, MA: The MIT Press).

—— (2009), 'Is the self a social construct?' *Inquiry* 52/6: 551–73.

—— (2010), 'Shame and the exposed self', in J. Webber (ed.), *Reading Sartre: On Phenomenology and Existentialism* (London: Routledge), pp. 211–26.

—— (2011), 'The experiential self: Objections and clarifications,' in M. Siderits, E. Thompson, and D. Zahavi (eds), *Self, No Self? Perspectives from Analytical, Phenomenological, and Indian Traditions* (Oxford: Oxford University Press), pp. 56–78.

PART IV

LANGUAGE,
THINKING, AND
KNOWLEDGE

CHAPTER 16

THE (MANY) FOUNDATIONS OF KNOWLEDGE

WALTER HOPP

FOUNDATIONALISM is a position concerning the structure of knowledge, according to which, every piece of knowledge is either:

(i) epistemically basic or immediately justified, or
(ii) justified, directly or indirectly, on the basis of epistemically basic pieces of knowledge.

If this is right, then if there is knowledge at all, then there is some immediate or foundational knowledge. Insofar as the foundationalist aspires to give an account of the structure of knowledge, he owes us an account of the nature of foundational knowledge.

In this paper I will not argue for the claim that every non-basic piece of knowledge is justified on the basis of basic knowledge. My purpose is to present the outlines of a phenomenologically-based account of immediate justification, according to which the facts or states of affairs towards which our beliefs are intentionally directed can sometimes serve as reasons or evidence for what we believe. On the view I defend here, there are cases in which one's reason for believing that, say, one is in pain is the fact that one is in pain. I will also argue that the sorts of empirical facts that can serve as reasons for non-inferentially justified beliefs are not confined to facts about one's own occurrent mental states, but include facts about the physical world as well. Right now, for instance, I know that I am in front of a computer, and my reason for believing that I am in front of a computer is the fact that I am in front of a computer. In many such cases, including the present one, such knowledge is epistemically foundational. Since at almost any given time we stand in a similar sort of relation to some local set of facts as I now stand to the fact that my computer is in front of me, and since we typically are exposed to a wide array of different facts even over short spans of time, foundational knowledge is both rich in content and easy to obtain. A large part of the paper will consist in trying to answer objections to this view.

1

One of the principal tasks of phenomenological inquiry is to provide a description of the conscious mental states and acts in virtue of which the entities that show up for us manage to show up for us, and in the precise ways that they do. An essential aspect of that task, at least with respect to any act that exhibits intentionality or directedness towards an object, is to 'ask it what it was aiming at and what it acquired' (Husserl 1969: 177). The preeminent way for an act to 'acquire' its object is for the act to render its object present to consciousness in the flesh. This is a familiar phenomenon. Think, for instance, about what it is like to experience a searing pain in your toe. Hopefully your mental act did *not* acquire its object in the manner that I have in mind, otherwise you will just have actually experienced a searing pain in your toe.

At least some acts of foundational knowledge are foundational in virtue of acquiring their objects in a very distinctive way. To give an example: right now I believe that my door is open. This is not because someone told me it is open. It is not because I examined the rest of my beliefs and found that the proposition <the door is open> coheres with them or that its negation does not. It is not because I know or believe some proposition <q> such that the proposition <the door is open> is probable given <q>. It is not because the proposition <the door is open> somehow just seems true. It is, rather, because (a) I am undergoing a perceptual experience that presents the door as being precisely the way that the proposition <the door is open> represents it as being, namely open, (b) I am thinking that proposition, and (c) my acts of thinking and perceiving are synthesized in a distinctive way. Note that I am not justified in believing <the door is open> because I believe that (a)–(c) are occurring. It is because they are occurring. This is a case of what Husserl calls 'fulfilment', and what I have elsewhere called 'primary epistemic fulfilment' (Hopp 2011: section 7.1). A great deal has been and remains to be said about this sort of act and its various types, but it is quite familiar: it is a matter of *finding* an object to be as one *thinks* it to be (see Willard 1995: 138–9).

In this act, as in any act of knowing, we can distinguish several different features and components. To keep things simple, consider first what any arbitrary act of knowing involves. The first obvious feature of acts of knowing is that they are intentional acts. That is, they represent the world as being a certain way. When I come to know that my door is open, my act of knowing represents my door, and represents it as being open. The door's being open is the *object* of that act—what the act is about. Note that the act does not merely represent the door. It also represents how things stand with the door. The property of being open is just as much a part of the full intentional object of my act of knowing as the door itself is (Husserl 1970: 579; Smith and McIntyre 1982: 6–9).

It would be tempting to conclude straightaway that what *I know*, when I know that the door is open, is the *fact* that the door is open. It is equally natural to say that what I know is the *proposition* <the door is open>. However, I do not stand in the same relation to the proposition <the door is open> that I do to the fact that the door is open. First, on any viable view whatsoever, propositions represent the world as being a certain way. But what I am thinking about when I think that the door is open does not represent the world as being a certain way. The fact that the door is open does not represent anything at all. Therefore, my act of thinking is not about a proposition.[1] Second, my act of thinking that the door is open represents the same thing that the proposition <the door is open> represents. But the proposition does not represent itself. So, my act of thinking does not represent the proposition.

In the case of any instance of knowledge, then, we can distinguish between (i) the act of knowing, (ii) the propositional content known, and (iii) the fact known (about). Only (iii) is the intentional object of an act of knowing. In the case of fulfilment, things are more complicated, since (at least) two acts—the fulfilling and the fulfilled acts—converge on the same object. That is, acts of fulfilment have two contents that are about the same state of affairs. That this sort of complexity is present in such acts becomes clear when we consider how the content of either the fulfilling experience or the thought that it fulfils can remain constant while the content of the other varies (Husserl 1970: 680). My thought that the door is open can be fulfilled on the basis of many experiences that differ in content from the one I am actually having. Were I three feet closer, or viewing the door from another angle, my experience would still fulfil my thought that the door is open. There is no proposition <p> such that having the thought that <p> fulfilled entails that I am undergoing just this type of perceptual experience. And I could fulfil a number of other thoughts on the basis of exactly this type of experience of the door, including thoughts with the propositional contents <this door is white>, <this door is taller than me>, <the door is over there>, and many others. There is no proposition <p> such that in virtue of having this perceptual experience, I am entertaining, believing, or judging <p>. Despite the multiplicity of contents in fulfillment, we are not therefore aware of two objects. Rather, 'the object, at once intended and "given", stands before us, not as two objects, but as one alone' (Husserl 1970: 291).

A further feature of acts of knowledge, and of beliefs generally, is that they typically do not simply arise out of nowhere, but are rationally motivated. We generally have reasons, or at least imagine ourselves to have reasons, for believing what we do. In the case of inferential knowledge and belief, we believe that the world is a certain way because of *other* ways we believe the world to be. I might believe that my wife is home because I believe (i) that her coat is on the hook and (ii) if her coat is on the hook, then she is home. In fulfillment, by contrast, we believe the world is a certain way because we are presented with that very portion of the world itself. In fulfillment, 'The object is

---

[1] Pollock and Cruz (1999) write: 'Objects of belief are called "propositions". For example, when I believe that there is a cat in the window, the object of my belief is the proposition that there is a cat in the window' (1999: 32–3). They then add: 'As we use the term, propositions are just possible objects of belief' (1999: 33). So their view does not contradict the view above, since, on this understanding of propositions, propositions might turn out to be facts. However, since the objects of belief are not always about something, it does run afoul of a basic truism about propositions, namely that they are always about something.

actually "present" or "given", and present as *just what we have intended it*' (Husserl 1970: 762). In primary epistemic fulfillment, the object must be present *in person*. Memory and imagination also present their objects, but not *in person*. With respect to empirical states of affairs, only perception does that.

Beliefs formed in this way are foundational or epistemically basic. My belief that <my door is open> is epistemically basic insofar as it does not epistemically depend on my having any more evidence than that which my present experience makes available to me, and what my experience makes available to me is the door's being open. While no empirical belief formed in this way is infallible or indefeasible, fulfillment is the only sort of intentional act in which we verify a proposition, not by consulting authorities, other propositions, theories, or even other parts of the world, but by turning to the portions of the world that those propositions represent. There are lots of good reasons to believe the proposition <the door is open>. One of the very best is the fact that the door is open. Because of the intentional relation I now stand in with respect to that fact—because that fact is directly present to me as I think it to be (but *not* because I believe that it is present to me)—that fact is my reason for believing that the door is open. It is my *evidence* for believing <the door is open>. More generally, fulfillment is that unique intentional act in which our evidence for a fulfilled proposition <p> is the fact which <p> represents.

I take the view that ordinary empirical facts sometimes constitute our evidence for what we believe to be very commonsensical, and I take that to be a *prima facie* virtue. The fact that my door is open is an excellent reason to believe the proposition <the door is open>; more generally, the fact that makes any proposition <p> true is an excellent reason to believe that proposition. And sometimes, facts of that sort are present to us in such a way that they can be *our* evidence. I also think that this view is phenomenologically defensible.

2

One straightforward objection to the view that mind-independent facts can constitute one's evidence for non-inferential beliefs is that the obtaining of such a fact plainly is not sufficient for one to believe, much less know, any propositions about them. The fact that my door is open does not entail that anyone knows it.

Richard Fumerton has an argument that the 'source of non-inferential justification' for a belief can never be 'the fact that makes the non-inferentially justified belief true' (Fumerton 2001: 11). The fact that Fumerton is in pain, for instance, is not the source of his non-inferentially justified belief that he is in pain. After all, 'When you believe that I am in pain, my pain does not justify you in believing that I am in pain...so there must be something different about my *relationship* to my pain that enters into the account of what constitutes my justification' (Fumerton 2001: 11). Similarly, then, the fact that the door is open cannot be my source of justification. My belief is justified because of the special relation I bear to that fact.

Suppose that one's *source of justification* were one's *evidence*. On this reading of the argument—which is not, I believe, the one Fumerton intends—the fact that Fumerton is in pain cannot be his *evidence* for his belief that he is in pain. Rather, his evidence is his special relationship R in which he stands to his pain. This version of the argument, how-ever, is flawed, and we can see so by using Fumerton's original argument to show that the special relationship R that Fumerton bears towards his pain cannot be his evidence that he is in pain. That relationship, which I believe to hold between Fumerton and his pain, does not justify *me* in believing that he is in pain. So, there must be something special about his *relationship* to R that justifies him in believing he is in pain. But then his rela-tionship R* to R cannot be his evidence either, since I am thinking, right now, that he bears R* to R (to the pain), and I am still no closer to knowing that he is in pain.

Since Fumerton obviously does know that he is in pain, and obviously knows this in part because of the special relationship R in which he stands to his pain, what shall we say? Well, we should abandon the assumption (which is not Fumerton's) that *the source of justification for a belief* is, or even supervenes on, *the evidence that one has for the content of the belief.*

There is an ambiguity involved in statements about what justifies our beliefs. A state-ment such as 'S's belief B that <p> is justified by M' could mean

(a) M is the evidence on the basis of which S believes <p>.

It could also be taken to mean

(b) M is one of the factors in virtue of which S's belief B that <p> is justified.

In (a), what justifies is evidence, and what is justified is the content of the belief: namely, the proposition <p>. Evidence is, in the first instance, evidence for *what* we believe, and what we believe are the sorts of things that can, for instance, appear as the conclusions of arguments. Those sorts of things are not token mental states, but propositions. If you prove the Pythagorean theorem, what you prove to be true is a proposition, not your state of believing it. If both you and Timmy prove it, there is only one thing that was proven. In (b), what justifies is some feature or fact concerning B itself, the state of believ-ing, and what is justified is the token act or state of believing. If you and Timmy are each justified in believing the Pythagorean theorem, then there are at least two things in the world that are justified.

The distinction between evidence and sources of justification, or between eviden-tial and non-evidential justifiers (Lyons 2009: 24), is also forced on us as soon as we recognize where evidence sits in the nexus of the intentional act. Earlier, I distin-guished the act itself, its content, and its object, or what it is about. Only the *objects* of consciousness—the things of which we are aware—can and do function as evidential justifiers. That evidence occupies the object position in the nexus of intentionality is often built into our talk of evidence: it is what we look for, discover, are presented with, examine, gather, and analyze. My evidence for the proposition <my door is open> is what my perceptual experience presents, and what it presents is the fact that my door is open. My perceptual experience, which is not about itself, is not the evidence of which I am conscious, but the consciousness of evidence.[2]

Since something can function as evidence only when made an object of our mental acts, we can frame a more general argument similar to Fumerton's own that the epistemic status of a belief never supervenes on the evidence of which one is aware. The single best way of acquiring empirical knowledge is to be in a situation in which the object one is thinking about is also present to one perceptually, and is perceived to be as one thinks it to be. Any object whatsoever can, however, be thought about emptily (Husserl 2001: 113). Anything that can be perceived, sensed, 'given', or introspected—including Fumerton's pain—can also be merely thought about without being perceived, sensed, given, or introspected. Since anything whatsoever can be emptily thought of, so can any piece of evidence. But those acts in which a piece of evidence is given in fulfillment have a greater epistemic status than those in which it is emptily thought of, as Fumerton's argument makes clear. Since both acts are of the same objects, the epistemic status of an act is not wholly determined by what it is the consciousness of, but also depends on the manner in which it lays hold of that object. Not all of the factors in virtue of which a belief is justified serve as evidence for the content of that belief.

This conclusion is evident for other, more familiar reasons as well. For instance, one obviously epistemically relevant factor involved in a belief's being justified is that it falls under a true epistemic principle as an instance. Consider this somewhat remote variation on Husserl's 'principle of all principles':

> POP: If something is intuitively present to consciousness as one thinks it to be, then the person to whom it is present is *prima facie* justified in believing it to be just the way it is presented as being.[3]

If this principle is a justifier, it is normally a non-evidential justifier, and it justifies not by serving as a piece of evidence that I use to justify what I believe, but by serving as a sufficient condition for my state of believing to have a positive epistemic status. If I perceive the door as being open, and think of it as being open, then, according to the principle, I am *prima facie* justified in believing that the door is open. I can, however, perceive and think about the door without recognizing that my doing so satisfies this or any other epistemic principle. 'If I call this intuited object a "watch", I complete, in naming it, an act of thought and knowledge, but I know the watch, and not my knowledge" (Husserl 1970: 837). I do not need to know, either occurrently or dispositionally, that my beliefs satisfy true epistemic principles in order for them to do so, and learning that

---

[2] See Pryor (2000, 519): '…your experiences give you justification for believing *p*, but it would be misleading to call these experiences your "evidence" for believing *p*. For saying that your experiences are your "evidence" for a perceptual belief suggests that your justification for that perceptual belief depends in part on *premises* about your experience—as if you were introspectively aware of your experiences, and your perceptual belief were based in some way on that awareness.'

[3] Husserl's version reads: '…every originary presentive intuition is a legitimizing source of cognition…everything originarily…offered us in "intuition" is to be accepted simply as what it is presented as being…but also only within the limits in which it is presented there' (Husserl 1983: 44).

they do does not, in general, give me any better reason to endorse the contents of those beliefs.[4] This is one reason why a successful educational system need not offer any course on epistemology or phenomenology. Students' knowledge of grammar, chemistry, and geography will not be compromised by their inability to identify the epistemically relevant features of their beliefs, nor will their knowledge of those subjects be improved by learning how to do so.[5]

If this is right, then we should endorse externalism about the sources of justification of our beliefs: sources of justification need not be internal to our minds in any sense of 'internal'—not as constituents of the stream of consciousness, not as contents of our mental acts, and certainly not as objects of those acts. Nothing said above, however, speaks against internalism about the evidence or reasons in virtue of which one justifiably believes the content of a belief; on my view, evidence must be 'internal', and must be internal in only *one* of the senses above, as an object of awareness (which does not entail that it is 'internal' in either of the other senses). We should reject State Internalism, but can happily accept Reasons Internalism.[6]

The trouble with many externalist views, such as unrefined versions of reliabilism, is that insofar as a reliabilist epistemology makes a belief's reliability, or something appreciably like it, sufficient for justification, and insofar as the consciousness of evidence is not necessary for reliability, such a theory entails that the consciousness of evidence is not necessary for justification. This is deeply objectionable, but only for reasons that support Reasons Internalism. It in no way supports the sort of internalism according to which 'all of the factors needed for a belief to be epistemically justified for a given person be *cognitively accessible* to that person, *internal* to his cognitive perspective' (Bonjour 1992: 32), since many of those factors—such as falling under a true epistemic principle—do not figure at all among the evidence on whose basis we believe ordinary propositions. Between the poles of epistemological reflection and theorizing, on the one hand, and differentially responding to promptings from the environment or its Continental cousin, 'skilful coping', on the other, lies a vast space of fully conscious, fully rational life, a space in which we *live through*, rather than examine, conscious acts, and in which we spend the overwhelming majority of our emotional and intellectual lives. A credible account of knowledge ought to depict us as acquiring knowledge in that space. Reasons Internalism does.

Distinguishing between evidential and non-evidential justifiers opens up another reading of Fumerton's argument on which it is unassailable, but does not threaten the view that facts can be evidence. On this reading, the source of Fumerton's justification for his belief that he is in pain is not the fact that he is in pain, but it might be his evidence

---

[4] Willard 2000: 33; Pryor 2000: 519. As Van Cleve argues, an epistemic principle 'is not a principle I have to *apply* to in order to gain knowledge; I need only *fall under* it' (Van Cleve 1979: 70).

[5] Compare Husserl: 'The existing sciences are essentially neither enhanced nor downgraded by the truths of critique of knowledge' (Husserl 2008: 186).

[6] See Hopp 2011: 94–5. In Hopp 2008, I call these views 'Strong' and 'Weak' Internalism, respectively.

that he is in pain, since it is what he is conscious of. But then, provided open doors are objects of perception, the fact that my door is open can also be my evidence that my door is open, even though it is not the source of justification for my belief.

3

One piece of evidence against my view is that we often say that someone has 'better evidence' or a 'better reason' for a proposition than someone else, even when there is no difference in the object of which they are conscious. If you just think that the door is open, you have much worse evidence than I do. How, then, can my evidence be identical with the object of which I am conscious.

The answer, I think, is rather simple: the claim that I have better evidence than you in this context means—has the same truth conditions and sense as—the claim that I have better access to the evidence than you do. Since the distinction between evidence and sources of justification is subtle, we can expect there to be a number of contexts in which the distinction is not expressly observed. We should even expect our ordinary way of talking to sometimes obscure it. Often, in characterizing something as someone's 'evidence' for what he believes, we imply that it functions *as* evidence for his *justified* beliefs, just as in characterizing something as 'perceived' we imply that it is related to some mind in some distinctive way. But just as it is not essential to something that is perceived to be perceived, so it is not essential to any piece of evidence for a justified belief that it function as someone's evidence for a justified belief. There are also plenty of contexts in which we speak of evidence as something thoroughly mind-independent in a way that sources of justification are not. If a scientist discovers a new meteorological phenomenon M that strongly indicates that widespread climate change is occurring, she will have discovered, not created, evidence that climate change is occurring. And it might be better evidence than M* for climate change—not because anyone has any better access to M than to M*, but solely because the probability of there being widespread climate change given M is greater than it is given M*.

4

A number of philosophers appear to hold that only *mental states* can function as evidence. This is often simply built into their definitions of epistemic concepts. Jack Lyons writes: 'An evidential justifier for a belief is any state that serves as part or all of the agent's justifying grounds, that is, evidence, that is, reasons, for that belief' (Lyons 2009: 23). Pollock and Cruz write: '… a state M of a person S is a reason for S to believe Q if and only if it is logically possible for S to become justified in believing Q by believing it on the basis of being in state M' (Pollock and Cruz 1999: 195).

In many cases, I suspect that the issue may be largely verbal—that what is infelicitously characterized as a 'reason' or 'evidence' is just what I would call the consciousness of a reason or evidence. Richard Feldman, however, explicitly argues that mental states, rather than ordinary facts, are evidence:

> While we might ordinarily say that your reason for thinking that the tree is a maple is that its leaves are a particular shape, the fact that the leaves are that shape is not part of your evidence. What you are going on in judging the tree to be a maple is your belief that it has leaves of particular shape, and perhaps ultimately you are going on how the tree looks to you (your perceptual experience). These are internal, mental states you are in. (Feldman 2005: 273)

The key to evaluating this argument is to understand just what 'going on' amounts to. Unfortunately, Feldman does not say. But under any plausible construal of it, the argument is defective. If what I am 'going on' is what I am conscious *of*, as an object, then this argument is flawed for two reasons. First, in having a perceptual experience of the shapes of the tree's leaves, I am conscious of the fact that the leaves are shaped in the way that they are—otherwise the experience would not be *of* the leaves being shaped as they are but of something else. Second, my judgement is not intentionally directed upon my own beliefs or mental states, so they are not part of what I am 'going on'. But since my evidence is what I 'go on', the shape of the leaves is part of my evidence, while my awareness is not.

If, on the other hand, what I am 'going on' is not the object of my acts of awareness but the acts of awareness themselves, then the argument is flawed for a different reason: my mental acts are the consciousness of evidence or reasons, not the evidence or reasons of which I am conscious, in which case what I am 'going on' is not my evidence or reasons. But then the argument does nothing to cast doubt upon the claim that my reason—my evidence—for thinking the tree is a maple is the fact that its leaves are shaped in a certain way. If, as is the case, my evidence is what I am conscious of, and if what I 'go on' is my consciousness of it, establishing that the shape of a leaf is not what I 'go on' does not establish that it is not my evidence.

5

So far I have defended objections to the view that facts can be evidence for non-inferentially justified beliefs by distinguishing evidential and non-evidential justifiers. I have also argued that facts concerning one's own mental acts are, typically, non-evidential justifiers. The fact that I see my door as being open is not my evidence for believing <the door is open>, even though it is a non-evidential source of justification for my belief.

One objection to this view is that in the process of justifying what we believe to others, we very frequently do appeal to facts about our own mental lives. If the proposition <the door is open> is challenged, I will provide an argument that it is true, one of whose premises will be that I see, or saw, that it is open. Not only that, but my inability to make such an appeal would render me incapable of justifying what I believe to others. In order to justify what I believe to others, I must present evidence that my state of believing it is justified.

This point is perfectly compatible with the view I am defending. If you call upon me to justify my belief that the door is open, I will take the request to imply that you do not have the same sort of access that I do to the relevant state of affairs. I assume that your access to the door is through my access to it (Alston 1989:163). I will accordingly attempt to establish that I know that the door is open, from which you may safely infer that the door is open. In order to establish the former claim, I will appeal to the fact that I stand or stood in an appropriate epistemic relation to the door—that is, that I see or saw it. That I justify my claim that the door is open by first establishing that I see (saw) and know that the door is open, however, does not show that I am verbally expressing a line of reasoning that led me to believe that the door is open; the proposition <I know the door is open> is not a premise I use to establish <the door is open>. Rather, <the door is open> is one of the premises I use to establish <I know the door is open>. Even if, as may be the case, I invariably know <the door is open> if and only if I know <I know the door is open>, I do not know the former *in virtue of* knowing the latter. This is one way that epistemic ascent works: what serves as a non-evidential source of justification for some non-epistemic belief that <p> serves as evidence for epistemic propositions such as <S knows that p>.

6

Even if my claims that facts can be objects of consciousness, that they can be our evidence, and that knowing about them does not depend on knowing one knows about them are all true, one might reject my claim that non-mental, worldly facts can be evidence for non-inferentially justified beliefs. In order for a fact to be evidence for such a belief, one must stand in a very intimate sort of intentional relation to that fact. According to a long tradition of thinking about sense experience and knowledge, however, we never do stand in that sort of relation to mind-independent entities.

The general line of reasoning here is familiar. I will choose an appropriately modified version of an argument presented by Richard Fumerton, whose theory of acquaintance is very similar in its structure to Husserl's theory of fulfillment:

1. In order for me to be non-inferentially justified in believing any proposition <p>, I must be *acquainted* with the fact F that <p> is about.[7]
2. In any (putative) act of fulfillment, if any component of the act does acquaint me with a physical fact, it is the perceptual experience E.

---

[7] Fumerton actually holds that it might be sufficient for one to be acquainted with a fact that is very much like the one that <p> is about (Fumerton 1995: 77). This premise is close enough for my purposes.

3. Acquaintance is a 'real relation'; necessarily, if S is acquainted with some fact F, then F obtains (and any proposition <p> which is true if and only if F obtains is true).[8]

4. For any veridical perceptual experience E, there is a possible indistinguishable non-veridical experience E* in which I am not acquainted with any physical fact.

5. Any experience E* which is indistinguishable from a veridical experience E is of the same determinate type as E.

6. If two experiences E and E* are of the same determinate type, then E is an act of acquaintance if and only if E* is.

7. So, no veridical perceptual experience E acquaints me with any physical fact.

8. So, no (putative) act of fulfillment with E as a constituent provides me with non-inferentially justified beliefs about physical facts.

A simpler way to express the worry is this: if we cannot directly perceive physical objects, then propositions about them cannot be *fulfilled* at all, and, as the possibility of hallucinations proves, we cannot directly perceive physical objects.

Still, I think it is problematic in a number of ways. In the first place, and as many disjunctivists would quickly point out, premise (5) of the argument above is not at all obvious. It is just as plausible to insist that perceptual experiences do, essentially, establish a real relation between us and a physical fact or object, and conclude that hallucinatory experiences do not belong to the same determinate kind as perceptual experiences.

This point is contentious, however, and there are several reasons I do not wish to rest my case against the argument above on it. First, even though I do not think that hallucinatory experiences can be of or about the same *individuals* that veridical experiences are about (Hopp 2011, section 6.4), they do still purport to present us with physical facts. Even if there is no actual individual which a hallucinatory experience is of, it does depict the world as containing an individual with such-and-such properties. What makes a hallucination an error is that there is no such individual.

Secondly, illusions are another type of non-veridical experience in which the individual presented does exist, but does not have some of the properties the illusory experience presents it having. But in that case, an illusory experience presents its subject with a fact or state of affairs that does not obtain; illusion is a species of hallucination with respect to states of affairs. Furthermore, illusory experiences and veridical ones can have precisely the same content. If I misperceive my white door as yellow, my experience presents *my door* as being *yellow*, and there is a possible veridical experience that would have exactly that same content. The possibility of such illusions—experiences with the same conditions of satisfaction and contents as veridical experiences—is enough for the argument's purposes.

I suggest that the real problem with this argument is the first premise, according to which in order for one to be non-inferentially justified in believing any proposition

---

[8] As Fumerton puts it, 'If *direct* epistemic access to the table is anything like a real relation, then it cannot be present when the table is not present' (Fumerton 1995: 165).

<p> about the physical world, one must be *acquainted* with the fact F that <p> is about. Fumerton holds not only that our knowledge of the world is *epistemically* indirect, but that it is invariably *intentionally* indirect. The reason, apparently, is that our perceptual states are not acts of acquaintance. 'When one is acquainted with a fact, the fact is there before consciousness. Nothing stands "between" the self and the fact' (Fumerton 1995: 76). It is fairly clear that Fumerton believes that only acts of acquaintance have this character, and because acts of perception are not acts of acquaintance, there *must* be something that does stand between them and the physical world. These are 'our past and present sensations' (Fumerton 1995: 161) or perhaps 'truths about the phenomenological character of my subjective experience and fleeting sensations' (Fumerton 1995: 32). We can, then, frame an argument for premise 1 of the main argument along the following lines:

(a)   In order for me to be non-inferentially justified in believing any proposition <p> about an object x, my access to x must be intentionally direct.

(b)   In order for my access to x to be intentionally direct, I must be acquainted with x.

In support of (a), consider the case above. Can my belief that the Matterhorn is snow-covered be non-inferentially justified on the basis of an experience of a photograph of it? No, it cannot. My justifiably believing that also depends on my justifiably believing that the photograph accurately represents the Matterhorn. But in that case, my belief that the Matterhorn is snow-capped is inferentially justified; it depends on my having justified beliefs about the accuracy of the photograph of which I am directly aware.

I am not convinced that this argument for (a) is sound. It seems quite plausible to claim, with the 'inferential externalist', that my justification depends only on the accuracy of the photograph, not on any beliefs I have about its accuracy. But I am not convinced that the argument is unsound either.

Premise (b), however, is pretty clearly false. Before saying why, let me say something about the notion of intentional or representational indirectness. According to one prominent conception, I see some object x indirectly just in case there is some other object y such that I see x in virtue of seeing y (Jackson 1977: 19–20). This does not capture what philosophers standardly mean in characterizing our access to an object as 'indirect'. For instance, if this were true of perception in general, one could only indirectly hear a sentence or a melody because one hears it only in virtue of hearing its words or notes. One could not hear a musical chord directly, since one hears it in virtue of hearing its constituent tones. Nor could one hear a tone directly, since one hears a tone in virtue of hearing its timbre, volume, and pitch. One could not even sense a visual sense datum directly, since one would sense it in virtue of sensing its properties and parts. If this is what is meant in saying that our awareness of something is 'indirect', then premise (a) of the argument is deeply implausible.

Husserl has a much better way of capturing something like the phenomenon Jackson describes by characterizing acts directed upon complex objects as *founded*. An act A is founded just in case:

   (i) A contains other acts a_1, a_2,...a_n as parts;

  (ii) A could not exist if those part-acts did not; and

 (iii) A is intentionally directed upon an object O which is not the object of any of a_1, a_2,...a_n (Husserl 1970: 788).

The hearing of a melody, for instance, is founded because it consists of acts directed upon the individual notes, could not exist if those acts did not, but has a different object—the entire melody—from any of those constituent acts. But it is not indirectly about the melody. Rather, consisting of such part-acts is precisely what is needed for it to be *directly* of the melody, just as hearing all of the words of a sentence is what lets you *directly* apprehend that sentence. In a standard case of hearing a sentence, neither the words nor the acts directed upon them 'stand between' your hearing and the sentence heard.

An act is indirectly about an object x, rather, just in case (a) the act is about x in virtue of representing some other object y *which in turn represents* x, and (b) the subject of that act uses y *as* a representation of x. Hearing a melody is not indirect, because the partial acts making up the hearing of the melody A are parts, not objects, of the act of hearing A, and neither they, nor the notes they represent, represent the melody. An example of an indirect act would be an act of apprehending the Matterhorn in virtue of perceiving a photograph of it. My consciousness of the Matterhorn is indirect because my perceptual act is directed upon a photograph, which in turn represents the Matterhorn, and I use the photograph as a representation of the Matterhorn. It is important that I use the representation in a certain way (Husserl 1970: 594). Being aware of something that just happens to represent x is not sufficient for being indirectly aware of x, since one might be aware of such a representation without being aware of x at all. A photograph of the Matterhorn might mean nothing to a cat, and a young child will probably not be image-conscious of Sarah Palin by watching Tina Fey's parodies.

Given this notion of indirectness, which seems quite close to the one Fumerton and other indirect realists rely upon, we can see why not every intentionally direct act is an act of acquaintance. When I just think about the planet Saturn while perceiving the layout of my living room, I am not indirectly aware of Saturn. There is no other thing that I am first representing which in turn represents Saturn. Certainly, a vague image of Saturn might float before my mind's eye. But it might not, and whether it does or does not is immaterial. Nor am I thinking directly of my idea or concept of Saturn. I am using the concept, but not representing it, just as, in speaking, I use words without talking about them. But my act of merely thinking about Saturn is hardly an act of acquaintance. An act can directly represent an object even when that object does not exist. False propositions represent states of affairs that do not obtain. My thought that Saturn is inhabited is directly of its object, but it represents something—Saturn's being inhabited—which does not obtain. We can even think of the god Saturn directly.

Since an act of mere thought can be directly of its object, why should we suppose that perceptual acts must be indirectly of theirs simply because they are not acts of acquaintance? I think we should not. In the first place, introducing mental objects to mediate between our mental acts and the world does nothing to explain how intentional acts can be erroneous or of objects which do not exist (Willard 1967: 517). Hallucinations, one might think, could not be *directly* of anything in the world, but they are directly of something, perhaps appearances or sensations. Are these appearances or sensations directly about any worldly objects? If so, then a representation's being directly about something does not entail that its object exists or that the representation is accurate, in which case the appearance explains nothing that we could not explain by appealing to an act which is *directly* about what does not exist. And if the appearance is not directly about anything in the world, then either (a) the appearance is not about anything at all, or (b) it is about another intermediary. If the latter, we face the same problem all over again. If the former, appealing to the appearance does nothing to explain how the hallucination is an error—that is, how it is a hallucination at all.

Hallucinations are not inaccurate merely because they do not represent the mind-independent world as it is. If that were a sufficient condition for inaccuracy, then everything that lacks representational properties altogether—mufflers, earrings, walruses—would be inaccurate, as would every intentional act that represents something besides the mind-independent world. They are inaccurate, rather, because they represent the mind-independent world as it is not. If my experience simply terminates in an appearance which exists and has the properties my experience presents it as having, then my experience is not mistaken about anything.

Furthermore, if my experience is hallucinatory or illusory, it is not mistaken because it can be factored into a veridical act directed at an appearance or a set of sensations and a mistaken inference from those to some proposition about the world. Hallucinations and illusions are *perceptual* errors, not mistaken judgements or inferences. As Mark Johnston puts it, 'being susceptible to visual hallucination is a liability that just comes with having a visual system' (Johnston 2004: 124). If hallucinations were faulty inferences, then, since faulty inference is a failure of rationality, hallucinations would appear to be failures of rationality. But hallucinations, like perceptual experiences, are neither rational of irrational; it just makes no sense to attribute those properties to them.

That perceptual experiences can be wrong about the world, and that hallucinations are, at least shows that both are about the world—that worldly states of affairs are, if not their direct objects, at least among their objects. That such acts are not *only* directed upon such things as sensations or sense data is clear from other phenomenological considerations as well. The basic characteristic of perception is that, unlike mere thought, memory, and imagination, it 'is that mode of consciousness that sees and has its object itself in the flesh' (Husserl 2001: 140). A perception of a sense datum or sensation is, or would be, what Husserl calls adequate or 'self-posing'. 'In the case of self-posing perceptions, the identity of the object and the identity of the perception are one and the same; I mean different perceptions have different objects' (Husserl 1997: 22). That is, any change in one's experience of such a thing is a change in the thing one experiences. One cannot take a closer or better look at a self-posed object, for instance, since in changing one's experience, one will simply encounter a different object. Nor can one perceive such an object in better or worse conditions, for the same reason. Sensations and sense-data are typically held to be, or defined into existence as, such objects.

Not everything we perceive has this character. At least some of the things we perceive—possibly *all* the things we perceive—are things one can take a closer look at or perceive under better or worse conditions. It might even be essential to our experience that we—or even our experiences themselves—strive for a 'maximal grip' on perceived objects (Kelly 2010: 152). As I walk towards the house, my perceptual experience changes, yet I continue to see the same thing, and what I see it gives itself perceptually *as* the same thing. The conditions under which I view it can improve or deteriorate, and, again, the perceived object not only remains the same, but is given *as* the same. Even properties such as colour, shape, and size are not self-posing, as the phenomenon of perceptual constancy shows. As the house gets closer, its intrinsic shape and size do not perceptually appear to change, even though my experience of them changes. I can try to get a closer or better look at the shape and colour of the house, which I could not do if the colour and shape were presented adequately.

So if hallucinatory and veridical experiences of such things as houses and colours are indirect, in what way are they indirect? Not, I think, in the way that being conscious of something by means of a sign is indirect. In sign-consciousness, not only is the signified object not present in the flesh (unless you have some *other* access to it not mediated by the sign), it is not present mediately by way of anything that is presumed to resemble it. Neither the written nor the spoken word sign 'dog' resembles a dog, and smoke does not resemble fire.[9] If perceptual consciousness were a kind of sign-consciousness, then we would not think that it matters whether the physical objects of which we are indirectly conscious resemble the objects that we directly perceive, since *its not mattering to us* is part of what makes something function as a sign. However, we do, most of us, think that physical objects resemble and must resemble the ones we perceive directly. Something that does not resemble what we see directly, when we see a tree, is not a serious candidate for being a tree.

A much more promising and historically popular answer is that perceptual experiences are indirect in the way that image-consciousness is indirect. However, neither hallucinating nor perceiving is anything like the consciousness of something by way of an image. The first problem with this suggestion is that in image-consciousness, the image-subject—the thing the image represents—is not given as present in the flesh. If I am looking at a picture of the Matterhorn while outdoors in Zermatt, I might believe, even very strongly and with psychological immediacy, that the Matterhorn is *present*— but that is a very different phenomenon from the Matterhorn's being present to me *in the flesh*. I do not thereby see *it itself*.

The second problem with this proposal is this: in order for an image to function as an image, it must resemble, and be apprehended *as* resembling, what it depicts. Sometimes images resemble what they represent by tricking our perceptual systems into representing them, the *images*, non-veridically. Consider how the aptly named *trompe l'oeil*

---

[9] A sign *might* resemble what it signifies, as in the sentence 'The first letter is "A"', but that is inessential to its being a *sign*. It does not become and function as an image or likeness just because of that. See Husserl 1970: Investigation 6, section 14a.

paintings work: they look realistic not because real violins, say, look flat, but because the painted violins do not. Similarly, a Necker cube is not a cube. It is something else, a schmube, all of whose parts are, but do not appear to be, situated on a plane. (The Gestalt-shift that occurs with Necker cubes could not occur if we were to see them veridically, or fully-veridically, since it involves an apparent shift in the distance-in-depth of its parts.) A Necker cube does not function as a good image of cubes because real cubes look, non-veridically, to be schmubical, but because schmubes look, non-veridically, to be cubical. Within limits to be discussed, a two-dimensional image functions as a good image of a three-dimensional object to the extent that the image does *not* look two-dimensional. After the discovery of perspective, but not before, competent painters could effectively 'trick the eye', and perspective does not do that by making the drawn images look flat. That is what previous artistic techniques accomplished. Of course, two-dimensional images rarely fool us into believing they are three-dimensional, and we can readily appreciate how far even expertly done paintings fall shy of looking genuinely three-dimensional when we contrast them with stereoscopic images, such as the famous photographs by T. Enami or, better still, by looking at the sorts of objects such images depict. Still, properly executed images can produce something like an illusion of depth by exploiting other, non-binocular depth cues, such as appropriate angular sizes, occlusion, and texture gradients. Our perceptual experiences of such images are partly non-veridical.

If, therefore, a two-dimensional sense datum or 'fleeting sensation' could serve as a good image of a cube or a violin, our perception of it would have to be non-veridical too. So, contrapositively, if sense data or sensations cannot be misperceived, then if there are accurate sensations that serve as images of cubes and violins, they are not two-dimensional. Infallibly and adequately perceived objects can only look like the three-dimensional objects they accurately depict if they *are* three-dimensional. This, however, raises a speckled-hen problem (Chisholm 1942). A three-dimensional object is one that could be seen from other points of view, from further or closer up, for instance. Even if we suppose that there is no volumetric perception of such an object—no consciousness of its solid shape—or any 'empty' intentions towards its unseen or occluded sides and parts, there is still the possibility of getting a better or worse view of it.[10] But with that possibility, as we all implicitly understand, comes the possibility of one's beliefs about it having greater or lesser grades of justification. My belief that something is thus-and-so is more justified when I see it in good conditions. Moreover, one reason a belief about, say, an object's shape is more justified when one sees it from the right distance and orientation is that one thereby rules out its having a shape that was not ruled out from an inferior viewing position. That is part of what makes a good condition good; by ruling out more possibilities than others, it carries more information. In sunlight we can rule out an object's having a number of colours that, as far as we could tell when viewing it under neon lights, it *might* have. If this is how things stand with sensations, then, assuming they have and must have determinate shape and

---

[10] For the difference between volumetric and three-dimensional perception, see Briscoe 2008: section 2.

colour properties, they cannot be perceived adequately, and various beliefs we have about their determinate properties will be defeasible. If, however, they do not have determinate shape and colour properties—if they are like the hen-sense-datum that has a lot of speckles but no determinate number of them—then it is hard to see how they have shape and colour properties at all. So, the dilemma: if sensations are accurate images which can only be perceived veridically, then they are three-dimensional, but if they are three-dimensional, then our perception of them must be inadequate.[11]

A third problem with construing perception as image-consciousness is that while an image must resemble what it represents, it cannot resemble it too closely (Husserl 2005: section 9). What sustains our ability to reckon differently with images than with the objects they represent—to not run away from images of lions or start up conversations with the people depicted on the movie screen—is that we grasp, whether correctly or not, various ways in which the image-object differs from the image-subject. The photograph on the table differs from the Matterhorn in all sorts of ways. It is only a few inches tall, and made of paper. If an object—the twin-Earth Matterhorn, say—resembles the Matterhorn too closely, image-consciousness would fall away, and we would have a straightforward act of perception aimed simply at that resembling object. The twin-Matterhorn might remind us of the Matterhorn, but being reminded of something is not image-consciousness. This is also why the extent to which an object can be given adequately is the extent to which image-consciousness of it is impossible. You cannot be image-conscious of a pain or an odour, since anything that resembles a pain or an odour closely enough to serve as an image of it would be painful or smelly, and so would present the thing itself in the flesh in a way that image-consciousness does not. The best we can do to represent, say, an odour by way of an image is to depict something that holds the promise of a certain olfactory experience, such as the heavy, noxious-looking cloud emanating from Pepé Le Pew's tail.

If, therefore, perceptual experiences of the physical world, whether veridical or not, were acts of image-consciousness, then we should be conscious of some objects besides the physical ones, and conscious of them functioning as images, and conscious, however marginally, of the ways in which those images both resemble and differ from the physical objects that they represent. But there does not seem to be anything like that occurring in perceptual consciousness, whether veridical or non-veridical. When I look at an open door I cannot find any object x of which the following is true: x has many of the properties that an open door has, but differs from the door too, and were x to resemble the door too closely, I would no longer be image-conscious of the represented door, but would have a straightforward perception that terminates in x. But that *is* true of every image of a door that can in fact function as an image.

The considerations above—together with the felt phenomenological openness to the world that virtually everyone agrees, however grudgingly, characterizes perceptual

---

[11] For a different and more detailed account of just how badly a sense-datum view handles the phenomenology of seeing three-dimensional objects and the sorts of errors that can arise with respect to them, see Siewert 1998, section 7.4.

consciousness—very strongly suggest that perceptual acts, including hallucinatory and illusory experiences, are intentionally direct *vis-à-vis* their terminal objects, and that their terminal objects are worldly ones. This at least gives us reason to reject the argument that because the hallucinator does not have 'direct access' to the world, 'you do not have direct access' either (Fumerton 1995: 165). The victim of hallucination does not have *access* to the world because he does not *successfully* perceive it. But his act is *directly* of the world. Veridical perception is also directly of the world. The difference is that in this case we *do* have access. So, we have *direct access* to the objects of veridical perception.

The question now is whether that sort of direct access is enough for our perceptual beliefs to be non-inferentially justified. The mere fact that perceptual acts are intentionally direct does not establish that beliefs based upon them are or can be non-inferentially justified or even justified at all. I might believe that Saturn is the second largest planet for no reason, or infer it from something else, all the while thinking about it directly.

Perceptual experiences, however, are not just intentionally direct, as we have seen. They *present* their objects as existing and bodily present, and are the only acts directed upon physical objects that do that. Does the presentational character of perception have any epistemic significance? Of course it does, just as the presentational character of sensation and introspection has epistemic significance. Suppose I have a perceptual experience of the door's being open, and that the experience fulfils my belief that the door is open, and that I have no additional reasons to believe that the door is open. If I were to replace the experience with an act of imagining that the door is open, or a mere thought that the door is open, my belief would become less justified. In fact, it would cease to be justified at all. Imagining and merely thinking that the door is open are not, by themselves, proper sources of justification of any degree or variety whatsoever for the belief that the door is open. Perceptual experiences are a source of at least some justification, of some type and positive degree, for beliefs about the states of affairs that they present.

My belief that <the door is open> is justified to some degree in the context of fulfillment. Is it *inferentially* justified? Only if fulfillment is inference. But it is not. Inferential or indirect justification involves believing one thing on the basis of *other* things. If my belief that <p> is justified on the basis of some set of propositions $p_1, p_2, \ldots p_n$, it cannot be the case that each of $p_1, p_2, \ldots p_n$ is about the very same state of affairs that <p> itself is about.[12] In fulfillment, however, the perceptual act and the thought it fulfils *must* be directed upon the same state of affairs (though the perceptual act will almost invariably be directed upon many *more* states of affairs). So, my belief that the door is open is, when fulfilled by a veridical perceptual experience directed upon that very state of affairs, justified, and non-inferentially so. Fumerton argues that it is not because, first, 'the victim of hallucination has the same kind of justification you have' (Fumerton 1995: 165), and 'in the non-veridical situation it is implausible to conclude that the jus-

---

[12] Though some of them might. For instance, one might conclude <Clark Kent flies> on the basis of i. <Superman flies> and ii. <Clark Kent = Superman>. The conclusion and premise i. are about the same state of affairs.

tification is non-inferential' (184). Contrary to Fumerton, however, fulfillment is a form of non-inferential justification even in matching non-veridical cases. It is perfectly plausible to suppose that the victim of hallucination has non-inferentially justified beliefs.

Of course, I *could* justify the proposition <the door is open> inferentially, just as you might offer an argument to yourself that you exist. I might, for instance, conclude that the door is open because (a) I am having an experience of the door-is-open-type (b) if I have a perceptual experience of that type, then (probably) the door is open. This is not, however, a superior source of epistemic justification than the original act of fulfillment. Whatever vulnerabilities my original, non-inferential belief possesses will simply accrue to the conjunction of (a) and (b). As a description of what we actually do, this is not remotely plausible. As a prescription for what we ought to do, it is not remotely attractive, promising, as it does, more labour for the same wage.

7

So, perceptual experiences provide non-inferential justification for the beliefs they fulfil. Furthermore, they can and very often do provide positive justification of a very high degree. The difference between merely thinking or imagining that <the door is open> and having that thought fulfilled by a suitably rich perceptual experience in favorable circumstances is not that in the latter case it is *just a little* more justified than in the former. It is massively more justified. It is also, in almost every suitably rich and clear case, more justified than it would be if based on hearing from a reliable source that the door is open, remembering that it is open, or inferring from other perceptual beliefs that it is open. If I heard that it was open from a reliable source, I would, if it really mattered to me, still feel some motivation to go see for myself. But if I saw for myself, clearly and distinctly, I would normally feel no motivation to consult the testimony of a reliable source ('Hey Dan, come and look at this door and tell me whether it is open') or infer it from any of my other beliefs.

The degree of justification that fulfillment confers on our true non-inferential empirical beliefs is high enough to allow those beliefs to qualify, in a wide range of cases, as *knowledge*. Consider a vivacious, clear, harmonious, and multi-faceted non-veridical experience of an open door, an experience that is subjectively indistinguishable, by a very capable and alert subject, from a veridical experience. Assuming, as I have, that this experience's content is the content of a possible veridical experience, what would we have to do to transform a belief fulfilled by it into a case of knowledge? One answer, which I find at least somewhat plausible, is that in addition to doing whatever is necessary to rule out Gettier cases—arranging things so there are no defeaters for my belief, for instance—we need simply to ensure that the world is in fact the way the experience depicts it as being—that there is an open door there—ensure that the perceiver's perceptual systems and sense organs are functioning properly, and establish a nomic, causal relationship between the open door and those systems. But if that is enough to transform such a belief into knowledge, then beliefs fulfilled by comparably clear, veridical perceptual experiences are cases of knowledge, since the modifications above simply transformed the hallucination into a case of veridical perception.

Non-inferential knowledge does not, on this view, have to be absolutely certain or indefeasible. If knowledge did have to be indefeasible, then the claim that we cannot non-inferentially know that any doors are open should be greeted with a yawn. Any theory of knowledge that renders our knowledge of open doors absolutely indefeasible has probably gone terribly wrong somewhere. As Husserl puts it, if the task of acquiring knowledge 'lies in the production of absolutely complete givenness, then it is *a priori* unsolvable; it is an unreasonably posited task. What we will conclude from this is therefore in the first instance the fact that the knowledge of reality cannot have this ideal, insofar as we may have confidence that knowledge accomplishes something actually rational and does so because it posits rational goals' (Husserl 1997: 114–15). The important point is that experiences of fulfillment have a degree of justification that is very high, and our justification for believing what we do on the basis of the presentational consciousness of states of affairs is not seriously undermined by the merely schematically imagined metaphysical possibilities to which sceptical arguments regularly appeal. Perceptual beliefs about the actual world can be undermined, but only by sources of justification comparable in strength, and the act of conceiving of the skeleton of a weird possible world is not such a source.

I cannot pretend that this argument would satisfy any sceptic. My position is dogmatic, in Pryor's sense,[13] insofar as I hold that the consciousness of an object in the flesh is, just in virtue of being what it is, a source of justification, and no sceptic, *qua* sceptic, would likely agree to that. I am not confident, however, that there is any single better answer to the sceptic, nor am I confident that the sceptic is someone who needs to be answered in terms of premises that he could or must accept. In any case, it is an undeniable empirical fact, and at one time a cause of some personal disappointment while I tried to provoke my students, that the majority of us are fairly unmoved, in our empirical beliefs, by sceptical arguments. Merely imagined—or, more properly, merely conceived of—possibilities simply do not in most cases provide any actual psychological resistance to the massive evidential and belief-motivating power of perceptual experience and the huge body of belief that it fulfils. This might be because we are constituted to be irrational. But I suspect thinkers such as Reid and Husserl are right in thinking that it is because we are constituted, within familiar limits, to be rational.

---

[13] 'When you have an experience as of p's being the case, you have a kind of justification for believing p that does *not* presuppose or rest on any other evidence or justification you may have' (Pryor 2000: 532).

References

Alston, W. (1989), 'Levels confusions in epistemology', in *Epistemic Justification: Essays in the Theory of Knowledge* (Ithaca: Cornell University Press), pp. 153–71.

Bonjour, L. (1992), 'Externalism/Internalism', in J. Dancy and E. Sosa (eds), *A Companion to Epistemology* (Oxford: Blackwell), pp. 132–6.

—— (2003), 'A Version of Internalist Foundationalism', in L. Bonjour and E. Sosa, *Epistemic Justification* (Malden: Blackwell Publishing), pp. 3–96.

Briscoe, R.E. (2008), 'Vision, Action, and Make-Perceive', *Mind and Language*, 23: 457–97.

Chisholm, R. (1942), 'The Problem of the Speckled Hen', *Mind*, 51: 368–73.

Conee, E. and Feldman, R. (2004), 'Internalism Defended', in *Evidentialism* (Oxford: Oxford University Press), pp. 53–80.

Feldman, R. (2005), 'Justification is Internal', in M. Steup and E. Sosa (eds), *Contemporary Debates in Epistemology* (Malden: Blackwell Publishing), pp. 270–84.

Fumerton, R. (1995), *Metaepistemology and Skepticism* (Lanham: Rowman & Littlefield).

—— (2001), 'Classical foundationalism', in M. R. DePaul (ed.), *Resurrecting Old Fashioned Foundationalism* (Lanham: Rowman & Littlefield), pp. 3–20.

Hopp, W. (2008), 'Husserl, phenomenology, and foundationalism', *Inquiry*, 51: 194–216.

—— (2011), Perception and knowledge: A phenomenological account (Cambridge: Cambridge University Press).

Husserl, E. (1969), *Formal and Transcendental Logic*. D. Cairns (trans.) (The Hague: Martinus Nijhoff).

—— (1970), *Logical Investigations*, J. N. Findlay (trans.) (London: Routledge & Kegan Paul).

—— (1983), *Ideas Pertaining to a Pure Phenomenology and to a Phenomenological Philosophy, First Book*, F. Kersten (trans.) (Boston: Kluwer Academic Publishers).

—— (1997), *Thing and Space*, R. Rojcewicz (trans.) (Boston: Kluwer Academic Publishers).

—— (2001), *Analyses Concerning Passive and Active Synthesis*, A. J. Steinbock (trans.) (Boston: Kluwer Academic Publishers).

—— (2005), *Phantasy, Image Consciousness, and Memory*, J. Brough (trans.) (Dordrecht: Springer).

—— (2008), *Introduction to Logic and Theory of Knowledge: Lectures 1906/07*, C. O. Hill (trans.) (Dordrecht: Springer).

Jackson, F. (1977), *Perception: A Representative Theory* (Cambridge: Cambridge University Press).

Johnston, M. (2004), 'The obscure object of hallucination', *Philosophical Studies*, 120: 113–83.

Kelly, S. D. (2010), 'The normative nature of perceptual experience', in B. Nanay (ed.), *Perceiving the World* (Oxford: Oxford University Press), pp. 146–59.

Lyons, J. C. (2009), *Perception and Basic Beliefs* (Oxford: Oxford University Press).

Pollock, J. L. and Cruz (1999), *Contemporary Theories of Knowledge* (New York: Rowman & Littlefield).

Pryor, James (2000), 'The skeptic and the dogmatist', *Noûs*, 34: 517–49.

Siewert, C. P. (1998), *The Significance of Consciousness* (Princeton: Princeton University Press).

Smith, D. W. and McIntyre, R. (1982), *Husserl and Intentionality: A Study of Mind, Meaning, and Language* (Dordrecht: D. Reidel).

Van Cleve, J. (1979), 'Foundationalism, epistemic principles, and the Cartesian circle', *The Philosophical Review*, 88: 55–91.

Willard, D. (1967), 'A crucial error in epistemology', *Mind*, 76: 513–23.

—— (1995), 'Knowledge', in B. Smith and D. W. Smith (eds), *The Cambridge Companion to Husserl* (Cambridge: Cambridge University Press), pp. 138–67.

—— (2000), 'Knowledge and naturalism', in W. L. Craig and J. P. Moreland (eds), *Naturalism: A Critical Analysis* (New York: Routledge), pp. 24–48.

CHAPTER 17

THE PHENOMENOLOGICAL FOUNDATIONS OF PREDICATIVE STRUCTURE

DOMINIQUE PRADELLE

WITHIN the logical and philosophical tradition the predicative structure of the proposition has enjoyed a certain form of privilege, which has been evident since the Aristotelian analyses of *De interpretatione* (Aristotle 2002: 21 b 9); each judicative proposition (*Aussagesatz*) is assumed to lead back to, or even to be reducible to, a predicative proposition of the type 'S is p', thereby attributing a predicate p to a subject S. It fell to Frege's analyses, and then Russell's, to call into question its paradigmatic character and to substitute for it a notion of function f( ) that is satisfiable or verifiable by an argument (Frege 1892: 193–5). Now, despite the evolution of formal logic that was driven by such analyses (the construction of a formal calculus of predicates in functional terms), Husserl continued to grant a paradigmatic or universal status to the predicative structure. On the one hand, a simple change in subjective attitude (*Einstellungsänderung*) allows all the forms of discourse to be traced back to the judicative or apophantic form 'S is p' (for example, from the direct wish 'may S be p!' to the judicative proposition 'I wish that S be p', and so on) (Husserl 1974: 27–8/23–4). On the other hand, the second section of *Experience and Judgement*, wholly devoted to 'Predicative Thought and the Objectivities of Understanding', begins with a chapter dealing with 'The General Structures of Predication and the Genesis of the Most Important Categorial Forms', making it clear that the predicative structure is the most fundamental of all the categorial forms (Husserl 1954: 231 *sq.*/195 *sq.*).

What is to be made of this primacy of the categorial structure among the discursive forms and the objectivities of the understanding? Can phenomenology provide evidence for the grounds of its legitimacy? And at what level of analysis is this foundation to be situated, along with the origin of the meaning of the 'is' in the predicative structure? Is it at the *psychic, or at a purely noetic* level of the subjective functions of thought? In such a case, the 'is' would correspond to a synthetic function, to an act establishing a link or separation between subjective representations, or still more profoundly, would correspond to a thematic orientation of cognizing subjectivity.[1] Is this foundation rather to be situated at the *syntactic* level of sense or ideal meaning, with the 'is' then designating an ideal formal nexus between the meaning-subject and the meaning-predicate, deprived of any real content? Finally, is it to be situated at the *ontological* level of the object, or of objectivity in a broad sense, where the 'is' can no longer be reduced to a meaning, but becomes an ideal, formal object which is given in a *sui generis* form of evidence?[2] In short, if phenomenology has to elucidate the genesis of the predicative structure, is it then led to a psychic, noetic, semantic, or object-related foundation?

Furthermore, if the 'is' does not refer to just one of these different levels, but simultaneously refers to all of them, what sort of hierarchy is there between them? Is it possible to claim that one of them constitutes the site (*Ursprungsort*) in which the other two have their origin? Does the categorial form 'is' have a univocal origin at a particular site? Is it a sensuous, external origin, referring to inherence of moments or of properties to the objects of external perception? Or is it an internal or reflexive sensuous origin, referring to reflection on the act of linking the subject and the predicate together in the judicative proposition? Ultimately, is it indeed a *sui generis* sort of origin—one no longer understood as production, but in terms of a bringing-to-the-fore or bring-into-view (*Hervor-Bringung*) or in terms of a retracing back to the intuitive fulfilment (*Erfüllung*) of the moment of the categorial form? In this way, one arrives at a general question regarding the very meaning of the notion of *Ursprung* or *Ursprungsort* of the categories in general; may there be talk of the genesis and origin of the formal categories? How so, if this does not come down to an empirical derivation on the basis of discrete data of experience?

1 THE HUSSERLIAN ANALYSIS
OF THE PREDICATIVE FORM AT THE LEVEL
OF MEANING

Does the predicative judgement legitimately hold a privileged position within the logical tradition? If such privilege is established by the elucidation of the evidence of states of affairs, is this also so at the level of meaning, due to analysis of the constitutive

---

[1] See Aristotle, *Metaphysics*, E, 4, 1027 b 30: 'But since it is in thought and not in things that synthesis and diairesis occur...for, with respect to a certain subject, thought conjoins to it or detaches from it either an essence, or a certain quality, or a certain quantity, or some other mode of being' (Aristotle 1998: 164). Translation changed by the author.

[2] See Aristotle, *Metaphysics*, Theta, 10, 1051 b2–5: '...with regard to entities, the alethes and the pseudos consist in a way of, from the beginning, holding-together and being-taken-separately, such that speaking the truth is taking what is separated in its being-separated, and taking what is held together in its holding-together.' Translation based on a free translation given by Heidegger (in Heidegger 1976: 165/138).

moments of the proposition's meaning? On the one hand, is predicative judgement the original logical construction—which is to say, the simplest proposition and the universal form from which, by way of transformation and composition, all propositional forms are derived? On the other hand, what is the meaning of the copula 'is' in such a propositional nexus of meanings?

To answer these questions, the Husserlian approach has to be contrasted with Brentano's and Frege's critiques of the primacy of the predicative proposition. Brentano denies that the essence of judgement in general possesses a synthetic and predicative character, which he justifies by a *method of reduction* of judgements. In his view, it is possible to translate every categorial judgement of the type 'S is p' (and its negative and quantified variants) into an existential proposition of the type 'there is an Sp'. Every predicative proposition is thus proven to be translatable into a kind of stance that either affirms or negates the validity of a complex representation comprising a subject and one or some predicates (Brentano 1971: 48 *sq.*; see Cobb-Stevens 1990: 109 *sq.*; Cobb-Stevens 2003: 151 sq.; Parsons 2004: 168 *sq.*).

As for Frege, his contribution lies in a critique of the notions of subject and predicate in logic, as well as in a conception of propositional unity as copulative liaison (thanks to the 'is') between a subject and a predicate. This decomposition in fact re-establishes the distinct logical function of the 'is', as well as the actual nature of the different parts of propositional meaning and their composition—namely, in terms of identity, which is reversible ('the morning star is Venus'), or in terms of subsumption of an object under a concept, which is irreversible ('the morning star is a planet'), or in terms of subordination of one concept to another, which is also irreversible ('every square is a rectangle'). The fundamental principle of compositionality of units of sense rests on the distinction between unsaturated and saturated sense that, at the level of denotation, refers to the distinction between concept and object, function $f(\ )$ or $p(S)$—and no longer 'S is p'— and argument or variable x. In this way, on the one hand, the predicative nature of the concept is not dismissed outright, but is assimilated with the unsaturated (*ungesättigt*) character of the function, to the extent that it is in need of a complement (*ergänzungs-bedürftig*) in order to designate a truth-value, thereby obviating the role of the copula 'is' as conjunctive element. On the other hand, this distinction between the saturated and the unsaturated is operative at the double level of sense (closed sense versus functional sense) and of denotation or reference (object-related versus conceptual) (Frege 1892: 193–5; see Cobb-Stevens 2003: 151 *sq.*; Mohanty 1982; Skarica 2004: 129 *sq.*).

What then, in this connection, does the Husserlian analysis consist in? What sorts of claim do the recourse to intuitive evidence allow him to make? Let us examine the different steps in Husserl's argument.

1) Meanings are from the beginning approached in terms of the formal–ontological distinction between *Selbständigkeit* (independence, self-subsistence) and *Unselbständigkeit* (dependence, non-self-subsistence). Being one particular sort of object—namely, ideal objects—meanings may be split up according to whether they are *concreta* or *abstracta*, that is to say according to whether they are independent or dependent contents.

Meaning of the first type is characterized by its *being-for-itself* (*Für-sich-Sein*) or its *being able to be given for itself* (*Für-sich-gegeben-können*). That is, such meaning meets the two Cartesian criteria of being a substance—namely, ontological independence (being in itself) and epistemological independence (being independently intelligible), which are then reformulated in phenomenological terms (able to be given independently). Meaning of the second type is characterized by how it may only be given in a larger context of meaning (*nur in einem umfassenden Bedeutungs-zusammenhang sein können*). By this means, the way the first type of meaning may be understood independently or in isolation is opposed to the way the second type of meaning can only be understood in a context of meaning. Now, strictly speaking, the *Selbständigkeit* holds true only for entire judicative propositions (Husserl 2003: 59; Husserl 1996: 102–4.). This results in a *principle of propositional contextuality* for every element of meaning; it is solely on the basis of entire assertoric propositions, and through the function of such elements of meaning in those propositions, that one can understand a semantic or syntactic constituent. The same then holds true *eo ipso* for the copula 'is'. As Frege states, one must start from the proposition and proceed to its analysis, rather than starting from the eventual constituents or atoms of meaning and attempting to build up the proposition through synthesis (Husserl 2003: 60; Husserl 1996: 104).

2) The analytic method makes it possible to distinguish between two senses of syntax and to clarify the notions of syntactic material and syntactic form. One can, in fact, approach the constituents (*Glieder*) of a proposition in two different ways. The first allows for the distinction between the material and the form of meaning (*Bedeutungsstoff* versus *-form*); a syntactic material (such as *Socrates, king, lion, green, fellow person*) comprises a reference to things (*Sachbezüglichkeit*) or to a kind of content tied to a thing (*Sachhaltigkeit*), meaning the relation to *Sachen* of a determinate domain. These materials are always given according to a determinate syntactic form: namely, the function of thought (*Denkfunktion*) which reverts to each within the whole proposition—that is, under the form of subject, of object, of predicate, of attribute, of preceding or ensuing proposition, and so on—where the same material can be something *ne variatur* across different syntactic functions (Husserl 1996: 106–8).

However, this process of analysis also results in the distinction between pure and formed material (*reiner und geformter Stoff*), as well as a distinction between nuclear material and nuclear form (*Kernstoff* versus *-form*). The analysis leads in the last instance to the ultimate constituents (*letzte Glieder*) that are simple or indivisible (*einfach, nicht mehr zu zergliedern*), and that are redistributed in different fundamental categories of syntagmata (substantivity, adjectivity, relationality: the three nuclear forms). As to the nuclear form, it designates the pure thing-content (*Sachgehalt*) in which the congruence of different nuclear arrangements resides (for example, the element common to the adjective *ähnlich*, to the substantive *Ähnlichkeit*, and to the relation *Ähnlichsein*, or indeed the one common to *rot* and *Röte*; Husserl 1996: 111–12). The first conception of syntax thus delineates the syntactic function in a proposition; the second indicates the ultimate formal elements which belong to a content of material meaning.

3) On the basis of the preceding, one can elucidate the decomposition of the proposition in function of this double syntactic level, and precisely define the traditional concept of *term*. Let us consider a traditional syllogistic form like Barbara:

> All Bs are C
> All As are B
> Thus all As are C

The term B, which appears once under the subject-form, and once under the predicate-form, designates the syntactic material common to those syntactic functions. However, at the deeper level of syntax, if the term B appears once under the substantive form, and at another point under the adjectival form, B then designates the nuclear material common to those nuclear forms. By consequence, the traditional logical concept of *terminus* has to be traced back to that of abstract nuclear material, completely deprived of syntactic form (Husserl 1996: 114). Moreover, with every nuclear form being a relatively independent unity of meaning, the resulting law of composition is the following:

> The simple propositional judgement [*propositional-einfaches Urteil*] has to be made up of at least two simple independent meanings [*aus mindenstens zwei einfach-selbständigen Bedeutungen gebildet sein*] in order to be a complete meaning of thought. (Husserl 1996: 130; author's translation)

On the basis of such a decomposition into ultimate materials, one can then understand the function of the copula 'is'; it designates the *Denkform* or *Verknüpfungsform*—that is, the form of thought and connection which is necessary for linking together nuclear materials that are closed in themselves, and which is specific to a type of proposition (*Satztypus*), whose terms belong to determinate syntactic categories: for example the form of connection between a substantive subject and an adjectival predicate, or again between a substantive subject, a relational predicate, and a substantive relative pronoun. The analysis of the proposition is thus to proceed as follows: S / is / p, S / is / R with respect to S', and so on—and not in the being-p(S) and the being-R(S, S'). Undertaking syntactic analysis with a view towards reaching the nuclear constituents deprived of syntax thus requires that the predicative copula 'is' take the form of a liaison between saturated elements.

4) A trivial objection comes to mind when considering this primacy of the copulative form; if there is a distinction between the ultimate syntactic functions—namely, the substantive, adjectival, and relational nuclear forms—is not this formal difference between elementary syntagms precisely what grounds the distinction between diverse propositional forms—for example predicative and relational propositions? In this way, is not the copula 'is' made unnecessary, or even redundant? If one considers the way that ultimate nuclear materials are always presented as having a nuclear form—and never in a state of total logical nudity—as well as the way that these nuclear forms themselves— or, as Husserl calls them in the Fourth Logical Investigation, the categories of meaning (*Bedeutungskategorien*)—dictate the laws of how they are to be strung together, is the 'is' not then made wholly superfluous?

Mindful of the possibility of such an analysis, Husserl distinguishes between two manners of looking at the predicate. In the one, the predicate comprises the whole predicate (*Vollprädikat*) 'is p'. In the other, the predicate is seen as a predicate in a narrow sense (*engeres Prädikat*), or as the predicate concept (*Prädikatbegriff*) 'p'. The former sense of predicate denotes everything that is uttered about the subject (*das Ganze von S Ausgesagte*), whereas in the latter, the predicate refers to the *terminus* in the traditional sense (Husserl 2003: 106, 194–5). Furthermore, Husserl suggests that the real break is to be found between the subject and the whole predicate, according to the schema 'S—is p' {'S is p'?} (Husserl 1996: 106). One would then seem to have a division into two levels (*Zweistufigkeit*)—namely, between the foundation constituting the subject or the *hupokeimenon*, and the *kategoroumenon* that is the ensemble of categorical utterance (*kategorische Aussage*). This observation would have been perfectly able to lead Husserl down the path taken by Frege, to a decomposition of the propositional structure into a saturated constituent (the *Subjekt-Glied* S) and an unsaturated constituent (the *Vollprädikat-Glied* 'ist p'; Husserl 2003: 195).

This is not, however, the course taken by Husserl. In his view, the function of the copula 'is' is not to indicate the synthesis between the saturated unity of meaning S and the unsaturated unity of meaning 'is p,' as would be the case in the Fregean model. Rather, in line with a quite classical conception, its function is to indicate the synthesis between S and p:

> ...the 'is p' cannot count for us as a representation, as if two representations, 'S' and 'is p' could together attain unity. Moreover, the synthesis that takes place is not one established between the more basic level [S] and the higher level ['is p']. It is rather a synthesis between S and p. (Husserl 2003: 106, author's translation)

Warrants for this traditional model of predication can be found in the structure of negative judgement. There are in fact three ways to present a negative judgement: 'S is not p', 'S is a non-p', and 'It is false that S is p'. In its first guise, one deprives a subject of a predicate (*ein Prädikat absprechen*). In the second, one attributes a negated predicate to a subject (*das negierte Prädikat zusprechen*), by incorporating the negation into the meaning of the predicate concept (Husserl 2003: 194–5). In its third guise, finally, one takes a stand against the predicate p, or more precisely, 'against the positing-as-p of S, and thus against the positing of the predicate' (Husserl 1996: 134; Reinach 1989: 110), in an antithesis. Now, given these three expressions of negation, is there one that is more self-sufficient or more original than the other two? Moreover, what are the consequences of this for the predicative structure?

There are two sides to Husserl's argument here. Starting with the first two forms of negative judgement, the first is the more original form, whereas the second is derived: '...the negative conceptual predicate implies the ideal possibility of the negative judgement'. The negative concept 'not-p' is not an original form of negation, but is a derived form of the negative proposition 'S is not p' through incorporation after the fact of the negation into the predicate. Within the order of derivation of meaning, the propositional or copulative negation precedes conceptual negation (Husserl 2003: 194–5). Let us then consider the consequence here for the predicative structure.

One could expect that the first guise of the negative judgement would provide more support for the primacy of the traditional predicative structure; if negation is incorporated into the predicate, it nonetheless leaves the predicative form 'S / is / (not-p)' intact. By contrast, if it affects the copula, the result is then two forms of copula, one affirmative and one negative, that can be expressed functionally as 'being p' and 'not being p'. This is not, for all that, the conclusion Husserl reaches. In the rudimentary form of the negative judgement, he writes, the *nicht* does not belong to the *Prädikatbegriff*. Instead, the *ist nicht* is taken to belong to the complete predicate (*ganzes oder volles Prädikat*). The *nicht* is thus not directed against the *Subjektvorstellung* S, but against the *ist p*, which is to say, against the predicative identification of S with p. The fundamental structure of negation is thus not a *negating copula* (*verneinende Kopula*: '*ist nicht*'), but rather a *negated copula* (*verneinte Kopula*: '*nicht / ist*'), that is a negated predicative identification (Husserl 2003: 196). As a result, the original structure remains the affirmative predicative form 'S / is / p', the negative declination of which is the derived form 'S / not (is / p)'.

The argument is strengthened by the disparity between the first and third guises of the negative judgement. The third conforms to a more traditional conception of negation; the fundamental form (*Grundform*) of the proposition is held to be the categorical judgement, which can be split up into equally fundamental and original forms (*gleichursprünglich*) of predication: namely, the affirmative 'S is p' and the negative 'S is not p'. According to such a view, if one were to start from the constituent-subject, the nominal positioning of the subject would come first, in its role as fundamental positing (*Grundsetzung*) or infrastructural positing (*Untersetzung*), followed by the superstructural positioning of the predicate. These two would then be bound together by the copulative interval, which is either affirmative or negative (Husserl 1996: 134).

This is, however, far from being a proper understanding of negative judgement! Negation is not formally *coordinated* with affirmation, but is a secondary and *subordinate* operation. It is an anti-thesis—an act of taking a stand after the fact against a thesis that was originally affirmative. It is an act of representing a thesis 'S is p' and of opposing a 'no' to it! Negative thought thus does not have one sole layer (*einschichtig*), as the affirmative might seem to, but is stratified (*geschichtet*) with a much greater degree of complexity (Husserl 1996: 134–5).

One might then expect Husserl to privilege the third guise of negative judgement, in which the negation is directed against the entire thought 'S is p'. Far from it, however: 'the "not" does not constitute a stance over and against the entire proposition "S is p"…The "not" remains exclusively on the side of the second fundamental constituent of judgement, namely the predicative constituent (*Prädikatglied*)' (Husserl 1996: 135). The first form of negative judgement is thus more original than the third. Negation affects above all the fundamental form of the predication 'is', to which it accords primacy. Yet something decisive may be added here; even if the two forms are equivalent as regards their truth, they do not have the same meaning. 'Plato was not Alexander's teacher' does not mean the same thing as 'Nicht Plato war der Lehrer des Alexander'. The latter claim, which may be read as 'it was not Plato who was Alexander's teacher', rectifies the initial hypothesis, according to which Plato had in fact been the teacher in question (Husserl 1996: 135).

On this basis one can clarify the meaning of the 'principle of all principles' (Husserl 1976: 51), which is to say the *phenomenological recourse to intuitive evidence*, which would here serve to ground the traditional primacy of the predicative structure. Evidence, in this context, is the givenness of meanings, but these are given in an *attitude that is attentive to discursive intentions*, and that is therefore attentive to the context of uttering a proposition. If the traditional predicative structure is then accorded a certain primacy within the domain of meaning, this is on condition that such primacy not be limited to the noematic examination of ideal meanings or to the truth-value of propositions. Rather, it must be extended to restituting an analysis of discourse in terms of its lived intentions, within the dimension of the *vouloir dire* attentive to the inflections of such discourse. Whereas Frege wished to strip back language's shell in order to reach its logical core—meaning the structures necessary for utterances about truth and falsity—Husserl shifts his gaze beyond that logical core, and instead focuses his analysis on the domain of the linguistic shell of the living word. That is, his interest lies in the grammatical shell of language insofar as it mirrors the lived intentions of the *vouloir dire*.

5) The preceding findings then set the stage for Husserl's direct critique of the Fregean decomposition of the proposition into an unsaturated conceptual function and a saturated object-related argument: '…it is not true that all judgements have arguments, or that they imply in themselves a function that, so to speak, would be endowed with a value according to its universal or singular validity' (Husserl 1996: 149). Husserl's argument plays out in an examination of the traditional conception of quantification, with its division of judgements into three co-original types: universal, particular, and singular.

This conception of quantification relies upon two suppositions. On the one hand it implies an *extensional* interpretation of universal generality, whereby it falls back on an idea of generality as extending over a set of individuals which is to be understood as a closed set ('all As'). On the other hand, such a conception assumes that singular judgements ('this A…') can be situated on the same level as the other two types of judgement. This tripartite division conceals, in Husserl's view, a more fundamental dichotomy, in which fixed judgements (*feste Urteile*) are opposed to functional ones (*Funktionsurteile*). The first sort presupposes the infrastructural positioning (*Untersetzung*) of a subject, on which is then erected the superstructural positioning (*Daraufsetzung*) of a predicate by way of the predicative copula. In 'the Emperor visited Prince Henry' and 'Berlin is a large city', the subjects are placed before the predication, in the sense that the nominal meaning or the *Subjektbegriff* is supposed to refer to a *Subjektgegenstand* about which one claims something (Husserl 1996: 148).

By way of example, let us consider the proposition 'an equilateral triangle is equiangular', which traditional logic would analyze as being reducible to the universal proposition '*every* equilateral triangle…'—which would hold true for the entire set of equilateral triangles. In this proposition ('an equilateral triangle…'), there is no anterior stance taken towards equilateral triangles. There is only a simple non-thetic function, deprived of any stance (*setzungslose Funktion*), whose meaning is determined by the sense of globality at stake in a blanket statement like 'in general'. The indefinite article '*a*' of 'a triangle' functions here as an empty placeholder (*Leerstelle*), as nondescript argument or term (*quidam-Glied*), or as bearer of the universal quantification of the *in general* (Husserl 1996: 148)—*every* x which is an equilateral triangle is equiangular, or *whatever* x *may be*, if...

The distinction between the two types of judgement is apparent in universal judgements, which have to be divided up into two classes: judgements about totalities (*Allheitsgedanken*), and judgements involving generality or universality (*Gedanken der Allgemeinheit, des Universellen überhaupt*; Husserl 1996: 166). Judgements about totalities are those that, in being related to a closed set of individuals, claim that all the individuals within the set possess a certain property. In the propositions 'all the trees in this forest are pines' and 'all the flowers in my garden are roses', the predication is referred to a closed, countable totality of singularities, in such a way that the general proposition here is made equivalent to a conjunction of singular propositions. It is a fixed judgement that presupposes an anterior stance towards the set of individuals considered. By contrast, in a mathematical proposition like 'for every [*jedes*] triangle, the sum of its angles is equal to two right angles', the *jedes* has the character of a general law (*Gesetzcharakter*), which holds true for any triangle whatsoever. However, this 'whatsoever' does not refer to any closed totality of triangles, since such a set of triangles, being infinite, cannot be given in a unitary representation (Husserl 1996: 168–9). The universal proposition is functional here, and not fixed. It does not presuppose any stance towards the subject, on account of the way the uncountable infinity of such subjects exceeds the potential for unitary representation of a totality. The *Leerstelle*, unable to support any *Setzung* here, is an argument for a functional proposition that harbours a universal quantification.

Thought dealing with nomological universality thus does not simply boil down to a sort of generality extending over a given set of objects. For the purposes of thought, such nomological universality solely functions as an expedient but secondary sort of instrument. Likewise, its order of derivation may be traced out as follows: from the universal evidence of 'every A is B', the next step is 'any As in general are B', after which comes 'within the totality of As there are none that are not B', and then finally 'within a universal generality, a multitude of As constitutes a totality of As that have the property B' (Husserl 1996: 170).

What conclusions are to be drawn here? One upshot of the preceding is that, in contrast with the Fregean view, *not all judgements can be equated with a nexus between a conceptual function and an argument*. That sort of understanding of judgements only holds true for judgements which involve subordination of one concept to another, and which are likewise not simple but composite forms of judgement—because of the presupposition they contain. By extension, such an understanding of judgement does not hold true for *feste Urteile*, which can be judgements of identification ('this is a raven') or judgements subsuming an object under a concept ('Berlin is a large city').

Husserl's focus thus lies in questions of whether the delineating domain of a function is finite, numerably infinite, or innumerably infinite, and whether the totality of objects under consideration is either a sort of totality able to be given in perception or an ideal, non-representable totality. In reality, however, such a focus makes Husserl's argument *weak*, since it has no bearing on the functional nature of the concept. The decisive distinction to be made here is not one that opposes actual and irreal totalities, but is rather one that establishes a difference between *bound* variables—considered within a clearly delineated domain—and *free* variables—with no restriction to any definite domain. Accordingly, what seems essential here is not the proof provided by, or the recourse to a phenomenologically irrefutable form of evidence, but Husserl's intention itself; why is it so *important* for him to uphold the import of the traditional predicative structure?

By virtue of the correlation between noesis and noema, there are ideal types of acts or forms of thought which correspond to the ideal types of syntactic *Verbundenheit* between subject and predicate (expressed by the copula 'is'). In similar fashion, the noetic plurality of functions of thought (*Denkfunktionen*) or of the forms of intentionality reflected (*spiegeln sich... wieder*) in grammar corresponds to the noematic plurality of formal meanings (*Formbedeutungen*) (Husserl 1996: 88): identification of two individuals, attribution of a property to an individual, expression of a universal law upon an infinite set, and so on. If it is then essential for Husserl to uphold the 'is' as the fundamental nexus of the proposition, this is for two reasons. On the one hand, it is for the sake of delineating *the noetic invariance of the synthesis as original form of consciousness* (*Urform des Bewußtseins*). At the same time, it is in the interest of specifying the different noematic types of syntactic nexus that reflect the various modes of the intention of meaning—that is to say, the types of acts in which one wants to say something about one or more objects. The predicative structure expresses the orientation of consciousness towards one or more objects taken as a theme of interest and utterance. Its syntactic declinations are *transcendental clues* which allow one to perceive anew, in the nexuses of the living word, the morphology of the synthetic acts of *Denken*. *The grammar of the 'is' opens the way to the morphology of thought.*

2 TRANSITION TO GENETIC PHENOMENOLOGY: TOWARDS A GENESIS OF SYNTACTIC FORMS

What would the adoption of a genetic phenomenological approach contribute to the preceding analyses? Does the genealogy of logic entail a reversal of the hierarchy of noematic and noetic forms? Does it also mean that the noetic functions of synthesis have to be accorded a kind of actual productivity with respect to the syntactic categories and forms? Is the concept of origin from then on to be understood no longer in terms of a path back to the source of evidence, but rather as a genuine form of *production* of the categories by acts of consciousness?

In fact, the genetic phenomenological perspective situates the question of the origin of predicative judgement within a much larger context, and in three ways.

1) The preceding considerations were largely guided by the concept of *foundation* (*Fundierung*) or *stratification* (*Schichtung*) of logic. Formal logic is made up, on the one

hand, of the formal laws of pure syntax, which act as a safeguard against formal non-sense—which is to say, against haphazardly stringing together elements of sense in a way that is inimical to the production of unitary meaning. On the other hand, formal logic is made up of the formal laws of validity (*Geltung*) or non-contradiction, which guard against formal counter-sense—that is to say, the analytic contradiction of propositional forms. Beyond these formal strata there is the domain of noetics, in its concentration on the differences between evidence and empty intentional aim (Husserl 1996: 77–80; Husserl 1974: 54–61/49–55). Now, these strata of formal logic are arranged in a relationship of foundation. On the one hand, it is possible to clarify the purely syntactic laws for creating a cogent chain of elements by abstracting from the level of the *Geltung*. Inversely, any clarification of the laws of non-contradiction and of analytic implications presupposes that one respect the laws of syntax. Similarly, any intuition of a categorial object presupposes that the laws of syntax and non-contradiction be respected, which themselves can be clarified without reference to any such intuition.

Once the genetic approach is adopted, however, Husserl's analysis is no longer centred on the singular consciousness of meaning (semantic or syntactic)—that is, on the two formal layers of logic. There is a *teleological and archaeological subordination of the problem of syntactic structures to the problem of the very possibility of knowledge of objects*. In fact, the propositional forms of judicative thought and the formal laws of non-contradiction are only *formal conditions* imposed upon the possibility of truth. On one side of the coin, they only have a function in view of knowledge of objects, and are subordinated to its endeavour (Husserl 1954: 8/16–17). On the other, these formal conditions have to be complemented with evidence (*Evidenz, Einsichtigkeit*) of the object, in order for knowledge to reach its goal (Husserl 1954: 8/17). From the point of view of knowledge, the propositional meaning 'S is p' can be seen to derive from a necessary form of mediation leading to the evidence of the state of affairs 'that S is indeed p' as the higher-order intentional object, as well as from the specification of those predicates inherent to the rudimentary object S.

Now, this teleological primacy of knowledge of the object is also an *archeo*-logical primacy relative to the forms of judgements. This entails that mere comprehension of propositional meaning is not some grounding, autonomous level of thought to which the possibility of truth or intuition is *merely* appended. *Rather*, acts of judging pure and simple (*bloßes Urteilen*) come about through a derivative intentional modification of judging on the basis of knowledge (*erkennendes Urteilen*) (Husserl 1954: 15–16/23). Judgement on the grounds of evidence, in which the object is given, possess an original or rudimentary character *vis-à-vis* judgements devoid of evidence, by which are meant judgements involving a mere comprehension of propositional meaning without any intuition of the object.

Such an archaeological primacy of knowledge amounts to a translation, in genetic terms, of the ancient thesis according to which propositional thought (matter, content) (*Satzgedanke, -materie, -inhalt*) proceeds by way of a neutralization of the judicative stance (in its thetic character). It occurs, in other words, through an irreal transposition into a quasi-judgement or through a substitution of mere comprehension for the act of judging. Put differently, any propositional content deprived of its thetic character is a 'dependent idea' (Husserl 1996: 54–6). The first sense of the *Ursprungsklärung* is thus that of *relating forms of meaning to the various types of evident judgements about objects*—tracing meanings back to the evidence of their respective states of affairs.

The essential consequence here is the *impossibility of making either formal logic* or the domain of meaning consciousness into *autonomous spheres*. It is equally impossible to sever the teleological and genealogical relationships that formal logic has with the cognitive intention. No level of intentional analysis can be radically disassociated with its teleological foundations and annexes. The forms of *Denkbedeutungen* and *Denkakte* are thus henceforth to be related to acts of synthesis brought into play by knowledge of the object. Is this then to say that the forms of cognitive consciousness ground syntactical forms? Is it to say that there is a primacy of noetic functions, and a sort of production (*Erzeugen*) of syntactic structures by those functions?

2) The *Ursprungsklärung* has a second sense as well; every act of judging bears on an object, as theme or substrate, and every act of true judicative thought about an object presupposes the antecedent givenness of that object. *The predicative evidence of the Sachverhalt* 'that S is p' *implies and presupposes* the intuitive *pre-predicative evidence* of the object or thematic substrate S (Husserl 1954: 11/19). By consequence, the logician's forms of judgement are not only purely analytic *Wahrheiten an sich*, but have to be fulfilled by syntactic materials (Husserl 1974: 230–2/223–5). They thus need to have a field of actual application—namely, in order to hold true with respect to that knowledge of a world of substrates that had preceded the predicative framing.

Logical knowledge (in a predicative sense) thus has a double relationship to pre-predicative knowledge. There is, on the one hand, a relationship of *foundation* (*Fundierungsverhältnis*), in the sense that the formation of the logical categories is built up on the basis of the world pre-given to perception (Husserl 1954: 13/20). There is between the two, on the other hand, a teleological relationship of *application* (*Anwendung*), in the sense that the analytic forms must serve as instruments for acquiring knowledge of the world of perceptual archi-objects (Husserl 1954: 13/20; Husserl 1974: 212–13/205). It is then necessary to investigate the mode of construction or assemblage (*das Wie des Sich-aufbauens*) of judicative evidence (*Urteilsevidenz*) whose structural foundations lie in object-related evidence (*gegenständliche Evidenz*). How can these syntheses of a higher order—in particular those of predication—be built up out of the syntheses proper to immediate evidence of perceptual objects (Husserl 1954: 14/21)? Does their structure depend on the structure of perceptual syntheses? Or is it indeed predetermined by the ontological structures of the objects given in perception? This is the fundamental question of logic when it is understood in the final analysis as world-logic (*Weltlogik*) (Husserl 1954: 36/39; Husserl 1974: 232–4/225–7).

3) This second sense of the concept of origin presupposes a *regressive method of elucidation*, which requires a return to the core of the formalizing act proper to formal logic. If in fact the forms of logical evidence, to the extent that they are purely analytic, leave syntactic materials indeterminate by replacing them with straightforward variables (various forms of substrate S, S', various forms of predicate p, q, various forms of relation R, R', and so on), one must not approach the analytical forms in terms of their atemporal validity.

Instead, they ought to be resituated within the history of meaning (*Sinngeschichte*), that is resituated within the order of operative transformations of meaning.

In this regard, within the assortment of logical substrates, two kinds in particular need to be distinguished. On the one hand there are substrates that harbour the sedimented result of an anterior syntactic framing from which they are derived by nominalization: for example, 'the red', derived from the judgement 'this is red' and from the adjective 'red', or 'the resemblance', derived from the judgement 'this resembles that' and the relationship 'resembling'. On the other hand there are the ultimate or original substrates (*letzte, ursprüngliche Substrate*): namely, the individual objects that bear no trace of either anterior judgements or acts of nominalization according to syntactic forms— this house, this rose, this bottle as objects of immediate experience that make perceptual judgements possible (Husserl 1954: 20/26; Husserl 1974: 209–11/202–4).

Husserl's account thus amounts to granting a *paradigmatic character to the theory of experience of ultimate individual substrates and to the theory of perceptual judgement*, particularly with respect to the theory of categorial judgement and the concept of logos in general. Paradoxically, the theory of pre-predicative—and thus infra-judicative, infra-linguistic—experience constitutes the first foundational level of the theory of judgement (Husserl 1954: 21/27; Husserl 1974: 216–20/208–12)! If Husserl's account has to be understood in this way, this is in virtue of an essential presupposition on his part: the act of judgement exhibits the *same fundamental structure* (*Grundstruktur*) throughout all the levels of knowledge and logical activity, no matter whether it is a matter of scientific or pre-scientific judgements (Husserl 1954: 59/58–9; see 241/205). This view then results in a kind of Cartesian precept concerning the transition from the simple to the complex; the theory of judgement has to begin with the most simple kinds of judgement—those of perception—because they ground all the more complex forms thereof and because they harbour the paradigmatic structures that are to be found throughout all the levels of logical activity (Husserl 1974: 216, 219/209, 211).

Moreover, instead of exploring the gamut of judgements of experience *in general*, Husserl limits his focus by taking the judgement of *external experience* as the paradigm for his account, where such experience is grounded in the perception of external bodies (Husserl 1954: 66/64). Despite the fact that the most commonly adopted attitude is not purely perceptual, but is rather practical (Husserl 1954: 67/64), one finds in Husserl a sort of methodological construction of a purely perceptual subject, uninvolved in practical evaluation and action (Husserl 1954: 68–9/66). Worse still, there only seems to be consideration for the particular case of static perception of an exterior object at rest. Why, then, would Husserl choose such a paradigm? Because of the methodological advantage of *greater simplicity* (Husserl 1954: 69/66). The most elementary structures of judgements will in principle be discernible within this simple example, because of how the external object is endowed with permanence, how an object at rest allows this constancy to be apprehended through a simple synthesis, and how no change in evaluation could ever come to disturb it.

All this leads, finally, to the ultimate level of explication, which traces perceptual judgements back to their source in external perception itself. It is a matter of bringing about *an enlargement of the traditional concept of judgement so as to include all the objectifying acts of the pre-predicative sphere* of perception, by showing that such a sphere already involves a way of logic already coming into force, and above all by showing that the objectifying *Leistung* founds the intelligibility of all the higher-order logical acts:

> ...logical activity is already present at levels in which it was not recognized by the tradition...it is precisely in these lower levels that the concealed presuppositions are to be found, on the basis of which the meaning and legitimacy of the higher-level self-evidences of the logician are first and ultimately intelligible. (Husserl 1954: 3/13; see 62–3/61; see Lohmar 1998: 229–31)

Yet, once again, what is the most crucial level in the genesis of the syntactic forms? Does that level consist in the noetic activity already present in perceptual objectivation? Or is it related to elementary ontological structures of the perceived object, in which one has to find the mould for the categories of formal ontology?

3 THE ORIGINS AND LEGITIMATION OF THE PREDICATIVE STRUCTURE

Let us recall what counts for Husserl as the *Grundstruktur* of categorical judgement. Instead of seeing the two forms of *synthesis* and *diairesis* as being two co-original and co-ordinated types, Husserl underlines the importance of the relation to the object (*gegenständliche Beziehung*) by breaking the categorical judgement down into two theses. First, there is the fundamental stance of a nominal type, which posits the *Subjektgegenstand*, the object-related denotation. Then, on top of this first thesis, there is a predicative stance that explicitly claims something as holding true for the object-substrate. The uttered claim is a true judgement if it is underpinned by a *Subjektgegenstand*, and not simply a *Subjektbedeutung* (Husserl 1996: 134, 138; Husserl 2003: 106–7); the proposition 'the present king of France is bald' is thus not a judgement, given that it has no object (*gegenstandslos*) (Husserl 2003: 195). The question for Husserl is then how to account for this stratified structure.

1) The most patent level of analysis is also the most well-developed; it is the analysis of the predicative liaison properly speaking, in its role in scientific knowledge of objects—that is to say, at a higher level of discursivity. The predicative structure of discourse is related to the predicative activity of knowledge, and this activity is, for its part, anchored in the fundamental noetic structure of knowledge and in the concept of object that correlates to it. The interest in knowledge properly speaking is in reaching a *Feststellung des Seienden*—an ascertainment of the entity in its mode of being and its essence (Husserl 1954: 231/197). That is, such interest lies in establishing *once and for all* (*ein für allemal*) the determinations of the substrate, as something that remains once and for all identical and forever more apprehendable, as a kind of enduring acquisition (*bleibender Besitz*) that holds true beyond the present of the current evidence and that can be reactivated at

any time by anyone (*intersubjektiv verfügbar*) (Husserl 1954: 232–3/198–9; see Lohmar 1998: 231–6).

The concept of object of knowledge is thus a categorial objectivity or an objectivity of the understanding, as substrate that incorporates all the determinations established with certainty by the *kategorein* and which is able to be given omnitemporal and intersubjective validity. It is grounded in the will to cognition (*Wille zur Erkenntnis*), understood as a noetic interest, which is not an anthropological constant anchored in human nature, but which is the *very structure of intentionality*—seeing that it tends towards fulfilment by evidence. This will to know is oriented towards the enrichment of the meaning (*Sinnesbereicherung*) of the substrate, meaning the progressive elucidation of the determinations that designate S as being p, q, and so on, and that belong not only to its infinite internal horizon, but also to its enduring and intersubjective character.

This will to know is then why the predicative activity has two facets. It is, on the one hand, a *productive spontaneity* of meaning (*schöpferische, erzeugende Spontaneität*), to the extent that the cognitive interest produces the categorial object as being p, q, r, and so on: that is, Spqr (an object having incorporated its attributes, which is thus syntactically framed) (Husserl 1954: 233/198–9). However, to the extent that the determinations p, q, and r are not created or invented, but rather revealed in evidence as belonging to the substrate S, the will to know is also a *pro-ductive spontaneity*, which draws the predicates directly from intuitive evidence or aims at *disclosing* S as *truly* being p, q, r. The predication thus has its source in the *deloun*, in the manifesting or the uncovering of the object as being this or that. The structure itself of the thematizing and uncovering comportment is what accounts for predication (see Lohmar 1998: 259 *sq.*).

One rediscovers here, in the activity of scientific objectivation, the dual structure (*Zweigliedrigkeit*) proper to predicative proposition. The additional capability provided by predication consists in establishing the synthesis of collection between the substrate S and the predicate p, and in steadfastly retaining (*festzuhalten*) the predicate as inherent to the meaning content of S—an S preserved in its identity, but also enriched as to its meaning (Husserl 1954: 242–3/206–7). Here, then, are both the *Untersetzung* of the *Subjektgegenstand* S, its preservation as focal point (*Brennpunkt*) of the cognitive interest, and the *darauf gebaute Setzung*, the enduring incorporation of predicates with the content of the object. This manner of tracing the syntactic forms back to their origin in a cognitive interest allows such various forms to be related to the specific modalities of that cognitive interest. Seen in this way, the difference between predication (S is p: the sky is blue) and attribution (Sp: the blue sky) is due to the hierarchy of determinations, which makes of the one a principle apprehension and of the other an adjunct apprehension. 'Sp is q' means the following: S, which is already determined as p, is so at present as q (Husserl 1954: 270–1/227–8). Linguistic structures are grounded in the *infra-linguistic modalities of interest*.

2) This synthetic *Zweigliedrigkeit* of predication nevertheless has *the same form as* the *specifying or explicative synthesis* (*Explikation*) which belongs to the perceptual and pre-scientific interest, which is not yet contaminated by any will to determine the object once and for all. The structure of the higher-order noetic activity of predication recalls

that of the lower-order noetic activity of perceptual examination. In this sense, the predicative connection has a noetic origin, a mooring in the lower levels of the activity of consciousness. It is only a reworking, at a higher level of activity, of the structure of the synthesis of specification of the perceptual object (Husserl 1954: 124/112).

In fact, the dual structure of the predicative proposition has its origin in the structural duality characterizing the orientation proper to the act of specifying examination of the perceptual object. This duality is comprised of the constancy of noetic orientation, by the gaze of consciousness, on one same object maintained as theme of attention, and the polythetic stringing together of singular apprehensions of moments of the object (Husserl 1954: 124/112–3). In the continuous examination of an object S, one finds the *unity of a predominant thematic interest* in the substrate S (*herrschendes Interesse an S*). This interest, as empty intention directed at the object's potential determinations, tends towards fulfilment. That is to say, it aims at the actualization of perceptual potentialities of the object, at the variation of its modes of subjective givenness which brings to evidence actual determinations and constant properties of the object. This constancy of the noetic interest grounds the polythetic unity of the process of determination of the object; because the *same* object remains as theme of attention, the course of the modes of perception is not a splintered collection of singular apprehensions deprived of relationships, but a unique 'developing consideration, a unity of articulated consideration' that grasps each property or determination 'as something in the object S, coming from it and in it' (*etwas* vom *Gegenstande S, etwas aus und in ihm*) (Husserl 1954: 126/113–4). A copper cup is determined by its integral roundness, then by a defect on one area of its surface, by its polish, by its dents, and so on (Husserl 1954: 130/ 117). The categorial form of the predication is in this way constructed upon the pre-predicative explicative synthesis, and originates in such a synthesis. The intentional function of the coherent interest in the thematic object, and its continuous fulfilment by the diverse modes of givenness of properties, transforms S into a substrate which is continuously being determined, and transforms the moments p, q, and r into predicates that determine S. Moreover, the intentional function with its fulfilment makes the 'is' into a name for the 'unity of coincidence' (*Deckungseinheit*) of the progressive explicative synthesis (Husserl 1954: 127/114).

The origin of predication thus seems to be wholly *noetic* in character. The structures of the act of synthesis ground the syntactic forms to which discourse gives expression. The various sorts of syntax are grounded in the structures of the transcendental subject. For all that, however, one ought not interpret this claim in a *subjectivistic* sense! The explicative interest is not an anthropological certitude or a tendency accorded to human nature which has to be accepted as a factual given. There is, on the contrary, a kind of genesis of interest that is enrooted in the object and its structure as perceptual horizon. The object does not spring up in isolation; its unknown properties are not totally indeterminate. Rather, it is apprehended on the basis of a pre-given and typified world, ordered according to types of empirical reality (plants, trees, shrubs, animals, mammals, fish, and so on). This entails that the object always appears with a familiar character (*Vertrautheit*), and that the unknown properties of the object are always already anticipated in function of the empirical type to which they are attached by association (Husserl

1954: 31–3, 124–5/35–7, 112–13; see Lohmar 1998: 236–44). What pushes the subject to unfurl the internal horizon of the determinations of the object according to its predetermined epistemic pathways is the empirical typification of the external horizon.

On such a basis, *the ontological foundation of predication* is laid bare. If the world of perceptual experience were not presented as a world of objects linked by similarities and disposed to being ordered in classes of similitude, there would never be anything like the typical character of familiarity that incites the recognition of the object *as being this or that*, and that pushes the subject to anticipate and verify the properties of the object. An infinitely changing, chaotic world, bereft of any sort of striking similitude, would not enable any specification, and thus would not lead to predication.

3) Let us explore the genealogy of predication all the way to its furthermost level: that of the perceptual experience of singularity. Are similar structures to be found there as well? Are these then noetic or ontological in character?

The explicative synthesis seems to be prefigured in the noetic structures of perception of an external object. In fact, instead of being limited to an immediate, actually present datum, the perceptual intention 'goes beyond the given and its momentary mode of givenness and tends towards a progressive *plus ultra*' (*hinaus tendiert auf ein fortgehendes* plus ultra) (Husserl 1954: 87/82, see 31/35; see Simons 1995: 127). If the intention exceeds the actually present datum, that is because the spatial object is from the start perceived *as* spatial object able to be given in an infinity of perspectives (from close by or far away, in such and such an orientation), and as an object belonging to a certain type determined by the horizon of familiar similitude. In this way, every actually present datum awakens, through its insertion into that which is typical of the world, a horizon of perceptual potentialities, as well as the tendency towards fulfilment of potential intentional aims. The potentiality spills over beyond the present givenness, and the 'tendency toward complete fulfilment' and the 'interest in the enrichment of the "self" of the object' spill over beyond the actually present sensation (Husserl 1954: 87–8/82–3; see Simons 1995: 130; Lohmar 1998: 255 *sq.*; Lohmar 2003: 105–15). Accordingly, there occurs what might be called, in Leibnizian terms, a passage from the *repraesentatio* to the *appetitio*. The perspectival givenness is at the same time consciousness of its own inadequacy, which motivates the tendency to multiply, via subjective kinaesthesis, one's perspectives on the object. Here it is a matter of a *perceptual drive* which is not yet connected with any explicative or thematising activity, while at the same time prefiguring synthetic traits within itself. It is *drive without will* in which predicative syntax acquires its most rudimentary form of foundation (Husserl 1954: 89/84).

Have we, then, arrived at the exclusive origin of predication? Does syntax have its unique origin in the noetic–noematic structures of the pure subject?

At first glance it would indeed seem so! For instance, the difference between substrate and determination seems purely relative to the noetic orientation of interest. Rather than there being absolute substrates and absolute predicates, every activity of explicative contemplation can relinquish its original substrate in favour of the latter's particular determinations as a new substrate. In front of a flower bed one may pick a particular bloom, making of it one's centre of attention, and then successively take an interest in its shape or its colour before turning one's attentions to those aspects of its stem, and so on (Husserl 1954: 147/130). The act of thematization blunts the distinction between *concretum* and *abstractum*—that is, between independent entity and dependent moment—in order to confer upon its object a relative form of independence and to make it into a substrate (Husserl 1954: 151/132–3). In that way, such an act prefigures the act of nominalization or of substantialization which can extract from judgements higher-order sorts of objects. Hence one can retrace the *genealogy of nominalization* back through the noetic layers; from nominalization to the substrate-forming thematization, and from there back to the act of turning oneself toward something.

Nevertheless, this softening of their distinction has its limits. The genetic point of view, applied to discourse, would lead to distinguishing between substrates that implicitly bear syntax and ultimate substrates, which for their part are of devoid of any syntactic framing (house, roof, flower, and so on). It would correspondingly lead to a clarification of ultimate adjectives (green, coloured, hard, flat) in opposition to syntax-bearing adjectives, as well as ultimate relations (left of... larger than... harder than...), as opposed to syntax-bearing relations. The history of meaning would thus be able to be deconstructed by working one's way back to the ultimate representatives of each syntactic category: ultimate substrates, ultimate predicates, and ultimate relations (Husserl 1974: 210–11/202–3).

Now, such a deconstructive or regressive undertaking can also be carried out in the lower-level layers of explicative contemplation and of pre-predicative experience. If every *explicatum* can be transformed into a substrate through interest, it should be equally possible to dismantle the chain of substrate-forming interests, in order to get 'finally and necessarily to substrates which do not arise from substratification' (Husserl 1954: 152/134)—that is, to absolute substrates. These are no longer those of discourse (irreducible to an anterior, non-substantive syntactic form), but those of experience (irreducible to any more rudimentary parts, properties, or relations of substrates). Absolute substrates are characterized by the classical notion of substantiality, yet where this is no longer understood as ontological independence (being in itself, cause of itself) or independent intelligibility (able to be thought by itself). Here, rather, it is rendered in terms of the capacity for something to be experienced directly and in isolation: '*An absolute substrate... is simply and directly experienceable, that is immediately apprehensible*' (Husserl 1954: 153/134).

Likewise, if every determination is the product of a process of determination and explicative synthesis of a substrate, and if such determinations fall under the classical characterization of *modes* translated in terms of experience (every determination is experienced *in* some thing, in a substrate), one must distinguish between derived and original determinations. The former are inherent to derived substrates; the latter, on the other hand, intrinsically belong to rudimentary substrates, in such a way that their essential form of determination is that of 'being-such of another being' (for instance, the colour or the shape of an external object) (Husserl 1954: 155–6/136). The difference between absolute substrates and absolute determinations thus corresponds to the ontological distinction between *concretum* and *abstractum*, being-in-itself and being-in-something-else in experience: '*absolute substrates are independent; absolute determinations are dependent*' (Husserl 1954: 155–6/136).

4) The foregoing then opens up the way to the ultimate foundation of the copula 'is'. This foundation is *ontological* and *no longer noetic*, and is relative to represented contents or objects of experience, and no longer relative to the modes of subjective interest. The diverse modes of possible predicative connections in the proposition originate in the diverse manners in which partial contents are included in the total object, meaning the different types of mereological relation between parts and wholes.

In fact, instead of being univocal, the identity of the copula 'is' acquires a number of different modes of connection between subject and predicate: inherence (the sky is blue), inclusion (the brick is part of the wall), and so on. All these modalities refer to a predicative synthesis possessing a specificity *vis-à-vis* other modes of synthesis. It is always founded on the 'coincidence according to the objective sense' (*Deckung nach dem gegenständlichen Sinn*; Husserl 1954: 128/115). If every synthesis, as 'synthesis of overlapping', owes its unity to the continuous activity of one same *ego*, the predicative synthesis is by contrast an *Identitätssynthesis* founded on the noematic unity of the object. It is neither a synthesis of similitude (resemblance of two colours) nor a synthesis of total identity (the morning star is the evening star), but a synthesis of partial identity—the congruence between the global apprehension of S and the partial apprehensions of p, q, r ... (Husserl 1954: 129/116).

What, then, is this *Partialdeckung* in the case of judgements of experience? It is congruence according to *the relationship of the whole to the part* in a broad sense. The structural origin of the predicative synthesis resides in the connection between the object and its moments or constitutive fragments. Furthermore, the diversity of modes of predication stem from the diversity of modes of connection between parts and wholes. One can accordingly distinguish, within a whole, between its dependent and independent parts. The white colour is *in* the paper insofar as it is inherent to that paper, and can be represented only through the paper, while the base of an ashtray is *in* the ashtray as a fragment that can be isolated on its own, as independently representable. The independent fragments are offset from each other while still being in connection with each other, while the dependent moments of an object are interpenetrated and are given as all affecting each other in one whole (Husserl 1954: 161–5/140–4).

In similar fashion one can distinguish between the mode of being-in of the quality and that of an immediate dependent moment; the boundary or surface delimiting a thing are inseparable moments of the thing, but are not qualities subject to intentional fulfilment, as colour or roughness may be. Moreover, although the form of connection of a part with the rest of the object does comprise a dependent moment of the object, it certainly does not constitute a quality of that object (Husserl 1954: 167–8/145–6). Finally, if strictly speaking only the world as absolute totality is an original substrate, all objects, in their capacity as finite relative substrates included in the world, are all connected with each other. All relational judgements that specify those objects' relations are ultimately grounded in the many ways that finite things have of *being in the world* according to diverse modes of connection (temporality, spatiality, causality, and so on; Husserl 1954: 156–8/136–8). All the syntactic modes of predication proper to ultimate judgements of experience are grounded in the modes of ontological and pre-predicative connection, which correlatively prescribe modalities of experience. *Pure grammar is ensconced within the formal ontology of wholes and parts, which for its part falls under the aegis of the material ontology of the forms of real connections.* The ontology of material connections and the elucidation of their mode of constitution has a determinative function for the implicit grammar of the 'is'.

4 THE IMPACT AND LEGACY OF THE HUSSERLIAN FOUNDATION OF PREDICATION

What are the reasons for primarily privileging the *Husserlian* foundation of predication in the foregoing? If the cardinal imperative of phenomenology is to return to the things themselves rather than hashing them out *de dicto*, would it not have been more appropriate to consider all the ways phenomenologists have attempted to tackle this subject, in order to assess their adequacy to the matters at hand? This disposition in our approach is due in part to the fact that few phenomenologists have taken an interest in this question (not one page in Sartre, Merleau-Ponty, Henry, Scheler, Ingarden, Schutz, etc. has been devoted to this question!). More important, however, is the fact Husserl almost completely exhausts the various options for grounding the predicative structure such as they are subsequently thematised by phenomenological thought.

1) Rather than being a mere explication of Husserl, our analysis has brought to light a central theme of phenomenology; the attempt *to ground anew a doctrine of the categories in the framework of a transcendental logic*. Such an attempt, in fact, has a double aim— elaborating an eidetics of syntactic operations, of the logical and ontological categories, and of the logical principles of consistency and truth, and then *grounding these structures through a noetic analysis* of the modes of subjective evidence that validate them.

Does the return to the things themselves then require an overhaul of traditional logic? The Husserlian analysis to the contrary exhibits a *conservative* character; there is no questioning of the commonplace grammar of language and of the predicative structure as basic building block of the judicative proposition; there is no inquiry into the logical core underlying the grammatical predicative shell in order to supplant it with either the existential proposition (Brentano), the connection of a function and of an argument (Frege), or the primacy of the relation to *n* terms (Carnap). In Husserl, the distinction between *Bedeutungslogik* and *Geltungslogik* grounds the primacy of the predicative structure. Any attempts to reduce it to something else only hold true at the level of validity (in the framework of a logical calculus), but not at the level of meaning. The phenomenological analysis does not stake out a logical overhaul of syntax, but rather offers an eidetic description of language, followed by an effort to ground it noetically; it is a *phenomenology of the living word or of the vouloir-dire*, and not just of logical validity.

The legacy of such analyses is thus less to be found in phenomenology than in the philosophy of language. For instance, in Strawson there is a nuanced distinction between the types of identification or insertion of a subject in the predicative proposition (reference to an individual, position of a second substance or an abstract universal), as well as between the types of intentional aims belonging to the *categoroumenon* that are masked by the formal identity of the predicative structure (aiming at predicates or at sortal or characterizing universals) (Strawson 1959: 168 *sq.*, 226 *sq.*). Such forms of inquiry are to be situated along the route plotted by Husserl's noetic analysis, but also indicate its ties to Aristotelian ontology (Cobb-Stevens 1990: 115–20).

2) The refutation of Locke's doctrine on the predicative structure results in the following upshot: the origin of the categories does not lie in the reflection of the mind on its own acts, but in the fulfilment of the propositional intention and in the contents of that fulfilment. That is to say, it lies in the *givenness of states of affairs* (*Sachverhalte*), which presupposes the predicative structure as one of its purely formal or categorial moments. Instead of being reduced to a syntactic meaning, the 'is' is a formal–ontological category able to be given in an intuition of a *Sachverhalt* (Husserl 1984, 669–70/278–80).

This analysis of the intuition of *Sachverhalte* has been expanded by Reinach in his 1911 article on negative judgements (Reinach 1989: 113 *sq./336 sq.*), which shows that states of affairs are intentional correlates aimed at by acts of judging, asserting, and believing, and which are only able to be the antecedent or consequences of a deduction. The predicative 'is' intervenes only at the categorial level of the *Sachverhalte*, and not at that of the perceptual *Gegenstände*. Mulligan, Simons, and Smith have explored the consequences of such analyses in identifying the *Sachverhalte* with *Truth Makers* that fulfil the categorial intentional aim (cf. Mulligan-Simons-Smith 1984), and then by comparing their status to that of objectives in Meinong and that of facts in Russell and early Wittgenstein (Mulligan 2003, 2006a, 2006b, 2007). Husserl's later descendants are thus to be grouped more within the ambit of analytic philosophy than any of his more immediate disciples.

3) One particular trait of the phenomenological analysis of predication and of language in general lies in the way the linguistic and noetic structures of *Bedeuten* are related to isomorphic structures of a pre-linguistic or pre-logical order. Predicative syntax is founded on the acts of synthesis of *Explikation* and of simple apprehension of the thing as being this or that. This amounts to a generalization of the Kantian thesis according to which the same forms of synthesis are at work in the discursive judgement and in the constitution of objects of experience (*KrV*, A 79/B 104). Put simply, in Husserl *the Kantian perspective is inverted*, for it is no longer a matter of framing the constituting synthesis in terms of the discursive categories of judgement. Rather, what is important is how such discursive categories are prefigured by the forms of pre-predicative experience on which they are founded.

Between the spheres of Bedeutung in a broad and in a narrow sense, a principle of isomorphism thus obtains; the same synthetic structures govern the syntheses of receptivity, the elementary forms of attention, and the complex forms of judgement. Within this framework Husserl attempts to explore the notion of *Noema* as meaning, and to see in the structure of horizon of intentionality the foundation of syntactic structures (see Follesdal 1969: 680 *sq.*; Simons 1995: 129–32).

4) Finally, in echoing the train of Aristotle's thought, this last area of focus on Husserl's part aims at the *ontological foundation of the predicative structure and of the concomitant*

categories of meaning, through a return to the formal–ontological structures of the singularities of sensuous experience. In this way, the syntactic *a priori* is founded on the material *a priori* of experience—which is to say, on the formal structures of concrete and abstract particulars: substrates, properties, and ultimate relations. The general principle in Husserl's approach is thus that *the formal–ontological structures* are not found *sub specie aeternitatis* in some sort of intelligible ether, *but are rather inherent to the domains of material reality. Formal ontology always comes second vis-à-vis material ontologies.*

Here, Husserl's thought verges on the Carnapian theme of protocol sentences relative to the *that there*, but from a different perspective; for Husserl the concern is not to reduce meaning and truths to atomic truths, but is a matter of uncovering the basis of the categories of meaning at a more primitive level—that of the ontological structures of sensuous archi-objects. If the first part of *Formal and Transcendental Logic* asserts that the apophantic and ontological categories run parallel, the second part arrives at an Aristotelian emphasis on material ontologies, or at a grounding of the logical categories on the ontology of perceptual objects.

There is an important link here to the Merleau-Pontian theme of the *primacy of perception*, but in Husserl this issue is considered from a perspective that was never taken up as such by Merleau-Ponty. Once more, this neo-Aristotelian stance has not been explored further by Husserl's direct disciples, but has been taken up by analytic philosophers who have analysed predicates and relations of individuals, and who have investigated the relationship between singular and universal predicates—notably, in the theory of tropes (see Mulligan-Hochberg 2004; Schnieder 2002).

At the beginning of this discussion we posed the question of whether the Husserlian foundation of the predicative structure is psychic, noetic, semantic, or ontological in character. The answer at which we have arrived is that while it is certainly not of a psychic nature, it can *simultaneously* be noetic, semantic, *and* ontological. Rather than severing them in favour of *one sole* mode of foundation, Husserl deploys, each in its own turn, the *manifold* options for grounding the predicative structure subsequently developed further by the analytic approach.

5 THE LIMITS OF THE HUSSERLIAN FOUNDATION OF THE PREDICATIVE STRUCTURE

Is the phenomenological analysis of predication strictly to be confined to one of the paths opened up by Husserl? If the principle guiding Husserl's analyses is a matter of *the inherence of formal structures in the concrete domains of entities*, eidetic variation upon these domains opens up four new lines of questioning.

1) For Husserl, the grounds of predication lie in the noetic structures of perception and the ontological structures of perceptual objects. Notably, such an understanding of predication relies upon the paradigmatic import accorded to external perception of

material bodies at rest, which is considered as the 'exemplary' case in which the 'paradigmatic syntheses' are to be uncovered (Husserl 1954: 66, 71). However, is sensuous perception truly the ground for our relation to entities, and are we entitled to accept the principle of isomorphism between the structures brought into play at all the different levels of relations to entities? In particular, is the relationship between an environing object (*Umweltding*) and the practical predicates reducible to the inherence of natural predications in the material thing?

One of the major themes of reflection in *Sein und Zeit* is the problematic character of the Cartesian ontology of the thing conceived as *remanens capax mutationum* and of the characterization of the mode of encountering the thing according to the paradigm of *Vorhandenheit* (in terms of the simple subsistence of the thing for sensuous perception). Far from being subsistent entities, bearers of permanent properties able to uncovered by sensuous intuition, the *Umweltdinge* are *pragmata*, equipment furnished to the gaze of *praxis* or to the *hermeneuein* of everyday life, which discovers them in their utility-for some use.

Sensuous perception of objects and their properties is neither the first nor even a fundamental or everyday mode of our being-in-the-world and of our relationship to entities. To the contrary, it is a secondary and derived mode of relating to entities, obtained by neutralizing our primordial involvement and our practical understanding; it is in fact in the act of hammering that I perceive the hammer as too heavy, and not in pure perception (Heidegger 1927: 66–101). By consequence, the original phenomenon of the *Als-Struktur* does not lie in the *apophantic as* (*apophantisches Als*)—that is, the declaration of this *as* being that and the *perceiving as*...that grounds the predicative structure. It rather rests upon the *hermeneutic as* (*hermeneutisches Als*)—namely, a modality of understanding as existential structure of being-in-the-world (Heidegger 1976: 143–61; Heidegger 1927: 148–60).

Once it is construed along these lines, the ultimate level of foundation of predication is no longer to be situated in the noetic analysis of perception and in the ontology of perceptual objects, but rather in the ontology of *Zuhandenheit* and the hermeneutic structures of *understanding*. The primacy of perception disappears, and along with it, that of the sensuous object.

2) In Husserl, the principle of inherence of formal structures in concrete ontological domains goes together with a partition of being into the following two fundamental domains: being as (relative) transcendent reality, and being as (absolute) constituting consciousness. This fundamental distinction requires that the doctrine of the categories also be split into two essential parts: on the one hand, the doctrine of worldly categories, and on the other that of the categories of absolute consciousness (Husserl 1976: 159). Given such distinctions, is it then legitimate to take perception of external bodies as the exclusive paradigm for formal–ontological analyses, while leaving the domain of consciousness out of the picture? Similar doubts may be raised about the way the ontological categories and syntactic structures, elaborated with respect to the example of the transcendent entity, are then implicitly transposed upon the transcendental subject. Such a line of thought seems to proceed under the pretext that language is the bearer of

formal structures of the 'something in general' that are applicable to every domain (Husserl 1976: 126). Yet does the transcendental subject fall under the auspices of each and every material body, in the latter's capacity as a substrate of constant properties?

In contrast with these implications of Husserl's thought, one can also find in Husserl the thesis of the *indescribability of the pure Ego*; rather than being a substance that bears properties, the pure Ego, as an abstraction of its modes of comportment, is 'completely empty of eidetic components' and has no horizon or 'explicatable content' (*keinen explikablen Inhalt*, Husserl 1976: 179). It is only in the context of the genetic analysis of the temporal self-constitution of the *Ego* and its *habitus* in a historical unity that the pure Ego regains the status of a sort of substance. It is, however, given in a particular sense— namely, within an immanent and productive temporality, in which the *habitus* are never given once and for all, but are dependent upon egoic comportments, and their assumption and repetition by the subject.

Heidegger went on to radicalize this partition within the doctrine of the categories, in exempting *Dasein*—that is to say, the being that bears the intentional structure—from any status as a substance, and from any relationship to permanent properties. If the predicative 'is' expresses the connection between a subject and its properties, a fundamental distinction needs to be made between *existentials* (ontological structures of *Dasein*) and *categorials* (structures proper to worldly entities other than *Dasein*). Because the existential properties are connected to existing as a mode of being or to transcending oneself, they cannot be construed as constant properties, and rather are manners of existing or transcending oneself, as well as being manners of relating oneself to…and of understanding the being toward which one transcends oneself. These are the possibilities that *Dasein* has *to be*, that it can live out in either an authentic or inauthentic manner, and to which it can comport itself in either an authentic or inauthentic fashion (Heidegger 1927: 41–5). In this way, the judgement 'Dasein is mortal' does not designate mortality as a natural and constant property of humankind—that is, as a trait of human nature—but rather points to being-toward-death (*Sein-zum-Tode*) as archi-factical possibility able to be properly assumed or repressed (Heidegger 1927: 237–40, 249–52). In its formal indifference, the predicative 'is' is thus the index of structures of connection which are radically different from the inherence of properties in substrates and from the containment of parts by a whole. In Heidegger, then, there is a more radical elaboration of the Husserlian thesis of the adherence of structures to the types of entities that underlie them.

3) With Brentano, Frege, Russell, and Carnap we have seen that the primacy of the predicative structure is called into question from the perspective of logic. However, is there also a way of calling it into question through *phenomenology*? If the 'is' remains attached to the types of entity dealt with in discourse, what happens when one leaves the domain of that which *is*? Must one then abandon the predicative structure of the *logos*?

Levinas' analyses of language and intentionality head in this direction. For Levinas, all intentionality has a thematizing or *kerygmatic* structure; the relationship of consciousness to the object always takes place through the mediation of an ideality, on the basis of intending (*Meinen*). This is because I can only intuit an object on the basis of an act of 'understanding' (*entendre*)—that is to say, on the basis of comprehension and pre-intending—something *as this or that* (Levinas 1974: 60–7; 1982: 217–22). 'Being shows itself on the basis of a theme' (Levinas 1982: 217). Intentionality rests upon an identification that makes a first *Meinen* possible (ibid.: 219). It is in this regard an understanding of meaning, in such a way that 'every phenomenon is discourse or a fragment of discourse' (ibid.: 221), and in such a way that experience is possible only on the grounds of the *logos* that harbours the predicative structure of identification.

Nevertheless, does all phenomenology solely come down to the reflective description of the intentionality of consciousness—which is to say, the description of the structure of the identifying *Meinen* that grounds manifestation? Levinas devoted his efforts to the question of the *revelation* of the Other as such, and of the fellow human being and the face, in an ethical experience which possesses neither an intentional structure nor the manifestation of a meaning: '... one's fellow human being precisely has an *immediate* meaning, prior to any meaning one could lend to them... the auto-significance *par excellence*' (ibid.: 228). The ethical relation to the other is thus not grounded in a *Meinen*. That is, it is not grounded in an identification of the other as being this or that, or in a posited ideality. Such a relation is rather about 'contact' or proximity to an absolute singularity (ibid.: 229) which occurs without mediation by a type or ideal meaning. Ethical experience is not intentionally aimed at a transcendent object by way of a meaning. It is rather a 'reversal of subjectivity' (ibid.: 225) or an inversion of the intentional structure.

Levinasian phenomenology thus entails a radical rethinking of the primacy of the predicative *apophansis*: while it might be sufficient for the thematisation of all intentional correlates and of entities as being this or that, it seems incapable of translating the original meaning of the fellow human being as non-entity, as situated *beyond being*. If the function of the *Said* (*Dit*) or of the *logos* is to express the being or the essence of the entity through apophansis, the original language is the *Saying* (*Dire*) of ethical responsibility. The Other denotes me as being responsible, *for the other*, and in this intrigue I am stripped down to being 'an unqualifiable *one*, the pure *someone*' (Levinas 1974: 78–85/50). This *ethical henology* deprives the predicative structure of its central status; such import may only be attributed to it within the context of ontology.

4) One last place where the predicative structure is called into question is in Heidegger's later thought. As we have seen, there are two central, interrelated themes of Husserl's eidetic analysis of the predicative structure; the one is the parallel between the syntactic categories of discourse and the ontological categories of the object in general (see Simons in this volume), and the other is the relativity of the latter to regional ontologies—notably that of the material thing which has traditionally been taken as the paradigm for all entities. This parallel between the discursive structure of the proposition and the ontological structure of the object (and thus of the thing) is what Heidegger interrogates when posing the following question. Is it up to the *Satzbau*, the predicative structure of judicative structure, to serve as the paradigm for conceiving the *Dingbau*— that is, the ontological structure of the thing as substrate of properties? Conversely, does the latter constitute the model for what the former is supposed to express? (Heidegger 1950: 8; Heidegger 1984: 44) Have humans deciphered the predicative structure within things, or has it rather been transposed upon them?

There can be no doubt about the response: neither the one, nor the other! Rather than one of the structures being the paradigm or the origin of the other, there is a reciprocal relationship (*Wechselbezug*) between the two, where they have a mirror-image structure (*spiegelbildlich gebaut*). In this reciprocal co-belonging they have the same provenance 'in a common, more originary source' (*entstammen... einer gemeinsamen ursprünglicheren Quelle*) (Heidegger 1950: 9; Heidegger 1984: 46).

What is this common source? It is the *Seynsgeschichte*, as the occurring of the reciprocal appropriation of the human and of being according to diverse modalities. Each epoch of Western thought is defined by a certain understanding of the being of the entity, which is expressed both in a certain structure of truth and in an understanding of the essence of the *logos*. The same holds true for the Platonic–Aristotelean epoch; there, the entity is disclosed and understood as *Herstand* that which is pro-duced (*hervor-gebracht*) or brought-into-view or led from withdrawal to non-withdrawal—and this on the basis of an implement thought of as an *ousia* possessing an *eidos*, or as a *hylè* having a *morphè*. This is why, at the same time, the thing is conceived as a substance bearing properties, and why the proposition is conceived as the judgement about predicates of a subject (Heidegger 1950: 7, 11–12; Heidegger 1954: 160). Similarly, in our contemporary epoch, the entity is accessible as a form of *Bestand*, which makes it grounds for exploitation and extraction of energy. The entity is thematized by science as *Bestand*, on the ground of a scientific project of total domination through calculus (*Berechenbarkeit*) and systematic domination of nomological relationships of cause and effect (Heidegger 1950: 76 *sq.*; Heidegger 1954: 20 *sq.*, 51 *sq*). Correlatively, language itself becomes an available tool, which logic thematizes in function of a project of calculability, in advancing toward the mathematization of the logical calculus of propositions and predicates; the predicative structure then makes way for the connection between functions and arguments, and for the calculus of propositional variables. The primacy and diminution of predication are thus situated within a joint history of the modes of understanding of the being of the entity and of the essence of language, where discursivity and ontology occur in each epoch of Being within a reciprocal relativity.

This is without a doubt the final lesson to be drawn from the phenomenological approach to the structures of discursivity: language can never be taken as an independent and autonomous dimension; its structures remain relative to diverse levels of thematisation, which refer to domains of the entity, manners of being, and modalities of revelation. It thus appears as a *general attempt towards deformalization*.

Translated by B. Vassilicos

REFERENCES

Aristotle (1998), *Metaphysics*, tr. H. Lawson-Tancred (London: Penguin).
—— (2002), *Categories and De Interpretatione*, tr. J. L. Ackrill (Oxford: Clarendon Press).
Brentano, F. (1971), *Psychologie vom empirischen Standpunkte* (Hamburg: Felix Meiner).
Cobb-Stevens, R. (1990), *Husserl and Analytic Philosophy* (Dordrecht: Kluwer).

—— (2003), 'Husserl's theory of judgement: A critique of Brentano and Frege' in D. Fisette, (ed.), *Husserl's Logical Investigations Reconsidered* (Dordrecht: Kluwer Academic Publishers).

Føllesdal, D. (1969), 'Husserl's notion of noema', *The Journal of Philosophy* 66: 680–7.

Frege, G. (1892), 'Über Begriff und Gegenstand', *Vjschr. f. wissensch. Philosophie* 16.

Heidegger, M. (1927), *Sein und Zeit* (Tübingen: Niemeyer).

—— (1950), *Holzwege*, GA 5, hrsg. v. F.-W. von Hermann (Frankfurt: Klostermann).

—— (1954), *Vorträge und Aufsätze* (Stuttgart: Neske).

—— (1976), *Logik. Die Frage nach der Wahrheit (1925)*, GA 21, hrsg. v. W. Biemel (Frankfurt: Klostermann, 1976); tr. T. Sheehan, *Logic: The Question of Truth* (Bloomington: Indiana University Press, 2010).

—— (1984), *Die Frage nach dem Ding (1935/36)*, GA 41, hrsg. v. P. Jaeger (Frankfurt: Klostermann).

Husserl, E. (1954), *Erfahrung und Urteil* (Hamburg: Glaassen & Goverts, 1954); tr. J. S. Churchill and K. Ameriks, *Experience and Judgment* (Evanston: Northwestern University Press, 1973).

—— (1974), *Formale und transzendentale Logik*, Hua XVII, hrsg. v. P. Janssen (The Hague: Martinus Nijhoff, 1974); tr. D. Cairns, *Formal and Transcendental Logic* (The Hague: Martinus Nijhoff, 1969).

—— (1976), *Ideen zu einer reinen Phänomenologie und phänomenologischen Philosophie*, Hua III/1 (The Hague: Martinus Nijhoff Publishers, 1976); tr. F. Kersten, *Ideas pertaining to a Pure Phenomenology and to a Phenomenological Philosophy* (The Hague: Martinus Nijhoff Publishers, 1982).

—— (1984), *Logische Untersuchungen*, Zweiter Teil, Hua XIX/2, hrsg. v. U. Panzer (The Hague: Martinus Nijhoff, 1984); tr. J.N. Findlay, *Logical Investigations* (New York: Humanities Press, 1970).

—— (1996), *Logik und allgemeine Wissenschaftstheorie 1917/18*, Hua XXX, hrsg. v. U. Panzer (Dordrecht: Kluwer Academic Publishers).

—— (2003), *Neue und alte Logik. Vorlesung 1908/09*, hrsg. v. E. Schuhmann, Hua Materialienbände, Band VI (Dordrecht-New York-London: Kluwer Academic Publishers).

Kant, I. (1996), *Kritik der reinen Vernunft (1781/1787)*, in *Kants gesammelte Schriften*, hrsg. von der Königlich Preußischen Akademie der Wissenschaften, 1900 sq., Berlin: Georg Reimer, then Walter de Gruyter; tr. W. S. Pluhar, *Critique of Pure Reason* (Indianapolis: Hackett, 1996).

Levinas, E. (2006), *Autrement qu'être ou au-delà de l'essence* (Den Haag: Martinus Nijhoff, 1974); tr. A. Lingis, *Otherwise than Being, or Beyond Essence* (Pittsburgh: Duquense University Press, 2006).

—— (1982), 'Langage et proximité', in Levinas, E., *En découvrant l'existence avec Husserl et Heidegger* (Paris: Vrin), 217–36.

Lohmar, D. (2003), 'Husserl's Type and Kant's Schemata', in D. Welton (ed.), *The New Husserl. A Critical Reader* (Bloomington: Indiana University Press), 93–124.

—— (1998), *Erfahrung und kategoriales Denken* (Dordrecht: Kluwer Academic Publishers).

McIntyre, R. (1987), 'Husserl and Frege', *The Journal of Philosophy* LXXXIV: 528–35.

Mohanty, J. N. (1982), *Husserl and Frege* (Bloomington: Indiana University Press).

Mulligan, K. (2003), 'Dispositions, their bases and correlates: Meinong's analysis', in K. Kijania-Placek (ed.), *Philosophy and Logic: In Search of the Polish Tradition* (Dordrecht: Kluwer), 193–211.

Mulligan, K. (2006a), 'Facts, formal objects and ontology', in A. Bottani and R. Davies, *Modes of Existence: Papers in Ontology and Philosophical Logic* (Frankfurt: Ontos Verlag), pp. 31–46.

—— (2006b), 'Ascent, propositions and other formal objects', *Grazer Philosophische Studien* 72: 29–48.

—— (2007), 'Facts', in *Stanford Encyclopedia of Philosophy*.

—— and Hochberg, H. (2004), *Relations and Predicates, Philosophical Analysis* (Frankfurt: Ontos Verlag).

—— and Simons, P., and Smith, B. (1984), 'Truth makers', *Philosophy and Phenomenological Research* 44: 278–321; reprint in J.-M. Monnoyer (ed.), *Metaphysics and Truthmakers* (Frankfurt: Ontos Verlag, 2007).

Ortiz-Hill, C. and Rosado Haddock (2000), *G. Husserl or Frege? Meaning, Objectivity, and Mathematics* (Chicago: Open Court).

Parsons, C. (2004), 'Brentano on judgment and truth', in D. Jacquette (ed.), *The Cambridge Companion to Brentano* (Cambridge: Cambridge University Press).

Reinach, A. (1989), '*Zur Theorie des negativen Urteils' (1911)*, in *Sämtliche Werke*, Band I (München: Philosophia Verlag, 1989), pp. 95–140; tr. 'On the Theory of the negative judgment' in B. Smith, 1982 (ed.), *Parts and Moments. Studies in Logic and Formal Ontology* (München: Philosophia Verlag), pp. 315–78.

Schnieder, B. (2002), *Substanzen und ihre Eigenschaften und Adhärenz: Bolzanos Ontologie des Wirklichen* (Sankt Augustin: Academia Verlag).

Simons, P. (1995), 'Meaning and language', in B. Smith and D. W. Smith, *The Cambridge Companion to Husserl* (Cambridge: Cambridge University Press), pp. 106–37.

Skarica, M. (2004), 'El juicio predicativo simple en Frege y Husserl: una confrontacion', *Annuario Filosofico* 37/1.

Strawson, P. F. (1959), *Individuals: An Essay in Descriptive Metaphysics* (London: Methuen).

CHAPTER 18

LANGUAGE AND NON-LINGUISTIC THINKING

DIETER LOHMAR

IN this chapter I will try to establish the concept of a 'system of symbolic representation'—a term which denotes a general idea of a type of performance of which our language is only a single case. Nevertheless, this general idea is best explained with the case of language. A system of symbolic representation should enable us to form an idea of a state of affairs or of an event without having the appropriate intuition of them. Usually this thinking occurs through the means of linguistic expression. But language is only one system of symbolic representation, and we can in principle conceive of other symbolic systems of representation that have the same or nearly the same performance.

I will argue for this claim by examining Husserl's theory of meaning which is based largely on his analyses of categorial intuition—that is, of the complex acts that fulfil the specific intentions of cognition. In my view, Husserl's phenomenology offers a refined theory of meaning that serves as a basis for understanding thinking, both that which is based on language and that which is not. In other words, this theory of meaning leaves open the possibility of systems of representation for cognitive contents which employ means other than language.[1] But first we must show that humans are capable of both modes of thinking.

It is easy to see that most humans are able to think in language. Language is a system of symbolic representation that enables us to conceive of objects, states of affairs, probabilities, and their consequences. But we are not so easily convinced that a non-linguistic system of symbolic representation for cognitive contents is also functioning in our consciousness. In my view, in our everyday thinking we simultaneously use different systems of symbolic representation, among which are language, gestures, feelings, and

[1] I would like to thank Dan Zahavi for critical remarks on a former version of this chapter, and Saulius Genusias and Jacob Rump for their efforts in improving my English text. I would also like to thank an anonymous referee at Oxford University Press for many hints concerning flaws in my presentation, and also for some very useful suggestions for clarifying my argument.

scenic images.[2] I will argue for this by providing a phenomenological analysis of the non-linguistic systems functioning in our consciousness. It is especially fruitful to investigate the scenic mode of thinking we usually identify with daydreaming which is a central form of the non-linguistic mode of thinking. This will turn out to be a phylogenetically old mode of non-linguistic thinking that is still operative in our consciousness.

We might immediately note one possible consequence of this last suggestion. It is highly probable that the non-human members of the primate group are able to think using the same non-linguistic systems of representation that we use. We might also gain some insight into the performative limits of non-linguistic modes of thinking by taking into account the cases of thinking available both to humans and to animals. But in my investigation this is only a secondary theme; primarily, I am interested in the mode(s) of human thinking.

1 Cognition, thinking, and meaning

Human thinking seems to rely on conceptual language. There are some very useful phenomenological descriptions of how we think with the help of concepts. Most basic in this regard is the insight into the function of acts that are dedicated to become the ground for intuitive evidence of states of affairs. Husserl names the intuitive ground(s) of cognition *categorial acts* (I will need to return to the details of these categorial acts later). There are other, further acts that serve to connect this intuition with elements of a representational system such as language. Categorial intuition is the source of meaning, and its meaning is transferred on a symbolic intention in what Husserl names *meaning-bestowing acts* (*bedeutungsgebende Akte*). This is already an important starting point, since it suggests that language by itself is not knowledge, and that knowledge does not have a linguistic character from the very beginning.

In explaining this claim we might begin with the better-known case of using linguistic expressions to express insights. In the complex interplay of meaning-bestowing and intuitive acts providing the evidence for categorial objects, the usual first problem is to adjust the expression to the intuition—that is, to find the right expression, the expression that 'fits'. Only the correct expression will later allow others to know what state of affairs one is intuiting.[3] Often we simply know how to express our insights, but this is not

---

[2] We might tend to interpret usual gestural languages as a form of language, which is quite appropriate for the forms of national gestural language that are highly conventionalized, such as ASL, and so on. But there are also elementary, non-conventionalized forms of gestural communication using only body-related gestures, onomatopoetics, pantomimics, and pictorial symbols based on similarity semantics. I will discuss this later as hands-and-feet communication.

[3] For Husserl's theory of meaning see the I. and VI. *Logical Investigation*, Husserl (2001), and concerning its connection to the present theme Lohmar (2008b). For the theory of categorial intuition see chapter 6 of the VI. *Logical Investigation*, Husserl (2001), and Lohmar (2002).

the result of following a clear-cut procedure or being guided by rules. In trying to adjust the expression to better fit the intuition we have had, we often only *feel* that one expression is closer to 'what I had in mind'. We usually learn about the use of words and phrases in the everyday contexts of our community, and therefore we often are unable to say exactly—that is, in a rule-governed or systematic way—why one wording better fits our intended meaning than another.[4]

Let us take a look at the expressive use of language. We are able to interpret the language used by others as words and sentences that point to the intuition usually connected with the sentences used. Through this process we can usually gain a clear idea of the state of affairs at which the words and judgements aim. We do not take this state of affairs for granted from the beginning, but we know from our own experience what we will have to do to gain the requisite intuition concerning these intentions. But this also suggests that language and the intuition of states of affairs are not inseparable. Language is a certain system for representation of states of affairs. This means that we are able to create—based on the rules of language use—a representation of the cognitive intention that can be used in our own further thinking about the situation as well as become the basis for a quite reliable communication with others regarding the same state of affairs. But a commonly shared intention is not yet intuition of the speaker's intended state of affairs. Categorial intuition is, in contrast to linguistic representation, more basic, originary, and independent. With the help of language we are able to conceive a state of affairs of which we have had a previous intuition, and in thinking this is possible even in the absence of a present intuition. This revitalization of cognitive intentions (together with the option to modify the intended state of affairs and its context) is, generally speaking, the *basic function* of a system of representation. If a system of representation also allows for communication—like language does—this is an additional feature in comparison to the system's basic function.[5] We should thus address systems of representation at their basic level—that is, on the level of solitary thinkers—without directing our attention to the communicative function.

---

[4] I will come back to this theme of 'rightness' of appropriate expression. As the sign-meaning relation is based on association (as well as the relation Anzeichen–Angezeigtes), the meaning is associated with the sign used for expression, and the connection is intuitively felt; see Husserl (2001, §4). The orientation of this process of adjusting language expression to intuition of states of affairs is easily grasped in the corrections of our language expressions in cases where they do not exactly fit what we mean.

[5] To give a first motivation for the claim that thinking and language are separable (I will argue for in the whole article), let me mention four connected arguments: Phenomenological analysis points out that the basic performance of cognition (categorial intuition) is functioning independent of language-based thinking. Therefore, cognition without language is possible. Today we know that many animals have the ability for complex cognitive performances, and as reductive explanation for this ability following Morgan's canon often turns out to be much more complicated and burden more assumptions than accepting animals 'lonesome', non-communicative thinkers, there must be thinking without language in animals. In the following I will show with phenomenological means that there is a non-linguistic system of representation for cognitive contents still working in human consciousness. Thus humans are able to think without language, and they still do so. This claim should also not deny that in humans there is usually a strong influence of communication on the forms of cognition and thinking. From a developmental point of view in humans, the communicative precedes the cognitive and shapes much of it, but this does not imply that non-language thinking is impossible without this communicative influence.

In opposition to the widespread opinion that thinking is closely bound to language, I would like to show that Husserl's analyses of the relation of intuition in knowledge (categorial intuition) and the connected act of meaning-bestowing (and eventually also the use of language based on meaning-bestowing acts) leaves room for alternative conceptions. In such cases I will speak of *non-linguistic systems of symbolic representation*.

My argument relies on Husserl's conception of cognition as an independent act of intuition (categorial intuition). Under normal circumstances, meaning-bestowing acts are closely connected to these acts of categorial intuition. However, in Husserl's view, meaning-bestowing acts are not a necessary element of cognition understood as an independent intuition. Thus there remains a difference, a gap, between categorial intuition and meaning-bestowing acts—and this applies even to the case of the use of language. This difference allows for the possibility of meaning-bestowing acts performed in other symbolic mediums of expression.

An easy way to indicate a state of affairs in a symbolic way is to intend it with the help of pictorial intentions.[6] For example, my favourite soccer club wins a game and I simply pictorially recall the decisive goal, the triumphant look of the winning team and the disappointment of the others. These are not only *pictures* of memory, which may also show up without our willing them and without the intention of the decisive victory; we can also use them as *symbols* to carry a particular meaning. We do not have to use pictorial elements merely as pictures of things roughly informing us about some of their essential features. We can also use them—in a way that exceeds their pictorial representation of simple objects of perception in favour of a symbolic representation—as symbols of state of affairs: I see the captain of the team carrying the trophy, and at the same time I have the feeling of a triumph. In this pictorially-based intention we are intending not only the depicted man and the trophy (this might also be possible for a fan of the other team, but accompanied with very different feelings). The symbolic meaning goes beyond the depicted contents. It is a pictorial symbol of my team's victory.

In Husserl's theory of cognition, categorial intuition is the source of the intuitiveness of categorial intentions. Categorial intuition is a fulfilled intention of states of affairs, of relations, of insights into the causal effects of events, or of the value of an object (or its use). This intuitive intention of cognitive contents entails two functions: The ability to intend a cognitive content and to have the same content intuitively. This characterizes thinking in the broadest sense—the sense in which I will be using the term for the remainder of this essay.

Let me shortly characterize Husserl's theory of categorial intuition as it is worked out as part of his theory of knowledge in the Sixth *Logical Investigation*. Husserl's account of categorial intuition clarifies how higher-order intentions—for example, of states of affairs—are fulfilled.[7] There are different forms of categorial intuition, each of which has

---

[6] For this suggestion, see Section 3 on similarity semantics.

[7] The most important sources on the theme of categorial intuition in Husserl are Tugendhat 1970: 111–36; Sokolowski 1981: 127–41; Lohmar 1989: 44–69; Seebohm 1990: 9–47; Cobb-Stevens 1990: 43–66; Lohmar 1998: 178–273, and Lohmar 2002: 125–45.

its particular type of synthetic fulfilment.[8] Husserl's analysis is based on the difference between simple acts, such as a perception of a book, and the complex founded categorical acts that we find in all forms of cognition. According to Husserl, the respective ways of fulfilment of simple and complex acts are also different. We might see a green book and have evident intuition of this simple object of perception ('I see the green book'). Yet this intuition cannot be identified with the higher-order intention 'I see that this book is green'. To gain categorial intuition of this state of affairs calls for a series of founding acts, which Husserl describes in Paragraph 48 of the Sixth *Logical Investigation*.

We have to start with the simple perception of the green book, and then concentrate on the green colour of the book. In the transition from the first to the second intention, a registered coincidence occurs between the respective contents of these intentions. The more implicit intending of the green colour in the case of the simple perception coincides in intention and in the aspect of sensual fulfilment with the concentrated intending of the colour in the second act. On this actively constituted basis—a basis that is not only sensual but rather is a synthesis of coincidence of intentional contents of founding acts—we are able to perform a new and intuitive intention of the book being green. This is the third decisive step of the process of categorial intuition (for more details, difficulties, and possible misunderstandings of the theory of categorial intuition, see Lohmar (2002)). Thus sense perception *can* contribute to the fulfilment of categorial intentions—at least in the most simple cases—yet it does not have to, because the decisive basis for intuitivity lies in the actively produced synthesis of coincidence between intentional contents of the founding, simpler acts. Thus many objects of fulfilled categorial intuition may have only a very loose connection with sense perception, as is the case in propositions in pure mathematics and algebra.

In the most common cases of thinking we have a categorial intuition already connected with a meaning-bestowing act and mostly also with an act of expression: that is, both are closely connected—one may even say 'melded together'. But this statistically normal connection of categorial intuition with a meaning-bestowing act using language does not imply the necessity of such a connection. Besides, language need not be the representing medium used in meaning-bestowing acts. Just as we may use a language other than our mother tongue for this function, so we can also use another symbolic medium entirely.

Thus, for Husserl, the relation of categorial intuition to meaning-bestowing acts is characterized by the difference between the intuition of states of affairs and empty intentions (in humans, mostly with the help of words, but possibly also with scenic phantasma).[9] Clearly, these two types of intention are not the same, which means that

[8] In the 6. *Logical Investigation* Husserl analyzes only some basic forms of categorial intuition (identification, relations, collections, eidetic abstraction) to show that the concept of categorial intuition is justified, and that these forms can serve as a pattern for analyzing the other forms (see Husserl 2001: §§47–52).

[9] Empty intentions of states of affairs are intentions that we can have only by understanding what precisely is meant by propositions—for example, when someone utters a sentence such as 'I see a pink elephant flying by the window'. A scenic image of a pink elephant may intend this object of perception emptily, for it is only a phantasma and not perception.

language should only be a *true and faithful expression* of categorial intentions ('*treuer Ausdruck*', Husserl 1984: 313). But already, the fact that I have to interpret this relation as a *norm* or a *rule* reveals that such truthfulness and faithfulness is not guaranteed in every case. Sometimes we distinctively realize the difficulty of adjusting judgements regarding language use to the evidence in intuition. Husserl coins a special concept of truth for exactly this relation between expression and intuition. We are striving towards *rightness* ('*Richtigkeit*'), which means appropriateness between categorial intuition and expression. Thus rightness designates the degree of appropriateness of an expression to the intuitively given cognition. (As a consequence we find a crucial difference from the prevalent way of considering such issues in analytical philosophy[10]: Cognition is here much more closely bound to intuition in the special form of categorial intuition than to the propositional forms characteristic of linguistic expression.) The aim of rightness of expression is a one-way striving: The expression should be made appropriate to the intuitively given cognition. This intuition is the guiding principle for my striving to rightness (see Husserl 1969: §46). In contrast to the dependent appropriate expression, categorial intuition is a primary and independent givenness.

The norm of rightness for expressions of intuitive cognition serves to guarantee the most important function of expression in my own thinking: The rightness of the appropriate symbolic expression of intuitive cognition should allow me to think about exactly the same insight on another occasion (and this time not intuitively but in the form of an empty intention). In regards to external and public communication, this norm demands that the right external expression would allow another person to *emptily* think exactly

---

[10]   An important exception is the impressive book of Bermudez (2008), which begins with the insight that there must be ways of representing cognitive contents in non-linguistic creatures. However, Bermudez's detailed theories of thinking in non-linguistic animals call for a more extended discussion, which I cannot provide in the present context (I have to refer to my forthcoming monograph *Denken ohne Sprache*). Here I will mention only a single item. Some of his theses about the principal limitations of non-linguistic thought seem to me not to be acceptable. He denies that there might be meta-representational thought in non-linguistic animals, because in his view there is no possible working alternative to symbolically represent it (no vehicle). The only alternatives he discusses are pictorial representations that revolve around the idea of analogical representation of states of affairs in something like mental models and mental maps (Bermudez 2008: 160–3). His interpretation of such pictorially-based alternatives for the representation of cognitive contents understands them as a covered version of linguistic metarepresentation—that is, he thinks the structure of this model is derived from linguistic thinking (Bermudez 2008: 163). His conclusion is that metarepresentation can be performed only by creatures who use language. This claim calls for the support of empirical evidence, suggesting that metarepresentation is possible for some animals (see Hampton 2001; Smith, Shields, and Washburn 2003; Smith 2009; and Hampton 2009).

Besides, the models for pictorial representation which Bermudez is discussing are too simple. The representation of cognitive contents cannot be done in single pictures, but asks for complex scenic phantasma, like video clips. The reason for this seems to me to lie in the complex structure of categorial intuition, which requires a series of different intentions. Another objection is that if you take feelings to be within the realm of possible symbolic functions, then the feeling of certainty/uncertainty accompanying a scenic-phantasmatic representation of a state of affairs can easily function as meta-cognition.

the same what I *intuitively* thought earlier. And most importantly, this norm not only holds for language but for every medium of expression.[11]

In regard to this last insight we seem to be allowed to make another step in generalizing the function of a true and faithful reestablishment of the cognition intended in all its single elements and traits. The symbolic expression of a cognition should allow one to once again *think* the same insight—either only by me in solitary thinking or, in the case of public communication, also by others. This quite general description of a principal function cannot determine whether it is language or another symbolic medium that has to be used to reach this aim. This allows us to recognize very clearly the basic, primary, and independent performance of categorial intuition.[12] Thus it turns out to be a question of second order, which particular symbolic medium is used to fulfil the demands for the function of thinking.

The expression of categorial intuition can use different means. I will address three types in terms of their function and their characteristic limitations. This list does not claim completeness.

1. Language and codified gesture languages (ASL...).
2. Non-codified gestures together with mimics and pantomimics—a kind of hands-and-feet communication system to which I will return soon.

These first two modes can be employed in communication as well as in solitary thinking.

3. Scenic phantasma of past and future events combined with feelings. These are suitable for the representation in solitary thinking, but they cannot be used for public communication.

Scenic phantasma are found in our nightly dreams as well as in daydreams (see Lohmar 2008a: chapters 9 and 12). In daydreams, as they occur in relaxed situations, scenic phantasma emerge like short video clips that give rise to feelings and co-feelings connecting short scenes in a kind of story. A close analysis will reveal that they are part of the non-linguistic system of symbolic representation still operative in humans. The emergence of scenic phantasma may be only momentary, like single views of something meaningful, but even then phantasma have narrative elements. They are scenic images or 'characteristic scenes' that are enriched by emotions and valuations; they entail intentions of co-present other persons, their valuations, and co-feelings of their emotions. For example, I may be immersed in my everyday activities with self-confident optimism and suddenly notice a phantasmatic appearance of my friend, looking at me skeptically

---

[11] This is also the case for other ways of expression. What is presupposed is a mutual interest in the communication of contents. Both sides must be oriented to such social norms, otherwise it will not work (see also Tomasello 2008).

[12] We might suppose that at least in the second step of a categorial intuition—for example, focusing on the colour of an object—the necessary function of language is already involved. This may often be the case with language-using subjects, but 'it ain't neccessarily so'. I tend to believe that the phenomenological analysis of categorial intuition is useful with humans and with non-linguistic creatures alike, in realizing, for example, that a fruit has a certain colour indicating that it is ripe and tasty.

as if he is going to say: 'this is not a good way to act; think it over.' Co-performing his emotional valuing, I correct my naively optimistic view of my inconsiderate plans and change my course of action. Scenic phantasma are not to be thought of as though they were objects of their own through which other objects are depicted; they are more like experiential scenes that appear in the same way as when the person is really looking at me. Thus—somehow—I am also there, right in the scene, but as the *spectator* who is incorporated, perhaps only implicitly, in his special perspective on that scene. Most scenic phantasma are not voluntary, as is easily seen when visual images suddenly impose themselves upon us.

Before I go into the details of non-linguistic systems of representation I would like to summarize what we know about the relation between the intuition of states of affairs and the different modes of symbolic representation which we might use to think about them.

Generally, the connection between language and thinking is not as strict and inflexible as we tend to believe. Not only can we express our insights in different languages while still thinking in the medium of our mother tongue, but we can also *think* in a language other than our mother tongue. Most of us are familiar with the following experience. After spending some days in a foreign country, where a foreign language is spoken with which we are well familiar, our thinking takes the form of this other language. This example suggests that the level of language is quite on the surface of the whole phenomenon of thinking, symbolic representation, and expression. This is in accordance with what we already know from the phenomenological analysis of cognition. The most basic level of cognition is intuition, and on the next level there are the meaning-bestowing acts and expressions.

Regarding the loose connection between thinking about cognitive contents and language, we might ask ourselves, counterfactually, that perhaps categorial intuition is primary and independent to such an extent that there is no real need for a symbolic medium to represent the information and to enable the hypothetical manipulation of intuitive cognition. But this is not the case. In fact, we can hold on to the intuition of states of affairs only for a short time. After this time we must have a symbolic medium to hold on to the contents of our cognition. In using a symbolic medium, the intuition transforms itself either into a firm conviction (which also obtains a symbolic form) that this state of affairs is the case, or into a modal modification of this conviction.[13] This is just as true for the hypothetical manipulation of future states of affairs, which we embark upon while thinking through our options. This characterizes the *narrow sense of thinking*.

We have seen that a symbolic carrier of a conviction is the presupposition for the three essential performances of thinking in this narrow sense: (1) the ability to awaken and to retain in mind the same object of cognition, (2) the ability to engender further cognitions stemming from this one, (3) the ability to manipulate our future possibilities (and also ponder different hypotheses concerning the course of history in the past). These

---

[13] Remember that both need not to have a linguistic form. A pictorial symbol combined with a feeling would work just as well.

central performances allow me to manipulate the possible future of an object or event in different situations, to ponder possible consequences of, and obstacles and solutions to, problems. Essentially, thinking is an active treatment of the contents of our cognition.

This requires that thinking has a medium of symbolic representation. The latter, however, need not be language. Yet language gives us a hint at the most important feature of such a system of symbolic representation. I must be able to produce the material carriers of symbols at any time: for example, I must be able to produce spoken or written words at any time either in public speech or in inner speech. I am only able to think if the symbolic carrier is ready at hand at all times. This carrier must achieve its meaning in a meaning-bestowing act based on the intuitive cognition. This is true for language as for all other non-linguistic systems of representation. In this regard also the use of non-linguistic symbols follows the pattern presented in Husserl's theory of meaning.

Thus we may conclude what we already know. Language is a useable carrier of cognitive meaning. It makes thinking and also public communication possible, because I can speak aloud (or write) at any time. And in regard to inner thinking, I can let my inner voice function as the carrier of thought. But our conclusions can also go beyond this trivial insight, because we now know at least one general feature of symbolic systems used in thinking. I must be able to produce the carrier of symbols at any time—either in inner or in outer sensibility. Thus there can also be internal carriers of meaning that allow for thinking but usually do not allow for public communication.[14] And there may also be symbolic carriers that allow for both, such as language, gestures, and pantomime. But it is obvious that language need not be the carrier in all these cases; there are always alternatives.[15]

2 A PHENOMENOLOGICAL ACCESS TO NON-LINGUISTIC SYSTEMS OF REPRESENTATION

What alternative symbolic carriers of meaning do we have? Our non-complete list was: codified gesture-language, non-codified gestures together with pantomime and onomatopoeisis (the hands-and-feet system of communication already mentioned), and

---

[14] We might suspect that sometimes this kind of internal phantasma may also allow for public forms of communication by allowing for the creation of a film, a picture, or a sculpture with this pictorial message.

[15] At other places I have discussed arguments supporting the idea that there must be necessarily non-linguistic systems of representation in humans and also in higher primates. The arguments go back to human evolution and dual-process theories designed to better understand the remarkable mental abilities of primates. This supports the hypothesis that humans and primates share a common low-level mode of thinking. Thus we feel the demand to make clear why humans have highly-developed culture, science, techniques, and computers, while primates do have cultures but no such refined techniques (see Lohmar 2010).

scenic phantasma together with emotions. In the following I will concentrate on the last two systems, and end by working out some striking similarities between them.

Let us start with the *hands-and-feet system of communication*. A simple example will show us that we usually underestimate our ability to communicate with gestures and pantomime. Imagine being in a foreign country, not being able to speak the local language, and having to go to the airport. I meet a taxi driver whom I need to inform about my urgent wish, but without the use of the local language. In a situation like this one, I immediately start communicating my wishes with the help of gestures, onomatopoetic means, and pantomime. I point to the driver and mimic turning the steering wheel, I imitate the sound of the car, and then, after pointing to myself, I pantomime running with luggage, and finally make the gesture and imitate the sound of a starting plane.[16]

This behaviour is quite revealing of our non-linguistic systems of representation. We start without any hesitation, literally without further thinking, and we are very certain about our attempt to communicate in this way. This unreflected certainty reveals that this non-linguistic mode of communication is all the time alive while we use language, for we do not have to wonder about the 'how' of this gestic–pantomimic–onomatopoetic communication.[17] We do not question whether it will work; we simply use it. Somehow we are behaving as if we have tacitly used this kind of communication all along. It works with people of other cultures, of higher or lower degree of development, and it can easily be corrected and refined because we are already in a context of common actions, which allows for an ongoing mutual correction. To understand our trust in our non-linguistic abilities of communication we might also think about the situation in which ethnologists meet a tribe that speaks an unknown language. In such a situation we begin with common human practices such as eating, drinking, and sleeping, allowing for mutual correction in such a way that there will be not much concern about the meaning of 'gavagai'.

Such non-conventionalized forms of preliminary communication are always exceptional and transitory; usually a codified system of communication will be established quite soon in common practice. Either gestures or elements of both languages will be used and mutually accepted, and thereby a new and connecting convention established. This is part of universal anthropology. Rules for everything are established spontaneously through communication in every community. Thus the non-conventionalized 'beginning' forms of communication quickly put an end to themselves. We will return to this theme later.

---

[16] The functioning of these natural gestures presupposes a big realm of commonly shared knowledge about our life-world. Tomasello (2008) gives a comprehensive overview of the rich functions and meanings of human natural gestures on the background of the human tendency to cooperate, and the framework of social norms that develops from this constellation.

[17] At this place it might be reasonable to draw a distinction between non-linguistic systems of representation for thinking and such systems for communication, but later we will see that they share a common similarity semantics. Moreover, if we inquire into the relation between them it seems likely that the more basic system is the scenic-phantasmatic system for solitary thinking, enabling us to use iconic gesturing and pantomimics for communication.

But this is only an example of a non-linguistic system of representation used for public communication. Now I would like to turn to non-linguistic modes of internal thinking that are only useful for solitary thinkers and that can unfold in the absence of any communication.

It seems to us that in daydreaming we are using scenic phantasma as expressions of our wishes and fears, and that they function as representations of cognitive contents. It is always a state of affairs that we wish for or are in fear of. But we do not simply express our preferences, our urgent wishes, and our views of the state of affairs by this means alone. It will turn out that daydreaming is also a kind of response to this problem, a mental action, a mental manipulation of the problematic situation that might lead to a solution until now unthought. In my view, daydreaming is a phylogenetically old mode of thinking which is still operative in our consciousness.

To work out this hypothesis we will have to ignore for a while numerous theories about the status of phantasy in daydreaming. We might object to this very reasonable interpretation of daydreaming from different points of view. From a *liberal-phantasy point of view* our phantasy is usually completely *free* in the formation of daydreams, and therefore cannot be of any use when it comes to the serious and important problems of everyday life. But some sobre reflection and self-observation will convince us that we are not completely free in the formation of our daydreams. From a *psychoanalytic point of view* we might suppose that all the contents of our daydreams are closely bound to our individual experiences and passions, just as our nightly dreams are *passively bound* to them. From a *part–part point of view* we might suspect that we are *free* in the formation of our positive and pleasurable daydreams, but *passive* in the formation of our daydreams about lasting fears. This is not the case either: in both cases we experience ourselves as bound.

In daydreams we are playing out possible solutions to a problem—that is, we are mentally testing our options, their usefulness for a solution, and their respective consequences. This life of scenic phantasma constitutes a great and important part of our conscious life, no matter how rarely we reflect on this fact. Here are a few examples known to everyone. Worries about urgent challenges or uncertainties arising in the form of worrisome scenes that make us sleepless at night. There are many phantasies of having success. I would also like to mention empirical–psychological research that suggests that most adult males periodically think of sex, and the mode of this thinking is definitely not conceptual. In these scenic episodes of our conscious life, the linguistic expressions fade into the background in favour of pictorial elements.[18] I am not denying that we can also think about our wishes and problems with the help of language and that in daydreams the linguistic and non-linguistic elements are often merged, but I want to stress that in daydreaming we are also using non-linguistic systems of representation.

We also know that most more highly developed mammals can dream. They show first signs of an attempt to act and of emotions in the phases of their sleep which we interpret

---

[18] See Cameron and Biber (1973); Hicks and Leitenberg 2001. The shifting background of language is also to be found in nightly dreams (see Symons 1993).

as dreamed episodes prolonging wakeful states of action and aims. Higher cerebralized mammals are also capable of daydreaming: they can identify events with relative precision and often visually replay difficult situations they were confronted with or they expect to be confronted with again in the future. But these theses need to be corroborated by empirical research, and I have to confess that I did not think it likely that there were serious researchers in neurology interested in the daydreams of animals. I was surprised to find out that in the last few years there has been some intensive research in this field, although daydreams have not been the explicit subject matter of this research from the very beginning. We might nonetheless take a look at recent research in the so-called *replay events* in the hippocampus of mammals (mostly rats) with the method of single neuron tracing. In the beginning, these investigations revolved around the hypothesis that short-term memory is somehow fixated or consolidated in long-term memory with the help of these replays in the hippocampus. But we will see that these experiments also allow for an interpretation of such replays in terms of daydreams and their careful modifications useful for planning future action.

The method of these experiments is single neuron tracing, which allows for a statistically reliable identification of some quite simple contents of conscious ideas. In most studies the neuronal activity in small regions of the hippocampus of rats seeking to orient themselves in different kinds of mazes is analyzed, for example, in simple mazes that have only few characteristic regions: A, B, C, and D. The first results emphasized that the factually experienced course of events is replayed in rats not only in dream states (Wilson and McNaughton 1994; Skaggs and McNaughton 1996), but also in relaxed wakeful states (Foster and Wilson 2006). The situation in which replay events occur was shown to be widely independent of the original occasion (Davidson *et. al.* 2009; Karlsson and Frank 2009). Further findings suggest that there is a synchronous parallel activity in visual centres, so that we might interpret the replays as a kind of visual replay activity (Ji and Wilson 2007)—a kind of daydreaming. More refined experimental arrangements show that the order of wakefully replayed events is not fixed; it can occur in the form of forward as well as backward replays (Foster and Wilson 2006; Diba and Buzsáki 2007; Davidson *et. al.* 2009). Thus a *modification* of such allegedly only reproductive 'replays' is possible (in my understanding this is something we have to expect from daydreams that are useful for planning). If the design of the maze was changed into a combination of two mazes overlapping in part, it was even possible to find (re-)plays (I think it is reasonable to avoid the reproductive implications of 'replay' from this point on) that referred to an alternative paths through the maze, and there were even (re-)plays of routes that the animals had never experienced before (Gupta *et al.* 2010; Derdikmann and Moser 2010). All of this is not a proof for the hypothesis that animals are using scenic visualization for thinking about and planning activities, but it does encourage this hypothesis, and offers a point of access for further research that might explore this question more closely.

We might therefore claim that a system of representation combined with scenic phantasma, and with feelings, is operative in dreams and wakeful states in higher cerebralized mammals up to primates in the same way as in humans. This claim, however, is only an important consequence of my investigations into the different systems of representation in humans. But nevertheless, this hypothesis about animal thinking is not mere fancy or an arbitrary phantasy, because, as the phenomenological analysis reveals, it characterizes an important dimension of our own thinking. Therefore, through these analyses we might find out in which ways we are still thinking like animals. In the present analysis I will not concentrate further on the theme of animal thinking. The evidence for such hypotheses stems not only from the phenomenology of human consciousness but also from other methods and other sciences.

We might also ask ourselves: is it still phenomenology? It might appear that we have strayed too far from the centre of phenomenological research. But a glimpse at Husserl's theory of pre-predicative experience makes it clear that we have not; one of the reasons why such experience is named pre-predicative is that we can have it without language (for a discussion of pre-predicative experience, see Lohmar 1998: pp. 6, 7).

Another important element of non-linguistic systems of representation are *feelings*, functioning, for example, in the framework of scenic phantasma. In my view we cannot interpret emotions as an independent system of representation, because we always have to presuppose another kind of representation in which we have in mind the things or (possible) events that are the object of feelings. Emotions can easily satisfy the most important requirements for a system of representation, for we can have them in an actual situation and we can also 'produce' them (although not arbitrarily) in the absence of the intuitive situation—that is, through the imagination alone. For example, the feeling of fury might move me violently in a certain situation; yet the same feeling can also reappear in my mere thinking of the same situation later on. In both cases the feeling 'tells' me something about the value of the event; it is a part of my inner 'expression', which has a certain meaning. In thinking about a nice experience, the pleasant feeling 'means' the desirable quality of the event.[19]

Let us take a short look at animals in this regard. Most animals have feelings as part of their systems of representation. Therefore, we might suppose that it makes no sense to have objects and properties of these objects if you do not have feelings with which to evaluate these objects and events, because this is the way to actively make use of your experiences with them. The limbic system which—as far as we know—processes most of our feelings lies in a layer between cerebellum and cerebrum. Thus from a speculative point of view inspired by brain physiology, we might suspect that feeling is part of the most basic system of representation—and that it is definitely phylogenetically more basic than language. But now back to humans.

Daydreams perform, in their own way, a consistent representation of our everyday longings, wishes, and fears. They somehow mirror our personal ordering of significance on the continuum between those events that should never happen and those that should happen at any cost. And they do not require a refined psychoanalytical hermeneutics.

---

[19] We should keep in mind that there is another aspect that can be partly expressed by feeling: the dimension of time. Fearing an event points to the future character of an event, regret to the past character.

Daydreams differ strongly from nightly dreams, in that they respect causality, the identity of objects, and their order in time. Also, from this point of view, they can be accepted as a 'reasonable' activity of thinking, dedicated to serious problems of past, present, and future reality.

The framework of our order of relevance for possible events also helps us to better understand why certain daydreams must be experienced over and over again as long as the urgent needs, tasks, and oppressing fears they reflect remain the same and unaltered. But daydreams do not repeat everything unaltered; we have to be attentive to small modifications in these repetitions that represent real options in real action.

To give an example: had I been pressed hard by an impertinent and aggressive person, and had I given way to his demands due to the circumstances, this annoying situation would re-emerge in my daydreams many times. But this repetition of daydreams is not always identical. Sober reflective self-observation makes me realize small variations of my behaviour, and quite slowly, with further replays, it can lead me to the right solution to get rid of his aggressive demands. This would have been the right reaction; had I done this, it would have stopped him! Although this insight is irreal, accompanied by a regretful feeling, and it cannot change the past, it nevertheless is a kind of action on future reality. It enables me in a similar situation, if it were to recur, to act appropriately and to resist the unjust demands.[20] The same is true for events that I am anxiously expecting.

Therefore, the scenic-phantasmatic mode of daydreams allows for an interpretation of daydreaming as a phylogenetically old but still operative mode of thinking. If I am worried in the mode of daydreaming, then things and persons are occurring in pictorial representations, and language is shifting into the background. The content of my worries is represented in scenic phantasma, but every time with small modifications. And in these modifications we sometimes realize successful solutions to our problems. For example, winning a lottery will easily solve pressing financial concerns—but it is unlikely to happen, and does not give me a feeling of confidence. Working hard or suffering for some time from some privations will work as well, and this idea gives me much more confidence in its success. This clearly shows the function of daydreaming as a nonlinguistic mode of thinking that can, so to speak, lead to solutions for everyday problems. Additionally, it points out that daydreaming should not be identified with an evasive regression to a childish mode of handling problems.[21]

---

[20] The result of this active manipulation of the future is a kind of ideal picture of the solution of problems such as this one under given circumstances. Nevertheless, the result of the sucessful manipulation of a flop (reframing) is often communicated afterwards untruly as a story to cover my failure to stand the unjust criticism of my boss, a confrontation in traffic, and so on.

[21] We might also stress that non-linguistic modes of thinking in the scenic-phantasmatic system are not as quick and effective as linguistic modes of thinking; it will always take some repetitions to find a way to solve the problem, even if the scenic representation of an event is running in a compressed speed-mode.

Despite my insistence on the reasonable character of non-linguistic modes of thinking, I do not deny that we, humans, in turning back from our inner life of scenic phantasma to other members of our group, immediately switch to a linguistic mode of communication. This shift, however, only expresses what was already found at the level of non-linguistic thinking.

Seen from a systematic point of view, there is only a limited set of themes that a given community—for example, primates living in groups—has to be able to think about. This list includes: 1) objects, their present and future states and use (for example as tools), as well as their value in my personal estimation and their value in the view of the community—that is, cultural value; 2) events in present, past, and future, their felt value, and their probable consequences; 3) other persons with their sensations, feelings, and convictions, and their practical intentions related to myself and other members of the group. I hope that I can leave it to you to find examples for the first two themes so that I can concentrate on the last group: that of the intentions of other persons.

It seems difficult to imagine a scenic image of a person's character and of his or her probable behaviour towards me, especially within complex constellations involving others. But scenic phantasma offer a simple solution to this apparent difficulty. In remembering a brutal former classmate, I see his face looking at me with evil eyes, with clenched fists, and ready to give me a beating. But this 'image' is not simply an image of him; it is a characteristic scene within which I am present, writhing with pain from his beating and in fear of his further beatings, and in the presence of a group of friends in the background not helping me. This scene presents central aspects both of his character and of his future behaviour within a social context.

Scenic presentation of the attitude and behaviour of a person need not be so one-dimensional as in the case mentioned, since normally there are multiple facets of the character of other persons that we are able to present. Thus the question arises: how can I think a multitude of (changing) attitudes in a scenic mode? Think of a colleague with whom you work together successfully in most cases, but who occasionally appears with an air of high-nosed arrogance. Both 'faces'—both aspects of his character—may be represented in a scenic phantasma, one after the other, or even as mixed in a changing way, which results in an uncertain basis for your plan-making. The modal character of possibility and uncertainty is thus present in the changing and merging faces of your colleague. We might interpret this changing image as a non-linguistic form of the logical 'or'. The colleague's attitude towards other persons and his options in a changing situation may be represented in a short but eloquent side-view to others, and so on.

Since the value and the usefulness of objects can change, this may also be reflected in characteristic scenes. For instance, if I own a car that usually breaks down and thus has to be towed away and repaired, the characteristic scene within which I am positively excited about my car is modified, and converted to one that is negative. The emotional aspects of this bad experience are especially mirrored in the scene characterizing the object: I no longer imagine the car with the joyful expectation of reliable use, but with the cheerless expectation of future harm, expense, and inconvenience. In this way, the variations of characteristic scenes—that is, characterizing persons, objects, or events—unfold by means of similar representations.[22]

So far I have discussed scenic phantasma in daydreams as a special system of representation and modification, characterizing this process as a still-functioning 'phylogenetically old mode of thinking' employed by humans and probably also by mammals up to primates. As a phenomenologist I cannot go further, for the empirical proof that primates are thinking in the mode of scenic phantasma must be provided by other sciences—for example, by experimental psychology or neuroscience.

Through our analyses the significance of language for human thinking is delimited in a clear way. Language is far from being the only possible means of thinking, and, moreover, it is not the only system of representation operative in human consciousness. It seems probable that the most basic performances of cognition and our conception of reality are based on simpler, non-linguistic systems of representation that are still operative in our minds. Public language and the concepts it uses turn out to be only a very superficial layer of the whole performance of thinking.

3 On similarity semantics in non-linguistic systems of representation

Allow me to add some further remarks to my theses concerning scenic-phantasmatic modes of thinking.

In this essay I have concentrated on establishing the idea of non-linguistic thinking in humans. But remember our other example—that of non-linguistic hands-and-feet communication using non-codified gestures, mimics, pantomime, onomatopoeisis, and other means such as hand-theatre. I would suggest that all humans are able to use these non-linguistic systems of representation. But then we may ask: is there a special way in which humans *learn* how to use these two non-linguistic systems of representation (that is, hands-and-feet communication and the scenic-phantasmatic system), or are these abilities somehow '*innate*'? Faced with the difficulties posed by these alternatives, it seems worthwhile to reflect on the common character of these two non-linguistic systems.

---

[22] Besides my emotional valuing of objects and events, I can also have a scenic phantasma which entails valuing reactions of others to my planned future actions. If I am pondering problematic plans for my future behaviour, suddenly close friends or relatives may show up in the characteristic scene, somehow looking sorrowfully at me, but also perhaps with sympathy. Through this, the valuation of my planned actions in the view of the community is articulated. This means that even persons sympathizing with me have serious considerations. Their expressions of sympathy and worry at the same time give me an important hint about the valuing and probable reactions of others with regard to my plans.

To start with, let us take a step back and try to find the common structure of these two systems of representation. We recognize that both ways of representing ideas have one important element in common: both use a *similarity semantics*. That is, all means of representation, all symbols in these two non-linguistic systems of representation, are somehow 'similar' to the objects they represent.

It is important to stress that not all non-linguistic systems of representation work on the basis of similarity semantics. There are also non-linguistic systems with a semantics based on conventions. From the age of a few weeks up to one year, human infants are starting to communicate intensively with the persons to whom they relate most closely—usually the mother. Daniel Stern has carried out some intriguing investigations into the mode of this early mother–child communication—that which serves as a base for all later forms of social interaction (see Stern 1977, and Stern 1990). During this early phase, mother and child are intensively engaged in simple social games such as peek-a-boo or tickling-the-belly-with-announcement and the like. Through this practice they are developing the basic patterns of communication which later will enable the child to initiate social interaction, to maintain it, and to modify it, but also to end it and to avoid it. The most important aspect of this form of communication is the extensive looking at each other. With the help of extensive mimicking, the modulation of the voice, and body movements, forms and contents of communication are learned: the invitation for play, the wish for prolongation, pretended surprise as a means to initiate a social interaction, affirmation, critique, scepticism, love, or a sorrowful frowning together with a turning away of the head that serves to end the interaction. In intimate mother–child communication, humans learn how to understand and how to use this pre-linguistic *language of the look*.

In later phases, after the first sixth months, this intimate interaction between mother and child will be extended to include more elements—mostly objects. The child looks at an object—for example, a hot flat-iron—which appears to him to be an attractive new toy, and then looks back to his mother to ensure that she is looking at and attending to this toy as well. In this second look (ensuring the shared attention on the object) the child can learn from the mother's facial expression about her attitude toward the object. Her look from the toy back to the baby may signal fear and concern, but if it is a harmless toy perhaps also encouragement to use the toy. If the mother is contracting her eyebrows and her nostrils are contracted, this signalizes that this object is dangerous. But perhaps she draws up her eyebrows and opens her mouth in pleased astonishment: You should try it!

We see that this object-directed communication entails a kind of triangularization between the child, the common object, and the mother. In this central mode of early communication on objects, new elements of meaning are first encountered. Most importantly, there are also valuations on the basis of the mother's own experiences, and there are also incorporated valuations stemming from the community. For example, if the mother nervously checks whether someone else is observing the behaviour of her child, this gives the clear message that this is not accepted by the others. Triangularization and the valuation of actions may rest upon on the semantics of early look-communication, but this ability is also a result of extensive training—of shared intentionality in the early forms of social interaction between mother and child.[23]

But let us now return to the two systems of representation based on similarity semantics, the scenic-phantasmatic system and the hands-and-feet system of communication. Admittedly, this is quite an unusual characteristic of semantics, which introduces an important difference that separates it from the semantics of natural languages. To clarify this point, I will turn to the very basics of semantics of usual languages. This characterization does not entail anything new.

In the normal semantics of national languages it takes a long time to *learn the connection* of a language sign and its meaning so as to be able to understand and to speak the language. *Learning* the normal semantics of usual languages rests on the relation of *contiguity*. As Hume puts it, contiguity is a relation established on several equal occasions where one object occurs together with another object in close temporal and/or spatial relations. This process might also be enforced by *normative activities* of a social group or a single person within this group. These normative activities are usually very simple. For instance, they correspond with the strong wish of a child to learn and adjust to the communication used by adults. As the child is learning the use of language, there may be several instances of seeing an object, upon each of which the parents name the object 'cow'. Perhaps they also correct the child for wrongly addressing the cow as a 'bow-wow'. Thus, normal semantics is always related to a community that agrees in *conventions* and acts in a *normative* way such that meanings are reliably connected with expressions. This *convention-and-contiguity semantics*, resting on agreement and conventions, is always to a certain extent artificial. It differs from neighbouring national (that is, related to the birthplace and the community) languages because of regional circumstances and also because it is part of our identity—that is, it is not only a distinct sign of my belonging to a particular community, but also indicates the difference of mine from the other communities. We have to *learn* all the semantic rules by heart before we are able to understand a particular language, and no single person could ever discover, in isolation, the concrete connections that bind words and objects.

By contrast, the *similarity semantics* of non-linguistic systems of representation neither rests on agreement nor on rules accepted by a communicating community.[24] In this

---

[23] Michael Tomasello has done much comparative research on the ability of joint attention in young humans and in primates (see Tomasello 1995; Tomasello *et al.* 2005; Tomasello and Carpenter 2007). The central characteristic of joint attention is that two persons are directed to an object or event and are informing one another about this object, and trying to be sure that the other is directed to the same object and is aware the other is aware of the object too. Tomasello wants to find a principal difference in the abilities of humans and primates, and what becomes obvious in his experimental research on joint attention is that this ability is very strong in human children—starting around the age of 9 months to a year—and quite weak in primates. But if we look at this difference from the point of view of Daniel Stern, this big difference may be more due to the fact that young human children have just undergone nearly one-year intensive training in joint attention.

[24] The relation of similarity seems to be very easy. We tend to believe that we are able to simply 'perceive' similarities—for example, between father and son, trees and sheep, and so on. As phenomenologists we are also convinced that this ability is the basic performance which establishes the intuition of common traces in a certain type of thing, as in trees (*Wesensschau*). But this does not imply

regard it is much more 'natural': it is based on the similarity of the sign to the object it designates.

Let us examine the hands-and-feet system of communication. If I imitate carrying a briefcase and running, it looks similar to the corresponding real event. If I imitate the sound and the movement of an aircraft it is similar to the sound and appearance of this event. This is the reason why I do not need to be trained in hands-and-feet communication. It rests on a *natural similarity semantics*, and not on *an artificial convention-and-contiguity semantics*.[25]

Let us now consider the system of scenic phantasma in thinking. We can see that the scenic-phantasmatic system of representation in solitary thinking (daydreaming) also uses natural similarity semantics. As we have already seen, this kind of thinking has either no, or only a few, linguistic elements, and is capable of directly (re)presenting its meaning. My daydreams imitate the actual event I am thinking of, as the following examples suggest.

The President of the Nobel Prize committee is approaching me, congratulating me, and handing over the award, and all of my colleagues are applauding and cheering (the last part, at least, will definitely never happen). But what about kissing Claudia Schiffer? I can almost feel her body, and even smell the new Lagerfeld fragrance in her hair—at least, it is quite similar. But now let us desist with the nice examples and come back to our systematic considerations.

Perhaps we should also take a look at the syntax side of these two non-linguistic systems of representation. For this task, the earlier example with the cab-driver may to be too simple. We should at least expect hands-and-feet communication to be able to tell a story of the past or future, of someone who is acting and another who is suffering. We can also indicate this in the hands-and-feet system. Think of a communication of two human hunters in the old days before the emergence of language—a classical genre even in our times. In this situation I may use my hands for pointing at the sun, to indicate to the other my hunting success in the early morning. I can indicate the time by moving my pointing hand from the present location of the sun backwards to the point where it rises in the morning. I can also use my hands as a kind of hand-puppets, indicating the rabbits I saw; and I can also pantomime my seeing the rabbits and the triumph of successfully shooting them with my bow, and so on.

This small piece of pantomime, onomatopoetics, mimics, and hand-puppet theatre will inform others very precisely about what has happened in the morning, what

that the facility of recognizing similarity is itself already established in children of the earliest age. This would also be a theme worth investigating in developmental psychology, which I cannot do here. My opinion in this regard is the following. We are able to establish our facilities to recognize and to actively use similarity through experience. That means that we can learn about similarity relations because we have some basic ability to recognize similar elements in different objects. But we do not have to learn from others how to use this ability.

[25] I agree that in this situation there is also presupposed a basic similarity of our life-worlds: for example, that there are airports, cabs, drivers, and so on. But I do not consider this to be problematic.

happened yesterday, or what will happen tomorrow. The function of syntax in a system of representation is to inform us about such issues as who the acting person is, on which object he is acting, who suffers from which action, when the action has happened or will happen, and so on. All these questions can be answered by means of non-linguistic hands-and-feet communication, on the basis of similarity semantics (and the same is true for the phantasmatic system of thinking to oneself). I can 'see' who is acting on what, even if this is mediated by similarity semantics. Moreover, as far as the dimension of time is concerned, we find a narrative structure capable of indicating the internal order of the phantasmatic scenes.[26] Thus the task of syntax is also fulfilled. And all these performances can occur on the basis of a quite simple similarity semantics.

We are always able to start communicating by means of hands-and-feet communication, because it does not rest on an artificial contiguity semantics. But—as already mentioned—we never remain in the transitory state of a beginning communication system, otherwise it would be difficult to understand why such a system has not been long established as a widespread and long-lasting, quite basic, but nevertheless universal, system of communication. What is the reason for this? The reason is simply the fact that communicating communities are always living in a realm of norms and values—that is, they strive to establish rules for all kinds of activities—including communication. Therefore, if communication is established in the mode of hands-and-feet communication (or in another way), then there will be conventions and rules established for it, enforced and conserved by tradition. That means that it will be transformed into a *regional gesture language* only understood here in this community, with a mixture of conventional signs and several elements that mirror its offspring in similarity semantics. This is the state of today's gesture languages. Thus, the use of the 'arch language' of hands-and-feet communication will change very quickly to a usual, normal, and codified language with partly artificial semantic rules. This is an unavoidable fate of hands-and-feet 'arch language' based on similarity semantics.

But now we have to solve another puzzle. If the 'arch language' of similarity semantics will always be overwritten in public communication and slowly change into a system of representation with a normal but artificial contiguity semantics, how could it have survived in humans at all? The answer is again quite simple: because our most basic form of non-linguistic thinking in the mode of scenic phantasmata uses this same kind of semantics. And now we might take a speculative step and argue that because the non-linguistic system of scenic phantasma survives (in the face of so many different artificial semantics we are also able to use), this fact alone proves that non-linguistic systems of representation are definitely much more basic than all kinds of linguistic systems.

---

[26] In regard to more distant events we have to take seriously into consideration the indication of time by the means of emotions. For example: if I am thinking of an event with deep regret, this emotion clearly indicates a value, but it also indicates that this event happened in the past. Phantasmatic pleasure, pre-pleasure, and anxiety point to the future, shame and past fury indicate the past, and so on.

References

Cameron, P. and Biber, H. (1973), 'Sexual thought throughout the life span', *Gerontologist* 13: 144–7.

Cobb-Stevens, R. (1990), *Being and Categorical Intuition: Review of Metaphysics* 44: 43–66.

Davidson, Th. J., Kloosterman, F., and Wilson, M. A. (2009), 'Hippocampal replay of extended experience', *Neuron* 63: 497–507.

Derdikman, D. and Moser, M.-B. (2010), 'A dual role for hippocampal replay', *Neuron* 65: 582–4.

Diba, K. and Buzsáki, G. (2007), 'Forward and reverse hippocampal place-cell sequences during ripples', *Nat. Neuroscience* 10: 1241–2.

Foster, D. J. and Wilson, M. A. (2006), 'Reverse replay of behavioural sequences in hippocampal place cells during the awake state', *Nature* 440/30: 680–3.

Gupta, A. S., van der Meer, M. A.A., Touretzky, D. S., and Dedisch, A. D. (2010), 'Hippocampal replay is not a simple function of experience', *Neuron* 65: 695–705.

Hampton, R. R. (2001), 'Rhesus monkeys know when they remember', *Proceedings of the National Academy of Sciences* 98: 5359–62.

—— (2009), 'Multiple demonstrations of metacognition in honhumans: Converging evidence or multiple mechanisms?', *Comparative Cognition and Behavior Reviews* 4: 17–28.

Hicks, T. and Leitenberg, H.: 'Sexual fantasies about one's partner versus someone else: Gender differences in incidence and frequency', *Journal of Sex Research* 38: 43–50.

Husserl, E. (1969), *Formal and transcendental Logic* (The Hague: Martinus Nijhoff).

—— (1984), *Logische Untersuchungen*. Husserliana XIX/1–2 (Den Haag: Martinus Nijhoff).

—— (2001), *Logical Investigations*. vols. I and II (London: Routledge).

Ji, D. and Wilson, M. A. (2007), 'Coordinated memory replay in the visual cortex and hippocampus during sleep', *Nature Neuroscience* 10/1: 100–7.

Karlsson, M. P. and Frank, L. M. (2009): 'Awake replay of remote experiences in the hippocampus', *Nature Neuroscience* 12/7: 913–18.

Knierim, J. J. (2009): 'Imagining the possibilities: Ripples, routes, and reactivation', *Neuron* 63 (Previews): 421–3.

Lee, A. K. and Wilson, M. (2002), 'Memory of sequential experience in the hippocampus during slow wave sleep', *Neuron* 36: 1183–94.

Lohmar, D. (1989), *Phänomenologie der Mathematik* (Dordrecht: Kluwer Academic Publishers).

—— (1998), *Erfahrung und kategoriales Denken*. (Dordrecht: Kluwer Academic Publishers).

—— (2002): 'Husserl's concept of categorical intuition', in D. Zahavi and F. Stjernfelt (eds), *Hundred Years of Phenomenology* (Dordrecht: Kluwer Academic Publishers), pp. 125–45.

—— (2008a), *Phänomenologie der schwachen Phantasie* (Dordrecht: Kluwer Academic Publishers).

—— (2008b), 'Denken ohne Sprache?', in F. Mattens (ed.), *Meaning and Language: Phenomenological Perspectives* (Dordrecht: Kluwer Academic Publishers), pp. 169–94.

—— (2010), 'The function of weak phantasy in perception and thinking', in S. Gallagher and D. Schmicking (eds), *Handbook of Phenomenology and Cognitive Science* (Heidelberg; New York: Springer), pp. 159–77.

Louie, K. and Wilson, M. (2001), 'Temporally structural replay of awake hippocampal ensemble activity during rapid eye movement sleep', *Neuron* 29: 145–56.

Seebohm, Th. M. (1990), 'Kategoriale Anschauung', *Phänomenologische Forschungen* 23: 9–47.

Skaggs, W. E. and McNaughton, B. L. (1996), 'Replay of neuronal firing sequences in rat hippocampus during sleep following spatial experiences', *Science* 271: 1870–3.

Smith, J. D. (2009), 'The study of animal metacognition', *Trends in Cognitive Science* 13/9: 389–96.

—— and Shields, W. E., and Washburn, D. A. (2003), 'The comparative psychology of uncertainty monitoring and metacognition', *Behavioral and Brain Sciences* 26: 317–3.

Sokolowski, R. (1981). 'Husserl's concept of categorial intuition', *Phenomenology and the human sciences. Philos. Topics* 12/Supplement: 127–41.

Stern, D. (1977), *The First Relationship: Mother and Child* (London: Open Books).

—— (1990), *Diary of a Baby* (New York, Basic Books).

Symons, D. (1993), 'The stuff that dreams aren't made of: Why the wake-state and dream-state sensory experiences differ', *Cognition* 47: 181–217.

Tomasello, M. (1995), 'Joint attention as social cognition', in C. Moore and P. J. Dunham (eds), *Joint Attention: Its Origin and its Role in Development* (Hilsdale NJ: Lawrence Erlbaum), pp. 103–30.

—— (2008), *Origins of Human Communication* (Cambridge: MIT Press).

—— and Carpenter, M. (2007), *Shared Intentionality, Developmental Science* 10: 121–5.

—— and Carpenter, M., Call, J., Behne, T., and Moll, H. (2005), 'Understanding and sharing intentions: The origin of cultural cognition', *Behavioral and Brain Science* 28, 675–735.

Tugendhat, E. (1970), *Der Wahrheitsbegriff bei Husserl und Heidegger* (Berlin: De Gruyter).

Wilson, M. A. and McNaughton, B. L. (1994), 'Reactivation of hippocampal ensemble memories during sleep', *Science* 265: 676–9.

....

CHAPTER 19

SHARING IN TRUTH: PHENOMENOLOGY OF EPISTEMIC COMMONALITY

....

HANS BERNHARD SCHMID

PAUL Grice's first conversational maxim of quantity requires people to make their contributions to discussions as informative as is necessary for the purpose of conversation (Grice 1975). In actual fact, however, many conversations tend to be surprisingly vacuous as far as the content of information is concerned. 'Nice weather!', one neighbour says to another over the fence, and she responds: 'Very nice indeed, and so much better then yesterday!', to which he then replies: 'Let's just hope it lasts for a while'—and so on, and so forth. These people just *state the obvious*, and do not share—nor aim at sharing—any real information. Each *knows* that the weather is fine, and each knows *that the other knows*. Neither of the participants has any reason to assume that what he says is news to the other. Thus one might think that such exchanges of words, especially where they are too long to be simple displays of neighbourly kindness or mere preludes to a real conversation, are just illustrations of how actual conversations between real people tend to fall short of how they *should* be. Griceans or Habermasians might even be tempted to go as far as to say that such idle twaddling and aimless chattering does not constitute a *real* conversation at all, but rather a *parody* or a *substitute* for proper conversations. After all, the weather is notorious for arising as a topic of conversation when people feel they *should* be conversing with each other, but do not really have anything to say. But such harsh judgements do not seem to do justice to the eminent role such exchanges of words play in our actual social lives. Under some circumstances such small talk appears to be just what is *needed* between people, and not merely a way of filling a lull in conversation; in these cases it would be *inappropriate* to start a 'real conversation' and trade information.

In one of his papers, Charles Taylor (1995: 189ff) makes a suggestion concerning what the exact contribution of such informationally vacuous conversations to our epistemic lives might be. What they do for us, Taylor claims, is not any improvement at the level of information, or the *contents* of beliefs, but rather a modification in the *way* the world is given to us, or in the *kind* of epistemic attitude involved. Such conversations *transform* epistemic attitudes of the *individual* kind into *shared* epistemic attitudes, or so Taylor argues. Before the conversation, the beauty of the weather was perceived by each of the neighbours *privately*, as it were; in conversation, it becomes something which is *shared* between them—something that is there for both of them *together*, something that pertains to them as a 'we'. One way of cashing out this claim is to say that this difference between individually held perceptual beliefs (which are communal between the participants only in a *distributive* sense) and genuinely *joint* perceptual beliefs is not just a matter of some warm fellow feeling of cognitive attunement, but rather the creation of some *new, collective type of epistemic commonality*. Taylor does not go into any further detail, but he suggests that commonality of this *collective* kind plays an important *epistemic* role, and is much neglected in post-Cartesian philosophy.

This paper aims at exploring this claim. Section 1 examines the idea of collective epistemic commonality suggested by Taylor's example, and contrasts it with a *distributive* notion of epistemic commonality to be found in much of the received literature. Section 2 briefly introduces and discusses a number of accounts of collective epistemic commonality both from the early phenomenological and the current literature. I shall argue that collective epistemic commonality is neither a matter of the *content* nor of the *mode* of the attitude in question, but requires a plural subject, which is not, however, a *corporate* subject. The concluding section argues that, contrary to what Taylor suggests, conversation is not constitutive of collective epistemic commonality as such, but rather *presupposes* basic forms of collective epistemic commonality. I shall claim, however, that conversation *widens* the scope, *deepens* the structure, and establishes a *higher* form of collective epistemic commonality, and is thus intimately related to our concern for truth.

1 THE COMMONALITY OF TRUTH

Taylor claims that the constitution of the type of epistemic commonality he has in mind is a *linguistic* matter, and that it comes about by means of *conversation*. It seems plausible to assume that this form of epistemic commonality is created where the participants agree with each other. If the other neighbour objects to the first and claims that the weather does not deserve to be called nice at all (for example, because of the gusty wind), the weather might still be established as something there for them *together*, as their joint focus of attention over which the participants disagree, but obviously not its being nice. Therefore, examining Taylor's claim requires of us to understand the nature of consensus and its place in conversation. Conversations are joint actions consisting of individual utterances, or speech acts, in which the participants express their views on—or attitudes towards—a given topic, and treat each other as peers. Like all actions, conversations may either succeed or fail. I take it to be intuitively acceptable to say that rational consensus is the condition of conversational success. A consensus is an agreed-upon attitude with regard to the topic of conversation, and a central part of its being rational is the participants only agreeing to propositions that seem to them to be *correct*. The rationality constraint means that consensus cannot be intended directly. You cannot have a real conversation with me if my sole aim is a consensus between us, regardless of what this requires me to accept. By the same token, however, there cannot be a conversation between people who do not think it is desirable, or believe it is possible, to reach *any* consensus. At first sight at least, it seems natural to assume that the consensus may well be to *disagree*. In any case, there is an important difference between a disagreement that is the result of a *failed* conversation (which is really a failure to reach, or a break-down of, mutual understanding), and a disagreement that is *consented upon*, and thus a result of a successful conversation. In the second case, the topic of conversation is the relation between the participants' attitudes concerning certain facts or propositions.

Taylor's remarks seem to suggest that it is insufficient to understand consensus simply as whatever proposition people rationally and openly accept in conversation. The point of Taylor's example seems to be that while it is true that consensus is a *social* rather than a merely *mental* fact, it has to be analyzed with an eye on how it affects the participants' mental attitudes. What conversation is all about is the *sharing* in the givenness of the world, the step from what each one perceives, believes, feels *individually* to what they perceive, believe, feel *together*: that is, the creation of joint intentional attitudes. In order to explore Taylor's suggestion concerning the structure and role of conversation, it is therefore necessary to understand what intentional attitudes are: what exactly is it that, according to Taylor's suggestion, is transformed from something individual to something shared in conversation? The following does not draw directly on the venerable sources of the phenomenological tradition from Brentano to Husserl, but picks up on more recent work on the intentionality of emotional and affective attitudes instead (Helm 2008). The emerging picture of intentional states is a structure of at least five features: subject, target, focus, formal object, and concern. These features will turn out to be useful to pinpoint the place of truth and its commonality in intentionality.

The *subject* is whoever *has* the attitude in question and to whom it is ascribed as its source or bearer—in the case of a consensus, a plurality of speakers, in the case of a simple intentional attitude, the good old singular subject (we shall return to this feature below). The *target* of an intentional attitude is that at which it is directed. If we agree that the weather is bad, the target of our agreed upon attitude is the weather; if I am afraid of a dog, the target of my attitude is that dog. The third feature is the *formal object*. Formal objects are usually defined as a quality implicitly ascribed to the target by the attitude that plays an important part in making it intelligible as the *kind of attitude* it is (Kenny 1994; Mulligan 2007). Another way of expressing this is to say that the formal object is what makes it *worthwhile having* an attitude as one of its kind. For example, it is the fact that my attitude ascribes the dog the quality of being *dangerous* that makes it intelligible as one of fear, and it is because the dog *is dangerous* that my fear is 'worthwhile' being had. If my attitude were to ascribe the dog the quality of being particularly *beautiful* instead, the attitude would rather be one of admiration, or perhaps enjoyment.

The formal object is particularly important because it determines the *mode* of an attitude, especially the difference between the four main modes of intentional attitudes: epistemic, practical, aesthetic, and affective. *Truth* is the formal object of *epistemic* (or factual, or doxastic, or cognitive) attitudes in the same way in which *desirability* is the formal object of volitive (or practical) attitudes. Thus, correspondingly, different kinds of *conversation* can be distinguished according to the kind of joint attitude that is agreed upon in consensus. A conversation is *epistemic* if the formal object of that attitude is truth. It is a *practical conversation* if its formal object is desirability. A conversation on the same target can be either epistemic or practical in the same way that a dog can be either feared or admired. If one person says 'it is raining', and the other agrees, the consensus might either simply be *that it is raining*, if the conversation is epistemic, or *that there is reason to do something*, if the conversation is practical (in the first case the raining is the target in its being true, in the second case in its being undesirable). The third kind is what might be called *expressive* conversations, where the conversation is about matters of taste, or some other epistemologically subjective issue. An example would be a conversation about a sunrise's being beautiful or kitschy. The fourth kind is affective conversation, which is about the affective evaluation of some target. I take it that there is no unifying formal object for the aesthetic and affective domains, but rather a *plurality* of formal objects. If there is one single formal object of which truth, desirability, and the formal objects of aesthetical and affective attitudes are special cases, it is probably something like *value*.

The formal object is a *relational* rather than an *intrinsic* property of the target. The fourth feature—the focus—answers the question of *in relation to whom* or *what* the target is ascribed the quality that is the formal object of the attitude. For example, if I am afraid of the dog, the target is the dog, the focus is its being dangerous, and the focus is on *me* insofar as it is by virtue of the dog's being dangerous to *me* that my attitude is one of fear. The focus is an essential component of intentional attitudes because it is *not determined by the subject, the target, and the kind of formal object of an attitude* alone. It is often forgotten in individualistic societies that a person's being afraid of a dog in virtue of its being dangerous does not *per se* involve a focus on *herself*, but might well be the matter of a different focus. A person may be afraid of a dog by virtue of its being dangerous to *somebody else*—for example, a child playing in the park—which that person observes from her window being approached by a big stray dog (this is Bennett Helm's example). Similarly, if we are conversing about how bad the weather is, the *target* of conversation is the *weather*, the *formal object* is the weather's being *unpleasant*, and the focus is on *us*, insofar as what we are really talking about is how bad the weather is *for us* (what is unpleasant for us may well be very beneficial to the vegetation, and welcome to the farmers). Or, if we are talking about whether the Tobin tax should be introduced, the target is the Tobin tax, the formal object is its desirability, and quite a bit of the success of our conversation will depend on our agreeing on the focus—that is, *for whom* exactly the introduction of the Tobin tax is or is not desirable.

This brings us to the final feature of intentional attitudes. A subject's perceiving the dog (target) as dangerous (formal object) for somebody else (focus) does not *per se* make intelligible his or her intentional attitude towards the dog as one of fear; just think of uncaring dog owners who seem to be taking pride in the threatening nature of their pet. In such a frame of mind, a dog's being dangerous may ultimately rationalize the attitude in question as one of enjoyment rather than one of fear. Obviously, there is an integral part missing in the structure. The relation between target, formal object, and focus rationalizes a subject's attitude as the kind of attitude it is only on the base of the subject's basic *concerns*. Only if other people's safety *matters* to them will people fear dogs for their being dangerous to somebody else. If they would rather have other people hurt, they will not fear the dog *for the others*; of course, such persons may still react with great fear where they themselves are in the focus. Likewise, it is only if people are concerned with other people's getting what they need that they will be moved to contribute to what is *desirable* for others. If they are entirely indifferent towards other people's wellbeing, no such practical attitude will be formed. Similarly for the case in which the focus is on the subject itself: in a suicidal frame of mind, what is dangerous may seem attractive, and for a person who has come to be distrustful of his or her own inclinations, what is desirable to himself might not rationalize a corresponding intention. It is only in the light of our concern for our own getting what we want that some state of affairs' being desirable for us rationalizes our attitude towards that state of affairs as one that has it as its success conditions.

It seems clear, however, that the epistemic, practical, aesthetic, and affective cases are not strictly parallel. In particular, there is something special about *epistemic* attitudes (and correspondingly, epistemic conversations) as compared to attitudes and conversations of these other kinds (perhaps with the exception of Kantian views on the structure of practical attitudes). There is a *fundamental difference* between the ways in which, by means of underlying concerns, different formal objects bring the target of an attitude into focus. This becomes obvious from the fact that epistemic attitudes (and conversations) *cannot go wrong* in a way practical, aesthetic, or affective attitudes always can. We may agree on the desirability of the Tobin tax, but fail in conversation for lack of agreement on the *focus*, if our underlying concern is different. It may always turn out that some target really *is* desirable or pleasant or dangerous, but not for *that* person or group. Yet the same does *not seem to be possible* in the epistemic case. There is a sense in which the 'for whom' question is *not open* where truth is concerned, which has no equivalent in the case of practical, aesthetic, or affective attitudes, and similarly for the corresponding types of conversation. Desirability, pleasantness, or some such formal objects have what one might call a *variable focus*. The same target might be judged pleasant for one person and not for another, or desirable for one group of people and not for another. If something is taken to be true, by contrast, the question as to *for whom* it is true does not arise in the same way. This is not to say that epistemic attitudes do not have a focus, but rather, that the focus is *fixed* instead of variable. True is true *for anybody*, or perhaps true for some qualified group such as 'anybody who adopts the same epistemic standards', or some such.

This is at the conceptual core of such folk-philosophical talk as truth being 'objective', 'absolute', 'public', 'universal', or 'communal', rather than 'subjective', 'relative', 'monological', 'individual', or 'private'. This is not to claim that a belief that happens to be held by one single individual only may not be true. Rather, the claim is that this individual cannot take the truth ascribed to the target of his attitude by his belief to be as something that is 'just for himself' in the same way as she or he may, in some cases at least, experience the desirability, pleasantness, or beauty of something as 'merely personal' or private. In some cases, people may come to experience the desirability, pleasantness, or beauty of something, as having a communal focus too, but it is only in the epistemic case that *universal focal commonality* is *essential*. If Nietzsche, or perhaps some of his followers, summons his readers to turn away from their herds and to find their own individual truth that is just for them and for nobody else, he obviously goes beyond the merely cognitive and asks us to base our quest for truth in some form of authenticity that really belongs to the *aesthetic* sphere. By contrast to this, it is a basic feature of purely epistemic attitudes that *commonality is always in the focus, and is unlimited.*

What is interesting about Taylor's remarks is that he seems to suggest that there are *two different ways* to spell out this basic claim. According to the *distributive view*, truth is common in the sense that if it is cognitively assumed that p, it is accepted that *everybody*, under suitable circumstances, could, or should, or would believe that p. On this view, the truth of my perceptual belief that it is raining commits me to the view that what I believe is simply what *anybody* would come to believe in my situation. This distributive understanding of the focal commonality of epistemic attitudes has to be carefully distinguished from a *collective* understanding. On this view, it is not just the case that in a group of individuals, each individual has (or should have) the belief that p *for himself or herself*, but that they have (or should have) that belief *together*. On this view, my perceptual belief that it is raining does not so much commit me to the view that in my role as a cognizer or holder of that particular belief, I am replaceable, as it were, by *any* single member of the general class of competent cognizers standing in my shoes (having the same evidence), but rather commits me to the view that the relation I have to the target of my attitude is *open to others* in such a way that any other competent cognizer could *join in* and participate in a way that makes the relation *our joint intentional attitude*. For a rough intuitive idea of what the distinction at issue here might be, one might say that in the first view, epistemic attitudes are essentially open to commonality in the way in which in a given population, individuals may share a particular hair colour, when each one has the same hair colour. In the second view, epistemic attitudes are open to commonality in something like a way in which people may share an apartment, when they move in together. The difference is in the way in which that which is shared between the individuals relates to the participating individuals. In the first case, that which is shared is a *type*, something *general* in which the individuals participate by means of individually *instantiating* particular tokens of the general type; in the second case, that which is shared is itself something particular, a token which is *jointly* constituted by the participating individuals. Distributive commonality is *general*; collective commonality is *joint*.

I think it is fair to claim that traditional epistemology has been largely preoccupied with *distributive* epistemic commonality. By contrast, the suggestion Taylor seems to be making points towards the idea that the focal commonality of epistemic attitudes should rather be understood in *collective* terms. It is widely agreed that truth is never a matter of some private isolated knower's attitude alone, as desirability and pleasantness may sometimes be, but something essentially communal. But it might be a mistake to conceive of the commonality of truth simply in terms of some privateness had by *everyone* instead of just one. Truth, one might say, is not had by each one *for himself*, but something that *connects us*, something that transcends our epistemic privacies, something genuinely *shared*, something that pertains to us not as an aggregate of singular egos, but as an encompassing 'we'. If this intuition is correct, 'collective epistemology'—a relatively new label for the study of the epistemic role of collectives (see Schmid, Sirtes and Weber 2011)—is not just a special branch of epistemology examining the particular epistemic virtues and vices of a certain sort of believers, namely groups, and studying the properties of some aggregated beliefs, as it is so often conceived, but rather the *much more fundamental* project of understanding the way in which truth is an *essentially* collective matter. In this view, epistemology is *per se* collective—or rather, to put it in more Taylorian words, something that has to be *overcome* if it is defined in non-collective terms.

Let me approach the distinction between distributive and collective commonality with an example. Edmund Husserl is often accused of having endorsed a monological, privatist, or even solipsistic conception of truth, in which truth is basically a matter of subjective evidence, or a matter of the relation between the ego's mental 'states' or 'acts' (see, for example, Tugendhat 1970b). Yet it is clear even to his critics that Husserl did not understand his analysis of the ego as an analysis of *his own* experience of evidence only, but claimed to be analyzing those evidences *in general* (in terms of *essences*)—that is, the way in which *anybody* (any particular instantiation of the essence 'ego') has them. Since the 'mental acts' in which something is 'given' as true have to be understood as *essences* rather than as facts, it is clear that 'truth is not the correlate of *my* particular act, but rather of *any* act of this species in *any* subject' (Tugendhat 1970a: 221). In his later work, however, Husserl became increasingly dissatisfied with this conception. He started to turn away from what he now called the merely 'logical commonality' of his essentialist generic account of epistemic commonality to something like 'intersubjective commonality' (Husserl 1973: 306; see Schmid 2000: 50–8). With this, the structure of *objectivity* becomes Husserl's central epistemological concern, and in his phenomenology of intersubjectivity as well as in his late philosophy of science, Husserl analyzes ways in which individual subjects *cooperate* in the pursuit of truth (see Kochan and Schmid 2011). Along these lines, Husserl ultimately ends up in something closely resembling Peirce's and Habermas' consensus theories of truth, in which the true transcendental subject is some universal 'we'—that is, the 'widest community of subjects' which is interconnected by mutual cooperation and critique and directed towards the ideal of universal unanimity (*Einstimmigkeit*; for example, Husserl 1993: 16; Schmid 2000: chapter 5, iii, 164ff).

Some consensus theories make agreements simply the *criterion* for the truth of cognitive attitudes (in the sense that agreements, reached under real or under ideal circumstances, are *indicators* of truth). This is usually combined with the view that communication plays an *instrumental* role in the process of belief formation (in this view, talking to each other should be seen as a *means* individuals use to modify and validate their beliefs). This is different in the view developed here. The basic idea is that truth, adequately understood, is *essentially* communal in that truth is the formal object of epistemic attitudes that are not just (potentially) distributively communal, but really (potential) *joint* epistemic attitudes. Wherever truth comes into play, even if it is evident for one single individual only, there is some sort of a 'we' involved. Of course, it is highly disputed among consensus theorists or epistemic communitarians what kind of 'we' this group of actual and possible epistemic peers might be, and what kind of cooperation may be needed between them. I will not pursue this question any further here, but instead concentrate on a basic question which is central to all of these conceptions, but that is rarely addressed and turns out surprisingly difficult to answer: what exactly does it mean for an epistemic attitude to be *jointly held*, and how exactly is this different from each participant's holding the corresponding view for himself or herself?

2 JOINT EXPERIENTIAL BELIEFS

Husserl's analyses put forward in his phenomenology of intersubjectivity seem to suggest that the right way to account for collective epistemic commonality is to elucidate the 'constitution of the other'—that is, the way in which one subject can become aware of another, and of the other's take on the world. This points towards a conception of collective epistemic commonality in which the prime subject is the *individual self*, and in which that self, by means of *empathy*, experiences another self as experiencing the same object, and experiences that other self as being empathically aware of him and of his experiencing the object, perhaps with some structure of further empathetic 'mirroring' between the self in the other. If we disregard, for the moment, the structure of empathy as opposed to belief, the basic picture that emerges along these lines is that for A and B to experience some x jointly, the following structure has to be in place: A experiences x, and believes that there is B, and believes that B experiences x, and perhaps has some belief that B believes that A experiences x. There are two objections against an account of this sort. First, it seems trivially true that *it takes at least two* for a belief to be held—or an experience to be made—*jointly*. It is not enough for one subject to *believe* that there is another subject who is in a suitable relation; that subject really has to *exist*. Insofar as Husserl's transcendental phenomenology is committed to the view that anything outside the individual's consciousness should be 'bracketed', it seems that Husserlian phenomenology simply cannot account for shared intentional states, but only for how it may *appear* to people to share an intentional state. Second, it seems that construing shared beliefs out of individual beliefs and some structure of reciprocal attitudes between the participants sets off an *infinite progress*. It is not enough for A to experience x and to know that B experiences x too, because if A does not know whether or not B knows that A knows that B experiences x, they do not seem to be sharing their experience at all (see Husserl 1973: 211). This is obvious in the case of conflicting higher-order beliefs: imagine the case where A and B are both observing the weather, but A is standing in B's back and mistakenly believes that B is not aware of his perceiving the weather. Similar but more complicated (and increasingly artificial) stories can be told about any higher-order level of mutual knowledge, so that it seems that the number of levels of mutual knowledge between A and B has to be infinite.

Another way of making the same point builds on how shared knowledge serves as a base for rational decision-making. The classical example is that of two allied generals residing with their armies in separate camps and able to prevail in battle only if they charge their common enemy at the exact same time. If only one strikes, or if the two strike at separate times, both armies will be annihilated. A sends a messenger to B, proposing to attack at t. B receives the message and likes the plan, but since the messenger had to pass enemy terrain on his way to B, B knows that A's commitment to attack at t is conditional on B's, he sends the message back to A that he agrees to the plan. Now A knows that B knows of the plan, but he has to assume that B has no reason to attack at t as long as he does not know that A knows that B accepted the plan. Therefore, the messenger has to be sent back to B again with the confirmation of the receipt of the previous message, and so on and so forth. Each round the messenger makes between the two creates a higher-order level of reciprocal knowledge, but there is no level which is *high enough*, so at time t, no reason will be created for either A or B to attack.

Along these lines we end up in what we may call the Nozick–Lewis–Aumann-account[1] (in short, the NLA-account) of shared epistemic attitudes. On this view, the experience of x is shared between A and B on the conditions 1–8:

1) A experiences x;
2) B experiences x;
3) B knows that 1;
4) A knows that 2;
5) A knows that 3;
6) B knows that 4;
7) B knows that 5;
8) …and so on and so forth *ad infinitum*.

Under the label 'common knowledge' (or 'mutual knowledge', as it is called in the semantic literature), the NLA-account has become something like the standard view of joint epistemic attitudes in the current debate. For example, a version of this seems to be appealed to in Raimo Tuomela's account of collective belief, where he makes 'mutual beliefs' concerning the participant's epistemic attitudes towards x and the entire complex of group belief, which includes a sort of 'acceptance', part of his analysis (see Tuomela 1992; 1995: chapter 7). Yet there are two basic criticisms directed against the NLA-account. First, it has been claimed that condition 8 cannot be *necessary* to shared

---

[1] For Lewis's version, see Lewis 1969. Robert Aumann has put this in a set theoretical framework (see Aumann 1976). In his last work, Robert Nozick (2001: 375ff) claimed the first analysis of the concept for himself.

experience, because experiences are shared between *finite* minds, and if condition 8 were correct, no finite mind would ever be able to share any experience, as finite minds can have only a limited number of beliefs, and in order for A to *know* that x A has to *believe* that x, or so it is assumed. The iteration, it is claimed, has somehow to be cut down to a manageable size. The second and more radical objection is that such a complex of beliefs (or some shortened version of it) would not be *sufficient* to constitute a case of genuinely *collective* experience, because individual experiences do not become collective just because they are somehow mirrored in each other (for example, Searle 1995). I will not go into any details of the recent discussion about common knowledge here, but rather present some early *phenomenological* analyses of joint experience, an alternative from the *joint attention literature*, and some inspirations from the analysis of *collective intentionality* in a blend of accounts, which in one way or other deal with the two objections levelled against the NLA-account.

The first analysis to mention is by the German phenomenologist Gerda Walther (Walther 1923: 45ff.). Walther's analysis suggests that of the above iteration, some form of numbers 1–4 are necessary (3 and 4 consisting of 'acts of empathy'), but that 5 and 6 consist of A's and B's respective 'acts of unification' (*Einigung*) with the other's experience, which then becomes, once again, the object of the other's empathic awareness. In Walther's view, this completes the analysis. Walther's account seems attractive because it addresses both worries concerning the NLA-account. It seems to have substantially more collectivity in it because it has the element of 'unification' (basically an affective act of affirmation; see Walther 1923: 42) included in the analysis. Also, Walther seems to avoid the infinite progress of attitudes. One might doubt, however, that Walther is successful in either respect. Acts of unification, just as the we-experiences of which they are a part, are 'wholly in the individual mind', as Walther claims (1923: 70), thereby adgering to 'Husserlian internalism'.[2] How could these attitudes, as purely internal facts about one individual mind, provide any real connection? (We shall come back to this worry below in the discussion of Searle's account). A second critical question is how Walther's analysis could avoid the infinite progress. Why does A not have to be somehow aware of B's empathic awareness of A's act of unification with B, and so on and so forth? It seems rather easy to make a strong case for this progress along the lines of the arguments made for the NLA-account, and I cannot find any argument to the contrary in Walther's analysis.

Perhaps something could be made with what Walther calls 'habitual' attitudes in the 'background' of intentionality (Walther 1923: 27ff.). Very much along the lines later developed by Searle, and much in tune with the phenomenological conception of the life-world, Walther insists that 'occurrent' intentional states have to be seen as involving presuppositions which are not themselves thematic. Every cognitive attitude involves a great deal of assumptions which are merely implicit rather than in the content of the

---

[2] The expression is in brackets because, as almost any philosophical interpretation, the view that Husserl is an internalist has also found its critics—one of whom is the editor of this volume (Zahavi 2004).

attitude in question; things that are simply 'taken for granted' or 'implied' as valid. It seems tempting to assume that the higher-order levels of reciprocal attitudes are not actually occurrent, but rather in the background—that is, perhaps in the way in which somebody who knows what equal numbers are knows *all* equal numbers without having to think about each of them. If common knowledge is taken to be of that sort, what is really meant by 'shared experience' is that it is a sort of experiential attitude that provides the participants with all the information needed to form whatever occurrent higher-order beliefs they please rather than requiring of them to actually *have* all those attitudes. This lowers the conceptual threshold substantially. In the light of recent work in developmental psychology, one might ask, however, if the threshold is lowered quite far enough. So far, this still requires of the participants some knowledge of the infinite *iterability* of their reciprocal attitudes—which is a rather demanding concept. Developmental psychologists suggests that the sharing of basic experiential attitudes or beliefs should be seen as not involving any developed theory of mind at all, and much less any grasp of infinite iterability of attitudes, as the corresponding practices of joint attention are displayed at an early stage in child development (Tomasello 1998).

In recent discussions about *joint attention*, the infinite progress is avoided by appealing to something like *mutually openended perceptual availability*. Appealing to *perception* rather than knowledge seems to render infinite iteration superfluous. If somebody sees something, and sees that the other sees it, and that the other sees that he himself is there and watching, the iteration seems to stop right there, and something like 'plain openness' or 'mutually open-ended availability' is established. No further, complex thought about what the other thinks one thinks he thinks one thinks, and so on, is required. Thus Christopher Peacocke (2005) proposes an analysis according to which *open perceptual knowledge* is established where the following three conditions are met:

a) x and y both perceive that p;
b) x and y are both aware that their perceptions that p are mutually open-ended; and
c) x and y are aware that they are both aware of this very awareness (a-c).

Here, the worry is with collectivity. When I perceive something as plainly visible to *anyone* who happens to be around and watching and become aware that *you* happen to be around and watching, this is clearly different from the case in which the two of us really are perceiving something *jointly*, as a 'we', and Peacocke's analysis does not cover the latter case, or so I would argue. Perhaps one might think that a simple *exchange of glances* is enough to establish genuine togetherness, but it seems to me that it would have to be a *significant* or *meaningful* one, not just any incidental meeting of eyes—that is, a proper *act of communication*, which involves a much more complex structure. Furthermore, not every meaningful meeting of eyes establishes a 'we': some meetings of eyes are meaningful in the sense that they create *isolation* rather than togetherness (think of Jean-Paul Sartre's famous examples). It might appear that Peacocke's analysis, just like the NLA-account, is just another attempt to pull the rabbit of epistemic jointness out of the empty hat of some complex of individual epistemic attitudes, with some structure of reciprocal awareness.

To my knowledge, Max Scheler was the first to come up with a *radically different* proposal. He claims that collective experience is *irreducible* to *any* set of individual experiences and reciprocal attitudes. 'Co-experiencing' something, Scheler claims, 'cannot be understood by saying: A experiences something that is experienced by B, and both, in addition, know of their experiencing it' (Scheler 2000: 516). Scheler argues against what he claims to be 'arbitrary constructions of a faulty science' which tries to construe collective epistemic commonality as some 'very complicated composition of experiences of single individuals, augmented by mutual knowledge or conjecturing that the other's experiences might be similar' (Scheler 1982: 272). What makes an experience (or, for that matter, a practical or affective attitude) a *joint* attitude is, Scheler claims, not a matter of the *content* of the participating individual's attitude, but rather a matter of 'a peculiar and ultimate *form* of that experience' (Scheler 1982: 273). In the context of his analysis of shared *affective* attitudes, Scheler gives an impressive illustration. He discusses a couple of parents standing at the deathbed of their child. The parents' grief, Scheler argues, is not a combination of each individual's attitudes towards the target of their emotion together with some awareness of the other's attitude. Rather, the commonality of their grief is in their grief itself—that is, that A's grief and B's grief are not separate, somehow interlinked mental facts, but 'phenomenologically *one and the same fact*' (Scheler 1974: 23f.).

Some years after Scheler, Martin Heidegger made the same point in one of his courses of lectures from the time shortly after the publication of 'Being and Time' (Heidegger 1996). Here he discusses the case of two hikers turning around a corner and being confronted with a breathtaking view. Heidegger claims that it is mistaken to analyze this case along the lines of A's experiencing the view, B's experiencing the view, and there being some sort of mutual awareness connecting the two experiences. Being totally *enrapt* by the view, Heidegger says, neither of the participants is aware of the other's presence in terms of the other being the target of any sort of intentional attitude. Heidegger argues that mutual (explicit) awareness is neither a necessary nor a sufficient condition of joint experience (1996: §13). By contrast to Scheler, Heidegger's discussion ties the idea of joint experience tightly to *truth*. It is *essential* for the kind of disclosedness or un-coveredness that is at the centre of Heidegger's idea of truth that it is *shareable* in the way illustrated by his example (1996: §14), and this also answers the question of the structure of *authentic* togetherness (Schmid 2009: chapter 9).

Other phenomenologists who have taken up the anti-reductionist idea that it might be wrong to construe shared intention by means of individual intentions and reciprocal attitudes include Jean-Paul Sartre and Dietrich von Hildebrand. In his *Metaphysics of Community* (von Hildebrand 1930: 39–45), Dietrich von Hildebrand argues that the way in which the participants sharing an experience (or some other kind of attitude) are in 'contact' (*Berührung*) with each other is not of the sort of being confronted with each other or facing each other in any way, but of a wholly different kind which von Hildebrandt labels 'we-contact' (*Wir-Berührung*). Sharing an attitude is not a matter of the *content* of individual attitudes, but has to be seen as a matter of the '*colouring*' (*Einfärbung*) which the participant's experience has by virtue of its being shared. Sartre's illustration is the joint experience of a play, where all members of the audience, being wholly focused on what is happening on stage, are *sharing* an experience without being the object of each other's attention. Sartre points out that whatever kind of awareness the participants in the shared experience have of each other is 'lateral' (Sartre 1991: 485) rather than 'thetic'.

The basic idea originally proposed by Scheler and elaborated further by Heidegger and other phenomenologists closely resembles John Searle's anti-reductionist claim which, in his latest book, he states rather cautiously, saying that 'not all occurrences of "we intend", "we believe", and "we desire" can be reduced to "'I intend", "I believe", and "I desire" and so on, plus mutual belief' (Searle 2010: 50). I think the view proposed by Scheler, Heidegger, and Searle is correct: collective epistemic commonality is not to be *reduced* to distributive collective commonality plus reciprocal attitudes. In itself, however, anti-reductionism is a purely negative claim. The question to be answered is: *how else* should collective epistemic commonality be conceived of if not in terms of some distributive and mutualist reduction? What is that special 'form' (Scheler) or 'colouring' (von Hildebrand) in which experiences are shared?

Searle's proposal is often taken to mean that the jointness of intentional attitudes is really a matter of a special *mode* of intentional attitudes. If this is taken literally, the suggestion would be that the difference between an individual experience of x and a joint experience of x is similar *in kind* to the difference between an individual's *fearing* that x and that individual's *intending* to x (fear and intention being different intentional modes). In a somewhat similar vein, Raimo Tuomela often uses the term 'we-mode', distinguishing it from the 'I-mode' (for example, Tuomela 2007: chapter 46). Whatever the merits and problems of this suggestion may be, Searle claims that the attitudes in question are realized wholly inside the individual minds of the participants, and are structurally independent of anything outside those minds (Searle 1990: 404), which is similar to Walther's claim cited above. Searle thinks that this is the only way to account for the irreducibility of we-intentional attitudes without ending up in some collectivist group mind conception, which he believes to be a 'perfectly abominable metaphysical excrescence' (Searle 1998: 150).

Even if we accept internalism for *individual* intentional states, however, it seems obvious that this cannot be true for the *collective* case. In the chapter on collective intentionality in his *Construction of Social Reality*, Searle presents two instructive figures—the one depicting the mistaken reductionist view, the other presenting his own proposal (Searle 1995: 26). Each of the two figures shows the outline of a pair of heads facing each other. In the first, 'reductivist' pair, 'I intend and I believe that you believe…' is written in each head, with 'we believe' written in the space between the two. In the second figure, 'we intend' is written in each head. Thus the we-intention placed *between* the participants in the reductive account becomes individualized in Searle's own analysis. It should be noted that the illustration in Searle's book is somewhat misleading because he has his individuals *facing* each other rather than facing the target of their joint intentional state, which conveys a sense of togetherness that is not there in the analysis. In actual fact there is no 'we' in Searle's analysis, and that is the basic problem of his account (Meijers 2003; Schmid 2003). If I have a thought of the we-form in mind, while by some coincidence and entirely unrelated to me you happen to have a similar thought in mind, this does not make our attitude a *shared* one. Rather, our thoughts need to be *related* in a suitable way to be collective. Thus I agree with Anthonie Meijers and other critics that collective intentional states are not only irreducible in *form* or *mode*, but genuinely *relational* phenomena too.

One way of putting this is to say that shared experiences are not simple aggregates of individual mental facts of whatever form or 'colouring'. Rather, they are *social facts*—something that is not inside individual minds, but *between* individuals—and the question is what *kind* of social facts they are. This is where Margaret Gilbert's analysis of joint intentional attitudes comes in (Gilbert 1989). Gilbert claims that for A and B jointly to believe that p (or intend that p, or to have a certain affective attitude towards p), they have to be *jointly committed* to believe, intend, or feel that p as a body (Gilbert 1987), which is the basic social fact. Joint commitments come about as a result of explicit or implicit communicative processes, by each member openly declaring his willingness to be jointly committed on the condition of the participation of the others. As the joint commitment is the group's, and not the participating individuals', the *subject* of the attitude in question is plural—hence the label 'Plural Subject Theory' for Gilbert's account.

Having discussed and criticized reductivist accounts of shared epistemic attitudes which place the plural element, the element of sharedness in the *content* of the attitude in question, and non-reductivist individualist accounts which place the element of togetherness in the *mode* or *form* of the attitude in question, we now finally arrive at the view that the plurality of the attitude in question is really a matter of the *subject*. Sharing an epistemic attitude, one might say, is neither a matter of *what* the participants experience, nor of *in what form* they experience it, but rather a question of *who they are*. Of course, the idea that the subject of the attitude in question might be plural rather than individual raises serious worries. I already mentioned Searle's reservations against the idea of a group mind, and similar (if somewhat weaker) statements can be found in Michael Bratman's and Raimo Tuomela's accounts. Similarly, in the phenomenological literature, Gerda Walther has stoutly rejected the idea that in we-experiencing something, there is 'a "we" standing "behind" or "above" the individuals' (Walther 1923: 70), and Edith Stein argues that 'the experiences of a community have in the final analysis their origin in the individual selves who belong to the community. A … "communal-self" is an impossibility … A communal subject as an analogue of the pure self does not exist' (Stein 1922: 120f.). By contrast to this, Husserl has for decades played with the idea of collective subjects and 'personalities of higher order' in his informal research manuscripts (see Schmid 2000: 17–26), and Scheler has repeatedly affirmed the idea of a collective subject or 'collective person' ('*Gesamtperson*') in his published work (see, for example, Scheler 2000). In recent philosophical research this issue has arisen again as a consequence of Philip Pettit's work on the *discursive dilemma*, where Pettit claims that some groups should be conceived of as having 'a mind of their own' (Pettit 2003). In my view, Pettit and Christian List have made a strong case for the existence of genuine collective subjects of epistemic and practical attitudes. Similar to Carol Rovane's related account (Rovane 1998), they deny that the collective mind involves any phenomenal aspect, or phenomenal consciousness, and Pettit/List suggest that beliefs which are merely 'common' or 'shared' among people should be distinguished from such 'corporate beliefs'. In communication, List has endorsed the NLA-account as necessary and sufficient for the analysis of shared epistemic attitudes, and I suspect that this might also be Pettit's view. For reasons mentioned above, I think that this is mistaken, and since the received individualistic versions of non-reductionism seem to be deficient too, Gilbert's claim seems attractive. The claim is that even in cases where this does *not* imply the solution of a discursive dilemma as the creation of an institutional, collective, Hobbesian *persona ficta*, the sharing of (epistemic) attitudes involves the creation of a plural subject. It seem worthwhile noting in passing that Gilbert's account seems to fit rather nicely with Charles Taylor's initial proposal concerning the creation of collective epistemic commonality by means of consensus. One might think that the role of vacuous conversations is just that: to create a plural subject of an attitude, which is different from two subjects having a corresponding individual attitude. Conversations transform something that is for *you and me*, severally, into what is for '*us*', collectively, by creating that 'we' that is the plural subject of the attitude in which it is given.

Yet there are at least three worries with this account. One, which I will mention only in passing, is with the normative force of these commitments (see Mathiesen 2006). The two other objections which I shall look at more closely are that this account a) is viciously circular, and b) sets off an infinite regress.

a) Raimo Tuomela (1992)—and, more recently, Deborah Tollefsen (2002)—have argued that explaining plural subjects by the expression of each individual's willingness to create a plural subject together with the others is circular, as this makes the *explanandum* a part of the *explanans*. Gilbert responds that this can be avoided by distinguishing between an intuitive folk-psychological (or folk-sociological) conception of joint commitment, and a full-blown or technical notion, and that expressions of willingness are *conditions of the formation* rather than parts of the analysis of joint commitments (Gilbert 2003). The first response, however, does not seem to square nicely with the very plausible idea (articulated in Gilbert 1989) that the 'technical' analysis articulates the conceptual core of the intuitive notion of what it means to share an intentional attitude. I believe that this idea should not be given up, especially since doing so charges us with the burden of providing an analysis of the folk-psychological, non-technical notion of sharing an intentional attitude, and seems to depart from the view accepted by Gilbert that the 'we' of joint attitudes has to be accounted for from the point of view of the participating individuals (Gilbert 1989: chapter 4). The second response raises deeper issues as to how conceptual analysis relates to questions of formation. In particular, other ways of arriving at shared intentional attitudes than via (implicit) expressions of willingness would have to be possible (if perhaps only theoretically), and given Gilbert's insistence on the formation of joint commitments through (implicit) expressions of willingness, some argument would be needed as to why this is the only way, or at least the preferred way, in which joint commitments are formed *among us*.

b) The second problem is that even where other ways of forming plural subjects are accommodated in the analysis, the claim that *in some cases* plural subjects are formed by the participating individuals' openly expressing their willingness to form a plural subject sets off regress, which may be infinite. Open expressions, however implicit they may be, are *communicative* actions. Communication, however, is a *joint action* involving joint intentional attitudes of the epistemic and practical kind. Therefore, the formation of a plural subject of the belief that x, or the intention to x, presupposes another plural subject: namely, the plural subject of communication—that is, the plural subject of what the participants are doing together if they (implicitly) openly express their willingness to be jointly committed to believe to x. The plural subject of the communication, in turn, involves a plural subject of the communication which constitutes the 'we' of the communication about the constitution of the plural subject of the belief that x, and so on and so forth.

Let me take a step back here. The issue at stake is the *kind of knowledge* which the participants must have of their having a joint epistemic attitude for this attitude to exist. In her general account of what it means to form a 'we', or a group, Gilbert appeals to Georg Simmel's view that for people to be a 'we', or a group, they need to *believe* to be a 'we', or a group. Gilbert conceives of this 'plural self-consciousness' in terms of a reflective attitude had by the individuals towards the group. This conception of the role of plural self-consciousness in the constitution of a plural self runs into the *same kind of problems* that have already been well-studied in the case of *individual self-consciousness*. The *circle* and *infinite regress* shown above are marks of what Dieter Henrich has called the 'reflection theory of self-consciousness' (Henrich 1968). If self-consciousness were to be of the kind of self-reflection, there would have to be a self *already in place* in order to be able to make itself the object of its reflective attitudes (the regress), and any attempt to provide an *explanation* of *that* self in terms of its being reflectively aware of itself would simply be circular. I take it to be well-established—by Henrich and other members of the Heidelberg school of self-consciousness (for example, Frank 1991)—that the basic way in which consciousness involves self-consciousness cannot be understood in the way of self-reflection—that is, in terms of some knowledge that is *about* oneself. By contrast to reflective self-consciousness, the basic kind of *self-awareness* is not a second, separate attitude with a different content, but rather part of the self or attitude of which it is aware. Jean-Paul Sartre has labelled this basic form of self-awareness 'conscience (de) soi', with the 'de' in brackets to emphasize that the consciousness in question is not a 'thetic', reflective consciousness—that is, consciousness *of* the self where the self is the content of that consciousness—but rather a 'non-thetic', pre-reflective type of self-awareness that *is* the self (Sartre 1948). For A to be aware of the sun's rising it is necessary for A to be aware of *his* being aware of the sun's rising, and this is a non-thetic and pre-reflective awareness that is not an additional attitude, but part of the very awareness of the sun's rising itself.

Herein finally lies the cornerstone of an adequate theory of which kind of attitude must be which individuals have for that attitude to be shared—what the 'form' or 'colouring' of that attitude is—and what the kind of awareness is they must have of each other—that is, what 'lateral' or 'we-contact' means. The claim is: for an attitude to be a shared attitude, the participants must be self-aware of their attitude—epistemic, practical, aesthetic, or affective—as had by *them* (plural) in such a way that their pre-reflective, non-thetic self-awareness is *plural* rather than individual, an awareness which equally relates the participating individuals to themselves, and to the other participants. For A's and B's being *jointly* aware of the weather, it is necessary for A and B to be non-thetically and pre-reflectively aware of *their* (plural) being aware of the weather, and this plural self-awareness *constitutes* the plural subject of the attitude, in whichever way it may have come about, in the same way individual self-awareness constitutes the individual self. In *plural self-awareness*, the participants are reciprocally *aware of each other* in the same way that they are *aware of themselves*—that is, in the same non-thetic, pre-reflective way.[3]

This conception of plural subjectivity finally allows us to understand one basic difference between the way in which a *plural subject* is involved in any sharing of attitudes from the way in which a *corporate subject* is formed in such complex cases of the creation of *personae fictae* as analyzed by Pettit. As opposed to the corporate subject, which is *different* from the participating individuals, the plural subject is no *additional subject* over and above the head of the participants, but rather a modification of *their own* subjectivity. If two people decide to form a political party, or some other goal-directed group of the kind Pettit has in mind, a new, *third subject* is formed. If two people go for a walk together, by contrast, there are *two* subjects acting *as one*, but certainly not three. The plural subject they form is a form of *their own subjectivity*, and not external to it in the way corporate subjects are, even though the plural attitude is not reducible to an aggregate of individual attitudes and some form of reciprocal knowledge. The simple sharing of attitude does involve a plural subject, but not a corporate subject 'over and above' the head of the participant individuals, and whether or not corporate subjects are just 'metaphysical excrescences', as Searle seems to suggest, or rather important elements of the social world, as Pettit claims, it seems clear that they are *different* from plural subjects, and that they *presuppose* plural subjects.

3 Conclusion: why state the obvious?

I have argued in the previous section that joint (epistemic) attitudes are irreducible, relational, and pre-reflective, and that such attitudes are joint in which the participants are aware of themselves as a 'we', which is a form of their own subjectivity rather than a corporate subject. Heidegger has argued that such sharing is essential to truth. Along the lines of the analysis developed in the first section, we might say that insofar as any of our

---

[3] This comes close to what Sartre called the 'nous-sujet' (Sartre 1991: 474ff.). Sartre, however, claims that this is not the basic ontological structure of human groups, but rather a merely psychological phenomenon. For a critique of Sartre's views, see Schmid 2005: §2, §12).

concerns pertains to truth, we are connected to each other in such a way as to be in the focus of our epistemic attitudes as beings potentially included in plural self-awareness. Plural self-awareness—which is pre-reflective—constitutes collective epistemic commonality.

If this is true, collective epistemic commonality is structurally on a par with individual cognition—that is, neither more fundamental, nor based in purely individual cognition. The constitution of the collective epistemic subject is of the same kind as the constitution of the individual epistemic subject, and there seems to be no reason to assume that individual self-awareness precedes plural self-awareness in the way Margaret Gilbert seems to assume that the 'I' precedes the 'we' (Gilbert 1989: 427). Collective epistemic commonality therefore seems to be a rather *basic* phenomenon. Michael Tomasello has convincingly argued that communication and the formation of joint commitments already *presuppose* joint epistemic attitudes. Thus there is a basic sense in which truth is shared in a *pre-consensual* sense, with no need for talk or even implicit communication. Martin Heidegger has the two hikers of his example being jointly enrapt by the view of the landscape without exchanging a single word about the matter. In fact, Heidegger even pokes fun at the idea that any talk between his two hikers might be necessary or even helpful for any genuine sharing of experience between them (Heidegger 1996: 86). The way truth is shared between them, Heidegger argues, tends to be *covered* up rather than *disclosed* by conversation, since it is *in the experience* rather than in any *talking about the experience* that the sharedness at issue between them resides. This brings us back to Taylor's suggestion, which seems to be mistaken: collective epistemic commonality does not presuppose conversation. Basic forms of collective epistemic commonality are not of the consensual kind. What role does this leave for conversation in the sharing of truth?

Note that until now our discussion of joint epistemic attitudes has been limited largely to joint *perceptual* beliefs—that is, to beliefs formed on the base of what is perceptually available to the participants. Such epistemic attitudes might be basic for our cognition, but in actual fact, very few of our joint epistemic attitudes are of that kind, and our epistemic lives would be rather poor if limited to perceptual beliefs. It seems obvious that conversation is needed to *broaden* the scope of epistemological collectivity beyond perceptual doxastic attitudes and simple inferential joint beliefs to non-perceptual or inferential beliefs of a more ambitious kind. We may share cognitive attitudes with regard to what is in our perceptual field without any consensus, and maybe share knowledge of obvious conclusions, but in order to share highly inferential beliefs we certainly need to appeal to some sort of consensus. Collective, highly inferential beliefs need some form of communication, and are probably really some form of joint commitment.

This *broadening of scope*, however, is irrelevant to our initial example of the two neighbours, since all they are talking about is what they see right before them, and do not make complex inferences. Should we therefore conclude that this is just *empty talk without any contribution to their epistemic commonality*? Are people who are talking about the obvious just pursuing non-epistemic purposes, or talking idly for no reason at all?

I see two ways in which this conclusion is mistaken. Conversation not only *widens the scope* of our epistemic collectivity; metaphorically speaking, it also enlarges it in the two remaining spatial dimensions by *deepening* it and by constituting a *higher form*, even in cases of conversations about shared perceptual beliefs. Consensus *deepens* collective epistemic attitudes by constituting shared content *under a description*. Heidegger's hikers may share their experience without losing any words about it, but in the case of our two neighbours it is not just the *experience* but also its *description* that they share, which deepens the collective experience. Second, consensus moves joint epistemic attitudes from the basic level of a simple social fact to the higher level of *social status*, or an *institutional fact*.[4] The conversation between our neighbours marks a step from their *sharing an experience* to their *counting as sharers of an experience*. The difference is a matter of status, along the lines analyzed by John Searle (1995): it is ontological, but it has normative consequences. By consenting on a view they acquire the status of joint believers in a similar way as a couple acquires the status of being engaged to each other by exchanging marriage vows. In our example the normative consequences are certainly much less dramatic. Turning the shared experience into something that connects us *by way of our status as joint knowers* may mostly have normative consequences for the way in which shared attitudes are made available for future reference. This becomes visible in the negative case. Sometimes people forget experiences which they shared with others. When they forget *shared views on which they consented*, they are not just met with disappointment, but with *stronger reproaches* from those whom they left alone with their memories, precisely because what they forgot was *consented* by them, and not just something they had. Thus part of what conversations such as the one between our neighbours do may be to create a shared past.

References

Aumann, R. (1976), 'Agreeing to disagree', *Annals of Statistics* 4/6: 1236–9.
Frank, M. (1991), *Selbstbewusstsein und Selbsterkenntnis. Essays zur analytischen Philosophie der Subjektivität* (Stuttgart: Reclam).
Gilbert, M. (1987), 'Modelling collective belief', *Synthese* 73/1: 185–204.
—— (1989), *On Social Facts* (London: Routledge).
—— (2003), 'The structure of the social atom: Joint commitment and the foundation of human social behavior' in F. Schmitt (ed.), *Socializing Metaphysics* (Lanham: Rowman), pp. 39–64.
Grice, P. (1975), 'Logic and conversation', in P. Cole and J. Morgan (eds), *Syntax and Semantics*, vol. 3, pp. 41–58.
Heidegger, M. (1996), *Einleitung in die Philosophie* (Frankfurt am Main: Klostermann).
Helm, B. (2008), 'Plural agents', *Nous* 42: 17–49.
Henrich, D. (1966), 'Fichtes ursprüngliche Einsicht', in D. Henrich *et al.* (eds), *Subjektivität und Metaphysik* (Frankfurt am Main: Klostermann), pp. 188–231.

---

[4] The idea of knowledge as institutional is developed in Kusch 2002.

Hildebrand, D. von (1930), *Metaphysik der Gemeinschaft* (St. Augustin).

Husserl, E. (1973), *Zur Phänomenologie der Intersubjektivität. Texte aus dem Nachlaß, zweiter Teil (1921–1928)* (Dordrecht: Kluwer).

—— (1993), *Die Krisis der europäischen Wissenschaft und die transzendentale Phänomenologie. Ergänzungsband, Texte aus dem Nachlaß* (Dordrecht: Kluwer).

Kenny, A. (1993), *Action, Emotion and Will* (Bristol: Thoemmes).

Kochan, J. and Schmid, H. B. (forthcoming), 'Philosophy of science', in S. Luft and S. Overgaard (eds), *Routledge Companion of Phenomenology*, (London: Routledge).

Kusch, M. (2002), *Knowledge by Agreement* (Oxford: Oxford University Press).

Lewis, D. K. (1969), *Convention: A Philosophical Study* (Cambridge: Cambridge University Press).

Mathiesen, K. (2006), 'Epistemic features of group belief', *Episteme* 2/3: 161–75.

Meijers, A. W. M. (2003), 'Can collective intentionality be individualized?', *American Journal of Economics and Sociology* 62/1: 167–183.

Mulligan, K. (2007), 'Intentionality, knowledge, and formal objects', in Hommage à Wlodek, electronic Festschrift for Wlodek Rabinowiz, http://www.fil.lu.se/HommageaWlodek/site/papper/MulliganKevin.pdf.

Nozick, R. (2001), *Invariances. The Structure of the Objective World* (Cambridge, MA: Belknap Press).

Peacocke, C. (2005), 'Joint attention: Its nature, reflexivity, and relation to common knowledge' in N. Eilan *et al.* (eds), *Joint Attention: Communication and Other Minds* (Oxford: Oxford University Press).

Pettit, P. (2003), 'Groups with minds of their own', in F. Schmitt (ed.), *Socializing Metaphysics* (Lanham, Rowman), pp. 167–94.

Rovane, C. (1998), *The Bounds of Agency* (New Haven: Yale University Press).

Sartre, J.-P. (1948), 'Conscience de soi et connaissance de soi', *Bulletin de la société française de philosophie* 42, 56–87.

—— (1991), *L'être et le néant. Essay d'ontologie phénoménologique* (Paris: Gallimard).

Scheler, M. (1974), *Wesen unçd Formen der Sympathie* (Bern: Franke).

—— (1982), 'Der Krieg als Gesamterlebnis' in M. Scheler, *Politisch-Pädagogische Schriften. Gesammelte Werke* vol. 4 (Bern/München: Franke), pp. 272–82.

—— (2000), *Der Formalismus in der Ethik und die materiale Wertethik. Neuer Versuch der Grundlegung eines ethischen Personalismus* (Bonn: Bouvier).

Schmid, H. B. (2000), *Subjekt, System, Diskurs. Edmund Husserls Begriff transzendentaler Subjektivität in sozialtheoretischen Bezügen* (Dordrecht: Kluwer).

—— (2003), 'Can brains in vats think as a team?', *Philosophical Explorations* 6/3: 201–18.

—— (2009), *Plural Action: Essays in Philosophy and Social Science* (Hamburg: Springer).

—— and Sirtes, D., and Weber, M. (eds) (2011), *Collective Epistemology* (Heusenstamm: Ontos).

Searle, J. R. (1990), 'Collective intentions and actions' in P. Cohen *et al.* (eds), *Intentions in Communication* (Cambridge MA: MIT Press), pp. 401–15.

—— (1995), *The Construction of Social Reality* (New York: Basic Books).

—— (1998), 'Social ontology and the philosophy of society', in *Analyse und Kritik* 20: 143–58.

—— (2010), *The Making of the Social World* (New York: Oxford University Press).

Stein, E. (1922), 'Beiträge zur philosophischen Begründung der Psychologie und der Geisteswissenschaften, zweite Abhandlung: Individuum und Gemeinschaft', in *Jahrbuch für Philosophie und phänomenologische Forschung* 5: 116–284.

Taylor, C. (1995), *Philosophical Arguments* (Cambridge MA: Harvard University Press).

Tollefsen, D. (2002), 'Challenging epistemic individualism', *Protosociology* 16: 86–117.

Tomasello, M. (1998), *The Cultural Origins of Human Cognition* (Cambridge, MA: MIT Press).

Tugendhat, E. (1970a), *Der Wahrheitsbegriff bei Husserl und Heidegger* (Berlin: DeGruyter).

——(1970b), 'Phänomenologie und Sprachanalyse' in R. Bubner *et al.* (eds), *Hermeneutik und Dialektik, Bd. II: Sprache und Logik, Theorie der Auslegung und Probleme der Einzelwissenschaften* (Tübingen: Mohr), pp. 3–23.

Tuomela, R. (1992), 'Group Beliefs', *Synthese* 91: 285–318.

——(1995), *The Importance of Us: A Study of Basic Social Notions* (Stanford: Stanford University Press).

——(2007), *The Philosophy of Sociality: The Shared Point of View* (New York: Oxford University Press).

Walther, G. (1923), 'Zur Ontologie der sozialen Gemeinschaften', *Jahrbuch für Philosophie und phänomenologische Forschung* 6: 1–158.

Zahavi, D. (2004), 'Husserl's noema and the internalism–externalism debate' *Inquiry* 47/1: 42–66.

PART V

ETHICS, POLITICS, AND SOCIALITY

CHAPTER 20

RESPONSIVE ETHICS

BERNHARD WALDENFELS

1 RESPONSIVE VERSUS COMMUNICATIVE ETHICS

Ethics has always revolved around the question as how to live and to act in the right way. This question can be answered in variant ways: with regard to aims and values, laws and norms, discursive claims to validity, or consequences. So we distinguish between a teleological, a deontic or a utilitarian ethics, represented by authors such as Aristotle, Hume, Kant, Habermas, or Mill. The special kind of responsive ethics which I propose is not apt to replace the other approaches, but is able to change the accent and to shift the relative weight in the field of ethics. 'C'est le ton qui fait la musique': similarly, it may be the tone which makes the ethics.[1]

The new tone will be named 'response'—that is, responding to the Other's demand or appeal. This sort of response has to be taken not only in the narrow sense of linguistic answers, but in the wider sense of responding on all registers of our bodily experience. There are various registers of response, similar to the registers on an organ. We respond by our senses, by our desire, by our memories and expectations, by our spatial orientation, by our speaking and acting, including diverse technical fittings. Besides, we can respond not only by words, but also by keeping silence; no answer is also an answer, as the proverb tells us. We respond by gazes and gestures, but also by acting and doing what the Other asks for. Often we carry on a conversation by hands. At all events, responding does not constitute a specific act such as giving information to a foreigner or answering to the doctor's inquiries. Quite similar to the process of meaning something, of aiming at something, or of following a rule, the process of responding has to be taken as a basic trait, present in all our behaviour towards things, towards ourselves, and towards others.

---

[1] For a comprehensive treatment of this issue, see Waldenfels 1994 (English translation forthcoming), 2002, 2006b, and the compact presentation of the basic theses in Waldenfels 2006a (Eng. tr. 2011).

It is precisely this basic trait that I call *responsivity*. Mostly it remains unnoticed and implicit. If you ask a chess player what he or she is doing he or she will certainly answer: 'I am just playing chess', or 'I just threaten the Other's queen', but only in special cases one would reply: 'I follow a chess rule'. A customer, setting about to balance an account, would rarely declare: 'I am performing an exchange act'. Precisely in the same way, we respond by saying or doing something; and only in special situations does responding get explicit such as in the phrase: 'I would answer ...'

Now, in contrast with other sorts of acts, responding is especially characterized by its starting *from elsewhere*. When responding, we are always incited, attracted, threatened, challenged, or appealed to by a somewhat or a somebody, before taking the initiative and aiming at something or applying certain norms. Of course, we are permanently involved in everyday situations to which we respond by recurring to certain 'stocks of knowledge', as Alfred Schutz puts it; there are always different types of answer at our disposal like the expressive repertoire of a skilled actor. But this changes when we stumble into situations for which we are not prepared and in which we do not feel quite at home. In addition to this, we have to raise the question as to whether there is any situation that is rid of all surprises, in which we were completely at home. This would only be the case if our behaviour were to be reduced to formal operations and the situation reduced to a set of manipulative data. Certainly, there are exceptional situations which overcome us such as the attack on the World Trade Center on 11 September. Still, the feature of *Fremdheit*, of otherness or alienness, in spectacular situations really catching our eyes, permeates all our experience in a tacit and inconspicuous way. Take the Other's gaze or word; it strikes us, whether welcome or not. We enter a field beyond liberty and constraint, beyond good and evil. A factor of otherness, of *heteron*, intrudes everywhere with the effect that traditional key figures such as *aisthesis*, *logos*, *nomos*, or *praxis* take on certain features of *heteroaisthesis*, *heterology*, *heteronomy*, and *heteropractise*, partly envisaged by Husserl. At the same time, we become aware of how the *logos* originates from a sort of *pathos*. Amazement and fear provoke our response which is neither, as Aristotle suggests, a *logos that a human being has* nor, as Heidegger suggests (1953: 134), a *logos that has the human being*. On the whole, a responsive ethics does not postulate new rules and new aims. Instead it raises the simple question: 'What are we struck by and what we are responding to while saying this or doing that?' This may be either something surprizing and overwhelming me or else somebody addressing me by a request, a promise, or an act of violence.

A responsive ethics starts from the Other's *demand* which arises here and now and always anew. So it goes deeper than the attempts of a communicative ethics and a rational morality, focused on common aims and universal norms. It goes back onto a *pre-final* and *pre-normative* level of experience. The Other's demand appears to be just as inspiring as the astonishment which Plato puts at the beginning of philosophical thinking (Plato 1900–7: *Theaetetus* 155 d). and it joins the power of the platonic *eros* (ibid.: *Phaedrus* 249 c–d). The *pathos* of astonishment can expand into sym-pathy, co-affection and sensible con-sensus, but not into a logical agreement. In this respect, platonic astonishment contrasts with Cartesian doubt; the former occurs to us, whereas the latter is chosen by us. Similarly, the singular demand, which I receive from the Other, differs from the universal claim to validity, which arises from everyone's assertion.

Such a sudden demand is able to extricate us from our habits and to shake our whole existence. Morality can no longer be taken for granted. The voice of amorality, invoked by Nietzsche, reveals the weakness of morality and what I call the 'blind spot of the moral' (Waldenfels 1995: ch. 22). No ethics and no morals are sufficiently supported by the aims, values, norms, and utilities which they invoke. What is the Good good for? Why should I obey to the law? Why should I first of all try to preserve myself? As system theorists like to argue, the difference at stake in the binary good/bad is not good itself. Morality either turns into a quasi-religious faith if it glosses over its own abysses, or it betrays itself, taking hold outside in the fields of nature, history, or culture. According to Husserl we need an *ethical epoché* which covers 'all acts referring to an absolute "ought" and everything that in this respect is relevant within the universal practical field' (Husserl 1959: 319). By practising this *epoché* we leave the ground of well-established morals without taking refuge in a sphere of pure morality or in a purely moral community. We are present at an estrangement of our normal seeing and speaking that allows for a genealogy of the moral. Literature offers good help here. Figures such as Raskolnikov, Madame Bovary, or Kafka's Mr. K. will protect us against the simplifications and artificial inventions of a mere handbook- or common sense-morals.

Such considerations open paths into the 'vast, distant and so hidden landscape of morals' (Nietzsche 1980: vol. 5, p. 254). In what follows I will restrict myself to three main topics: first, the traditional role of responsibility; second, responding as its counterpart; and third, the possible connections between response and responsibility. These connections will be examined through two motives: the advance of trust and the surplus of the extraordinary in relation to the Third Party.

2 BEING RESPONSIBLE FOR SOMETHING TO THE OTHER

The idea of responsibility comes from the sphere of juridical law, and has a theological touch. The German term *Verantwortung* is documented from as early as the fifteenth century, followed in the eighteenth century by the French and English words *responsabilité* and *responsibility*. In Greek, it is the dialogical term λόγον διδόναι which is the nearest; and it echoes in the German expression *Rede und Antwort stehen*. The process of 'giving' and 'taking' the *logos* reflects the interchange of the *dia-logue*; yet by its concentration on a single and homogeneous logos, the classical dialogue tends to become a monologue with assigned parts. Thus dialogical responsibility is dominated by two motives. On the one side it functions as a *calling to account* and a *giving account* by means of arguments; on the other side, as an *imputation* of actions. This is well known from legal practises in court, including a forum for the discussion of moral issues. The process of becoming and making responsible shows three essential traits.

(1) One becomes responsible *for something* that one has said or done, whether of one's free will or by negligence. The readiness to extend the responsibility to what exceeds one's own intentions distinguishes an ethics of responsibility from a mere ethics of conviction.[2] In any case, one remains in the perspective of the *past* which Aristotle already attributes to the genre of speech in court. The judgement of the court refers to existing facts in ways similar to historical or moral judgements.

(2) One becomes responsible *to* or *before somebody*, whether a court occupied by individual office-holders or an anonymous forum such as the public, society, or history. Kafka's text *Before the Law* depicts this situation in all its depth. The perspective here shifts to the neutrality of the *Third Party*. The paradigm figure is the judge who stands between the parties, blind-folded, without any respect of persons. By separating the role of complainant, of defendant, and the judge, the law suit sharply contrasts with an open debate between persons who are on a par with each other. Thus Plato (1900–7: *Rep.* 398 b) emphasizes that the philosophical dispute needs no judge because everybody appears as speaker and judge in one person. But even in this case the Third Party is not lacking completely. The *logos* of the dialogue, in which all interlocutors participate, constitutes the Third. In modern terms the part of the Third Party can be defined as transsubjective; only the initial search for arguments takes on intersubjective features, but not the final evaluation of statements and proposals.

(3) One justifies *oneself*. Without a doer or a perpetrator to whom the action is ascribed in order to avow or to disavow, the subject to be judged is a mere matter of fact which might be described and explained, but not a deed waiting to be justified. Responsibility is especially important for the status of the modern 'subject' who does not only appear as the bearer of responsibility, but rather as its essence. Responsibility, based on sanity, is the precondition for being qualified as a legal or a moral person. Someone who is unable to be called to account for something, neither passes for a legal person, endowed with rights and duties, nor for a normal citizen. Thus the third perspective we are considering is that of the doer.

The classical paradigm of responsibility we have outlined so far appears as clearly limited. It needs to be revised under all its aspects.

(1) Responsibility turns up *post festum* after the deed has been accomplished. The subsequent assessment does not tell us what we have *to do* now and in the future. Somebody may object that our acting must in itself be defined as responsible or irresponsible. However, this responsibility *in actu*, clearly different from the responsibility *post actum*, is by no means homogeneous. It includes the observance of rules, the consideration of

---

[2] Max Weber's famous distinction has long since had to be altered. By the planetary tele-effects of our actions, operating in climatic change, in the consumption of raw materials, in the proliferation of destructive weapons, and on the exchange market, we are forced to redefine the limits of responsibility; anyone who would be held responsible for everything would be responsible for nothing.

circumstances and consequences, and the coordination of individual actions. The special weight we attribute to our responding to the Other's demand does not come forth so long as we do not conceive acting itself as responsive.

(2) Further limits appear when we regard the standards to which our actions are submitted. Whoever defends himself or herself against Others does so by referring to a given political, legal, or moral order. Now, we presume that every order whatsoever is contingent from the beginning (Waldenfels 1987). 'Contingent' does not mean arbitrary as the debates between modernists and post-modernists often suggested. Not unlike linguistic orders, all practical orders can be other than they are, but not completely other. The simple interpretation of an action as a larceny presupposes an existing proprietary right. If citizens who are evading high sums of taxes, or managers who are taking high bonuses after grave mismanagements are not ranked as thieves or swindlers, this is due to a moral book-keeping by double entry. The qualification of acts of violence, whether as first- or second-degree murder, whether as a fight for liberty or as a terrorist act, raises similar questions. Certain actions are called theft or murder, as Hobbes argues (1987: 6, 16). Practical judgements are certainly based on reasons, but never on *sufficient* reasons, unless we are living in the best of all worlds.

(3) Lastly, responsibility shows its limits when we consider the agent's role. Giving account without any restriction requires a self-supporting subject that completely masters its own speaking and acting. Such a subject would be, according to Kant's well-known definition of liberty as the 'power of beginning a state spontaneously' (1966: vol. 2, 488). But if we admit that our actions are our own only to some extent and that they are influenced by unconscious and involuntary forces, we must concede that we are not the 'master of our own house' and that we are affected by *Fremdheit*, by alienness or otherness, in our inmost part. Therefore every attempt to offer an account of our actions meets with something *incalculable* amidst all calculations and imputations. Even moral book-keeping has void entries.

The classical conception we have presented suffers from a permanent erosion that is reinforced by systemic constraints. In his novel *The Man without Qualities* Robert Musil predicts a 'world filled with qualities without man...of lived experiences without somebody living them...', as if 'the friendly burden of personal responsibility would be revolved into a formula system of possible meanings' (Musil 1978: 150). But he plays down misleading expectations by conceding to the hero certain 'incalculability' and a 'feeling of insufficient reasons' against which the 'public persecutors and security chiefs of logic' cannot do anything (ibid.: 17, 35, 47). Who is still responsible to whom? This question is all the more important insofar as our life-world is approaching a state of sub-systems that are maintained only by the functional imperatives of system preservation, seeking nothing more than connectivity as such. It is not so astonishing to see that system theorists have little to do with alienness or otherness. If it is really true that everybody is alien in his or her own way, then nobody will be alien. Our man without qualities will end as a man without otherness. Does this mean that Marxism will gain a late victory by the abolition of alienation?

3 RESPONDING TO THE OTHER'S DEMAND

The situation abruptly changes when we start no longer from our own speaking and doing, but from responding. Responding to the Other's demand means much more than accounting for one's own deeds. A scene taken from Herbert Melville's short story *Bartleby the Scrivener* may illustrate what is at stake. Bartleby is a clerk, working as a law-copyist in the office of an honorable lawyer at New York. After having done his work for a long time, he refuses his service from one moment to the other, and he does so in a rather strange way. To the lawyer's request to copy the documents as usual he simply answers with a 'rarely soft, fast voice': 'I would prefer not to'. This stereotypically repeated 'no' is a no without 'ifs' or 'buts'. In my book *Antwortregister* I have interpreted this story as a case of response refusal (1994: 587–9).

Obviously this conversation definitively fails, but it does not fail, because the usual standards of intentionality, of communicability, or of utility are neglected. The cited sentence can be easily understood; the meaning shows up rather clearly. No practical rules are violated; for who stops serving does not offend against a regulation like a common striker who walks out, but remains ready to negotiate. At last, the conversation does not fail because what is said does not suit the circumstances; there are no appropriate circumstances for this escape from the usual. Indeed, this escape appears as a verbal anticipation of suicide with which the story finishes. Taken to a house for vagrants, the former clerk refuses eating and literally passes away. Such a kind of communicative refusal shows that all attempts to resolve the situation, such as those made by hermeneutics, discourse analytics, or pragmatics, fail. True, there is a dialogical remainder left, but this farewell to dialogue consists only in saying 'no'. It happens in the paradoxical form of a negative speech act such as: 'I am saying nothing'. The speaker says what he does not do, and he does not do what he says. Linguistic pragmatists are inclined to disqualify this linguistic slip as a case of performative contradiction; however, the speaker is really involved in a lived conflict, a *Widerstreit*, or *différend*. Not even the attempt to retreat into silence would suffice to resolve the paradox, since silence itself becomes eloquent as soon as somebody has entered the stage of communication. Whoever keeps silent continues to participate in the conversation, if only as a dark shadow. What the story tells us pertains to a deep dimension that has already been announced under the title of *responsivity*.[3]

The special kind of responding at stake here splits into the *given answer*: the propositional content which fills in a lacuna of knowledge, and the process of *giving an answer*

---

[3] The only equivalent, showing German roots, would be the word *Antwortlichkeit*; but this is as unusual as the corresponding Russian word *otvetnost*, introduced by Mikhail Bakhtin in his many-voiced conception of literature, and rendered in English with *responsiveness* (Bakhtin 1981: 346) or *answerability* (see Bakthin 1990; see also Waldenfels 1999: 168). The term *Responsivität*, which stems from the German nineteenth-century school medicine, is systematically used by Kurt Goldstein to characterize manifestations of the organism which meet the requirements of the milieu (Goldstein 1934: 265–82, and Waldenfels 1994: 457–9).

or *replying*—that is, the process of engaging with the Other's demand or evading it. The case of the scrivener demonstrates that the event of giving exceeds what is given. What is given may have a pecuniary value, whereas the event of giving has not. In a similar way, what is said may have a predicative truth-value, whereas the event of saying has not. Giving is an event which only lives on by a sort of re-giving, just as the event of saying depends upon a sort of re-saying, of *redire*, as Levinas puts it. Given answers may become sediments, habits, or a symbolic capital, but not so the event of giving an answer that happens here and now.

The doubling of responding, on the side of the respondent, corresponds with a doubling of the demand, on the side of the addressee. So we distinguish between the *claim to something* and the *appeal to somebody*—both called *Anspruch* in German. Let us imagine someone complying with a request. At first sight this seems rather simple, yet it has to be understood in a double way. On the one side, one can comply with a request by giving what is requested; on the other side, the act of requesting can be complied with only if reduced to a mere state of lack. Or consider the situation of thanking. Thanking somebody for something means more than an empty phrase or a mere accessory; it finds its place in the fissure that separates the given from the giver and the giver from the receiver. Nobody has grasped this crucial issue better than Giuseppe Ungaretti in his two-line poem: 'Tra un fiore colto e l'altro donato / l'inesprimibile nulla' ('Between a flower picked up and the other given / the inexpressible nothing'). The double event of demand and response turns out to be the incorporation of a peculiar *logos*, joined with a certain *ethos*. Once more we can distinguish three aspects showing how the logic of response exceeds the logic of responsibility.

(1) The first aspect concerns the *temporality* of responding. The Other's demand resists being reduced to normatively warranted rights which are pre-given and can be claimed at any moment. Everything that addresses us in terms of incitation, look, or appeal does not come from ourselves, but comes to us. This difference of orientation is decisive. What appeals to us reaches us from a distance; it arises too early, compared with our own initiative, whereas our response is too late, compared with what happens to us. This does not mean that *something* precedes our initiative, such as a stimulus which causes a reaction; rather, we precede *ourselves*. This can be expressed paradoxically, taking as a pattern Plato's (1900–7: *Parmenides* 141 c–d) characterization of being in time: *I am younger and older than myself*. Simultaneously, we are faced with an originary form of precedence and of posteriority. Thus our speaking and acting are never totally up to date. Our responding is separated from what we are responding to by a hiatus. I use the ancient term *diastasis* to characterize this peculiar sort of time-lag.

There are cases of increased experience which bring to light this temporal deferment. Let us first take the shock that is caused by a perplex event; as Descartes remarks, it makes our body as immobile as a statue (1988: art. 73). Shocks play a special role in modern aesthetics like that of Walter Benjamin. Moreover, there are traumatic events, only to be grasped by their after-effects. In his analysis of the Wolfsmann Freud speaks explicitly of on original sort of *Nachträglichkeit*, of deferment or posteriority. In the meantime, the loss of language from which traumatic patients suffer pertains to everyday therapeutics. Yet, beyond pathological effects, we should consider scientific discoveries and artistic inventions, which surprise not only contemporaries, but first of all the researchers and the artists themselves. The history of science, studded with shifting paradigms, shows plenty of innovations which had to wait for their recognition. Let us lastly refer to the foundation of political or religious orders. Incisive happenings, such as the foundation of Rome, the birth of Christ or Buddha, the Reformation or the French revolution, are only *après coup* changed into dated events, inserted into the chronologies of history. Phrases such as Lichtenberg's 'It thinks' or Foucault's 'There is order' indicate events of foundation (*Stiftung*) which come to light only by a series of post-foundations (*Nachstiftungen*). Every festival, leaving behind simple routine and economic exploitation, takes on traits of a symbolic re-event.

(2) The second aspect constitutes the *inevitability* of responding. Influenced by certain traditions, we spontaneously tend to ask whether what happens or appeals to us is a matter of descriptive facts or prescriptive norms. Our answer is: neither one nor the other. The standard distinction between 'is' and 'ought', between individual facts and universal norms, fails in the face of the Other's demand. Situational demands, such as a request for help or a simple inquiry as to the right direction, do not amount to mere facts that we register, nor do they come under general law. Some philosophers like to push up such simple incidents into the field of everyday morals which matters only for sociologists or historians. But by such abstinence, moral gets deprived of its humus. Paul Watzlawick formulated the thesis: 'One cannot not communicate.' This double 'not' suggests a sort of *being forced*, of *Müssen*, which constitutes a practical form of necessity. The communicative trap, suggested by Watzlawick, passes into a responsive trap. The double bind generated by commands such as 'Do not listen to me!' refers to an inner compulsion, not to be confused with an outer causation. 'We feel compelled', as we say, and this does not by any means express a lack of liberty. In Proust's *Recherche* (1989: vol. III, p. 693) it is the dying writer Bergotte who invokes 'unknown laws which we obeyed, because we bore in ourselves their instruction, without knowing who had them inscribed there.' This last minute insight is not provoked by the look into a moral text-book, but by an inconspicuous motive—namely, the 'little yellow brick' in Vermeer's 'View of Delft'. Levinas approaches the same insight when he stresses the disturbing and troubling quality of the Other's demand and defines the ethical as a kind of *non-indifference*, previous to any argument (Levinas 1974: 105).

(3) The third aspect contests the status of the so-called subject or self, as I prefer to say. Certainly, the liberty of an autonomous being, acting from itself, does not vanish under the Other's demand and command; yet it will be transformed into what may be called *responsive liberty*. That means that being an agent *I start*, but being a respondent *I start from elsewhere*—that is, from a place where I am not, where I have not yet been, and where I will never be. Hereby I make my appearance in two ways: as a patient to whom something happens, and as a respondent who responds to this. One's self is a divided self, as Lacan and others put it. Nevertheless, answers are not presented as coins on the counter. The answers I give must be invented, or more precisely, they are found (*finden sich*) by coming to us. Once again we are running into a paradox. Like the lover in Lacan's

view, the respondent gives what he or she does not have. Brecht's *Legend of the Rise of the Book Taoteking* ends with the following lines: 'One must first tear the wisdom from the wise. / So the costumer should be thanked too / He has demanded it from him—*er hat es ihm abverlangt*.' This duet of demand and response, of challenge and response, leaves room for overtones and dissonances. This would yield a better model of history than do goal-orientated processes and rule-governed actions.

4 Advance of Trust

Now we have to face the question as to how a responsive ethics, starting from the Other's demand, is connected with the common aims of a communicative ethics and with the universal norms of morality. If there were no connection at all, our common life would be confined to an oasis, far from society and history, and the relation to the Other would be restricted to a dyad of Me and You. Our search for social cement, connecting otherness and sociality, will start with the motive of trust.

Trust, called πίστις in Greek, *fides* or *fiducia* in Latin, has first of all to do with the Other. In this respect it resembles justice, which in Aristotle's view constitutes a virtue in relation to the Other (πρὸς ἕτερον) (Aristotle 1894: V, 3). One gives credence to somebody or proves to be credible. In the great tradition of practical philosophy, trust plays only an incidental part since its binding force arises from elsewhere. This shows up in an exemplary way in Aristotle's and Hobbes' conception of social life.

In the view of Aristotle, trust is a natural element of every community that is held together by common aims in life. Its proper locus is the area of *friendship*. Becoming friends with another presupposes that the Other can be trusted in every respect and that one can rely on him or her, especially in precarious situations. Friendship constitutes a sphere of confidence and familiarity which grows out of a process of living together, including the proverbial eating salt together. In addition to it, *public speech* is supported by trust, since the orator will not persuade his audience unless he proves to be trustworthy by his *ethos*, by his way of life (Aristotle 1959: I, 2). By contrast, mistrust prepares a fertile soil for enmity, splitting the political community into isolated parts and driving it into violent conflicts with other states. In book IX of Plato's *Politeia* and in book V, 11 of the Aristotelian *Politics* the Tyrannis is depicted in the glaring colours of an all-pervasive mistrust and suspicion. But apart from such a degeneration of personal and political life, trust is omnipresent like the air we are breathing. As an ingredient of sociability, pregiven by nature, it seems so self-evident that it does not even appear on current lists of virtues.

This social tableau changes in the modern era. Thomas Hobbes describes the natural state, as we know, as a permanent war, nourished by the fear of death. The self-preservation of the individual functions as an asocial impulse, excluding any common good. It engenders on the one side a nucleus of *self-confidence*, relying on one's own forces, on the other side a fundamental *mistrust with regard to the Other*. Both are part of our human condition. Symptomatic of this is the situation of travelling which brings us in contact with unknown and foreign people. Whereas Aristotle downplays the dangerous aspects of this situation, referring to a wide-spread philanthropic impulse (Aristotle 1894: VIII, 1), Hobbes gathers from the same situation clear signs of a spontaneous mistrust (Hobbes 1987: 1, 2). This makes us lock the door before going to sleep and carry a sword when travelling. The whole society seems covered by an atmosphere of mistrust; so we do well to leave a party last in order to make sure that nobody will talk bad about us (ibid.). A chance to conquer the mistrust and to compensate for the missing bond of friendship seems only to be given in drawing up an artificial contract. But even a contract will never completely eradicate the mistrust, which will only be delayed. Mistrust penetrates the contract because everybody has to pay an advance of trust when the contract is going to be concluded. In contrast with secondary contracts, which are supported by an existing contract law, the primary contract, known as the social contract, is based on unfulfilled promises, whose precedence generates a time-lag, similar to the above mentioned one.[4] To be sure, one can calculate certain risks like the required advancement of trust, but this will not enable the contract to ensure itself. *Do ut des*—I give so that you give, but how can I make sure that you will really give? Trust and faith appear to be the bond of contracts (Hobbes 1987: 2, 18), but a trust regulated *by institutions*, does not coincide with a trust *in institutions*; the former is not a sufficient safeguard against the breakdown of institutions. In order to warrant stability the state recurs to control measures. 'Explorers' and 'listeners', reduced to mere instruments of the tyrant in the view of Aristotle (1957: V, 11), become members of the civil service in Hobbes' state, comparable to the beams of sun and to spiders' webs (Hobbes 1987: 13, 7). As precursors of the Big Brother, they pertain to the pre-history of espionage and secret service. Through latent or open mistrust, separating not only citizens from citizens, but the ruled from the ruler too, the normal state takes on features of a surveillance state. Notwithstanding various doubts, we must admit that this state model is instructive in its own way. We really learn that trust has to be taken neither as a gift of nature, nor as a 'tacit trust', which spontaneously arises between the governed and the governors, as Locke assumes (1970: XV, 171). Trust rather emerges from contingent acts of trust building (*Vertrauensstiftungen*) that respond to specific risks and dangers. The permanent recourse to situations of insecurity reinforces the impact of time. Trust does not simply exist or not exist; it lasts. To Foucault's basic fact that 'there is order', corresponds the likewise basic fact that 'there is trust'. This fact can neither be transformed into a stock of trust nor banked as moral capital.

In the course of time, a lot of partial solutions have been tested. One reserves trust for a friendly intimacy where we open the heart to each other (see Kant 1966: vol. IV, pp. 156ff), while delivering the public to a sort of 'wholesome suspicion'. How easily

---

[4] Concerning the temporality of concluding a contract and giving a promise see *Schattenrisse der Moral* (Waldenfels 1996: ch. II, 6). In our argumentation it does not matter whether the conclusion of a contract is taken as a construct or as an historical event.

vigilance turns into surveillance has already been shown. More dangerous is the claim to 'realise' trust, just as for Hegelians reason has to be 'realized'—up to the consequences of a bloody fight for fraternity. Today a patchwork prevails. The concept of trust often consists in a confused array of readiness for cooperation, of sentimental proximity, and of risk calculation, close to financial operations and stock-jobbery. The system theory provides more sophisticated tools. In his treatise on *Vertrauen* (1968), Niklas Luhmann characterises trust as the 'reliance upon one's own expectations'; we expect that something will not happen although it might happen. In this sense trust pertains to the mechanisms of reducing social complexity, based on a risky form of advance payment.

My own proposal is focused on the question: in which way and to what extent can and must we admit a special sort of *responsive trust*? Such a responsive approach in no way excludes institutional and professional forms of trust, but it does go beyond them. As already indicated, trust is generally founded by responding to special challenges. What is extremely important in this context is the *ambivalence of alienness*, oscillating between friendly and hostile alienness, between incitation and menace. Confronted with ambivalent situations, we are forced to evaluate, putting our cards on the table. Trust, in the fight against mistrust, seems to be a *primary response* to the Other's demand. Grey neutrality, suggesting that the Other does not matter, has to be taken itself as a response in the mode of refusal. But how is the demand, coming *from the Other*, transformed into a trust that takes place *between us*? On the whole, the phenomenon of trust refers to the *bond*, the *nexus*, which holds together the members of a community, creating the requisite solidarity. Solidarity does not mean something like an affective fusion, a racial homogeneity or a fixed common good; it simply means that one does not separate one's well-being from that of the Others. What is at stake here is the *syn-*, the *con-*, or the *mit-*, without which there would be nothing like a *koinonia*, a community or society: in short, there would be no *living-together* (συζῆν), no *Mitsein*. On the one hand, the simple contract does not suffice; it comes too late to generate social relations. On the other hand, nature constitutes a dubious bond. As is well-known from our common history, numerous things are imputed to nature: for example, an ethnic sort of barbarism, the existence of slaves by nature, the natural subordination of women, a natural hierarchy of races and so forth. Nature seems to be passive like paper. Responsivity, our leading motive, points in another direction. We have to assume a genuine hiatus between *you* and *me*, between the alien and the own. A synthesis emerges only on the level of aims which *we* share, on the level of norms to which *each of us* is subordinated, or on the level of habits which *one* has embodied. Arising from the double event of demand and response, trust has to be considered as a pre-final and pre-normal *syn* or *with*. It simply comes out, but how does this happen?

Let us inspect the phenomenon of trust more precisely. In general terms, trust can be understood as a practical *attitude* towards Others. In contrast to single acts such as promising, trust arises in an implicit and tacit way as something like an unlimited credit. We might call this a sort of *Fremdglaube*, a belief in Others, which like Husserl's

Weltglaube precedes any explicit form of yes and no.[5] When Levinas emphasizes the command: 'You will not kill me' he invokes a borderline experience which highlights the risk of any normality. The *breech of trust* shows what trust means.

Viewed from an eidetic or structural standpoint, trust clearly differs from simple forms of belief by referring to somebody as to its *addressee*. To believe that something is the case is to engage in a diminished form of knowledge, which allows for probability calculations. But trust goes beyond this. It means that I believe in Others, carried by the conviction that they mean what they say, that they do not deceive me and that their utterances are free from any *arrière pensée*,[6] that they will keep their promises; in short, that they are well-disposed to me, even in cases of conflict. Traditionally speaking, trust includes *benevolence* (see Aristotle 1894: IX, 5). In keeping with my existence, far from being absorbed in the actual instant, trust displays its temporal horizons, extended to the future by promising, to the past by fidelity and forgiving. But trust is really effective here and now in our words, deeds, and gestures. Trust that does not prove to be trustworthy would remain ineffectual. Yet *proofs of trust* do not furnish any sort of irrefutable evidence. People become trustworthy precisely in the same way as the public orator obtains this quality in the course of time. Trust grows and vanishes like friendship and love. It gets stabilized by official and personal *rituals of trust*, among them the multiple expression of the smile. Smiling is preformed in gestures of appeasement, and is even performed by animals such as dogs. An exclusive humanizing of trust would be at the cost of its embodiment. Finally, I want to mention the *pledge* as an incorporation of the social bond in the field of things (Mauss 1960: 263–5).

But it is more difficult to show in which way trust is shaped by the crucial event of demand and response. Does trust primarily mean something that I give and owe to the Other, or something the Other offers to me, or something that is going on between us? It strikes me that Levinas' ethics of the Other, seems nearly to neglect the phenomenon of trust.[7] It is not so difficult to say why this is so. The unconditioned demand, arising from the Other's face, cannot be derived from a 'natural benevolence' (see Levinas 1974: 142, 160). It excludes even more any attempt to make my own response dependent upon the benevolence of the Other. Provided that the same is to be expected from the Other, nothing would move between us in case of conflict. In the end, we would stumble into the vicious circle of mutual distrust which feeds on itself. At the best, others would concern me as my own friends, companions, or co-citizens. Alienness that exceeds any common order would be suppressed. Trust would be nothing more than an enlarged form of self-confidence, just as for Aristotle friendship ultimately amounts to an enlarged form of

---

[5] Concerning a pre-predicative *Urglaube*, on the lines of Hume, see Husserl 1950: §§103–6; for my own, I have proposed to divide Husserl's *Glaube* into the variants of *Weltglaube*, *Selbstglaube* and *Fremdglaube* (Waldenfels 1971: 333).

[6] However, trust does not require telling all that one has in mind. Such openness would fail, because behind each thought there are hiding further thoughts.

[7] Concerning my strong but not uncritical relation to Levinas, I refer to the numerous chapters on Levinas in Waldenfels 1995 and 2005—among them, my contribution to the *Cambridge Companion to Levinas* (2002), edited by Simon Critchley and Robert Bernasconi.

self-friendship. This may be the reason why Levinas starts from the abrupt command: 'You will not kill me'. This harsh command, formulated in the future tense, and which is due to the fact that Hebrew does not have a negative imperative, is based on an ethical resistance from which every confidential approximation bounces off. The unconditioned demand speaks out of the murderer's face as well. Imposing on it any restriction, we would return to the limits of a friendship ethics or a law-like moral system. The Other's alienness would be overrun by established forms of ethics and morals that refuse being contested.

In the end, trust does not originate from what we expect from Others, but from the confidence we *give*. Like every sort of giving, which consists in offering presents and exceeding the mutual exchange, giving credence too means giving in advance. Nobody can lay claim to being trusted. Responsive trust only occurs in terms of *the advance of trust*, full of risk; whoever gives will never be sure whether something comes back. Mistrust precisely means that the advance is refused or only given with hesitation; one tries to avoid disappointments by adopting a wait-and-see attitude. Mistrust is not the same as hostility, but it leads to it, unless our legitimate suspicion is governed by a certain trust. One may tolerate the refusal of trust as an attitude of prudence which takes into account human weakness and malignity. But prudential rules do not allow us simply to refuse trust, as if one could get rid of the inevitability of response by pre-judging the Other's demand. We would commit the logical error of a *prius posterius*. Does this mean that there is no bond between us, except by distributing duties and chances in the name of the Third Party?

This question leads us to the *reciprocity* of trust. A perfect form of reciprocity would require a previous comparison, according to the golden rule. At this point Levinas seems to be right, but is this all? Indeed, giving confidence includes *inspiring* or *inducing confidence*. Inducing does not mean producing something, but making something happen, as by calling for someone's attention. Usually, inducing is not performed by an explicit act; rather, we induce the Other's trust *by* saying or doing something. I appear as a creditor by giving confidence, precisely in the same way as I appear as a respondent by responding. Using means of persuasion (Greek, πίστεις) pertains already to a reflected rhetoric, analysed by Aristotle. By contrast, the inducing of trust is part of an elementary genealogy, previous to the calculation of effects. I would be simply unable to place confidence in somebody's behaviour, if I would expect the Other to misuse it and finally to kill me. My gesture of confidence would loose its addressee. Consequently, our expression of confidence does not only contain the promise; 'I shall not kill you', but also the expectation: 'You will not kill me'. In accordance with Levinas, I prefer such extreme utterances in order to take account of the extreme point of enmity, instead of sticking to innocuous situations. However, trust does not consist in running against the wall of an ethical resistance, nor in being possessed by the Other in terms of a hostage; it rather makes something going on between us. It is just in this way that obligation, pronounced as 'you shall (not)', enters into social relations. Inducing confidence does not mean to produce trust, nor simply to wait for it. To the extent that trust is responsive, it is creative too, since it involves a response which makes something new flourish between us.

Due to its own logic, trust passes into specific *trust conditions*, even though the initial uncertainty is not abolished. The original asymmetry between the Other's demand and my own response does not vanish; on the contrary, it is multiplied. It is significant that the Greek word πιστός—'trustworthy', or 'reliable'—is used both in the active and in the passive voice, as if trust were wandering from the one to the other. The structure of reciprocity can be illustrated by the reciprocity of gaze, wherein my own gaze and that of the Other are intertwined like the lines of a chiasm, but without leading to a common gaze.[8] While responding to the Other's gaze, I see myself in the Other's eyes, even if the Other's look changes into an evil look. Let us once again take up Hobbes' animal example. If the Other would really have qualities of the wolf—that is, of a being threatening me to death—I would never be able to conclude a contract with such a dangerous being. I could only protect myself against its attacks, just as Locke concedes to the defendant that when confronted with somebody who by his aggression returns to the state of nature: '...one may destroy a Man who makes War upon him, or has discovered an enmity to his being, for the same Reason that he may kill a Wolf or a Lyon...' (Locke 1970: III, 16). I neglect the fact that the quality of wildness or savageness looks like a caricature which by no means suits the peculiarity of the animal's sociality and the reciprocal habituation of man and animal. In the end, it is true that the intertwining of one's own and the Other's confidence clearly differs from conditions of trust that are based on institutional rules; we are arrested at a threshold we will never leave behind definitively.

The term 'trust' or 'confidence' should not primarily read as a substantive, but as a verb or as the derivative of a verb. The bond, which underlies the reciprocal trust, depends on the dynamic of a *binding in actu*. Trust tends to evaporate and dissolve, unless it is renewed again and again. Our expression of confidence is not confined to what is said, it is performed by acts of saying; similar to the act of giving, mentioned above, it is dependent upon repeated acts of re-saying. In this respect it conforms to the performance of speech acts which cannot be replaced by the presentation of documents. Further, trust is connected with feelings which transgress the borders of social attitudes and utility calculations. Still, everything depends upon how feelings are understood. As long as we reduce feelings to subjective states, we do not reach the level of social bonding. Things change when we consider trust, like other feelings, as a *pathos*, happening to us and affecting us, which, in case the trust is breached or lost, can shake us in the core. Trust belongs to the vulnerability by which we are exposed to each other. This is the grain of truth in the old dictum: *homo homini lupus*, which is repeated by Freud in his *Civilization and its Discontents* (part V).

Trust entails a *history of trust*. The foundation of trust goes back to the life experience of the little child. This has been shown by the investigations of René Spitz or John Bowlby, focusing on the bodily dialogue between the baby and its main caretakers, as is found especially in the child's attachment to the mother. Quite similarly, Erik H. Erikson's

---

[8] Concerning the contrast between Merleau-Ponty's idea of *entrelacs* with Levinas's idea of *separation*, see Waldenfels 1995: ch. 20.

psychology of development starts from a kind of social zero—namely, from a 'basic trust' and a primary conflict between primal anxiety and primal hope. Such a *primary trust*, accompanied by the dark shadows of a *primary distrust*, should not be interpreted as a naturalistic phenomenon, but as the premature phase of a history by which the self grows up, in permanent exchange with 'significant Others'.[9] Part of the social history is the early smile of the child, which has been often commented on with reference to Virgil's *risu cognoscere matrem*. The initial differentiation of familiar and unfamiliar figures is marked by a peculiar form of becoming alien which in German is called *Fremdeln*. The smile appears as a primary response, announcing the trust in the benevolence of the so-called 'good-enough mother' (see Winnicott 2008). Obviously, the smile turns out to be more than a neuro-physiologic reaction, to be described on the base of behaviour observations and neurological studies. Only if we adopt the participant's perspective can we understand how a specific relation to the Other comes up, exceeding the mere satisfaction of natural needs. The smile manifests a responsive surplus which can be expressed in various ways, while being awakened by the Other's demand and appeal. Responsive forms of trust never arise in terms of a simply spontaneous confidence, literally *placed* in the Other; it rather constitutes the *echo* of a gift one receives. This gift may be missing or poisoned. Early distortions, affecting the relation to the Other, are not only known from wrecked families, but as a specific form of hospitalism too. It is difficult to imagine that the high command 'you will not kill me' will have something to say for persons, lacking the full experience of being trusted by Others. The genesis of trust is permeated by elements of what Freud describes as drive destiny (*Triebgeschick*) and what Jean Laplanche (1997) derives from the Other's originary 'implantation' in me. An un-conditioned demand, arising from the face of the Other or from a categorical law, cannot skip over concrete conditions; it only exceeds and contests them. Such conditions are not only conditions of realisation, but conditions of susceptibility too, including the impact of trust.

A last problem concerns the expansion of trust into a wider *trust sphere*. We refer to such a sphere whenever we place our trust in the world, in humankind or in God, or make use of simple devices such as '*Alles komt terecht*', adopted by the Dutch publisher Martinus Nijhoff. As long as trust is associated with friendship, one tends to a universal philanthropy, opposed to misanthropy. But we should guard against such trends toward universalism; they often make us shy away from rigorous proofs. Hence mistrust may be used as a remedy against a blind confidence that in case of emergency all too easy turns into hostility. Paul Ricœur assembled Nietzsche, Marx, and Freud in a 'school of suspicion'. Apart from such healthy doubts, on its own trust resists being integrated into a universal horizon of mankind. When Levinas claims that in the face of the Other the whole of humankind regards us (1961: 188, 282), he does not treat the Other's demand as *pars pro toto* or as the beginning of an ethics of mankind; but he really regards it as the

---

[9] See Erikson, *Childhood and society* (1950). In Merleau-Ponty's *Sorbonne Lectures* (1988) we find further materials concerning the development of the self in relation to the Other.

place where the destiny of mankind and humanity is at stake, like a permanent *Hic Rhodus hic salta*. Nevertheless, what we have in mind goes further. Transforming responsivity into an institutional trust means that I trust you *as somebody*; thus the acts of giving, arousing and receiving confidence are transferred into legitimate expectation. So we enter the domain of the Third Party.

5 THE ORDINARY AND THE SURPLUS OF THE EXTRAORDINARY

Our final reflections on the ordinary and the extraordinary bear on the position of the Third Party. The figure of the Third, already mentioned above in connection with the classical concept of responsibility, has been explicitly introduced by various authors such as Simmel, Sartre, and Levinas, and it also touches the super-ego of psychoanalysis (see Bedorf 2003). But all this is not something additional. It is involved in every word we pronounce, in every skill we exercise and in every feeling we experience. It constitutes our being and living together. This dimension is spread out in a cultural and intercultural *Zwischensphäre*, an intermediary sphere. This sphere contains co-affections, cooperation, life rhythms, social techniques, relationships, value tables, norm systems—shortly, everything that can neither attributed exclusively to myself nor exclusively to Others. In one of my early books, I called this a *Zwischenreich*—that is, an intermediary reign. This common sphere becomes specifically articulated by a responsive trust that is articulated along institutional lines.

Everything that belongs to me is in various ways intertwined with what belongs to the Other. Thus, in each case I meet the Other as *somebody*, as a man or a woman, as old or young people, as German or French, as a layperson or an expert, as a friend or as a rival, and so on. In a similar way, anything that surrounds us, being either useful or troublesome, comes to meet us *as something*. Nevertheless, the Other is always more than the member of a group or as an element of a whole. The otherness of the Other, like the otherness of myself, transgresses the frame into which we are integrated; to some extent the same holds true for the otherness of the various things that pertain to our world. Provided that every order, even the moral one, represents a certain perspective and shows a specific filter, it follows that each order bears a surplus of what is *extraordinary*. What is literally extraordinary—that is, out of order—pertains to a special dimension of otherness, apart from the otherness of Others and of myself. Ordering means, according to Nietzsche, 'equalizing what is unequal' (1980: vol. I, p. 880), just as jurisdiction, designed to making equal (ἰσάζειν, see Aristotle 1894: V, 7), means, according to Levinas (1974: 202), 'comparing the incomparable(s)' as. Consequently, justice does not represent a higher form of right, beyond the legal rules, but originates in the midst of right taken as a surplus of justice. Other orders function in a similar way. Whether we take politics, economy, art, or religion, they all release specific forms of the extraordinary. In the end, the response we give is just as little separated from our social responsibility as the extraordinary is separated from the ordinary.

However, the relation between the ordinary and the extraordinary forms an internal tension full of controversies. We see a permanent trend to prefer either what is normal, common and regular to what is anomalous, singular, or exceptional. The two trends—the one aiming at a stable mean, the other oscillating between extremes—may be characterized as normalism and extremism. A synthesis between both is excluded, unless we pay the costs of a violent totality. Hegelian dialectics, the first candidate for such a synthesis, fail, faced with differences such as present and past, here and there, figure and ground, male and female; none of them can be reduced to a contradiction without losing what is proper to it. By contrast, we are invited to perform acts of balance on the margins of normality. They will leave room for a plurality of life-forms and life-worlds. On the borderlines of the different orders emerge *transitional figures* (*Übergangsfiguren*) which, like Winnicott's 'transitional objects', are placed neither inside nor outside. Let us give some examples. The interpreter moves between different languages without hope for a universal language. The victim of violence suffers from violations which are taken *as* infringements of law, but which are more than this. Similarly, the patient's pains and diseases are treated as typical forms of sickness. Without attempts to transform the inflicted justice into legal cases and to convert painful sufferings into medical cases, public institutions such as the court and the clinic would simply not exist. Yet, all these professional procedures stumble on thresholds of alienness or otherness. If we neglect these thresholds we run the risk of a total legalisation or medicalisation of life. Similar consequences are to be feared when economics degrades into a capitalistic economism, respecting nothing more than exchange value and profit. The economic process of 'equalizing the unequal', which according to Marx defines the function of money (1953: 80), would amount to a simple process of equalizing the equal. At this point we are reminded of the transitional action of *giving*, which is characterized by respect for what has no price within the sphere of economic exchange (see Hénaff 2002).

These considerations might be continued. They suggest expanding the ethics of otherness to a politics of otherness or alienness. Such an attempt would culminate in what I call a sort of unsociability within sociability, as adumbrated by the Atopia of Socrates. As a citizen, Socrates belonged to Athens, but not completely because he liked to place in question what was taken for granted. Indeed, whenever someone says 'we', it is myself, you, or somebody else who speaks, not we. Every 'we', whether representing family, people, church, class, or society, is a broken 'we'; it turns into a Tyrannis who will not tolerate deviates and dissidents. What is alien or strange is never a simple failure we should get rid of, but rather a stimulus that is able to wake us up from the sleep of normalization. The responsive ethics I propose could function as a permanent corrective. Concerning the contrast between response and responsibility, from which we started, this means, in the words of Maurice Blanchot (1973: 168): 'Responding to what escapes our responsibility.'

References

Aristotle (1894), *Ethica Nicomachea*, I. Bywater (ed.) (Oxford: Clarendon Press).

—— (1957), *Politica*, W. D. Ross (ed.) (Oxford: Clarendon Press)

—— (1959), *Ars Rhetorica*, W. D. Ross (ed.) (Oxford: Clarendon Press).

Bakhtin, M. M. (1981), 'Discourse in the novel', in *The Dialogical Imagination*, tr. C. Emerson and M. Holquist (Austin: University of Texas Press).

—— (1990), *Art and Answerability: Early Philosophical Essays* (Austin: University of Texas Press).

Bedorf, T. (2003), *Dimensionen des Dritten* (München: Fink).

Blanchot, M. (1973), *Le pas au-delà* (Paris: Gallimard)

Descartes, R. (1988), *Les passions de l'âme*, G. Rodis-Lewis (ed.) (Paris: Vrin).

Erikson, E. M. (1950), *Childhood and Society* (New York: Norton).

Goldstein, K. (1934), *Der Aufbau des Organismus* (The Hague: Martinus Nijhoff); *The Organism* (Boston: Beacon Press, 1963).

Hénaff, M. (2002), *Le prix de la vérité* (Paris: Du Seuil).

Heidegger, M. (1953), *Einführung in die Metaphysik* (Tübingen: Niemeyer).

Hobbes, Th. (1987), *De cive*, H. Warrender (ed.) (Oxford: Clarendon Press).

Husserl, E. (1950), *Ideen zu einer reinen Phänomenologie und phänomenologischen Philosophie*, Book I (Hua III) (The Hague: Martinus Nijhoff).

—— (1959), *Erste Philosophie*, Part 2 (Hua VIII) (The Hague: Martinus Nijhoff).

Kant, I. (1966), *Werke in sechs Bänden*, W. Weischedel (ed.), (Darmstadt: Wissenschaftliche Buchgesellschaft).

Laplanche, J. (1997), *Le primat de l'autre* (Paris: Presses Universitaires de France).

Levinas, E. (1961), *Totalité et Infini* (The Hague: Martinus Nijhoff); tr. A. Lingis, *Totality and Infinity* (Pittsburgh, Pa.: Duquesne University Press).

—— (1974), *Autrement qu'être ou au-delà de l'essence* (The Hague: Martinus Nijhoff); tr. A. Lingis, *Otherwise than Being, or Beyond Essence* (The Hague: Martinus Nijhoff).

Locke, J. (1970), *The Treatises of Government*, P. Laslett (ed.) (Cambridge: Cambridge University Press).

Luhmann, N. (1968), *Vertrauen* (Stuttgart: Enke).

Mauss, Marcel, 'Le don', in *Sociologie et anthropologie* (Paris: Presses Universitaires de France, 1950).

Marx, K. (1953), *Grundrisse der politischen Ökonomie* (Berlin: Dietz)

Merleau-Ponty, M. (1988), *Merleau-Ponty à la Sorbonne. Résumé de cours 1949–1952* (Grenoble: Cynara).

Musil, R. (1978), *Der Mann ohne Eigenschaften* (Reinbek: Rowohlt).

Nietzsche, F. (1980), *Studienausgabe* (Berlin: de Gruyter).

Plato (1900–7), *Opera*, J. Burnet (ed.) (Oxford: Clarendon Press).

Proust, Marcel, *À la recherche du temps perdu*, ed. J.-Y. Tadié, vol. III (Paris: Pléiade, 1989).

Waldenfels, B. (1971), *Das Zwischenreich des Dialogs. Sozialphilosophische Untersuchungen in Anschluß an Edmund Husserl* (The Hague: Martinus Nijhoff).

—— (1987), *Ordnung im Zwielicht* (Frankfurt: Suhrkamp); tr. D. J. Parret, *Order in the Twilight* (Athens: Ohio University Press, 1996).

—— (1994), *Antwortregister* (Frankfurt: Suhrkamp).

—— (1995), *Deutsch-Französische Gedankengänge* (Frankfurt: Suhrkamp)

—— (1999), *Vielstimmigkeit der Rede* (Frankfurt: Suhrkamp).

—— (2002), 'Levinas and the face of the other', in *The Cambridge Companion to Levinas*, S. Critchley and R. Bernasconi (eds) (Cambridge: Cambridge University Press).

—— (2005), *Idiome des Denkens. Deutsch-Französische Gedankengänge II* (Frankfurt: Suhrkamp).

——– (2006a), *Grundmotive einer Phänomenologie des Fremden* (Frankfurt: Suhrkamp) tr. A. Kozin and T. Stähler, *Phenomenology of the Alien: Basic Concepts* (Evanston: Northwestern Press, 2011).

—— (2006b), *Schattenrisse der Moral* (Frankfurt: Suhrkamp).

Winnicott, D. W. (2008), *Playing and Reality* (London and New York: Routledge).

CHAPTER 21

··

TOWARDS A PHENOMENOLOGY OF THE POLITICAL WORLD

··

KLAUS HELD

ANY introduction to the phenomenology of the political faces a certain difficulty: namely, the contributions of those figures considered central to the phenomenological tradition have not generated the impression that their mode of thinking is particularly well-suited for a philosophical treatment of this subject matter. Edmund Husserl, the founder of phenomenology, believed no doubt with a certain *naïveté* in a renewal of Plato's *politeia* with phenomenologists acting as spiritual leaders (see Schuhmann 1988). Martin Heidegger, who undertook the first revolutionary revision of phenomenology, became the object of very legitimate criticism for his attempt to justify National Socialism philosophically (see Heidegger 2000). Jean-Paul Sartre—another important figure whose thought was at least early on in his career phenomenologically oriented—abandoned his phenomenological origins when he began to address political questions. And even if Maurice Merleau-Ponty in his book *Humanism and Terror* convincingly criticized the Stalinist terror and, thus, there and elsewhere did take up a position on the political problematic, this taking of a position hardly qualifies as a genuinely phenomenological part of his work. Thus, there has so far been no established 'political phenomenology' on which an introduction such as this one could rely.

Indeed, in the estimation of this author, only Hannah Arendt has an approach out of which a genuine phenomenological philosophy of the political might be developed, despite the fact that she does not understand herself as a phenomenologist. From Arendt's political thinking, it is possible to construct a bridge to phenomenology precisely because she interprets the political as a 'world' and because her understanding of world can be given a systematic form with the help of the Husserlian and Heideggerian interpretation of the world as horizon. In any case, this can only be successful if the phenomenology in question follows Eugen Fink, a student of both Husserl and Heidegger, in recognizing the world as its most fundamental theme. With this step, phenomenology would depart from Husserl as well as from Heidegger, insofar as phenomenology of the former orbits around consciousness while for the latter it places Being at its centre.

In their respective projects, both Husserl and Heidegger connect their phenomenology to the philosophical canon. Husserl takes a position in relation to the tradition inaugurated by Descartes, and Heidegger to one that extends back to Aristotle. Over against these approaches, a phenomenology of the world must turn its attention to that early thinker who first recognized the world as a fundamental philosophical theme, Heraclitus. Indeed, it was Heraclitus as well who for the very first time made the political an object of philosophical reflection, the political understood specifically as the civic order of the Greek *polis* (Diels and Kranz 2004/2005: 22 B 44, 114, 121). For a phenomenology of the world and of the political world, it is, however, simply not enough here to refer to Heraclitus. On account of the above-mentioned connection to Hannah Arendt, any such phenomenology must take into consideration Kant's conception of 'reflective judgement' as political 'common sense', as the return to this idea is indispensible for any understanding Arendt's political thinking.

The preliminary considerations sketched here should lead phenomenology to a self-critical insight: It must admit that it has not yet succeeded in producing a systematic, well-grounded reflection on the political. Phenomenology must, therefore, get underway initially with an analysis of the political world. (Indeed, it is for just this reason that the present essay bears the title '*Towards* a phenomenology of the political world'.) Because phenomenology stands before a new beginning here, it cannot yet proceed as if it is simply entitled to subject to phenomenological investigation various traditional or contemporary problems in political philosophy. *If* and, if so, *how* such problems are able to become themes for phenomenology must first be decided. And it must decided based upon whether the political as world finds for itself any place at all in a phenomenology of the world and, if so, how it can be systematically determined. For this reason, the following introduction limits itself to considerations devoted to that task. In order to take up the task in as unprejudiced a manner as possible, four fundamental questions should first be posed and answered.

(1) With what justification can the proper object—that is, the proper *Sache* or 'subject matter'—of political philosophy be defined, in stark contrast to traditional terminology, as the 'political world'?

(2) What is the reason for such a departure from the generally accepted terminology?

(3) To what extent is the phenomenological approach specifically suited to thematizing or foregrounding the 'political world'?

(4) Why does the thematization of the political world fall among the essential tasks of phenomenology in general?

1

(1) The object of political philosophy

Among English- and German-speaking thinkers it is common to use the term 'political philosophy' or '*politische Philosophie*'. Seen grammatically, the adjective 'political' functions here as an attribute of the substantive, 'philosophy'. However, it is not actually philosophy as a way of thinking that is here being predicated with the property of being 'political'. Rather, the attribute is being applied to the object, the subject matter, to which the area of philosophy thus characterized relates.

If 'political' were a property of the way of thinking in this discipline, the execution of this mode of philosophizing itself would be a political activity. One can indeed in some cases put forth such an interpretation, for which Marxism would be the most well-known example. But normally with the conceptual construction, 'political philosophy', what is meant is that the philosophizing or the carrying out of philosophy in this area of thought, which need not itself have a fundamentally political character, is devoted to an object the essence of which consists in its being 'political'.

The question then presents itself, however, as to what this object might be. One can offer an immediate answer to this question, if one simply, as was possible for the first time in ancient Greek, adds an article to the adjective and converts it into a substantive: 'the political'. This substantive presents itself to us quite strikingly at the very beginning of political philosophy, in those of Aristotle's lecture notes that have been passed down to us under the heading, '*Ta politika*'. This Greek title is commonly translated into English as Aristotle's *Politics*. This Anglicization with a substantive allows one to recognize that the word *politika* is actually the plural of an adjective, namely the adjective *politikos*, 'political'. The adjective appears here in the neuter. That situates us once again before the question as to the substantive to which this adjective corresponds as an attribute.

The most common translation of *ta politika* in German and English reads '*politische Angelegenheiten*' or 'political affairs'. As a substantive, 'affair' or '*Angelegenheit*' is thus added. If translated back into Greek this word would be *pragma*, which shares the root *prak-* with '*prattein*', 'to do or set', and the related substantive, '*praxis*'. In Latin this was translated as '*res*'. '*Res*' is the subject matter or *Sache*—not, however, in the sense of an inanimate or indifferent thing or object, but rather as a task or problem that demands human action or doing. The latter would be an 'affair' or an '*Angelegenheit*'. It is in this sense that one speaks in German, for example, of a *Sache* being handled before the court of law.

'*Sache*', understood thus as a substantive term for the political, we find for the first time in the political philosophy of Cicero, who elevated the expression '*res publica*' to a philosophical concept. This expression was the term commonly known to every Roman for their communal existence. Therefore, it is common today to translate '*res publica*' in German with '*Staat*' or in English with 'republic'. Literally translated, however, '*res publica*' is the *Sache* of the *populus*, the 'people'. What concerns all members of a people and therefore must be handled before their eyes is called *publicus* (an adjective derived from the word *populus*), from which come modern terms such as 'public' and 'publicity'. In this sense, '*res publica*' means most properly a 'public affair'.

Not all inhabitants of a given territory belong to a given *populus* or people, but rather only those who are free enough to take part in shared activity—that is, the 'citizens'. Accordingly, the phrase 'a people'—in Greek, *dêmos*—when used in the political sense, means the 'citizenry', or in Latin from '*civis*' or 'citizen', '*civitas*'. In Greek, the citizen is called '*politês*'. From this the word '*politikos*' is derived, which also focuses on one's citizenship and one's being engaged in acting as a citizen. The 'political' is that which constitutes the shared and thus public *Sache* or 'affair' for the activity of citizens, the *res publica*.

With this we have found in the ancients an expression for 'the political', which includes a substantive, *res*—or, translated back into Greek, a *pragma*. But our guiding question of the appropriate substantive, to which the attribute 'political' applies, is not yet satisfactorily answered. We sought a substantive as a mark for the *Sache* of political thinking. We have come to a word thereby, *res* or *pragma*, which indeed means *Sache*. As the *Sache* of political philosophy we have identified something that is labelled 'public'. However, we seem to have come not one step further, for we have only replaced the first attribute of the *Sache*, political, about which we are concerned, with another, its being public. But perhaps we will find that we have advanced a bit, if we ask what it might mean, that a *Sache* is understood as an affair that is 'public'.

In order to answer this question we turn in the second step of our considerations to the fact that the term 'political' can be connected with many substantives. In English at any rate, language allows one to speak of 'political events', 'political institutions', 'political situations', 'political personalities', 'political opinions', and so on. Given the difference in among that which is referred to here, the various occurrences in human life that can all be referred to as 'political', the initial impression arises that we are equivocating when we apply this attribute to such different things. If there is a unity and togetherness here in what we refer to with the attribute 'political', it obviously does not lie in the fact that everything we refer to in this way shows forth some corresponding feature. The concept is thus not univocal.

In his *Metaphysics* (Aristotle 1984: *Met.* IV.1003a33–b4, XI.1061a1–6), Aristotle draws attention to the fact that, using the classic example of the word 'healthy', the unity in an attribute's usage can be based upon its analogous (rather than its univocal) application—which is to say, on the fact that there is a first or an initial instance, to which the attribute is primarily related, and that every variation in secondary usage receives its meaning from that primary instance. A parallel case of word-usage, which could be instructive for the case of the 'political', is found in the employment of 'childish' in expressions such as 'childish toy', 'childish behaviour', 'childish clothing', and so on. If we search for a primary instance, from which these possibilities of expression derive their sense, only the fact that all the above belong to what we might call 'the world of the child' presents itself as an explanation. That first, to which the attribute 'childish' is related, should thus be understood as a *world*.

Just as one can speak of, in a parallel sense, the world of sports, the world of the office, the world of the family, the European or Asian world, and countless others, it is in many modern languages possible, without further clarification, to employ an expression amounting to 'the political world'. Given this, it is easy to assume that such expressions as 'political event' or 'political contribution' derive their sense from the fact that what makes them likewise (and yet not simply in the same sense) political is their belonging to a 'political world'. If the unity of the 'political' consists in the fact that everything that we denote with this term belongs in respectively different ways to a political world, we have with this found an answer to our question of what the character of the *Sache* or subject matter of political philosophy might be. The term for this *Sache* is the 'political world'.

After following the first path of our considerations above, the question remained open as to what is expressed in saying that political philosophy's *Sache* is *res publica* and, thus, a matter that is 'public' and thus touches the whole of the citizenry. Here the initial answer that has presented itself is that the *Sache* we characterize as 'political' is nothing other than a world.

(2) The term 'political world'

Before we address more precisely the relation between the concept of world or worldliness and the openness of the political, a passing examination of the common, modern suggestions for the object of political philosophy, above all the concepts of 'society' and 'state', might be instructive. We come now to our second leading question. Why is it advisable for political philosophy to avoid referring to its object in the common or traditional terms? The answer is that concepts such as 'society' and 'state' are simply less expedient than 'political world' because they effectively reduce or constrain the varying usage of the attribute 'political', of which examples were provided above. Certain variations of this usage will be unsuited for political philosophy from the outset if the political is identified with something like 'state' or 'society'. If the 'political' and that which concerns the 'state' are the same, how can, for example, someone's mere opinion be labelled 'political'?

The employment of the concept 'political world', by contrast with such concepts as 'state' and 'society', is more uninhibited. It allows for all the various ways in which one uses the attribute 'political'. The modern narrowing of the problematic of 'political philosophy' to that which is denoted by 'state' and 'society' relates back to a certain interpretation of the 'political' in the history of political relations in modern Europe. 'State' first entered into the discussion in the sixteenth century with Jean Bodin, and 'society', in its current meaning, first came upon the scene with G. W. F. Hegel in the nineteenth century.

If one uses one of these concepts, one makes his or her philosophical analysis of the 'political' unavoidably dependent upon these respective interpretations, and their fundamental representations thereby come to function as presuppositions taken over without examination—that is, as prejudices. 'Science', however, earns its name only so long as the striving for liberation from prejudice remains constitutive for its kind of knowing. Using the term 'political world' is preferable to using the traditional terms because it is, in short, less burdened by prejudice.

(3) Phenomenology and the political world

With the attempt to study the political in the least prejudicial manner, we arrive at phenomenology. Edmund Husserl introduced it as a method that would allow one to make good on ancient philosophy's claim to engage in non-prejudicial thinking, but in a radically new way. Indeed, we encounter Husserlian phenomenology when we press further with that same line of thought which led us to the concept of the 'political world'. We are thus able to respond directly to the third introductory question. To what extent is phenomenological thinking especially appropriate for the thematization of the 'political world'?

In such phrases as 'political world' or 'child's world', it is possible to replace 'world' with 'horizon'. But that is indeed only meaningful if we understand this concept with the sense that it was given by Husserl and through which it became a fundamental term for phenomenology. It must here suffice to recall the Husserlian sense of 'horizon' in summary form. 'Horizon', in its phenomenological sense, means a context of meaningful references, an encompassing order, which is normally not a conscious theme to which we turn our attention, but rather through which it is indicated what futural possibilities for comportment open up themselves for us in a situation through our actual enacted comportment. When we seize possibilities of comportment we are not determined to choose a certain possibility by our horizon, but rather it is only through its referential contexts that we come to know the *possible* paths that we can take in our futural comportment.

As mentioned above in the introduction, the guiding impulse toward the clarification of the *Sache* of political philosophy as political world stems from Hannah Arendt, who, in her employment of the concept of world, does not make use of the phenomenological conception of 'horizon'. For this reason, as has often been remarked, her political thought lacks a satisfactory systematicity. A secondary aim of the present reflections, then, might be understood to be finding, by phenomenological means, a systematic groundwork for Hannah Arendt's idea of the political world.

(4) The thematization of the political world as the task of phenomenology itself

With this, we have arrived at an answer to the fourth introductory question: Why is the thematization of the political world among the essential tasks of phenomenology itself?

This amounts to a preemptive response to the possible objection that the task at hand is something to which the perspective of phenomenological thought applies only externally. In order to answer, it is necessary to be responsive to the ambiguity in the concept of 'world'. Up to this point we have spoken only of the many 'worlds'—that is, those various horizons of which we have considered a few examples. However, it is also possible to use world as a, in grammatical terms, *singulare tantum*—a word that can be used only in the singular. We can do so when we, with Husserl, acknowledge that the references in question do not only bind together the occurrences within a given horizon, but also bind the various horizons together. When we say 'the world' we refer thereby to the one and singular referential context, the interminable 'and so on' of the innumerable horizons, which Husserl calls the 'universal horizon'.

It is fundamentally important for the phenomenological concept of horizon, as introduced by Husserl, that each respective referential context normally withdraws itself from our attentiveness. The horizons remain for us in the background, they lie so to speak in the shadows and every occurrence to which we turn our attention steps out from the darkness of these shadows. Only in this way can it become so to speak a pole toward which we direct ourselves with one of our modes of comportment. Insofar as something comes forward out of the shadows of the horizon and enters into the lighted region of our attention, it becomes in Husserl's terms a *Thema*—a 'theme' or a 'topic' for us—and horizons constitute for us an 'unthematized' background.

With the horizon's remaining unthematized, we must observe phenomenologically a fundamental distinction. Although normally we pay no attention to each respective horizon, it can become known to us occasionally that we are orienting ourselves within a specific horizon. For example, when making a judgement about a given subject matter, we can remark in the presence of other human beings, or even by ourselves, that our horizon, is 'too narrow'. However, it is quite different in the case of the one and singular world. It remains, normally speaking, always unthematized. The one world is thematized as the universal horizon for the first time in phenomenological philosophy. This is not to say that world was, as universal horizon, previously unknown to us. We are already, before any philosophy, familiar with the one world in a fundamental way. With unquestionable self-evidence, we rely upon the supposition that the all-encompassing 'and-so-on' of the various references will never break down. In this sense, we are already, before philosophy, certain that 'there is' a world. But we never remark on the existence of the world as such, before the world becomes our phenomenological theme or topic as the universal horizon.

Husserl calls this relation to the world the 'natural attitude'. 'Natural' here means that the attitude in question exists or arises 'from nature' or 'from itself', whereby it is indicated that, in contrast to other attitudes, we need not actively take it over as our own. It is so self-evident for us that we do not once even remark that we find ourselves within a given attitude. Nonetheless, we live in an uninterrupted familiarity with the existence of the unthematically familiar world, because there is for us the possibility of overstepping each individual horizon that determines our thought and activity to another horizon. But in this case, the world never becomes as such a theme or topic because we do not ask what allows for or makes this overstepping possible. Because the world remains hidden from us as the enabling ground for our mobility between horizons, we have a tendency to remain in our own habitually familiar horizons, in our particular worlds which form respectively our standard. We orient ourselves in our comportment in these particular worlds, or '*Sonderwelten*' (Husserl 1954: 459 ff.) to use a fortuitous concept from the later Husserl, and we dim or obscure the other horizons.

This confinement in our respective particular worlds appears concretely in that we tend towards one-sidedness and prejudice when making judgements in the natural attitude. However, on account of the unthematized familiarity with the one world, we have some inkling always already even in the natural attitude that there are horizons beyond our own particular worlds. On account of this, we can restrict the validity of the judgements that we make in conversation with others by means of such expressions as 'it seems to me', or 'in my opinion', and so on. Such gestures of restraint, of which there are numerous examples in at least all Indo-European languages, express in conversation that the horizons of others, which reach out beyond our own, are nonetheless somehow present together with ours. Of course, as long as the natural attitude remains entirely intact, we are not especially interested in visualizing these horizons. This disinterest has the consequence that we constantly talk past one another and do not really listen to one another.

The situation described above occurs often enough in everyday communal life, but it is nevertheless a limit case of the natural attitude—namely, the extreme possibility that we remain prisoners of our particular worlds. Nonetheless, this limit case is what first drew philosophical attention of Heraclitus and Parmenides at the turn of the sixth to the fifth century BC. In the fragments of their writings that remain we find the first consideration of the kind of insight that we identify since Plato as 'science': *epistêmê*—that is, a 'knowing' in the emphatic sense, of oneself. For this reflexive consideration it is necessary to distinguish in an essential way this epistemic knowing from that kind of knowing possessed by human beings in their everyday ordinary comportment.

It is above all Heraclitus who in his thought fundamentally and polemically turns himself against those he calls the 'many' or the 'majority' and whom he compares to those who are asleep. Whoever sleeps lives in his or her own dreamworld and is thereby cut off from the shared world of all human beings (Diels and Kranz 2004/5: 22 B 89). As long as the natural attitude holds us under its spell, we are not able to open ourselves for 'the common', to *xunon* as Heraclitus expresses it (see Held 1980: 244 ff.). However, when considered in terms of the thing itself, this 'common' can only be the one world that encompasses all horizons, because that from which one might close oneself off in making a judgement is nothing but the horizons of others.

The most common Greek equivalent of the above-mentioned gestures of restraint is *dokei moi*. From the stem *dok-* of the verb '*dokein*' that appears here, the word '*doxa*' (= *dok-sa*) is derived, which we translate with 'opinion'. In the tradition of Heraclitus and Parmenides, Plato too refers to the natural attitude as *doxa* and sets *epistêmê* over against it. When it was stated above that the one world first becomes a theme with the birth of phenomenology, that was a bit of a simplification. Phenomenology stands in the tradition of *epistêmê* or of 'epistemic knowledge', and thus its interpretation of the world did not materialize out of thin air. Already at the point when *epistêmê* came into its own by distinguishing itself from *doxa* the one world lost that self-evidence which characterizes human beings' familiarity with it in the natural attitude. At that historical moment there arose the first explicit opening for the one world. The linguistic evidence for this is not accidentally found in the work of Heraclitus. After having no word for the whole of the one world, it was likely he who introduced the word *kosmos* in this sense, a word that had in everyday Greek previously denoted not 'world', but only something like 'ornamental order'.

In his 1936 *Crisis of the European Sciences*, Husserl explicitly recalls the Greek beginning through which epistemic knowledge was introduced in its original sense. The sense of this *Urstiftung*, as Husserl puts it, or 'inauguration', was, however, the *doxa*-critical opening for the one world, the bursting open of the confinement in the horizons of particular worlds through which our prejudices are determined. Phenomenology relates itself to this inauguration, in that it oversteps the natural attitude through the thematization of the world as universal horizon and strives to liberate itself in a new way from prejudices. Thus, phenomenology might be characterized as an explicit resumption of the most ancient self-conception of philosophical/scientific *epistêmê*. This is the very reason that, so long as it is carried out in the spirit of its original maxim 'To the things themselves' and thus wishes to be more than a scholastic interpretation of its own classic figures, phenomenology is not possible without hermeneutic recourse to the history of philosophy and science. More precisely, without reflecting on what became of the inaugural sense of *epistêmê* in its subsequent development.

If one allows oneself to begin reflecting upon the meaning of the inauguration of epistemic knowledge with the *doxa*-critical opening for the one world, one confronts a fundamental difficulty. As Heraclitus's polemic against the 'many' indicates, *epistêmê* or epistemic knowledge showed itself in the inauguration of its self-conception as a radical break with the natural attitude, which in the view of *epistêmê* was presented in an extreme form—that is, as complete confinement to particular worlds. The radicality of this break has had a disastrous consequence already for *epistêmê* at its historical beginning, but also for the phenomenological renewal of the significance of *epistêmê's* inauguration: namely, how it is even possible for humans to accomplish a disclosedness for the one world from out of their confinement in particular worlds becomes inexplicable.

If one sets out, in the spirit of Heraclitus, under the assumption that humans living out their lives in *doxa* know nothing other than their respective particular worlds, then it follows that they are fundamentally in no position to understand the philosophical critique of *doxa's* limitation. They could only then understand the one world, thematized by *epistêmê*, as yet another particular world. The right by which philosophy could claim a superiority to *doxa* would have to remain inconceivable for them. This means that *epistêmê's* frontal assault on *doxa*, carried out by Heraclitus, can never lead the many toward opening themselves for the one world. *Epistêmê's* unmediated confrontation with the natural attitude makes an unsolvable riddle out of how the human beings that live within this attitude would ever bring themselves to turn away from it.[1]

The one possible solution to the problem is to abandon the notion of an unmediated confrontation of the natural and the philosophical attitudes. We must presume some 'middle', some 'mediator', between them that would then explain how it is possible to arrive at the philosophical attitude from the natural attitude. This would be a precursor to the opening of the human being for the one world, which must already within the natural attitude itself open up the possibility of transcending its particular horizons toward the unity of the world. *Doxa* must itself already be situated, even before the actual transition to the thematization of the world in philosophy and science, to open itself for the one world.

Given that *doxa* is adequately represented as a confinement of the human faculty of judgement within particular worlds, there must be a use of judgement that remains *doxa*-like, but nonetheless is already characterized by a disclosedness for the one world. That is, there must be a world-open form of *doxa*, which is not yet *epistêmê*. The answer to the fourth introductory question is: in order to explain the possibility of its own grounding attitude, phenomenology must thematize the political world as the mediator between the natural and the philosophical attitudes. And it can only take up this task concretely, if it describes a use of judgement that is world-open and at the same time *doxa*-like. Hannah Arendt, however, has discovered, with the help of a return to Kant's *Critique of Judgement*, just such a use of judgement, and therein lies her true significance for the phenomenology of the political world (see Arendt 1982).

2

For our further considerations the first task that arises is to take up phenomenologically the just-mentioned special use of the faculty of judgement, making specific reference to Kant as well as to Hannah Arendt. As indicated above, the complete confinement within particular worlds criticized by Heraclitus is merely a limit case and not the normal condition of the natural attitude. *Doxa* does not hold us completely under its spell. It allows us the freedom to proceed from the unthematized empathetic awareness of the horizons of others, as expressed in the above-discussed gestures of restraint ('it seems to me', and so on), to the explicit visualization or making-present of those horizons. Kant describes how this is possible in his *Critique of Judgement*, §40,

This section concerns those human beings who possess an 'extended way of thinking', or who are in a position to set themselves outside of the 'subjective, private conditions of judgement', 'within which so many others are as though trapped'. Kant writes

---

[1] It might be remarked here, as an aside, that this is probably the reason that, in his innumerably many reflections on the motivation for phenomenological reduction (collected for the first time in 2002 in a historical–critical edition), Husserl never seems to move on and accomplish his aim.

'*eingeklammert*', which in modern German can be understood as '*eingeklemmt*'—'stuck', 'jammed', or 'trapped'. It is unnecessary here to go into what Kant understood as 'private conditions'. For our purposes it is sufficient that we interpret these private conditions phenomenologically, and indeed that we do so in terms of being bound to particular worlds. As long as we are, in Kant's term, 'trapped' in our particular worlds—that is, as long as the confinement or bias of the natural attitude has not slackened, not even in a preliminary way—the possibility of moving back and forth between our own and other horizons is known to us but not pursued.

This 'extended way of thinking' stands for the possibility of freeing oneself from such immobility and opening oneself in this way for the one universal horizon. It is the capacity of humans to become explicitly conscious of their own mobility between horizons, thus to 'reflect upon' this mobility. Kant can thus, with a view to this state of affairs, speak of 'reflective judgement'. Reflection consists here in being able to 'put' oneself 'in someone else's place' when making a judgement. This means phenomenologically that I make present or visualize for myself the horizons that constitute the background for their judgements.

One who judges reflectively subjects his or her own judgements to self-control, insofar as he or she poses the question: how can I even survive with my opinions in the competition with the other diverging opinions of other particular worlds? It is first with this consideration that one brings about the chance of making one's opinion truly heard. This gives one's judgement the form through which, as Kant expresses it with a particularly apt German term, one is able to '*ansinnen*' or 'address' others with it. That is, one is then able to make the claim that the others at least attend to one's judgement and take it seriously. Whether or not they agree is a question that arises only afterwards.

It is decisive now that *doxa* is not yet abandoned in the reflective use of the faculty of judgement. The essential bond or the natural attitude to the various individual horizons, each of which provides a measure for judgement, is not completely abolished. This only occurs with *epistêmê*, which would like to free itself completely from *doxa*. Contrarily, for the 'extended way of thinking' it is true that the one who endeavours to bring about the 'addressability' of his judgements knows that his or her judgements are always conditioned through his own horizons, from which the making of judgements must continue to depart. Otherwise, the problem of addressability would never arise. The 'extended way of thinking' is not a complete liberation from the bond to the particular worlds. If the judgements of participants in a discussion did not remain determined by their origin in the horizon of a particular world, the 'extension' of one's way of thinking would be unnecessary from the outset and the danger that one would not really listen to others wouldn't exist.

In §40 of his *Critique of Judgement*, Kant characterizes this extended way of thinking as '*Gemeinsinn*'—in Latin, *sensus communis*, or in English, 'common sense'. In this there is a directive that points toward the phenomenology of the political world. At all times and in all cultures it has been possible for human beings, when they spoke with one another and when they expressed their divergent opinions to one another, to reflectively employ their powers of judgement. But it is first with the Greeks that this employment took on the character of 'common sense' in the more narrow, or political, sense of this concept.

This became possible through the fact that the 'many', in the same historical period that they were subjected to Heraclitus's critique on account of their blindness—as mentioned above—to the 'common', discovered a new form of communal life. This occurred when the Greek city-state, the *polis*, became a democracy. The many found their commonality in precisely that which Heraclitus had polemically attacked—namely, in the bond between their opinions and the horizons from which their judgements originated. What unified them into a community was the discovery of a common interest, an interest in doing justice to this bond and remaining 'many'.

Concretely, this means that the many recognized one another as citizens, and as such as members of the *polis* who possessed the same right to participate with their judgements in the discussion of communal affairs. Thus, 'democracy' was not historically the first name for this form of communal life; it was, rather, *isêgoria*, or 'equality in public speech' for all citizens. In the compound, *iso-agoria* there is the verb *agoreuein*, or 'public speaking', which is related to the word for the *polis* central market area: the *agora*. Aristotle's *Politics* begins with the fundamental thought that every human being is determined to live as a citizen with equal rights, *politês*, in a civilly ordered *polis* with other citizens (*zôon politikon*), because a human being is a being capable of speech (*zôon logon echon*) (Aristotle 1984: *Pol*. 1253 a1–18). This observation is well known, but what is less often realized is that Aristotle does not understand *logos* in this formulation as any given kind of linguistic ability. Rather, what is intended is, when *agoreuein* or 'speaking in the market-place' in a circle of human beings, all of whom are under the form of *isegoria* equal to one another, the capacity to 'give account' or *logon didonai* for one's judgement on a matter that concerns the entire citizenry.

As is indeed well known, 'democracy' stems from the word *dêmos*, the 'people', whereby 'people' are to be understood as the totality of the citizens, the *civitas*, as indicated above. The citizenry, thus understood, constitutes itself through the granting of equal rights for public or open speech. The citizens, the *politai*, are no one other than the many, whom Heraclitus attacked, who explicitly grant one another the right to preserve what makes them 'many'—that is, to preserve in the use of their judgement the right to set out from their many various, particular worlds.

Thus, democracy is the many's way of living together as many. It is that kind of human community, the meaning of which is to guarantee that no citizen is obstructed from presenting his or her opinion from his or her own horizonal point of view. The birth of democracy, its 'inauguration'—to use the concept of the late Husserl once again— consists in the institutionalization of a 'free-space' that extends this guarantee to every citizen. This assumes that everyone is in a position to open him or herself by way of an 'extended way of thinking' for the opinions of others. That is, to use one's faculty of judgement reflectively and with common sense and in this way to win the attention of listeners in public speech.

This connection between an 'extended way of thinking' and the inauguration of democracy situates us for taking the next step in our considerations—the discussion of the connection between world and openness in the political, as introduced in the discussion above. First, a misunderstanding must be warded off: we cannot imagine the above-mentioned free-space for the many's freedom of speech as some kind of empty container, which already existed before it became full so to speak with the freely expressed opinions of the many citizens. The free-space is nothing other than the free-play of the exchange of citizens' world-open opinions, which is made possible through 'common sense'. The institutionalization of free-space for the freedom of speech and the world-open *doxa*, through which the many recognize one another as fellow citizens, are one and the same.

It was this state of affairs through which the communal life in the Greek *polis* became a 'political world'. The political living-space, the possibility of which is attested 'to by its becoming a reality, does not exist independently of the freely expressed political opinions that fill it. It is not there before the citizen's open, public discussions with one another. The political world is nothing other than the correlate of the many opinions that open up this living-space. It exists only insofar as it is spoken by the citizens, making judgements according to their common-sense opinions. As far as we know, this constellation emerged for the first time in world-history in Athens near the turn of the sixth to the fifth century BC. Thus, the object of political philosophy, the 'political world', has not existed at all times, in all cultures. Rather, it is a consequence of an 'inauguration', which is historically dateable and geographically localizable. This is actually the reason that 'political philosophy' cannot be pursued independently of history, and indeed, more specifically, not independent of European history.

In our considerations of the first introductory question, the question of the *Sache* of political philosophy, the problem remained unresolved as to how the open or public character, the publicity of the 'political', fits together with the fact that the political constitutes a world. Now, an answer to this question presents itself. Because the political world only exists insofar as it presents itself in being spoken by the great mass of the many, the people of the citizenry, it has the character of openness or public-ness.

But what does this mean in concrete, phenomenological terms? What makes the political world a world—that is, what makes it a space that provides a place for many horizons is the many-ness of the particular worlds, through which the many opinions are possible, which then for their part lend this world its character of openness or public-ness. In the language of Husserl, the political world 'constitutes itself' by advancing into appearance in being spoken through the many opinions that refer to it. Therefore, the political world is thoroughly characterized by the fact that the 'worldly' character of the world itself comes to be and to appear with it. The appearing of the political world lets itself appear in the form of its being publicly or openly spoken through the many. The political world, in this peculiar sense, has the character of appearance. What is particular to it is its 'phenomenality'—a term of Ernst Vollrath, who among German scholars first and most decisively took up and extended the insights of Hannah Arendt (Vollrath 1977, 1987, 2003).

With this last observation there arises an answer to a question that, although not yet explicitly posed, is not far removed from our discussion so far, as long as the 'political world' is understood as the proper subject matter of political philosophy and the concept of 'world' is viewed in light of phenomenology's notion of horizon. The question is that in the sense of this notion of horizon, there are many worlds. But they certainly do not all deserve to be the subjects of their own branches of philosophy. If the political world is to be singled out as a special topic over against these many other particular horizons that can also be called 'worlds', then it is necessary to prove that it deserves, because of its special character, to be made an object with its own branch of philosophy. Indeed, we have already generated such a proof: the political world distinguishes itself through its phenomenality, and that makes a proper 'political phenomenology' a meaningful pursuit.

The many, as employing judgement with common sense, transcend with their world-open *doxa* their confinement in particular worlds, without thereby achieving *epistêmê*. The political world is 'more' and other than the many horizonal worlds, because it constitutes itself through this transcendence and because even in this its phenomenality is announced. This line of thinking is at the same time the solution to the problem that arose in the preliminary response to the fourth introductory question above, as to why the thematization of the political world is among the essential tasks of phenomenology. The thesis was that there must be something that enables the transition from the natural to the philosophical–scientific attitude.

Since the inauguration of the political world, there is an answer to the question of whether there is some middle term or intermediary between *doxa's* confinement in particular worlds, or its closure to the one world, and the world-openness of *epistêmê*. For human beings in the natural attitude, life in the phenomenal political world, appearing as it does as world, already holds within itself the possibility for transcending the particular worlds, even without the one world ever having been philosophically–scientifically thematized. The one world appears already as world, because it has the character of phenomenality as political world and yet has not yet become an object of *epistêmê*.

This thought has essential consequences for a comparison of the reflective employment of the faculty of judgement, through which the political world opens itself, with that particular employment of judgement required for the pursuit of science, *epistêmê*. Thus, a closer look at the distinction between the political and the scientific employment of the faculty of judgement is now required. This grants us the opportunity to make a remark on the relation of the Frankfurt School to the 'political'. Although Jürgen Habermas is surely taken, at least in Germany, as a leading political philosopher, the question arises in light of the above considerations whether or not he has missed decisive aspects or elements of the political world, even given his tremendous learning.

If there were only the plurality of opinions that granted the political world its phenomenality, one could not properly speak of a *unity* of this world. Why do the political opinions in their plurality simply not disintegrate into a disconnected variety? They do not do so only because there is something that binds the citizens together. This is, however, the fundamental interest, common to all of them, in preserving the manyness of the departure points, which are bound to their various horizons. This involves a fundamental interest that unfolds itself precisely in the preservation of this plurality.

Now, there is also something in *epistêmê* that binds together the many judgements of philosophers and scientists. The binding element here, however, is a unity, free of all plurality. In the employment of judgement in *epistêmê*, there is—at least ideally—a complete liberation from the confinement to particular horizons. Contrarily, with common-sense, world-open *doxa*, the bond that connects reflective judgement back to the respective particularity of the various horizons from which they have arisen remains intact. In principle, it is true here that judgement can never achieve an absolute universality, with which the particularity and plurality of the various horizons would be definitively overcome.

The world as political world is only accessible to the citizens in such a way that they open themselves for the many horizons of others. Science must consider this nothing but a detour, for it strives for something that is binding independent of the particularity of judgement's various horizonal departure-points. The bindingness here is grounded in the unity of the scientific universal, wherein all participants alike agree and in the light of which the particularity of the many individual horizons in principle loses its significance. What, contrarily, binds the citizens of a political world together cannot be the same as scientific arguments' compulsory rational uniformity of vision—a 'universal obligation or bindingness'. The arguments that I present to my fellow citizens in political discussion are the results of the reflective employment of my power of judgement, with which I can then only 'address' my fellow citizens. That is, I cannot mentally compel them with such arguments. I can only put upon them to listen to me and possibly to make my argumentation their own on the basis of the use of their own reflective judgement. But there is no guarantee that they will do so. My judgement remains a *dokei moi*—it remains a judgement that 'does seem so, but I cannot make an utterly compelling claim that it is so.'

The Greek *polis* became a civic, democratic world in the very same period that this people opened up the world as world, as *kosmos*, in *epistêmê*. That was no mere historical coincidence, however. Rather, these two events belong together essentially. On account of this relationship, it is from a philosophical perspective easily assumed that the inauguration of the political world and the world-disclosedness of *epistêmê* became possible through the same use of the faculty of judgement.

The first to make this assumption, with unforeseeable effects on the whole of European history, was Plato. As a consequence of making this assumption, Plato could put forth the thesis that the authoritative advocates of *epistêmê*, the philosophers, would be the best-suited to take over the leadership of the political world of the *polis*, and that they should thus be its 'kings'. Because for Plato it is in principle the exact same world-openness that enables human beings to possess philosophical/scientific knowledge of the world and to live together in the *polis*, he had no need of a distinct political philosophy. For this reason it is a mistake to refer to Plato as the founder of this branch of philosophy. It was Aristotle who first—a critical turn against his teacher—inaugurated political philosophy insofar as he elevated the 'political' to the subject matter of its own series of his lectures; he made it the subject of its own *pragmatiê*, the *Politics*.

In his *Nicomachean Ethics*, Aristotle uses the word *phronêsis* to denote common-sense, world-open *doxa*—a word later translated into Latin with *prudentia* and into

English with 'prudence or practical wisdom'. But as groundbreaking as Aristotle's distinction between *phronêsis* and *epistêmê* in the sixth book of this work is, a question remains unanswered: what is peculiar about the openness for the world as world in which we nevertheless do not depart from *doxa*? It was Kant who first pointed the way toward answering this question in the above-mentioned section of his *Critique of Judgement*, and it was Hannah Arendt who first fully realized the political significance of this text in her later lectures on judgement.

Plato's blindness to the peculiarity of the common-sense, reflective power of judgement passed down through the entire history of ideas in Europe all the way to the conception of the 'ideal communication society', developed by Apel and taken over by Habermas, in which all participants could ideally, not factually, become united with one another.

Epistêmê presumes, more or less explicitly, that the scientific contributions to the understanding of the world are in principle intelligible to all human beings, because they are directed by and towards reason, which is universal. One is convinced, with complete self-evidence, that this universal reason is independent of the plurality of the various judgements conditioned by their origin in particular worlds. For *epistêmê*, no role is played in principle by the difference between the horizon from which my judgements arise and the horizons of others that I must reflectively visualize or make present for myself. But it is by way of precisely this difference that the individual citizen differentiates him- or herself from the other citizens in a given political world. That is, the plurality of the many human beings, making common-sense judgements, depends upon this difference.

This plurality emerges through the specific differentiation that occurs when each individual experiences the horizons of fellow citizens as other than his or her own. I cannot visualize or make present for myself the horizons of others in the same way that I can, for example, remember the horizons of past periods of my own life. Between my view of others, with their respective horizons, and others' view of me, with my horizons, there exists an unconquerable asymmetry. As a result of this asymmetry, the horizons of others, and thus their worlds, always remain foreign to me. In this sense, Husserl later in his career spoke of the '*Fremdwelt*' or 'foreign world', and distinguished this from the '*Heimwelt*' or 'home world', or the horizons in which I feel at home because they are accessible 'from myself' or, as it were, 'from within'. Through phenomenology's further development in France, above all with Sartre and Levinas, this Husserlian insight has been deepened. However, if this fundamental idea were in part as radicalized as some 'post-modern' phenomenologists believe, there would only be the plurality of those many worlds conditioned by asymmetry and the *one* world of which we are certain in the natural attitude would be a mere deception. Any such verdict concerning the original certainty of the natural attitude, however, contradicts the very spirit of phenomenology. This spirit demands that one does justice to the natural attitude in reflections concerning it.

Although this extreme position is thus phenomenologically untenable, this alters nothing concerning the insight of phenomenology, that there is an unconquerable difference between home-world and foreign-world, upon which depends the plurality of the many judgements made in a political world, and thereby the plurality of the many citizens who make these judgements. *Epistêmê* hopes to make itself independent of the plurality conditioned by the asymmetry between the horizons of the home-world and the foreign-world. It strives for a uniform knowledge, free of such plurality, wherein the distinction between my horizon and those of others plays no role in the end. The many-ness of human beings, with their various horizons, does not ultimately interest *epistêmê* in the least.

Thus, a theory such as the ideal communication-society, allowing itself to be guided in principle by an *epistêmê*-based representation according to which citizens in a democracy should be incessantly striving to unify themselves, cannot at its core be interested in maintaining the plurality of the participants in the communication. That is, when viewed in the light of day, what makes a community or a society what it is—namely, the plurality of its members—is simply not the concern of such a theory. As long as one applies *epistêmê's* standard of bindingness to political judgement, one is in principle and from the outset not in a position to entertain a conception of the political whereby the manyness of individual human beings is accepted and respected.

Science's confidence that it can achieve a knowledge free of all horizonal plurality, according to Husserl, is among the most fundamental prejudices that phenomenology endeavours to overcome. Given that confidence, science disregards the fact that every human mode of comportment can allow the occurrences to which it relates to appear only out of a given horizon. Scientific research is itself a mode of human comportment, and thus *epistêmê* cannot in truth liberate itself from the relation of its form of knowing back to the horizons from which it arises. Pre-modern philosophy and science therefore did not attempt to become independent of every horizonal bond. But, for reasons that have their first origin in the Greek's inauguration of *epistêmê*, this character has been fundamentally altered in modern science—an alteration led by modern natural science. The denial of the bond between judgement and its horizon is characteristic of the fundamental attitude of modern science.

Modern science strives to achieve an objectivity in its knowledge of the world, with which its research would become fully independent of the horizons from which its scientific judgements have arisen. It is concerned with grasping the world as it is 'in itself', or 'objectively'—which is to say, without any connection to us human beings or to our respective horizons. In his *Crisis of the European Sciences*, Husserl characterizes this belief in a horizon-free, scientific access to the world as 'objectivism'. The occurrences of the world, as they appear to us outside of science, we encounter as undeniably imbedded in a horizon. In order to emphasize, against the objectivism of modern science, the bond between every appearance and its horizon, Husserl in the *Crisis* introduces his own term for the world understood as a horizonal, rather than objective, world—'*Lebenswelt*', or 'life-world'. Objectivism is the forgetting of the life-world.

As a consequence of its growing forgetting of the life-world, philosophy from Plato to Habermas has attempted, ever more decidedly, to interpret the political world from the perspective of *epistêmê*, and has thereby lost sight of its proper and essential character to a greater and greater degree. With its analysis of the horizonal character of appearance, phenomenology has, since Husserl, hoped to overcome the forgetting of the life-world. For this, however, it is unavoidable that it devotes its particular attention to the relationship of our judgement back to the horizon from which it arises. We experience this relationship as such—that is, reflectively—when we make 'common sense' use of our faculty of judgement. Thus, phenomenology must consider the significance of the inauguration of the political world, in order to break the spell of the forgetting of the life-world.

As indicated above phenomenology is the decided present renewal of the most ancient idea of *epistêmê*. But precisely in order to accomplish this renewal, phenomenology must make the very kind of world-openness that does *not* have the character of *epistêmê*, the common-sense openness for the political world, a central area of investigation. If indeed, according to the thesis of Hannah Arendt that has stimulated the foregoing discussion, traditional political philosophy has from Plato to Habermas broadly missed its proper subject matter—namely, 'the political'—then the actual cause of this is, from a phenomenological perspective, the forgetting of the life-world.[2]

References

Arendt, H. (1982), *Lectures on Kant's Political Philosophy*, R. Beiner (ed.) (Chicago: University of Chicago Press).

Aristotle (1984), *The Complete Works of Aristotle Vol. 2* (Princeton: Princeton University Press).

Diels, H. and Kranz, W. (2004/2005), *Die Fragmente der Vorsokratiker*, 3 vols. (Hildesheim: Weidmann, unveränderte Neuauflage 2004/2005 der 6. Aufl. 1951/1952).

Heidegger, M. (2000), 'Die Selbstbehauptung der deutschen Universität', in: *Reden und andere Zeugnisse eines Lebensweges* (Frankfurt a.M.: Vittorio Klostermann, Gesamtausgabe, vol. 16), pp. 107–17; tr. K. Harries: 'The Self-Assertion of the German University', *Review of Metaphysics* 38, 1985: 470–80.

Held, K. (1980), *Heraklit, Parmenides und der Anfang von Philosophie und Wissenschaft: Eine phänomenologische Besinnung* (Berlin: De Gruyter).

Husserl, E. (1954), *Die Krisis der europäischen Wissenschaften und die transzendentale Phänomenologie* (Den Haag: Martinus Nijhoff), Beilage XVII. This appendix is not included in David Carr's English translation: *Edmund Husserl, The Crisis of European Sciences and Transcendental Philosophy* (Evanston: Northwestern University Press, 1970).

Schuhmann, K. (1988), *Husserls Staatsphilosophie* (Freiburg i. Br.: Alber).

Vollrath, E. (1977), *Die Rekonstruktion der politischen Urteilskraft* (Stuttgart: Klett).

——(1987), *Grundlegung einer philosophischen Theorie des Politischen* (Würzburg: Königshausen and Neumann).

——(2003), *Was ist das Politische?* (Würzburg: Königshausen and Neumann).

[2] I would like to express my thanks to Sean D. Kirkland (DePaul University, Chicago) for translating this essay.

CHAPTER 22

OTHER PEOPLE

SØREN OVERGAARD

THE 'problem of other minds' has been of central concern to philosophers for at least two centuries. One thing that makes this problem interesting is that it has been a central problem not only within analytic philosophy, but also within phenomenology. Phenomenologists such as Edmund Husserl, Max Scheler, Edith Stein, Maurice Merleau-Ponty, and Jean-Paul Sartre, to mention just a few, have taken a keen interest in something remarkably similar to what analytic philosophers know as 'the problem of other minds'. Yet similar problems need not imply similar solutions, and in fact many phenomenologists have advocated a solution that most analytic philosophers have deemed implausible (Hyslop 2010).[1] Briefly put, phenomenologists such as Scheler and Merleau-Ponty have argued that, in *some* cases, we can know about other people's mental states by directly *perceiving* them. And they have held that such a perceptual account of our knowledge of other minds renders *inferential* accounts superfluous.

It is important to distinguish between what we might call the 'descriptive' and the 'epistemological' (or normative) problem of other minds (see Goldman 2006: ch. 1).[2] The former concerns the cognitive processes and mechanisms that are involved when we attribute mental states to other people, regardless of whether the processes are ever sufficient to rationally justify these attributions. By contrast, the epistemological problem is not about how people actually arrive at their beliefs that other people possess minds and mental states, but about the extent to which those beliefs can be justified. One does not have a knock-down argument against an attempted solution to the descriptive problem if one can show that the cognitive processes the solution attributes to us fail to yield knowledge or rational justification; for it could be that we just rely on faulty reasoning when we attribute mental states to others. Nor is it a knock-down argument against an attempted solution to the epistemological problem that it invokes an inference

---

[1] Most, but not all. See Austin (1979), McDowell (1982), Wittgenstein (1980), and more recently, Green (2010) and Pickard (2003) for views in line with those advocated by the phenomenologists.

[2] Many philosophers have also been concerned with the so-called 'conceptual problem, how I can *understand* the attribution of mental states to others' (Nagel 1986: 19; see Avramides 2001: 4).

people rarely or never actually make; for here the question is not what sorts of inferences people make, but what sorts of inferences (if any) they *could* make that would warrant their beliefs about other minds.

The aim of the present chapter is to develop and defend a perceptual solution to the *epistemological* problem of other minds, relying on central ideas from Merleau-Ponty's phenomenology. The descriptive problem does not completely disappear off the radar, however, since I take it that a perceptual account of our knowledge of other minds must be phenomenologically as well as epistemologically plausible. The chapter is divided into three sections. In the first section I give a more precise characterization of what I take the epistemological problem of other minds to be, and I contrast two different strategies for addressing it, both of which aspire to be perceptual solutions. In the second section I argue that a perceptual account of our knowledge of others' emotions is phenomenologically and psychologically plausible. Importantly, however, I also suggest that, of the two perceptual solutions to the other minds problem outlined in Section 1, only one meets the phenomenologists' desideratum of offering an alternative to inferential solutions. Finally, in Section 3, I respond to various objections to the non-inferential account.

1 TWO PERCEPTUAL SOLUTIONS

Consider the following question. How is it possible to know that another person is bald? Some answers to this question are so obvious that the question itself seems hardly worth raising. We can *see* or *feel* that another person is bald. The question becomes more interesting, however, the moment difficulties are raised about our ability to detect baldness through visual (or tactile) means. If heads with hair can look or feel just like heads without hair, then it becomes less obvious that we can detect baldness by exclusively visual or tactile means, and the question of how we *can* detect it becomes correspondingly interesting.

This example is intended to illustrate some points that Quassim Cassam makes in his recent book *The Possibility of Knowledge* (2007). Questions such as 'How is it possible to know that another person is angry?' and 'How is it possible to know that another person is bald?' are examples of what Cassam calls 'how-possible questions'. Such questions, he says, 'are *obstacle-dependent* questions. We ask how x is possible when there appears to be an obstacle to the existence of x' (Cassam 2007: 2).[3]

---

[3] Some philosophers might dispute this. In the tradition of transcendental philosophy, it is perfectly legitimate to inquire into the conditions for the possibility of something—for example, perceptual experience of physical objects—without there being any obvious obstacle to its existence. Nothing turns on this issue here, however, as it seems obvious that the question about our knowledge of other people's mental states *is* fuelled by the idea that there is a serious obstacle to our having such knowledge.

One important reason why the question concerning our knowledge about another's anger[4] has struck many philosophers as more interesting and important than the question of how we can know about someone's baldness[5] is that there are some familiar obstacles in the former case that do not seem to apply to the latter case. While hairs (if a person has any) are the sort of thing that one can see (and feel), it is less clear that anger is the sort of thing that one can either see, feel, or in any other way detect by perceptual means alone. This seems to present us with a formidable obstacle to our knowledge in the other minds case that is not there with respect to our knowledge of other bodies. As Dretske puts it:

> Some philosophers seem to think that there is a special difficulty about other minds because, to put it roughly, we cannot see other minds. They are unobservable. You can see the smile (at least the upturned mouth), but not the thought 'behind' it. You can see the perspiration, the flushed face, the wrinkled forehead, the squint, the jerky motion of the arms, the hunched shoulders, the clenched fist, and the trembling lips, but you cannot see the fear, the embarrassment, the frustration, the desire, the pain, or the anger that the other person (presumably) feels. (Dretske 1973: 36)[6]

If emotions are unobservable, then it might seem as if a perceptual model of our knowledge of other minds is ruled out. In other words, it might seem as if the answer to the how-possible question concerning our knowledge of other minds cannot be that we can sometimes know 'by looking'. According to Cassam, there are two basic strategies for handling a how-possible question: 'The first is to deny the existence of the obstacle which gave rise to the question. This is an *obstacle-dissipating* strategy' (Cassam 2007: 2). The second approach accepts the existence of the obstacle, but maintains that it can be overcome—hence the name '*obstacle-overcoming*' strategy (ibid.). In the context of the other minds problem, the latter strategy has tended to dominate. Most philosophers have accepted that, at best, perceptual experience can furnish us with behavioural data from which we may *infer* the obtaining of mental states in others.

One might think that perceptual solutions to the other minds problem would have to be obstacle-dissipating. Certainly, Merleau-Ponty advocates a perceptual model of this sort:

> I do not see anger or a threatening attitude as a psychic fact hidden behind the gesture, I read anger in it. The gesture *does not make me think* of anger, it is anger itself. (Merleau-Ponty 2002: 214)

---

[4] I am only concerned with how we may know that another person is in the grip of an emotion—for example, anger. A further question, which I shall not consider, is how we can know what others are angry *about*.

[5] Obviously, there are various ways in which difficulties may be raised about our ability to know about baldness by perceptual means (for example, if this is understood as a version of the problem of the external world, or if one questions just when a person counts as bald). I shall ignore these, as the other minds case is usually taken to involve special additional difficulties, and it is with the latter that the present chapter is concerned.

[6] Dretske agrees that one cannot literally see another person's anger, desire, or pain, but denies that this creates a special difficulty about other minds.

I perceive the grief or the anger of the other in his conduct, in the face or his hands, without recourse to any 'inner' experience of suffering or anger, and because grief and anger are variations of belonging to the world, undivided between the body and consciousness, and equally applicable to the other's conduct, visible in his phenomenal body, as in my own conduct as it is presented to me... (ibid.: 415)

We must reject that prejudice which makes 'inner realities' out of love, hate, or anger, leaving them accessible to one single witness: the person who feels them. Anger, shame, hate, and love are not psychic facts hidden at the bottom of another's consciousness: they are types of behavior or styles of conduct which are visible from the outside. They exist *on* this face or *in* those gestures, not hidden behind them. (Merleau-Ponty 1964a: 52–3)

I know unquestionably that that man over there *sees*, that my sensible world is also his, because *I am present at his seeing*, it is *visible* in his eyes' grasp of the scene. (Merleau-Ponty 1964b: 169)

In various different works, Merleau-Ponty consistently defends the view that the mental itself may, on occasion, be visible in others people's conduct and expressive behaviour. On his view, therefore, we can see that another person is angry by seeing that person's *anger itself*.

It is important to Merleau-Ponty, as it is to like-minded phenomenologists such as Max Scheler, that this perceptual model of our knowledge of other minds constitutes a genuine alternative to inferential accounts of the same. Others' experiences are 'given for us *in* expressive phenomena... not by inference, but directly, as a sort of primary "perception"' (Scheler 1954: 10; see Merleau-Ponty 2002: 410). The great value of the perceptual account is precisely that it lets direct perception do the work other accounts assign to inferences of one sort or another. If another's anger is visible, then it is not something whose presence I need to infer.

Yet there are other, more sophisticated ways of construing a perceptual model of our knowledge of other people's emotions. In a recent paper, Joel Smith tries to account for our ability to see that others are angry by relying in part on Husserl's work on 'horizon intentionality'. When we look at a book lying on our desk, it is not just the front cover facing us that is perceptually present, but also, in some sense, the back cover and the pages between the covers. Similarly, we 'see' the desk as being present beneath the book: we don't see the book as somehow hanging suspended atop a gap in the desk. In Husserl's terminology, the back cover and the occluded parts of the desktop are 'co-presented'.

Note that 'co-presented' does not mean 'seen'. Occluded back covers and tabletops are not actually seen; if they were discoloured or full of holes, we would not be able to notice. On the other hand, however, 'co-presentation' is a perceptual phenomenon. It is not adequately explained by saying that we *believe* or *think* that the tabletop, for example, continues in a gapless fashion underneath the book. This can be made clear by looking at simple geometrical figures. If you draw a 'pacman' such that the angle of its mouth is exactly 90 degrees, and add a square such that one of its corners merges with the pacman's mouth, it will look as if the square is partially occluding a circular disc (see Smith 2010: 737). Given that you know that these are two-dimensional drawings on a piece of paper, you have no inclination to judge that the square really occludes anything; but that does nothing to alter the fact that it *looks* as if it does.

An important reason why we have no inclination to judge that the disc has a hidden part is our understanding that there is no confirmatory presentation to be had of it. That is, there is no such thing as *removing* the square to see the occluded bits of the disc; there is no *moving around* the displayed figures so that the disc would now occlude the corner of the square, and so on. In the case of the book partially occluding the desktop, we have a sense of such confirming experiences being possible, however. Hence, in this case, unless we have reason to suspect otherwise, we do believe that the desktop is actually present under the book.

Now, Smith's suggestion is that

> the way in which other minds are present in experience is like the way in which the rear aspect of the book is. Might it be that whilst only behaviour is presented in visual experience mentality is co-presented? Just as the rear aspect of the book is visually present without being visually presented, so another's misery is visually present even though only their frown is visually presented. (Smith 2010: 739)

As he is quick to emphasize, however, if only behaviour can be presented and '[t]he mentality of another is never any more than co-presented' (ibid.: 740), then there seems to be a problem about how, if at all, these co-presentations can be confirmed in experience. Smith's solution is an idea he claims to derive from Husserl:

> …what is anticipated in the case of co-presented mentality are further presentations of behaviour that co-present related mentality. For example, if your frown co-presents misery then I will *anticipate further behaviour* that co-presents appropriately related states, such as for example self-pity. In this way, a co-presented horizon can be verified in another's 'changing but incessantly harmonious behaviour'.[7] We can regard one's co-presentations of another's mentality to be fulfilled *not*, as with the rear aspect of the book, *by the co-presented becoming presented*, but by the co-presented and presented taking part in a harmonious experience. (Smith 2010: 740–1; my emphases)

It is clear from this that Smith's solution to the other minds problem is obstacle-overcoming. That is, unlike Merleau-Ponty, Smith accepts the idea that another person's misery as such *cannot be seen* (cannot 'become presented'). We can have a perceptual sense of its (co-)presence; and if a person's perceived behaviour unfolds in a way that harmonizes with such co-presence, we see that the person is miserable. But the misery itself is not something we can see.

If we have two perceptual models to choose between, the question is which model to choose. Towards the end of the next section I suggest that it only the Merleau-Pontian, obstacle-dissipating model that yields an alternative to traditional, inferential accounts of our knowledge of other minds.

---

[7] This is a quote from Husserl (1995: 114). I shall not discuss whether Smith's reading of Husserl is correct.

2 PERCEPTION VERSUS INFERENCE

In saying that we can sometimes know that others are angry by seeing that they are, the defender of the perceptual model should be understood to oppose the view that we can always only *infer* that another is angry. An inference being the process of drawing a conclusion from some set of assumptions, the contrast between perception and inference is intuitively clear enough. If I am told of a person whom I have never met that he is trying on a new wig, I am likely to infer that he is bald. But if I meet the man and he is not wearing his wig, I have no need for inferences. Given adequate lighting, intact visual abilities on my part, and various other conditions being met, I can *see* that he is bald.

In this section, however, I suggest that the relation between perception and inference is less simple than this example might lead us to think. To see this, we need to distinguish between the claim that our access to the minds of others is *phenomenologically* perceptual and the claim that it is *epistemologically* perceptual.

(a) Phenomenology

To address the phenomenological side of things first, a model is perceptual (in terms of phenomenology) if and only if it claims that it sometimes seems to us that we see that other people are in the grip of various emotions. An inferential model would deny this and add that it always seems to us as if we *infer* others' emotions.[8]

I think that the phenomenological question is easily settled in favour of the perceptual claim. As Scheler famously puts it,

> we certainly believe ourselves to be directly acquainted with another person's joy in his laughter, with his sorrow and pain in his tears, with his shame in his blushing, with his entreaty in his outstretched hands, with his love in his look of affection, with his rage in the gnashing of his teeth, with his threats in the clenching of his fist, and with the tenor of his thoughts in the sound of his words. If anyone tells me that this is not 'perception', for it cannot be so, in view of the fact that a perception is simply a 'complex of physical sensations', and that there is certainly no sensation of another person's mind nor any stimulus from such a source, I would beg him to turn aside from such questionable theories and address himself to the phenomenological facts. (Scheler 1954: 260)

If someone would be prepared to deny that it ever seems to us as if we see that another is angry, say, and instead claim that it always seems to us that this is something we infer from behavioural clues, it is not easy to see how one could convince them otherwise.

---

[8] Other models are possible. One could deny the perceptual claim without insisting that we need always experience that we *infer* what others are feeling. But I shall ignore such alternatives.

Perhaps the best one could do is draw their attention to how some autistic persons experience that they have to make complicated inferences where the rest of us have a much more direct grasp of others' emotions. Thus, consider the experience of Temple Grandin, who as a child felt that:

> Something was going on between the other kids, something swift, subtle, constantly changing—an exchange of meanings, a negotiation, a swiftness of understanding so remarkable that sometimes she wondered whether they were all telepathic. She is now aware of the existence of these social signals. She can infer them, she says, but she herself cannot perceive them, cannot participate in this magical communication directly, or conceive the many-levelled kaleidoscopic states of mind behind it. Knowing this intellectually, she does her best to compensate, bringing immense intellectual effort and computational power to bear on matters that others understand with unthinking ease. (Sacks 1995: 259–60)

Surely, there are situations—perhaps a great many of them—in which those of us who are not autistic *do not* experience that we have to make any 'intellectual effort' to work out what another person is feeling. Situations, that is, in which it seems to us that we directly perceive or pick up another's emotional state, effortlessly. Sometimes the 'phenomenological facts' are precisely the way Scheler claims: it seems to us that we *perceive* that others are angry, sad, or happy. In the following discussion, I will call such cases 'P cases', and I will assume that their phenomenology is beyond dispute.

Everyone who accepts that we can sometimes be wrong about our own minds, however, must be prepared to accept the possibility that we could be making inferences even though it seems to us that we are not. If so, there is a question about how much support the indisputable perceptual phenomenology lends to the perceptual account of other minds. Just to have a name for it, let 'psychology' refer to whatever is actually going on in the mind of someone detecting another person's emotion.[9] The possibility to be considered is that the perceptual phenomenology of P cases is compatible with inferential psychology.

Suppose it is suggested that in P cases we infer, rather than perceive, that another person is angry; however, since these inferences are habitual and very fast, say, we do not notice that we make any inferences (which would explain the 'perceptual' phenomenology). Consider an example. Since raindrops are not always easy to see through a window, a common way of figuring out that it is raining out is by seeing that streets and sidewalks are wet. In this sort of case, do we *see* that it is raining, or do we *infer* that it is? I think most of us would be inclined to say that this is an example of a (fast, habitual) inference being made on the basis of relevant perceptual information; it is not an example of perception doing all the work by itself.[10] One thing that seems particularly important to our reaching this conclusion is that what we 'perceive' here is directly sensitive to other information that we have, or take ourselves to have. If you have just been informed

---

[9] This is purely stipulative and may not map onto any of the normal uses of the word 'psychology'.

[10] Though this example does meet Dretske's conditions for 'secondary epistemic seeing' (except, of course, in the fire hydrant variant). See the next section.

that someone has opened a fire hydrant in your street, the wet asphalt may not strike you as evidence of rain. In the words of Zenon Pylyshyn, this example shows 'cognitive penetration' at work (Pylyshyn 1999: 343). This is precisely what you would expect of an inference: that it would be possible for us to inhibit it if, for example, we have conclusive evidence against the conclusion being true. Habitual inferences may be difficult to block, but it is hardly impossible to do so.

According to Pylyshyn, it is characteristic of at least what he calls 'early vision' that it is cognitively *im*penetrable. Simply put, what you see is not affected by any non-visual information that you have. Consider, for example, the famous Müller-Lyer illusion. Once you have measured the two lines, you will know (and hence believe) that they are the same length. Yet you still see one line as longer than the other. What you know has no effect on what you see. Of course, knowing what you know, you will not *judge* that one line is longer than the other; but that does nothing to change the fact that one line *looks* longer.

Now consider the case where you are looking at the paradigm expression of anger, complete with clenched fists, exposed teeth, and the characteristic angry glare. The question is whether in such a case, you perceive a wrinkled forehead, and so on, and *infer* that the person is angry, or whether you perceive not only (or even primarily) that the person's forehead is wrinkled, but (also) that the person is angry. Given what we have just said about the cognitive impenetrability of (early) vision, the perceptual model does not seem implausible.[11] Can you refrain from judging that the person you see is angry? Easily—if you know that the person is an award-winning actor rehearsing for a part in a movie, for example. But you cannot make the angry *look* go away. Regardless of what you know, the person will look angry to you.[12] If this is true, then it seems plausible to say that cognitive impenetrability applies to some cases of detecting others' emotions by visual means. And if so, it seems reasonable to say that in those sorts of cases, the emotions are detected *perceptually*, not inferentially. You see the person as angry(-looking), whether or not you believe him or her to be angry. It is not an inference that leads you to apply the emotion term 'anger' to this person: you *see* that the term is applicable, though you may not—depending on what other information you have—end up *judging* that the person is angry.

It seems, then, that some P cases may be genuine cases of perception rather than inference. This conclusion is in line with the views of phenomenologists such as Scheler and Merleau-Ponty: they do not merely claim that it sometimes *seems* to us as if we perceive

[11] Note that I am not suggesting that a psychological process cannot be perceptual unless it is cognitively impenetrable. Rather, I am suggesting that if the psychology of a P case—that is, a case in which it seems to us that we *perceive* another person's emotion—is cognitively impenetrable, this is a strong reason for thinking that the psychology in this case is perceptual, rather than inferential.

[12] This claim needs to be modified somewhat, as I take it there are no clear-cut borders between the expression of anger and certain closely related negative emotions. Depending on the background information you have, the person may strike you as vengeful, hateful, or perhaps even disgusted. Yet all these are variations of the fundamental hostility expressed by the person, and I doubt there is any information you could be given, which would make the person *look* happy.

that another person is angry or sad; they also maintain that this is what *in fact* goes on in some P cases.[13] Yet perhaps this conclusion seems hard to reconcile with the fact that numerous researchers in social cognition have emphasized the 'inferential' nature of the processes by which we go about attributing emotions (and other mental states) to others.[14] Such research, it might seem, contradicts the point I have just tried to make; and the abundance of such research would seem to cast serious doubt on the psychological viability of the perceptual model.

However, I think the contradiction is more apparent than real. Many vision scientists accept (or used to accept) Helmholtz's view that perceptions are 'unconscious inferences' from sensory input (for example, Gregory 1997: 2; Rock 1977).[15] On this sort of view, the idea is not that the *person* who perceives unconsciously infers the real shape or size of an object, for example. This would be the idea I have just suggested should be rejected—both with respect to the Müller-Lyer illusion, and with respect to some cases of emotion detection. Rather, the claim is that there are processes 'analogous to (syllogistic) reasoning', or 'inference-like processes', going on in 'the visual system' (Rock 1977: 358, 368-9: see Green 2010: 49)—processes that we might call 'inferences' (in scare quotes). So, when you are looking at the Müller-Lyer lines, *you* need not (and *will not*, once you have measured the lines) infer that one is longer than the other; yet that does not prevent your 'visual system' from making precisely that 'inference'. And this accounts for the fact that, regardless of what you know, believe and judge, one line keeps looking longer than the other.

If visual phenomena that nobody would dispute are perceptual are also 'inferential', then there is every reason to think that P cases of emotion detecting must be 'inferential' as well, even if they are perceptual. But this does not jeopardize the phenomenologists' idea of offering a genuine alternative to inferential solutions to the other minds problem. What matters is that the processes in virtue of which the episodes count as 'inferential' should be *sub-personal* processes. The 'inferences' in question should not be made *by* the person who perceives—that is, the perceiver should not *reason* to the other person's emotion—though they would obviously occur 'in' the perceiving person. Indeed, insofar as the 'inferences' involved in P cases of emotion detection are made in some part of the visual system (however this question is to be decided),[16] this would be a reason *for*—not against—regarding those episodes as perceptual. The phenomenologists' perceptual approach to other minds is inconsistent with *personal*-level inferentialism, if this is understood as the view that *we* (as opposed to some part of our cognitive machinery) always infer others' emotions. But the approach is consistent with sub-personal 'inferentialism', and it would be unwise of phenomenologists to suggest otherwise.[17]

---

[13] See the quotes from Merleau-Ponty given in the previous section.

[14] For various examples, see the essays collected in Malle and Hodges (2005).

[15] Pylyshyn concedes that there is a broad sense of 'inference' such that his theory attributes inferences to the system of early vision (Pylyshyn 1999: 407).

[16] See Scholl and Tremoulet (2000) for an argument that we may perceive agency and animacy.

[17] *Pace* Gallagher (2008: 537) and Ratcliffe (2007: 123-4).

(b) Epistemology

In the preceding subsection we were concerned with determining whether there might be *some* genuine cases of perceiving another's emotional state.[18] To that extent, we were in fact addressing what I have called the *descriptive* problem of other minds. When we inquire into the *epistemology* of P cases, however, we are not so much interested in what is going on in the psyche of a subject having such an experience, as in the epistemic grounding that the subject has for claims about another person's emotional state.[19]

As Currie and Ravenscroft (2002: 56) stress, we must 'distinguish two senses of "dependent on inference"'. In one sense, my belief is dependent on inference 'just in case I actually go through a process of inferring it' from certain premises (ibid.). A belief that meets this condition is *psychologically* inferential. The other sense of 'dependent on inference' is 'dependent on inference for a justification of your belief' (ibid.). A belief of this kind is *epistemologically* inferential. Though questions of psychology are sometimes run together with the question of justification (see Pargetter 1984), it is fairly obvious that they should be kept apart. It is one thing whether or not people actually infer (consciously or not) the mental states of others and, if so, what sorts of inferences—analogical, inferences to best explanation, or whatever—they make. Another question is whether inferences are needed to justify our beliefs about others' mental states and, if so, what sorts of inferences (if any) are up to the task (see Melnyk 1994: 483).[20]

Note that this point cuts both ways. If the absence of actual inferences does nothing to rule out an inferential account of our knowledge or justification for believing that others feel, think, and so on, the *presence* of personal-level inferences does not rule out a perceptual account of our justification either. If this point is not immediately clear, it is helpful to briefly look at an example. Suppose that a perceiver with excellent colour vision looks at a yellow banana (under normal viewing conditions, and so on), and that the perceiver *sees* that the banana in front of her is yellow. On any acceptable account of perceptual knowledge, this ought to be a prime example of such knowledge; the perceiver's knowledge that the banana is yellow is perceptual, not

---

[18] Some have made considerably stronger claims. Shaun Gallagher, for example, maintains that 'for the most part, in most of our encounters in everyday life, direct perception delivers sufficient information for understanding others' (Gallagher 2008: 540). But for the purposes of addressing the epistemological problem of other minds it is sufficient that we *sometimes* have perceptual access to *some* mental states of others.

[19] In this section I rely on Dretske (1969) and McNeill (2011).

[20] Alec Hyslop (defending the argument from analogy) relies on this distinction. Discussing the view that 'we see the outer as expressive of the inner. No inference is in question' (Hyslop 1995: 127), Hyslop remarks that it 'might well describe accurately our psychological response to human figures. However, that is as far as it goes... If any sort of justification was aimed for, it is not forthcoming' (ibid.: 128). Hyslop obviously takes the question of whether we *actually* do or do not infer others' mental states as being of little relevance to the question concerning our justification for believing that others have such states.

inferential.[21] At the same time, there is nothing to prevent our perceiver from (consciously or, perhaps, unconsciously) going through a process of reasoning along, for example, the following lines: (i) that banana is the same colour as lemons; (ii) lemons are yellow; (iii), therefore, that banana is yellow. If so, this would be relevant to the psychological story of what is going on in this case. But it would be irrelevant to the epistemological question of how she knows that the banana is yellow (see Dretske 1969: 120–1). Her belief that the banana is yellow does not depend for its justification on her belief that lemons are yellow. For suppose she believed (falsely) that limes, too, are yellow, and adjusted her inference accordingly. If she spoke the inference out loud, a listener might point out that limes are green. She could obviously accept this point without being any less justified in believing the banana to be yellow.[22] For what justifies her belief that the banana is yellow is her seeing that it is, not her inference via beliefs about the colours of lemons or limes. The inference, though psychologically real enough, does no justificatory work.

If it is true that we can sometimes see that others are angry then that would be the justification we would have in those situations for believing other persons to be angry. At the same time, we *could*, in those situations, supplement our seeing with a bit of reasoning along such lines as: this person's forehead is wrinkled; wrinkled foreheads usually signal anger; therefore, this person is probably angry. We *could* do that, but in many such situations this activity would be doing no justificatory work.

As already indicated, it also seems possible for knowledge to be epistemically inferential although, as far as psychology and phenomenology are concerned, no process of inferring or reasoning is involved. Some defenders of inferential solutions to the other minds problem emphasize this possibility, as we have seen (footnote 20). Since this point is of some relevance to the question concerning the precise articulation of the phenomenological response to the other minds problem, I will dwell a bit on some of its consequences. As we will see, it is important to ascertain precisely when a belief is inferentially (as opposed to perceptually) justified.

Consider an example of what Dretske calls 'secondary epistemic seeing'.[23] This time our perceiver cannot see the banana, for it is hidden inside the fruit bowl. She can,

---

[21] This is an example of what Dretske calls 'primary epistemic seeing'. According to Dretske, S sees that b is P in a primary epistemic way only if: (i) b is P; (ii) S sees$_n$ b (that is, S sees b non-epistemically); (iii) the conditions under which S sees$_n$ b are such that b would not look, L, the way it now looks to S unless it was P; and (iv) S, believing the conditions are as described in (iii), takes b to be P (Dretske 1969: 79–88). By the way, even though one cannot see that b is P unless one has certain beliefs, it should not be supposed that this point contradicts what I said above about cognitive impenetrability. If you do not believe conditions are such that the banana would not look the way it looks (yellow) unless it was yellow—say you believe someone has manipulated the lighting—then you do not see *that* the banana is yellow; indeed, you may not even believe that it is yellow. But this is perfectly compatible with cognitive impenetrability as defined above: because, regardless of whether or not you believe the banana to be yellow, it still *looks* that way to you.

[22] Assuming that she is not confused or in doubt about what colour that thing in front of her is.

[23] S sees that b is P in a secondary epistemic way if and only if: (i) b is P; (ii) S sees$_n$ c ($c \neq b$) and sees (primarily) that c is Q; (iii) Conditions are such that c would not be Q unless b were P; and (iv) S, believing conditions to be as described in (iii), takes b to be P (Dretske 1969: 153).

however, see (in a primary epistemic way) that fruit flies are hovering over the fruit bowl. Suppose that fruit flies only hover over ripe bananas. Knowing (or truly believing) this, our perceiver sees in a secondary way that the banana in the bowl is ripe. Is her justification for taking the banana to be ripe purely perceptual in this case, or is it based on inference? Remember that Dretske's observation that 'secondary seeing does not, any more than primary seeing, involve a reasoning or inferring that b is P on the basis of what one has seen to be the case' (Dretske 1969: 159) is irrelevant here. We are not interested in how our perceiver actually reaches her belief that the banana is ripe, but in what justification her visual perception gives her for holding it. And, surely, what she sees in a primary epistemic way (that fruit flies are hovering) gives her *no* justification for believing the banana to be ripe independently of her belief that connects fruit-fly hovering with ripeness. Unlike the limes and lemons case we considered above, she cannot abandon her belief about fruit flies and still be justified, on the basis of what she sees, in believing the banana to be ripe. If so, then our perceiver's justification is ultimately inferential, rather than perceptual. There is a justificatory gap, so to speak, between her (primary epistemic) seeing that fruit flies are hovering and her (secondary epistemic) 'seeing' that the banana is ripe, which must be filled by a belief that connects fruit-fly hovering with ripeness.

Next, consider a variation of our example that falls somewhere between the two versions we have discussed so far. Suppose our subject sees a ripe yellow banana in plain view, and suppose bananas are only yellow when ripe. Believing this, our subject takes the banana to be ripe. In Dretske's classificatory scheme, this is another example of primary epistemic seeing.[24] The banana is ripe; the perceiver sees the banana; conditions are such that the banana would not look the way it now looks to her if it were not ripe. And finally, the perceiver, believing conditions to be as just specified, takes the banana to be ripe.

Yet is her taking it to be thus justified on purely perceptual grounds, or does she need a connecting belief as in the case we just considered? It seems there are two ways we might go with this example, and the way we go determines the answer we will have to give to the question just asked. The crucial issue is whether or not we will want to say that the banana's ripeness is itself a seen feature of the banana. Suppose it is. In this case, the example is parallel to the first banana example we discussed. Our perceiver has no need for inferences. Suppose ripeness is *not* a seen feature of the banana. In that case, our perceiver sees the banana and its colour (yellow), but not its ripeness as such. But this means, surely, that her visual perception can only warrant her belief that the banana is ripe given a belief that connects a visible feature of the banana (its yellow colour) with the invisible feature of ripeness. If so, her justification is inferential, rather than purely perceptual. Independently of the connecting belief that yellow bananas are ripe bananas, she has no justification, on the basis of her perception alone, for taking the banana to be ripe. In general, 'you may primarily see that b is F by seeing F, or by seeing some distinct

---

[24] Insofar as the perceiver's background beliefs are not faulty in certain ways (see Dretske 1969: 113–17).

feature of b and knowing how it relates to b's being F... Only in cases where you see that b is F by seeing F do you get non-inferential knowledge. Cases where you see that b is F by seeing some other feature can secure only inferential knowledge' (McNeill 2011: 11).

The upshot of this discussion for the two perceptual models—Merleau-Ponty's obstacle-dissipating model and Smith's obstacle-overcoming one—should now be obvious. If anger can be visible, as the obstacle-dissipating response would have it, then you can see a person and you can see her anger[25]; both are visible features of the scene. On this sort of picture there is no room for a justificatory gap to open up between the features of the person that you see and your belief that the person is angry—for the seen features include *her anger*. Obstacle-overcoming responses, on the other hand, accept that another's anger is not a visible feature of the person. Insofar as they hold that it is nevertheless possible to see *that* a person is angry, they must maintain that one sees this by seeing some other feature(s) of the person—such as her wrinkled forehead. But this does leave a gap between what your visual perception *itself* warrants believing (that the person has a wrinkled forehead) and the belief that the person is angry—a gap which can only be filled by a connecting belief to the effect that when people wrinkle their foreheads they are (usually) angry.

On Smith's view, we see that another is angry when her behaviour co-presents anger, and when the co-presentation is confirmed by further presented behaviour. Perhaps it might be suggested, in defence of Smith, that if anger is visually co-presented and we thus see that someone else is angry, then his anger *is* a seen feature of the scene. How else are we going to decide what is or is not a seen feature than by reference to what we see? And on Smith's view, we precisely see that the person is *angry*. This defence does not work, however. For, as pointed out in Section 1, what is co-presented is not actually seen: if the co-presented bit of the tabletop underneath my coffee cup was discoloured I would not be able to notice. Nor can it be concluded from the fact that we see (in a primary epistemic way) that someone else is angry that then her anger itself is something seen. One of McNeill's examples brings this out (McNeill 2011: 13). In the example, a normally sighted person sees that the traffic light is glowing red by seeing the red light illuminated. A colour-blind person also sees that the light is glowing red, but she sees this by seeing that the top light (which she knows to be the red light) is illuminated. Both see, in a primary way, that the traffic light is glowing red. But only the former person sees this *by seeing the light's redness*. So it does not follow from the fact that, on Smith's account we may see that another is angry, that on this account the person's anger is itself a seen feature. On the contrary, Smith's co-presentation analysis seems to rule this out. Thus, according to Smith, we see that another is angry by seeing, *not her anger*, which can only ever be co-presented, but her behaviour (understood as distinct from her anger). But then we can only be justified in believing another to be angry if we have a connecting

[25] 'See' here means 'see non-epistemically'. Just as you do not need the concept of a person, or any beliefs about persons, to see a person, you do not need the concept of anger, or beliefs about anger, to see another's anger.

belief to the effect that behaviour of *this* sort means anger. Hence Smith's is clearly an inferential account.[26]

Smith would obviously deny that on his view, people infer others' emotions—and he would be right to do so. But this point is relevant only to the phenomenological and psychological stories, and it leaves intact the point that if we know about others' emotions the way Smith proposes, then our knowledge must be inferential. What is more, given that Smith's story concentrates on the phenomenology and psychology of P cases, it leaves the precise nature of the inference unexplained.

3 Objections

If the argument offered in the previous section is on the right lines, it seems that if we want a perceptual as opposed to an inferential account of our knowledge of other people's emotions, then we have to follow Merleau-Ponty in adopting an obstacle-dissipating response. That means defending the view that emotions can be visible. No doubt this will strike many as a radical thesis that is open to serious objections. In this section I suggest that the thesis can be defended against a number of such objections. Replying to these will help me put more flesh on the Merleau-Pontian proposal.

(a) Asymmetry

Alec Hyslop has recently launched two connected objections against the idea that we can directly experience others' mental states. The first turns on a self-other asymmetry that he claims is 'at the heart of the problem of other minds' (Hyslop 2010). According to Hyslop, we often, though not always, know directly whether we are in a particular mental state. But 'what is striking is that we never have direct knowledge that other human beings are in whatever mental state they are in. It is this stark asymmetry that generates the epistemological problem of other minds' (Hyslop 2010). If the obstacle-dissipating model is true, however, it seems to follow that 'the dreaded asymmetry between ourselves and others does not exist. This has generally been seen as implausible' (ibid.).

---

[26] This criticism does not imply that we never see three-dimensional objects. To see a three-dimensional object is to have some aspects of it presented and others co-presented. But my criticism of Smith *does* imply that one's justification for believing *that* the seen object is three-dimensional is inferential in cases in which none of the co-presented aspects become presented. For such cases, *if* I am justified in believing that the seen object is three-dimensional and not merely a two-dimensional facade, this must depend on my having a connecting belief to the effect that objects that appear three-dimensional are rarely mere facades. By contrast, when various different aspects of an object are presented to me, my justification for believing that it is three-dimensional may be *non*-inferential. These implications, however, seem intuitively plausible.

Hyslop is surely right to suggest that most philosophers have believed the denial of a stark self-other asymmetry to be implausible. But of course, the majority view is not necessarily the right view, and some might feel that Hyslop does not do enough to establish that it is in this case. I do not think, however, that the defender of the obstacle-dissipating model ought to press this concern in responding to Hyslop's criticism. It is surely hopeless to deny that there is a fundamental difference between the sorts of access I may have to my own emotions, say, and the access I have to the emotions of another person. Although, as Hyslop correctly notes, we may not always have an immediate first-person awareness of our own mental states, it remains true that we often do. And Hyslop is also right to suggest that when we do, the sort of access we have to our own mental states is one we do not—do not *ever*—have to the mental states of other people. In other words, that there is a basic self-other asymmetry is, I think, undeniable.

But it is far from obvious that a defender of the obstacle-dissipating model is committed to denying the asymmetry. Merleau-Ponty, for one, emphatically insists on the reality of the asymmetry: 'The grief and anger of another have never quite the same significance for him as they have for me. For him these situations are lived through, for me they are displayed' (Merleau-Ponty 2002: 415). Indeed, Merleau-Ponty goes as far as to say that there is a sense in which 'the truth of solipsism is there', insofar as 'I am necessarily destined never to live through the presence of another to himself' (ibid.: 419, 424).[27] I cannot 'live through' another's grief or anger the way the other does, just as others cannot live through my grief or anger the way I do. In the case of other people's anger, I am, as we might put it, necessarily confined to a very limited and one-sided view.

What Merleau-Ponty does not say, and what the defender of the obstacle-dissipating view should avoid saying, is that this essential asymmetry must be cashed out in terms of the *directness* of the knowledge involved. For on the perceptual view, another's anger may, in some cases, be visible; thus in such cases, I can know that another is angry by seeing her anger. In my own case, I can presumably know that I am angry by 'feeling' angry. These ways of knowing about anger are essentially different, so the basic asymmetry is accommodated. But since both ways of knowing involve an awareness of the anger itself, it is not clear what it would mean to say that one type is more direct than the other. So, the perceptual model involves a rejection of Hyslop's construal of the self-other asymmetry in terms of essentially different degrees of directness, but it is fully compatible with other ways of conceiving of it.

(b) The poverty of telepathy

Hyslop's second criticism is closely related to the first. According to him, even if I were 'able to observe the mental states of another human being that would not mean that I did not have a problem of other minds. I would still lack what I needed. What I need is the

---

[27] For an argument that it is wrong to regard this insight as illustrating the truth of solipsism, see Overgaard (2007: ch. 5).

capacity to observe those mental states as mental states belonging to that other human being' (Hyslop 2010). He illustrates the problem by imagining telepathic subjects 'who are as it were "plugged in" to another's mental states' (ibid.). Even such subjects, Hyslop claims, 'would need what they do not have, direct knowledge that what they are "plugged in" to is, indeed, the inner life of another' (ibid.).

This objection seems to work with a very specific notion of what it would be to 'directly observe' another person's mental state. Hyslop seems to think that the only way to make sense of this suggestion is by interpreting it as attributing to us the ability to 'live through' someone else's inner life. Indeed, if this is how the perceptual model is to be interpreted, then it is difficult to see how the perceived inner life could be experienced as another's life at all—let alone that of a *particular* other person. But as we have just seen, this is precisely not Merleau-Ponty's view. According to him, I perceive another's anger 'in his conduct, in his face or his hands' (Merleau-Ponty 2002: 415). And if so, then surely there is no problem about explaining how we may observe the anger as belonging to a particular other person: we typically perceive the anger as belonging to the person in whose conduct it is expressed.

(c) Behaviourism

Suppose we ask why, precisely, the Merleau-Pontian obstacle-dissipating response does not assume an epistemological 'gap' the way the obstacle-overcoming response does. After all, short of postulating telepathic or introspective types of access to others' emotions, to see another's anger must mean something along the lines of: to see it *in her wrinkled forehead, flushed cheeks, clenched fists*, and so on. For Merleau-Ponty, the crucial point is, though, that *in the right circumstances*, the wrinkled forehead, clenched fists and so on *are* the anger (or part of it)—they are not features *distinct* from the anger. So there is no gap or distance between an awareness (in those circumstances) of those features and an awareness of the anger.

But surely, it might be said, the problem with claims of this sort is that they seem to imply a pretty crude form of behaviourism (Jacob 2011): emotions are (partially) identified with patterns of observable behaviour (forehead-wrinkling, and so on).[28] And that is simply not plausible, for one thing because such forehead-wrinkling, first-clenching, and the rest, can occur in the absence of anger.

On what I think is Merleau-Ponty's considered view, however, emotion is 'a variation in our relations with others and the world' (1964a: 53). Or again, 'grief and anger are variations of belonging to the world, undivided between the body and consciousness' (2002: 415). To paraphrase slightly, one might say that grief and anger are ways of coming to grips with the world, or engaging with the world, as sad or infuriating. When the other person is angry, this is what her wrinkled forehead, her glare, and her threatening

---

[28] Merleau-Ponty explicitly says that anger and shame are 'types of behaviour or styles of conduct' (1964a: 52).

gestures *are*: a way of coming to grips with some part of her environment as galling, say. By contrast, when a person merely pretends to be angry, those gestures, that glare, and so on, are something altogether different. They are still not *mere* bodily movements—as they might perhaps be if a person had a series of ticks that happened to look exactly like a fit of anger. But they are not ways of coming to grips with the galling character of the world either.

So when Merleau-Ponty says that the angry gesture 'is' the anger (2002: 214), he is not identifying anger with mere bodily movement. On the contrary, he is *denying* that the gesture, in this sort of case, is a mere bodily movement. This is confirmed by the sentences that immediately follow the passage in question: 'However, the meaning of the gesture is not perceived as the colour of the carpet, for example, is perceived' (ibid.). The point is not that, unlike the colour of the carpet, another person's anger is not a visible feature of the scene: as we have seen, Merleau-Ponty consistently affirms that emotions can be visible. Rather, his claim is that anger should not be identified with colours or shapes, or the movement of coloured shapes. More generally, Merleau-Ponty's point is that the behaviourism objection implicitly works with a dualism of disembodied mind versus mindless or 'soulless' body such that, if mental states are said to be visible, then all this can mean is that they are identified with states of the ('soulless') body. And it is precisely this dualism that we need to reject: 'incarnate significance is the central phenomenon of which body and mind... are abstract moments' (ibid.: 192).

This response to the behaviourism objection brings with it a commitment to a *disjunctive* account of behaviour.[29] On this account, the difference between the person who genuinely vents her anger and the person feigning anger is not that in the former case, there is the angry behaviour plus a feeling of anger, while in the latter case, there is only the behaviour (or rather, that plus an intention to deceive, say). Rather, even if the two behaviours are movement-for-movement indistinguishable to an outside spectator, they are *different kinds* of processes. In the one case, the visible behaviour is a person's coming to grips with the world as infuriating; in the other it is not. This disjunctivism ties in nicely with the fact that, 'from the inside', the fake and the genuine expression of anger are very different phenomena. The genuine expression often 'takes us over', as it were, and may be almost impossible to curb. The fake expression, by contrast, is something we deliberately bring about, and we need much practice if we are to become any good at it.

(d) Arguments from illusion

The disjunctivism just outlined not only helps to address the accusation of behaviourism; it also helps prevent that a version of the argument from illusion is brought to bear on the obstacle-dissipating model I have outlined. The argument in question might be formulated as follows: We can imagine a pair of cases in which I am witnessing a person

---

[29] See McDowell (1982). See also Stout (2010) for an argument that genuine and fake expressions of anger are different processes.

wrinkling her forehead, clenching her fists, and so on, such that the only difference between them is that in one case, the person is angry, and in the other she is not. If so, it seems that what I see, what my visual experience reveals to me, makes me perceptually aware of, must be the same in such a pair of cases. I am aware of the person's behaviour—her forehead-wrinkling, and so on—but surely not of her anger as such. The conclusion follows that even in the best possible case—the case in which the person *is* angry—her anger is beyond reach of my perceptual awareness. The Merleau-Pontian perceptual model, therefore, must be rejected.

The disjunctive view of behaviour blocks this argument by denying the crucial premise. It is simply not true that if the behaviour of the genuinely angry person is indistinguishable from the behaviour of the person faking it (or having a series of ticks), then in either case the most we can be perceptually acquainted with is mere behaviour compatible with the absence of anger. In the case where the person is genuinely venting her anger, her behaviour is *not* compatible with the absence of anger, for it *is* her anger made visible.

(e) A sceptical rejoinder

Let me, by way of concluding, consider a final objection. The objection is simply that seeing another's anger is insufficient to warrant a belief that the other person is angry. Before such a belief can be justified, it might be said, I need to *know that I am seeing her anger* as opposed to a fake expression of anger. The trouble is, however, that if fake and genuine expressions can be indistinguishable, it is not clear how I *can* know that I am seeing anger in any given case. And this means that, even if it is true that I can see another's anger, this doesn't help us address the epistemological problem of other minds. For regardless of whether anger is visible, I cannot know that another is angry unless I can know that she is not faking anger; and the (surely unavoidable) concession that fake and genuine expression can be indistinguishable seems to ensure that no such knowledge can be had.

The parallels between this objection and certain sceptical arguments about our knowledge of the external world should be obvious (see Overgaard 2011). It is also clear that not everyone accepts the crucial premise that I cannot know something unless I am able to rule out the classical sceptical hypotheses.[30] Yet it would take us too far afield to enter into these debates. But nor do we need to, for it is in fact possible to accept the sceptical argument as just formulated and still claim that the Merleau-Pontian perceptual account does constitute an answer to the epistemological problem of other minds. In the way I introduced this problem above, it was shaped by the idea that there was a fundamental obstacle to our finding out about others' mental states—an obstacle that does not arise when it comes to finding out about their baldness. The

---

[30] Reliabilists would deny this.

obstacle was that another's mental state is not something one might directly perceive. But the Merleau-Pontian account precisely dissipates this obstacle, thereby solving— or rather dissolving—the epistemological problem of other minds.[31]

REFERENCES

Austin, J. L. (1979), 'Other minds', in J. O. Urmson and G. J. Warnock (eds), *Philosophical Papers*, (Oxford: Oxford University Press), pp. 76–116.

Avramides, A. (2001), *Other Minds* (London: Routledge).

Cassam, Q. (2007), *The Possibility of Knowledge* (Oxford: Clarendon Press).

Currie, G. and Ravenscroft, I. (2003), *Recreative Minds* (Oxford: Oxford University Press).

Dretske, F. (1969), *Seeing and Knowing* (London: Routledge & Kegan Paul).

—— (1973), 'Perception and other minds', *Noûs* 7/1: 34–44.

Gallagher, S. (2008), 'Direct perception in the intersubjective context', *Consciousness and Cognition* 17: 535–43.

Goldman, A. I. (2006), *Simulating Minds* (New York: Oxford University Press).

Gregory, R. L. (1998), *Eye and Brain: The Psychology of Seeing*, 5th edn. (Oxford: Oxford University Press).

Green, M. (2010), 'Perceiving emotions', *Proceedings of the Aristotelian Society Supplementary Volume* 84: 45–61.

Husserl, E. (1995), *Cartesian Meditations: An Introduction to Phenomenology*, trans. D. Cairns (Dordrecht: Kluwer Academic Publishers).

Hyslop, A. (1995), *Other Minds* (Dordrecht: Kluwer Academic Publishers).

—— (2010), 'Other minds', in E. N. Zalta (ed.), *The Stanford Encyclopedia of Philosophy* (autumn 2010), http://plato.stanford.edu/archives/fall2010/entries/other-minds/.

Jacob, P. (forthcoming), 'The direct-perception model of empathy: A critique', *Review of Philosophy and Psychology*.

Malle, B. F. and Hodges, S. D. (eds), *Other Minds* (New York: The Guilford Press).

McDowell, J. (1982), 'Criteria, defeasibility, and knowledge', *Proceedings of the British Academy* 68: 455–79.

McNeill, W. E. S. (2011), 'On seeing that someone is angry', *European Journal of Philosophy*, DOI: 10.1111/j.1468-0378.2010.00421.x

Melnyk, A. (1994), 'Inference to best explanation and other minds', *Australasian Journal of Philosophy* 72/4: 482–91.

Merleau-Ponty, M. (1964a), *Sense and Non-Sense*, tr. H. L. Dreyfus and P. A. Dreyfus (Evanston: Northwestern University Press).

—— (1964b), *Signs*, tr. R. C. McCleary (Evanston: Northwestern University Press).

—— (2002), *Phenomenology of Perception*, tr. C. Smith (London: Routledge).

Nagel, T. (1986), *The View from Nowhere* (New York: Oxford University Press).

[31] Previous versions of this material were presented at the 2010 Copenhagen Summer School in Phenomenology and Philosophy of Mind, at a seminar in the Department of Philosophy at Boğaziçi University, and at the 9th Annual Meeting of the Nordic Society for Phenomenology, University of Iceland. I am grateful to all audiences for helpful discussion. Special thanks are due to Thor Grünbaum, Joel Krueger, Camilla Serck-Hanssen, Lucas Thorpe, Bill Wringe, Dan Zahavi, and an anonymous reviewer.

Overgaard, S. (2007), *Wittgenstein and Other Minds* (London: Routledge).

—— (2011), 'Disjunctivism and the urgency of scepticis', *Philosophical Explorations* 14: 5–21.

Pargetter, R. (1984), 'The scientific inference to other minds', *Australasian Journal of Philosophy* 62/2: 158–63.

Pickard, H. (2003), 'Emotions and the problem of other minds', in A. Hatzymoysis (ed.), *Philosophy and the Emotions* (Cambridge: Cambridge University Press), 87–103.

Pylyshyn, Z. (1999), 'Is vision continuous with cognition? The case for cognitive impenetrability of visual perception', *Behavioral and Brain Sciences* 22: 341–423.

Ratcliffe, M. (2007), *Rethinking Commonsense Psychology* (London: Palgrave Macmillan).

Rock, I. (1977), 'In defense of unconscious inference', in W. Epstein (ed.), *Stability and Constancy in Visual Perception* (New York: Wiley), 321–73.

Sacks, O. (1995), *An Anthropologist on Mars* (London: Picador).

Scheler, M. (1954), *The Nature of Sympathy* (London: Routledge & Kegan Paul).

Scholl, B. J. and Tremoulet, P. D. (2000), 'Perceptual causality and animacy', *Trends in Cognitive Sciences* 4: 299–309.

Smith, J. (2010), 'Seeing other people', *Philosophy and Phenomenological Research* 81/3: 731–48.

Stout, R. (2010), 'Seeing the anger in someone's face', *Proceedings of the Aristotelian Society Supplementary Volume* 84: 29–43.

Wittgenstein, L. (1980), *Remarks on the Philosophy of Psychology*, vol. II, G. H. von Wright and H. Nyman (eds.), tr. C. G. Luckhardt and M. A. E. Aue (Oxford: Blackwell).

PART VI

··

TIME AND HISTORY

··

CHAPTER 23

EXPERIENCE AND HISTORY

DAVID CARR

PHENOMENOLOGY differs from its nearest neighbours among the philosophical disciplines, metaphysics and epistemology, by the kinds of questions it asks. Metaphysics asks what exists, how it exists and sometimes whether it exists (God, nature, human beings, universals, and so on), and epistemology asks how we know what exists. Phenomenology is more likely to ask, of anything that exists or may exist, how it is given, how it enters our experience, and what our experience of it is like.

So also with history. Rather than asking 'What *is* history?' or 'How do we *know* history?', a phenomenology of history inquires into history as a phenomenon, and into the experience of the historical. How does history present itself to us, how does it enter our lives, and what are the forms of experience in which it does so? The purpose of this essay is to outline a distinctively phenomenological approach to history. History is usually associated with social existence and its past, and so we shall be asking about the experience of the social world and of its temporality. As we shall see, experience in this context connotes not just observation but also involvement and interaction. We experience history not just in the social world around us, but also in our own engagement with it.

Philosophers have asked both metaphysical and epistemological questions about history, and some of the best-known philosophies of history have resulted from this questioning. The phenomenological approach is different, but it is not unrelated to these traditional philosophical questions, and later we will turn in some detail to how phenomenology may connect to them. To begin, however, I want to say something about recent work in the philosophy of history, in order to show the need for a phenomenological approach.

1 REPRESENTATION, MEMORY, EXPERIENCE

The philosophy of history has been dominated in recent years by two themes: *representation* and *memory*. These preoccupations arise primarily from epistemological considerations and respond to a traditional question in the philosophy of history: how do we know the past? The first answer is that we represent it, and for philosophers of the twentieth century this meant *linguistic* representation. In keeping with the 'linguistic turn' in both analytic and continental philosophy, the way to understand knowledge is to examine the language in which it is expressed. As for history, the primary linguistic form in which the past is represented is generally agreed to be narrative, and narrative is, or so Hayden White (1987) has argued at length, altogether different in form from the reality it purports to represent. One does not have to be as sceptical as White to recognize the problem that such representation poses: how to bridge the gap between the representation and the represented.

Memory, in its turn, while it may seem to provide a more direct link to the past, nevertheless seems to presuppose a gap of its own. For it can be argued that in order to be remembered, something must first be forgotten. Most of our words suggest this: *re*-member, *re*-call, *re*-collect, and so on. Memory seems to consist in bringing back something that has been lost. History is often portrayed as an operation of salvage or retrieval against forgetfulness, or at least of holding on to what otherwise would be lost to the present. History is often called 'society's memory', and for this to make sense memory has to be detached from its usual psychological sense, tied to the individual, and made collective. But even if this difficult feat is successfully performed, the separation between memory and the past remains.

On both of these accounts, then, history is divided by a gap from what it seeks to find or wants to know, and its activity is seen by philosophers as that of bridging this gap. This constitutes the *problem* to which the philosophy of history addresses itself: how does history bridge the gap, overcome the distance, which separates it from its object, the past? It is against this background that a phenomenological approach suggests itself: before it is *re*-presented, history must be presented, before it is remembered, the past must be experienced. So the phenomenological questions, mentioned above, suggest themselves: how do we encounter history directly, how do we experience it, how does it enter our lives?

Stated in this way, however, there seems to be something paradoxical about a phenomenology of history, especially if we think of it as a description of *experience*. This term has meant many things to philosophers, but one thing that all its meanings have in common is that experience is rooted in the present. It is in the present and of the present; it opens us to the present. But if 'history' means 'the past', as suggested above, then experience seems excluded as a mode of access to it. Representation and memory suggest themselves as our mode of access to history precisely because history is not available to our experience.

One of the accomplishments of phenomenology, however, and one of the tasks of this essay, is to dismantle the prejudices expressed in the last paragraph. One such prejudice is the simple picture that experience (or perception) relates to the present while memory connects us with the past. The phenomenological account of temporality, starting with Husserl's lectures on time-consciousness, recognizes that the experience of time is much more complex than this simple picture would suggest. The past turns out to be intimately involved, as we shall see, with our experience of the present. Another prejudice that needs to be examined is that history is exclusively about the past. The discipline of history, and the knowledge sought by historians, is about the past, but even our ordinary language allows that present events can be 'historical'. One of our aims will be to understand the historical as something broader and deeper than what counts as the object of historians' knowledge.

2 TEMPORALITY

One of the best-known accomplishments of phenomenology is its description of lived or experienced space, as distinguished from objective space. Merleau-Ponty (1962) draws on Husserl's account of the role of the body in perception and emphasizes the oriented, practical space of its surrounding world. The phenomenological account of experienced time, as opposed to objective time, constitutes a similar accomplishment. Like the phenomenology of space, that of time draws on a first-person account. Just as I am not merely in space as an object in a container, so I am not in time in the sense of occurring at a particular moment, or as a sequence of moments. It is true that I exist in an ever-changing Now, and in one sense my experience is a sequence of Nows. But like the Here in relation to the space that I perceive and inhabit, the Now is a vantage point from which I survey a kind of temporal field (Husserl 1991: 6) encompassing past and future. Husserl used the terms 'retention' and 'protention' to describe the grasp of past and future which, together with that of the present, make up our on-going temporal experience. Past and future in this sense constitute the horizon or background against which the present stands out; together they give meaning to the present in which I experience or act. I hold onto the past as I project a future.

Husserl uses the example of hearing a melody, note by note. Even though the past notes have elapsed, they must be retained in order to frame the note that is sounding now. The present note is nothing by itself; it has its significance, and is heard, as part of a larger temporal *Gestalt* that includes its past and its future horizons. These temporal features are essential, not accidental to human experience. It is not that I exist in the present and have the capacity occasionally to think about the future and remember the past. Human experience just *is* a kind of temporal reach or stretch, as Heidegger (1977: 343) called it. Husserl distinguished this retentional–protentional reach of time-consciousness from acts of explicitly 'envisaging' the future or 'recollecting' the past.

If we keep in mind the temporal field constituted by retention and protention, and think of it as a horizon or background for what occurs in the present, the 'past' takes on a special sense. Again the comparison with perceived space can be useful. The perception of things always involves a combination of the given and the hidden. Objects have their hidden sides which nevertheless belong to their perceived sense. They are also surrounded by a spatial background that contains other things and extends into the indefinite distance. What do I experience here? My perception is focused on one thing or another, but it also 'takes in' the background and the indefinite horizon. In perception I take the object to exist; but I take it to exist in its larger spatial context which exists as well, even if I do not perceive all the details.

So also with time. What 'takes place' in my experience, what is taken to occur or to be real, 'takes the place' of what came before (note the continued use of spatial metaphors), and I must be conscious of both. It can only be real, or be really occurring, if its background is equally real for me. The temporal field, then, is a field of reality for me. Like the spatial field, it fades into the indefinite distance, but it provides the background that allows the present to stand out and be distinct from it. The very sense of the present, then, as I experience it, requires that it bring its past along with it, even if the details do not remain distinct. What do I experience? Not just the punctual event, but the whole field that makes its presence (now in the temporal, rather than the spatial sense) possible. This includes the future as well. The horizon of protention is in many ways different from that of retention—for one thing, what occurs may differ from what I expect and thus surprise me. But it could not surprise me if I did not anticipate a more or less definite future for what is happening now. This future horizon also fades into indistinctness—the indefinite future—but it is just as essential to the constitution of my temporal experience as is the horizon of the past.

These considerations allow us to see that 'experience' not only can but must encompass the past, provided that we understand the peculiarly horizonal or background sense of the past (and future) we have outlined here. It might be thought that this analysis is too small-scale and too formal to be of use in the understanding of history. Terms like horizon and background may be thought to refer to 'immediate surroundings' only, and this not to extend very far. But remember that these surroundings have their own surroundings, and the idea of *indefinite extension* is crucial to the phenomenological understanding of these concepts. As for their formal character, it is true that we are talking here about the general framework for the experience of time. But we do not experience time 'as such' any more than we experience empty space. We experience space by perceiving particular things, and we experience time by encountering actual events that occur.

3 INTENTIONALITY AND THE WORLD OF THE NATURAL ATTITUDE

This last point reminds us of an essential feature of experience that phenomenology has brought to light: its *intentionality*. Experience is always experience *of* something. So far, in speaking of space and time, we have mentioned *things* and *events*. But in order to arrive at the experience of history we need to be much more concrete than this.

Our account of the spatiality and temporality of experience belong to the description of what Husserl called the 'natural attitude' or 'natural standpoint' (Husserl 1983: section 27). Heidegger referred to 'everydayness' (Heidegger 1977: 41). Both were trying to capture consciousness or human experience in its 'natural' or naïve state, that is, prior to its adoption of theoretical interpretations and agendas deriving from science, philoso-phy, or religion. Both thought that experience had been distorted and misdescribed because of these agendas, so they were trying to recapture or return to something that had been lost, at least to philosophy. Husserl also spoke of the 'world' of the natural atti-tude (Husserl 1983: section 27), and Heidegger of 'being in the world' (Heidegger 1977: 49). In their work the peculiarly phenomenological concept of 'world' emerges, a con-cept that has been one of its most influential legacies. The world in the phenomenologi-cal sense is not simply the totality or collection of all the things there are; it is the meaningful and organized whole of what is experienced *as* it is experienced. Just as experience is always *of* something—of things or other entities and ultimately of the world—so the world, in the phenomenological sense, is always world *for* an experienc-ing subject. To speak of the world of the natural attitude, or the world of the everyday, is to refer to the world as it presents itself in our naïve and pre-theoretical experience.

How to describe the world of the natural attitude? In his early attempts, Husserl devoted much attention to the spatiality and perspectival givenness of *things* in percep-tion, though he noted that some things are also 'goods' that have practical value. Other persons also belong to the world of the natural attitude. He also explicitly refers to the 'temporal horizon' (Husserl 1983: section 27) we mentioned above: the world is given temporally as well as spatially. Heidegger, in search of the 'being of beings encountered in the surrounding world', insists that such beings are encountered *not* originally as mere things but as practical equipment, not merely 'on hand' but as 'handy'. (Heidegger 1977: 67) The world of the everyday is not just the horizon of spatial perception but the organi-zation of the surrounding work environment into complexes of equipment determined by practical tasks and projects. Only a secondary act of reflection, in which we take a distance from our practical engagement, allows 'mere things' to emerge, shorn of their embeddedness in complexes of equipment. Heidegger obviously believes that his description is much more concrete, and comes closer to the 'naturalness' of the natural attitude than Husserl's does.

But Husserl's own thinking on the world of the natural attitude changed after his ini-tial attempts. He points out that we must distinguish the 'natural' from the 'naturalistic' attitudes (Husserl 1989: 190). The latter is guided by the modern, scientific concept of nature, and focuses on those aspects of our surroundings that are susceptible to scien-tific treatment—for example, seeking out causal regularities that are measurable and are expressible as laws. The naturalistic attitude overlooks or ignores everything that does not fit this model—so-called 'secondary qualities'—but also practical and aesthetic properties. The naturalistic attitude arises out of the natural attitude, and has made modern natural science possible, but it represents an impoverishment compared to the richness of the world we actually experience.

Husserl introduces this distinction between the 'naturalistic' and the 'natural' atti-tudes because he wants to distinguish the natural sciences from the human sciences, or humanities. As sciences, both are activities that arise out of the natural attitude and its world, but each concentrates on different aspects of the world: the humanities focus not on physical events but on human events, and these involve fundamentally different concepts and principles from those of the natural world: not things and causally related events but persons and their actions, thoughts, experiences, emotions and motivations. Persons interact not causally but socially, acting in light of their awareness and understanding of the actions of others. They aggregate not into collections of mere things in space and time but into groups and communities founded on attitudes, projects, intentions, and feelings. These sciences rest not on the 'naturalistic' but on what Husserl calls the 'personalistic' attitude. Just as the naturalistic attitude corresponds to the world of 'material nature', the personalistic attitude corresponds to what Husserl calls the human world (*die geistige Welt*) (Husserl 1989: 181).

But Husserl realizes that this personalistic attitude is more 'natural' than the naturalistic attitude; rather than comprising a narrowing of focus, like the naturalistic attitude, in order to develop a science, the personalistic attitude is exactly our naïve and pretheoretical way of being in the world.[1] It is true that the human 'sciences' take up a theoretical stance toward the human world, and that disciplines like sociology, anthropology, and literary studies look at different aspects of the human world in order to understand them in systematic ways. But they draw more directly on our pre-scientific understanding of the world than the natural sciences do. The natural attitude is itself that of social interaction and communication, and the world of the natural attitude is the social and human world. In a sense, Husserl goes a step beyond Heidegger's critical emendation of Husserl's original description: if our encounter with the 'handy', the world as practical equipment, is prior to our encounter with mere things, as Heidegger says, it is because we are engaged originally with others in the social organizations and structures of the world. It is these that constitute the tasks and projects that give these entities their practical meanings. To use Heidegger's famous example of the hammer: this item of equipment is immediately understood by us because we live in a social world in which tasks like carpentry and construction exist, and in which complexes of equipment like hammers and nails are manufactured for their purposes. The 'handiness' of the hammer, and of other entities of our surrounding world, derives from their embeddedness in the social world.

4 THE HUMAN WORLD AND THE HISTORICAL WORLD

We noted that Husserl arrived at his revised conception of the world of the natural attitude by examining the constitution of the human world in relation to the human sciences. We mentioned sociology, anthropology, and literary studies, but failed to mention

---

[1] In more recent parlance this would be described as the sphere of 'folk psychology'; but this term tacitly suggests that, like 'folk medicine', this primitive approach will eventually be supplanted by a scientific psychology. For Husserl, the personalistic attitude is not a deficient, aspiring science, but is no science at all.

history, which is sometimes classified as a social science, sometimes counted among the humanities, but in any case counts preeminently among the human sciences. If, as we claimed, the various disciplines focus their attention on certain aspects of the human world with theoretical intent, then we can also ask this question: on what aspect of the human world does history focus its attention? This question may provide clues in the pursuit of our primary concern here, which is to understand the experience of the historical in its pre-theoretical form. To posit the question in another way: how does the historical manifest itself in our ordinary experience, before it is taken up by the disciplined inquiry of historians?

When Husserl uses the term 'personalistic attitude' (and sometimes the 'personalistic world'), and then goes on to identify this with the natural attitude (Husserl 1989: 190), he suggests that 'persons' are the basic entities of this human world, just as 'things' are the basic entities of the naturalistic world. We have already mentioned some of the features of persons that distinguish them from things: actions, thoughts, experiences, emotions, intentions, and so on. We encounter persons, and persons encounter each other, not as things interacting causally but as subjects of experience and as agents motivated to act on their surroundings, and with or against their fellows. Their surroundings are not merely such as to interact causally with their bodies, but constitute a meaningful environment that can be perceived as a situation calling for certain actions. As we said before, pluralities of persons constitute not just collections but groups and communities based on mutual recognition and joint plans and actions. To encounter a person is not just to identify a person as such—as opposed to a mere thing—but to recognize man or woman, friend or foe, stranger or familiar, subordinate or superior, and so on. It is these kinds of relations, and not merely causal and spatial relations, that make up the human *world*. We inhabit that world not merely as perceivers and observers but primarily as agents seeking our own purposes and objectives. It is in terms of these that the world and its constituents have meaning for us. Since this is true of my world, it is also true of the world of every other person I encounter, and the human or social world is consequently one of overlapping and interlayered worlds. Every act of communication and understanding with another person is an act of entering into that person's world—or at least that is its intention. Another way of putting this, in order to avoid a monadological fragmentation of the social world, is to say that persons are essentially points of view, which means that persons are not so much possessed of their own worlds as they are differing perspectives on the world we share.

At this point we need to add a word about this important term 'attitude' or 'standpoint'. Describing the 'personalistic' attitude as taking *persons* as its fundamental constituents does not mean that it focuses on persons to the exclusion of everything else. The personalistic or human *attitude* corresponds to a human *world* in the sense that it views the whole world in human terms. This means that 'things'—that is, entities that are not persons—appear here too, but construed in human terms. This is where Heidegger's description of the 'being of entities encountered in the surrounding world' finds its place. That is, the surrounding world of persons is a world *not* of 'mere' things, as they might be construed from a scientific point of view, but of items and complexes of equipment, objects of value and enjoyment. Even 'nature', as Heidegger recognized (Heidegger 1977: 66–7), appears here with all its human significance: as cultivated, as formed and structured to suit human purposes. The forces of nature—climate, water, wind, and so on—are experienced here with their practical values, providing the resources and materials for our nutrition and habitation. And the 'man-made' surrounding world extends far beyond the tools and implements that figure in Heidegger's account to include the dwellings and other buildings, the streets and walks, the cars and other means of transportation that surround and envelop us in the everyday, modern urban world.

The human world is the *whole* world, then, experienced from the human point of view. And Husserl is quite right to identify this world with the natural attitude in the sense that it corresponds to our naïve and unmediated way of being in the world. The 'naturalistic' attitude, by contrast, is a special undertaking that results for us in the world of 'mere things' and thing-like properties, the world of 'nature' in the scientific sense. But this attitude too is a standpoint on the *whole* world, not just a focus on certain kinds of things to the exclusion of others. Persons too—indeed, every aspect of the human and animal existence—are treated as items belonging to material nature. This attitude has made possible not only the theoretical and technological mastery of the material world, but also the biological, chemical, and physiological understanding of animals and humans that has led to modern medicine.

These references to technology alert us to the existence of important points of intersection between the naturalistic and human worlds, and between the attitudes that underlie them, and we shall return to this point later. But first we must take up the question posed at the beginning of this section: how does the historical manifest itself in our ordinary experience, before it is taken up by historical inquiry? If the historical belongs to the human world, what aspects or features of this world constitute our 'natural' encounter with the historical? We have already suggested that temporality is the key, but now we must approach temporality, not merely from the standpoint of my individual experience. In other words we must inquire into the specifically social features of temporality. What is social temporality?

5 SOCIAL TIME AND THE EXTENDED
PAST AND FUTURE

The social or human world, as we described it above, is made up, most importantly, of persons acting and experiencing. This means that what was said about my individual experience, described from the first person point of view, applies also to the persons I encounter in the world. Their pasts—and futures—are not merely a series of elapsed now-points, but constitute a meaningful retentional–protentional background, horizon, or context for their present action and experience. Many cases of action in the social world are not individual but collective actions, and these will involve shared past and future horizons. Thus the social world is made up not only of overlapping pasts (and futures) belonging to individuals but also of overlapping *shared* pasts (and futures) belonging to groups and communities. The temporality of the social world is thus very different from the temporality of the naturalistic world, because it involves the experienced time of subjects and agents.

We said before that we encounter persons as part of a structured world involving gendered, social, and affective dimensions and differentiations. But this structure involves important temporal dimensions as well. Alfred Schutz (1967: 208) pointed to the difference between 'contemporaries' and 'predecessors'. But our contemporaries are older and younger, and their lives and experiential backgrounds may not completely overlap with my own. In addition to the many other ways the social world is structured and stratified, it is also divided into *generations*, and this distinction turns out to be crucial for our understanding of how the historical is experienced. It is primarily in our encounter with *older people* that the reality of the historical past is experienced, just as our encounter with *younger people* opens up a future that can be called historical as well.

The reason for saying this is that we usually think of the *historical* past (leaving the future aside for the moment) as the past which extends beyond the reach of my direct experience, and thus also beyond the reach of my memory, in the usual sense of memory. It thus includes, crucially but not exclusively, what happened before my birth. In the usual senses of both memory and experience, there is no way that the time before my birth could have been experienced or could be remembered by me. Nevertheless, I want to claim that, in the sense of experience and social temporality that we are developing here, the historical past in just this sense does indeed enter into my experience.

The best way to understand this is to return to the comparison with experienced space. We noted that space as perceived is a combination of the presented and the hidden; the things I see have their hidden sides, and are present to me within a spatial horizon or entourage which includes other things and recedes into the indefinite distance. This is the nature of the spatial reality that is available to me in and through each thing that I perceive. As it shades imperceptibly from my visual field into the indefinite distance, this spatial reality is also largely hidden from my view. It extends far beyond my capacity to perceive it; yet it is as real to me as is the small part of it that I perceive at any given moment. *What* it contains is partly determinate for me, thanks to past experience supplemented by knowledge; but it is mostly indeterminate in its detail.

As we saw, Husserl speaks of a *temporal field* that can be compared in many respects to our experience of space. My experience now, and the events I experience now, constitute a kind of core of presence (in the temporal sense) standing out from a temporal background which is the dual horizon of retention and protention. Like the elapsed and prospective notes of the melody I hear, this horizon contributes to the significance of the present. Can we not say that this temporal horizon, like that of space, extends into the indefinite past and future? Like the spatial reality of visual perception, this horizon extends far beyond the limits of my own experience; yet it constitutes the indispensible background for what I do experience. But the 'limits of my experience' in this temporal context are precisely my birth and my death.

If we now recall the interlayered and overlapping horizons of the other persons and groups that make up the social world, and especially those of persons older and younger than I, we get a much more concrete sense of how pasts and futures, beyond the limits of my birth and death, are encountered in my own experience. But the temporality of the human world extends beyond the lives of persons. The non-human aspects of the human world have their own temporality. The natural world I inhabit is vastly older than I am, and even its cultivation has a history that extends beyond my individual experience. The built environment of our towns and cities reveals the same temporal extension, this time overlaid with the plans and projects of those who built them. Houses and streets, cities, and their configurations and traffic patterns, their neighbourhoods and landmarks, have their own sort of pasts that are part of what they are as I experience them. Though they rise and fall, sometimes within the reach of our experience of them, the skylines and contours of our cities and towns obey a different time-scale than that of the human individuals that inhabit and use them. We count on them as a more or less stable background for our activity, and their sudden destruction deprives us of more than just shelter. Our social stability, our orientation and sense of place, are linked to the stability of our built environment. Those of us who walk the streets of cities know the sense of massiveness and permanence that is conveyed by the buildings, streets, and neighbourhoods that were there long before we were. This permanence can also extend beyond the purposes of their construction: as artifacts, they were constructed for some purpose, but over time they can be diverted to other purposes as persons and groups, often of later generations, change their projects and their needs.

We feel this clearly when we walk through the ruins of ancient and restored cities. The streets, paths, doors, and enclosed spaces may be full of tourists, but they are empty of what gave them their origins: namely, the people who pursued their interests and projects, sought shelter in the protection of home and family, and assembled for public gatherings. The existence of archeological sites and restorations, the very idea of wanting to know how people lived in the past, derive from the historical consciousness of recent times. But one of its unexpected benefits, not noticed by most of those who look on in fascination today, is what these experiences can tell us about own (as yet) non-ruined and (not yet) archaeologically excavated cities and buildings. Trying to imagine the Roman, Greek, or Cambodian inhabitants of these splendid ruins can lead us to see our own living and working cities as if we were historians and archaeologists. This kind of distancing is a version of the phenomenological reduction that Husserl practiced, allowing us to see for the first time something that is otherwise too close for us to observe.

The time-scale that extends back before our birth is given in our experience not only of the persons and the built and natural environments that make up the human world; it is present also in the institutions and practices, rules and regulations that govern our social existence. Some of these derive from legal and collective actions or decisions, others simply grow up as human practices and customs. In either case they belong to the fabric of our social world, and are as real to us as the persons and objects that make up our surroundings.

6 PARTICIPATION AND MEMBERSHIP

This reference to institutions and practices reminds us that our account of the 'experience' of the historical must not be limited to the kind of subject-object encounter that is traditionally associated with perception. Persons and things are of course objects of our perception, and we experience them, as belonging to the human world, with all their social and cultural meanings attached, as we have seen. But we must not think of this as a kind of observation at a distance. Even perception itself, as Husserl and Merleau-Ponty have shown, is a special kind of interaction, in which the world reveals itself to us thanks to the movements and orientations of our bodies. When it comes to the institutions and practices of the social world, we relate to them not as external observers, as if we were anthropologists or sociologists, but as participants in the group or community to which they apply. Institutions and practices, conceived in the normative sense as rules and social prescriptions, are always associated with some group or other, and I am subject to them as a member of such a group, whether these rules have the force of law, applying to citizens or inhabitants of a particular state, or whether they are no stronger than social norms and counsels of prudence.

I participate in these practices, then, insofar as I belong to the group to which they apply. My membership accounts for some of the ways I relate to other individuals: as fellow citizens or fellow members in my particular group, or indeed as strangers and outsiders. But my relation to the group itself is that of membership. Very often the sign of membership in a group is my use of the first-person plural, the 'we', as the subject of actions and experiences in which I participate. It is also used as the subject of beliefs in which I share. The notion of the collective subject is controversial, and may be very questionable if conceived as an independently existing entity. But it certainly functions as a pervasive feature of our social existence at the level of experience. It is the way we express our adherence to the groups and communities that govern our lives. Each of us belongs to multiple groups: citizenship, profession, religion, family, and even leisure activities, envelope us with stronger or weaker bonds. Sometimes membership is chosen, sometimes we simply grow into it without ever making a choice. In any case it is an important feature of what we have been describing as the experience of the social or human world.

The concepts of participation and membership permit us to see how this experience of the social world is also the experience of the historical. Just as we inhabit a world made up in part of persons and things that are older than we are, so we participate in groups, communities and institutions that have been ongoing since before our birth. Growing up, coming of age, is marked in many religious communities by ceremonies of 'confirmation' in which the individual, already a member though family upbringing since birth, is expected to affirm his or her adherence or allegiance to the community now as a mature person making a conscious and informed decision. In doing so the individual joins an ongoing entity that exists for thousands/hundreds/dozens of years and thus becomes the heir of a tradition and a member on whom rights, privileges, and responsibilities are conferred. With this sort of initiation the individual's relations to others, as we have noted, are transformed. With respect to a particular community, others are now either insiders or outsiders, believers or non-believers, colleagues or laymen, and so on. Because the group that the individual joins has its own history, this community of insiders may include many that are long gone.

The 'experience of the historical' thus involves the awareness of the temporality of the persons, things—natural things and artifacts—social organizations, institutions, and practices that surround us in the human world—a temporality that extends beyond the limits of our own life-span. But it is also the experience of our own involvement and interaction with this social world as we take up traditions, join in ongoing organizations and collective projects, and see ourselves as the bearers of a past that we inherit. Heidegger writes of the notion of *heritage* as something that is handed down to us (*überliefert*) (Heidegger 1977: 350–1), but then points out that this heritage can be either passively assumed or actively chosen. One may add that one can actively reject one's heritage as well, though this often turns out to be much more difficult than it seems. But in any of these cases one's insertion in the historical world is an unavoidable aspect of human existence.

7 HISTORICITY

Heidegger makes these points in a chapter of *Being and Time* entitled 'Temporality and Historicity' ('*Zeitlichkeit und Geschichtlichkeit*') (Heidegger 1977: 341). Temporality, as the unity of pastness, presentness, and futurity, has been at the centre of his analysis of human existence. Now he expands this temporality to include the role of predecessors, generations, traditions, and heritage in the temporal synthesis that makes up the individual. To this he gives the name 'historicity'.

But this is a concept that derives primarily from Wilhelm Dilthey, whom Heidegger credits as a source for his treatment of historicity. Husserl, too, draws inspiration from Dilthey, and himself often uses the term 'historicity'. Though Dilthey is not normally considered part of the phenomenological tradition (he died in 1911), his work is valuable in articulating what it means to experience the historical. In a late text Dilthey (2002) expresses in a few words the sense of the historical world that we have been trying to capture: 'The distribution of trees in a park, the arrangement of houses in a street, the handy tool of the artisan, and the sentence propounded in the courtroom are everyday examples of how we are constantly surrounded by what has become historical' (Dilthey 2002: 169). In another passage Dilthey comes close to capturing the sense of historicity:

The historical world is always there, and the individual does not merely contemplate it from without but is intertwined with it... We are historical beings before we are observers of history, and only because we are the former do we become the latter. (Dilthey 2002: 297)

Two things are expressed in this last passage that are important for the purposes of this chapter. The first is the claim that we are 'historical beings', and the second concerns the relation between 'being historical' and being an 'observer of history'. I will take up these two points in turn.

First, what does it mean to say that we are 'historical beings'? We began this essay by distinguishing between the knowledge of history and the experience of history. We have been trying to answer the questions we posed at the outset: how do we encounter history, how does it enter our lives, and in what forms of experience does it do so? Our account has moved inward, we might say, from the historical aspects of the human or social world around us to our participation and membership in that world. What this itinerary reveals is that the world is historical, our experience of it is historical, and finally that the subject of experience is also historical. In sum, subjectivity is itself historical, and historicity is an essential feature of subjectivity itself. This is ultimately what the phenomenologists mean by historicity: just as subjectivity is essentially temporal, intentional, embodied, intersubjective, and world-constituting, so it is also essentially historical.

One question that suggests itself here is this: does historicity in this sense imply historical relativism? Historicity means that the subject always finds itself embedded in a concrete historical situation, heir to certain traditions and practices, and so on, as we have seen. Historical relativism goes a step further, however, by claiming that the subject can never extricate itself from its situation, can never rise above the prejudices of its historical context. The possibility of scientific and moral objectivity—indeed, the possibility of human freedom—seems threatened by this form of relativism. If historicity is an essential feature of subjectivity, could its accomplishments ever be more than a contingent expression of its time, a perspective on the world that can never hope to be independent of its situation? In his earlier writings Husserl struggled against historical, psychological, and other forms of relativism and scepticism, arguing that they contradict themselves by claiming a truth for their own assertions whose possibility they deny in principle. His argument was part of the larger claim that philosophy, in the form of phenomenology, could become a 'rigorous science' (Husserl 1962). Yet in his later writings he embraced the thoroughgoing historicity of subjectivity. Was he now contradicting himself? Is it a contradiction to assert that subjectivity is 'essentially' historical and at the same time to claim that it is capable of arriving at trans-historical truth?

Perhaps the best way to deal with this problem is to acknowledge that along with historicity and situatedness go the urge and the desire to surmount them, to achieve an unprejudiced point of view in science or philosophy, and to be capable of a free act in the moral sphere. Are these not just as essential to subjectivity as historicity? Note that we are speaking here only of aspirations and desires. Whether as subjects we are actually capable of this kind of freedom or objectivity, whether in any particular case we have actually achieved it, is not something that philosophy can decide. Philosophy cannot deny the possibility in principle, as we have seen, without contradicting itself. Questioning the objectivity of particular scientific claims is a matter for scientific argument, not for philosophy. Even philosophical claims can only legitimately be challenged by philosophical counter-claims. As to the freedom of my individual act, I would argue, with Kant, that I can never know for sure, but I can also never deny its possibility in principle.

8 HISTORICITY AND HISTORICAL KNOWLEDGE

This discussion of the relation between historicity and objectivity leads us to the question of historical knowledge. How do historicity, and in general the experience of history we have been at pains to describe here, relate to the knowledge of the past we associate with the discipline of history? This discipline, insofar as it aspires to knowledge, claims a form of objectivity that rises above its own historical situation and lays hold of the truth about the past. It is here that we become 'observers of history', in Dilthey's phrase, and not just participants in it.

History in this sense, as is well known, did not always exist, and is itself a product of particular historical circumstances. History as a genre or form of writing, which long predated it, was prized more for the moral lessons it could derive from the past than for its accuracy in portraying it. It was precisely in reaction to this 'edifying' approach to history that Leopold von Ranke uttered the much-quoted dictum that the aim of history is 'merely to show how it really was'. His false modesty hides the fact that figuring out what happened, evaluating conflicting claims and interpreting disparate sources, and arriving at a convincing account, is a laborious process. He expressed the views of a generation of early nineteenth-century scholars who developed rigorous methods and sought to be strictly unprejudiced in their research. Thanks to them, history acquired a place in the academy, took on the trappings of what the Germans called a *Wissenschaft*, and established an ethos of objectivity that governs the discipline to this day.

The capacity of the 'science' of history to live up to this ideal picture has often been questioned, and sometimes denied outright. When compared with other cognitive endeavours, especially mathematics and the natural sciences, history seems to come up short, incapable of the kind of agreement supposedly found there, and never able to surmount the subjective and ideological biases of its practitioners. But this is not the issue for us here. Given that the ideals of historical objectivity undeniably exist, and are embodied in an existing academic discipline, how do these relate to what we have described as the experience of history and the notion of historicity? Dilthey says that we are 'historical beings' *before* we become observers of history. What is the sense of this 'before'?

It is clear that the experience of history, as we have described it here, does *not* constitute a scientific grasp of the past, or in general of the events we encounter in our experience. In relation to a scientific attitude it can be described as pre-scientific or pre-theoretical. More to the point, it consists of a passively received and unquestioned complex of beliefs. It is our view of our community and our social surroundings derived from a combination of upbringing, school-learning, and popular mentality. It is the past that bears down upon us in the buildings and streets, the farms and villages of our physical surroundings. Above all it lives in the particular groups—family, religion, region, state, profession—with which we identify ourselves. It is handed down by word of mouth, by folktales and songs, by public commemorations and monuments. This is the lived history of everyday experience that we have been trying to describe in this essay.

If 'historicity' in this sense is indeed essential to human experience and human existence, as Dilthey and others have claimed, then it also constitutes the background against which the project of objective knowledge arises. The historian, as an inheritor of the modern idea of objectivity, often sees himself as a check on the public or popular memory. The historian's questions do not arise out of nowhere, but emerge out of a professional scepticism regarding the received view of the past. Thus every historian, just in virtue of existing in a certain social and temporal context, inherits a view of the past. But as an historian he must take a critical stance toward that view. It is often said that 'all history is revisionist history'—meaning that historians always begin with an account by their predecessors of their subject-matter, and then go on to criticize, improve upon, or replace it. But according to what we have said, there is a deeper sense to this revisionism. All historical accounts constitute a revision, not only of previous historians' accounts, but of the popular sense of the past in the society at large.

The historian is, in Dilthey's word, an historical being, but also one who wants to become an 'observer' of the past 'as it really was'. Scepticism toward received opinion is the mark not only of historians but of other scientists and of anyone who wants to think independently. It is no contradiction to note that this scepticism toward popular views of the past, in the case of history, is itself an historical tradition that exists before the individual historian takes it up. Nothing follows from this about her capacity to achieve the objectivity that is sought here. Whether or not she does so is for other historians to decide.

9 THE HISTORICITY OF SCIENCE

This brings us to a point we made earlier about the distinction between the 'natural' and the 'naturalistic' attitudes. After recognizing the existence and character of the 'naturalistic' attitude, which reduces the whole world to material objects and events, as the basis of modern science, Husserl also recognizes that this attitude has its own history. It derives from what he calls the mathematization of nature, initiated by Galileo and other innovators of the early modern period, and passed down through Descartes to the whole modern age of science and philosophy (Husserl 1970). It is thus actually an historical accomplishment. It institutes new ideas of reality and objectivity, where what counts as real is what can be measured in mathematical terms. Just as every historian takes up an idea of objectivity that derives from a particular tradition of thought, so every natural scientist draws on a rich tradition consisting not only of ideas and concepts but also of ideals and norms for the evaluation of research.

What is forgotten in this process is that this scientific interpretation of the world presupposes what Husserl, in his late work, calls the 'pre-scientific life-world' (Husserl 1970: 103ff) of everyday experience. 'Life-world' is another expression for what Husserl earlier called the world of the natural attitude. We can contrast this pre-scientific world with the scientific world, but we must recognize that they also interact in interesting ways. As we noted earlier, the technological innovations that derive from the scientific interpretation of the world flow back into the life-world and become part of its fabric.

But there is another interesting connection that now emerges between the life-world and the scientific world. We have seen how our everyday experience in the natural attitude constitutes an experience of history, and an involvement in history. What we see now is that even our departures from the natural attitude, when we take up the quest for objectivity in the natural and the human sciences, have their own historicity. The ironic result is that this quest for objectivity, which is an attempt to escape our historicity, is itself an historical project—one that constitutes a tradition taken up by every scientist who enters the profession and begins to theorize.

If we ask, then, as we did at the beginning, how history is experienced, how it enters our lives, then we shall have to say that it does so not only in the pre-scientific life-world of everyday experience, but also in scientific activity. But this is because science is a human activity, and as such partakes of the thoroughgoing historicity of everything human.

10 THE METAPHYSICS AND EPISTEMOLOGY
OF HISTORY

We began by distinguishing the phenomenology of history from traditional philosophies of history, which we identified as asking metaphysical and epistemological questions about history. We said that the phenomenological approach is distinct from these traditional approaches, but not unrelated to them. It is time to state more clearly what those differences and relations are; this will explain better how the phenomenological approach fits into the array of philosophical theories of history.

As we have seen, the phenomenology of history asks how history is experienced. Put in another way, this is a question about the *meaning* of history. But meaning is meaning *for* someone, so the reference to our experience is, as it were, built into the question. Now it is important to distinguish such a question from the classical inquiry into what is often called meaning *in* history. The traditional philosophers of history, from Augustine to Hegel, Marx, Toynbee, and Spengler, wanted to know not just what history means to us, but what it means 'in itself', independently of our experience and involvement. For these philosophers meaning in history was the direction and even purpose in history, the intentionality, if you will, of a divine plan or a hidden reason which functions independently of, and sometimes contrary to, human experiences and purposes. For our purposes the point to be made is that this approach is metaphysical rather than phenomenological. It asks not how history is experienced or given, but what it is in itself. Does human history consist in a disconnected series of events and actions, or is there an order to its progression? Does it constitute an advance toward some goal, a decline from a golden age, or does it move in a circle? This approach is often linked to the idea of 'theodicy', in which the 'slaughterbench of history', as Hegel called it, had to be reconciled with divine providence and benevolence.

Sometimes called the substantive or speculative philosophy of history, this approach has very much gone out of fashion, having been debunked, in the second half of the twentieth century, by thinkers as diverse as Karl Löwith, Arthur Danto, and Jean-François Lyotard. Löwith (1949) tried to unmask the philosophy of history as religion in disguise; Danto (2007) denounced it as conceptual confusion; and Lyotard (1984) branded it a totalizing *grand récit* with an ideological agenda. However it may stand with the legitimacy of these classical theories, it is clear that their questions are not phenomenological ones.

It is possible, however, that phenomenology can consider these questions, not in order to answer them but to cast light on why they are asked. I see a certain parallel here to Kant's transcendental philosophy. For Kant it was just as important to explain why traditional metaphysical questions are asked as to show why they could not be answered. He claimed that our reason demanded the kind of satisfaction that could be provided only by the ideas of God, freedom and immortality. Similarly, perhaps our sense of history calls for the kind of wholeness and closure that the classical theories sought to provide. We want history as a whole to 'make sense': that is, we want it to form a large-scale narrative with a beginning, a middle, and an end. Given the temporality of our experience, it seems a natural illusion—perhaps even a 'transcendental illusion' in Kant's sense—that we view the past as a series of steps preparing the way for the present. On this scenario, the present is the culmination and conclusion of a process, as it was for Hegel. Or alternatively, in a more Marxist perspective, the present is experienced as a decisive turning point or crisis in relation to an imminent goal, calling for immediate action. In either case, these ideas often express popular views about the destiny or mission of a particular group—religious, political, economic, or ethnic—and are often more about the future than about the past. And, as their critics say, they often embody political or ideological programs rather than theoretical claims. The idea of the End of History retains its appeal. As recently as the 1990s, it was revived, briefly and implausibly, by Francis Fukuyama, in a book published in 1992 called *The End of History and the Last Man* (Fukuyama 2002). This work too was attacked as masking an ideological agenda. But it revealed the persistence of an idea that seems not to go away.

Contrasted with the classical metaphysics of history, the epistemology of history constitutes a different tradition of inquiry, and one that is more closely tied to phenomenology. Since the end of the nineteenth century, when Dilthey, the neo-Kantians, and others explored the differences between the *Geisteswissenschaften* and the *Naturwissenschaften*, philosophers have asked questions about the status, scope, and objectivity of historical knowledge, especially when compared with the supposed paradigm case of the natural sciences. As we noted, Husserl was also interested in these questions. The nature of historical evidence and inference, the role of causality in history, the distinction between explanation and understanding or interpretation, between nomothetic and ideographic inquiry, and so on, were topics that were raised again in post-World-War-II Anglophone 'analytic' philosophy of history. What is the relation between the phenomenology and the epistemology of history?

These epistemological questions are directed at the discipline of history—that is, the organized academic inquiry that tries to determine the objective truth about the past. In Section 8 we discussed the relation between historicity and historical knowledge, and we set aside some of the traditional epistemological questions about history in favour of a phenomenological account. The emphasis there was on how history as a 'science' emerges out of the background of historical experience. This already contributes to the epistemological understanding of historical knowledge by placing such knowledge in its broader human context. Epistemological theories which focus on the discipline of history alone are somewhat abstract. They create the misleading impression that the sense of the past and the role it plays in our lives is entirely the responsibility of the historical profession, that 'our' knowledge of the past consists solely of what the historians tell us. This is parallel to the philosophy of science, where 'our knowledge of nature' is conceived strictly in terms of the latest and most sophisticated physical theory, which most of us do not even understand. While this approach may be acceptable in the philosophy of natural science, it seems to me entirely inappropriate in connection with history. As we have seen, in virtue of our historicity as human beings and particularly as social beings, we have a very full and concrete sense of what that past is in our own lives and in that of the communities to which we belong. Our sense of who we are, whether as individuals, as families, as institutions, as societies, or even as nations, is very much a function of our sense of where we have come from and where we are going.

It is only in the context of this lived sense of the past that the cognitive and critical interest associated with the discipline of history, as it currently exists, can arise. This is the background against which questions can arise about what really happened and how and why it happened. This is the framework in which the methods, procedures and goals of an academic discipline have been developed. Historians are too often conceived by philosophers as if their task were to construct *ex nihilo*, as it were, by reading documents or looking at monuments and heaps of ruins—a past with which they have no direct acquaintance. But awareness of the past, as we have noted, always already exists in the form of the public or popular narratives associated with such issues as group, regional, ethnic, or national identity. It is also found in the speculative excesses and *grands récits* that are encouraged by the rhetoric of political leaders. As we have seen, part of the task of the professional historian is to look at this popular history with a watchful and sceptical eye.

11 CONCLUSION

We have tried to show how the metaphysical and epistemological questions associated with the traditional philosophies of history differ from those of a phenomenology of history. Phenomenology can contribute to the understanding of these philosophies, not by offering answers to their questions, but by showing how these questions emerge out of our experience of history. Phenomenology can also explore how the search for knowledge of the historical past, knowledge that we associate with the discipline of history, arises out of our experience. But it is the experience itself, the encounter with history, that forms the main focus of the phenomenology of history.

At the beginning we contrasted the phenomenology of history with the recent and contemporary focus on representation and memory. There is no doubt that these concerns have revealed much about history, but, as we argued, they need to be grounded in a much broader experiential approach. Linguistic representation, especially in the form of written narratives, reposes on a background of pre-linguistic temporal experience, without which it becomes unmoored and spins off into a self-enclosed universe of intertexuality. Memory, important as it is for history and all human existence, likewise refers back to an original experience which it revives. Philosophies of history based on representation and memory are not so much incorrect as incomplete if they fail to return to experience.

We began by asking: how does history present itself to us, how does it enter our lives, and what are the forms of experience in which it does so? We have seen that the experience of history is our passive and active involvement with the social world, and in particular with the temporality by which it exceeds and extends beyond the temporality of our individual lives. Through this involvement we are not just social but also historical beings, understanding ourselves as participants in the historical panorama. History is accessible to us not just through representations or memories of the past, but as an historical world that we directly experience and inhabit.

REFERENCES

Danto, A. (2007), *Narration and Knowledge* (New York: Columbia University Press).

Dilthey, W. (2002), *The Formation of the Historical World in the Human Sciences*, R. Makkreel (ed.), *Selected Works, vol. III* (Princeton: Princeton University Press).

Fukuyama, F. (2002), *The End of History and the Last Man* (New York: Perennial).

Heidegger, M. (1977), *Being and Time*, tr. Joan Stambaugh (Albany: State University of New York Press).

Husserl, E. (1965), 'Philosophy as rigorous science', in Husserl, E., *Phenomenology and the Crisis of Philosophy: Philosophy as a Rigorous Science, and Philosophy and the Crisis of European Man*, tr. Q. Lauer (New York: Harper & Row).

——— (1970), *The Crisis of European Sciences and Transcendental Phenomenology*, tr. David Carr (Evanston: Northwestern University Press).

Husserl, E. (1983), *Ideas Pertaining to a Pure Phenomenology and Phenomenological Philosophy*, First Book, tr. Fred Kersten (The Hague: Martinus Nijhoff).

——(1989), *Ideas Pertaining to a Pure Phenomenology and Phenomenological Philosophy*. Second Book, tr. R. Rojcewicz and A. Schuwer. (The Hague: Martinus Nijhoff).

——(1991), *On the Phenomenology of the Consciousness of Internal Time (1893–1917)*, tr. J. Brough (Dordrecht: Kluwer Academic Publishers).

Löwith, Karl (1949), *Meaning in History* (Chicago: University of Chicago Press).

Lyotard, J.-F. (1984), *The Postmodern Condition*, tr. G. Bennington and B. Massumi (Minneapolis: University of Minnesota Press).

Merleau-Ponty, M. (1962), *Phenomenology of Perception*, tr. Colin Smith (New York: The Humanities Press).

Schutz, A. (1967), *The Phenomenology of the Social World*, tr. G. Walsh and F. Lehnert (Evanston: Northwestern University Press).

White, H. (1987), *The Content of the Form* (Baltimore: Johns Hopkins University Press).

CHAPTER 24

THE FORGIVENESS OF TIME AND CONSCIOUSNESS

NICOLAS DE WARREN

1 PARADOXES OF TIME AND FORGIVENESS

In our everyday dealings with offenses committed against ourselves or by ourselves against others, the refrain that forgiveness requires time and that time sustains forgiveness—that the transfiguration of time goes hand in hand with the transaction of forgiveness to affect even the most egregious of wrongdoings and soften even the most stubborn of resentments—is not uncommon. Such commonplaces attest to a robust bond between time and forgiveness; there is a proper time for forgiveness (we cannot ask for forgiveness too early nor should we seek forgiveness too late); there is a temporal dynamic to forgiveness for both offender and victim, each charged with her own, yet interdependent transformation; most importantly, there is the forgiveness of time itself, as released from a bondage to a past, a purgatory in a present, and a foreclosure of any genuine future. Whether anchored in an Abrahamic tradition or in a secular discourse, these judgements collectively register an underlying intuition that the performance of forgiveness is essentially shaped in as well as a shaping of time itself.

The bond between time and forgiveness is apparent in various widely acknowledged paradoxes. As Arendt broadly defines: 'The possible redemption from the predicament of irreversibility—of being unable to undo what one has done though one did not, and could not, have known what he was doing—is the faculty of forgiveness' (Arendt 1998: 237). What is *prima facie* puzzling is how forgiveness unfetters the person forgiven, but also the person who forgives, from the past without thereby severing the past from the present. Forgiveness institutes a rupture with the past that does not amount to its forgetting, excusing, or erasure. But neither is the force of forgiveness merely the function of an altered perspective that would conveniently suppress or deny one image of the past in favour of selectively fashioning another. In forgiving, a past wrongdoing is acknowledged as irreversible in the name of responsibility, and yet through the grace of forgiveness, the past becomes equally seen as reversible; its present claim on the offender and the victim becomes meaningfully superceded, its time unhinged. Expressed thus, the exceptional character of forgiveness involves a suspension of a 'common view of time' according to which time is represented as a linear succession of instants (Levinas 1969: 283). Forgiveness operates within a different and more fundamental order of time, specific to its performance and expressive of its character as an ethical transaction. In its own manner, the question of forgiveness poses the question of time anew: insofar as we cannot take the past for granted, as over and done with, as settled once and for all, we are compelled to ask what, then, is time, and so confront the meaning of our temporal existence in relation to others.

In addition to paradoxes of temporal discordance and concordance, we find further puzzles in specifying *who, or what*, is to be forgiven: the deed or the person? And even if, as Arendt contends, '*what* was done is forgiven for the sake of *who* did it', we are still left with the pointed issue of who—in a temporally specifiable sense—is the recipient of forgiveness: the offender's past self who committed the wrongdoing or the offender's present self who asks for forgiveness? If, as commonly understood, the offender must repent her ways in seeking forgiveness, she must sincerely repudiate her past self while promising to become a person who, retrospectively, would not have acted as she did, had she been the person she has now committed herself to becoming. Self-repudiation in view of a future self-image runs in tandem with assuming responsibility for a past wrongdoing in the name of one's present self. The offender must paradoxically own up to her own past doing while disowning her own past self. This complex of repudiation and responsibility entails an emphatic conversion or 'change of heart/change of mind', as enshrined in Luke 17:3–4: 'And if he trespass against thee seven times a day, and seven times a day in turn against to thee, saying, I repent; thou shall forgive him.' Repentance is here called *metanoia*, or conversion; it must first issue from the offender herself. Such a project of self-transformation cannot, however, be fulfilled by the offender alone, as the axis of her conversion turns in the hands of the Other. An offender cannot forgive herself, but must seek and receive forgiveness from the Other, whom she has wronged. Forgiveness is both singular and plural as a 'face-to-face' encounter; as such, the transaction of forgiveness undermines any strict difference between a subject's 'inner' temporality and inter-subjective temporality. Forgiveness is a time that I can only give but cannot only give to myself.

In light of these various paradoxes, my present aim is to explore forgiveness through a phenomenological inflected analysis of its temporal constitution as an inter-subjective self-constitution; my subsidiary intention is to showcase how the resources of phenomenological thinking—here broadly construed and diversely represented—are exceptionally suited for developing just such an understanding. A central claim to phenomenological thinking, differently explored in Husserl, Heidegger, and Sartre, is the recognition of temporality as fundamental to the constitution of human subjectivity, and as concretely experienced across the wide spectrum of possible activities in terms of which the world and Others becomes meaningfully constituted. But if, in this manner, temporality is inseparable from subjectivity, it is equally imperative to grasp this phenomenological insight as proposing a project of descriptive investigation into specific forms of temporalization that operate within different forms of human experience. To be a subject can be said and experienced in many ways, much as to exist in time can be said and experienced in many ways. A phenomenological analysis of any given phenomenon—the transaction of forgiveness, for example—must attentively describe the complex ways in which the various 'moments' or 'dimensions' that constitute forgiveness are fundamentally constituted temporally—that is, as reconfigurations of temporality, and thus as reconfigurations of subjectivity itself. In this manner, as I hope to develop presently, forgiveness is a complex phenomenon composed of various strata or sedimentations of concrete 'acts' (as I shall argue in detail: shame, guilt, resentment, and so on), such that each of these acts possesses its own temporal form; the constellation and orchestration of these various temporalizations contribute to the constitution of forgiveness, and which, specifically, I argue turns on the two dimensions of responsibility and transformation. Temporality is not an abstract or inert form; it is, instead, as Husserl, Heidegger, and Sartre explored, each in their own way, the warp and woof of subjectivity itself. In my own analysis here, my intent is to develop an argument into the constitution of forgiveness that crtically responds to contemporary theories of forgiveness, that relies on a greater appreciation of the temporality of forgiveness in view of its component emotions and attitudes, and that advances in greater detail and depth into the complex weave of forgiveness as a reconstitution of an individual's subjectivity in relation to the subjectivity of another. In this manner I propose to enrich our conception of forgiveness through phenomenological means while broadening phenomenological thinking through the means of forgiveness. Keeping my sights on the 'things themselves'—that is, forgiveness—I employ different phenomenological frameworks without reducing or reconciling them, nor without losing sight of their respective differences. I shall, moreover, not offer here an exhaustive treatment of forgiveness, but limit my analysis to forgiveness as a temporal form of self-constitution, with a special emphasis on the constitution of responsibility and self-transformation, as decomposed through the prism of attending emotions such as shame, guilt, and resentment. Most significantly, the narrative dimension of forgiveness is excluded from the compass of my reflections, and thus a host of issues dealing with how the time of forgiveness is dialectically related to the narrative of forgiveness, such that the action of forgiveness becomes meaningful through narrative emplotment, while in turn, the narrative of forgiveness attains significance in conditioning temporal existence.[1]

---

[1] I am here thinking of the relation between time and narrative as formulated by Ricouer (1983).

2 FORGIVENESS AS TRANSFORMATION AND RESPONSIBILITY

It is widely accepted that forgiveness is an intersubjective and ethical transaction between two individuals, the offender and the victim of a wrongdoing; each individual must strive to transform herself in view of the other; it is to the offender to ask for and thus initiate forgiveness; it is to the victim to tender forgiveness (Levinas 1969; Griswold 2007). I will not address here the complex and contentious issue of whether, as put forth differently by Jankélévitch and Derrida, 'forgiveness is there to forgive precisely what no excuse would know how to excuse' or, more pointedly, that 'forgiveness forgives only the unforgivable' ('*le pardon pardonne seulement l'impardonnable*') (Jankélévitch 2005: 156; Derrida 2000: 108). Given my focus on the temporal constitution of forgiveness as a transaction between offender and victim, the question of what kind of wrongdoing even calls for forgiveness is left in suspense. However one decides whether forgiveness exclusively responds to evil (the unforgivable) or inclusively speaks to mundane moral violations, it stands that forgiveness, under whatever circumstance, must minimally be distinguished from excusing and condoning, as well as clemency and political pardons. And even if drawing the line between forgiveness and excusing, for example, is hard won without a commitment to the question of what warrants forgiveness, I nonetheless claim that my own analysis of its temporality, as centred on the issue of self-constitution, does not depend on any specific commitment on this issue. My stress falls on the dual dimensions of *responsibility and transformation* without which the transaction of forgiveness would have little meaning and force; both of these dimensions define forgiveness as a 'conversion', 'change of heart/mind', or *metanoia*.

Whereas excusing an offender's wrongdoing makes light of her responsibility and abdicates the victim's own responsibility to hold the offender accountable for her misdeed, condoning an offender's action silently sanctions her wrongdoing. In both cases, the demands of responsibility and transformation that define forgiveness are lacking. Both excusing and condoning often mistakenly pass in everyday practice as forgiveness, since each does not necessarily exclude acknowledging an offense as a moral wrong; yet each falls short of passing judgement of moral blame on the offender as a responsible subject. This common slippage between excusing and condoning, on the one side, and forgiveness, on the other, brings into relief the distinction between the wrongdoing as an act and the self, or subject, who bears responsibility for that act. It is not uncommon to hear vociferous protests of innocence along with louder declarations of the wrongdoing's blameworthiness among those who defend themselves against responsibility. The pride we take in ourselves disposes us to have it both ways: to claim our own innocence while holding forth our own deed at arm's length from ourselves as the sole object of moral criticism, including, self-servingly, our own.

Expressed as a form of intentionality, forgiveness—the act of forgiving the Other— takes as its primary object the offender as a subject responsible for her conduct. The wrongdoing itself can be seen as a secondary object, equally intended, but differently, in light of which the offender is forgiven. This dual-object of forgiveness reflects Arendt's prescription that '*what* was done is forgiven for the sake of *who* did it' (Arendt 1998: 241). Yet, I would suggest reversing the intentional poles of act and self: a person is forgiven in light of what she did. More significantly, I shall argue that the distinction between act and self becomes itself configured in different ways, in a specifiable temporal sense, within the transaction of forgiveness, and in an asymmetrical manner for offender and victim. The offender's subjectivity becomes reconstituted around a newly forged relationship between her wrongdoing and her self, between what she did and who she is, and is to become. Likewise, but along different, yet intersecting lines, the victim's subjectivity, insofar as she tenders forgiveness, becomes reconstituted around a newly minted distinction between the offense committed against her, the offender's self, and her own self, freed from her own resentment.

3 THE OFFENDER: THE CONJUNCTION OF REPUDIATION AND RESPONSIBILITY

In thus distinguishing forgiveness from excusing and condoning, we have seen that the intentionality of forgiveness targets the offender as its primary object in view of her past wrongdoing. From the position of the offender, the double-intentionality of warranting forgiveness crystallizes around the conjunction of two apparently contradictory demands: the offender must assume responsibility for her past wrongdoing as well as repudiate her past self. Whereas repudiation ruptures her present self from her own past while projecting a novel conception of herself, assuming responsibility for her past wrongdoing incorporates it into the present, for one assumes responsibility for what one did in the present and on behalf of one's present self. Repudiation and responsibility thus define the offender's self-transformation with a threefold temporal structure, yet what is distinctive of this three-fold temporalization is how the dynamic of repudiation and responsibility appear at cross-purposes with each other, as if each flowed against the temporal grain of the other. This circumstance that the offender assumes responsibility for her wrongdoing and repudiates her past self—but not the wrongdoing (for if this were the case, the offender would not be taking responsibility for what she did)—involves 'the conjunction of a seeming impossibility' (Griswold 2007: 50). As Derrida and Kolnai have separately questioned, if the offender repudiates her past self and thus no longer conceives of herself as the same person who committed the wrongdoing, is she still effectively constituted in the present as an offender (as *the* offender) who could be forgiven (Derrida 2000: 113; Kolnai 1973: 98)?

If the problem at hand turns on the dual requirements that the offender repudiate her past-self and assume responsibility for her past wrongdoing, it will not do to claim that in repudiating her past self from the stand-point of her present self, the offender could also, without further qualification, assume her past wrongdoing in the present. For, in fact, it would prove impossible for the offender to assume her wrongdoing in the present without also recognizing that wrongdoing as her own, as committed by her in the past— which would be precluded if, concurrently, she repudiated her past self, breaking in other words, any *meaningful* identification between her present and past self. This inability to assume a past deed as mine in the present without tacitly recalling my past self points to a constitutive feature of remembrance in general, without which self-repudiation and self-responsibility could not be possible. And yet, merely to recall that I did something in the past does not in itself entail or amount to a repudiation of my past self, nor the assumption of any responsibility for what I did.

Clarity can be sought on this issue by turning to Husserl's analysis of remembrance and its temporal structure. As Husserl argues, the intentionality of remembrance is two-fold: in remembering a past event in my lived experience, I recall directly the object of my experience (I can describe the flight of the bird seen yesterday; I can describe what I did to you last week, and so on) but also thereby implicitly recall myself—my past self— as having originally experienced the recalled event in a living present, my own (Husserl 1991). To express this thought in Husserl's vocabulary, the past self is pre-reflectively implicated in the intentional directedness towards the thematic object of my remembrance. Indeed, I recall an event from the past as an event that *I* once experienced. If I did not implicitly recall myself as the subject of that lived experience, I would not be able in the present to claim this experience as something I had originally experienced as present, as *mine*. On the one hand, my past self becomes 're-lived' in the present in which I remember myself as having done such and such; on the other hand, this time and self regained are given to me at a distance, as constituted in a temporal difference between the present in which I remember and the past that is remembered. If this constitutional difference between the re-lived past self and the remembering present self were somehow abolished, I would be in the spell of a delusion, as I would believe that this presumptively past experience were actually happening to me *now*, as if for the first time.

The insight to be retained here is two-fold. First: the distinction between act and self cannot be entirely suppressed since the foundational structure of remembrance entails both: recalling what I did and recalling implicitly that I did it. Second: though the past self is implicated in any act of remembrance, it is only once it becomes objectified, through an act of reflection or other attitudinal stance towards my past self, that the past self appears to me thematically. How my past self becomes objectified, as when I begin to question what I was feeling yesterday, depends on the kind of self-objectification performed. The 're-living' of my past self within the field of remembrance presupposes a differentiation, and thus spacing, between past self and present self; within this distance towards oneself, the relationship between past and present self can be variably conceived and experienced.[2] The phenomenological lesson to be drawn is that a resolution to the

---

[2] I cannot pursue this further, though it bears noting that, on Husserl's analysis, the constitution of remembrance is in turn based on an original time-consciousness within the occurrence of lived experience itself and its threefold structure of retention, original impression, and protention (Husserl 1991).

'seeming impossible conjunction' of repudiation and responsibility cannot take the form of severing the distinction between wrongdoing and self, nor can its temporal constitution as a distinction be taken for granted. To recall the problem at hand, the conjunction of repudiation and responsibility plays itself out along two intersecting distinctions: between act and self, and between the past and present/future. The present is itself divided, both one and two: it is the joint of discontinuity with the past (self) as well as the locus of incorporation of the past (wrongdoing).

4 SHAME AND SELF-REPUDIATION

In this light, repudiation and responsibility, in their conjunction within the transaction of forgiveness, must be understood as forms of self-objectification. With repudiation I see myself for whom I *was* in light of what I did, and through this self-objectification I am able to repudiate my past self. In the case of forgiveness, this self-repudiation and temporal self-constitution has its genesis in shame in light of the victim's resentful gaze towards the offender. Yet, insofar as shame is primarily self-regarding, it provides the basis for self-repudiation without thereby being sufficient to motivate responsibility, which, for its part, cannot be assumed without directly regarding the victim. Guilt, as primarily victim-directed, along with the call of conscience, underpin the genesis of the offender's self-responsibility; shame and guilt are compounded together as underlying constituents in the conjunction of self-repudiation and self-responsibility.

Shame has long been recognized as essential to ethical life. In Aristotle's *Nicomachean Ethics*, shame exercises a substantial role in ethical self-development in accounting for the formation of virtuous motivation prior to the acquisition of a virtuous disposition. In its most general features, shame is an internalized awareness, or self-awareness, of being seen in a blameworthy manner by the Other such that the Other's critical disposition towards me becomes revealed to me. Shame takes the form of an 'internalized figure' of the Other's gaze, of the Other as 'witness', in light of which the offender becomes directed adversely towards herself, and specifically towards her own failing, inadequacy and 'loss of power' (Williams 1993: 220; 222; Sartre 1984: 340ff). The internalized Other can be any number of possible subjects: an individual; a social group; an imaginary Other; ethical principles (Williams 1993: 84). In the case of forgiveness, the internalized Other is the victim of my offense who has installed herself, as it were, as witness to my offense, just as my own shameful self-awareness. Shame is, in other words, a form of self-recognition as self-objectification in which the Other becomes registered within me as looking at me. In the transaction of forgiveness, the offender's sense of shame and the victim's resentful gaze are inextricably entwined.[3] To speak metaphorically, the resentful light in which the victim sees the offender does not shine on the offender from the outside, but illuminates

---

[3] I leave aside the question of individuals who are not disposed to shame: for example, the magnanimous man, or 'great soul', in Aristotle or clinical psychotics.

or reveals the offender to herself from within. Insofar as the offender comes to see herself through the victim's resentment and comes to feel ashamed as thus exposed, the victim's resentment objectifies the offender for herself. The offender's shame is the living evidence of the Other's resentment in the experienced form of her own adverse self-awareness. As I shall subsequently examine, in resenting an offender, the victim equally internalizes the offender within her own consciousness and thus comes to define, or affect, herself in her resentment; the offender in this manner comes to haunt the victim from within to the degree that the victim becomes ensconced in her own resentment to which she is liable, with time, to fall victim: the lure of resentment resides in its proclivity for self-victimization. Remaining here with the perspective of the offender, the internalization of the victim as witness to the offender's wrongdoing constitutes the offender in a specific temporal form: the victim's resentment places a temporal lien on the offender's existence such that she becomes mineralized in time, held hostage to her past wrongdoing and thus fore-closed of any genuine, renewable future. Thus conceived, shame is an inner exposure to the victim's resentment who is thus acknowledged as constituting *who* the offender is in a specific temporal manner (as a specific form of self-temporalization to which the offender remains beholden *despite herself*) *and* as directing the offender's awareness adversely against herself—her past self in light of her past wrongdoing. As Sartre argues, shame is a 'unitary apprehension with three dimensions: "I am ashamed of *myself* before the *Other*"' (Sartre 1984: 385). In the present context, these three dimensions correspond to three temporal dimensions, distributed across the distinction between act and self *as well as* the distinction between offender and victim. My present self is ashamed of my past self, in light of my past wrongdoing, before the presence of the Other—my victim.

Prior to the formation of shame, the offender's relation to her past self and past wrong-doing can be described in contrast to Sartre's classic example of spying through a key-hole in *Being and Nothingness* (Sartre 1984: 347ff.). In this example, a voyeur is spying through a key-hole at a scene on the other side of the door that she clearly should not be viewing. Her consciousness is thoroughly absorbed by the spectacle she is observing; while she is directed towards the object of her visual indiscretion, the voyeur remains aware of herself, but only in a pre-reflective and 'non-thetic' manner—that is, without any explicit and objectified self-awareness. As Sartre writes: 'I am a pure consciousness *of* things, and things, caught up in the circuit of my selfness, offer to me their potentialities as proof of my non-thetic consciousness (of) my own possibilities' (Sartre 1984: 347). In thus becoming caught up in the objects of her consciousness, the voyeur remains unable to know herself—to become aware of her indiscretion in any direct or objectified manner—given her 'non-thetic' self-awareness. She is entirely encircled in her situation and lacks any internal distance towards her own activity. In Sartre's example, footsteps, however, are suddenly heard; our indiscrete voyeur is seized with surprise and, in feeling ashamed at being caught, comes to see herself as being seen, and thus exposed in her indiscretion, by the Other.

In the case of self-repudiation within our present concern with forgiveness, the self-objectification of shame functions differently, and primarily because the shame here in question is mediated through a specific gaze—the victim's resentment. As significantly, the self of which I become ashamed, as well as the past wrongdoing in terms of which I become adversely aware of my self, are *of the past*, and not, as with the voyeur example, of the present. Prior to the formation of being ashamed in light of the Other's resentful gaze, the offender's present self is alienated, as it were, from her past misconduct; she is not mindful of her past waywardness; she is not captivated by her past wrongdoing, even though she nonetheless remains implicit aware of her past self. But precisely because her past self remains non-thetically self-aware despite her own directedness towards her wrongdoing (or precisely because of such unthinking directedness), she is unable to know herself, but not, as with the voyeur, because she is absorbed in a current spectacle, but on contrary, because she remains entirely obliviousness to her deed *as a wrongdoing* (for, indeed, an offender may know that she acted so and so without admitting that her act constituted a wrongdoing against her victim). This form of indifference may take different forms: either as if the past wrongdoing never occurred (denial) or as if it were not at all a wrongdoing, strenuously rationalized away (excused, special pleading, and so on). The offender may well recognize her past deed as a wrongdoing and yet, given the non-objectified condition of her past self, which she retains in the present, or even as she recalls what she did, she is still able to have it both ways: blame her deed, not herself. Having placed herself in such a condition of bad faith, the offender—to adopt Sartre's description of bad faith—is non-thetically aware of her past self as the offender precisely in order to hide her past self from her present self, and thus institute a 'disintegrating synthesis' between past and present self. Under such circumstances, the offender proffers excuses for herself even as she recognizes her wrongdoing: the act had to be done, I was made to do it, and so on.

On this interpretation of shame within the etiology of self-repudiation, being ashamed at one's past conduct and past self objectifies the offender for herself, thus inciting the offender to distinguish between her past and present self in the negative light of the victim's resentment. This distinction between past and present self is itself constituted for the offender just as her consciousness of shame: her present self is ashamed of her past self; she is adversely self-aware of her past self. The gaze of the Other (the victim) divides me temporally from myself and delineates, in the form of her internal presence within my self-awareness as witness to my past misconduct, an internal distance of reflection and motivation for self-repudiation. I come to recognize not only what I did as wrong; I also recognize my past self as the subject of that wrongdoing who *now* warrants repudiation and condemnation *by me*. In seeing myself objectified in the gaze of the Other in this manner, my adverse self-regard towards my past self is coupled with a self-regard towards a future image of myself as detached from my past self, in the presence of which I am currently ashamed, and in light of the Other's presence.

5 GUILT AND RESPONSIBLE CONSCIENCE

If the self-objectification and temporalization of shame thus accounts for self-repudiation, it does not, however, provide a sufficient basis and motivation for responsibility. As just argued, whereas repudiation is adversely directed towards exorcising my past self from the compass of my present self, coupled with a future self-image to which I aspire, responsibility entails the incorporation of my past wrongdoing into the present. The distinction between past wrongdoing and past self, originally constituted together in the lived experience of my misconduct, must become *re*-temporalized at crossed purposes, against the grain of each other, in such manner that I leave my past self behind while retaining my past wrongdoing. Indeed, the common conflation between repudiation and responsibility is largely understandable as the misconstrued sufficiency of shame for responsibility. In desiring to be seen differently from my past self, I repudiate the object of my embarrassment and so come to believe that this act of self-repudiation suffices to dispel the Other's resentful gaze. I thus attempt to act *on* the victim's resentful gaze by acting on myself, yet fail to recognize that no amount of self-repudiation will change her sentiment until I recognize her as my victim; her resentment is not simply against my past self, but against my present self, as held hostage to my past. The victim's resentful gaze constitutes me in such a temporal manner that my subjectivity becomes immobilized in the amber of my past wrongdoing. Undoing this fusion of self and deed in the eyes of the victim does not require simply that I repudiate my past self, but that, in taking responsibility for my deed, I assume this deed in the present: I speak on its behalf. Responsibility, as the counter-part of repudiation, turns me towards my victim as well as towards myself in the specific sense of *assuming* my past wrongdoing in her presence as well as mine.

If shame provides the underlying motivation and temporalization for self-repudiation, guilt and the call of conscience jointly function as the form in which the offender crystallizes into a responsible subject. Whereas in shame 'the viewer's gaze draws the subject's attention not to the viewer, but to the subject himself', guilt turns the subject's attention towards the victim, and primarily in terms of 'fear *at* anger', as opposed to the 'fear of anger' (Williams 1993: 219). As Bernard Williams remarks: 'What I have done points in one direction towards what has happened to others, in another direction to what I am . . . guilt looks primarily in the first direction, shame looks primarily to what I am' (Williams 1993: 92). Resentment and anger are, of course, not identical; yet resentment reveals to the offender the aggrieved condition of the victim such that that the victim's moral and self indignation at having been wronged provoke unpleasantness, or fear in this sense, for the offender—namely, in view of the victim's retributive passion of resentment.

In turning the offender towards her victim through guilt, the offender must also, in order to fully constitute her responsibility, heed to the call of her own conscience. As Heidegger developed in his analysis in *Being and Time*, the call of conscience is self-revelatory in its disclosure of the self (more accurately for Heidegger: Dasein) as irrevocably responsible for its own singular and irreversible existence (or what Heidegger compacted into his term of art *Jemeinigkeit*). This self-revelatory character of conscience sets it apart from the mediated character of shame (as the internalization of the Other as witness) as well as guilt (as directedness at the Other's anger). As Heidegger describes, the call of responsible conscience (*Gewissen*) dawns from above me; it speaks silently within me without any identifiable origin (Heidegger 1996: 252). This non-specifiable origin of my own responsible conscience (or alternatively, my conscience of responsibility) and its directive of responsibility is primarily directed towards the future, and which Heidegger defines as the horizon of my 'being-towards-death'. As Heidegger argues, the call of responsible conscience 'summons' my existence (Dasein) to its 'ownmost potentiality-of-being' (Heidegger 1996: 252). In thus owning up to the singularity and irreversibility of its own death, subjectivity authentically crystallizes as a responsible subject.

In the circumstance of forgiveness, however, this call of responsible conscience becomes deflected away from the primary horizon of one's own finitude towards the death of the Other—the victim—without forfeiting entirely the summons of one's own existence to self-responsibility. In this manner, forgiveness gives credence to Levinas' claim that 'responsibility is not at first responsibility of myself for myself' and that 'I am responsible for the death of the other to the extent of including myself in that death' (Levinas 1987: 114). This directedness of responsibility towards the Other is not only guided through the victim directedness of guilt. The responsibility that I am called to assume is inseparable from a relation to the Other, insofar as this call of responsibility is heard in light of my wrongdoing against the Other and refracted in the internalization of my victim *as* my guilt. The victim's resentment functions as a summons to responsibility to which the offender responds through the summons of her own conscience.

This responsibility for the Other's death is manifest in the *tact* required of the offender in asking for forgiveness, neither too early, nor too late. Tact is a prudential judgement regarding the proper time for acting as well as adroitness in approaching my victim. One should not ask for forgiveness too soon after a wrongdoing, yet no measure of time prescribes in advance and in abstract how much time must elapse before which seeking forgiveness would be premature. Undoubtedly, the degree of injury and the standing of the victim (a friend, a stranger, and so on) contribute to the tact of knowing when is the right time to begin the turn of forgiveness. It would clearly make little sense, and in fact, would be judged as a further offense, to ask for forgiveness immediately on the heels of an egregious wrongdoing. But if there is a sense in which one should never ask for forgiveness too soon, is there a comparable threshold by which forgiveness can be too late? If forgiveness is essentially an ethical relation between offender and victim, the horizon of time that defines the time for forgiveness, as initiated by the offender, is the death of her victim: the offender cannot seek forgiveness once her victim has passed. The summons of the offender's responsible conscience is inscribed within the horizon of her victim's death and, in this sense, can be said to issue from or as a responsibility for her mortality. Likewise, the horizon of the offender's own death, insofar as the offender is hostage to the summons of her victim's death, calls for the seeking of forgiveness. Forgiveness must be sought before death, whether that of the offender who seeks it or that of the victim who grants it.[4]

---

[4] This summons of forgiveness beholden to the horizon of mortality, whether the offender's or the victim's, is often depicted in literature (for example, Charles Dickens' *Bleak House*, or Elizabeth Gaskill's *Mary Barton*).

The offender's responsibility towards her victim is nonetheless entwined with a responsibility for herself, and in the specific form of incorporating her past wrongdoing into the compass of her present self. Whereas she must repudiate her past self, she must incorporate her past wrongdoing. This assumption of her wrongdoing runs in tandem with a purification of the present self that resulted from her self-repudiation and aspiration to a future self-conception. Understanding how a past wrongdoing thus becomes assumed can be extracted from an insight advanced by Levinas. For Levinas, forgiveness acts on the past instant and conserves the past in the purified present (Levinas 1969: 283). I take this to mean that the past wrongdoing becomes retained *at the expense* of the past self who committed this original offense. This conservation of a past wrongdoing is a form of repetition, but not, however, a 're-living' of the past deed or its remembrance; for in the case of remembrance, as already discussed, the past is still held as past, at a distance from the present in which it is remembered. In speaking, however, of 'conserving' or 'retaining' the past wrongdoing, one is here to understand the incorporation of the deed into a present purified of the past self, or, in other words, as assumed by a renewed or purified self. This renewed self, as the consequence of the repudiation of one's past self, assumes the past wrongdoing, shorn of the self who had committed this wrongdoing. In taking responsibility for this past, I must speak for it from the present and in my name so as 'to be as though that instant had not past on, to be as though he had not committed himself' (Levinas 1969: 283). The past wrongdoing is thus retained within the compass of the self who now no longer commits herself to her past commitment and, accordingly, is able to expresses remorse and regret at having in the past thus committed herself in her wrongdoing.

An example for this assumption of a past wrongdoing *along with* the repudiation of a past self can be gleaned from an observation by the film-maker Anne Aghion. In an interview recounting her experiences in Rwanda, Aghion recounts how one of her acquaintances, who had long been involved in Rwanda, once had the opportunity to visit the detention centre for the International Criminal Tribunal for Rwanda in Tanzania. As this individual recounted, the majority of detainees were directly implicated in the Rwandan genocide; of these sixty offenders, only three had confessed. As Aghion explains: 'They did more than say "I am sorry". Unlike those who managed to convince themselves that they did nothing wrong, these three have begun to come to grips with what they did and what they must live with. The rest of the prisoners were reported to be in a chatty mood, talking about Rwanda as if nothing had happened. The three who confessed acted as if they continued to carry a heavy burden—not as if the burden had been lifted by the confession' (Aghion 2009: 148).

The assumption of responsibility by the offender does not break with the past wrongdoing. On the contrary, the offender must render her offense present to herself, confront it from the standpoint of her present self, and thus enlarge the compass of her present self by her past wrong. In an important sense, the offender over-comes her past self while conserving her past wrongdoing, and this lived and present irreconcilability, indeed, incomprehension, between past deed and present self just is the project of responsibility and repudiation in terms of which she begins again, but not in terms of the self she once was. In this threefold structure of her transformed temporality, the past self is repudiated, the present self incorporates a past wrong, and the future is directed towards the presence of her victim, from which she seeks forgiveness in order to invent herself anew, as other than the self she once was and would never want to become again.

6 THE VICTIM: RESENTMENT AT CROSS-PURPOSES WITH ITSELF

Numerous accounts of forgiveness attribute to the moderation and eventual forswearing all together of resentment (along with revenge) a central role in the transaction of forgiveness (Butler 1896; Arendt 1998; Griswold 2007). Whereas the offender must repent her past waywardness, assume responsibility for her wrongdoing and commit herself to self-renewal, the victim's conversion centrally turns on relinquishing her resentment towards her offender. Resentment is a retributive passion, distinct, though not opposed to anger; it is deliberative, not impulsive (Butler 1896: 139). In resenting an offender's wrongdoing, her character and action are judged blameworthy; resentment is part and parcel of the victim's exercise of her own responsibility. A victim failing to resent an offender would in turn become morally blameworthy. As Griswold reminds us, following Adam Smith, resentment attests on the part of the victim to a respect for the moral norms of her community as well as to her own self-esteem as a moral agent. Resentment combines the third party perspective of the impartial spectator *and* the first-person perspective of an impacted victim (Griswold 2007: 42). As already introduced, resentment is essentially manifest as a resentful gaze (idiomatically registered in the common expression 'the negative light in which a victim perceives her offender') in terms of which the offender becomes constituted and objectified, for herself as well as for others. The victim's resentful gaze issues an implicit demand to be recognized as justified in her resentment as well as a summons on the offender to own up to her misconduct. As an intersubjective relation, resentment is also a form of self-constitution on the part of the victim, which must be transformed and overcome so as to come of age into forgiving her offender.

Resenting an offender performs a double temporalization of her (the offender's) subjectivity in terms of which the victim comes to affect herself. The constitutional relationship between act and self (past wrong doing and past self) becomes inverted; and consequently, a temporal lien is placed on the existence of the offender such that her subjectivity, centered on her present self, becomes barred from temporal renewal—her subjectivity becomes suspended in the amber of her past wrongdoing, thus foreclosing her temporal existence from any genuine future. As Husserl argued in his phenomenological analysis of time-consciousness, what it is to be a subject is to constitute one's lived experiences temporally on the basis of an awareness of oneself as a constituting subject that is both implicated and temporalized along with the objects of one's experiences. To abbreviate this complex insight: an action in the life of subjectivity is constituted by a subject who 'knows', as it were, the difference between who one is and what one does. It is in this sense that the self is responsible for its actions insofar as, transcendentally speaking, an act can only be constituted for me on the basis of a pre-reflective self-awareness of *my own* activity of self-constitution. Within this constitutional schema, the victim's resentment constitutes the offender by *inverting* the relationship between her (constituted) past wrongdoing and her (constituting) past self. This inversion retrospectively suppresses, as it were, the constitutional sovereignty of the offender's self over her own actions by interjecting the sovereignty of the victim's (resentful) agency. Specifically, in resenting the offender for her wrongdoing, her past self comes to be exhausted through her past wrongdoing; her past self is suspended in the amber of her action. The offender's past wrongdoing is worn as a scarlet letter that marks, and so objectifies, her entire self in the eyes of the victim, and as further reflected in the eyes of the moral community. Indeed, the victim may seek to make public her resentment of the offender and reveal to others the corrosion of the offender's self by the acid of her wrongdoing. This is the sense in which a resentful gaze holds the offender's wrongdoing against her—indeed, holds it exhaustively and untiringly *as her*.

This aspect of resentment runs tandem with another aspect of temporal contraction. Insofar that the offender's past self becomes captive to her past wrongdoing, resentment further imposes a temporal lien on the offender's temporal existence *as such*. Her subjectivity becomes effectively foreclosed of a time and of a self other than the time of her past self and the self of her past offense. In this manner, her subjectivity is barred from within through the imposition of my resentment. The point is worth stressing: the renewal of the present, which Husserl and Bergson had independently argued as the vital gravity in the self-constitution and self-temporalization of subjectivity, becomes foreclosed; it is as if the offender's self becomes suspended in a purgatory of suspended time from which she is barred from renewing herself by the subjectivity—and hence sovereignty—of the victim. The retributive passion of resentment against the offender exercises a lien on her temporal self in such a manner that the temporality of the offender's existence becomes sequestered into the temporality of the victim's resentment. As just suggested, the offender's self is encompassed by a single past wrongdoing, and on this basis, condemned to an eternal recurrence of herself as so defined and damned; this damnation of the Other to the perpetual past of her wrongdoing comes to define the offender. It is to reduce her alterity to the identity of an eternal past instant: she will forever be what she has done to me.

An example of this dynamic of resentment can be found in Charlotte Brontë's *Jane Eyre*. The orphan Jane Eyre is resented by her aunt, Mrs Reed, who begrudgingly promised her dying husband (Jane's uncle) to adopt Jane as a child. Mrs Reed, however, favours her own children immensely and blindly, and repeatedly faults Jane for various misdeeds and wrongdoings, unfairly. On one particular occasion, Jane is wrongly accused of a transgression against Mrs Reed's spoiled son; Jane is locked up in an attic, pleads forgiveness from her aunt, is refused, and is eventually packed off to a dour boarding school. When the headmaster appears to take away his new charge, Mrs Reed proclaims to Mr Brocklehurst *in the presence of Jane* that she, Jane, is a liar and not to be trusted—that her subjectivity is irredeemably defined by past wrongdoings. This public scene of constituting the young Jane through the resentful eye of her aunt is repeated at the boarding school when the headmaster announces the same about Jane in front of the students. The point illustrated here is how Mrs Reed's resentful gaze has suspended Jane's subjectivity in time, damned her to the perpetual repetition of her past wrongdoings. In the character of Mrs Reed, Brontë crystallizes how resentment exercises a temporal lien on the offender's subjectivity that forecloses, in the eyes of the moral community, the victim, and most importantly of all, the offender herself, the promise of becoming different and other in the future. Jane Eyre will always be a liar, and indeed, Jane comes to doubt herself in light of her aunt's self-proliferating resentment.

This lien of past wrongdoings (imaginary or otherwise, as the case may be) placed on the offender in resentment is meant to secure *in retrospect* a respect and recognition that the offender did not offer in the past to the extent that she committed a wrongdoing against the victim. The lien of resentment forecloses time itself for the offender in order to secure an obligation due to the victim in the past, but not given. Yet in foreclosing the offender of a genuine future in which she could be different than how she has been fossilized in her past, resentment both seeks recognition and accountability in the future while at the same time foreclosing that future for the offender by condemning her to a perpetual past. In the eyes of Mrs Reed, Jane Eyre will always be a liar, and she will always fail to respect her. In its most viral form, resentment places a lien on the offender precisely in order to prevent forgiveness; resentment is counter-purposive to its own intention. The point is worth stressing. Resentment places a lien on the offender in order to obtain the respect that the victim should have given. Yet, given that the offender *did* commit a wrong, and thus fail in her obligation towards the victim to respect her, the victim now holds the offender in distain and resentment. Resentment can, in this regard, run itself to infinity—since the lien of resentment is meant to secure recognition that paradoxically could only have been given in the past, it tends to fester without end, running in circles after itself, and chasing its own tail, only to devolve into self-pity. To pity oneself is for one's own resentment to make an end run against itself.

What Brontë perspicuously examines in *Jane Eyre* is how resentment appears to be at cross-purposes with itself: resentment is a demand for respect and recognition that resentment itself bars the offender from offering in damning her to a past abjection. To draw this contradictory and revelatory paradox into fuller clarity: resentment can be seen as oscillating between two opposing poles that divide the resentful self from within, and with contradictory impulses. The *challenge* of forswearing resentment in the name of forgiveness resides in struggling against the inertia and self-affection of one's own resentment. On the one hand, as noted, resentment is a demand for recognition and respect of the victim's aggrieved subjectivity. As argued above, resentment summons the offender to responsibility and recognition of her wrongdoing, her wayward past self, and the suffering caused by her actions; in this regard, resentment induces forgiveness insofar as the offender becomes ashamed at herself, feels guilty, and so on. On the other hand, resentment is a self-constitution in terms of which the victim sets herself apart from and over, as a constitutional sovereign and moral witness, the offender's subjectivity. In resentment, the victim places herself beyond reach in reaction to having been offended. This sovereignty over the offender is expressed in terms of the lien placed on her temporal existence and foreclosure of her temporality. An outline of this thought, I suggest, is discernible in Adam Smith's suggestive observation that 'resentment seems to have been given to us by nature for defense... [for] the safeguard of justice and the security of innocence' (Smith 2002: 92). This mechanism of safeguarding justice and producing a *cordon sanitaire* sequesters the offender in a foreclosed temporality, and sets apart the victim in a locus of moral standing and constitutional sovereignty. Resentment secures the victim against the offender. Resentment is thus often indistinguishable from indignation at being wronged, and which can veer to the extreme of disbelief: the incredulity at having at all been wronged. In this sense we hold the offender in resentment in order to hold ourselves a part and hold onto ourselves and our innocence against the offender: we hold ourselves against the offender in holding ourselves apart, even beyond and against forgiveness itself.[5] The retributive character of resentment resides in this affirmation of the victim's alterity as sovereign over the victim's subjectivity at the expense of her own alterity, insofar as the victim has placed a lien on the offender's existence in light of her wrongdoing. The inherent proclivity of resentment consists in ensnaring the victim within her own resentment so as to revictimize the victim from within, and by her own means—the injunction 'Never forget!' is a manifest expression of a latent self-victimization through an untiring and untouchable resentment. In this sense, resentment is the capacity to victimize myself to eternity.

7 THE GENEROSITY IN FORGIVING

This cross-purposiveness of resentment accounts for a constellation of diverse and opposing conceptions of the relation between resentment and forgiveness. Different aspects of resentment's contradictory demands are reflected in different conceptions of

---

[5] This force of resentment to retain itself in its self-affection can lead to the subterfuge of instrumentalizing, or 'weaponizing', the act of forgiving itself, as my colleague Lisa Rodensky once aptly termed it (and who first observantly drew my attention to *Jane Eyre*). This, indeed, is a key to the penultimate scene between Mrs Reed and Jane in *Jane Eyre*. Jane returns to Gateshead to visit the dying Mrs Reed, who, in classical Victorian style, seeks forgiveness for her mistreatment of Jane on her death-bed. Jane appears to tender forgiveness in uttering the words 'Love me, then, or hate me, as you will, you have my full and free forgiveness: ask now for God's; and be at peace', as Mrs Reed slowly dies. And yet despite this ritual pronouncement of forgiveness, Jane remains unchanged, for she has in fact not forsworn her resentment against her aunt, as the reader comes recognize shortly after this enactment (Chapter XXI). The aunt is dead, and Jane does not shed a tear—neither for her aunt's death, nor, we might infer, for her own play of forgiveness in the name of her resentment. That Mrs Reed, in her dying stupor, failed to recognize the presence of Jane at her bedside and spoke of Jane in the third person and of her regrets at mistreating her further, underlines how until the end, Mrs Reed refused to recognize Jane in her individuality—hence the withholding of Jane's own forgiveness in order to affirm retributively her individuality against Mrs. Reed own mineralized resentment. Mrs Reed and Jane are mirror images of each other: each holds onto their resentment, and against each other, and against forgiveness.

forgiveness—three of which, for my purposes, will allow for a triangulation towards a resolution to the dilemma at hand. One tendency, represented by Jean Améry, but anticipated in *Jane Eyre*, consists in affirming the justice of resentment *against* forgiveness (Améry 2002); another tendency, represented by Jacques Derrida, 'dreams' of an innocent and pure forgiveness, without sovereignty, modelled, one may presume, on the figure of the 'holy fool' in Dostoyevsky (for example, Prince Myshkin) (Derrida 2000); and yet another tendency, represented by Charles Griswold, envisions the requirement of sympathetic understanding between offender and victim as the necessary supplement to the insufficiency of the forswearing of resentment so as to preclude any affirmation of the victim's moral superiority (or sovereignty, as I am here calling it) against the victim (Griswold 2007). The point I want to make in view of this constellation of different positions on the relationship between resentment and forgiveness is that each of these positions—Améry, Derrida, Griswold—turns on the instability of resentment; each exploits or reacts to one aspect of its unstable mixture and contradictory dimensions.

When seen within the prism of resentment's cross-purposiveness, Améry represents the collapse of resentment's internal tension in favour of affirming the justice of resentment *against* forgiveness. According to Améry, resentment constitutes the victim as a moral witness so as to incarnate the moral truth of the offense committed against her. Through this materialization of resentment, the offender is perpetually confronted with the moral truth of her transgression (Améry 2002: 131). As Améry observes, 'the time sense of a person trapped in resentment is turned upside down and unhinged [*verdreht, ver-rückt*] ... for it desires two impossible things: regression into the experienced past and annulment of what happened' (Améry 2002: 128 (my translation)). Améry's insight reiterates an insight gleaned above from *Jane Eyre*: resentment sets the victim apart and against the grain of time, but also, and crucial for his thinking, against social and political pressures for reconciliation *and forgiveness*. In fixing the victim and the offender to the past, resentment expresses a desire for its annulment, since the victim, insofar as she continues to suffer from the wrong, adopts the posture of resentment as both proof of her innocence and as a locus of defense against her wrong, as if to counteract the force of its aggression (hence the *retributive* nature of resentment). But resentment also expresses a desire to retain the past wrongdoing as perpetually present, on the cross of which the offender is nailed—as Améry strikingly phrases it. Améry further considers resentment as a self-affection (as captured in the French *ressentiment*) in terms of which the victim 'singularizes' herself: resentment sets the victim apart and against the offender in 'the solitude and abandonment of her condition' (Améry 2000: 131). If resentment thus constitutes the victim as moral witness to the truth of the wrong committed against her, the victim is charged with the responsibility of an unending vigilance. On this notion, Améry insists on the justice of resentment against forgiveness. If forgiveness entails, as Améry believes, reconciliation and integration into a moral community, the retention of resentment staves off the 'deindividualization' produced in forgiveness, and thus keeps the victim's conscience both restless and sleepless.

Derrida's conception of the 'madness of forgiveness' as unconditional and absolute represents a collapse of resentment's paradox in the opposite direction. For whereas

Améry affirms resentment against forgiveness, Derrida's position can be seen as a vision of forgiveness entirely purified of any resentment, including the positioning of the victim as sovereign in claiming for herself the right and *power, or possibility, to forgive*. The absolute and unconditional character of forgiveness precludes any conditions, including the condition of having a purpose, function or meaning. And yet forgiveness must succumb to conditions in order to be effective; hence the *aporia* of forgiveness as 'divided' between the unconditional and the conditional, both indissociable yet incompatible. Derrida thus 'dreams' of forgiveness in an absolute innocence that would amount to 'forgiveness without power' and without sovereignty (Derrida 2000: 133). How can the victim proclaim 'I forgive you' without thereby affirming her sovereignty? Between Derrida and Améry, we find a middle ground in Griswold, who proposes a supplement to resentment in order to stabilize and resolve its inner tensions. The concern is that the victim could sincerely forswear her resentment all together and yet still constitute her forgiveness as an affirmation of moral superiority. The standing of the victim as set apart and against the offender through resentment may survive the suppression of resentment itself, and become transformed into a heightened sense of moral superiority in forgiving, as an act of magnanimity, for example. One could even imagine that forswearing one's resentment and forgiving one's victim would amount to taking pity ('a noxious and insulting sort of tribute' in the apt words of Mr Rochester in *Jane Eyre*) on the victim. In Griswold's scheme, the conjunction of sympathetic understanding *and* the recognition of shared human imperfection are called upon as a safeguard against this instability of resentment and affirmation of moral sovereignty. On this argument, the victim, in arriving at a sympathetic view of the circumstances in which the offender committed her wrongdoing, is unable to claim the possibility that under similar circumstances she would not have acted differently. Once I recognize the circumstances in which the offender acted against me and further recognize my own human condition as imperfect, I cannot in good faith claim that I would have not also succumbed to committing this wrongdoing, given comparable circumstances, and given that I, too, am an imperfect being: this possibility of wrongdoing cannot be foreclosed. In thus forgiving, I cannot hold against my victim my own moral superiority, or perfection.

The constellation of these contrasting views generates the desideratum of conceiving the act of forgiving as 'innocence', without forfeiting the distinction of the victim as moral witness—in other words, as standing apart and against the victim, but not from the height of sovereignty. This possibility of forgiveness without sovereignty or reconciliation would also not appeal to the supplement of sympathetic understanding. Although forgiveness does not preclude sympathetic understanding, it is not required for forgiveness. Sympathetic understanding must ensue in light of forgiveness, but forgiveness is of a spontaneity that does not *necessarily* turn on understanding (for example, Jane first forgives Mr Rochester—'I forgave him at the moment, and on the spot'—*so as to be able* to listen sympathetically to his confessional narrative of atonement); or else the requirement for sympathetic understanding is itself perverse. Would we demand of a holocaust victim to say to herself: in sympathetically understanding my offender I cannot thereby rule out that I, too, would have not been acted thus under similar circumstances?

As a candidate for this desideratum I propose that the tendering of forgiveness to an offender who warrants forgiveness is an act of *generosity* that forecloses the victim's own position of moral superiority, but not at the expense of diminishing the victim's standing as a moral witness, as standing apart and singular, and thus as irreconcilable with her offender.[6] In forswearing resentment the offender renders time back to the victim by relinquishing her temporal lien and revoking the foreclosure of the victim's own constitutional sovereignty over her temporal existence. Generosity consists in giving back to the offender the alterity of her own temporality. I am in a sense withdrawing my sovereignty that has barred your own subjectivity and self-presence; and in so withdrawing you can become yourself anew, without thereby abdicating my position as set apart and against you, as the truth of your wrongdoing, as the moral gravity of our shared past.

Generosity can be broadly understood as a movement towards the Other without direct return to the self nor without direct renouncement or negation of the self. As Jankélévitch insightfully distinguishes, whereas generosity indirectly looks away from the self who gives in affirming the Other directly, humility is primarily self-regarding while only indirectly affirming the Other (Jankélévitch 1986: 315).[7] Expressed as a form on intentionality, generosity intends as its primary object the Other, who becomes affirmed and recognizing as Other, as the person to whom I give without demand and precondition; and thus regard myself as a secondary object, indirectly and non-thetically, as the subject who gives. The generous person forgets herself in giving—withdraws, as it were, from the scene of the transaction without thereby denouncing or abasing herself. Generosity is also not charity: charity gives *to infinity and without limit*, 'operates *ex nihilo*, from the nothingness of humility', and gives even when I have nothing to give or spare; generosity, on the other hand, is 'vitality', not an instrument or means, but an innocence that does not deprive the person who gives (Jankélévitch 2000: 316). In this sense, generosity is not to be confused with Levinasian fecundity and devotion to the Other, which he argues as the accomplishment of forgiveness, and in which the self looks up to the height of the Other. To think of forgiveness as generosity involves, in contrast, an act that affirms the Other without placing the Other above me—without devotion—and without renouncing my own distinction as not your moral equal. The act of teaching is, in this regard, quintessentially an act generosity: one gives without proclaiming oneself sovereign over what one teaches without thereby renouncing the difference and distinction between teacher and student, between the

---

[6] Is this conception of forgiveness as generosity another way to claim that forgiveness is love? I think not, but cannot fully develop the differences here. Suffice to say that I follow Descartes in thinking that generosity does not necessarily require love, although love cannot do without generosity.

[7] What is the relation between Jankélévitch's conception of forgiveness and his ethics of generosity? The question is intriguing, but cannot be engaged here. A brief discussion of forgiveness can be found in *Les vertus et l'amour* (Jankélévitch 2000: 245–73).

position of a witness to the truth of what is said and the position of the one to whom this truth is unconditionally presented, or given. If the act of forgiving is generosity, the victim, in receiving forgiveness, is not humbled or humiliated, but is called in turn to gratitude. Generosity is not tendered in exchange for gratitude; it is in this sense gratuitous, even though the person forgiven must express gratitude: one should only thank as well as forgive once, never twice.

8 CONCLUDING REMARKS: THE GIFT
OF TIME RENEWED

As I have argued in this paper, in its directedness towards the offender and in its form of 'other-constitution', resentment summons the offender to responsibility and demands of the offender that she recognize and respect the victim. As an objectification of the offender's self that is structured along the dual-temporalization outlined above, resentment forecloses the power of the offender's own self-constitution and self-temporalization; in the eyes of the victim, and more broadly, in the eyes of the moral community, but most poignantly even in her own eyes, resentment installs the sway of the victim's constitutional sovereignty *over* the offender. The sovereignty of the victim as moral witness in her resentment places an extra-ordinary lien on the offender's temporal existence in light of her wrongdoing—an offense that forfeits, in the resentful eyes of the victim, temporal self-renewal. The time of the Other becomes unhinged. This demand for recognition as resentment becomes fulfilled with the offender turning to seek forgiveness from her victim on the basis of her self-repudiation and self-responsibility through shame, guilt, and the call of responsible conscience. The sincerity of transformation and accountability, coupled with her request for forgiveness, apology, and remorse warrant the victim's forswearing of resentment and the granting of forgiveness. And yet resentment also possesses a dynamic of self-constitution in terms of which the victim defines herself as moral witness and sovereign, as set apart and against the offender. When seen from this aspect, the transaction of forgiveness can appear to run against the grain of the integrity and singularity of the victim's sovereignty. What is called for is an act of forgiveness granted in innocence, without the continued affirmation of sovereignty, and yet without forfeiting the victim's singular standing as moral witness—as the only one who can forgive.

In response to this dilemma I have proposed thinking of forgiving as generosity. Once granted, the act of forgiving and the warranting of forgiveness, as two poles of conversion, twin stars spinning on their own axis yet each in orbit around the other, allows for the coming of age of forgiveness as an asymmetrical transfiguration of time and subjectivity. The victim forgives me and introduces a discontinuity between my wrongdoing and myself, while I establish a continuity between past wrongdoing and present self; on the side of the victim, her foreswearing of resentment means that she renews my temporal existence in withdrawing her lien on my existence; generosity is here the gift of time itself—of a time over which the offender has regained her own renewed sovereignty.

Whereas the victim releases the offender from her past in forswearing resentment against her, the offender, in assuming responsibility for her past wrongdoing, comes to live with her past deed in the present. It is as if the burden of the wrongdoing has been passed from the victim back to the offender, thus transforming the offender into a moral witness to the truth of her own wrong. The offender accepts the burden of her past wrong into the compass of the person she is today and thus becomes the living questionability of her own wrongdoing. In being forgiven by the victim, the offender regains alterity and sovereignty over her own temporality; the victim gives to the offender the unpredictability and openness of her future—and which was precisely foreclosed through the victims' resentment, whose gaze fossilized the offender's subjectivity in the amber of her past wrongdoing. To forgive is thus to bid farewell (we were never so close as when I resented you), without any demand or expectation—not even of reconciliation or understanding. It is only through this generosity of relinquishing sovereignty over and against the offender that, in saying farewell, the future becomes *open* for us to begin anew, but not from where we last began. This is not to claim the final word on the accomplishment of forgiveness. It is, however, to suggest how to consider forgiveness in its temporality, without which the words 'please forgive me' and 'I forgive you' cannot be said in good faith or without implicitly proclaiming oneself sovereign over its graceful transformations.

REFERENCES

Aghion, A. (2009), 'Living together again, in Rwanda', in A. Wagner and C. Kuoni (eds), *Considering Forgiveness* (New York: The Vera List Center for Art and Politics), pp. 141–9.

Améry, J. (2002), *Jenseits von Schuld und Sühne*, in I. Heidelberger-Leonard (ed.), *Jean Améry. Werke*, II (Stuttgart: Klett-Cotta), pp. 11–177.

Arendt, H. (1988), *The Human Condition* (Chicago: University of Chicago Press).

Butler, J. (1896), 'Upon resentment', in W. E. Gladstone (ed.), *The Works of Joseph Butler*, vol. 2 (London: Clarendon Press), pp. 136–67.

Derrida, J. (2000), 'Le siècle et le pardon', in J. Derrida, *Foi et Savoir* (Paris: Gallimard), pp. 103–33.

Griswold, C. (2007), *Forgiveness: A Philosophical Exploration* (Cambridge: Cambridge University Press).

Heidegger, M. (1992), *The Concept of Time* (Oxford: Blackwell).

—— (1996), *Being and Time* (Albany: State University of New York Press).

Husserl, E. (1991), *On the Phenomenology of the Consciousness of Internal Time (1893–1917)* (Dordrecht: Kluwer Academic Publishers).

Jankélévitch V. (1986), *Les vertus et l'amour*, II (Paris: Flammarion).

—— (2005), *Forgiveness* (Chicago: University of Chicago Press).

Kolnai, A. (1973), 'Forgiveness', *Proceedings of the Aristotelian Society* 74: 91–106.

Lévinas, E. (1969), *Totality and Infinity* (Pittsburg: Duquesne University Press).

Lévinas, E. (1987), 'Diachrony and representation', in E. Levinas, *Time and the Other* (Pittsburgh: Duquesne University Press), pp. 97–120.

Ricouer, P. (1983), *Temps et récit*, I (Paris: Éditions de Seuil).

Sartre, J-P. (1984), *Being and Nothingness* (New York: Washington Square Press).

Smith, A. (2002), *The Theory of Moral Sentiments* (Cambridge: Cambridge University Press).

Williams, B. (1993), *Shame and Necessity* (Berkeley: University of California Press).

CHAPTER 25

....

HERMENEUTICAL
PHENOMENOLOGY[1]

....

GÜNTER FIGAL

1

In phenomenology there is a tendency, perhaps even a necessity, to be hermeneutical. In this sense, Paul Ricœur speaks of a 'hermeneutic presupposition' of phenomenology, stating that the phenomenological method has to be conceived as *Auslegung* (Ricœur 1986: 69).[2] An evidence for this statement is to be found in the work of the founding father of classical phenomenology himself. In his *Cartesian Meditations*, one of his most important programmatic writings, Husserl takes up a key term of hermeneutics, 'explication' (*Auslegung*), in order to characterize phenomenological reflection and thus the method of phenomenology itself. Phenomenology reflects upon intentional experiences, cognitions, or sensory perceptions, in order to conceive their correlates *as such* and so as phenomena. As Husserl says, this does not mean to reiterate the original experiences. It rather means 'to contemplate' (*betrachten*) and 'to explicate' (*auslegen*) what can be found in them (Husserl 1950a: 72–3s). 'Intentional analysis' (*intentionale Analyse*) is an 'explication' (*Auslegung*), 'elucidation' (*Verdeutlichung*), and 'clarification' (*Klärung*) of what is intended in intentional experiences; thus it is an attempt to conceive their 'objective meaning' (*gegenständlicher Sinn*) (Husserl 1950a: 83–4). Intentional analysis explicates intentional experiences just like readers explicate texts.

In Husserl's work, the hermeneutical dimension of phenomenology remains at the margins. There may be found traces of hermeneutical reflections in Husserl's conception of meaning in the first *Logical Investigation* and also in Husserl's conception of intersubjectivity as it is developed in the fifth *Cartesian Meditation* (see also Ricœur

---

[1] I am grateful to my wife Antonia Egel, to David Espinet, and to Dan Zahavi, for helpful comments on this chapter.

[2] If not otherwise indicated, all translations are my own.

1986: 69–81). Husserl also touches upon the hermeneutical character of sense percep-tion, stating that perception includes a 'fore-conception' (*Vorgriff*) insofar as it also refers to the aspects of something that are not actually perceived but only implicitly intended (Husserl 1959: 45). But Husserl never discussed the hermeneutical aspects of his conception of phenomenology; he never clarified what precisely he meant by 'expli-cation', and how it should be practiced. Despite his meticulous methodological reflec-tions, Husserl was rather unconcerned about the status of phenomenological analysis. Quite often he calls this analysis 'description' (*Deskription*), but the linguistic character of description remains unclear. At least one reason for this is what may be called the dominance of the optical paradigm. For Husserl, phenomenology is primarily an act of *seeing*, and accordingly, the phenomenological attitude is that of a spectator. Phenomenological reflection is not conceived as what it really is: namely, as the descrip-tive clarification of what one is doing. Husserl rather understands it as the beholding of intentional acts, mainly of cognitions and of sense perceptions (see Husserl 1950a: 72; see also Figal 2009: 138–9). In the *Cartesian Meditations* the 'phenomenologically meditating ego' (*das phänomenologisch meditierende Ich*) is called 'an uninvolved self-spectator' (*unbeteiligter Zuschauer seiner selbst*) (Husserl 1950a: 75).

Husserl's understanding of the phenomenological attitude is closely related to his understanding of phenomena. Once the phenomenological attitude is adopted, phe-nomena are just there. They are given in intentional experiences, insofar as these experi-ences are no longer simply performed and thereby refer to something factual. Phenomena are, more precisely, the correlates of consciousness, as they are contem-plated in phenomenological reflection and thereby not taken as something factual. Phenomena in this sense may be vague or clear; they are just there. No further attempt to disclose them *as* phenomena is necessary. They are disclosed as soon as the phenom-enological attitude is adopted. Then they are plainly given, and because of this they can be described and explicated. Although, according to Husserl, the description and expli-cation modifies the phenomena that are described and made explicit because of its reflective character (see Husserl 1959a: 72–3), the explication does not affect their dis-closedness. Thus the hermeneutical dimension of phenomenology is not essential for phenomenology as such.

This changes as soon as the dependency of disclosedness on explication is taken into account. Then phenomena as such cannot be understood without their description and explication. It was Heidegger who took this route. In *Being and Time* he developed a concept of phenomenon which makes the hermeneutical dimension of phenomenology obvious.

In order to clarify the meaning of 'phenomenon', Heidegger goes back to the Ancient Greek origin of the word. As Heidegger writes, *phainomenon* means 'what shows itself', it is 'the self-showing, the manifest' (*das Sichzeigende, das Offenbare*), or more precisely, 'what shows itself in itself' (*das Sich-an-ihm-selbst-zeigende*) (Heidegger 2010: 27; Heidegger 1977: 38). Read in the context of Husserl's work, this characterization seems not to be all too innovative. Rather, it alludes to Husserl's conception of givenness, espe-cially to the 'givenness of something as itself' (*Selbstgegebenheit*), which for Husserl is essential already in his early *Logical Investigations* (Husserl 1950c: 597) and which he again discusses in the first book of his *Ideas* (Husserl 1976: 141–2). But Heidegger's conception differs from Husserl's in a decisive respect: whereas for Husserl, evidence is a 'mode of intentionality' (*Weise der Intentionalität*) (Husserl 1974: 168), the self-showing in Heidegger's sense is self-disclosure for intentionality. Thus phenomena are no longer understood only as the immanent correlates of consciousness—as 'subjective phenomena'. They are no longer 'appearances', which, as such correlates, can be taken as in their subjective 'appearing' (Husserl 1950b: 14). According to Heidegger's conception, the appearing of the appearances is not to identify with the very givenness for consciousness and, accordingly, with the 'bracketing' of their factual existence as it is effected by the phenomenological *epoché*. Rather, the appearing of a phenomenon is, although not a matter of fact, an actual appearing. It is, to say it with a term which later became central for Heidegger, an 'event' (*Ereignis*) (concerning the notion of *Ereignis*, see already Heidegger 1987: 75; see also Heidegger 1989; Heidegger 2007).

In respect to the hermeneutical dimension of phenomenology, this conception of phenomenon is only the first step. Heidegger's understanding of phenomena as 'self-showing' is clearly revealed as hermeneutical not until Heidegger completes his conception by considering the linguistic character of phenomenological research. Phenomenology in Heidegger's sense can only be sufficiently understood if both the essence of phenomena as well as the essence of the phenomenological *logos* are considered.

In order to clarify the meaning of '*logos*', Heidegger goes back to the Greek verb *legein*, which, as he says, means '*apophainesthai*'; *logos* 'lets something be seen' (φαίνεσθαι); *logos* 'lets us see', from itself (ἀπὸ), what is being talked about (Heidegger 2010: 30–1; Heidegger 1977: 45). *Logos*, understood in this way, is no autonomous discovery—as if it were the sufficient condition for something to be present. What a *logos* lets see is not *made* present; it *comes* to presence by showing *itself*. But this self-showing, as it seems, is not possible without a *logos*. Something cannot show itself without, howsoever, being shown. Showing and showing itself belong together in what may be called the *deictic correlation*. According to Heidegger, this correlation defines phenomenality.

Heidegger explains his understanding of this correlation by referring to the particular task of phenomenology, and he thereby renders his understanding of phenomena more precise. His way of doing this is puzzling, and could even seem paradoxical. According to the pertinent passage of *Being and Time*, phenomena need to be shown by *logos* because they do mostly *not* show themselves. Mostly they are '*concealed* in contrast to what initially and for the most part does show itself' (Heidegger 2010: 33; Heidegger 1977: 47). Heidegger is even clearer in his discussion of the concept of phenomenon some pages before. According to a distinction that Heidegger introduces there, phenomena show themselves, but they do not 'appear' (*erscheinen*): 'appearing is a *not showing itself*' (Heidegger 2010: 28; Heidegger 1977: 39). Appearances, understood in this way, form a kind of surface; they are presences for the first glance—presences under the dominance of the prejudices of everyday life. Appearances of this kind *conceal* phenomena. As Heidegger says, concealment is 'the counterconcept' (*Gegenbegriff*) to phenomena (Heidegger 2010: 34; Heidegger 1977: 48). Accordingly, phenomena can only show themselves if their concealment by appearances is overcome. As phenomena, they are then unconcealed in an emphatic way. In the event of their unconcealment—as it is indicated by the Greek word *aletheia* in its literal meaning—they are phenomena.

Heidegger complements this conception of phenomenon hermeneutically. Discussing the 'phenomenological method of the investigation' of *Being and Time* (Heidegger 2010: 26; Heidegger 1977: 36), Heidegger defines the 'methodological meaning of phenomenological description' as 'explication' (*Auslegung*). In the same context he introduces the term 'hermeneutics', stating that the *logos* of phenomenology has to be understood as *hermeneuein* (Heidegger 2010: 35; Heidegger 1977: 50).[3] But a reader of these statements who expects a more extensive and detailed discussion, in which the explicative and thereby hermeneutical character of the phenomenological *logos* would be clarified, will be disappointed. Heidegger leaves the concept of explication as unclear as the concept of hermeneutics. As to hermeneutics, this holds true for the rest of *Being and Time*, whereas Heidegger discusses the concept of explication quite detailed in a later section of the book. So as to hermeneutics one has to rest content with Heidegger's statement that 'hermeneutics' means the 'work of explication' (*das Geschäft der Auslegung*) (Heidegger 1977: 50; see Heidegger 2010: 35: 'the work of interpretation'). Further clarification of the hermeneutic dimension of Heidegger's phenomenology must be expected from his discussion of explication.

Heidegger devotes the whole of section 32 of *Being and Time* to this discussion. But his considerations in this section are quite enigmatic. Heidegger does not discuss what might be expected—namely, the work of exegesis and interpretation as it is known from theology as well as from the humanities. Rather, he speaks of *Auslegung* in respect to the use of tools and other 'useful things'.[4] This concept of explication cannot really be understood if taken alone. It must be clarified by going back to Heidegger's earlier discussion of explication and hermeneutics. Heidegger knew very well the theological tradition and the importance of hermeneutics for the humanities, which emerged from it. The theological tradition is even the key for Heidegger's understanding of *Auslegung* and of hermeneutics—a key, however, which cannot be found in *Being and Time*. It is to be found in the work of his early Freiburg period, especially in his lecture course held in summer 1923.

This lecture course is devoted to hermeneutics, and here Heidegger gives a precise and comprehensive outline of the hermeneutical tradition. But Heidegger also makes clear that he is not interested in this tradition in order to understand and to discuss the methodological problems of interpretation. Rather, his motive is 'existential': Heidegger is interested in a kind of discourse which is essentially integrated in human life—in *Dasein*, as he says since his programmatic text *Phenomenological Interpretations with Respect to Aristotle (Indication of the Hermeneutic Situation)* from 1922.[5] Heidegger finds this kind of discourse in the hermeneutics of (Jewish and Christian) religion, for which the exeget-

---

[3] Heidegger 2010 has 'interpretation' for '*Auslegung*'.

[4] This is the translation of *Zeug* in Heidegger 2010.

[5] I follow Heidegger 2010 in leaving the term '*Dasein*' untranslated.

ical work with the holy texts has always been—or should have been—a self-clarification of religious life. From this understanding of hermeneutics to Heidegger's it takes only a single step. Religious life has only to be generalized to life as such and thus to *Dasein*. But in this generalization the existential aspect of religious life, which for Heidegger had been so essential, must not be lost. Consequently, *Dasein* has to be understood as radical individuality—as *Dasein* that is in actual existence, as life that is actually lived. Heidegger calls this the 'facticity' (*Faktizität*) of *Dasein*. According to Heidegger, this facticity is at issue for hermeneutics. If hermeneutics is the 'work of explication' (*das Geschäft der Auslegung*), and if explication is essential for discourse or even is itself the discourse in which *Dasein* in its facticity is articulated, then hermeneutics can be defined as the 'self-explication of facticity', (*Selbstauslegung der Faktizität*) (Heidegger 1988: 14). For Heidegger, hermeneutics is only interesting as such a hermeneutics of the self.

In discussing the status of self-explication, Heidegger is especially anxious about a possible misunderstanding. Although the results of self-explication may appear as statements about a matter of fact or something objective, they must not be understood in this way. Heidegger admits that *Dasein* as 'theme' of contemplation has the status of an 'object' (*Gegenstand*). But, as he adds, this does not mean anything for the question whether *Dasein* must be an object for the 'kind of experience' (*Erfahrungsart*) in which it is 'there' (*da*), and in which the analysis takes place (Heidegger 1988: 47). This consideration makes the crucial problem of a hermeneutics of facticity in Heidegger's sense very clear. As self-explication, which is articulated linguistically, hermeneutics cannot avoid making statements about *Dasein*; all sentences that are no mere expressions are 'about' what Heidegger calls their 'theme', and are thus objectifying. But for Heidegger, *Dasein*, understood as the immediate process of being, is not accessible as an object. Therefore, every statement 'about' *Dasein* is as such a concealment of what it is 'about'.

There is only one way out of this difficulty. The explication of *Dasein* must cross out the objectifying effect that it cannot avoid. It must make clear that this effect is inappropriate, and only due to the linguistic appearance of the explication; sentences as such can only be 'about' something. According to Heidegger, this crossing out is established by characterizing the kind of statements in which *Dasein* is explicated, as 'formal indication' (*formale Anzeige*). Heidegger uses this term for the first time in his review of Karl Jasper's book *Psychologie der Weltanschauungen*, which he wrote between 1919 and 1921 (see Heidegger 1976). He discusses it extensively in his lecture course *Introduction to the Phenomenology of Religion*, which was held in winter 1920/21. As Heidegger says here, the task of formal indication is to keep free the 'relation' (*Bezug*) to the phenomenon, and to do so in a negative sense, as it were, as a warning. A phenomenon, as Heidegger adds, must be given in such a way that the 'sense of reference' (*Bezugssinn*) is kept in 'suspense' (*Schwebe*). According to him, the formal indication is a 'defense' (*Abwehr*), a 'protection in advance' (*vorhergehende Sicherung*), so that the 'actualization character' (*Vollzugscharakter*) is kept free (Heidegger 1995: 63–4; see Makkreel 1985).

What Heidegger says about formal indication can be read as a commentary in advance to his conception of phenomenology in *Being and Time*. According to this commentary, the phenomenological *logos* must not occupy and dominate the phenomena so that they can show *themselves*. A phenomenological *logos* that does not keep distance from the phenomena will not *let them be seen* but rather be an appearance that conceals them. Thus the phenomenological *logos* is by no means capable to support the self-showing of phenomena in a positive way. It can only let it happen.

The problematic character of this conception is obvious. Although the phenomenological *logos* is related to the self-showing of phenomena, it can only fulfil its particular task in keeping open the *difference* between itself and the phenomena. In other words, the deictic correlation between *logos* and phenomenon breaks apart; it is only a difference and no correlation. Correlation is, indeed, impossible without difference. Without difference, nothing could be *related* to something else; if it could be distinguished from something else at all, the distinction would only refer to two aspects or parts of the same. So in order to be a correlation, the difference must go along with a conjunction. If this holds true for the relation between *logos* and phenomenon, *logos* must—in whatever way—be 'about' the phenomenon. Otherwise it could be no explicational or hermeneutic *logos* at all.

Heidegger must have realized this aporia in this early conception, otherwise it would be difficult to explain why he might have decided not to restrict the term *Auslegung* to hermeneutical articulation in the discussed sense. For the first time in his lecture course from summer 1925, and then extensively in *Being and Time*, Heidegger develops a conception of *Auslegung* as a general aspect of *Dasein* as 'Being-in-the-World' (*In-der-Welt-sein*). *Auslegung* in this sense is the enactment of understanding. In the context of *Being and Time*, 'understanding' is the intuitive comprehension of possibilities, in which *Dasein* has its own 'potentiality of being' (Heidegger 2010: 144; Heidegger 1977: 197). In explication (*Auslegung*) these possibilities are explicated in the literal sense of the word; they are developed and thereby realized as particular possibilities. This can happen without any linguistic articulation. As an example Heidegger mentions the use of a hammer 'too heavy' for the work that is to be accomplished with it. This experience can be accompanied by a sentence such as 'The hammer is too heavy'. But already to put the hammer away 'without wasting words' is an act of explication (Heidegger 2010: 152; Heidegger 1977: 209).

The strategic purpose of this move is obvious. Heidegger wants to conceive explication in such a way that linguistic articulation can be embedded in the very being (understood in a verbal sense) of *Dasein*, and thus he wants to find a possibility of linguistic articulation, which is in not objectifying at all. Accordingly, linguistic explication is contrasted to 'statement' (*Aussage*), which in section 33 of *Being and Time* is defined as a 'derivative mode of explication' (*abkünftiger Modus der Auslegung*) (Heidegger 2010: 149; Heidegger 1977: 204).

According to Heidegger, explication in the sketched sense is not restricted to the use of tools and other practices of everyday life. It is supposed also to cover the phenomenological explication and thus to make possible a non-objectifying, not only prohibitive or protective linguistic articulation of phenomena. But Heidegger's strategy fails. He admits this indirectly when he says that 'the circumspectly *spoken* explication' (*die umsichtig ausgesprochene Auslegung*) is 'not already necessarily a statement' (Heidegger

2010: 152; Heidegger 1977: 209). That means that it *can* be a statement, and as such it is objectifying. As it seems, linguistic articulation as such has the tendency to objectification, and then it can never be completely embedded in the enactment of *Dasein*.

This assumption is not at least supported by the fact that, according to *Being and Time*, the 'authentic' linguistic mode of *Dasein* is silence (see Heidegger 2010: 284; Heidegger 1977: 393). So it is not by chance that Heidegger reverts to his conception of formal indication in order to clarify the 'hermeneutic situation' and the 'methodological character' of the 'existential analytic' as it is developed in *Being and Time* (Heidegger 2010: 297; Heidegger 1977: 411). The central question in this context is how the 'self-explication' (*Selbstauslegung*) which belongs to the being of *Dasein* can be able to articulate *Dasein* in its 'authenticity' (*Eigentlichkeit*). This question is especially urgent because, according to Heidegger's 'existential analytic', *Dasein* has in itself the strong tendency to conceal its own being in explicating this being in orientation to the world. This 'falling prey' (*Verfallen*) is—at least amongst others—Heidegger's version of what Husserl calls 'natural attitude' in contrast to the 'phenomenological attitude'. Accordingly, in authenticity, *Dasein* is transparent for itself in a phenomenological, or to be more precise, pre-phenomenological way. In authenticity *Dasein* shows itself to itself. But if authenticity is essentially silence, one must ask how the 'existential analytic'—ergo the book *Being and Time*—can be an explication of authenticity.

Heidegger's answer to this question is twofold. First, the phenomenological explication of authentic *Dasein* has the character of a presupposed 'idea of existence' (*Idee der Existenz*). And second, this presupposition is in truth a 'projection' (*Entwerfen*), which linguistically articulates that what is explicated so that *Dasein* 'may decide of its own accord, whether, as this being [*Seiende*], it will provide the constitution of being for which it has been disclosed in the projection with regard to its formal indication' (Heidegger 2010: 301). In other words, *Dasein* must 'decide' whether to understand itself according to the formal indication or not. But according to Heidegger's conception, this decision, which is identical with the showing-itself of *Dasein* to itself, cannot be discussed and examined phenomenologically. It must be enacted in silence.

2

After Heidegger, the question of how to conceive the relation between phenomenology and hermeneutics has remained a challenge. This is not mainly due to the fact that Heidegger's answer in *Being and Time* remained aporetic. Heidegger's aporia would have become marginal if the question bound to it would not be of real philosophical interest—for phenomenology as well as for hermeneutics. As to phenomenology, a convincing answer to the question would integrate philosophy of language, which has become of increasing importance in modern philosophy, into phenomenology, in such a way that the central role of language could become intelligible in respect to the conception of phenomenon and thus to the basic task of phenomenology. As to hermeneutics, the philosophical claim of phenomenology to overcome all presuppositions as well as its methodical scrutiny would be helpful in order to establish hermeneutics as true systematic philosophy. Thus hermeneutics would be more than a limited and occasional reflection of interpretation and understanding.

It was Gadamer who understood hermeneutics in this way. Gadamer's project of 'philosophical hermeneutics', which is mainly developed in his main work *Truth and Method*, is essentially bound to 'the diligence of phenomenological research' (*die Gewissenhaftigkeit phänomenologischer Deskription*) (Gadamer 1986a: 5; see my essay 'Gadamer als Phänomenologe' in Figal 2009: 277–90). Gadamer's intention to overcome the orientation of the humanities to the methodical ideal of natural science owes much to the phenomenological tradition. For Gadamer, the attempt of 'overcoming the epistemological question by phenomenological research' is decisive for philosophical hermeneutics (see Gadamer 1986a: 246–69), and accordingly he devotes a whole section of his book to this theme. But Gadamer's philosophical hermeneutics is not only dependent on phenomenology; although it was not intended as a contribution to phenomenology, his work is of interest for the phenomenological discussion. It offers a new hermeneutic version of the phenomenal or deictic difference as Heidegger had introduced it to the phenomenological discussion. In doing so, Gadamer finds his own version of Heidegger's hermeneutical thinking, which he was acquainted with when he attended Heidegger's lecture course on the hermeneutics of facticity in 1923.

In the conception of understanding that Gadamer develops in *Truth and Method*, at least three of Heidegger's thoughts can be discerned. When Gadamer says that everything has 'its being in its presentation' (*in seiner Darstellung sein Sein*) (Gadamer 1986a: 480), this statement obviously is in the line with Heidegger's definition of phenomenon as 'showing itself'. But there is also a remarkable difference. 'Showing itself' is immediate, whereas 'presentation'—Gadamer also speaks of 'self-presentation' (*Selbstdarstellung*) (Gadamer 1986a: 113–4)—has an aspect of mediation. Gadamer illustrates this by a helpful example. According to him, portraits—especially the portraits of rulers, statesmen, or heroes—are no depictions. Rather, the ruler himself is present in his portrait, and he must be present in such a way because he has 'a being in self-showing' (*ein Sein im Sichzeigen*) (Gadamer 1986a: 147). If an analogous characterization holds true for every being, then every being *is* what it is only in its presence. In becoming present it obtains the 'determinacy of itself' (*die Bestimmtheit seiner selbst*) (Gadamer 1986a: 479).

Gadamer develops this consideration further in the third part of *Truth and Method*, devoted to the topic of language. Here, Gadamer wants to show that in respect to understanding, self-presentation has to be conceived as linguistic presence. In presenting itself, something which is not language comes to its presence in language. This linguistic presence is 'total mediation' (*totale Vermittlung*) (Gadamer 1986a: 125). It is no mere symbolization or representation of something by a system of signs which are different from the represented. Rather, something finds in language its own presence. It 'comes to language', as Gadamer says; 'coming-to-language' (*Zur-Sprache-kommen*) (Gadamer 1986a: 478) is a self-manifestion in language. This is so because it becomes understandable. For Gadamer, being is essentially being intelligible and as such being-in-language. Or, as Gadamer expresses it with the key sentence of his book: 'being that can be understood is language' (*Sein, das verstanden werden kann, ist Sprache*) (Gadamer 1986a: 478).

Gadamer's step beyond Heidegger's conception of phenomenon has a decisive advantage. For Gadamer, there can be no gap between self-showing and language, because self-showing *is* language. Nonetheless, Gadamer does not neglect the difference between self-showing and letting see as Heidegger had introduced it. For Gadamer too, self-showing must be allowed; there must be a disposition for it. But unlike Heidegger, Gadamer conceives this disposition not only in a negative way. For Gadamer the condition for self-showing to take place is not the defense of inappropriate objectification. Rather, it is prejudice (see Gadamer 1986a: 275–90), which is the disposition of non-understanding as well as of understanding. Prejudices allow the first access to something understandable, and they also conceal it, at least to some degree. Prejudices are not necessarily inadequate. But they must prove to be adequate or inadequate, and this can only happen in understanding, in which the prejudices are 'at stake' (Gadamer 1986a: 304). As Gadamer claims in explicit reference to Hegel, understanding is a process of 'experience' (*Erfahrung*), in which the appearance of something in prejudice is step-by-step overcome by self-showing. Prejudices that are more or less inadequate are modified, while the self-manifestation of what is to be understood becomes dominant.

Gadamer describes this process in more detail in silent reference to Heidegger's conception of *Auslegung*. In *Being and Time*, Heidegger distinguishes three structural aspects of *Auslegung*: 'fore-having' (*Vorhabe*), 'foresight' (*Vorsicht*), and 'fore-conception' (*Vorgriff*) (Heidegger 2010: 145–6; Heidegger 1977: 199–200). In order to explicate something—both with or without linguistic articulation—one must first be familiar with what is to be explicated; Heidegger calls this *Vorhabe*, but also an 'appropriation of understanding' (*Verständniszueignung*) (Heidegger 2010: 145; Heidegger 1977: 199). Explication needs, secondly, an orientation in respect to which something can be discovered as explicable; this is *Vorsicht*. And every explication is, thirdly, guided by a preliminary conception, *Vorgriff*, of what is to be explicated. Gadamer reformulates this structure in the context of his conception of prejudice (see Gadamer 1986a: 271). Understanding a text always needs a preliminary acquaintance with what is to be understood. But this acquaintance is only the necessary condition of understanding; being an initial appearance of the correlate of understanding, it does not immediately and completely discover what is to be understood. What is understandable—Gadamer calls it 'the meaning [*Sinn*] of the text'—must therefore be 'projected'. As soon as some first meaning 'shows itself' in the text, the meaning of the whole text is preliminary presented in projecting (*Entwerfen*). The projected meaning becomes concrete insofar it is elaborated or conceptually explicated in the process of understanding. As Gadamer stresses, this is an open process. Along with the partial success of understanding, the preliminary project (*Vorentwurf*) of meaning again and again must be revised. In this process the meaning of a text more and more comes to show itself.

It is not by chance that Gadamer speaks of the 'self-showing' of meaning. The phenomenological character of his conception of understanding and explication is obvious when he says that every true explication has to 'orient its view to the things themselves' (*den Blick 'auf die Sachen selber' richten*) (Gadamer 1986a: 271). Accordingly, Gadamer conceives the fulfilment of understanding as 'evidence' (*Evidenz*). As to this, he could have referred to section 24 of Husserl's *Cartesian Meditations*, where evidence is explained as the 'self-presenting' (*Sich-selbst-darstellen*) and as the 'self-giving' (*Sich-selbst-geben*) of something (Husserl 1950a: 92). And he could have combined this with Heidegger's understanding of phenomenality as self-showing, to which he alludes in his conception of explication and understanding. But Gadamer takes another way. He explains the conception of phenomenality as evidence by referring to Plato's conception of the beautiful.

According to Gadamer's interpretation of this conception, beautiful things are purely and immediately evident in their appearance, and their appearance is binding. The beautiful wins favour with those who experience it; one can only be caught and convinced by it. As Gadamer says, this is the same with 'the meaningful' (*das Sinnvolle*). If we understand a text, the meaning of the text wins favour in the same way as the beautiful does. The meaningful wins favour 'before someone who experiences it, so to speak, regains consciousness and is able to examine the claim of "meaning" [*Sinnanspruch*] that is addressed to her or him' (Gadamer 1986a: 494). Just like the experience of the beautiful, the experience of the meaningful is without any distance. Gadamer emphasizes this with respect to the beautiful by speaking of 'aesthetic non-differentiation' (*ästhetische Nichtunterscheidung*) (Gadamer 1986a: 122). The meaningful manifests itself in the experience of explication and understanding so that this experience can no longer be distinguished from what takes place in it.

Gadamer has developed this thought more extensively in respect to the understanding of tradition. According to him, tradition cannot really be distinguished from present as past. Rather, tradition is effective history (*Wirkungsgeschichte*). It is past as well as present, the all-encompassing process of history as such. But this process can only be experienced if a text that represents the tradition first appears as belonging to a past age, and thus, as Gadamer says with Husserl's term, to a different 'horizon'. The 'historic horizon' in Gadamer's sense is the particular openness of a traditional text in its meaning, from which the particular openness of present understanding is distinguished. Historical understanding is as such only possible in this tension of two horizons, which is the 'tension between text and present' (*Spannungsverhältnis zwischen Text und Gegenwart*) (Gadamer 1986a: 311). But as Gadamer adds, the projecting of a historical horizon that is different from the horizon of the present can only be a 'phase' (*Phasenmoment*) in historical understanding (Gadamer 1986a: 312). If one really wants to understand a traditional text one must not reduce it to a document of past times, but rather be open for what it has to say. In this openness for being addressed by a text, the text can become manifest as meaningful. Thereby, the two horizons fuse, and it becomes obvious that there is only one tradition that encompasses also the present (see Gadamer 1986a: 321–3). History, as Gadamer says, does not belong to us, but rather we belong to history. The individual historic consciousness that regards itself in difference from the past is only 'a flicker in the closed electrical circuit of historical life' (*ein Flackern im geschlossenen Stromkreis des geschichtlichen Lebens*) (Gadamer 1986a: 281).

Historical understanding, as Gadamer conceives it, is thus not possible without taking distance to the past in projecting an historical horizon. But the distance of understanding cannot be reduced to this projecting. Before the distinction between two historical horizons can be made, there must be something that initiates the intention of understanding—something that is meaningful and not self-evident in its meaning. What is initially there is a text. Texts are the true representatives of tradition. As Gadamer says, they are no relics of a past world but rather belong to the 'sphere of meaning' (*Sphäre des Sinns*). They are like messages sent to unknown addressees that, because of the 'ideality of the word' (*Idealität des Wortes*), can reach someone in later times and be understood. So texts are situated between foreignness and familiarity. They could be called 'the true place of hermeneutics' (*der wahre Ort der Hermeneutik*) (Gadamer 1986a: 300).

But Gadamer does not draw this consequence. Rather, he characterizes writing as 'self-alienation' (*Selbstentfremdung*) (Gadamer 1986a: 394), and accordingly, the understanding of a text as 'retransformation of signs in speech and meaning' (*Rückverwandlung der Zeichen in Rede und Sinn*) (Gadamer 1986a: 397). Gadamer's reason for doing so is quite clear, otherwise he could not have maintained his conception of understanding as the total self-presentation of the meaningful. Written or printed texts do not present themselves, and they do not absorb their readers in 'total mediation'. Rather, they are, and essentially remain, different from reading; as real correlates of understanding they allow reading again and again. Whereas according to Gadamer's conception the deictic correlation is only a 'phase' in understanding, the hermeneutical and phenomenological orientation to texts could recognize it as the basic structure of hermeneutical phenomenology.

3

Ricœur has made a step in this direction. As he argues, Gadamer has underestimated the 'hermeneutical function of distanciation', and has therefore not done justice to the hermeneutical importance of the text. For Ricœur, distanciation—that is, as he says, his own contribution to the phenomenological and hermeneutical school (see Ricœur 1986: 7)—is essential for understanding. The meaning of linguistic articulations can be encompassed only if one is not caught up in the event of language but rather able to be attentive to what is meant—to the '*noema* of the saying' (Ricœur 1986: 119), as Ricœur says with Husserl's term. According to Ricœur, we do not want to understand the event of language but its signification. Whereas the event is ephemeral, what is meant remains, and therefore can be understood not only by the speaker but also by someone else (see Ricœur 1986: 117).

The latter consideration may sound familiar from Gadamer's discussion of the 'sphere of meaning' and the 'ideality of the word'. But whereas Gadamer conceives this ideality as the very possibility of tradition, Ricœur sees it essentially realized in texts. Texts are set free from the contexts of normal conversation, and open up a sphere that is in distance to it. They give access to the 'ideal meaning' (*sens idéal*) that in normal conversation remains tacit because it is bound to the situation of the speakers and to the reality to which they are referring (Ricœur 1986: 157). This has also a phenomenological consequence. Texts do not belong to the natural attitude, but rather allow an understanding of the 'life-world' as such (Ricœur 1986: 127). Going along with this, they allow self-understanding. In texts, the reference to particular matters of fact—Ricœur calls this 'first-order reference' (*reference de premier degree*)—is suspended. So they can refer, 'second order', to the 'horizon of our life' (*horizon de notre vie*) and to our 'being-in-the-world' (*être-au-monde*) (Ricœur 1986: 58). This does not mean that texts are a mirror of a particular life-world. In this case, the 'meaning' (*sens*) they offer could not be 'ideal'. Rather, they confront with 'imagined variations' (*variations imaginatives*) of oneself (Ricœur 1986: 131). What, asks Ricœur, would we know about love and hate, moral sentiments, and, in sum, all that we call 'self' (*soi*) if all this had not been articulated by literature (Ricœur 1986: 130)—that is, in ideal meaning? The constitution of the self and that of meaning (*sens*) are 'simultaneous' (*contemporaines*) (Ricœur 1986: 171).

Ricœur's conception, as sketched, has some plausibility, but it is also ambiguous in different respects. First, his conception of text itself is unclear. Mostly Ricœur speaks of text in general without any qualification, defining it as the disruption of normal reference and as the opening-up of the ideal meaning (see Ricœur 1986: 157). But this is obviously problematic. Many texts—for example, instructions for use and travel guides—do refer to something particular in the world. Consequently, Ricœur's definition could hold true only for a certain kind of text, and in this sense Ricœur refers to 'the works of culture' (*les œuvres de culture*) (Ricœur 1986: 130) and also to 'literature'—what may include scientific, philosophical, and religious texts—and especially to fiction and poetry (Ricœur 1986: 127). But Ricœur does not clarify the difference between normal texts, and 'eminent texts', as Gadamer calls them (Gadamer 1986b: 348). Rather, he maintains that the essential quality of 'literature' is made possible by the very nature of the text (see Ricœur 1986: 127). But texts do not in general open up ideal meaning, and thus cannot, as such, be as important for self-understanding.

Ricœur's conception of self-understanding is as such problematic. Ricœur does not really clearify how self-understanding can be rendered possible by texts. To be confronted with 'imagined variations'—that is, with possibilities of human life—can at least be a necessary condition for self-understanding. Ricœur, as it were, thinks that texts quicken a sense for the possibility of life as such, and he also assumes that they confront with particular life-projects. As he says, texts suspend subjectivity: they let subjectivity become unreal, and make it potential (see Ricœur 1986: 130–1), and he seems to understand this as pure potentiality. But the text also is called a 'suggestion of a world' in which I could live and project my most authentic possibilities (Ricœur 1986: 130), and this must be a particular world. In the context referred to it remains unclear what kind of 'world' it is that is opened up by a text—whether it is the world of the reader or, as Ricœur also says, the 'world of the work' (*le monde de l'œuvre*) (Ricœur 1986: 130).

This ambiguity indicates another one: namely, the ambiguity of Ricœur's conception of understanding. On the one hand, Ricœur says that self-understanding has to take place before the work (*devant l'œuvre*) (see Ricœur 1986: 129), and that in order to understand oneself one has to be a 'pupil of the text' (*disciple du texte*) (Ricœur 1986: 60). On the other hand, Ricœur calls the text a 'medium' of self-understanding (Ricœur 1986: 130), a support of communication in and through distance (see Ricœur 1986: 57). The domination of self-understanding in his conception makes it very likely that Ricœur takes the latter alternative more seriously. Consequently, the understanding of texts cannot be more than a mediation (*médiation*), which leads through distance to appropriation (see Ricœur 1986: 57). It is only important in respect to the self—even if the self may be modified or changed by this mediation.

This point can be generalized. Although Ricœur's declared intention is a hermeneutically revised version of phenomenology, he has not elaborated a conception of phenomenon. For him, the only phenomenological presupposition effective in hermeneutics is that every question with respect to a being whatsoever is a question of 'meaning (*sens*)' (Ricœur 1986: 61). For Ricœur, neither Husserl's conception of self-givenness or evidence nor Heidegger's characterization of the phenomenon as self-showing, which are both so decisive for Gadamer, have any importance. Ricœur's hermeneutical phenomenology has no phenomena.

4

Hermeneutical phenomenology cannot do without texts; it even has to give them a prominent position.[6] Texts are the correlates of hermeneutic experience—not all texts, but texts that challenge understanding. The phenomenal character of these texts is hermeneutically evident. They show themselves, and they do so not only when the attempt to understand them is successful. The self-showing of a text is not necessarily and not essentially the event of the meaningful in Gadamer's sense. Rather, a text shows itself to hermeneutic experience in its initial challenge—as something that is to be understood. A text also shows itself continuously during the process of hermeneutic experience; its presence leads and motivates this experience again and again. With eminent texts, hermeneutical experience will never come to an end. Their understanding cannot be completed. It can be ended only for the time being. There will always remain an irreducible remainder: in rereading a text, something may for the first time be realized, or something that had appeared to be known will show itself in a new light.

If eminent texts can show themselves in such a way, they must be essentially *different* from the diverse attempts of understanding, and they are, in fact, experienced in this difference, otherwise different attempts to understand a text would be impossible. In this difference, texts show themselves as *definite*; nothing can be added nor erased without

[6] For the following cf. Figal 2010b (German edition Figal 2006).

destroying them. In their definite character, texts are *stable*, while the diverse attempts of understanding them change. In their stability, texts prescribe, in some way, how to approach them; not every attempt of understanding them can be successful, because not every approach is appropriate. Eminent texts, in sum, are *objective (gegenständlich)*; they are true counterparts for interpretation. They have *phenomenal objectivity*, or, *to be more precise: objectity*. This objectity is essentially self-showing for experience. Phenomenal objectity is truly correlational; although it is related to interpretation, it is not dependent on it. Phenomenal objects 'stand over and against' as the exterior correlates of hermeneutic experience. The German word *Gegenständlichkeit* says this in a more concrete way. *Gegenstand* is something which *stands* there. Phenomenal objects are *gegen-ständlich* in the literal sense of the word. Their objectity has not been 'thrown over', *ob-jected*; it is independent of such a subjective project. Rather, it affects subjects as a challenge, and this challenge is answered by interpretation.

Phenomenal objectivity or objectity, this may already have become clear, is different from the objectivity of factual things. Because of its phenomenal character one cannot adequately refer to it by propositions. The aspects of phenomenal objects cannot be stated as if they were matters of fact. The text, and every phenomenal object, can always be interpreted otherwise, and therefore no interpretation can be simply true or false. Interpretation always articulates only a possibility of the text, and thus indicates its priority. It confirms its self-showing. In showing itself a text is always richer and more complex than its particular interpretations

Nevertheless, texts—phenomenal objects in general—can, and in order to do justice to them, must be *shown*. Their self-showing is not the overwhelming event of evidence that Gadamer describes, but rather an address to be answered. Such an answer is given in *presenting* phenomenal objects. Although self-showing, they do not present themselves. Without presentation, their self-showing would remain initial; it would be a mere potential of meaning.

In order to become actual, this potential must be realized by presentation, and presentation is never without alternatives. These alternatives are, at least to some degree, prescribed by the texts themselves. Texts are primarily present in reading, and reading is not 'about' a text. Reading follows the text, but is not embedded in it or absorbed by it. Reading is essentially different from the text that is read. Being attentive on some aspects and regarding others as more or less marginal, every reading presents the text in a certain way. Reading, to say it with one word, is *interpretation*. It is, more precisely, the basic form of interpretation—just a mimetic presentation without commentary. But reading is already reflective; in reading, one may ask how a sentence fits into its contexts or reread the previous pages in order to understand a passage of a text in its meaning. Reflection of this kind is a necessary condition for interpretation in a narrower sense. In this sense, interpretation is either *explicative*—in explication, understood in the strict sense of the Latin word *explicatio*, a text is unfolded—or it can have the mode of clarifying (*Deutung*), by which the meaning of a text is summarized and more or less brought to conceptional clarity. In any case, interpretation is *reflected*. One cannot develop an interpretation of a text without at least a certain consciousness of what one does. In reflection, the particular steps of an interpretation may be revised or confirmed. Examining whether they fit together with other interpretations can test their appropriateness and make clear whether they offer a concise and coherent presentation of the text.

This sketchy characterization of interpretation anticipates in some respects a more concrete conception of text. Text is not only a written discourse. Rather, it should be understood as a more or less complex and consistent meaningful order. This understanding can be confirmed by the literal meaning of the word. The Latin word *textus* literally means 'fabric' or 'weave'. In ancient rhetoric it signifies the order of speech; in this meaning, the word is a translation of the Greek word *logos*—which does not primarily mean 'speech', but rather the said in its meaningful order that can also be expressed 'in other words'. But *logos* is not restricted to language. Pictures or buildings and pieces of music also have a meaningful order.

In any case, the order of *logos* must be *fixed*, otherwise it could not be a definite order but only a state in a process or even the more or less vaguely structured process itself. As fixed, the order of *logos* or text is *simultaneous*. Of course, it can only be experienced and interpreted successively, but the succession of interpretation is not a quality of the interpreted text. An evidence for this is interpretation itself. A novel, for example, is normally to be read from the first to the last page, but its explication and clarification is not bound to this procedure. Rather, explication and clarification normally discover simultaneous correspondences all over the work. The more this is the case, the more sophisticated is an interpretation, and the more the work can be understood.

In this context, understanding means that a text is experienced as showing itself in such a way that its order is evident and, in its evidence, intelligible. The intention of understanding is this evidence—the text itself. Understanding, conceived in this way, is no self-understanding; it is only an understanding by oneself so that, more or less explicitly, the interpretative experience of texts will modify or even change the dispositions and the character of a person. To turn to oneself in order to understand oneself can only mean to experience one's own life like a text (see Figal 2009: 119–20). The life of a person is not fixed in its order like a building, a picture, or a literary work. But as a set of dispositions, attitudes, relations, and experiences, it is a kind of logical or textual order. Accordingly, the attempt to understand the life of a person must fix it at least to some degree. It is not by chance that the attempt to understand the life of a person is elaborated in biography.

This consideration is of decisive methodological importance. What is true for the lives of persons must consequently be true for everything that has to be described and understood as an order. Like in the life of a person, this order is mostly not clearly given. Unlike in a produced text—let it be painted, built, composed, or written—the order has not been established. It is not definitely textual, but rather pre-textual—embedded in the perceptible in its complexity, and thus often hardly to be discerned in the process of experience. The description has therefore a more demanding task than in hermeneutical clarifications; it must fix the order that is to be described in explicating it.

This is the situation of phenomenological description in general. Phenomena as Husserl conceives them are never given in isolation. Rather, everything phenomenal is embedded in a 'horizon' of complements, modifications, and potentialities. A building as phenomenon, for example, can only be adequately described if its different aspects, such as front, backside, outside, and inside, are taken into account. Phenomenological analysis must always go beyond particular experiences and 'explicate' (*auslegen*) the 'correlative horizons' In such an explication, the experiences are positioned in the 'thematic field' of those that function constitutively for them (Husserl 1950a: 85)—in other words, a particular experience, and thus also its correlate is only what it is in the context of others, actual as well as potential. The explication of phenomena is tantamount to the presentation of a phenomenal order that is a system of modes of givenness. Only as belonging to such a system, an experience and its correlate have meaning.

But, as has been stressed in the discussion of Ricœur's conception, meaning as such is not phenomenality. In order to be phenomenal, meaning must show itself. Self-showing, in turn, can only be experienced as such if it is realized as different from experience itself. A self-showing of meaning in this sense is given when a fixed text is there as intelligible in its objectivity. Meaning that shows itself must be the meaning of something objective. It must 'stand there' in true correlation, essentially different from interpretation and understanding. But it must not be in absolute otherness. What is in absolute otherness can only be recognized, but never be understood.

The notion of phenomenal objectivity may in the first moment appear to be incompatible with Husserl's conception of phenomenology. But, as one should remember, it is Husserl who devotes phenomenological analysis to the clarification of 'objective meaning' (*gegenständlicher Sinn*) (see above). In the context of Husserl's work, the objectivity of this meaning could best be conceived with respect to sense perception. Although Husserl does not restrict phenomenological analysis to phenomena given in sense perception, but rather stresses the importance of imagination and even 'fiction' (Husserl 1976: 147; see Figal 2010a: 87–90), there can be no doubt about the founding character that sense perception has for him. 'Originally giving perception' (*originärgebende Wahrnehmung*) is regarded as the basis for 'phenomenological statements of essence' (*phänomenologische Wesensfeststellungen*) (Husserl 1976: 146). In a text from the early 1920s Husserl develops this position further by stressing the objective character of perception. He maintains the priority of objects that are 'pre-given to the experiencing subject in passivity' (*dem erfahrenden Subjekt passiv vorgegeben*). Everything intelligible—*Denkgegenstände, geistige Gebilde*—is, as he adds, possible only because there are 'other objects pre-given by receptivity' (*andere Gegenstände durch Rezeptivität vorgegeben*) (Husserl 1966: 291).

Meaning, as one may conclude, must be bound to the perceptible. This does of course not mean that there must be a one-to-one relation between the perceptible and the intelligible aspects of something. The perceptible and the intelligible belong together in a complex order. Mostly they complement each other, as is the case with the visible front of a building and the invisible rear of the building. Phenomenality is never plain presence. It is more like a pattern of transparence and obscurity, of surface and depth, of denseness and distinctive structures. For phenomenological analysis, all this belongs to its objective meaning. But its self-showing cannot be reduced to meaning. Meaning, as bound to the perceptible, is always 'there'. It may not be the meaning of a phenomenal object, but it always has the character of phenomenal objectity. Therefore, phenomenological analysis has its paradigm in the interpretation of phenomenal objects. In this sense, it is hermeneutical.

References

Figal, G. (2006), *Gegenständlichkeit. Das Hermeneutische und die Philosophie* (Tübingen: Mohr Siebeck).

—— (2009), *Verstehensfragen. Studien zur phänomenologisch-hermenutischen Philosophie* (Tübingen: Mohr Siebeck).

—— (2010a), *Erscheinungsdinge. Ästhetik als Phänomenologie* (Tübingen: Mohr Siebeck).

—— (2010b), *Objectivity: The Hermeneutical and Philosophy*, tr. T. George (Albany: State University of New York Press).

Gadamer, H.-G. (1986a), *Hermeneutik I. Wahrheit und Methode: Grundzüge einer philosophischen Hermeneutik*, Gesammelte Werke, vol. 1 (Tübingen: Mohr Siebeck).

—— (1986b), *Hermeneutik II. Wahrheit und Methode: Ergänzungen und Register*, Gesammelte Werke, vol. 2 (Tübingen: Mohr Siebeck).

Heidegger, M. (1976), *Anmerkungen zu Karl Jaspers 'Psychologie der Weltanschauungen'*, in Gesamtausgabe, vol. 9 (Frankfurt a.M.: Vittorio Klostermann), pp. 1–44.

—— (1977), *Sein und Zeit*, Gesamtausgabe, vol. 2 (Frankfurt a. M.: Vittorio Klostermann).

—— (1987), *Zur Bestimmung der Philosophie I: Die Idee der Philosophie und das Weltanschauungsproblem*, Gesamtausgabe, vol. 56/57 (Frankfurt a. M.: Vittorio Klostermann).

—— (1988), *Ontologie. Hermeneutik der Faktizität*, Gesamtausgabe, vol. 63 (Frankfurt a. M.: Vittorio Klostermann).

—— (1989), *Beiträge zur Philosophie (Vom Ereignis)*, Gesamtausgabe, vol. 65 (Frankfurt a. M.: Vittorio Klostermann).

—— (1995), *Einleitung in die Phänomenologie der Religion*, in Gesamtsausgabe, vol. 60 (Frankfurt a.M.: Vittorio Klostermann) pp. 1-156

—— (2007), *Zeit und Sein*, in Gesamtausgabe, vol. 14 (Frankfurt a.M.: Vittorio Klostermann), pp. 3–30.

—— (2010), *Being and Time. A Translation of* Sein und Zeit, tr. J. Stambaugh, rev. and with a foreword by D. J. Schmidt (Albany: State University of New York Press).

Husserl, E. (1950a), *Cartesianische Meditationen und Pariser Vorträge*, Husserliana 1 (Den Haag: Martinus Nijhoff).

—— (1950b), *Die Idee der Phänomenologie. Fünf Vorlesungen*, Husserliana 2 (Den Haag: Martinus Nijhoff).

—— (1950c), *Logische Untersuchungen II.2*, Husserliana 19.2 (Den Haag: Martinus Nijhoff).

—— (1959), *Erste Philosophie (1923/24), Zweiter Teil: Theorie der phänomenologischen Reduktion*, Husserliana 8 (Den Haag: Martinus Nijhoff).

—— (1966), *Analysen zur passiven Synthesis: Aus Vorlesungs- und Forschungsmanuskripten 1918–1926*, Husserliana 11 (Den Haag: Martinus Nijhoff).

—— (1974), *Formale und Transzendentale Logik. Versuch einer Kritik der logischen Vernunft*, Husserliana 17 (Den Haag: Martinus Nijhoff).

Husserl, E. (1976), *Ideen zu einer reinen Phänomenologie und phänomenologischen Philosophie I*, Husserliana 3.1 (Den Haag: Martinus Nijhoff).

Makkreel, R. (1985), 'The feeling of life: Some Kantian sources of life-philosophy', *Dilthey-Jahrbuch* 3: 83–104.

Ricœur, P. (1986), *Du texte à l'action. Essais d'hermeneutique II* (Paris: Seuil).

PART VII

ART AND RELIGION

CHAPTER 26

SOMETHING THAT IS NOTHING BUT CAN BE ANYTHING: THE IMAGE AND OUR CONSCIOUSNESS OF IT

JOHN BROUGH

IMAGES are peculiar and perplexing phenomena, highly complex and capable of representing things entirely different from themselves, a feat beyond the reach of ordinary objects. They have intrigued philosophers since the time of Plato, and have played what some take to be a quite pernicious role in epistemology, particularly in the understanding of perception. Phenomenology approaches images and imaging from a variety of perspectives. The images I will be concerned with in this essay are those we actually see—the sort encountered regularly in museums and movie houses, in newspapers and magazines, and on the stage. My focus will be on the nature of the image as it presents itself in our experience, with its remarkable capacity to represent within itself people, events, emotions, and many other things, and with its place in art. What I have to say will be influenced by Edmund Husserl's understanding of phenomenology, and particularly by his phenomenology of image consciousness. The Husserlian perspective has many affinities with more recent investigations of images, such as those of Richard Wollheim and Robert Hopkins, among others.

1 THE THREE MOMENTS IN IMAGING

Image consciousness is a kind of perception, but a peculiar kind in that it is mediated, which ordinary perception is not. We usually think of perceiving as the straightforward awareness of something in the world: a glass of red wine on the table in front of me, a train slowly entering a station. In such cases, no image intervenes between the act of consciousness and its object. Memory and phantasy in the sense of visual imagination, on the other hand, would seem to be more complicated. If I imagine a satyr, a mythical creature who is clearly absent, there is a strong temptation to say that I am directly conscious of a present image serving as a vehicle giving me access, indirectly, to the absent satyr. Since what I remember or imagine is not actually there, so the reasoning goes, there must be something present in my mind—the image—standing in for the missing object. Memory and phantasy would then involve two objects: the internal image of which I am immediately aware, and the absent object that I reach only through the image. Phenomenologically, however, this is not the case. My awareness of the remembered or imagined object is just as straightforward as my awareness of the perceptual object. It is true that the satyr I imagine is not present in person, as it would be if I were perceiving it; but it is also true that what I imagine is the satyr itself, not a picture of it tacked to the wall of my mind. I can, of course, imagine a painting depicting a Satyr, but that is to imagine a painting, not a satyr, except indirectly. Furthermore, if I do imagine the painting, I imagine the painting itself, not an image of it. Both perception and phantasy present the object itself; the difference between the two is that perception presents its object as actually there, while phantasy represents its object only 'as if' it were present. Images do not intervene between consciousness and its object in phantasy and memory. They are not modes of imaging. Where, then, are images to be found?

The brief answer is: in image consciousness, which is a mode of awareness fundamentally different from perception or phantasy. It is in image consciousness alone that one encounters images in the authentic sense—paintings, sculptures, films, and the like— and becomes aware, in a single integrated conscious act, of more than one 'object'. Indeed, in seeing an image such as a painting or photograph, as many as three objects are involved. There is first the representing or depicting image, which is what I immediately see when I stand, for example, before Manet's *Bar at the Folies Bergère* at the Courtauld Institute in London. The image is an object; it is what I actually encounter when I look at the painting. The image can also have a subject, what it represents and depicts—in this case, a bar at the famous Parisian music hall. The depicting image-object often has multiple image-parts or moments representing a variety of things, such as the bottles of Bass ale and the glass dish filled with oranges in Manet's painting. The notion of the subject of an image is more ambiguous and complex than might at first appear. The subject can be obvious, as is in the case of the portrait of a famous person, but it can also be elusive. Some writers, for example, find in Manet's painting a commentary on the alienation and perhaps exploitation of working-class women in late nineteenth-century Paris. We shall discuss the issue of whether images must always have a subject, and what the range of subjects might be, later in this essay. The third element involved in image consciousness is the physical support that undergirds the image. Although the image and its subject will be my main concern in this essay, the physical dimension deserves careful consideration, since it plays a fundamental role in imaging and has been largely neglected by philosophers, though not by artists.

2 THE PHYSICAL SUPPORT

A physical thing serves as the support or substratum for the image I see. The material support is not the image itself, but without it there would be no image. In the case of images that are two-dimensional, the support might be canvas and pigment or paper and ink. Images, however, can also be three-dimensional, such as sculptures, or the props and even the actors in a play. The physical support in such cases would then be three-dimensional as well, formed from bronze, stone, wood, or any other material capable of being shaped into something with breadth, width, and depth. Like all physical things, the image's support fits into the environment of the real world. It can hang on the wall of a house, or sit on a pedestal in a gallery. It interacts causally with other physical things, and thus can be damaged by fire or moisture.

There are further important aspects of the physical support. It is an artefact made by an image-maker precisely in order to excite the experience of a specific image, which by extension is itself an artefact. If the substratum has been properly constructed, then the image it supports will appear to the spectator more or less as the maker intended it to appear. The support also ensures the intersubjective and public character of the image it founds, and endows it with a stable and abiding content that can be experienced at different times and, in many cases, in different places. Throngs of people may line up in one city to see an exhibition of paintings by Vermeer, and then, a month later, thousands more will visit the same exhibition in a place halfway around the world. This contrasts with the objects of phantasy, which are irreducibly private and tend to be fleeting, unstable, and relatively indeterminate with respect to colour and other qualities. Only I can experience what I visualize in imagination; it would be absurd to expect others to stand in line to contemplate my phantasies.

Since the physical support is an object in actual space, it can be seen from a variety of orientations or perspectives. It cannot, however, be seen from just any orientation if the appropriate image is to appear. A painting, for example, considered as a physical thing, has a 'normal position' in which the image shows itself (Husserl 2005: 586). The support obliges the spectator to view it from the particular perspective and distance that will instigate the appearance the image-maker intended the painting to have. An ordinary physical thing carries no such obligation. A stone can be seen appropriately from any perspective one chooses. The presence or absence of motion can also be a characteristic of the experience of the substratum. The support for a photograph, for example, is supposed to be unchanging and at rest. Turning it too far to the side or moving it about rapidly will frustrate the emergence of the image it is intended to excite. On the other hand, in the case of a moving image such as a film, the appropriate image fails to appear when the physical support abruptly ceases its motion. The frozen appearance left behind on the screen is usually not what the filmmaker intended to appear. 'Moving' pictures and 'still' pictures are therefore rooted, respectively, in the motion or rest of their physical supports. This does not mean, however, that an image that does not move could not depict motion. Degas' paintings of racing horses do not themselves move, but one certainly sees motion in them.

Although there can be no image without a physical substratum, what I see in image consciousness is the image, not its support. The support is concealed or integrated into the experience of the image in such a way that it tends to disappear or be suppressed as an object in its own right. Indeed, the appearance of the image depends on the disappearance of its support; or, more accurately, the image emerges when the support goes underground or retreats into the background. I remain conscious of it, but not as a second object on the same level as the image. Indeed, I must be aware of the support if I am to be aware that what I am experiencing is an image. Consciousness of the image never quite eclipses the awareness of the support, leaving a tension between the two that is essential to image consciousness.

The image and its physical substratum are so tightly interwoven that if one tries to focus one's attention on features of the latter—the texture of canvas, for example, or the direction of a set of brush strokes—it is extremely difficult to suppress the appearance of the image altogether. The intertwining of the two also means that aspects of the material support, such as passages of raw canvas in paintings or the grain of the wood from which a sculpture is made, can seep into the image, showing themselves in subtle ways and contributing to the image's unique character and aesthetic effect. The physical support is not aesthetically neutral.

The substratum plays interlocking roles in image consciousness: underpinning the image, instigating its appearance, and securing its public status. Through its relative permanence and stability, it also embeds the image in time, making possible the history of art. It grounds critical commentary about size, shape, colour, texture, and other features of the image that depend on a work's physical dimension and that are important historically and aesthetically.

3 THE IMAGE

When I look at a painting or photograph, it is the image that truly and fully appears, not its subject and not its physical support, even though the image could not appear without the latter. The support, as we have seen, tends to be concealed in image consciousness, and although the subject is meant and announces itself in the image in ways to be seen, it does not appear in person, as present here and now. The image, on the other hand, taken just it appears, is present in person. Since perception is the mode of consciousness that presents something as actually there, image consciousness is a kind of perception, and its object is genuinely perceived. I perceive the little grey image-figures in a photograph with the 'full force and intensity of perception', just as I do the cup on my desk (Husserl 2005: 62).

The image, however, differs from an ordinary perceptual object in important respects. It is exhausted in its appearance, for example, unlike the object of straightforward perception, whose spatial horizons can always be explored further. The image is a figment, a semblance, a 'show'. In fact, all imaging, not just theatre, can be described as 'show business'. As such, the image, unlike its physical support, is not an actual physical thing placed in the midst of the world and related causally to other physical things. The image itself cannot be burned up, even if the canvas and pigment supporting it can be. One can touch the cold, unyielding surface of a bronze sculpture or inhale the aroma of fresh oil-paint, but one cannot touch or smell the image itself. In that respect, the image is an 'ideal' object, as Husserl puts it (Husserl 2005: 647), or 'irreal', as Sartre says (Sartre 2004: 125). It has its own space and time set apart from the space and time of reality. It embraces a world internal to it and discontinuous with the reality around it. Its physical support may attach it to the time and space of the world—Manet's *The Bar at the Folies Bergère* hangs at this moment in the Courtauld Institute in London—but the image as such resists assimilation into its surroundings, which are made up of real walls, floors, light-switches, and museum guards. The image is 'in' the world but not 'of' it. Manet's painting and all of its image components are nevertheless perceived; they are public objects, intersubjectively available and not privately phantasied. Thanks to its physical substrate, which locates it in space, I can ask you to follow me into the room at the Courtauld Institute where it hangs. Both of us will then see the painting, though neither of us will be tempted to take what we see in it to be real. Our awareness lacks the belief in existence that marks ordinary perception. Image consciousness simply lets the image appear, but appear as something that is not real; it does not support the positing of its image-object as actual. Thus I can see appearing bottles and fruit and people and much else in the image, but I cannot step into the imaged scene and order a drink from the young woman behind the bar. She is an image person, not a real person, and the bottles arrayed in front of her are image bottles. She cannot actually pour from them, or drop and break them. They do not fit into the spatiotemporal horizon of the gallery room in which they appear.

There are, of course, instances of visual deception in which one takes an image, such as one of Duane Hanson's hyperrealistic sculptures, to be real, although the deception is usually only temporary and dissipates with closer observation. Images, however, are not illusions of this kind, which are in fact the antithesis of authentic imaging, since they trick us into believing that they are real objects, effectively masking their being as images.

The peculiar status of the image as sheer semblance explains why, although it is genuinely perceived, it can be described as a 'nothing', a 'nullity' (Husserl 2005: 50, 51). To say that it is 'nothing', however, is not to say that it has no being at all. It is rather to point to its odd ontological status. Its being is unique: not real being, but what might be called 'image being'. It may be 'nothing' in the sense that it does not fit comfortably into the spatial and temporal structures of the world, but it is a nothing that nonetheless appears. The image's lack of real being in the world, however, should not be construed to mean that it exists inside the mind. If the painting I see were a mental image, assuming for a moment that there are such things, it would be as fleeting as a twinge of feeling or passing psychic act, enjoying a brief moment of existence before being swept away in the stream of subjective time. It would lose its full-fledged perceptual presence and public availability. Images are unique among beings precisely because they exist neither inside the mind nor outside it, and yet are available to everyone endowed with the capacity to perceive them. Furthermore, because they are not real things but nevertheless appear, they can be hospitable to a degree that only human minds can approach, embracing, disclosing, and, in the mode of imaging, becoming the things they are not—that is, the things they represent. René Magritte's *The Treachery of Images*, the various versions of which picture a pipe with the words 'Ceci n'est pas une pipe' painted below the image of the pipe, is justly famous because it captures this odd status of the image and the difference between two ways of being present. If someone standing before the picture were to ask 'what is this?' it would be perfectly reasonable to respond: 'This is a pipe.' On the other hand, it is a painting of a pipe, not a real pipe. It both is a pipe—an image-pipe—and is not a pipe—a real pipe. It is the nullity of the image that lets it represent a pipe—that is, be a pipe without really being one. 'Things are in pictures,' Robert Sokolowski notes (Sokolowski 1977: 21), and we can add that they are in sculptures, plays, and other kinds of images too. Things leave behind their real being and enter into the accommodating nothingness of the image, where they enjoy image-presence. We can then see them in the images.

4 IMAGE CONSCIOUSNESS AS SEEING-IN

If the image does not present itself as a real thing existing in the world or as a mental picture, how does it present itself? It appears before me as exhibiting or displaying something. Real things just are what they are; they do not exhibit anything, except accidentally and superficially, as when a cloud formation looks like a castle. The image, however, is made to display something other than itself. Its physical support is an artifact, we noted, made precisely to excite the consciousness of a particular image in the perceiver. Manet employed his pigments and brushes to make something that would represent a woman, fruit, bottles, and much more, all in the fashion his creative imagination demanded. But how is the image able to represent? Certainly a necessary condition for having a depictive image is the capacity to recognize something as an image—that is, one must be capable of image consciousness, which Husserl describes as 'a unique and absolutely primitive mode' of awareness (Husserl 2005: 18). One could no more be conscious of images without that capacity than one could be conscious of the past without memory.

The uniqueness of image consciousness resides in its ability to see something in something else—a bottle in a painting, for example, or a human figure in a photograph. The notion of 'seeing-in', understood as an essential moment of representation, has gained wide currency in Anglo-American aesthetics, particularly through Richard Wollheim's *Painting as an Art* (Wollheim 1987). It is an idea also present in Edmund Husserl's texts from early in the last century, although its importance in his phenomenology of imaging has not been adequately exploited. Wollheim approaches seeing-in through the notion of 'twofoldness': one is visually aware of a marked surface, and one sees in that surface a figure or a face, for example, although it could just as well be a geometrical form (Wollheim 1987: 21). Wollheim contrasts seeing-in with seeing 'face-to-face', which occurs in ordinary perception in which one simply sees something straightforwardly without seeing anything in it. In phenomenological terms, the awareness of the surface and the awareness of something in the surface are not two separate experiences, which would be the case if an act of perceiving were simultaneous with or followed by an act of phantasying. They are, rather, two distinct but inseparable moments of the single act of seeing-in. This act, as Robert Hopkins says, is 'a phenomenally integrated whole' (Hopkins 1998: 17).

Seeing-in is more complicated than might initially appear. Husserl's remarks about imaging suggest that it is possible to distinguish two levels of seeing-in (Husserl 2005: 21, 30). Wollheim does not seem to make this distinction, instead focusing exclusively on what I take to be the first of the two levels. In this first kind of seeing-in I see something in the image's physical support—that is, in the lines drawn in ink on a piece of paper, in the carved marble of a sculpture, or in the coloured forms on the surface of a photograph. In the lines and bounded grey and black areas of a photograph by Henri Cartier-Bresson, for example, I see the face and the upper body of a woman who stands next to a building fronting on a street along which three pedestrians can be seen walking in the distance. It is this act of seeing the human figures, the street, and the building in the lines and patches of grey distributed across the surface of the photograph that transplants me from the realm of ordinary perception, in which I would see just paper with a mottled grey surface, into the realm of images. If I restrict myself to what actually appears when this first level of seeing-in has done its displacing work, what I see are people, a street lamp, and buildings, all image-parts of a larger image-whole, and all small and grey.

The second level of seeing-in involves seeing something in the image rather than in its physical substratum. Here the subject of the image comes into play: I see the subject in the image. Thus in the small grey figure of a woman that I perceive in Cartier-Bresson's photograph, I see a specific person, Simone de Beauvoir, standing on a street in Paris. Only images can have subjects; an oak tree may have majesty and a screwdriver may have a purpose, but neither has a subject. The image-person I see in photographic colours appears perceptually, but the subject I see in the image does not; that is, Simone de Beauvoir is not actually present to me in person when I look at the photograph, nor am I consciousness of her through phantasy or memory, although seeing her in the image could trigger both. As long as I stay within the boundaries of image consciousness, the subject does not offer itself in a second appearance, whether memorial or imaginative, distinct from the image.

To the degree that I do see the subject in the photograph, I must see her in the traits of the image: 'The subject looks at us, as it were, through these traits' (Husserl 2005: 31). There is a kind of doubling of consciousness at work here. One is aware of both the image and the subject of the image in two moments of a single complex act. In Cartier-Bresson's photograph the image with its small grey figures does appear perceptually, but, unless we are absorbed in the image as a work of art, it is usually the subject that we mean, as when we say to someone 'This is a photograph of Simone de Beauvoir.' The perceptually present image exhibits Simone de Beauvoir. We take the image to be the image of a particular person, and we mean that person within the limits of the image exhibiting it, although, as we shall see later, this does not entail the perfect coincidence between the features of the image and those of its subject. Indeed, insofar as an image appears, there will not be, and must not be, complete agreement.

One might be tempted to claim that seeing-in in both of its forms is really the same as 'seeing-as'. Why can I not say, in looking at the photograph, that I see certain shapes on the surface of the paper as a woman and that I see this woman as Simone de Beauvoir? It would certainly make sense to say that about a piece of driftwood with patterns that in some respects resemble a woman's face and even Simone de Beauvoir's face. Another person, however, might see the same patterns as a rabbit's head, or not see them as any particular thing at all; or perhaps seeing the patterns as a woman's face, see it as Simone Signoret's face rather than as Simone de Beauvoir's. Seeing-as, because it can be exercised on virtually anything given perceptually, is arbitrary and subjective in a way that seeing-in is not. Seeing-in, as it is understood here, involves only images, and, more precisely, only images made by a human agent in such a way that the observer is supposed to see something definite in them. The creator of the image may have considerable freedom in producing the image, but the spectator has much less. In Richard Wollheim's terms, a standard of correctness governs the image-experience (Wollheim 1987: 48). Seeing-in is therefore pinned down in a way that seeing-as is not. Cartier-Bresson does not have it in mind that I see just anything I might wish in his photograph: his intent is that I see a woman's face, and in that face see Simone de Beauvoir. In following the demands the photographer has embedded in the image, I do not see what is represented in the photograph as a woman's face or see the face as Simone de Beauvoir's face because what appears to me is a woman's face and is meant to be Simone de Beauvoir's. It is true that I can be mistaken about what I see, but that is because what I am supposed to see in the image is not left up to my whim.

I also think that it would be off the mark to claim that seeing-in amounts to seeing something through an image in the sense of seeing it by means of the image. As we shall see in the discussion of symbolic consciousness in the next section, the image is not an instrument prompting me to think of something else—that is, of something not actually seen in the image or in what the image-maker has put down on the surface of the support. If the image were a means in that sense, other means might serve equally well to summon up the representation—a possibility that would sever the intimate bond between the image and its physical support and between the image and its subject.

That there are two senses of seeing-in suggests that we should speak of 'threefoldness' rather than 'twofoldness' in image consciousness: on one level I am aware of the surface of the physical support; on another I see something in it, giving me the image; and on the third I see the subject in the image.

There can be more complicated instances of seeing-in than those we have been considering, especially in the case of images with 'tricks' built into them. It is precisely seeing-in that makes the tricks work. Giuseppe Arcimboldo's composite portraits illustrate this in interesting ways. Arcimboldo builds up portraits of human faces by ingeniously combining images of fruit, vegetables, flowers, mammals, or fish. When one encounters one of his polysemous paintings, one normally sees a human face. The appearing face, however, bristles with knobs and protrusions and curious combinations of colours. The experience of conflict it provokes compels the spectator to examine the image more carefully. One then sees meticulously rendered flora and fauna in the paint-covered surface of the support: one realizes that the nose is a pear; the lips, cherries; the rosy cheeks, apples; and the eyelids, pea-pods. The image of a human face dissolves into an assemblage of images of non-human things. It would be tempting to claim at this point that the pear image, for example, has a kind of foundational priority and that one sees the nose in it. It would seem more accurate, however, to say that one sees the nose in a shape painted on the surface of the support that is sufficiently 'nose-like' in form and also related to other shapes on the surface in such a way that one can see in them eyes, a mouth, ears, and so on, together forming the appearance of a face in which the nose appears in its appropriate location. One sees the pear, on the other hand, when one isolates the same shape and considers it apart from its relations to the other shapes on the surface. The pear, then, appears when the shape is considered by itself, while the nose appears only when the shape plays a specific role in a relational whole. If the 'nose' as painted by Arcimboldo were cut from the canvas and hung on the wall, one would not and could not see a nose, but only a pear. As it is, in looking at Arcimboldo's painting one alternates between seeing a face with a large nose and rosy cheeks and seeing apples and pears, all in the same surface. The painting is unsettled. A radical change in images takes place, challenging the spectator and inviting exploration and discovery. Seeing what is in it becomes as much an intellectual as a sensuous experience.

Since Arcimboldo's images are portraits, they also provoke the second kind of seeing-in. In one painting, for example, the subject is Vertumnus, the Roman god of the seasons and vegetation, but one also sees the Emperor Rudolf II, since the portrait depicts Rudolf as Vertumnus—assuming, of course, that one is not absorbed in the images of fruits and vegetables that make up the head, in which case there is no portrait (Ferino-Pagden 2010: 18). Arcimboldo also made reversible pictures that in one position show, say, a still life of vegetables in a bowl, but when turned upside down show a face—a phenomenon that confirms in dramatic fashion the importance of the position of the physical support in determining what can be seen and how adequately it can be seen.

Arcimboldo's paintings may be tricks, but they show how rich and diverse the phenomenon of seeing-in and imaging can be. Their surfaces support images of flora and fauna, but also images of the human face in which one can see a Roman god and an emperor. All of this occurs within the few square centimetres of a wooden panel covered with pigment, which is not itself any of the things whose representation it makes possible.

5 SYMBOLIC CONSCIOUSNESS

Before examining further aspects of seeing-in as well as features of the image that make it possible, it will be helpful to note the differences between image consciousness and symbolic or signitive consciousness, which is also a form of mediated awareness.

An image represents internally; one sees something in the physical support and in the image itself. In symbolic or signitive consciousness, what is signified is neither seen in the sign nor presented in an appearance distinct and separate from the sign. Rather, it is indicated as something absent and external to the sign that I am given in perception. 'The symbolizing function represents something externally; the imaging function exhibits its subject internally, seeing it in the image' (Husserl 2005: 89). Unlike the image, the sign does not exhibit, make intuitable, or pictorialize what it symbolizes, except incidentally. In perceiving the sign I am instead carried by association or convention to its referent, which is not itself perceived. If it were, there would be no need for the sign. It is such signifying consciousness that lets me understand highway signs or icons in airports directing me toward the nearest bar or luggage carousel. Appearing in their own right, such signs point externally, usually in an anticipatory way, to something that does not appear. When what is signified actually occurs and is experienced, sign consciousness evaporates in the face of perceptual fulfilment. Image consciousness, on the other hand, is not anticipatory. When I see something in an image, I become absorbed in the image and do not see beyond it. It is fulfilled in the present for as long as seeing-in continues to occur.

Despite the difference between sign and image, sign consciousness, or something like it, can arise on the basis of image consciousness. I can immerse myself in the photograph of a friend, for example, but the photograph might also trigger memories and encourage phantasies that lead me away from what I see in the image to other appearances. One might also stipulate arbitrarily that a certain image will serve as a sign. In that case, the function of the image would not be to invite seeing-in but to give directions or serve as a warning about something not yet perceived. A full-blown image, however, would seem to be less effective in meeting such pragmatic requirements than a conventional schematic sign. If Manet's *Bar at the Folies Bergère* were suspended from the ceiling of an airport concourse to indicate the location of a bar, passengers might well become so immersed in the sign/image that they would never find the bar, or, if they did find it, would feel disappointed that it does not resemble what they saw in the image. Of course, if small reproductions of Manet's painting were universally accepted in airports as the sign for bars, then the painting's stipulated function as a sign would trump its status as an image. Similarly, if the purpose of a sign is to indicate an unseen turn in the road ahead, a yellow, diamond-shaped marker with a curved black arrow on its surface would be more effective than André Derain's painting, *The Turning Road, L'Estaque* (1906), in which one sees the turn in the image, and much else besides, all in the wild hues of Fauvism. Travel on winding roads would become more risky, not less, if the signs warning of approaching curves consisted of elaborate paintings like Derain's. They would invite seeing-in, a delightful activity to pursue in an art museum, but a dangerous distraction on the road, since when one sees in, one does not see beyond. Signs demand 'seeing-out' rather than 'seeing-in' for good reason.

6 RESEMBLANCE, DIFFERENCE, AND SEEING-IN

Granted that we are able to see images as representing something, that is, that we are capable of seeing-in in the two senses we have described, what is it about the image itself that brings image consciousness and seeing-in into play?

A common answer is that images are able to represent through resemblance. This reply has often been challenged. The principal criticisms are that images do not resemble their subjects and that the reputed resemblance between image and imaged is arbitrary and ultimately a matter of convention. These criticisms are misguided. First there is, phenomenally, at least some degree of resemblance between an image and what it images, as we shall see shortly. Furthermore, there must be some resemblance if we are to experience an image and not just a sign, which does not have to resemble what it signifies. The kind of resemblance at work in image consciousness, however, differs from resemblance as it is commonly understood, which involves an external relation. The resemblance in imaging is instead an internal matter bound to 'seeing-in'; it makes possible seeing something in a physical support or a subject in an image.

Normally, when we say that one thing resembles another, we have in mind comparing different things—identical twins, for example, or two buildings—and noting their similarities. The comparison can be made between present things, between absent things, or between something present and something absent. I can compare the identical twins standing in front of me right now and see that they resemble each other perfectly, or nearly so. That, however, does not make one twin the image of the other. Even two pictures or two sculptures, which are already images—two prints of Cartier-Bresson's photograph of Simone de Beauvoir, for example—can resemble one another without either being the image of the other. As Husserl succinctly puts it, 'the resemblance between two objects, however great it may be, still does not make one into the image of the other' (Husserl 1970: 594). One might respond to this that in imaging I do not compare two present things but something that is absent with something that is present, and that it is precisely the resemblance between what is present with what is absent that makes the former the image of the latter. Richard Wollheim refers to this as the 'resemblance view', which identifies the experience of the image 'with that sort of experience in which the spectator compares...what is in front of him with something that is absent' (Wollheim 1987: 77). But even this would not account for imaging. A painting that is present to me now does not become an image simply because a comparison shows its resemblance to something absent, anymore than the resemblance between a twin I am seeing now and her absent sibling makes the present twin the image of her sister. Furthermore, resembling taken as an external relationship is reciprocal, while imaging is not. David's painting of Napoleon in his study may be an image of the emperor, but Napoleon himself is not an image of the painting.

A corollary to the resemblance view is that something becomes an image because it is a copy or imitation of what it represents. Copies, however, are not images. They are separate objects that duplicate or reproduce other objects, and, as Rebecca West is reported to have said about the imitation theory of art: 'A copy of the universe is not what is required of art; one of the damned things is ample.' Images, whether works of art or not, fulfil their purpose by representing, not by reproducing or replicating.

The objections I have outlined above are not fatal to the claim that resemblance plays a fundamental role in image consciousness, for the resemblance in imaging is not an external relationship established by comparing two separate objects or appearances. There is only one appearance in image consciousness: the appearance that is the image itself. What the image represents does not have a separate appearance of its own. Since image consciousness offers only a single appearance, the awareness of the resemblance that makes depicting possible cannot be a matter of comparing one appearance with another. It is rather a question of seeing-in: seeing-in and the resemblance underlying it are inseparable moments internal to image consciousness. I see the resemblance and through it recognize or see something in the image. This can happen because of the unique ontological status the image enjoys. It is, as we have seen, nothing real. Its whole being is to show, to represent, to exhibit, that is, to let something be seen in it through resemblance.

The resemblance to what the image depicts is inherent in the image, then, intentionally produced there by the image-maker. This is not the case for ordinary things, which may incidentally resemble other things, but do not have to. In saying that the image must resemble what it depicts if we are to see something in it, we are claiming, in a sense, that we see the resemblance of the thing with itself, but with itself in the image, not outside it; or better, that we recognize and identify the thing in its image. Resemblance in the case of imaging involves the being of something in the image, its 'image being' or representational being as opposed to its real being. It is still the same thing in both cases, however, although in its image being it is not present in person, as it would be if it were actually being perceived.

This notion of a resemblance that shows itself internally as opposed to resemblance as an external relation must defend itself against two criticisms: first, that it is obscure; and second, that images are not based on resemblance in any sense. I shall consider the second objection first. Nelson Goodman takes works of art, and by extension images generally, to be symbols or signs that denote, and argues that they are independent of resemblance. Resemblance is neither necessary nor sufficient for reference, Goodman claims, since 'almost anything may stand for almost anything else' (Goodman 1976: 5). That may be true of signs, which do not involve seeing-in and do not have to resemble their referents, but it certainly does not seem to be true of images. Images do not 'stand for' things; rather, things are in images and are seen in images. Paraphrasing Goodman, it would be more accurate to say, as far as images are concerned, that 'in almost anything one cannot see almost anything else.' In the absence of resemblance in any sense, it is difficult to see how seeing-in and therefore imaging could occur at all. As Robert Hopkins observes: 'Representations are only able to represent aspects of the world by maintaining some connection between how they represent it as being and how it really is' (Hopkins 1998: 34).

This brings us to the second objection. What does 'internal resemblance' really mean, and how does it make seeing-in possible? This is an especially acute question with respect to the first sort of seeing-in. If resemblance in imaging depended on comparing two appearances, then I would see a human figure in a photograph by comparing the appearance of the physical support—a piece of paper with patches of grey on its surface—with the appearance of a human being, noting the resemblance between the two. However, as we have seen, I do not in fact have a separate appearance of the physical support that I could compare with the appearance of a human being. The seeing of the support and the seeing of the human figure in it are fused. There must nevertheless be some resemblance between what is seen in the image and the features of the physical support; that is, the lines, shading, colour, and so on, must be such that I can see something in them. The source of this resemblance, I would argue, resides in an 'idea' of what I see in the image. The idea 'human being', for example, comes into play when I see a human figure in the support. This idea 'prescribes certain possibilities for perception: a human being is something that has a certain look in perception' (Husserl 2005: 585). If what I see in the physical support displays this 'look', I experience the image of a human being. The idea is not an appearance with which I compare what I see. Rather, it radiates from what I see, animating it internally. This assumes, of course, that I am acquainted with the 'look' of whatever is supposed to be seen in the image. Seeing something in a representation, Robert Hopkins writes, 'essentially requires a knowledge of how things look' (Hopkins 1998: 34). Resemblance and seeing-in are therefore mediated by the cognitive resources of the spectator. If I lack the appropriate 'idea', the embedded acquaintance with the 'look', I will be incapable of seeing the corresponding object in the support.

Resemblance in this sense serves as a check on seeing just anything I want to see in an image. I cannot see a giraffe, for example, in Cartier-Bresson's photograph of Simone de Beauvoir because I know what a human being looks like, and the visible form present on the surface of the physical support sufficiently resembles what I know to demand that I see in it a human being, while there is nothing at all there to make me see a giraffe.

To defend the role of resemblance in image consciousness is obviously not to claim that the resemblance must be perfect. In fact, the opposite is the case. The resemblance must precisely not be perfect; it must be paired with and permeated by difference and even conflict. 'A consciousness of difference must be there', Husserl writes, if we are to experience an image' (Husserl 2005: 22). If the resemblance were perfect in every respect, ordinary perception or seeing-face-to-face would displace image consciousness. The image would be mistaken for what it represents, producing an illusion rather than an image. Although a standard of correctness is at work in image consciousness, it demands difference as much as it demands similarity.

The possible differences touch every aspect of imaging. Perhaps the most obvious of these is an outright conflict with the perceptual surroundings of the image. The image's physical support thrusts it into the world, but what appears in the image does not really belong there. A street represented in shades of grey in a photograph does not fit into the room where the photograph hangs. If I look to the right or left of the image, I do not see a continuation of the represented street, as I would if it were part of my actual environment. Instead I see the red wall of my living room and a table with a vase full of flowers. There is nothing I can do to fill the empty horizons of the photograph. This disjunction between surrounding world and image is just one of the ways in which resemblance falls short and combines with difference to signal that it is an image I am experiencing, not an actual street. Another is the conflict within the image itself between what actually appears and what is represented. The face of a woman I see in the photograph appears as small and grey, but I know that women's faces are not grey and that women do not occupy a grey world and are not just a few inches high. The image does not present the woman in her real colour and size, and I am aware of that. However, I do mean her with her real qualities when I look at the image. This difference between what appears in the photograph and what I mean again makes me aware that what I am perceiving is an image and not actually the reality the image internally represents. To 'mean' the real features of what is depicted, it is important to note, is not to imagine or intuit them in separate acts of phantasy or memory. I could do that, of course, but then I would have left image consciousness behind and taken up residence in visual imagination, which is a different kind of experience and does not involve seeing-in.

Given the differences that attend them, the resembling features of an image might best be described as 'analogous' to the features of what is represented in the image, with 'analogous' understood in its standard meaning of resemblance in some respects between things that otherwise are different. The image can be rich or poor in resembling traits. The only limit to the poverty is that a certain minimal level of resemblance must be present if a physical object is to be depicted. Robert Hopkins finds this in what he calls 'outline shape' (Hopkins 1998: 53), and Husserl locates it in 'plastic form' (Husserl 2005: 90). Beyond that there seem to be no hard and fast rules governing the degree of analogy, or of resemblance and difference, required for seeing-in. An image might, as in a spare drawing by Matisse, simply outline a human face with a single continuous black line. This would be enough to let me see the face in the shape traced by the line, but I would be aware that the complex tonal contrasts of the face are absent. The same idea of the human face that lets me see a face in the drawing also tells me how much is missing from the image. Relative poverty in image-content need not be an aesthetic flaw, of course; it might, in fact, contribute to the aesthetic force of the work. At the other extreme, a painting by Raphael might offer the full human figure in colours analogizing the tones of skin, hair, lips, eyes, garments, and much else besides. Still, no matter how rich the resembling content in the image might be, differences must remain if image consciousness is not to give way to perceptual illusion.

There can, to be sure, be instances in which features appearing in the image can be perfectly faithful to what the image depicts. In the case of a sculpted bust, for example, the image-shape of a head and the physical substratum supporting it can be identical to the actual shape of the subject's head. I would see the shape of the head in the image without difference or conflict. This perfect resemblance in one respect, however, is interwoven with other traits that analogize less perfectly, or perhaps not at all, as would be the case with respect to colour if the head were made of white porcelain. Such differences keep the image-appearance firmly planted in the realm of semblance, despite the faithfulness of this feature or that.

To say that certain traits analogize imperfectly is not to make a value judgement. Aside from the fact that their deviation is necessary to the constitution of the image as something distinct from reality, their very 'imperfection' may tell us that the image is a work of art and contribute essentially to its aesthetic value. In such cases I do not take the deviant features as occasions to abandon image consciousness and turn to phantasies or memories that might fill the gaps and correct the distortions. Instead I contemplate the image aesthetically, immersing myself in it, distortions and all. Picasso's *Guernica*, for example, whose subject is the bombing of the Basque city during the Spanish Civil War, is an image in black and white and shades of grey in which I see, among other things, a bull, a horse, men, women, children, a light bulb, all appearing in the distorted forms familiar from Picasso's work. The event and presumably Picasso's reaction to it are seen in the sombre tones, and in the truncated and fractured figures strewn across the canvas in physical and emotional agony. Because it is an image, the painting can contain the event in its fury and express Picasso's vision of how the people it engulfed experienced it. The overall appearance of the image, the distorted faces and forms I see in it, the grey palate, may not be 'faithful' depictions of human beings or of a city under bombardment, but their deviations from the literal not only contribute to the constitution of the image but express something much deeper than ordinary resemblance could hope to convey.

7 DEPICTION, THE SUBJECT, AND SEEING-IN REVISITED

The notions of depiction, seeing-in, the subject, and even the image are more fluid than I have suggested. In this final section I take a further look at these aspects of imaging, starting with the subject and focusing on nonobjective or abstract art.

Some images represent specific historical persons or events; others represent particular fictional or mythological beings. This is one sense of the subject. Another is a painting's or sculpture's motif taken in very general terms—sunflowers in a work by van Gogh, a kiss in a sculpture by Rodin. For many artists, however, particularly nonfigurative artists from the last hundred years or so, these notions of the subject would be much too restrictive. The Abstract Expressionists, for example, far from denying that their works had subjects, insisted, as Mark Rothko and Adolf Gottlieb wrote, that 'the subject is crucial and only that subject matter is valid which is tragic and timeless' (Johnson 1982: 14). Rothko's mature paintings are not depictive images in the ordinary sense, that is, they do not have manifest subjects—a mountain, a horse, a satyr—drawn from the perceptual or fictional worlds. Even Picasso, who engages in a considerable degree of abstraction in *Guernica*, intends us to see recognizable things in his picture. Indeed, seeing them in their distorted forms is essential to grasping the meaning of the painting. Rothko intends us to see something in his paintings as well, but not something that we can so readily identify.

Barnett Newman, Rothko's contemporary and fellow abstract painter, also held that subject matter is central to art, but Newman presents a somewhat perplexing case. Richard Wollheim, for example, thought that Newman's mature works do not permit seeing-in. Wollheim did not claim that images must be figurative, but he did think that they must represent something, and that representation requires seeing 'things three-dimensionally related' in a marked surface (Wollheim 1987: 21). On this basis, a signature painting by Rothko, with its rectangular planes of colour floating in front of a background, would be an image, while Newman's huge *Vir Heroicus Sublimis*, which is a flat, rectangular expanse of red punctuated from top to bottom by a few thin lines or 'zips', would not be. One sees nothing three-dimensional in its surface. Husserl thought that 'without an image, there is no fine art' (Husserl 2005: 41)—a debatable proposition for which I will not argue here—but I will attempt to show that it is still possible to preserve the connection between image, seeing-in, and subject in Newman's painting, the absence of three-dimensionality notwithstanding. A first step would be to take seriously the artist's claim that the work has a subject, as the title indicates. Even if one does not see anything three-dimensional in its surface, it may still be true that one sees something there. Specifically, Newman claims that what one sees in the painting has a metaphysical significance. 'My painting is physical and . . . my painting is metaphysical', he wrote; it has an 'intellectual content' and is therefore 'philosophic' (Newman 1990: 280, 155). Since intellectual contents are 'of an abstract nature', artists such as Newman who sought to embody them in their work were led inevitably to the creation of forms 'that by their abstract nature carry some abstract intellectual content' (Newman 1990: 140). Although these statements are redolent of Abstract Expressionist rhetoric from the 1940s and 1950s, they still tell us much about the possibilities of artistic imagery generally and about Newman's images in particular.

This turn to the abstract did not reflect a belief that abstraction automatically guarantees the presence of serious subject-matter. In fact, Newman thought that much twentieth-century abstract art had ignored the subject and become 'decorative'. Newman and his contemporaries, on the other hand, insisted that their paintings, colourful and visually enticing as they often were, would nonetheless 'insult anyone who is attuned to interior decoration' (Johnson 1982: 14). They knew that decoration was ultimately inimical to imaging, or at least to imaging with serious content. Decoration absorbs the art work into its surroundings, compelling it to submit to a larger decorative scheme and obscuring the conflict with its environment that is essential to its being an image. Paintings selected primarily with an eye to decorating a room, for example, probably will not provoke much interest as images. The point in selecting them is to have them harmonize with the other things in the room. The image becomes, in effect, an ordinary object, like the couches, chairs, rugs, and wall coverings surrounding it. It becomes a moment in a pleasing ensemble, chosen not because of what can be seen in it—its content—but because it harmonizes with its exterior environment, just as one might select books with fine leather bindings for one's library because they contribute to the room's overall aesthetic effect, not because they contain important ideas between their covers. The thrust of decoration, then, is toward environmental harmony rather than the environmental conflict that marks imaging. The Abstract Expressionists, on the other hand, sought to 'reveal truth' (Johnson 1982: 14), which, they thought, involves resistance to the ordinary. Their aim in resorting to abstraction was revelatory, not decorative. It is not surprising, then, that Newman said that his paintings 'are hostile to the environment' (Newman 1990: 307). It is this 'hostility' that lets him sow in his paintings the ideas that move and deeply concern him (Newman 1990: 254).

Granting that images intending to be serious art must have serious subjects and must stand out from their environment, the question remains about what it means to say that their content is metaphysical. Indeed, it might be argued that metaphysical content is incapable of exhibiting itself in a visual image. This view, however, represents much too narrow a conception of what can be seen in a work of art. Newman, with his more expansive notion of 'intellectual' or 'philosophic content', agrees with Husserl's claim that the image in art is an 'intellectually mediated semblance' and not merely sensuous (Husserl 2005: 172). Artistic semblances are mediated because they can embrace a broad array of beliefs, feelings, and events that can appear in an image and yet transcend immediate sensuous presentation. As Husserl observes, 'art can be philosophical, metaphysical, elevating one to the idea of the good, to the deity … to the deepest world-ground, uniting one with it' (Husserl 2005: 654). It is true that bare perceiving, the so-called 'innocent eye', will not suffice to open up such philosophical or metaphysical content. Image consciousness, however, does not have to be naive; it can and should be as sophisticated as the image of which it is aware. Newman, of course, knew this. His paintings demand what I would call a 'mediated seeing-in' capable of penetrating the intellectually mediated image. The image in art, after all, is a cultural phenomenon, created within a distinct historical horizon and capable of embodying meanings flowing from the religious, philosophical, artistic, and social consciousness of the age. This is particularly true of Newman's paintings, which reflect not only their maker's feeling but also his relation to the tumultuous course of modern art and to a world transformed by war and profound social change. Truly to see Newman's *Vir Heroicus Sublimis*—to see in it its content—involves bringing to it a fund of knowledge and insight about the subject and its way of being presented that straightforward perception may not be able to offer. As Thomas Hess said of the depiction of the crucifixion in the *Eisenheim Altarpiece*: 'If you don't know the New Testament, you can't even see the Eisenheim Altarpiece' (Hess 1978: 187). Mediated seeing-in will not dispel the ambiguity of Newman's painting, which in any case is a condition of its strength and presence, but it can deepen our understanding of it. One must live with the work, becoming absorbed in it over time and getting to know it as one might get to know another person.

What, then, are the ideas carried within the abstract form of *Vir Heroicus Sublimis*? Newman said that the titles of his works often furnish a clue to the meaning they embody. *Vir Heroicus Sublimis*—'man heroic and sublime'—is a case in point. The title is intended to suggest 'that man can be sublime in his relation to his sense of being aware' (Newman 1990: 258). The abstract image gives this intangible idea reality. Jonathan Fineberg observes that the painting 'projects a metaphysical absoluteness': its vast expanse of red 'evokes the universe, the infinite... The zips, on the other hand, convey the painter's presence and spatially establish the relation of the individual to the wider order of things' (Fineberg 1995: 103). The zips in Newman's paintings thus have an analogizing force. They divide and connect, giving the spectator a sense 'of his own individuality, and at the same time of his connection to others, who are also separate' (Newman 1990: 257–8). Through its form, one sees in the painting these divisions and connections, its 'metaphysical' ideas. Stephen Policari adds that *Vir Heroicus Sublimis* 'renders the joy and sublime heroism of humanity through the rhythmically accented dazzling red' (Policari 1991: 202). The spread and the size of the painting exhibits an expansive idea of human nobility in an image that transcends the particular and lets the spectator see in it something of the nature of a universal condition, the sublimity and heroism of humanity. It is this that the work exhibits and that can be seen in it by the informed and sympathetic spectator. In Arthur Danto's formulation, which is quite congenial to phenomenology, *Vir Heroicus Sublimis* is 'about' something, 'embodies' what it is about, and 'shows' it (Danto 2000: 132, 133).

8 CONCLUSION

Mark Rothko said that 'there is no such thing as a good painting about nothing' (Johnson 1982: 14). Paintings that matter are about something that matters. But it is precisely because the painting itself, as an image, has the peculiar nature of being 'nothing' that it can be about something. Images enrich our experience by folding into themselves the world and our relation to it, our feelings and our beliefs, offering them to our contemplation and bringing their truth before us, moving and delighting us. Though images may be nothing real, nothing embraces reality better.

REFERENCES

Danto, A. (2000), 'Art and meaning', in N. Carroll (ed.), *Theories of Art Today* (Madison: University of Wisconsin Press).

Ferino-Pagden, S. (2010), Brochure accompanying the exhibition 'Arcimboldo, 1526–1593. Nature and Fantasy', National Gallery of Art, Washington, 2010–11.

Fineberg, J. (1995), Art since 1940: Strategies of Being (New York: Harry N. Abrams).

Goodman, N. (1976), *Languages of Art* (Indianapolis: Hackett Publishing Co.).

Hess, T. (1978), 'The stations of the Cross: Lema Sabachthani', in Carmean, E. (ed.), *The Subjects of the Artists* (Washington: National Gallery of Art).

Hopkins, R. (1998), *Picture, Image, and Experience* (Cambridge: Cambridge University Press).

Husserl, E. (1970), *Logical Investigations, Volume II* (New York: Humanities Press).

—— (2005), *Phantasy, Image Consciousness, and Memory (1898–1925)* (Dordrecht: Springer).

Johnson, H. (ed.) (1982), *American Artists on Art from 1940 to 1980* (New York: Harper and Row).

Newman, B. (1990), *Selected Writings and Interviews* (New York: Alfred A. Knopf).

Policari, S. (1991), *Abstract Expressionism and the Modern Experience* (Cambridge: Cambridge University Press).

Sartre, J-P. (2004), *The Imaginary* (London and New York: Routledge).

Sokolowski, R. (1977), 'Picturing', *The Review of Metaphysics*, XXXI/1: 5–28.

Wollheim, R. (1987), *Painting as an Art* (Princeton: Princeton University Press).

....

CHAPTER 27

PHENOMENOLOGICAL AND AESTHETIC *EPOCHÉ*: PAINTING THE INVISIBLE THINGS THEMSELVES

....

RUDOLF BERNET

THE present volume demonstrates well enough that phenomenology is not only concerned with the visual perception of 'things'. In addition to things, empirical or ideal states of affairs and mental states of all sorts show themselves from themselves. And all that shows, appears, manifests, discloses, gives, intimates, or announces itself does not rely for this on 'visual perception'. Other kinds of sensuous perceptions involving touch, hearing, smell, and taste have been widely explored by phenomenologists. Such non-visual perceptions also make one realize that not all that is perceived needs to be a thing or an 'object' of some kind and that even perceived things and objects are of different sorts, can be given in a manifold of ways and present themselves on the basis of non-thingly experiential dimensions. Accordingly, and without transcending the limits of sensuous experience, phenomenologists have investigated supra-thingly and infra-thingly phenomena and their relation to things. They have exposed how space, without being a property of things, still needs things to become manifest. Similarly they have been led to admit that sensuously experienced feelings, despite their difference from things perceived, can be perceived under the form of an emotional 'colouration' of things.

It is also necessary to do away with the prejudice that a phenomenology of perception necessarily involves some kind of 'intuitionism' or 'metaphysics of presence'. One must emphasize, instead, that not all that shows itself to a perceiver lends itself to an explicit perception and that all that appears intuitively is surrounded by the shadow of unapparent and absent moments. There is, indeed, no such thing as an adequate visual perception of a thing because all things appear through partial 'adumbrations' (*Abschattungen*) and within a 'horizon' that extends far beyond what is actually perceived. This well-known Husserlian insight can be further articulated in terms of a 'lack' and an 'excess' that characterize all intuitive givenness of perceptual things. Such a lack and excess make that the relation between a perceiving subject and a perceived thing is never 'quite right'. Despite their intentional 'correlation', perceiver and perceived never perfectly match or mirror one another. This non-coincidence or difference is what Husserl means by the 'inadequate intuitive fulfilment' of all thing-perception. This is to say, on the one hand, that the perceiver always intends more than what she really sees. She intends the entire thing and not just fleeting and partial adumbrations of it. According to this first scenario, the lack is entirely on the side of the givenness of the thing perceived and the excess on the side of the intentions of the perceiver. On the other hand, however, what shows itself to the perceiver is always more than what she can grasp. The thing shows qualities and meanings the perceiver did not expect and its shining appearance carries a 'comet tail' of other possible appearances and other things possibly appearing. In this second scenario, the lack is thus on the side of the perceiver and the excessive richness on the side of the appearing phenomena.

According to Husserl, both kinds of interplay between lack and excess in visual perception are usually overlooked and are thus in need of a phenomenological eye in order to be properly noticed and attended to. Ordinary perception serves our orientation in a familiar world, and it does so most efficiently when the handling of useful things and tools is not held up by our wondering about their way of appearing. In order to be noticed or to appear as such, ways of appearing are in need of what Husserl calls a phenomenological *epoché*—that is, a suspension of the normal course of perceptual life. Thus, the 'things themselves' attended to by phenomenology are not ordinary things, but things in their mode of givenness, the 'pure phenomena' disclosed by the phenomenological *epoché*. The suspension of natural life allows for a new form of perceiving and, more generally, of experiencing. Instead of being drawn, like the ordinary perceiver, from one thing to the next by the needs and concerns of practical life, the phenomenological perceiver takes advantage of an (actively produced or passively undergone) interruption of this life to pay attention to the intentional correlation between the things in their way (or their 'how') of appearing to her and her way of apprehending these appearances of things.

It is thus only a phenomenological *epoché* of natural life that makes the phenomenologist aware of the interplay between lack and excess that characterizes the intentional correlation between a perceiver and a thing perceived. Depending on her specific interests, the phenomenologist will then behave according to the first or second scenario described. A phenomenologist, whose main concern is to critically measure her perception and understanding of things against the extent and mode of their intuitive appearing, will emphasize that she perceives more than what is actually given to her. Localizing the lack on the side of givenness of the thing, she will require further thingly givenness to confirm her views and to make certain that her perception is correct. This first phenomenologist will, like Husserl himself, consider perception to be a kind of *knowledge*, the truthfulness of which is in need of being critically examined. Phenomenology of perception thus becomes a branch of a 'theory of knowledge' (*Erkenntnistheorie*). Another phenomenologist, more interested in the things themselves and the wealth of their modes of appearing, will be inclined, instead, to pay careful attention to the excess in thingly givenness and to her own lack of preparation for it.

A paper dealing with the possibility and nature of a phenomenology of artistic painting need only be concerned with this second phenomenologist. The *first* and most obvious question to be asked is then whether performing or submitting oneself to a kind of phenomenological *epoché* is necessary (and sufficient?) to become an amateur of paintings or a painter. Linked to this is then the further question of whether a phenomenology of painting provides a mere illustration for a phenomenological mode of perception or whether a phenomenologist can also learn something new from closely studying paintings. More insidiously, one must ask whether Merleau-Ponty's account of Cézanne is more than an application of his phenomenology of bodily perception and whether Henry's account of Kandinsky is more than an application of his phenomenology of pure self-affection. Needless to say, however, neither Merleau-Ponty nor Henry would go so far as to claim that Cézanne and Kandinsky were basically just good phenomenologists. Hence our *second* question: what is it that makes the ways of perceiving of these painters unique and how is this mode of perception related to what and how they paint? What is needed to transpose a pictorial mode of perception into a painted image on a framed canvas? Did Cézanne and Kandinsky just paint what they had already seen or did their paintings make something visible (for themselves and others) that otherwise can never be seen? If the latter were the case, then we could not avoid asking also what this *invisible* that only painting can make visible is like and how it relates to what we normally see, to what phenomenologists see, and to what painters see. Asking this *third* question properly means that one does not presuppose that the invisible made visible in paintings is of the same nature as the visible in which it is made to appear.

In his book on Francis Bacon, Deleuze agrees with Henry that the main object of the art of painting is the action and expression of invisible 'forces' and not the 'enigma of the visible world' (Merleau-Ponty). Even if their understanding of the nature of the invisible forces active in the paintings of Bacon and Kandinsky differs substantially—just as does their account of the possibility or impossibility to make them visible in a painting—Deleuze and Henry also agree that the art of painting is as much a matter of affectivity as of visibility. More precisely, the art of painting becomes for them a matter of perceived visible figures and felt affects that are commanded by invisible forces rather than by mundane or psychological laws. But if the act of painting does not have its ultimate origin in the enigma of the visible world, and if painted images operate a de-formation of the visible world rather than its exquisite transformation, then paintings become a very peculiar kind of phenomenon. Consequently, both the task and method of a phenomenology of painting need to be carefully reconsidered.

1 The phenomenological and pictorial *epoché* of visual perception

It was Husserl himself who, in a now famous letter to the Austrian poet Hugo von Hofmannsthal (Husserl 1994: 133–6), first compared the attitude of the phenomenologist to the attitude of an artist. Both the phenomenologist and the artist consider things, persons, events, and the entire world from a distance and with wonder. Compared to ordinary people (or with themselves in ordinary life), phenomenologists and artists have both lost and gained something at the same time. What they have lost is their familiarity with the surrounding world, their spontaneous understanding of the meanings of things, and their capacity to immediately see what needs to be done in all circumstances of practical life. What they have gained is a perception of the world freed from the need of orientation, a non-instrumental relation to things, and a consideration of worldly events and situations for their own sake. Phenomenological and artistic perceivers have thus exchanged their own know-how about things and their knowledge of the world for the discovery of the coming forth or 'birth' of both things and the world out of a manifold of ever changing appearances. It would be wrong, however, to view this transformation that is brought about by the suspension or *epoché* of natural life as a turning away from objectivism or naturalism in favor of a mere subjectivism. It is true that appearances always appear to someone. However, it is no less true that artists and phenomenologists wish to overcome their personal opinions, presuppositions, and preferences in order to open themselves as much as possible to the beauty and lessons of the phenomena as mere phenomena.

It goes without saying that attending to the shining beauty of appearances and attending to what they can teach us about the true nature of things is not the same. But no painter would deny that the contemplation of the beauty of the fugitive formations of clouds in a late afternoon light enriches her knowledge of a landscape. And it is possible that no phenomenologist would deny that describing the multiple 'adumbrations' of an ashtray for the sake of making correct perceptual statements first made her aware of the beauty of this thing. It also goes without saying that a *pictorial epoché* and a *phenomenological epoché* suspend different sorts of prejudices. The painter will have to overcome a schematic seeing of familiar shapes and their distribution in a geometrical space in order to perceive colours just as colours, light and shadows, or empty spaces. The phenomenologist will have to forget all scientific theories about the nature of perception and the physical world in order to see a web of interrelated appearances where others can only see solid things existing in and by themselves. But it is equally true that the painter and the phenomenologist both turn towards a world that is still in the making and to a making of the world that owes nothing to familiar concepts, scientific theories, and logical laws.

Doubting whether this realm of a primitive experience under *epoché* could still be called a 'world', Merleau-Ponty has referred to it as 'brute Being' and has untiringly explored the 'dimensions' of its 'sensible *logos*'. Characteristically, Merleau-Ponty's account of the *pictorial epoché* always has both a negative and a positive side. On the negative side we find his lengthy critical discussion of Descartes's theory of visual perception as a spiritual inspection of coloured shapes that are localized in an homogeneous extended space. Descartes' philosophy of mind and the Renaissance doctrine of drawing according to the rules of perspective are shown to be equally guilty of an intellectual reconstruction that overlooks the simplest phenomena of bodily perception. On the positive side of the pictorial *epoché* we find Merleau-Ponty's stress on the 'ambiguity' in the appearing of things, on 'the gaze of things', on the sensible logic of a 'seeing according to' (*voir selon*), and on a perceiving and painting that is in tune with 'the invisible' in the visible things and landscapes. Let us look at these elements of a phenomenology of pictorial perception one by one.

Ambiguity in visual appearances can be illustrated by the fact that we can see both the foliage of a tree and an infinite variety of leaves, both apples with round volumes detached from a table and the same apples with uncertain contours mixing with the flat surface of the table, both a mountain far away and the same mountain as part of the surrounding things we can grasp with our hands. In Merleau-Ponty's view, Cézanne, like no other painter, has been able to render these perceptual ambiguities in his paintings. This is not only to say that his painted apples, trees, and Montagnes Sainte-Victoire appear in a way that is as ambiguous as the actual things and landscape. It also means that, as a 'visible of the second power' (Merleau-Ponty 2004: 296), his paintings make us aware of the uncertain and changing modes of appearing belonging to the ordinary things of our perception. We can now see the real mountain as Cézanne has painted it and we are led to see things that are unknown to him as he would have painted them. When we leave the museum, people and even streets and cars can look ambiguously Cézanne-like to us.

Merleau-Ponty's theory of perception is also known for having emphasized that seeing is a matter of bodily movements, that our seeing body is simultaneously a body seen (by us and by others), and that—far from perceiving things as objects in front of us—we perceive things from a place 'among things' (*du milieu des choses*) (Merleau-Ponty 2004: 295) and 'from the inside' (*du dedans*) (Merleau-Ponty 2004: 309, 317) of a mundane connection of things. Since we are also seen bodies, no things seen by us can be completely foreign to us. Whether we perceive our own body or the things around us, perceiver and perceived are always 'cut from the same cloth' (*taillés dans la même étoffe*). They are not different by nature but become different only by the very process of perception that introduces a 'distance' (*écart*) in what naturally hangs together. There is thus, in principle, no good reason why 'the reversibility' that characterizes the relation between my touching hand and my hand touched (which can, in turn, touch the first hand) would not also apply to the relation between my perceiving body and the things perceived by me (and others). This is to say that what I see can also be experienced (by me and not by itself) as seeing me and as making me feel seen by what I see. Between the perceiver 'and the visible the roles are reversed' (Merleau-Ponty 2004: 299).

But is such an experience of feeling seen or even gazed at by a perceived table or knife not a pathological—that is, schizophrenic—experience? This would be the case only if the things that see me were to look at me as other human persons do. Clearly, this cannot be what Merleau-Ponty has in mind. By quoting painters such as Cézanne and Klee at length, he rather wants to make us understand that things, in their ambiguous gazes or looks, invite the painter to have a closer look at them. He also wants to stress that the invitation into this dialectical exchange of looks comes from the things and not from the painter. It is thus a dialogue that begins with a question, and where the first question is put to the painter by the things. For us all to share this experience, it suffices to submit our ordinary perception to a *pictorial epoché*: to let all recognition, understanding, and seeing-as of things go, and to allow ourselves to feel puzzled, irritated, or interrogated by the things we see. Things then begin to look at us by 'letting themselves be seen' in a way that invites us to have a second, third, fourth…look at them.

Time and again, while looking for hours at the mountain with which he had been familiar since early childhood, Cézanne was struck by the 'enigma of its visibility' (Merleau-Ponty 2004: 297). He felt there was a 'lack' (*manque*) (Merleau-Ponty 2004: 297) of coherence in the improbable juxtaposition of patches of colour and a lack of unity binding the 'incompossible' (Merleau-Ponty 2004: 298) elements of stone, sky, trees, and houses together. But he also felt that there must be some hidden sensible logic in the composition of the whole landscape. According to Merleau-Ponty, there was no other way for Cézanne to find out if this was the case than by using his hand, brush, and paint. It was like the mountain had taken hold of his hand and that the painter and the motif were forming one body breathing together in one rhythmic movement of 'inspiration' and 'expiration' (Merleau-Ponty 2004: 299). Painting the 'internal equivalent' (Merleau-Ponty 2004: 296) of the interrogative gaze of the landscape, Cézanne's reply to its mystery was little more than a handing over of the enigma of the invisible in the visible to the spectator of his paintings. We need to return to how he managed to do this.

Merleau-Ponty tries to get a better hold on the 'sensible logic' of the visible, the appearance of which is both ambiguous and enigmatic, through his notion of a '*seeing according to*' (*voir selon*) (Merleau-Ponty 2004: 296). In *Eye and Mind* he describes how one can see not only the bottom of a swimming pool but also the cypresses in the garden, the surrounding landscape, and the sky 'according to' the element of the water, or better, according to appearance of the sunlight reflected by the water (Merleau-Ponty 2004: 313). Such a seeing 'according to' replaces the ordinary seeing 'as' where what is seen is subsumed under some kind of schema, concept, or category and thereby immediately recognized and understood in the common way. On the contrary, when one sees trees according to the mode of appearance in which the water presents or shows itself, one exchanges the common understanding of the nature of trees and of their difference from water for a new aesthetic experience of a 'radiation of the visible' (Merleau-Ponty 2004: 313)—that is, the resonance between different fluid colours vibrating in the hot summer light. Just imagine what Monet could have made of this. Expressed in philosophical language, the aesthetic seeing 'according to' means that every thing—or better, every kind of appearance of something that is not a thing any longer—can inaugurate a new mode of seeing related to the entire visible world.

Most importantly, a perceiving of the world under *epoché* completely changes the meaning of the relation between what we call '*visible*' and '*invisible*'. We have seen that a *phenomenological epoché* already makes us aware of the fact that the perception of a visible thing necessarily includes an awareness of invisible aspects of the same thing. More precisely, the awareness of visible 'adumbrations' of a thing is inseparable from the awareness of the sides of the thing that are merely 'co-intended', but not intuitively given. In other words, without the awareness of the invisible sides, there are no adumbrations at all. The visible and the invisible are so interwoven that it makes perfect sense to speak, with Husserl, of an 'improper *appearing*' (*uneigentliche Erscheinung*) of the invisible. Thus, the not yet visible sides of the thing are not just perceived as possibly becoming visible in the further course of experience, they have a visibility of their own from the beginning.

An aesthetic and especially a *pictorial epoché* considerably enriches the range of appearances that make visible the invisible of the visible. Painters not only see and paint perceptual ambiguities, the interrogative gaze or look of things, the rhythmic resonances between different colours and material elements, the unity of a composition in juxtaposed appearances, and so on. They also see and paint the ordinarily overlooked *conditions* of these appearances: light and shadows, reflections, empty spaces, what is behind and masked by the visible things, how things seen feel when they are touched, the sound they make when they are hurt by another thing... There is something 'magical' (Merleau-Ponty 2004: 298) about the art of painting and, like magicians, painters make everything out of almost nothing. But unlike magicians pulling rabbits out of their hats, painters do not just make absent, 'ghostlike' (Merleau-Ponty 2004: 298), and non-existent things present; painters assemble, distribute, and paint invisible no-things such as the density of a particular material, the trembling of the light, and the ever-receding dimension of 'depth'. The magic art of painting thus suspends the common difference between things and the non-thingly conditions of their visibility, between the visible and the invisible. As the invisible shines through the visible and as visible things give way to the reflections of light, the difference between the visible and the invisible becomes 'undecidable'. Or, as Merleau-Ponty's image of the 'chiasm' or of a Moebius strip suggests, the difference between the visible and the invisible results from a torsion of the same fabric or 'flesh'.

For the ordinary perceiver, this amounts to no less than a complete revolution of her way of seeing and of the ontological nature of what is seen by her. For what is seen, the ontological difference between things and their mode of being becomes just as uncertain as the difference between the visible and the invisible. And in her new seeing of visible things through the medium of ordinarily invisible conditions of their visibility, forms will dissolve in shapes, shapes will become patches of colour, patches of colour will assemble and separate in a ballet dance to a yet unheard musical rhythm. Thus, transformed in her way of seeing the world by her seeing of art, she also sees painted works of art differently. Sensitive to an overall proximity between the visible and the invisible, when visiting an art museum she will pass from the contemplation of figurative paintings to the contemplation of abstract paintings without noticing the difference.

However, and despite what all painted works of art have in common and what philosophers too hastily call 'the essence of painting', each painting is a small world of its own with its own rules of perception, its own sensible logic, and its own ontological categories. Just think of a painting by Klee. It is thus about time that we address the issue of the singularity of works of art and also of what it takes to turn a perception under aesthetic *epoché* into a painting. This will also sharpen our awareness of what distinguishes a perception of the world under a *phenomenological epoché* from the way in which a painter perceives his 'motif' under a *pictorial epoché*.

2 PERCEIVING AND PAINTING THE INVISIBLE OF THE VISIBLE

In order to understand what it means to paint, we need not only account for how the painter transforms her perception into a work of art, we must also return to the difference between the mode of perceiving belonging to the painter and to the phenomenologist. This is necessary to avoid confusing a phenomenological description of the nature of (particular) painted works of art with a (general) account of a phenomenological perception of the world. Actually, there are good reasons to think that what distinguishes the perception of the painter from the perception of the phenomenologist is precisely the fact that the painter *wants to paint* (and not to describe) what she sees. The painting must somehow already be present in the painter's seeing of the brute and savage Being of the things and of the world even before she starts painting.

But how 'somehow'? It certainly cannot mean that the painter sees the landscape she wants to paint already as an image or even that she sees in the landscape what her painting will look like when it is finished. Everything that we have learned from Merleau-Ponty about the 'interrogative gaze' of the Montagne Sainte Victoire, its 'lack' of coherence and need for 'restitution', its taking hold of Cézanne's 'hand' and 'inspiring' the 'expressive' dance of his brush on different parts of the canvas simultaneously, explicitly contradicts such a view. If the painting to be painted announces itself in the way the painter perceives his motif, it can thus never be as a visual anticipation but only as the stimulation to begin painting. Actually, Cézanne and Bacon both emphasize that the origin of their paintings lies in a ruin of the harmonious order of the perceived world, in a kind of 'catastrophe', in their exposure to 'inhuman' and 'chaotic' forces. Thus, compared to the perception of the phenomenologist, there is less image-like coherence in the perception of the painter, not more.

It is thus not entirely unproblematic to ascribe an image- or work-like and bodiless seeing to the painter and to account for the content of her perception as a 'texture' waiting to be 'translated' into the 'work' of a painted image (Figal 2010: 206–30). Even if it seems reasonable to think that painters see differently and see 'more' and than other people, such acuity of perception (they actually share with connoisseurs) is insufficient to turn them into painters. Painters must also see 'less' than other people in order to feel the need or desire to paint. And if there is, indeed, a close relation between their way of seeing and of painting, this is more a matter of a sense lacking than a pre-given image-like sense to be translated and further articulated. Rather than realizing a possible work or painting a pre-given perceptual motif, the painter lends her hand to *chance* and to its distortion of all subjective intentions and perceptual phenomena preceding the act of painting. The very act of painting can bring about a new and unforeseen way of perceiving, which Deleuze calls '*haptique*'.[1] He quotes Bacon saying that as soon as he begins painting, his perceptual 'clichés' and projected images undergo a complete alteration (Deleuze 2003: chap. 11). As a consequence, the painter is the first one to be surprised by her work and to like or dislike it. Giving room to 'chance' (*hasard*) and manipulating 'probabilities' until they give birth to 'improbable Figures', the act of painting is taking the 'risk' that the hand produces works of which the eye of the artist disapproves.

Admittedly, the amount of room given to chance and to a painting hand that is out of subjective control changes from artist to artist and even from work to work. In his book on Bacon, Deleuze provides a helpful classification that goes from absolute chance in 'abstract expressionism' or 'Action Painting' (Pollock) to a seemingly absolute control in 'abstract painting' (Kandinsky, Mondrian). In this scale, Bacon and Cézanne with their manipulated chance or '*chaos germe*' hold the middle (Deleuze 2003: chap. 12). Bacon's manual 'diagrams' and arbitrary strokes, his erasing and blurring what he had already painted never cover the entire surface of his paintings. They thus become regions of the canvas invested with particularly intensive 'forces'. Diagrams destroy recognizable humane forms and change them into 'figures' expressing invisible 'sensations' and 'forces'. Controlled abstract painting in Kandinsky or Mondrian is just another way to do this. It is more radical by departing even further from perception—natural, phenomenological, and pictorial. It is less radical by leaving no room for chance. The geometrical forms and 'compositions' of abstract painting are governed, instead, by the 'necessity' of a 'digital' code and the logic of binary oppositions. Pollock's 'abstract expressionism' represents, on the contrary, an extreme form of celebrating mere chance in the expression of completely chaotic forces. Underlying the difference between necessity and chance and between degrees of abstraction from the perceptual world, there is, however, a common emphasis on the expression of forces shared by these three kinds of painting. For Deleuze, they are all 'non-figurative' because they do not 'represent' the visible world, but rather make visible the invisible forces active in the world, in the universe, or in ourselves. It is thus tempting to view the difference of the forces expressed as the true reason for all the other differences between the three sorts of contemporary painting. This is what we shall attempt to show in our next section.

Cézanne's and Bacon's, Kandinsky's and Pollock's turning away from the still 'figurative' painting of the impressionists was thus less motivated by their will to further explore the new possibilities offered by a pictorial abstraction from ordinary perception than by their decisive experience of invisible forces that do not lend themselves to an expression under the form of some sort of 'figurative' painting. Their new way of painting was thus

---

[1] 'Finally, we will speak of the *haptic*…when sight discovers in itself a specific function of touch that is uniquely its own, distinct from its optical function' (Deleuze 2003: 155).

forced on them by these forces and it is the difference between the forces experienced that explains the difference between their painting—and not the other way around.

However, even so-called 'figurative' paintings actually owe much less to a mere perception of the world than one is often inclined to think. A perception—even under *pictorial epoché*—is at best a necessary but never a sufficient condition for producing a painting (of whatever sort). In addition to perceiving light and shadows, reflections and colour, empty space and depth in the real world, even a figurative painter creates an imaginary world on her canvas. It suffices to think of a painter like Ingres to realize that, strictly speaking, there can be no such thing as a 'realistic' art of painting. The painter's turning way from reality begins already with her choice of a *motif*. A motif is something cut out and isolated from its perceptual context in the real world. Even if the choice of her motif may be forced on the painter by the interrogative gaze of what she perceives, and even if the chosen motif often changes or disappears in the process of painting, the painter nevertheless starts painting something that is more in her mind than in outer reality. Better still, the motif is neither in her mind nor in the external world. Being an 'inner equivalent' of reality, as Cézanne aptly calls it, the motif to be painted is both outside of the mind and buried inside the depth of the world. Unlike what is inside the mind, it can be visually perceived, and unlike what belongs to the external world, not everybody but only the painter can see it.

A second step in the painter's turning away from reality is accomplished by her concern for the *composition* of an artistic image. The composition of a painted image—whether figurative or abstract—has constraints that are completely foreign to the context of real things in the perceptual world. Composition is about the construction of the totality of a unique image that has its own artificial coherence and visual unity. The totality of a particular painted image is thus essentially different from the natural and general evidence belonging to visual 'forms' or '*Gestalt*' and their spontaneous organization through the perceptual schema of the contrast between figure and background. A painting can thus have many centres of interest or none, it can disclose itself immediately in one global gaze or require a long wandering exploration.

Finally, paintings are also unlike the real things of the perceptual world because of the imaginary or *fictional* character that separates them immediately from the realm of real things. It is the frame of a painted image that marks the line of separation or transition between its unreal inside and its real outside. All paintings must have some kind of frame and frames realize the phenomenological miracle of making the ontological difference between an imaginary world and the real world appear as a visual phenomenon. It seems, however, that those phenomenologists who have described the frame of a painted image as some kind of 'window' leading out to the real world were wrong. Indeed, unlike what one sees through an ordinary window, all one sees through the frame of a painting is unreal and not real. The painted image as well as its motif or 'image subject' (*Bildsujet*) (as Husserl would call it (Husserl 2005: no. 1, ch. 2ff)) are essentially and irremediably affected by the frame and therefore remain purely fictional. The fact that some paintings suggest that what is in the painting continues in the real world outside of its frame or that the frame itself is something painted and therefore unreal does not make these paintings more realistic; quite to the contrary, it makes them surrealistic. Just think of Magritte. Similar techniques of an en-framing as well as of a de-framing of the painted image have been part of the art of painting for centuries, and they certainly do not make images more real. Rather, they make reality look more unreal or fictional.

The same can actually be said of the techniques—already practiced with great virtuosity by the Greeks—of painting a *trompe-l'oeil*. A painted *trompe-l'oeil* never quite deceives an aesthetic eye to the extent that one would take the painted image for something real. The grapes painted by Zeuxis only deceive the eyes of birds, and they are really meant to be a source of admiration for his colleague and rival Parrhasius. Parrhasius's way of painting a veil on the wall that makes Zeuxis wonder what other painting might be behind this veil is even more impressive and certainly more subtle. Because what Parrhasius paints is an image that evokes the presence of another even more unreal image. And what his painting eventually suggests is not that something real can be included in a painted image, but rather that all we take to be real is actually mediated in its appearance by imaginary constructions. Pictorial illusions that undo the ontological difference between what is real and what is unreal always work, in the end, to the disadvantage of reality. They also always involve some kind of manipulation of the frame of the image, which constitutes the visual guarantee of the non-coincidence between the imaginary and the real.

Instead of coinciding with the perceived world or 'representing' it 'realistically', paintings, as framed images, rather interact or resonate with both the outer reality and the reality of its 'inner equivalent'. Paintings change our way of perceiving real things, and they make us aware of unknown dimensions of our mind. Unreal and merely imaginary in the ordinary sense, paintings have, however, a reality of their own. They are fictions we can perceive—that is '*perceptual fictions*'—as Husserl most appropriately names them (Husserl 2005: no. 18). As *perceived* images, paintings are not mere dreams or projections of mental images. As perceived *fictions*, however, paintings and their motifs are separated from all ordinary perceptual reality. This is to say, that they require a specific mode of perception one must learn and develop by means of a long practice of artistic contemplation. What one cannot learn, however, is what the contemplation of a particular painting does to each of us and what these emotions or sensations can teach us about its pictorial signification.

The limits of what one can and cannot learn about a proper way of looking at paintings also weigh on the achievements of a *philosophical phenomenology of painting*. One often has the impression that phenomenologists are much more successful in their accounting for the 'essence of painting' than in their description and interpretation of concrete painted artworks. At the same time, their account of this essence of painting is often little more than a mere application of their general phenomenological doctrine. It thus falls painfully short of the close attention particular artworks require and deserve. Every act and kind of painting is, indeed, a singular fact and all paintings are somehow, as Bacon claims, about particular 'matters of fact'. A phenomenology of painting thus cannot limit itself to an exploration of the necessary conditions of the act of painting or of the essential constituents ('elements') of a painting: point, line, colour, pictorial space, frame, imaginary existence, and so on. It must also remain attentive to the singularity of the work of art and the particular matter of fact it is about.

It is true that a familiarity with the essential elements or necessary constituents common to all paintings is of great help when describing a particular painted work of art. It opens one's eyes for its composition and doesn't need to make one blind for the ways in which the general pictorial elements are handled and modified by each particular painting. At the same time, such an *a priori* knowledge implies, however, a true danger of a merely schematic and technical contemplation of paintings. In such an approach, unfortunately common among professionals, identifying the artist and recognizing the style of a particular period of his creative work can become prominent and get in the way of the possibility of losing oneself in the contemplation of a singular painting just of its own sake. The interest in some kind of general knowledge about painting and the interest in what makes each painting unique must rather go hand in hand. And it is eventually always a particular painting in its uniqueness that determines what general knowledge and how much of this knowledge is helpful and compatible with the grasp of its singular signification. Thus, whether in addition to the pictorial elements of point, line, colour, space, composition, and so on, 'meaning' is something to be looked for in the interpretation of a particular painting needs to be decided by the work under consideration itself. And if notions such as 'sensation' or 'force' seem to have a more general relevance for the description especially of non-figurative modern paintings, these notions are still in need of further qualification and specification to match what different painters and different paintings by the same artist let one see.

Building further on Kant's distinction between determinative and reflective judgements, one can say that the interpretation of a painting requires a reflective judgement that works with a very small amount of familiar *a priori* categories and a very large amount of new categories directly derived from the empirical contemplation of singular works of art. In addition to the priority of the empirical or descriptive categories over the *a priori* (but equally 'sensuous') categories, the use of the latter must also always be measured against the phenomenon of the particular work of art under consideration.

3 PAINTING INVISIBLE FORCES AS AN INVISIBLE REALITY

The more a painting moves away from a re-presentation of the perceived reality of things and the world, the more prominent its task of presenting the hidden 'forces' that inhabit and govern painted things and the world becomes. It should come as no surprise that philosophers who take the real world to be a battlefield of antagonistic forces are also particularly sensitive to the forces that manifest themselves in paintings and other artworks. Schopenhauer, but also Hegel and especially Nietzsche, immediately come to mind as possible examples. They all take for granted that the essence of art is metaphysical and that art has the privilege of *making visible* the same metaphysical forces operating in the phenomenal or objective world that philosophy tries to *think conceptually*. As Hegel's philosophy of art shows with particular clarity, such a view involves the risk of turning art into some kind of 'representation' again. Instead of representing outer reality by means of a resembling imitation of its external appearance, painting now becomes a symbolic representation of the hidden metaphysical forces and true essence of reality. The art of painting runs the risk of appearing as a mere servant to a metaphysics that only philosophical thought and reflection can properly comprehend. If one wishes to avoid this consequence, and if one also wishes to preserve the metaphysical relevance of painting, then a new kind of phenomenological or empirical philosophy of painting is required. We shall limit ourselves here to a short presentation of two examples of such a strategy: Henry's book on Kandinsky (Henry 2009) and Deleuze's book on Bacon (Deleuze 2003).

Making extensive use of Kandinsky's theoretical writings, *Henry* aims to show that for Kandinsky the metaphysical forces presiding over reality and the 'spiritual' forces expressed in his paintings are identical. Well aware of how close this brings him to Hegel's position, Henry also puts great emphasis on the fact that the forces experienced and their mode of experience are identical in reality and in painting. Thus, paintings do not just illustrate or represent metaphysical forces that could be more directly experienced in another symbolic medium and also better understood by conceptual thought. Paintings rather contain the metaphysical forces they express, and there is only one way to experience these forces—namely, by feeling them in a 'pathetic' form of affectivity. Actually, according to Henry's 'radical phenomenology', the being of these metaphysical forces coincides with their self-manifestation or phenomenalization. Kandinsky and Henry both call what manifests itself to itself and to us in our pathetic feelings, the forces of 'life'. We can feel these spiritual forces of life in our ordinary lives, but even better by contemplating artworks that are made especially to express them. For Henry, all human forms of experience of the forces of life must, however, be understood as participating in the archi-experience that archi-life has of itself. Being a movement of affective self-manifestation, life is the (immanent and self-affective) archi-phenomenon we can affectively experience both in art and in our lives.

Henry's phenomenological–metaphysical system can thus aptly be rendered and summarized through the following series of relations of identity: (1) life is identical with its *manifestation*, the metaphysical reality of life coincides with the way it manifests itself to itself. The metaphysical essence of life consists in being a phenomenon for itself. Life is therefore always aware of itself; life is the 'archi-subject'. (2) This self-manifestation of life consists in an *affective and passive experience of itself*, an intimate joyful or painful feeling itself and having to bear itself with no possible escape. (3) *All living beings participate in this original life*; their individual lives are in essence not different from the archi-life. There is only one life in all lives. (4) From this identity between life and lives follows the further *identity of their experience*. Just as archi-life experiences itself and its own dynamic forces through the pathos of a self-affection, living beings experience their own life in feeling alive—that is, in the pathos of undergoing the dynamic forces governing their lives. It is through the force of their 'drives and affects' that humans experience their own life as an expression of the forces of the archi-life. They feel the life in their lives and they feel the forces of life in the force of their passions. (5) Just as the forces of archi-life express themselves in human lives, they express themselves and can be *affectively felt in the paintings of Kandinsky*. The forces that govern all the pictorial elements and their composition must therefore be identical with the forces that govern the human passions of love and hate, the human affects of joy and sorrow. Being identical means that Kandinsky's paintings do not just represent or illustrate human feelings; they are these same feelings. 'Colours' do not imitate an 'affective tonality' (Henry 2009: 35 *et passim*); they *are* 'cold and warm, bright and obscure'. When painting 'our drives, our affects, our force', Kandinsky makes us actually feel them.[2]

In the present context it is only the two last relations of identity that are of interest to us: the identity between the experience of affective forces in our lives and in Kandinsky's paintings, and also how both experiences identically derive from the metaphysical reality of a self-affection of the forces of archi-life. What is difficult to understand in this double identity is not that Kandinsky (like most other contemporary painters and especially Bacon) wants to paint ('spiritual') forces, but that the forces contained in his paintings are said to be identical with the force of our affects and that they both must be understood as an expression of the pathetic self-manifestation of archi-life itself. What makes the difficulty look insurmountable is especially Henry's (and not Kandinsky's) claim that the art of painting is in its very essence nothing else than a mode of this self-affection or intimate self-manifestation of archi-life that is said to owe absolutely nothing to visibility, to the conditions of visibility, or to anything visible such as the appearance of things in perceptual adumbrations. After having tried to make good sense of the claim that painters attempt to make the invisible visible, we now find ourselves confronted with the most implausible claim that Kandinsky's paintings are about an *invisible expression* of the forces of an invisible life.

This is, indeed, the claim that Henry makes. For him, true painting must be 'abstract painting' because it belongs to the 'essence of painting' to paint what is, in essence, 'invisible'. Thus, the essence of a painted colour is said to consist in what it makes us feel like and not in something we perceive or in what it makes us see beyond itself. The same holds for all the other pictorial 'elements' such as point, line, '*plan*' or space, and so on. The less figurative their use is, the better, because their true essence consists in nothing else than an 'affective tonality' to be felt and never to be seen. If painting is essentially about the invisible in the sense of something that never lends itself to visual perception, then everything that we have called 'conditions of visibility' also disappears from the art of painting. Painters painting light and shadow are thus unfaithful to the essence of their art. They are guilty of fixing our attention on the visible rather than helping us to abstract from it. The paintings by true painters make us forget about things and the world, they

---

[2] 'Kandinsky's genius is not only to have taken this capacity to paint the invisible—our drives, our affects, our force—to a hitherto unattained level, but also to have provided an explanation of this extraordinary capacity' (Henry 2009: 26).

concentrate on our pathetic feeling of the forces of life. The forms and colours we see on their canvases become mere *occasions* for us to feel the 'affective tonality' belonging to the 'dynamic forces' of life. As such, they are, however, not mere visible signs or symbols representing these forces, they really and invisibly contain them in themselves. The presence and affective experience of the invisible forces of life is so strong in the pictorial elements used by Kandinsky that we completely forget about their visibility. The meaning of Kandinsky's paintings is thus not only 'spiritual' for Henry; it must be called religious. The way in which these paintings make the invisible really present as invisible can best be compared to the *'presentia realis'* of God and his saints in religious icons, or to the invisible real presence of Christ in the Eucharist.

But if what the art of painting is about owes nothing to the visible and can be equally felt in the way we are aware of our own life or of the life in us, then what are paintings still good for? We can break down Henry's answer to this intriguing question into two parts. *First*, painting does not just *express* an inner experience we already had of our own life and of archi-life, it *is* such an experience in its own right. Also, the two experiences are not only equiprimordial, they are essentially experiences of the same and therefore only accidentally different. Just as our experience of archi-life through the pathetic-affective experience of our own life is not psychological, so the presence of archi-life in the affective tonalities of colours is not empirical but spiritual. *Second*, painting and the other arts *add*, however, something substantial both to the self-manifestation of archi-life and to our pathetic-affective experience of life in our lives. Henry never falls short of qualifications for what art adds to life and to its modes of self-manifestation and pathetic experience: 'fulfilment' (*accomplissement*), 'exaltation', 'endless renewal', 'expansion', 'intensification', 'growth' (*accroissement*) of its forces, 'creation of new forces', and so on (Henry 2009: 19 f., 121 ff.) Paintings thus come from life, paintings remain in life, and paintings return to life while contributing to its renewal, reinforcement, and enrichment.

The price Henry's phenomenology of art pays for making painting a matter of a real presence and of a creation of the invisible forces of life is extremely high. *First*, this view estranges painting completely from the realm of the *perception* of something *visible*. For Henry, far from making visible the wild being of the flesh of the world that remains invisible for common perception, far from expressing and refiguring the new phenomena disclosed by a phenomenological and pictorial *epoché*, the phenomena of painting have nothing in common with any kind of perception of any kind of mundane phenomenon. *Second*, for Henry, the forces expressed in paintings are and *remain invisible*—also in the paintings themselves! If painting means making something somehow visible, then strictly speaking Kandinsky does not paint the spiritual forces his paintings are about. *Third*, the identification of these spiritual forces with the forces of a life that we also feel in ourselves entails that all paintings are about forces we humans can possibly feel either by ourselves or by empathy. Henry thus excludes from painting all concern for *infra- or inhuman animal and material forces*. If paintings can contain some sort of non-human spiritual forces, then these must be supra-human or 'cosmic' for Henry (Henry 2009: 125).

Although published seven years before Henry's book on Kandinsky, Deleuze's book on Francis Bacon—despite agreeing with Henry that painting is about 'sensations' and 'forces'[3]—can actually be read as a successful endeavour to avoid the three inconveniences of Henry's view on the 'essence of painting' we have just mentioned. We must limit here our presentation of Deleuze's philosophy of painting to these issues—well aware that we are thus far from doing justice to the rich content of his book, and especially to his careful interpretation of many paintings by Bacon. There is also no need for us to return to what we already said about Bacon's way of painting with 'diagrams' and by means of a 'manipulation of chance', or on how his 'modulation' of the relation between 'eye' and 'hand' results in a 'haptic' dimension that make his works essentially different from the 'abstract' paintings by Kandinsky.

In Deleuze's view, rather than transcending all visual perception (as Henry would have it for Kandinsky), Bacon's paintings introduce a new way of seeing and feeling related to new sorts of bodies. What we see in Bacon's paintings is essentially a 'deformation' or de-figuring of human bodies by invisible forces. These forces of de-formation 'dissolve' all visible 'forms' (Deleuze and Guattari 1994: 173). They annihilate all resemblance of the painted bodies with the perceptual forms of human bodies and turn them into mere 'figures'. These figures are a purely pictorial element in an art of painting that is not 'figurative' any longer and that has left behind all concern for a 'resembling representation' of outer reality. As non-figurative figures, Bacon's painted human bodies are in essence not different from the 'round area, the ring' (le rond, la piste) that rotates around them and from the uni-form and neutral background or 'aplat' behind them. The 'athletically' or 'diagrammatically' deformed human bodies we see in Bacon's paintings are bodies that express and make visible nothing else than the invisible forces that act on them. They show the process of 'becoming animal' of human bodies that are exposed to inhuman forces. The 'meat' (viande) falling off the 'bones' makes visible how physical forces of gravity or acceleration work on human bodies, the animal shadows of deformed human bodies show the beastly suffering caused by injuring forces, the widely open mouth of a pope is a head screaming under the torture of unbearable moral forces.

Strictly speaking, Bacon does not actually paint deformed bodies or invisible forces, but what Deleuze calls 'sensations'. Are we then back to Henry's account of non-figurative paintings expressing how we human beings feel the invisible forces of life in the mode of a pathetic affection that has nothing in common with the perception of mundane manifestations? Not at all. Deleuze's 'forces' and 'sensations' are very different from what Henry calls by these names. Bacons 'forces' are not spiritual forces of life and harmony, but material forces of destruction and dissonance. They also do not remain invisible and merely felt, but they become visible through visible sensations. Bacon's works thus consist of visible 'blocs of sensations' that invisible forces create in the very 'material' (matériau) of painting: 'canvas support, paint-brush or equivalent agent, colour in

---

[3] See also Deleuze and Guattari 1994: 181f: 'And this, first of all, is what makes painting abstract . . . making the invisible forces visible in themselves.'

the tube' (Deleuze and Guattari 1994: 166). Artworks 'are' such 'blocs of sensations': they 'create' them and they 'preserve' them forever; they make them 'stand by themselves' (*tenir debout tout seul*) by means of the pictorial material and the 'composition' by the artist. Needless to say, then, that such 'sensations' existing 'in and by themselves exceed any lived experience [*vécu*] of them' (Deleuze and Guattari 1994: 164 (modified translation)). 'Sensations' made visible and becoming a pictorial element, refer to other, different sensations and to other, different pictorial elements, but they never refer to *absent* invisible forces nor to an invisible '*sense*' or meaning behind them.

To better explain the nature of these 'blocs of sensations' and the way we experience them in Bacon's paintings, Deleuze divides them into what he calls 'percepts' and 'affects'. *Percepts* are the sensations as we perceive them in the material of the paintings. Neither perceived bodies nor felt sensations, they are materialized sensations and matter made sensible. Percepts are what remains of perception when neither an object perceived nor a perceiving subject is left over. Bacon's way of painting 'attendants' (*témoins*) (Deleuze 2003: ch. 10)—that is, deformed bodies watching the deformation of other bodies—illustrates well what happens also to the spectator of his paintings. *Affects*, on the other hand, are the sensations as they affect material bodies—not in how they look, but in how they feel and are changed in their nature by these feelings. Unlike internally felt affections, these affects are about how invisible forces affect painted figures and how these forces make 'humans become non-human' suffering animals (Deleuze and Guattari 1994: 173). Bacon's paintings are thus about a de-objectivation of perception and a de-subjectivation of affection: 'By means of the material, the aim of art is to wrest the percept from perceptions of objects and the states of a perceiving subject, to wrest the affect from affections as the transition from one state to another' (Deleuze and Guattari 1994: 167). This is precisely what happens to the 'hysteric' bodies painted by Bacon (Deleuze 2003: chap. 7). Such hysteric bodies or 'bodies without organs' are bodies that have lost not only their human form but also all their natural organic capacities. They are blocs of excessive sensations, pure expressions of the overwhelming presence of the invisible forces to which they are subjected. The pope's mouth *is* the scream—not made 'flesh', but 'meat' and bone/teeth.

Put in a very schematic way, one can say that Deleuze and Henry agree in their disagreement with Merleau-Ponty but that they completely disagree about the proper way to depart from philosophy of painting based on a phenomenology of perception. They agree that the 'invisible forces' a non-figurative art of painting is about do not belong to 'the flesh of the world'. But they totally disagree about what and where they are instead. For Henry the invisible forces belong to life and not to the world, they can only be felt in us and not seen in paintings, they are spiritually human or supra-human. Deleuze, on the contrary, thinks that paintings can make visible invisible forces, but that this requires a complete transfiguration of perception, of the perceiver, and of the perceived. To perceive how invisible forces act on bodies, the bodies must be subjected to a violent deformation of their recognizable forms and to a blurring of their human signification. Merleau-Ponty's 'flesh is too tender' (Deleuze and Guattari 1994: 179); it lacks the 'bones', the physical resistance and the structural stability to express and preserve the sensations caused by a traumatic exposure to the violence of inhuman forces.

What Bacon paints instead of the abstract forms painted by Kandinsky or of the invisible texture of the visible world painted by Cézanne, are 'affects' and 'percepts'— that is, materialized 'sensations' of bodily 'figures' exposed to chaotic and destructive forces. He paints their 'spasms', their 'contraction' on themselves or their 'escape' from themselves—that is, visible forces caused by invisible forces. What we see and what affects us in Bacon's paintings is animal meat suffering[4] from forces that are physical instead of spiritual, that belong to matter instead of life, that come from a 'chaosmos' instead of a cosmic harmony. This 'chaosmos' is a chaotic reality in which humans have no proper place. What Bacon's paintings are thus about is what happens to humans in an inhuman and cruel reality—a reality without spiritual meaning and without transcendence or escape.

This is not the place to further develop the differences between Deleuze's and Henry's philosophies of radical immanence (and their reading of Spinoza). And there is no need to return to their common insistence on 'forces' that do not constitute the invisible *of a visible world* and to how this makes them both reluctant to embrace the underlying metaphysics of Merleau-Ponty's analysis of the art of painting. Deleuze's account of painting differs radically, however, from Henry's through its effort to reduce all reference to subjectivity to an absolute minimum. More precisely, Deleuze denies the creative painter and the spectator of her work any form of transcendence and turns them both into immanent moments of the painting. He also considers the painted work to be a singular and therefore empirical metaphysical event. Such a pictorial event is not given *to* an external perceiver; just as Bacon's 'attendants' (*témoins*), the spectator is involved in the painting and intimately concerned by it. Her 'affects' are, however, inseparable from her 'percepts', and they belong to the painted work and its invisible forces as much as they belong to her. For Deleuze, the abolition of the work of art as an externally transcendent object necessarily also entails the abolition of the artist and the spectator as an internally (or intimately) transcendent subject. A painting of invisible forces can thus retain its natural relation to perception on the condition that this perception is not ascribed to an autonomous or even 'absolute' subject. Similarly, paintings can retain their composition of visible figures, rings, and *aplats* if these are not treated as (representations of) mundane objects but as pictorial elements created by the action of invisible forces. For Deleuze, the phenomenon of painting thus requires a new kind of phenomenology that takes phenomena just as phenomena—without a thing-in-itself *behind* them, and without a subject *for* whom they are how they appear *to* it.

REFERENCES

Deleuze, G. (2003), *Francis Bacon: The Logic of Sensation* (London: Continuum).
——— and Guattari, F. (1994), *What is Philosophy?* (New York: Columbia University Press).
Figal, G. (2010), *Erscheinungsdinge. Ästhetik als Phänomenologie* (Tübingen: Mohr Siebeck).

[4] 'Pity the meat!' (Deleuze 2003: 23).

Henry, M. (2009), *Seeing the Invisible on Kandinsky* (London: Continuum).

Husserl, E. (1994), *Briefwechsel, Band VII* (Dordrecht: Kluwer Academic Publishers).

—— (2005), *Phantasy, Image Consciousness and Memory (1898–1925)* (Dordrecht: Springer).

Merleau-Ponty, M. (2004), 'Eye and mind', in Merleau-Ponty, M., *Basic Writings* (London: Routledge), pp. 290–324.

CHAPTER 28

....

EVIDENCE IN THE PHENOMENOLOGY OF RELIGIOUS EXPERIENCE

....

ANTHONY J. STEINBOCK

To what extent is a philosophical account of religious experience possible? If perceptual objects are perceived according to their own structure, does anything that falls outside of perceptual givenness fail to be given? After Kant, for example, there can only be a philosophy of religion in the sense of a rational religion or 'morality', and there can never be a philosophy of religion in the sense of a rigorous account of religious experience. I argue, however, that religious experience has its own integrity such that it is irreducible to a perceptual or an ethical order, and that it is accessible to phenomenological philosophy.

In this chapter I first take up Kant and the potential impasse of any philosophical account of religious experience. Second, I address the issue of limit-phenomena: namely, those matters that are on the limit of experience in order to broach the question of a phenomenology of religious experience. Third, I discuss various attempts within phenomenology to broaden the notion of givenness and evidence beyond the parameters of object-givenness. Finally, I point to a phenomenology of religious experience as an irreducible sphere of human experience, and consider its unique style of evidence and modalizations.

1 KANT AND THE PHILOSOPHY OF RELIGION

....

Having identified Reason as prior to its own historical revelation (or any historical revelation, for that matter), Kant implicitly places himself—insofar as he is a rational being—at the origin of philosophy. In this respect, Kant establishes any rigorous philosophy as a 'critical' philosophy of experience. In order to introduce the issues relating to the nature of experience and how it relates to the religious sphere, allow me to give a brief account of this concern as it is situated in Kant, beginning with the problem of givenness.

To be given is to be an object of knowledge. What can be experienced is that which can be presented in a spatiotemporal manifold as actively synthesized by the categories of the understanding. A given object unfolds in a causal nexus of objective time order, and to this extent it can be said to be determined by natural laws such that what counts as given and hence as something experienced and experiencable is what appears. What appears as the object of knowledge is *made to appear*; thus representations or objects of experience are the product of the understanding's activity on the manifold.

We only know how the world appears to us, not the things in themselves, even though this does not stop us from making practical use of appearances as if they were things in themselves (for example, this is why we can have success in the natural sciences). The point, however, is that in this appearing, the human being is the *active* source, and the givenness, the object of knowledge, is *our* doing since anything that has the structure of an object is dependent upon the subjective conditions of knowledge. The transcendental unity of apperception expresses the fact that there can be no objects that are not the representations of the one who has them, that is, the one 'who' makes them possible by bringing the unity of synthesis (which the imagination constrains on the spatiotemporal manifold) to concepts. Hence, the 'I think' must be able to accompany all my representations (Kant 1956: A 119).

While reason can function speculatively, and in this sense have any object it pleases merely as an object of thought, it cannot enjoy it as an *object of experience*. Reason acts, not reacts, and in its practical capacity it is able to determine the will in a purely autonomous manner: in a manner that is rational—that is, universally necessary, and as the same for everyone. Accordingly, a pure morality is to be established only when the rational agent's acts determines its own action by legislating and freely (spontaneously) adhering to the imperative that is categorial, which the rational agent itself holds subjectively as a maxim and legislates universally, objectively as a law.

Thus, we have in Kant a distinction between (1) what can be known and is made known by the understanding, and is made to be given in a temporal manner as an experience, and (2) what holds universally for all times, for everyone and everywhere, in a rational manner. Morality would be an example of the latter. Let me turn now to the question of 'religion' and evidence in the religious sphere.

With the distinction between epistemic experience and the universal validity of pure (practical) reason, Kant's foray into matters of religion unfold in the following way. He distinguishes between a religion that is founded on revelation—that is, historical revelation, which is propounded by ecclesiastical faith (*Kirchenglauben*)—and a pure 'faith of religion' (*Religionsglaube*) that is grounded in reason. Historical faith is based on revelation understood '*as an experience*' (Kant 1989: 126/105). As empirical experience, it has only a particular validity for those who happened to have access to the historical period, location, or to historical records upon which that faith rests. Historical faith can become an ecclesiastical faith, of which there can be several. But only the pure faith of religion, which bases itself wholly upon reason, can be accepted as necessary and universal. On the one hand, there is revealed religion and historical faith, which strictly speaking is not experienced (that is, an object of knowledge), and on the other, a 'pure religion of reason', which is nothing other than moral reason. This distinction is paramount in the *Conflict of the Faculties*, because it is here that Kant wants to preserve the autonomy of philosophy as a critical discipline and as able to adjudicate the meaning of the theology (Kant 1992: 62–5, 110–11; 42–3). In short, the freedom of reason is expressed as reason's freedom over the temporal/historical realm (Kant 1989: 119/100f.).[1]

Given the assertion of pure rational religion over ecclesiastical faith, is there a place for a philosophical account of religious experience? The dimension of the 'religious' entails some kind of relation or interaction with God. According to Kant's *First Critique*, God is an idea that purely speculative reason can think, but not determine according to its objective validity. There is no evidence, no experience of the religious. When we do *think* God, we do not really extend our knowledge (that is, experience) beyond the limits of objects of possible experience (Kant 1956: A 674–5). God as transcendent is not knoweable, *not experienceable* (see Kant 1956: A 685–6, A 580, A 676; Kant 1992: 76–7).

This presumptuousness of experiencing God is in part the reason for Kant's chastisement of the mystics and mysticism. Referring to mysticism as fanaticism, as merely allegorical, and as the killer of reason, Kant warns against 'a pious feeling of supernatural influence', since it yields no objective principle and is valid only subjectively (Kant 1989: 145/121; Kant 1992: 54–5, 78–9, 106–7). To avoid mysticism, writes Kant, one must anchor 'the supersensible (the thought of which is essential to anything called religion)' in determinate concepts of reason; otherwise fantasy becomes lost in the transcendent where religious matters are concerned; this can lead to Illuminism—that is, supernatural inspiration in which private, inner revelations rule, with no public touchstone of truth (Kant 1992: 80–1, 108–9). It is only by the concepts of reason that we can recognize the (putative) divinity of a teaching promulgated to us (Kant 1992: 104–5, 80–5). But strictly speaking there can be no positive appeal to evidence in matters of religion since feelings are not knowledge, and they cannot yield the presence or evidence of a mystery; the mystery of revelation is simply incongruous with our power of comprehension and ability to experience (Kant 1992: 114–15; Kant 1989: 154, 159/129, 133).

While there are varieties of belief in divine revelation and its teachings, there are not different religions. There is only *one* religion, and this springs from reason (Kant 1989: 117/98; Kant 1992: 60–1, 78–9, 92–3, 114–17). What, then, is religion if it is not somehow correlative to religious experiencing? Religion is not the cult that develops from divine insight or religious experience; it is not the ensemble of ritual and liturgy that aids one in disposing oneself to God. For Kant, the religion of 'divine worship' or cultus is rooted in arbitrary precepts rather than universal reason. Instead, genuine rational religion is the sum of our moral duties *regarded as if* they were divine commands and our fulfilling

---

[1] The function of philosophy in relation to the three 'higher' faculties (theology, law, and medicine) 'is to control them and, in this way, be useful to them, since *truth* (the essential and first condition of learning in general) is the main thing, whereas the *utility* the higher faculties promise the government is of secondary importance.' (See Kant 1992: 44–5, 60–1, 122–3).

them as such (Kant 1989: 115–16, 170–1/97, 142). But this is to say that the *domain of religion is essentially the domain of morality*, and the distinction between religion and morality is merely a formal one. 'As far as its matter or object is concerned, religion does not differ in any point from morality, for it is concerned with duties as such' (Kant 1989: 105–6, 134–5, 123/90–1, 112, 103; Kant 1992: 78–9, 86–7).[2]

To sum up, then, since God does not correspond to an experience and cannot be an object of knowledge shareable by all human beings and for all times, and thus susceptible to evidence, the supposition of a revealed religion and ecclesiastical faith must yield to a pure rational religion and pure faith of reason. Religion is purely moral, and philosophically there is nothing higher than inter-human—which is to say, intra-rational—morality. For Kant, consequently, experience is restricted to one mode of givenness in which objects of knowledge are actively constituted with the direct implication that one cannot meaningful speak of a religious experience.

2 LIMIT-PHENOMENA

To some extent this conception of givenness—that there is only one way of being given and that it concerns perceptual and categorial knowing—is carried through in the phenomenological tradition. Let me explain. Already, beginning with Husserl's Fifth Logical Investigation, phenomenology has been trained on the following two aspects of description (Husserl 1968: esp. section 17). On the one hand, phenomenology wants to inquire into *how* something is given, its modes or manner of givenness (sense, meaning). On the other hand, it wants to examine *what* something is, the thing, the subject, the world, and so on; its being, its essential structures. As phenomenology developed it was able to see both the constitutive questions (the how of givenness, and so on) as *leitmotifs* for ontological questions (concerning the being of things), and ontologies (essential structures, and sciences of the latter) as leading clues to constitutive ones (Husserl 1952; Husserl 1954; Husserl 1956; Husserl 1959; Husserl 1993; Steinbock 1995).

No matter 'what' the thing is—object or subject—a phenomenological perspective does not simply assert its being, but holds in abeyance the pre-posited, pre-supposed acceptance of being, allowing one to comport him or herself differently, from a changed attitude, focusing now on how 'it' appears, the modes of giving and the multifarious ways of meaning-accepting (Fink 1933). Thus, rather than taking things for granted, phenomenology strives to inquire into its way of givenness and the power and limits of the process of meaning-giving.

---

[2] Kant censures those who would worship, act, or pray in this way: 'It does not enter their heads that when they fulfil their duties to men (themselves and others) they are, by these very acts, performing God's commands and are therefore in all their actions and abstentions, so far as these concern morality, *perpetually in the service of God*, and that it is absolutely impossible to serve God more directly in any other way (since they can affect and have an influence upon earthly beings alone, and not upon God)' (Kant 1989: 111–12/94).

Understandably, this comes up against important limits: namely, limits of givenness and potential 'limit-phenomena'. For example, it is one thing to ask how a perceptual or epistemic object is given. Husserl's earlier analyses concerning the ways in which spatial objects are presented perspectivally, how temporal objects are given in the present, with a retention and with a protention, how objects are constituted actively in judicative assertions, how essences are given and founded in simple perceptions, how facets of objects and horizons are given in passive syntheses with an affective prominence, how the structure of intentionality forms a constitutive duet of sense. All these analyses explicate meaning within a certain register of givenness. I have called this particular register of givenness, 'presentation' (Steinbock 2007).

Accordingly, if *presentation* is our operative model of givenness, there will be phenomena that remain essentially on the limit of givenness. Presentation is a type a givenness that is more or less dependent upon my power to usher things into appearance, either through the power of my 'I can' or my 'I think'. When I intend an object, an object gives itself (whether or not it is the object I intended) in such a way that it points further on to new themes and new horizons. There is, of course, nothing wrong with this mode of givenness; it concerns a genuine dimension of our experience that bears on the relative givenness of things in the economy of appearing and concealing. It describes our relation to the world as one of immediate or mitigated belief in its being. But it is another matter to take presentation as the only mode of givenness.

How, then, does something become a limit-phenomenon for phenomenology? By limit-phenomena I understand those matters (*Sachen*) that are on the edge of accessibility in a phenomenological approach to experience, and not simply those matters that have historically been at the border of phenomenological discourse. I characterize limit-phenomena as those 'phenomena' that are given as not being able to be given. The question of limit-phenomena relates to the question of religious experience because it is generally assumed that the sphere pertaining to the religious is not able to be experienced, and likewise, is susceptible neither to a philosophical, critical perspective, nor to the question of evidence.

In order for something to be constituted as a limit-phenomenon, a certain order of givenness or methodological approach has to be presupposed in a phenomenological inquiry. Thus there can be many 'phenomena' given at the limit of experience, depending upon how one approaches these very phenomena. For example, within a static phenomenology which is restricted simply to present experiences, sleep and fainting are given as limit-phenomena. However, they are given as phenomena within the genetic phenomenology—that is, when the scope includes the process of self-temporalization; now sleep, for instance, is integrated into an overarching concordance of meaning. Alternatively, birth and death are given on the limits of experience within a genetic phenomenology, but are 'constitutive'—phenomenological—events within a generative phenomenology: that is, when phenomenology treats the movement of historicity as it unfolds over the generations. Animals can be understood as on the limit of experience, but within a generative phenomenology Husserl sees in certain cases the possibility of the liminality of human and animal life being exposed as inessential—that is, when they become home-comrades as co-constituting a home-world (Steinbock 1998).

Now, within a genetic phenomenology, when Husserl inquires into the experience of the alien (*Fremderfahrung*), he has to ask how the otherness of the other, the other as alien is given or is accessible to me. While an object can be given with a foreground that is present and a backside that is not present now but can in principle be present, the otherness of the other in its radical alienness can never be given; it can never become present, not just factually but in principle. When Husserl inquires into how the alien is given, he writes that the alien is given as not being able to be given, accessible in the mode of inaccessibility and incomprehensibility (Husserl 1973: 631). The alien is in this way a limit-phenomenon and on the limit of being given.

Within a generative phenomenology, there is a similar, but distinctive issue when we speak about the limits of homeworld and alienworld. By homeworld, I mean a normatively significant lifeworld, and by alienworld, a lifeworld that is experienced as normatively atypical, unfamiliar, and non-optimal for experience (Steinbock 1995: Chapters 12–14). The limits peculiar to the home and alien arise because the alien is not given to the home in a way that the home is given to itself. Even phenomenology and the phenomenologist, Husserl asserts, is situated within the historical density of the home. This means, that the phenomenologist can never completely objectify the limits of home and alien—that is, stand above home and alien or control generativity—since the phenomenologist himself or herself is located within the generative process, describing the structure of generativity as it is generating. Moreover, generativity is 'given' as the structure home/alien. But the 'whole' home/alien structure is only experienced as such from within the liminality of the home in relation to the alien, and in this regard given with a certain liminality.

From these examples and the analyses of previous work, we can say the following about limit-phenomena. First, limit-phenomena are not arbitrary in the sense that just anything can become a limit-phenomenon. Second, limit-phenomena are relative determinations, relative, that is, to a certain methodological approach. Third, limit-phenomena are necessary or 'essential' when they pertain to a certain order of experience. Within that order of experience, there will necessarily be these or those limit-phenomena, even if they are relative to a certain order of experience. Fourth, in some instances phenomena will be given as limit-phenomena, while in others they will not. But are there not some limit-phenomena that are *essentially* limit-phenomena: for instance, 'God'?

We can meaningfully approach this question only by recognizing that the observations regarding limit-phenomena presuppose as a standard a particular mode of givenness. If presentation is our operative model of givenness, then we can assert that there are phenomena constituted as not being able to be given, and that hence remain essentially on the limit of givenness. However, this assumes, at best, that one model of givenness is operative—presentation—and, at worst, that there is only one kind of givenness, which is presentation. However, if phenomenology is open to all kinds of givenness (no matter which ones they are) according to how the things give themselves, then not only does the very tenor of phenomenology shift, but the status of liminality concerning certain phenomena does as well.

Let me return to the manner of givenness that qualifies presentation. Presentation unfolds along the axis of intention and fulfilment, and is generally understood as the structure of intentionality or the noesis–noema relation, sense giving, and sense givenness. A givenness is said to be 'fulfilled' in adequate or inadequate evidence according to whether the given corresponds to the way in which it is intended or meant. If I 'see' (or 'intend') a squirrel on the branch outside my window and the squirrel is co-evally given, the perception is fulfilled, even if the perception simultaneously opens up new perspectives and points to futural ways of being given which are not yet given, but 'empty'. If upon closer inspection the squirrel turns out to be leaves on a branch, then something new is precisely *given*—even if it is not what I initially intended. Now the leaves are presented such that in and through this, the squirrel-intention is 'disappointed', 'crossed-out', and replaced with a new experience. The leaves on a branch are given, as they simultaneously forecast new kinds of givenness that will fulfil the global perception.

The recognition of the experience of limit-phenomena—or as we might say, the non-experience of these non-phenomena (depending upon how we understand experience and phenomena)—attest to the simple fact, as Kant saw, that 'God' is not given like an object. For this reason, God does not have to correspond to my idea of God in order to be given in evidence. The dynamic of intention and fulfilment, which does apply epistemically and perceptually to eidetic and perceptual objects, does not characterize my relation with God.

Does this mean, then, that we can have no experience of God, that there is no 'religious experience' strictly speaking, and that it is impossible to speak of evidence where the religious sphere is concerned? More generally, does the noesis–noema structure exhaust experience such that what does not fall into its domain remain outside of experience and the question of evidence?

While presentation describes a dimension of our experience of the relative givenness of things, and while it describes our belief-relation to the world with respect to its being, the problem has been that presentation captures the dominant model of givenness for us and has been allowed to efface other legitimate modes of givenness. But why should phenomenology, in order to reflect *within* the very experiencing itself, not open itself to *all* kinds of 'givens' *in the distinctive manner that they give themselves*? Is it not arbitrary to limit in advance the ways in which givenness can take place?

3 PHENOMENOLOGIES OF RELIGIOUS EXPERIENCE

Precisely because presentation has defined what gets counted exclusively as a matter of experience, other dimensions of experience that differ from presentation have been left virtually out of philosophical and specifically phenomenological accounts. There are, however, contemporary attempts to grapple with these issues stemming for the most part from phenomenological inspirations. They implicitly concern the constitutive questions of givenness, and are distinct from philosophers of religion such as Henry Duméry, who submitted the idea of God to rational criticism (Duméry 1957). For example, Adolf Reinach, an early phenomenologist, recognized quite early (1916) that religious experiences have their own integrity. From the perspective of perceptual experience, of course, religious experiences 'cannot be "understood". They are not "motivated".' But this means all the more that we need to respect the sense that religious experiences have of their own accord, 'even if [their sense] leads to enigmas'; (Reinach 1989: 593). Such an openness can be found in Jean Hering's phenomenological study of the unique nature of religious consciousness (Hering 1926: see 87–140). Kurt Stavenhagen, too, conducted his research into the possibility of an absolute personal comportment *vis-à-vis* an absolute, that is, religious sphere (Stavenhagen 1925).[3] Otto Gründler's work is also a good example of the problematic attempt in early phenomenology simply to apply a phenomenology of presentation to 'religious' phenomena (see Gründler 1922). Though not phenomenological in name, Rudolf Otto could also be linked to this tradition to the extent that he investigated religious experience as the experience of being before 'an overpowering, absolute might of some kind', the experience of the presence of that 'Something' that Otto calls the 'numinous' and that is experienced as *mysterium tremendum* in awe (Otto 1958: 10).

The early part of the twentieth century and following saw other kinds of inquiry into 'religion'. By contrast to the constitutive approach, these can be understood as materially and/or formally eidetic, for example, describing the variety of religions and religious experiences—whether to catalogue their types or to advance a philosophy of religion. These approaches typically include James' investigation into the kinds of religious experience (James 1961), van der Leeuw's typification of religion, and Heiler's inquiry into the manifestation and nature of religion (Van der Leeuw 1956; Heiler 1961).

In the phenomenological tradition, however, Max Scheler was not only the earliest most influential force, but the most profound. From the very outset he maintained that there was nothing more disastrous for philosophical inquiry, and indeed for all epistemology, than to operate methodologically with a 'too narrow, restrictive concept of experience', to equate the whole of experience with one particular kind of experience, and then to refuse to admit into evidence and deny categorically anything that could not be reduced to this one kind of experience (Scheler 1954: 250).

This openness enabled him to identify two different ways of givenness, on the one hand, what he termed *Offenbarkeit* or manifestation (what I have called above, 'presentation'), and *Offenbarung* or 'revelation', which has its own style of evidence, as well as deceptions, and breaks in givenness (Scheler 1966; Scheler 1973). Scheler was able to do this because he recognized a broader order of evidence, not just one that was founded in

---

[3] I would like to thank Jim Hart for this reference. The kind of questioning raised here would not be unfamiliar to Kierkegaard, who understood the religious dimension as an absolute relation to an absolute, at least in *Fear and Trembling* (Kierkegaard 1983). See also Kierkegaard's *Works of Love*, in which loving is directed toward the neighbour as in accordance with the absolute character of the movement of love oriented toward God (Kierkegaard 1998).

reason. Going back to Pascal, Scheler worked out phenomenologically the philosophi-cal import of an *ordo amoris*, or order of the heart. For Scheler this means that the 'heart' has a 'logic' all its own, and does not take it from the understanding or reason. It is not without sense or direction, simply vague or chaotic, without meaning, or merely a 'sub-jectively human' matter of fact (Scheler 1957). Sensitivity to this order demands a 'culti-vation of the heart' that is independent of the cultivation of the understanding, without succumbing to a slovenliness in matters of feeling, and without surrendering the entire emotional life, and specifically religious experiencing to psychology or to myth and superstition.

Other works that build directly and indirectly on these insights include Martin Buber (who contrasted the I–It word pair ('experience' that is appropriate to objects) with the I–Thou word pair ('relation'); he accounted for different manners of givenness that per-tain, each in their own way, to God, the other person, and nature (Buber 1965). More squarely in the phenomenological tradition is Michel Henry's monumental, *L'essence de la manifestation*. Here he criticizes as 'ontological monism' this kind of limitation of givenness to one kind of being (= monism), and which understands the very essence of manifestation to be revelation (Henry 1990; Henry 1996, Steinbock 1999). Following in this tradition is also Jean-Luc Marion, who draws a similar distinction between mani-festation and revelation in his work *Dieu sans l'être* (Marion 1991; Marion 1997). Going even further, however, Marion offers an expanded description of givenness with a detailed account of 'saturated phenomena', phenomena that are distinctive from the poor or common phenomena (Marion 1997, Marion 2001; Steinbock 2010). This is con-sistent with Emmanuel Levinas's insight that 'the noesis–noema structure is not the pri-mordial structure of intentionality' (Levinas 1961: 271/294). What Levinas means by this is that the 'Other' is not simply a differently interpreted noema. To go back to Husserl's early terminology, it is *not* the case that the face-to-face with the Other is simply a non-objectivating act. That is, if an objectivating act is that intentional act which 'refers' to an object in and through a certain sense, then the relation with the Other does not depend upon, is not founded in objectivating acts in order for the Other to be given. Instead, it has a wholly unique structure that is peculiar to the interpersonal experience. This is why we must, for Levinas, revise phenomenological concepts according to the experi-ence, and not force the experience into predefined or at least presupposed structures (see Steinbock forthcoming).

Indeed, it is Levinas who at once profoundly opens up the question of givenness and evidence in phenomenology, and brings us back full circle, as it were, to the difficulties of the like we encountered in Kant concerning evidence of a religious nature. The diffi-culties in accounting for a phenomenology of religious experience in Levinas are too complex to enumerate here, though it is possible to outline the problematic (Steinbock 2009).

On the one hand, it goes to the great credit of Levinas not to have limited givenness, experience, relation, intentionality, and so on, to the mere *disclosure* of pre-objects or full-fledged objects, either perceptual or categorial. He discerns in our very lives another kind of givenness that is irreducible to disclosure: namely, the *revelation* of the Other as an 'absolute experience'. It makes sense to speak of an 'absolute experience' as an experience of an absolute: namely, the 'absolutely Other', because it is not the case that the 'I' simply encounters a different 'object'—in this case, the Other. Rather, in the 'experience' of the Other as revelatory, the very tenor of the experience is transformed; it is not mere experience (as disclosure), but absolute experience as revelation (Steinbock 2005).

Still, the question of God arises (at least in part for Levinas) precisely *because* the face of the Other is the trace of God. Thus, even if we wanted to stay only on the level of the face of the Other, as it were, we would still be confronted with the 'question of God' in the face of the Other through which 'God' takes on meaning (Levinas 1988: 216). The *meaning* of God then has to become an experiential issue *in some sense* for Levinas. Just as Levinas does not *a priori* reduce intentionality to the *noesis–noema* correlation; just as he does *not restrict* experience to disclosure, he also leaves open the possibility, phenomenologically, that the inquiry into meaning is not limited to the meaning of being peculiar to philosophy. For Levinas, the meaning of God, the God of the Bible, escapes the restrictive meaning of being to which it has been limited in philosophy; this is why he queries whether 'God' signifies 'in an *unlikely manner*' the beyond of being—that is, signifies as transcendence and without analogy (Levinas 1992: 95). 'Our question', writes Levinas, 'is whether, beyond being, a meaning *might not show itself* whose priority, translated into ontological language, will be called *prior* to being' (Levinas 1992: 96, my emphasis added). So, even if there is nothing more basic than the inter-human face-to-face which is 'religion', the meaning of God is at least an experiential issue, as it is revealed in the demand coming to me from the face of the Other. In even this way, Levinas opens the question of *religious* experience.

It is not that Levinas refrains from speaking of an 'encounter' with God, since God is always already given as Desirable. God, however, is not the Other, but 'other than the other' (Levinas 1992: 112–5). This means for Levinas that even if we are oriented toward God, God is not the 'end' of this orientation, for according to Levinas, God immediately turns us toward the Other. This means that the orientation toward holiness is immediately 'good deeds', social justice, righteousness, and charity (*tzedakah*). Accordingly, the 'religious' is inescapably and directly an '*ethical turnabout*' (*retournement éthique*) (Levinas 1992: 114). If there is an impossibility of a religious encounter without Others, there is also an impossibility of ethics without the religious—that is, the impossibility of the face of the Other without God.[4]

So, while Kant limits experience to the 'disclosure' of objects, Levinas opens up givenness/experience to the revelation of the Other. But in his own way, Levinas also limits modes of givenness other than disclosure to just one other mode, revelation (the givenness of the face) without due consideration to other modes of givenness that also do not share the same assets as disclosure. This other mode (the mode of the otherwise than the Other) would be a mode of givenness peculiar to religious experience, what I have

---

[4] 'The goodness of the Good—of the Good that neither sleeps nor slumbers—inclines the movement it calls forth to turn it away from the Good and orient toward the other, and only thus toward the Good' (Levinas 1992: 114).

termed elsewhere, 'epiphany', irreducible to disclosure and to revelation (Steinbock 2007). Thus, even if concretely one is turned by God to the Other, we should ask: what is the phenomenological sense of this very *being turned toward* the Other by God? Phenomenology in its concreteness *must dwell with the meaning of such being turned toward* as an irreducible dimension of religious experience.

This is not merely a theoretical point, but an experiential one. And one experiential resource available to describe this kind of religious experience—the one which both Kant and Levinas disavow—can be found in the lives of the mystics.

In relation to this dimension of experience, we cannot discount examples of these religious experiences, living examples *within human experience* found in the Jewish, Christian, and Islamic mystics. The mystics, particularly within the Abrahamic tradition, often have more in common with each other, guided by their experiences of the Holy, than do the respective mystics with those of their own faith traditions which are guided indirectly by cult and liturgy ('religion'). Again, I am not suggesting that there are two separate ways of encountering God, like two possibilities from which I could choose. The mystics themselves also insist through their experiences along with the likes of Kant and Levinas that loving God is service to others. My point is that there is a phenomenologically distinctive sphere of experience with its own unique style of evidence that is itself interpersonal, but is irreducible to the moral sphere.

4 PHENOMENOLOGICAL METHOD
AND EVIDENCE IN THE RELIGIOUS SPHERE

Recent phenomenology has been characterized as having undergone a 'religious turn' (see Janicaud 1991; Janicaud 1998). However, what this brief overview should help to make clear is that although there has been more attention of late to the question of religious experience, it is more an expression of a steady and persistent occupation than it is a turn. If anything, we might say that through existentialism, structuralism, post-structuralism, deconstruction, and post-modernism, there is a reappropriation of religious questions and themes. But within phenomenology and phenomenological inquiry in thinkers such as Scheler, Reinach, Stavenhagen, Hering, Ricoeur, Henry, Levinas, Marion, and others, there is steady pattern of interest in phenomenology of religious experience. My own work develops these earlier insights in phenomenology in order to account for different kinds of experience/givenness. In this way, phenomenology is a philosophical style that can be attentive to religious, moral, and ecological evidence without reducing that experience to the presentation of objects (Steinbock 2007).

Phenomenological method begins as a special disposition toward the matters (what Edmund Husserl terms the 'reduction') that allows the matters to appear as they give themselves; it is an attitude that strives to be attentive to the unique ways in which they give themselves, and to be attentive to the particular ways in which we contribute to sense-emergence, be it active meaning constitution or accepting sense-givenness. In this reflection within the experiencing itself, phenomenological method also attempts to describe the givenness and the giving without prejudice as to what it is that is given, what can be given, or more to the point, the very how or modality of givenness. It does not want to limit in advance the appearing nor occlude the giving by accrued prejudices of mind and habit. Where others are concerned, the phenomenologist's effort is to evoke, not provoke, the given so that others too can more readily 'see' for themselves.

In this way, phenomenology can in principle be open to religious experience and its unique kind of evidence, as well as the disappointments, illusions, and self-deceptions that can accompany the sphere of religious experience. Certainly, phenomenology appeals to experience from a first-person perspective, or at least from what is experienced from a first-person perspective. But it is not clear that the description of our own first-person experiences demand any less examination than the description of the first-person description by others. Even my own descriptions of my first-person experiences are distanced reflections on my own experiences, and to this extent they can coincide with other's reflections on my experiences. It is true that my descriptions of my bodily movements are distinct from others' descriptions of their bodily movements. But phenomenology never excluded others' first person's account in an effort to clarify the phenomena. Instead, it did not wish for third person, ostensibly objective accounts of our lifeworld to wear the mask of truth to dominate the field of lived-experiences. I do not have to have had the experience of a phantom limb, as in Merleau-Ponty's *Phenomenology of Perception*, in order to give a phenomenological account of it as an ambivalent presence in the global kinaesthesis of the lived body and my being in the world (Merleau-Ponty 1945: 95ff). Access to myself, even to my so-called bare freedom, is already mediated (Merleau-Ponty 1945: 511). This is why it is possible to appeal to the accounts of religious experience given by others, and why the mystics above all can be privileged in this regard.

Mystical experience is a discrimination of experience within religious experience; the latter, which as Rudolf Otto has clarified (Otto 1958: 10) can be indeterminate experience, the experience of being before 'an overpowering, absolute might *of some kind*.' Human beings can have a religious stirring outside of any established religious tradition; a religious sense may arise out of a striking existential situation; it may come upon one as a vague feeling of 'ultimate reality'. Religious experience should not be confused with 'religion'. Religion, as noted above, concerns the dimension of cult and ritual which springs from religious experiences. The former can become an institution expressive of practices that dispose one toward (but do not produce) religious experiencing.

Mystical experiences, however, are to be characterized here by *special intimacies* of the presence of the Holy. These special intimacies are not restricted to, but can include, intimacies more commonly associated with such experiences such as 'union'. I draw on mystical experience to clarify religious experience (and thus the structure of epiphany) because mystical experience refines the evidence already given in the religious sphere. Mystical experience can do this because it lives the immediate Person to person movement that may only be (but not need be) implicit in religious experiencing as such.

In this way, the mystics can become exemplary of religious experience by highlighting the 'evidence' of epiphany, the 'Personal' evidence, as a distinctive vertical mode of givenness. Accordingly, as paradigmatic of religious experience, mystical experiences are always religious experiences, but not all religious experiences are mystical ones. By epiphany being clarified through mystical experience, we can say that religious experiences are so many ways of living out the interpersonal sphere. Religious experience can be clarified as interpersonal through lived-experiences and practices of various mystics. Admittedly, this makes religious experience less 'general' in the sense that it does not pretend to cover every 'spiritual' tradition, West or East; but by the same token, it makes it all the more distinctive.

The appeal to the mystics is an appeal to the authority present in the mystics by virtue of their experiences—an authority that is given *in and through* the experiences and their lives lived, and not from a commitment to a philosophical theory or by theorizing about the nature of God. From the accounts provided by the mystics we can discern basic structures of experience and relate other descriptions of mystical experiences to them, without having 'to put myself in the place of the other' (which, by the very structure of the uniqueness of personal, 'religious', experience is impossible).

There have been attempts to take the mystics and their experiences seriously such that they could be relevant philosophically. For example, Augustin Poulan, in his classic treatise *The Graces of Interior Prayer* (*Des graces d'oraison*, 1910), distinguished between a 'speculative school' which attempts to systematize all the givens theologically, and as a consequence remains basically static, and a 'descriptive school'. The descriptive school, to which he adheres, takes mysticism as 'forward-moving', and is able to accommodate itself to this dynamic element by becoming more and more exact, for example, in distinguishing one experience from another as the mystics themselves become more sensitive to the subtle differences in experiences (Poulan 1950: see xiii-xiv and 539–49).

More concretely in the phenomenological tradition is Gerda Walther. Not wanting to share in the prejudices peculiar to psychologism or empiricism, not wanting to reduce spiritual phenomena to quantifiable facts in the natural sciences, Walther remained faithful to the early sense of phenomenology in Husserl and Pfänder. Guided by the experiences of several mystics, she recognized in her *Zur Phänomenologie der Mystik* (Walther 1923) 'a mode of givenness that is fundamentally different', an irreducible 'spiritual givenness' that is peculiar to the 'primordial phenomenon' of mystical experience as the primordial source of religious experience. In so doing, she brought to light basic structural features of mystical experience and examined how such experiences are possible.

Another, more contemporary approach in this vein is provided by Nelson Pike in his work focusing on Christian mysticism. Despite the use of the term 'phenomenology' in the title, he characterizes his approach as 'phenomenography', because it is the study of the phenomena (the givens in mystical experience) as they are reported, and thus understands what he is doing to be a branch of hermeneutics (Pike 1992: 166–8).

While there are many works on mysticism that deal, ultimately, with mystical experiences, and evoke a phenomenological discourse (for example, Carl Ernst in his works relating to Rūzbihān Baqlī; Ernst 1985, 1996), and others that deal with mystical 'fact', but are not phenomenological (Underhill 1974), there are approaches that reduce mystical experience to psychodynamics, psychoanalytic object-relations, cognitive psychology, and sociological constructs (Bellak 1949; Henry 1949; Deikman 1982; Hunt 2003). Again, just because the mode of givenness does not conform to the givenness of presentation, or to the way objects are given, which are in principle able to be ratified intersubjectively, does not mean that mystical experiences (be they experiences of rapture, quiet, delight, ecstasy, visions, locutions, and so on) are aberrant mental states.

What the medical, psychological, psychoanalytic, and sociological diagnoses and analyses miss is that a religious experience is given with its own structure, immediacy, and 'order', and as such does not need to conform to a narrow, restrictive view of experience in order to count as a different kind of evidence. Bergson wonders, for instance, how the mystics could ever have been grouped with the mentally ill once we grasp the internal movement of their lives and spirit. Admittedly, we live in a situation of unstable equilibrium whereby the health of mind and body as well as their pathologies are not easily defined. Yet, he continues, there is an exceptional mental healthiness—what Husserl would call 'hyper-normality'—that is readily recognizable; a healthiness that is expressed in the penchant for action, in the faculty of adapting and readapting oneself to circumstances, and in the spirit of simplicity that triumphs over complications: 'And could this not serve as the very definition of intellectual verve' (Bergson 1984/1932: 242–3)?

This should not suggest that one cannot be deceived or that one cannot suffer from self-delusion; it does not mean that there are not sociological, historical, and cultural matrices in which the mystics live. In fact, the mystics themselves are the first to admit this. Indeed, it is a legitimate question to ask whether or not there is a lived, phenomenological difference between, say, mystical experience and what we understand today as psychopathology. When the mystics attempt to sort out a genuine experience from a deception or from a malady, they appeal to operations *on or within that level of religious experiencing*, and do not reduce the religious, say, to the psychological or vital level of experience; and they appeal to the historical efficacy of the experience and to the interpersonal 'confirmation' unique to a master/confessor/exemplar relation. The fact that they are able to pose the question concerning a delusion and attempt to distinguish it from a genuine experience of Divine presence, and to see these experiences within a religious tradition, presupposes a unique kind of givenness; and most importantly, it calibrates the problems they encounter in their own terms and within that sphere of evidence. There are those who maintain that mystical experiences are everywhere; and some even go so far as to assert that 'we are all mystics' (Soelle 2001). Such a claim is understandable; it is based on the insight that epiphany, which qualifies an experience as religious, transpires in everyday experience, and that these experiences are 'open' to everyone. I agree that the religious dimension of experience is a fundamental component of human experience—that is my point. I also agree that mystical experience should not be limited to the 'spiritual zenith of contemplation' (Soelle 2001: 14). Even if many of the mystics within the Abrahamic tradition, for example, could be called contemplatives, the mystical life is not to be equated with the contemplative life, because what qualifies the mystics as such are their experiences, not the fact that they engage in contemplative practices. It is further clear that mystical elements can also be present in ordinary forms of experience, such as the experience of nature (Soelle 2001: 15). Mystical experiences take on various forms, and it would be premature on our part to assert in advance that they are just in the reach of a few privileged individuals. But this does *not* mean that everyone is a mystic. Rather, strictly speaking, it means that mystical experiences are not *within anyone's reach* because they are not correlative to our efforts in the first place, as would be the case in the field of presentation; they are experienced as 'gifts'. One can always strive to dispose oneself to the Holy, and one can always engage in rigorous spiritual exercises and try to live a 'religious' life in this way, but it is not a foregone conclusion that mystical experiences will come about.

I would further add, as we will also see below, that mystical experiences are in no way limited to experiences of union, and moreover, union is not even the point of the mystics' lives; rather, it consists in service to God, the redemption of the world, and the participation in establishing loving and justice. We lose the distinctiveness of mystical experiences when we run all spiritualities, traditions, and religious experiences together; we fail to appreciate the radical nature of self-abandonment, the moral rigour required for spiritual and material non-attachment, the unique demands placed on a life *oriented* in this way (and not just occasionally) that affords little time for squander or pause—and all this without any guarantee that something will come of it. Not everything is a mystical experience, even if mystical experiences reveal what is most characteristic of a religious experience.

My own approach focused on the mystics of the Abrahamic tradition, and in particular on three exemplary mystics: St Teresa of Avila, in the Christian tradition, Rabbi Dov Baer of Lubavitch, in the Jewish mystical tradition, and Rūzbihān Baqlī, a sufi in the Islamic mystical tradition (Steinbock 2007). It is not that there are not other religious traditions that have the notion of person generally speaking, nor even spiritual traditions that do not unfold on the basis of person at all—Zen Buddhism in the later case. Although it would be simplistic to lump all spiritual and religious traditions together and to speak of a unified mystical tradition, Judaism, Christianity, and Islam can be regarded as a whole because of their 'Abrahamic' character. In this respect, as a whole, they are essentially distinctive from, say, Zen Buddhism, Taoism, Hinduism, Shamanism, and so on—even though we can productively undertake comparative analyses between them and find striking similarities among them. Indeed, the latter have their own dimensions of spiritual practices and directednesses that are irreducible, and there is certainly no point in blurring their differences in the enthusiastic recognition of some common structures.

But it is peculiar to the Abrahamic religious traditions that the *experience* of the absoluteness of the Holy (sometimes expressed as the 'Oneness' of God) is expressly cultivated. Because they live from the experienced Oneness of God, the mystics often share *more with each other*, even though they spring from different religions and religious backgrounds—something we witnessed in the early Middle Ages between the Jewish, Christian, and Islamic mystics—than do the mystics and 'believers' who belong to the same confession. Among the mystics we can see a true ecumenical dialogue taking shape without any attempt to be ecumenical.

Thus, when we compare a seemingly cross-cultural experience like the 'loss of self', we cannot be too quick to assert that it is experienced in the same way as voidness of own being, like we find articulated in Zen Buddhism. In the latter it would be grasped as a realization of the non-being of the self on the hither side of its being or non-being (*sunyata*). In the Abrahamic tradition it is a matter of self-surrender, self-abandon with a positive orientation toward the Holy, or an experience that comes to me ultimately from the Holy. These are phenomenologically distinctive and irreducible experiences (see Zaehner 1961; Otto 1970). Even Foucault, who is more interested in 'religion' as an instrument of 'power', recognizes such a fundamental experiential difference in spiritual orientation: Zen and Christianity are incommensurable, for while the former is geared to attenuating the individual, the latter, in its emphasis on loving between God and the individual, is trained on individuation (Foucault 1999: 112). Such a phenomenological and experiential position goes against the claim, made for example by Soelle or Stace and Smart, that there is no experience of the Holy that is ultimately distinctive from other mystical or spiritual traditions or that it is basically the same experience in widely different cultures, only 'interpreted differently' (see Soelle 2001; Smart 1965; Stace 1960a, 1960b).

In the Abrahamic religious traditions, the interpersonal dimension becomes the specific determination of religious experience. Let me emphasize that this perspective on religious experience is not an attempt to give a global narrative of 'the sacred'. In this respect it cannot be 'comparative' in the sense that it deals with all religious traditions or various types thereof (Otto 1979; Zaehner 1961). It is not an attempt to survey all spiritualities from a putative neutral nowhere. The abstention from a surveying attitude does not arise, because there is such a vast *quantity* of religions that it would be impossible to do so. Rather, focusing on the Abrahamic mystics emerges from the singular integrity of sets of experiences. Further, just because there are religious possibilities that have been revealed other than the Abrahamic ones does not mean that the Abrahamic interpersonal reality is somehow 'arbitrary'—a designation that William James would misleadingly give it (James 1961: 40–3).

It is not possible to provide a case study here given restrictions of space. On the basis of their descriptions, it was possible to show (Steinbock 2007: Chapters 3–5) how a givenness in the religious sphere is distinguished in terms of its internal clarity, power and authority, and depth, as coming-from-elsewhere; its immediate, sudden, non-anticipatable quality such that each experience is given as 'complete', full, 'absolutely'. No matter what the level of experience, each givenness—understood as prayer—for example, prayer of quiet, prayer of spiritual delight, or the prayer of rapture (St Teresa of Avila), ecstasy—at the level of ruach/רוח or *chayyah*/חיה, or *yechidah*/יחידה (Rabbi Dov Baer), or unveiling—be it the station of laughter or annihilation (*fanā*/ فنا] or subsistence *baqā*/ بقا) (Rūzbihān Baqlī)—is experienced as 'overabundant'—suggesting a different kind of presence. The Holy is not partially given in the experience, not present and absent like the presentation of the front side and reverse side of an object, but given 'fully'. Indeed, if we wish to equate fullness with objects of presentation, then we would have to say that epiphanic givenness peculiar to religious experience generally and mystical experience specifically is 'over-full', superabundant, and as in the refrain of the mystics, 'without measure'.

To say that this presence is experienced absolutely and fully, however, does not mean that the Holy is exhausted in this experience; but if the experience is surpassed by an ever deepening presence, or if it is renewed, it takes place uniquely. Furthermore, these kinds of presence are qualified as sudden, coming on of their own accord, spontaneous, creative, immediate, without any sense of our being able to anticipate or control them. It is God who is 'active' in relation to which our participation in the experience is 'passive': we do not cause or provoke epiphanic givenness; it is experienced as grace; our 'activity', as it were, is receiving. But the Holy is 'received' in such a way that this reception *alters the structure of experience itself*, and this makes a qualitative difference in how we live with others and in the world.

Furthermore, regarding the evidence peculiar to this sphere of experience, an investigation of first-person descriptions by the mystics of the Abrahamic tradition shows a unique style of givenness that cannot be reduced to the presentation of objects or the other person. It shows that the mystics do not reduce God to an object of knowledge; they do experience God as a perceptual or theoretical object, a representation, or an absent present. It would reveal a 'relation' that is not a correlation.

In and through the very experiencing itself that the mystics report, pervasively, a 'cross-cultural' distinction (within the Abrahamic mystics at least) between (a) what correlates to the provocation of my efforts (passive or active) as what can be 'acquired' as an experience, *and* (b) the experience of the Holy that is essentially beyond my efforts, which cannot be acquired as an experience and which is experienced as 'infused', as 'divine', as by 'grace', or as a privileged 'station'. This 'beyond my efforts', however, is not to be confused with a waiting around, as if passivity would be a negation of activity. One's efforts are expressed as study, meditation, vocal prayer, as well as an ardent 'going out toward' God and neighbour. But if my efforts or my activities are called into question, it is not because I stop them; rather, it is because they are 'stilled' from the outside, held in check by having been *occupied in another way*—in this case, by God.

The virtue of such descriptions lies in the attempts to show that there is 'something else' going on here, beyond the presentation of objects. But it is a sign of capriciousness to assume that one must equate 'experience' and 'presence' with the presentation of objects—that is, with a 'having' of things, perceptually or epistemically, or with an accomplishment initiated by the self. It is an insidious form of positivism to force all experiences into the noesis–noematic logic of appearance and fulfilment under the rubric of being true to 'evidence'. It only highlights the prejudice that presentation exhausts experience, and that presentation somehow comes first and gets to claim experience for itself. If we take givenness seriously, then it would go against the very grain of the given itself to hold that, for example, God is not 'experienced' just because 'it' is given in a radically different way.

Religious experience is not immune to what we might call 'modalizations' of that experience. Indeed, having its own difficulties is what also makes it a unique sphere of experience. In this case, one might undergo experiences of self-deception or self-delusion, temptations, self-doubt or pride, distractions and concessions that creep in little by little, and so on. Examples of corroborating evidence include a confessor or spiritual master (the role of which we find in all three mystical traditions), or the historical efficacy of the experience, or again, Scripture, the service of God, love of neighbor, humility, and so on.

The recognition of the different quality of givenness in religious experience has, as suggested, important implications for the matter of religious evidence. When we think of evidence in the modern world-view, we appeal to its ability to be repeated, not just by me, but by others. As such, evidence as a mode of ideality becomes an aspect of justification, something that I can explain and something that I or others can redo. In religious experience, self-evidence does not exhibit this structure of ideality and corroboration. In the first place, it is nothing 'I' accomplish or there for *me* or another subject to redo. Even though it is given, it is not there anytime we want it. In the second place, since the experiences are spontaneous, creative, unique, owing to 'person' and the personal nature of loving, there is nothing 'to redo' or that could be repeated like an ideal object. This does not mean that this evidence lacks a structure all its own or that we cannot see commonalities across cultures within the Abrahamic tradition, or again, that we cannot pursue a similar path. But if there is any kind of interpersonal 'ideality', it would be found in the structure of exemplarity—that is, in living *as* another, past, present, or future, and not *like* another. Consequently, the corroboration of religious evidence in the mode of self-evidence occurs within the style of religious experiencing itself, and cannot be expected to conform to a style of confirmation alien to it, like when the geometer appeals to the ideality of self-evidence in repetition.

One can certainly submit an experienced presence, the givenness of the Holy in the form of 'prayer', 'ecstasy', or 'unveilings' to interpretation. Such religious experiences are embedded in a religious tradition and in the individual's personal relation to the Holy. St Teresa of Avila, for instance, constantly attempts to 'test'—after the fact—whether a particular givenness (say, a prayer of quiet, a prayer of spiritual delight, a prayer of rapture) is actually from God or from another source, such as self-delusion. One way of testing cited by her looks for what we can call the 'historical efficacy' of prayer—namely, if the experience leaves one 'calm', rather than frustrated, if the virtues flourish, and so forth. There is also an imperative interpersonal dimension to understanding prayer in St Teresa's writings, ecstasy in Rabbi Dov Baer, and unveilings in Rūzbihān Baqlī—namely, in the form of relating and discussing the experiences with a confessor or master. This can be understood as an interpersonal hermeneutical endeavour.

The danger, however, is to say that hermeneutics at this level is employed in order to ascertain the evidence of prayer, ecstasy, and unveiling (something that we find constantly at stake in the mystics); to say that religious experience given 'at the pleasure of God' is nuanced by the richness of the historical context is to my mind different from saying that the presence of God emerges only from a dialectical interplay or negotiation of meaning (passive or active). One can identify an epistemological feature here insofar as there is a concern with what we would call evidence; but this does not mean that God is experienced as an epistemological object. The interpretation of the presence of the Holy is a formidable undertaking, if one wishes to call the practice of what is known generally as the 'discernment of spirits' an interpretative enterprise, then I would concur (see Ignatius 1991: 113–214). I only hedge calling this 'hermeneutics' if one identifies the hermeneutics of experience as a process of dealing with perceptual or epistemic objects. What we must avoid at all costs is a new type of positivism that creeps in under the name of hermeneutics. In this case, givenness could only be a relative givenness dependent upon and subject to my interpretations, and what is given would have to fit into the logic of appearance and fulfilment in order to count as 'true' experience. A hermeneutics of religious experience must itself be situated and relativized *by* religious experience, its unmistakable features made salient by a givenness that it is incapable of producing.

Evidence peculiar to the religious sphere (like the evidence in the moral sphere, say, of the love of another person) is only given with a 'logic' or a 'style' that is intrinsic to that dimension of experience, and in and through that concrete experience. It cannot be adjudicated by mutual agreement, for example, coming from a shared perceptual life, by making the experience 'accessible to all', by explaining it in terms of physiological or psychological abnormalities, or by 'measuring the spiritual'. One cannot make a religious experience happen like one cannot make another person love. In this respect, one cannot 'access' God. Being disposed toward an experience or even evoking an experience is not the same a producing or provoking an experience.

But if religious experience is so 'singular', one may wonder whether the so-called idiosyncrasy of the mystics is really not just a sign of their pathology, or whether psychoses are not really just what religiously inclined folks want to call mystical experiences. The writings of the famed Dr Schreber, analyzed and popularized by Freud, highlight some of the difficulties in discerning differences in such experiences (Freud 1963: 103ff). For example, Dr Schreber writes lucidly from his first-person perspective about being in direct communication with God, of having a mission to redeem the world and to restore it to its lost state of bliss, of being the recipient of divine miracles ('rays of God'), of becoming God's wife, of assuming passivity in relation to God, of bodily functions being evoked miraculously by God, of regarding 'God Almighty' as his ally, of suffering and privation for God, and so on. He also notes that his experiences exceed human understanding; the 'divine revelations' cannot be expressed adequately within the confines of human language, and for this reason he must resort to 'images and similes' (Schreber 2000). Are these not religious experiences and attempts at expression like any other we have encountered?

There were of course 'nuances' to these experiences. For example, Dr Schreber describes, in an attitude of both rebelliousness and reverence, God not needing to be acquainted with living human beings, since he only needed to have intercourse with corpses; he maintains that God is only 'nerve'; he writes of his emasculation by God as a precondition for a new race of humans being created, of his 'voluptuousness' as a taste of bliss, of his right to scoff at God—a right that belongs to him alone and not to others— and of his identification with Jesus Christ.

We must note several things here. First, the attempt to evaluate these descriptions, to the extent possible, is the attempt often referred to, within a religious context, as the discernment of spirits. Is not Freud himself attempting this, if only in an ambivalent way or against his intentions? On the one hand, Freud immediately situates Schreber's writings within the framework of psychopathology—due in some part, perhaps to Schreber's own self-diagnosis. His ideas are said to be of a pathological origin; he is assumed to be a paranoiac and delusional.

Second, within the context of religious experience the relation between the mystic and 'religious paranoia' may not always be clear for us. If the mystics, as I mentioned above, are 'hyper-normal', then what it means to be normal, as it is unfolding within human experience, is still in the process of *becoming normal*, in the process establishing norms within experience. The religious life is in this sense optimalizing, normalizing, in the dynamic sense (Steinbock 1995: Sec. 3). There is not a final sense of normality already worked out in advance, outside of human experience that we could then apply to that experience. If there is a difference between the 'normal' in the sense of optimalizing, and the pathological, it is a difference that lies in the integrity of the religious experience itself, and is not in its conformity to a stock set of external standards. Furthermore, we cannot rule out the possibility that one could have religious insights, mystical experiences, and then lose them, misunderstand them, or misinterpret their significance, not just intellectually, but at the core of one's being. It is entirely possible that psychoses be taken as mystical experiences, mystical experiences as psychoses, or genetically speaking, that mental pathologies had originated as mystical experiences.

Religious experience as I have been explicating it, is fundamentally open, 'generative' (optimalizing), and not closed. It is not susceptible to a definitive clarity. Does this mean, then, that phenomenology must abandon any and all critical perspective of 'discernment'? Although one cannot discern, say psychoses from mystical experiences with absolute clarity and definitiveness (since the experiences arise within Generativity and have to be taken up *within* 'it'), we can note some clues for discernment, clues suggested by these mystics' experiences, but nevertheless clues that do not provide a final key for dispelling the mystery in which we find ourselves. For example, to repeat some of the features disclosed by the mystics and on the basis of the authority of their experiences (the mystics—whom, I admit, I identify on the whole *as* having mystical experiences or who live a religious life—an unavoidable hermeneutical problematic), we could ask: are the experiences expansive or narrowing? Do the experiences lead one to embrace all levels of reality or to shrink back from existence? Are the 'effects' of prayer that one live in the service of God, love of neighbor, welcoming the stranger, or do they yield the shunning of others? Is there a devotion to God more than the devotion to the idea of God? Is one left cold, frustrated, indifferent, or with a sense of calm and 'interior peace'? Do the experiences open one to deeper values, or limit what can appear as value? Is the attitude toward 'nature' a devaluation of it through *ressentiment*, or a revaluation of it in relation to spirit? Does a later experience or insight disclose something about a former one? Is one left humble or prideful? Is one left fixated on the 'communications', 'visions', 'locutions'? Is there service or devotion despite the 'gifts'?

Do the experiences tend toward the abandonment of self, or toward the attachment to self and to things?

These kinds of questions and orientations to experience do not set out to prove the validity of one experience over another, but only suggest the issues that pertain to this sphere of experience. The main point is that religious dimension can meaningfully be described as an experience that it has its own style of evidence and modalization that is discernible only within that sphere.

5 Conclusion

Since Kant, the question of the philosophical accessibility of God and of a 'religious experience' has been thrown into relief by delimiting the religious (and God) from experience, and by equating experience with having an object of knowledge. Presupposing the presentation of perceptual and categorial objects as the parameters of experience, phenomenology has exposed the limits of this mode experience. In effect, it has exposed the limits of experience which take place on a featured model of givenness, and simultaneously opened phenomenology to what is beyond this style of givenness. In being attentive to givenness—to the matters in the ways in which they given themselves and are given—phenomenology opened itself to modes of givenness that do not necessarily conform to the presentation of perceptual and categorial objects, but to kinds of givenness that nevertheless count in human experience. In this way, phenomenology has been obligated to give constitutive and structural account of these experiences, and to the extent possible, without prejudice. This article has been concerned with religious experience. And although we all might have a peculiar access to this kind of experience, it is with the help of the first-person description of mystical experiences that give us our first clue to the unique order of givenness, with its inherent difficulties and pitfalls and which outline its own style of evidence, irreducible to other kinds of human experience.

In this openness, we could actually find several kinds of givenness that go beyond the presentation of objects, what I have called elsewhere 'vertical' givenness. They include not only the epiphanic givenness peculiar to the religious sphere, but the 'revelation' of the other person, the 'manifestation' of the product as the icon of cultural production, the 'disclosure' of the Earth as earth-ground, and the 'display' of elements. It is the broader task of phenomenology to give an account of these unique kinds of evidence with its own irreducible sphere of experience, and as well, the ways in which they are intertwined and enhance one another in human experience.

References

Bellak, L. M. D. (1949), in Gordon. H. L., *The Maggid of Caro: The Mystic Life of the Eminent Codifier Joseph Caro as Revealed in his Secret Diary* (New York: Shoulson Press).

Bergson, H. (1984/1932), *Les deux sources de la morale et de la religion* (Paris: PUF).

Buber, M. (1965), 'Ich und Du', in *Das dialogische Prinzip* (Heidelberg: Lambert Schneider).

Duméry, H (1957), *Le problème de Dieu en philosophie de la religion* (Paris: Desclée de Brouwer).

Ernst, C. W. (1985), *Words of Ecstasy in Sufism* (New York: SUNY Press).

—— (1996), *Rūzbihān Baqlī: Mysticism and the Rhetoric of Sainthood in Persian Sufism* (Richmond: Curzon Press).

Fink, E. (1933), 'Die Phänomenologische philosophie Edmund Husserls in der gegenwärtigen kritik', in *Kant-Studien* 38: 321–83.

Foucault, M. (1999), *Religion and Culture*, J. R. Carrette (ed.) (New York: Routledge).

Freud, S. (1963), *Three Case Histories*, P. Rieff (ed.) (New York: Colllier Books)

Gründler, O. (1922), *Elemente zu einer Religionsphilosophie auf phänomenologischer Grundlage* (Munich: Kösel & Pustet).

Hering, J. (1926), *Phénoménologie et philosophie religieuse* (Paris: Felix Alcan).

Heiler, F. (1961), *Erscheinungsformen und Wesen der Religion* (Stuttgart: W. Kohlhammer).

Henry, G. W. M. D. (1949), in Gordon. H. L., *The Maggid of Caro: The Mystic Life of the Eminent Codifier Joseph Caro as Revealed in his Secret Diary* (New York: Shoulson Press).

Henry, M. (1990), *L'essence de la manifestation*, second edn. (Paris: PUF).

—— (1996), *C'est moi la vérité: pour une philosophie du christianisme* (Paris: Seuil).

Hunt, H. T. (2003), *Lives in Spirit: Precursors and Dilemmas of a Secular Western Mysticism* (Albany, NY: SUNY Press).

Husserl, E. (1952), *Ideen zu einer reinen Phänomenologie und phänomenologischen Philosophie. Drittes Buch: Die Phänomenologie und die Fundament der Wissenschaften.* Husserliana Vol. V, W. Biemel (ed.) (The Hague: Martinus Nijhoff).

—— (1954), *Die Krisis der europäischen Wissenschaften und die transzendentale Phänomenologie. Eine Einleitung in die phänomenologische Philosophie.* Husserliana Vol. VI, W. Biemel (ed.) (The Hague: Martinus Nijhoff).

—— (1956), *Erste Philosophie (1923/24). Erster Teil: Kritische Indeengeschichte. Husserliana Vol. VII*, R. Boehm (ed.) (The Hague: Martinus Nijhoff).

—— (1959), *Erste Philosophie (1923/24): Zweiter Teil: Theorie der phänomenologische Reduktion.* Husserliana Vol. VIII, R. Boehm (ed.) (The Hague: Martinus Nijhoff).

—— (1968), *Logische Untersuchungen. Band II: Untersuchungen zur Phänomenologie und Theorie der Erkenntnis*, I. Teil (Tübingen: Niemeyer).

—— (1973), *Zur Phänomenologie der Intersubjektivität. Texte aus dem Nachlaß. Dritter Teil: 1929–1935*, Husserliana Vol. XV, I. Kern (ed.), (The Hague: Martinus Nijhoff).

—— (1993), *Die Krisis der europäischen Wissenschaften und die transzendentale Phänomenologie: Ergänzungsband. Texte aus dem Nachlass 1934–1937.* Husserliana Vol. XXIX, Reinhold N. Smid (ed.). (Boston: Kluwer).

Ignatius of Loyola (1991), *The Spiritual Exercises and Selected Works*, tr. and ed. George, E. Ganss, S.J., et. al. (Mahwah, NJ: Paulist Press).

James, W. (1961), *The Varieties of Religious Experience* (New York: Collier Books).

Janicaud, D. (1991), *Le tournant théologique de la phénoménologie française* (Combas: l'éclat).

—— (1998), *La phénoménologie éclatée* (Combas: l'éclat).

Kant, I. (1956), *Kritik der reinen Vernunft, Raymund Schmidt* (ed.) (Hamburg: Meiner).

—— (1989), *Die Religion innerhalb der Grenzen der bloßen Vernunft*, Karl Vorländer (ed.) (Hamburg: Meiner); tr. Th. M. Greene and H. H. Hudson, *Religion within the Limits of Reason Alone* (New York: Harper and Row, 1960).

—— (1992), *The Conflict of the Faculties/Der Streit der Fakultäten* (Bilingual edition), tr. Mary J. Gregor (Lincoln: University of Nebraska Press).

Kierkegaard, S. (1983), *Fear and Trembling*, tr. and ed. H. V. Hong and E. H. Hong (Princeton: Princeton University Press).

—— (1998), *Works of Love*, tr. and ed. H. V. Hong and E. H. Hong (Princeton: Princeton University Press).

Levinas, E. (1961), *Totalité et infini* (The Hague: Martinus Nijhoff); tr. A. Lingis (Pittsburgh: Duquesne University Press, 1969).

—— (1988), *En découvrant l'existence avec Husserl et Heidegger* (Paris: Vrin).

—— (1992), *De Dieu qui vient à l'idée* (Paris: Vrin.)

Marion, J.-L. (1991), *Dieu sans l'être* (Paris: PUF).

—— (1997), *Étant donné. Essai d'une phénoménologie de la donation* (Paris: PUF).

—— (2001), *De surcroît: Études sur les phénomènes saturés* (Paris: PUF).

Merleau-Ponty, M. (1945), *Phénoménologie de la perception* (Paris: Gallimard).

Otto, R. (1958), *The Idea of the Holy*, tr. J. W. Harvey (New York: Oxford University Press).

—— (1970), *Mysticism East and West: A Comparative Analysis of the Nature of Mysticism*, tr. B. L. Bracey and R. C. Payne (New York: The Macmillan Company)

Pike, N. (1992), *Mystic Union: An Essay in the Phenomenology of Mysticism* (Ithaca: Cornell University Press).

Poulan, R. P. A. (1950), *The Graces of Interior Prayer: A Treatise on Mystical Theology*, tr. L. L. Yorke Smith, corrected to accord with the 10th French edn. (St Louis: Herder).

Reinach, A. (1989), *Sämtliche Werke*, K. Schuhmann and B. Smith (ed.), (Munich: Philosophia).

Scheler, M. (1954), *Vom Ewigen im Menschen*, Gesammelte Werke, Vol. 5, M. Scheler (ed.), 4th edn. (Bern: Francke).

—— (1957), 'Ordo Amoris', in *Schriften aus dem Nachlaß*. Vol 1. Gesammelte Werke, Vol. 10. M. Scheler (ed.), (Bern: Francke), pp. 345–76.

—— (1966), *Formalismus in der Ethik und die Materiale Wertethik*, Gesammelte Werke Vol. 2, M. Scheler (ed.), (Bern: Francke).

—— (1973), *Wesen und Formen der Sympathie*, Gesammelte Werke, Vol. 7, M. Frings (ed.) (Bern: Francke, 1973).

Schreber, D. P. (2000), *Memoirs of My Nervous Illness*, tr. I. Macalpine, *et. al.* (New York: New York Review of Books).

Smart, N. (1965), 'Interpretation and mystical experience', in *Religious Studies* I: 75–87.

Soelle, D. (2001), *The Silent Cry: Mysticism and Resistance*, tr. Barbara and Martin Rumscheidt (Minneapolis: Fortress Press).

Stavenhagen, K. (1925), *Absolute Stellungnahmen: eine ontologische Untersuchung über das Wesen der Religion* (Erlangen: Philosophischen Akademie).

Stace, W. T. (1960a), *Mysticism and Philosophy* (Philadelphia: Lippincott).

—— (1960b), *The Teachings of the Mystics* (New York: New American Library).

Steinbock, A. J. (1995), *Home and Beyond: Generative Phenomenology after Husserl* (Evanston: Northwestern University Press).

—— (1998), 'Limit-phenomena and the liminality of experience', *Alter: revue de phénoménologie* 6: 275–96.

—— (1999), 'The problem of forgetfulness in the phenomenology of life', in *Continental Philosophy Review, The Philosophy of Michel Henry*, A. J. Steinbock (ed.), 32/3, pp. 271–302.

—— (2005), 'Face and revelation: Levinas on teaching as way-faring', in *Addressing Levinas*, E. S. Nelson *et. al.* (eds) (Evanston, IL: Northwestern University Press), pp. 119–37.

Steinbock, A. J. (2007), *Phenomenology and Mysticism: The Verticality of Religious Experience* (Bloomington: Indiana University Press).

—— (2009), 'Reducing the One to the Other: Kant, Levinas, and the problem of religious experience', in *Levinas Studies: An Annual Review* 4: 127–56.

—— (2010), 'The poor phenomenon: Marion and the problem of givenness', in *Words of Life: New Theological Turns in French Phenomenology*, B. E. Benson and N. Wirzba (eds), (New York: Fordham University Press), pp. 120–31.

—— (forthcoming), 'The distinctive structure of the emotions', in *The Continuing Impact of Husserl's 'Ideas'* (Dordrecht: Springer).

Underhill, E. (1974), *Mysticism: A Study in the Nature and Development of Man's Spiritual Consciousness* (New York: Penguin Books).

Van der Leeuw, G. (1956), *Phänomenologie der Religion* (Tübingen: J. C. B. Mohr. Paul Siebeck).

Walther, G. (1923), *Zur Phänomenologie der Mystik* (Halle: Niemeyer).

Zaehner, R. C. (1961), *Msticism: Sacred and Profane* (New York: Oxford University Press).

INDEX